Chevrolet & GMC Vans Owners Workshop Manual.

333p ill. 27 cm

by J H Haynes
Member of the Guild of Motoring Writers
and P G Strasman

Models covered 1968 thru 1985.

Chevrolet
G10, G20, G30 Series, Chevy Van and Sportvan, including Custom, Deluxe and Beauville versions

GMC
GE/GS 1500, 2500 and 3500, including Rally and Vandura versions

Covers 230, 250 and 292 cu in 6 cylinder in-line engines and 305, 307, 350 and 400 cu in V8 engines. Manual and automatic transmission

ISBN 1 85010 123 X

Haynes Publishing Group
Sparkford Nr Yeovil
Somerset BA22 7JJ England

Haynes Publications, Inc
861 Lawrence Drive
Newbury Park
California 91320 USA

Acknowledgements

Thanks are due to the Chevrolet Motors Division and GMC Truck and Coach Division of the General Motors Corporation for their assistance with technical information and the supply of certain illustrations. Castrol Limited provided lubrication information, and the Champion Sparking Plug Company supplied the illustrations showing the various spark plug conditions. The bodywork repair photographs used in this Manual were provided by Lloyds Industries Ltd who supply 'Turtle-Wax', 'Dupli-colour Holts,' and other Holts range products.

Lastly, thanks are due to all those people at Sparkford who helped in the production of this Manual. In particular, these are Brian Horsfall who carried out the mechanical work, Les Brazier who took the photographs, Ian Robson who planned the layout of each page, and Pete Ward who edited the text. ·

About this manual

Its aim

The aim of this Manual is to help you get the best value from your van. It can do so in several ways. It can help you decide what work must be done (even should you choose to get it done by a service station or dealer), provide information on routine maintenance and servicing, and give a logical course of action and diagnosis when random faults occur. However, it is hoped that you will use the Manual by tackling the work yourself. On simpler jobs it may even be quicker than booking the Van into a service station or dealer, and going there twice to leave and collect it. Perhaps most important, a lot of money can be saved by avoiding the costs the service station or dealer must charge to cover its labor and overheads.

The Manual has drawings and descriptions to show the function of the various components so that their layout can be understood. Then the tasks are described and photographed in a step-by-step sequence so that even a novice can do the work.

Its arrangement

The Manual is divided into thirteen Chapters, each covering a logical sub-division of the vehicle. The Chapters are each divided into Sections, numbered with single figures, eg 5; and the Sections into paragraphs (or sub-sections), with decimal numbers following on from the Section they are in, eg 5.1, 5.2, 5.3 etc.

It is freely illustrated, especially in those parts where there is a detailed sequence of operations to be carried out. There are two forms of illustration: figures and photographs. The figures are numbered in sequence with decimal numbers, according to their position in the Chapter: eg, Fig. 6.4 is the 4th drawing/illustration in Chapter 6. Photographs are numbered (either individually or in related groups) the same as the Section or sub-section of the text where the operation they show is described.

There is an alphabetical index at the back of the Manual as well as a contents list at the front.

References to the 'left' or 'right' of the vehicle are in the sense of a person sitting in the driver's seat facing forwards.

While every care is taken to ensure that the information in this manual is correct no liability can be accepted by the authors or publishers for loss, damage or injury caused by any errors in, or omissions from, the information given.

Contents

134546

Three quarter front view of the Chevrolet Sportvan

Use of English

As this book has been written in England, it uses the appropriate English component names, phrases, and spelling. Some of these differ from those used in America. Normally, these cause no difficulty, but to make sure, a glossary is printed below. In ordering spare parts remember the parts list will probably use these words:

English	American	English	American
Aerial	Antenna	Layshaft (of gearbox)	Countershaft
Accelerator	Gas pedal	Leading shoe (of brake)	Primary shoe
Alternator	Generator (AC)	Locks	Latches
Anti-roll bar	Stabiliser or sway bar	Motorway	Freeway, turnpike etc
Battery	Energizer	Number plate	License plate
Bodywork	Sheet metal	Paraffin	Kerosene
Bonnet (engine cover)	Hood	Petrol	Gasoline
Boot lid	Trunk lid	Petrol tank	Gas tank
Boot (luggage compartment)	Trunk	'Pinking'	'Pinging'
Bottom gear	1st gear	Propeller shaft	Driveshaft
Bulkhead	Firewall	Quarter light	Quarter window
Cam follower or tappet	Valve lifter or tappet	Retread	Recap
Carburettor	Carburetor	Reverse	Back-up
Catch	Latch	Rocker cover	Valve cover
Choke/venturi	Barrel	Roof rack	Car-top carrier
Circlip	Snap-ring	Saloon	Sedan
Clearance	Lash	Seized	Frozen
Crownwheel	Ring gear (of differential)	Side indicator lights	Side marker lights
Disc (brake)	Rotor/disk	Side light	Parking light
Drop arm	Pitman arm	Silencer	Muffler
Drop head coupe	Convertible	Spanner	Wrench
Dynamo	Generator (DC)	Sill panel (beneath doors)	Rocker panel
Earth (electrical)	Ground	Split cotter (for valve spring cap)	Lock (for valve spring retainer)
Engineer's blue	Prussian blue	Split pin	Cotter pin
Estate car	Station wagon	Steering arm	Spindle arm
Exhaust manifold	Header	Sump	Oil pan
Fast back (Coupe)	Hard top	Tab washer	Tang; lock
Fault finding/diagnosis	Trouble shooting	Tailgate	Liftgate
Float chamber	Float bowl	Tappet	Valve lifter
Free-play	Lash	Thrust bearing	Throw-out bearing
Freewheel	Coast	Top gear	High
Gudgeon pin	Piston pin or wrist pin	Trackrod (of steering)	Tie-rod (or connecting rod)
Gearchange	Shift	Trailing shoe (of brake)	Secondary shoe
Gearbox	Transmission	Transmission	Whole drive line
Halfshaft	Axleshaft	Tyre	Tire
Handbrake	Parking brake	Van	Panel wagon/van
Hood	Soft top	Vice	Vise
Hot spot	Heat riser	Wheel nut	Lug nut
Indicator	Turn signal	Windscreen	Windshield
Interior light	Dome lamp	Wing/mudguard	Fender

Miscellaneous points

An 'oil seal' is fitted to components lubricated by grease!

A 'damper' is a 'shock absorber', it damps out bouncing, and absorbs shocks of bump impact. Both names are correct, and both are used haphazardly.

Note that British drum brakes are different from the Bendix type that is common in America, so different descriptive names result. The shoe end furthest from the hydraulic wheel cylinder is on a pivot; interconnection between the shoes as on Bendix brakes is most uncommon. Therefore the phrase 'Primary' or 'Secondary' shoe does not apply. A shoe is said to be 'Leading' or 'Trailing'. A 'Leading' shoe is one on which a point on the drum, as it rotates forward, reaches the shoe at the end worked by the hydraulic cylinder before the anchor end. The opposite is a 'Trailing' shoe, and this one has no self servo from the wrapping effect of the rotating drum.

Introduction to the Chevrolet/GMC Van

The vans covered by this Manual are vehicles capable of simple customizing with the minimum of outlay.

They are available with a wide variety of engine, transmission and other factory-installed options and in consequence, used examples offering the precise specification required are easily obtainable.

The production run has been so long that spare parts are plentiful and easily obtainable, and any early troubles have long since been rectified or eradicated.

Repairs and maintenance are simply carried out by the DIY owner as the vehicle is ruggedly constructed and has good accessibility to all components and assemblies.

Buying spare parts and vehicle identification numbers

Buying spare parts

Spare parts are available from many sources, for example: Chevrolet/GMC dealers, other dealers and accessory stores, and motor factors. Our advice regarding spare part sources is as follows:

Officially appointed Chevrolet/GMC dealers — This is the best source of parts which are peculiar to your vehicle and are otherwise not generally available (eg; complete cylinder heads, internal transmission components, badges, interior trim, etc). It is also the only place at which you should buy parts if your vehicle is still under warranty — non-GM components may invalidate the warranty. To be sure of obtaining the correct parts it will always be necessary to give the storeman your vehicle's engine and chassis number, and if possible, to take the 'old' part along for positive identification. Remember that many parts are available on a factory exchange scheme — any parts returned should always be clean! It obviously makes good sense to go straight to the specialists on your vehicle for this type of part for they are best equipped to supply you.

Other dealers and auto accessory stores — These are often very good places to buy materials and components needed for the maintenance of your vehicle (eg, oil filters, spark plugs, bulbs, fan belts, oils and greases, touch-up paint, filler paste etc). They also sell general accessories, usually have convenient opening hours, charge lower prices and can often be found not far from home.

Motor factors — Good factors will stock all the more important components which wear out relatively quickly (eg, clutch components, pistons, valves, exhaust systems, brake cylinder/pipes/hoses/seals/shoes and pads etc). Motor factors will often provide new or reconditioned components on a part-exchange basis — this can save a considerable amount of money.

Vehicle Identification numbers

Modifications are a continuing and unpublicised process in vehicle manufacture. Spare parts manuals and lists are compiled on a numerical basis, the individual vehicle numbers being essential to identify correctly, the component required.

Service Parts Identification Plate

This is located on an inner body panel, and lists the vehicle serial number, wheelbase and the options specified at the time of production.

Vehicle Emission Control Information

This is given on later models in the form of a decal or sticker, and should be referred to whenever engine tuning is to be carried out.

Vehicle Identification Number and Rating Plate

This is attached to the dash and toe-panel.

Engine Number

This is located on a machined surface on the cylinder block.

Transmission Number

On 3-speed manual units, the number is located on the lower left side of the case.

On 4-speed units the number is stamped on the rear of the case above the output shaft.

On automatic transmission units, the number is located on the right rear vertical surface of the oil pan.

Rear axle numbers

On Series 10 and 20 vehicles the number is stamped on the front of the right rear axle tube.

On Series 30 vehicles (except those with dual rear wheels) the number is stamped on the forward upper surface of the carrier.

On vehicle with dual rear wheels, the number is stamped on the front of the right axle tube.

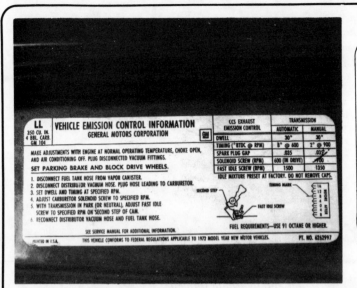

Typical Vehicle Emission Control Information Decal

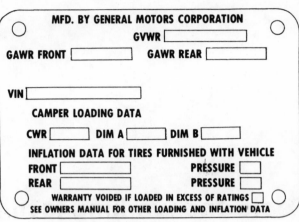

Vehicle Rating Plate

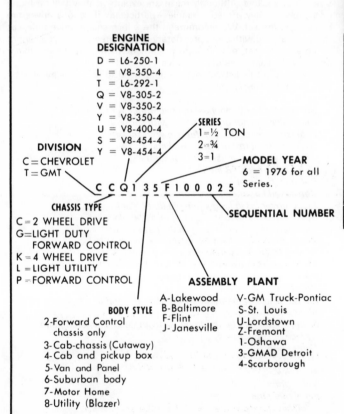

Vehicle Identification Number Plate

SERVICE PARTS IDENTIFICATION

V.I.N. [_____] W/BASE [____] SE [____]

V.I.N. — VEHICLE IDENTIFICATION NUMBER

NOTE: THE SPECIAL EQUIPMENT LISTED BELOW HAS BEEN INSTALLED ON THIS VEHICLE. FOR PROPER IDENTIFICATION OF REPLACEMENT PARTS BE SURE TO SPECIFY THE APPLICABLE OPTION NUMBERS.

OPTION NO.	DESCRIPTION	OPTION NO.	DESCRIPTION

IMPORTANT: RETAIN THIS PLATE AS A PERMANENT RECORD

Service Parts Identification Plate

MFD. BY GENERAL MOTORS CORPORATION

GVWR

GAWR FRONT   GAWR REAR

VIN

INFLATION DATA FOR TIRES FURNISHED WITH VEHICLE

Shown on Vehicle Certification Label

WARRANTY VOIDED IF LOADED IN EXCESS OF RATINGS

MFD. BY GENERAL MOTORS CORP.

	08/77		
	GVWR	GAWR FRT	GAWR RR
LB/kg	14000/6350	4000/1814	10000/4536
TIRES	10.5 X 16.5D	10.5 X 16.5D	10.5 X 16.5D
RIMS	16.6 X 9.75	16.5 X 9.75	16.6 X 9.75
PSI/kPa	36/243-42/290	36/248	42/290

THIS VEHICLE CONFORMS TO ALL APPLICABLE FEDERAL MOTOR VEHICLE SAFETY STANDARDS

IN EFFECT   ON THE DATE MANUFACTURE   SHOWN ABOVE
  CG601681100001   BUS - NOT SCHOOL BUS

SEE OWNERS MANUAL FOR ADDITIONAL INFORMATION.

Later type Vehicle Identification and Rating Plates

Tools and working facilities

Introduction

A selection of good tools is a fundamental requirement for anyone contemplating the maintenance and repair of a motor vehicle. For the owner who does not possess any, their purchase will prove a considerable expense, offsetting some of the savings made by doing-it-yourself. However, provided that the tools purchased are of good quality, they will last for many years and prove an extremely worthwhile investment.

To help the average owner to decide which tools are needed to carry out the various tasks detailed in this manual, we have compiled three lists of tools under the following headings: *Maintenance and minor repair, Repair and overhaul,* and *Special.* The newcomer to practical mechanics should start off with the *Maintenance and minor repair* tool kit and confine himself to the simpler jobs around the vehicle. Then, as his confidence and experience grow, he can undertake more difficult tasks, buying extra tools as, and when, they are needed. In this way, a *Maintenance and minor repair* tool kit can be built-up into a *Repair and overhaul* tool kit over a considerable period of time without any major cash outlays. The experienced do-it-yourselfer will have a tool kit good enough for most repair and overhaul procedures and will add tools from the *Special* category when he feels the expense is justified by the amount of use these tools will be put to.

It is obviously not possible to cover the subject of tools fully here. For those who wish to learn more about tools and their use there is a book entitled *How to Choose and Use Car Tools* available from the publishers of this manual.

Maintenance and minor repair tool kit

The tools given in this list should be considered as a minimum requirement if routine maintenance, servicing and minor repair operations are to be undertaken. We recommend the purchase of combination wrenches (ring one end, open-ended the other); although more expensive than open-ended ones, they do give the advantages of both types of wrench.

Combination wrenches - $\frac{3}{8}$ to $\frac{11}{16}$ in AF
Adjustable wrench - 9 inch
Engine sump/gearbox/rear axle drain plug key (where applicable)
Spark plug wrench (with rubber insert)
Spark plug gap adjustment tool
Set of feeler gauges
Brake adjuster wrench (where applicable)
Brake bleed nipple wrench
Screwdriver - 4 in long x $\frac{1}{4}$ in dia (flat blade)
Screwdriver - 4 in long x $\frac{1}{4}$ in dia (cross blade)
Combination pliers - 6 inch
Hacksaw, junior
Tire pump
Tire pressure gauge
Grease gun (where applicable)
Oil can
Fine emery cloth (1 sheet)
Wire brush (small)
Funnel (medium size)

Repair and overhaul tool kit

These tools are virtually essential for anyone undertaking any major repairs to a motor vehicle, and are additional to those given in the *Maintenance and minor repair* list. Included in this list is a comprehensive set of sockets. Although these are expensive they will be found invaluable as they are so versatile - particularly if various drives are included in the set. We recommend the $\frac{1}{2}$ inch square-drive type, as this can be used with most proprietary torque wrenches. If you cannot afford a socket set, even bought piecemeal, then inexpensive tubular box wrenches are a useful alternative.

The tools in this list will occasionally need to be supplemented by tools from the *Special* list.

Sockets (or box wrenches) to cover range $\frac{7}{32}$ to $\frac{11}{16}$ in AF
Reversible ratchet drive (for use with sockets)
Extension piece, 10 inch (for use with sockets)
Universal joint (for use with sockets)
Torque wrench (for use with sockets)
Self-grip wrench - 8 inch
Ball pein hammer
Soft-faced hammer, plastic or rubber
Screwdriver - 6 in long x $\frac{5}{16}$ in dia (flat blade)
Screwdriver - 2 in long x $\frac{5}{16}$ in square (flat blade)
Screwdriver - 1$\frac{1}{2}$ in long x $\frac{1}{4}$ in dia (cross blade)
Screwdriver - 3 in long x $\frac{1}{8}$ in dia (electricians)
Pliers - electricians side cutters
Pliers - needle nosed
Pliers - circlip (internal and external)
Cold chisel - $\frac{1}{2}$ inch
Scriber (this can be made by grinding the end of a broken hacksaw blade)
Scraper (this can be made by flattening and sharpening one end of a piece of copper pipe)
Center punch
Pin punch
Hacksaw
Valve grinding tool
Steel rule/straight edge
Allen keys
Selection of files
Wire brush (large)
Axle stands
Jack (strong scissor or hydraulic type)

Special tools

The tools in this list are those which are not used regularly, are expensive to buy, or which need to be used in accordance with their manufacturers' instructions. Unless relatively difficult mechanical jobs are undertaken frequently, it will not be economic to buy many of these tools. Where this is the case, you could consider clubbing together with friends (or an automobile club) to make a joint purchase, or borrowing the tools against a deposit from a local repair station or tool hire specialist.

The following list contains only those tools and instruments freely available to the public, and not those special tools produced by the vehicle manufacturer specifically for its dealer network. You will find occasional references to these manufacturers' special tools in the text of this manual. Generally, an alternative method of doing the job without the vehicle manufacturer's special tool is given. However, sometimes, there is no alternative to using them. Where this is the case and the relevant tool cannot be bought or borrowed you will have to entrust the work to a franchised dealer.

Valve spring compressor
Piston ring compressor
Balljoint separator
Universal hub/bearing puller
Impact screwdriver
Micrometer and/or vernier gauge
Carburetor flow balancing device (where applicable)
Dial gauge
Stroboscopic timing light
Dwell angle meter/tachometer
Universal electrical multi-meter
Cylinder compression gauge
Lifting tackle
Trolley jack
Light with extension lead

Buying tools

For practically all tools, a tool factor is the best source since he will have a very comprehensive range compared with the average repair station or accessory store. Having said that, accessory stores often offer excellent quality tools at discount prices, so it pays to shop around.

Remember, you don't have to buy the most expensive items on the shelf, but it is always advisable to steer clear of the very cheap tools. There are plenty of good tools around at reasonable prices, so ask the proprietor or manager of the shop for advice before making a purchase.

Working facilities

Not to be forgotten when discussing tools, is the workshop itself. If anything more than routine maintenance is to be carried out, some form of suitable working area becomes essential.

It is appreciated that many an owner mechanic is forced by circumstances to remove an engine or similar item, without the benefit of a garage or workshop. Having done this, any repairs should always be done under the cover of a roof.

Wherever possible, any dismantling should be done on a clean flat workbench or table at a suitable working height.

Any workbench needs a vice: one with a jaw opening of 4 in (100 mm) is suitable for most jobs. As mentioned previously, some clean dry storage space is also required for tools, as well as the lubricants, cleaning fluids, touch-up paints and so on which soon become necessary.

Another item which may be required, and which has a much more general usage, is an electric drill with a chuck capacity of at least $\frac{5}{16}$ in (8 mm). This, together with a good range of twist drills, is virtually essential for fitting accessories such as wing mirrors and back-up lights.

Last, but not least, always keep a supply of old newspapers and clean, lint-free rags available, and try to keep any working area as clean as possible.

Care and maintenance of tools

Having purchased a reasonable tool kit, it is necessary to keep the tools in a clean serviceable condition. After use, always wipe off any dirt, grease and metal particles using a clean, dry cloth, before putting the tools away. Never leave them lying around after they have been used. A simple tool rack on the garage or workshop wall, for items such as screwdrivers and pliers is a good idea. Store all normal spanners and sockets in a metal box. Any measuring instruments, gauges, meters, etc., must be carefully stored where they cannot be damaged or become rusty.

Take a little care when the tools are used. Hammer heads inevitably become marked and screwdrivers lose the keen edge on their blades from time-to-time. A little timely attention with emery cloth or a file will soon restore items like this to a good serviceable finish.

Wrench jaw gap comparison table

Jaw gap (in)	Wrench size	Jaw gap (in)	Wrench size
0·250	$\frac{1}{4}$ in AF	0·944	24 mm AF
0·275	7 mm AF	1·000	1 in AF
0·312	$\frac{5}{16}$ in AF	1·010	$\frac{9}{16}$ in Whitworth; $\frac{5}{8}$ in BSF
0·315	8 mm AF	1·023	26 mm AF
0·340	11/32 in AF; $\frac{1}{8}$ in Whitworth	1·062	$1\frac{1}{16}$ in AF; 27 mm AF
0·354	9 mm AF	1·100	$\frac{5}{8}$ in Whitworth; $\frac{11}{16}$ in BSF
0·375	$\frac{3}{8}$ in AF	1·125	$1\frac{1}{8}$ in AF
0·393	10 mm AF	1·181	30 mm AF
0·433	11 mm AF	1·200	$\frac{11}{16}$ in Whitworth; $\frac{3}{4}$ in BSF
0·437	$\frac{7}{16}$ in AF	1·250	$1\frac{1}{4}$ in AF
0·445	$\frac{3}{16}$ in Whitworth; $\frac{1}{4}$ in BSF	1·259	32 mm AF
0·472	12 mm AF	1·300	$\frac{3}{4}$ in Whitworth; $\frac{7}{8}$ in BSF
0·500	$\frac{1}{2}$ in AF	1·312	$1\frac{5}{16}$ in AF
0·512	13 mm AF	1·390	$\frac{13}{16}$ in Whitworth; $\frac{15}{16}$ in BSF
0·525	$\frac{1}{4}$ in Whitworth; $\frac{5}{16}$ in BSF	1·417	36 mm AF
0·551	14 mm AF	1·437	$1\frac{7}{16}$ in AF
0·562	$\frac{9}{16}$ in AF	1·480	$\frac{7}{8}$ in Whitworth; 1 in BSF
0·590	15 mm AF	1·500	$1\frac{1}{2}$ in AF
0·600	$\frac{5}{16}$ in Whitworth; $\frac{3}{8}$ in BSF	1·574	40 mm AF; $\frac{15}{16}$ in Whitworth
0·625	$\frac{5}{8}$ in AF	1·614	41 mm AF
0·629	16 mm AF	1·625	$1\frac{5}{8}$ in AF
0·669	17 mm AF	1·670	1 in Whitworth; $1\frac{1}{8}$ in BSF
0·687	$\frac{11}{16}$ in AF	1·687	$1\frac{11}{16}$ in AF
0·708	18 mm AF	1·811	46 mm AF
0·710	$\frac{3}{8}$ in Whitworth; $\frac{7}{16}$ in BSF	1·812	$1\frac{13}{16}$ in AF
0·748	19 mm AF	1·860	$1\frac{1}{8}$ in Whitworth; $1\frac{1}{4}$ in BSF
0·750	$\frac{3}{4}$ in AF	1·875	$1\frac{7}{8}$ in AF
0·812	$\frac{13}{16}$ in AF	1·968	50 mm AF
0·820	$\frac{7}{16}$ in Whitworth; $\frac{1}{2}$ in BSF	2·000	2 in AF
0·866	22 mm AF	2·050	$1\frac{1}{4}$ in Whitworth; $1\frac{3}{8}$ in BSF
0·875	$\frac{7}{8}$ in AF	2·165	55 mm AF
0·920	$\frac{1}{2}$ in Whitworth; $\frac{9}{16}$ in BSF	2·362	60 mm AF
0·937	$\frac{15}{16}$ in AF		

Routine maintenance

Maintenance is essential for ensuring safety and desirable for the purpose of getting the best in terms of performance and economy from the vehicle. Over the years the need for periodic lubrication – oiling, greasing and so on – has been drastically reduced if not totally eliminated. This has unfortunately tended to lead some owners to think that because no such action is required the items either no longer exist or will last for ever. This is a serious delusion. It follows therefore that the largest initial element of maintenance is visual examination. This may lead to repairs or renewals. Neglect results in unreliability, increased running costs, more rapid wear and more rapid depreciation of the vehicle in general.

The service intervals and the procedures given are basically those recommended by the vehicle manufacturer. The major service intervals have always been given in multiples of 6000 miles for vehicles manufactured up to 1974, but from 1975 an extended interval in multiples of 7500 miles has been introduced.

This longer service interval may be safely applied to earlier vehicles provided that the latest high quality recommended lubricants are used.

Where any vehicle is used under very arduous conditions, in very dusty atmospheres, in continual stop/start conditions or where the engine does not have a chance to thoroughly warm up, engine oil should be changed at intervals of 3000 miles. The vehicle manufacturers do not recommend supplemental oil additives, and only recommend oils of SE designation (GM specification 6136-M 1972).
Note: Where an item is referred to in the routine maintenance table, and that item is not applicable to a particular model, it is to be ignored.

Every 250 miles or weekly – whichever comes first

Steering
Check tire pressures.
Examine tires for wear or damage.

Brakes
Check master cylinder fluid reservoir.
Check parking brake operation.

Lights, wipers and horn
Check that all light bulbs are working.
Check wipers, washers and horns.

Engine
Check engine oil level.
Check coolant level.
Check battery electrolyte level.

Every 6000 miles (through 1974) or 7500 (1975 on)

Steering
Lubricate suspension.
Check power steering fluid level (where fitted).
Inspect all suspension and steering components for wear.

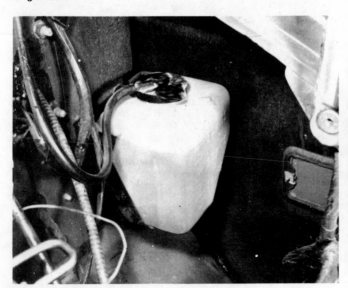

Washer fluid reservoir

Topping up engine oil

Rotate position of roadwheels to even-out tire tread wear.

Brakes

Check disc pad wear.
Check brake lines and hoses.
Check and lubricate parking brake cables.

Engine

Check drivebelt tension.
Renew engine oil and filter.
Clean and re-gap spark plugs.
Clean contact breaker points; check gap and dwell angle.
Check operation of temperature-controlled air cleaner.
Check operation of choke.
Check operation of manifold heat-valve (early models).
Check and adjust engine idling speed.
Check ignition timing.
Check all emission control systems for security of hoses and wires.

Transmission

Lubricate universal joints and propeller shaft slip joint.
Check and adjust clutch.
Check rear axle fluid level.
Check transmission fluid level.

Every 12 000 miles (through 1974) or 7500 (1975 on)

Brakes

Check rear drum linings.
Clean exterior of radiator and air conditioning condenser.

Engine

Renew carburetor fuel filter.
Renew PCV filter.
Clean EGR valve.

Check condition of exhaust system.
Renew spark plugs.
Renew contact breaker points.
Renew air cleaner element.
Check ignition timing.

Steering

Check front wheel alignment and steering angles.

Every 24 000 miles (through 1974) or 30 000 miles (1975 on)

Steering

Clean and repack the front wheel bearings.
Check steering gear for wear or leakage of oil.

Engine

Check and adjust valve lifters.
Renew antifreeze mixture and check hoses.
Check engine cylinder compression.
Renew distributor lubricator.
Renew evaporation control filter.

Transmission

Renew automatic transmission fluid.
Lubricate clutch cross-shaft.
Renew rear axle oil (fully floating axles).
Adjust rear hub bearings (fully floating axles).

Every 50 000 miles (or three years)

Renew the brake system hydraulic component seals.
Bleed the brake system and renew the fluid.
Renew brake booster air filter.

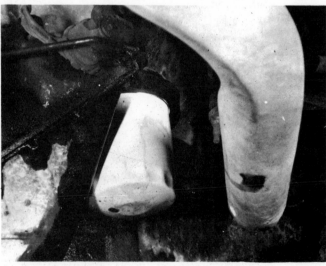

Engine oil filter location

Jacking and towing

The jack supplied with the vehicle varies in design according to the date of vehicle production. On earlier vehicles, the jack is positioned beneath the bumpers. On later models, the jack should be positioned under the suspension lower control arm or under the rear axle housing.

Only use the early-type bumper jack for highway emergency wheel changes. For repair work always use a hydraulic or screw jack, and then supplement it with axle stands.

If the vehicle needs to be towed or pushed, make sure that local laws are observed. If the vehicle is equipped with automatic transmission, restrict towing speed to 30 mph and distance to 25 miles; otherwise disconnect and remove the propeller shaft. Failure to do this may result in damage to the transmission.

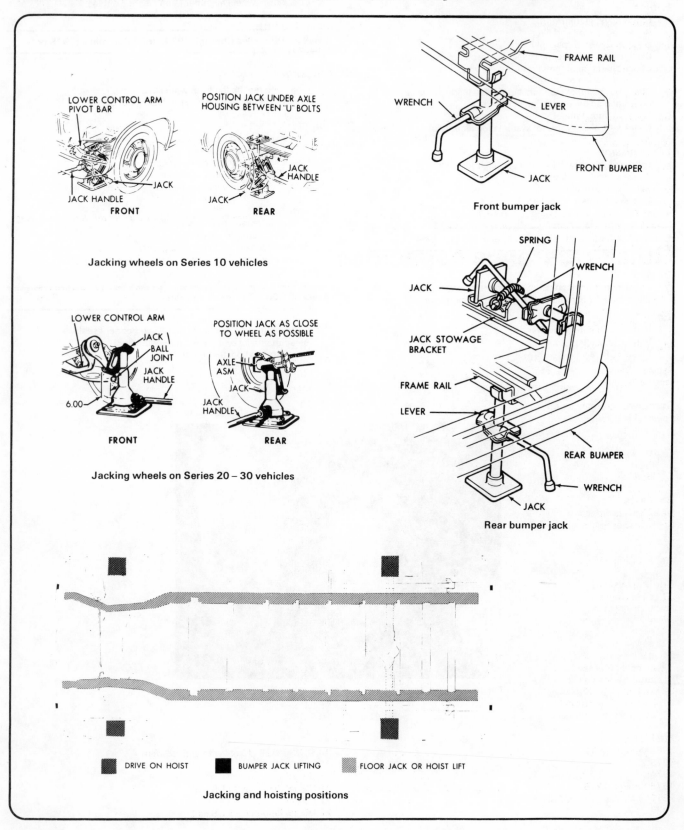

Jacking wheels on Series 10 vehicles

Jacking wheels on Series 20 – 30 vehicles

Front bumper jack

Rear bumper jack

Jacking and hoisting positions

Recommended lubricants

Component	Lubricants
Suspension and steering joints	Chassis lubricant
Wheel bearings	Wheel bearing lubricant
Brake master cylinder	Delco Supreme No. 11 or DOT 3/DOT 4
Manual transmission	GL-5
Automatic transmission	Dexron II or equivalent
Universal joints	Chassis lubricant
Propeller shaft slip joint	Chassis lubricant
Rear axle	GL-5

Note: *The above are general recommendations only. Lubrication requirements vary from territory to territory and depend on the vehicle usage. Consult the operators handbook supplied with the car.*

Quick reference capacities

Engine
Engine oil with filter change . . . .   5 US qts
Engine oil without filter change . . . .   4 US qts

Manual transmission
Warner 4-speed . . . .   6 US pints
Saginaw 3-speed . . . .   3.2 US pints
Muncie 3-speed . . . .   4.6 US pints

Automatic transmission
Powerglide 2-speed
   Refill . . . .   4 US pints
   From dry . . . .   16 US pints
Turbo Hydra-matic 350 or CBC 350
   Refill . . . .   5 US pints
   From dry . . . .   20 US pints

Rear axle
$8\frac{1}{2}$ in Dana or Salisbury . . . .   4.25 US pints
$8\frac{7}{8}$ in Dana or Salisbury . . . .   3.5 US pints
$9\frac{3}{4}$ in Dana . . . .   6.0 US pints
$10\frac{1}{2}$ in Dana . . . .   7.2 US pints
$10\frac{1}{2}$ in Chevrolet . . . .   5.4 US pints

Cooling system
230 cu in engine . . . .   13 US qts
250 cu in engine
   manual transmission . . . .   15 US qts
   automatic transmission . . . .   15.2 US qts
292 cu in engine . . . .   14.8 US qts
Small V8 engines (305, 307, 350 cu in)
   manual transmission . . . .   17.9 US qts
   automatic transmission . . . .   17.7 US qts
Large V8 engine (400 cu in)
   manual transmission . . . .   18.2 US qts
   automatic transmission . . . .   19.9 US qts

Fuel tank
1968 through 1972 . . . .   24.5 US gal (22 US gal with anti-overfill)
1973 . . . .   21 US gal
1974 . . . .   21 US gal
1975 through 1976 . . . .   21 US gal (optional 36 US gal)
1977 . . . .   22 US gal
1978 . . . .   22 US gal (optional 33 US gal)

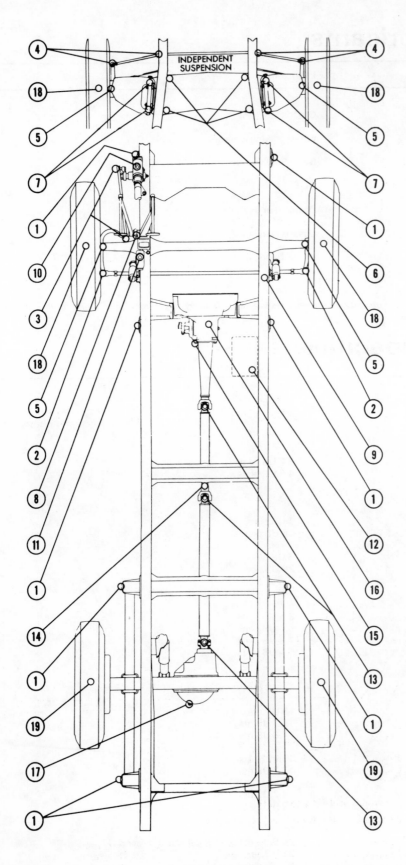

INDEPENDENT SUSPENSION

Lubrication chart 1968 through 1971

1 Spring shackles and brackets
2 Steering tie rod ends
3 Steering drag link
4 Steering outer links
5 Steering knuckles
6 Steering knuckle lower arm pin
7 Steering knuckle upper arm bracket
8 Clutch and brake pedals
9 Vacuum cylinder air cleaner
10 Steering gear housing
11 Brake master cylinder
12 Battery terminals
13 Propeller shaft U-joints
14 Propeller shaft slip joints
15 Speedometer adapter
16 Automatic transmission
16 Manual transmission
17 Rear axle
18 Front wheel bearings
19 Rear wheel bearings

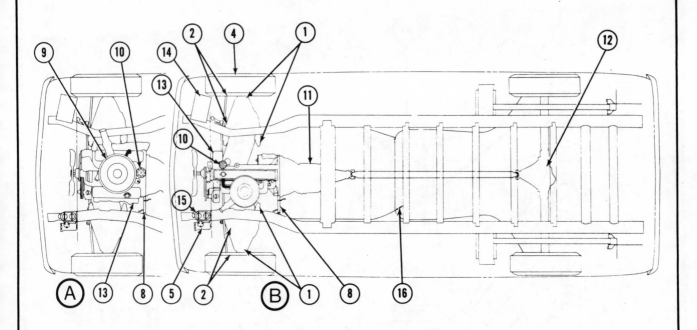

Lubrication chart 1972 through 1974

A   V8 engine   B   6-cylinder in-line engine

1 Control arm bushings and balljoints	5 Steering gear Clutch cross-shaft	9 Air cleaner element	13 Oil filter
2 Tie rod ends	8 Transmission control shaft	10 Distributor	14 Battery
4 Wheel bearings		11 Manual transmission	15 Brake master cylinder
		12 Rear axle	16 Parking brake linkage

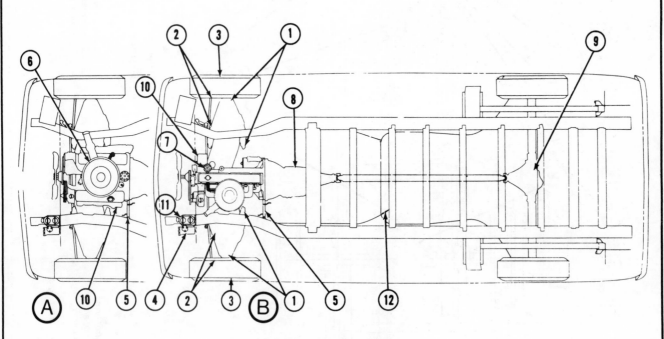

Lubrication chart ½ ton 1975 on

A   V8 engine   B   6-cylinder in-line engine

1 Control arm bushings and balljoints	4 Steering gear Clutch cross-shaft	6 Air cleaner element	9 Rear axle
2 Tie rod ends	5 Transmission control shaft	7 Distributor	10 Oil filter
3 Wheel bearings		8 Automatic transmission	11 Brake master cylinder
		8 Manual transmission	12 Parking brake linkage

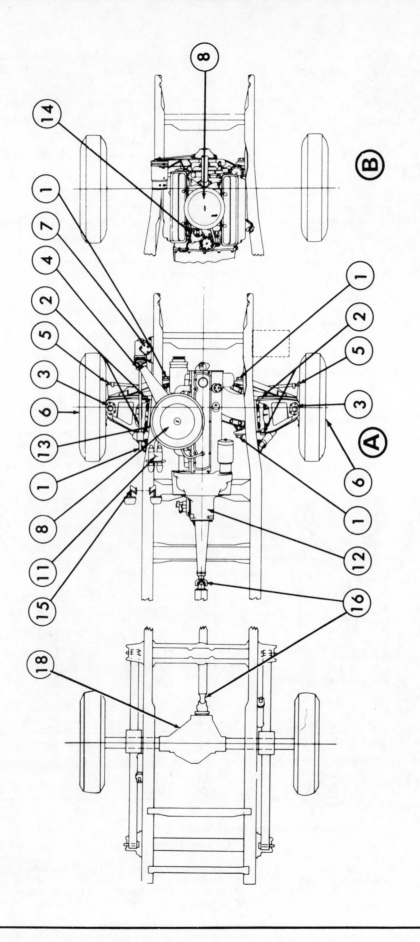

Lubrication chart ¾ and 1 ton 1975 on

A   6-cylinder in-line engine   B   V8 engine

1 Lower control arms	5 Tie rod ends
2 Upper control arms	6 Wheel bearings
3 Upper and lower control arm	7 Steering gear
balljoints	8 Air cleaner element
4 Intermediate steering shaft	

11 Master cylinder	14 Carburetor linkage
12 Automatic transmission	15 Brake and clutch pedal
12 Manual transmission	springs
13 Throttle bell crank	

16   Universal joints
17   Propeller shaft slip joint
18   Rear axle

Chapter 1 Engine

Contents

Specifications – general

Engine application chart

Year	Vehicle series	Standard engines	Optional engine
1968/1969	G10, G20	230 cu in 6-cyl	250 cu in 6-cyl *OR* 307 cu in V8
1970	G10, G20	250 cu in 6-cyl	307 *OR* 350 cu in V8
1971 thru 1973	G10, G20, G30	250 cu in 6-cyl	307 *OR* 350 cu in V8
1974	G10, G20, G30	250 cu in cyl	350 cu in V8
1975 thru 1978	G10, G20, G30	250 *OR* 292 cu in 6-cyl *OR* 350 cu in V8	305*, 350†, 305‡ *OR* 400 cu in V8

*Available from 1977, except California vehicles
† Engine with 2-barrel carburetor
‡ Engine with 4-barrel carburetor

Specifications – In-line engines

(All dimensions in inches unless otherwise stated)

Engine – general

		6 cylinder, in-line, overhead valves	
Type			
Displacement	**230 cu in**	**250 cu in**	**292 cu in**
Bore	3·875	3·875	3·875
Stroke	3·25	3·53	4·12
Compression ratio *	8·5 : 1	8·5 : 1	8·0 : 1
Compression pressure at cranking speed, throttle wide open*	130 lbf/in^2	130 lbf/in^2	130 lbf/in^2
Permitted difference in compression pressure between cylinders	20 lbf/in^2	20 lbf/in^2	20 lbf/in^2
Horsepower @ rpm	140@ 4400	155 @ 4200	170 @ 4000
Torque @ rpm	220 lbf ft	235 lbf ft	275 lbf ft
Firing order		1 – 5 – 3 – 6 – 2 – 4	

Cylinder bore

Diameter	3·8745 to 3·8775
Max. out-of-round	0·0005
Max. taper	0·0005

Pistons

Clearance between pistons and cylinder wall
230/250 engines	
Production (new)	0·0005 to 0·0014
Service (max)	0·0025
292 engine	
Production (new)	0·0026 to 0·0032
Service (max.)	0·0045

Piston rings

Groove clearance (compression rings)
Top compression: 230/250 engines	0·0012 to 0·0027
Top compression: 292 engine	0·0020 to 0·0040
Second compression: 230/250 engines	0·0012 to 0·0032
Second compression: 292 engine	0·0020 to 0·0040
End gap	0·010 to 0·020

Groove clearance (oil control)
230/250 engines	0 to 0·005
292 engine	0·0005 to 0·0055
End gap	0·015 to 0·055

Piston pins

Diameter	0·9270 to 0·9273

Clearance in piston
230/250 engines	0·00015 to 0·00025
292 engine	0·00025 to 0·00035
Fit in connecting rod (interference)	0·0008 to 0·0016

Crankshaft

Diameter (main journal)	2·2983 to 2·2993
Max. out-of-round	0·001
Max. taper	0·001

Running clearance (main bearings)
230/250 engines	0·0003 to 0·0029
292 engine	0·0008 to 0·0034
Maximum clearance	0·004
Crankshaft endfloat	0·002 to 0·006

Diameter (crankpin)
230/250 engines	1·999 to 2·000
292 engine	1·999 to 2·100
Max. out-of-round	0·001
Max. taper	0·001

Running clearance (connecting rod bearings)
230/250 engines	0·0007 to 0·0027
292 engine	0·0007 ιο 0·0027
Maximum clearance	0·004
Connecting rod side clearance	0·0085 to 0·0135

Camshaft

Lobe lift
230 engine	0·1896
250 engine	0·2217
292 engine	0·2315
Journal diameter	1·8682 to 1·8692

Runout (max.) . . . . 0·0015

Valves
Face angle . . . . 45°
Seat angle . . . . 46°
Seat width
   Intake . . . . $\frac{1}{32}$ to $\frac{1}{16}$
   Exhaust . . . . $\frac{1}{16}$ to $\frac{3}{32}$
Stem clearance
   Intake . . . . 0·0010 to 0·0027
   Exhaust . . . . 0·0015 to 0·0032
Valve lash . . . . One turn down from zero lash
Valve spring installed height
   Intake . . . . $1\frac{21}{32}$
   Exhaust
      230/250 engines . . . . $1\frac{21}{32}$
      292 engine . . . . $1\frac{5}{8}$

Oil capacities
Without oil filter change . . . . 4 US qt
With oil filter change . . . . 5 US qt

Compression ratios, compression pressures and engine torque may vary according to date of vehicle production and type of emission control equipment installed. Consult the vehicle decal for additional information.

Specifications – V8 engines

(All dimensions in inches unless otherwise stated)

Engine – general

Type	8 cylinder, V configuration, overhead valves			
Displacement	**305 cu in**	**307 cu in**	**350 cu in**	**400 cu in**
Bore	3·736	3·875	4·0	4·125
Stroke	3·48	3·25	3·48	3·75
Compression ratio *	8·5 : 1	9·0 : 1	8·5 : 1	8·5 : 1
Compression pressure at cranking speed throttle wide open *	130 lbf/in²	150 lbf/in²	150 lbf/in²	150 lbf/in²
Permitted difference in compression pressure between cylinders	20 lbf/in²	20 lbf/in²	20 lbf/in²	20 lbf/in²
Horsepower @ rpm	170 @ 4000	200 @ 4600	255 @ 4600	See decal
Torque @ rpm	275 @ 1600	300 @ 2400	355 @ 3000	See decal
Firing order	1 – 8 – 4 – 3 – 6 – 5 – 7 – 2			

Cylinder bore
Diameter
   305 engine . . . . 3·7350 to 3·7385
   307 engine . . . . 3·8745 to 3·8775
   350 engine . . . . 3·9995 to 4·0025
   400 engine . . . . 4·1246 to 4·1274
Maximum out-of-round . . . . 0·0005
Max. taper . . . . 0·0005

Pistons
Clearance between piston and cylinder wall
   305/350 engines
      Production (new) . . . . 0·0007 to 0·0017
      Service (max.) . . . . 0·0027
   307 engine
      Production (new) . . . . 0·0005 to 0·0011
      Service (max.) . . . . 0·0025
   400 engine
      Production (new) . . . . 0·0014 to 0·0024
      Service (max.) . . . . 0·0035

Piston rings
Groove clearance(compression rings)
   Top and second compression:
   305/350/400 engine . . . . 0·0012 to 0·0032
   Top compression: 307 engine . . . . . . 0·0007 to 0·0027
   Second compression: 307 engine . . . . . 0·0012 to 0·0032
   End gap: 305/350/400 engine
      Top ring . . . . 0·010 to 0·020
      2nd ring . . . . 0·010 to 0·025
   End gap: 307 engine
      Top and second rings . . . . 0·010 to 0·020

Oil control ring groove clearance
    305/350/400 engine . . . .   0.002 to 0.007
    307 engine . . . .   0 to 0.005
    End gap: all engines . . . .   0.015 to 0.55

Piston pins
Diameter . . . .   0.9270 to 0.9273
Clearance in piston
    305/350/400 engines . . . .   0.00025 to 0.00035
    307 engines . . . .   0.00015 to 0.00025
Fit in connecting rod (interference) . . . .   0.0008 to 0.0016

Crankshaft
Diameter (main journal)
    305/350 engines
        No. 1 journal . . . .   2.4484 to 2.4493
        No. 2, 3 and 4 journals . . . .   2.4481 to 2.4490
        No. 5 journal . . . .   2.4479 to 2.4488
    400 engine
        No. 1, 2, 3 and 4 journals . . . .   2.6484 to 2.6493
        No. 5 journal . . . .   2.6479 to 2.6488
    307 engine
        No. 1, 2, 3 and 4 journals . . . .   2.4484 to 2.4493
        No. 5 journal . . . .   2.4479 to 2.4488
Max. out-of-round 0.001
Max. taper 0.001
Running clearance (main bearings)
    305/350/400 engines
        No. 1 bearing . . . .   0.0008 to 0.0020
        No. 2, 3 and 4 bearings . . . .   0.0011 to 0.0023
        No. 5 bearing . . . .   0.0017 to 0.0032
    307 engine
        No. 1, 2, 3 and 4 bearings . . . .   0.0008 to 0.0024
        No. 5 bearing . . . .   0.0010 to 0.0026
Maximum clearance
    No. 1 bearing 0.002
    All other bearings 0.0035
Crankshaft endfloat
    305/350/400 engines . . . .   0.002 to 0.006
    307 engines . . . .   0.003 to 0.011
Diameter (crankpin) . . . .   2.199 to 2.200
Max. taper 0.001
Max. out-of-round 0.001
Running clearance (connecting rod bearings)
    305/350/400 engines . . . .   0.0013 to 0.0035
    307 engine . . . .   0.0007 to 0.0027
Connecting rod side clearance
    305/350/400 engines . . . .   0.008 to 0.014
    307 engine . . . .   0.009 to 0.013

Camshaft
Lobe lift
    Intake
        305 engine 0.2485
        307 engine 0.2658
        350 engine 0.2600
        400 engine 0.2600
    Exhaust
        305/350/400 engines 0.2733
        307 engine 0.2658
Journal diameter
    305/307/350 engines . . . .   1.8682 to 1.8692
    400 engine . . . .   1.9482 to 1.9492
Runout (max.) 0.0015

Valves
Face angle . . . .   45°
Seat angle . . . .   46°
Seat width
    Intake . . . . $\frac{1}{32}$ to $\frac{1}{16}$
    Exhaust . . . . $\frac{1}{16}$ to $\frac{3}{32}$
Valve lash . . . .   One turn down from zero lash
Valve spring installed height
    305/350/400 engines
        Intake . . . . $1\frac{23}{32}$
        Exhaust . . . . $1\frac{19}{32}$

307 engine
   Intake . . . . $1\frac{21}{32}$
   Exhaust . . . . $1\frac{21}{32}$

Oil capacities
Without filter change . . . . 4 US qt
With filter change . . . . 5 US qt

* Compression ratios, compression pressures and engine torque may vary according to date of vehicle production and type of emission control equipment installed. Consult the vehicle decal for additional information.

Torque wrench settings	lbf ft
In-line engines	
Connecting rod cap nuts	
230/250 engines	35
292 engine	40
Flywheel housing bolts	30
Thermostat housing bolts	30
Main bearing cap bolts	65
Flywheel bolts	
230/250 engines	60
292 engine	110
Torsional damper bolt	60
Cylinder head bolts	
1st stage	35
2nd stage	60
Final stage	95
Oil pan drain plug	20
Spark plugs	25
Oil filter center bolt (early type filter)	45
V8 engines	
Oil filter center bolt (where applicable)	25
Spark plugs	15
Flywheel bolts	
305/307/350 engines	60
400 engine	65
Camshaft sprocket bolts	20
Main bearing cap bolts	
305/307/350 engines	80
400 engine	110
Torsional damper bolt	
305/307/350 engines	60
400 engine	85
Flywheel housing bolts	30
Torque converter housing bolts	30
Connecting rod cap nuts	
305/307/350 engines	45
400 engine	50
Cylinder head bolts: 305/307/350 engines	
Stage 1	30
Stage 2	45
Final stage	65
Cylinder head bolts: 400 engine	
Stage 1	30
Stage 2	50
Final stage	80
Oil pump bolts	65
Oil pan drain plug	20

PART 1 – ENGINES GENERAL

1 General description

1   The engines used may be of six cylinder in-line or V8 type, according to vehicle model.

2   The engine capacity varies according to the year of production; also the engine size may be selected as a factory-fitted option.

3   All the power units are of conventional overhead valve design, and incorporate hydraulic valve lifters.

4   The cylinder block and heads are of cast iron construction.

5   On six cylinder in-line engines, the crankshaft is supported on seven main bearings with end-thrust being taken by No. 7 bearing. On V8 engines, the crankshaft is supported on five main bearings.

6   The camshaft is gear-driven from the crankshaft on in-line engines, and by chain on V8 engines.

7   The V8 engines used in the range of vehicle covered by this manual are known as *small* V8's with the exception of the 400 cu in unit which is known as *large* or Mk IV.

2 On-vehicle repairs

1   The following operations may be carried out without having to remove the engine from the vehicle.

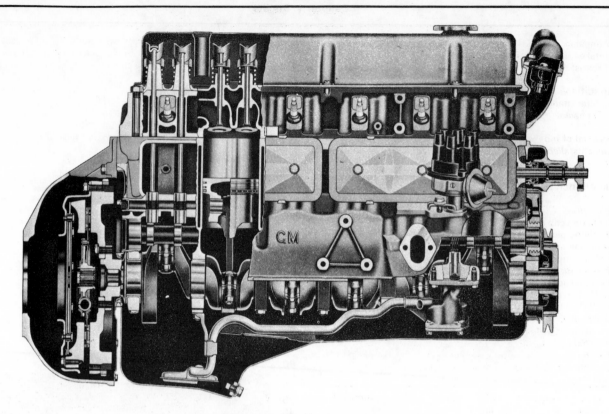

Fig. 1.1 Cutaway view of a six cylinder engine

Fig. 1.2 Cutaway view of a V8 engine

a) *Removal and installation of the cylinder heads.*
b) *Removal and installation of the intake and exhaust manifolds.*
c) *Removal and installation of the camshaft and timing gear.*
d) *Removal and installation of the piston/connecting rod assemblies.*
e) *Removal and installation of the oil pan and oil pump.*
f) *Renewal of the crankshaft rear oil seal.*

2   Removal of the crankshaft and flywheel, and renewal of the main bearings should be carried out after withdrawing the engine from the vehicle.

3   Engine – methods of removal

1968 through 1970
1   On these vehicles, the engine complete with transmission is removed from below the vehicle.

1971 through 1973
2   On these vehicles, the engine complete with transmission is removed in conjunction with the front suspension assembly.

1974 through 1976
3   On these vehicles, the engine complete with transmission is removed through the front of the engine compartment. *From 1977 onwards,* the removal method is similar except that the engine can be removed leaving the transmission in the vehicle.

4   Engine/transmission (1968 through 1970) – removal and installation

1   Position the vehicle over an inspection pit, or raise the front end on ramps or stands.
2   Drain the cooling system and disconnect the battery.
3   Remove the engine splash shields.
4   Disconnect the coolant hoses from the radiator.
5   Disconnect all electrical wires from the engine and transmission. If there is likely to be any doubt about their reconnection, mark them with a piece of tape.
6   Disconnect the accelerator linkage.
7   Disconnect the manual choke cable.
8   Disconnect the heater hoses.
9   Disconnect the fuel lines from the fuel pump.
10   Disconnect the engine-to-frame ground straps.
11   Disconnect the exhaust downpipes and move them to one side.
12   Remove the fan and pulley.
13   Disconnect the clutch actuating assembly from the transmission.
14   Disconnect the speedometer drive cable from the transmission.
15   Remove the propeller shaft (Chapter 7).
16   Disconnect the shift linkage from the transmission.
17   *On automatic transmission vehicles,* disconnect the automatic transmission fluid cooler lines, and plug the lines and openings.
18   Support the engine/transmission on a trolley jack, take the weight and then disconnect the engine front and rear mountings at the rear crossmember.
19   Make a final check to see that all connecting wires, pipes and controls have been detached, then lower the engine/transmission and withdraw it to the rear to clear the front suspension crossmember.
20   Installation is a reversal of removal but remember to refill the engine with oil and coolant, adjust the clutch free movement and top-up the transmission oil.

5   Engine/transmission (1971 through 1973) – removal and installation

1   Working inside the vehicle, remove the engine cover (photo).
2   Disconnect the battery.
3   Drain the cooling system.
4   Disconnect the heater hoses and the radiator hoses.
5   *On automatic transmission vehicles,* disconnect the fluid cooler lines from the radiator and plug them.
6   Remove the fan guard and radiator.
7   Disconnect all electric wires, connector plugs, and controls from

the engine and transmission. Identify each one as an aid to installation.
8   Disconnect all hoses and electrical leads from the engine which are part of the emission control system. Identify each one as an aid to installation later.
9   Disconnect the power brake vacuum line from the intake manifold.
10   Disconnect the fuel line from the fuel pump.
11   Disconnect the engine ground straps.
12   Disconnect the leads from the starter motor.
13   Disconnect the exhaust downpipe from the exhaust manifold and then remove the exhaust system complete.
14   Disconnect the clutch actuating mechanism from the transmission.
15   Disconnect the gearshift control from the transmission.
16   Remove the propeller shaft (Chapter 7).
17   Raise the front of the vehicle and support it securely under the bodyframe side rails. Leave the roadwheels still in contact with the ground.
18   Disconnect the mounting from the crossmember at the rear of the transmission.
19   Disconnect the front stabilizer bar from the frame brackets.
20   Disconnect the front shock absorber lower mountings and move the shock absorbers out of the way.
21   Disconnect the brake fluid line which runs to the front brakes at the 'T' union.
22   Disconnect the brake fluid line which runs to the rear brakes, at the right-hand bodyframe rail. Disconnect the steering idler arm and

Fig. 1.3 Removing engine/transmission on a support cradle

5.1 V8 engine with cover removed

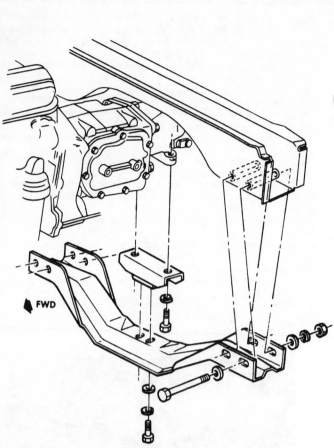

▲ FWD

Fig. 1.4 Engine/transmission rear mounting components

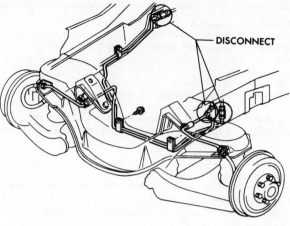

DISCONNECT

Fig. 1.5 Brake line disconnection points (1971 through 1973)

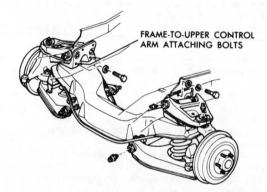

FRAME-TO-UPPER CONTROL ARM ATTACHING BOLTS

Fig. 1.6 Front suspension upper control arm attaching bolts

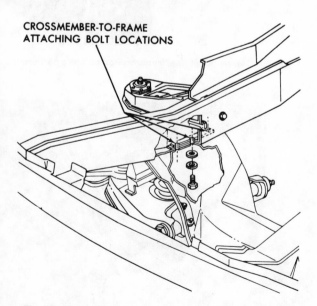

CROSSMEMBER-TO-FRAME ATTACHING BOLT LOCATIONS

Fig. 1.7 Front suspension crossmember attaching bolts

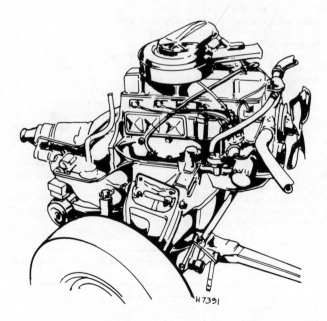

H7391

Fig. 1.8 Removing engine/transmission and suspension (1971 through 1973)

the Pitman arm.

23 Remove the bolts from the suspension upper control arm inner pivots. These are the bolts which attach the control arms to the front crossmember.

24 Remove all the bolts which attach the front crossmember to the bodyframe side-rails.

25 Support the transmission on a jack and then insert a block of wood between the oil pan and the front crossmember to prevent the transmission dropping when the support crossmember is unbolted from the side-rails. This should now be done.

26 Slowly raise the jacks under the side-rails until the vehicle is sufficiently high to enable the engine/transmission complete with front suspension assembly to be rolled out from under the front end.

27 Using a suitable hoist, the engine/transmission can be lifted off the suspension once the front mountings have been disconnected.

28 Installation is a reversal of removal but remember to refill the engine with oil and coolant, adjust the clutch free movement, top-up the transmission oil, then top-up and bleed the brake hydraulic system.

6 Engine/transmission (1974 through 1976) – removal and installation

1 Extract the screws from the radiator grille and remove the grille.

2 Drain the cooling system and disconnect the radiator and the heater hoses.

3 *On vehicles equipped with automatic transmission,* disconnect the fluid cooler lines and plug the pipes and the openings.

4 Remove the fan guard and the radiator.

5 Remove the radiator support and tie-bar.

6 Disconnect the battery cables.

7 Disconnect all electrical leads from the engine. Identify each one as an aid to installation.

8 If an oil pressure gage is fitted, disconnect the pipe from the engine.

9 Disconnect the fuel lines from the fuel pump.

10 Disconnect the engine ground straps.

11 Disconnect the speedometer drive cable from the transmission; also the shift linkage.

12 Disconnect the exhaust downpipes from the manifolds and then remove the exhaust system.

13 Disconnect the accelerator control.

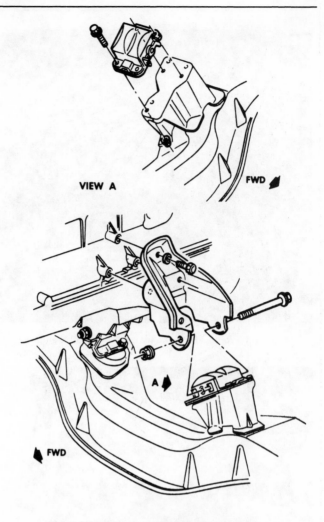

Fig. 1.9 Six cylinder engine front mountings

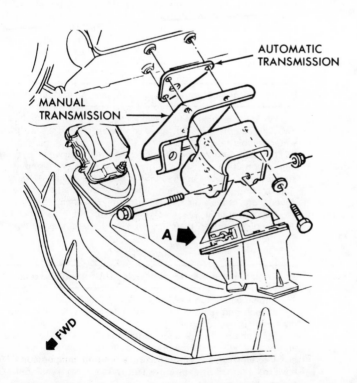

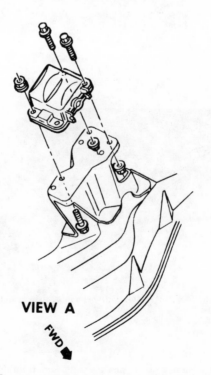

Fig. 1.10. V8 engine front mountings

Fig. 1.11 Typical lifting chain attachment to V8 engine

Fig. 1.12. Typical boom-type hoist

Fig. 1.13 Removing engine/transmission from front of vehicle (1974 through 1976)

14 Disconnect the clutch actuating linkage and remove the air cleaner.
15 Disconnect the spark plug leads and position them to one side.
16 Disconnect and remove the ignition coil.
17 Disconnect the vacuum hose for the power brakes from the intake manifold.
18 Remove the propeller shaft (Chapter 7).
19 Working inside the vehicle, remove the engine cover.
20 The weight of the engine/transmission should now be taken on a boom-type (cantilever type) hoist. Disconnect the engine front and rear mountings, remove the rear mounting crossmember and withdraw the engine/transmission forward from the vehicle (photo).
21 Installation is a reversal of removal but remember to refill the engine with oil and coolant, adjust the clutch free movement and top up the transmission oil.

7 Engine (1977 onward) – removal and installation

1   The operations are very similar to those described in Section 6 but nothing need be disconnected from the transmission as this is remaining in the vehicle. The following additional work must be carried out however.
2   *On vehicles equipped with power steering* unbolt the pump and lay it to one side.
3   Remove the starter motor.
4   Remove the flywheel or torque converter housing cover.
5   *On vehicles with manual transmission,* remove the bellhousing-to-engine bolts.
6   *On vehicles with automatic transmission,* working through the aperture now open by removal of the cover plate, unscrew each of the converter-to-flexplate bolts. The engine will have to be turned in order to bring each bolt into view. Also mark the relative position of the flexplate to the converter.
7   Support the transmission on a jack and then take the weight of the engine on a suitable boom-type (cantilever type) hoist.
8   Disconnect the engine front mountings, raise the front of the engine at an angle and then withdraw it forward from the vehicle.
9   Installation is a reversal of removal but if the clutch has been disturbed, it must be centralized as described in Chapter 5 before the engine can be fitted to the transmission.
10 *On automatic transmission vehicles,* do not allow the torque converter to fall forward when removing the engine, but secure it with a tool as described in Chapter 6. When refitting the engine to the automatic transmission, push the torque converter fully rearwards and turn it to ensure that the tangs are engaged with the oil pump drive.
11 Refill the engine with oil and coolant, adjust the clutch free movement and then top up the transmission oil.

8 Engine/manual transmission – separation and reconnection

1   With the engine/transmission removed from the vehicle, clean away all external dirt. Do this using kerosene and a stiff brush, or a water-soluble solvent.
2   Unscrew and remove the bolts from the flywheel housing and then, supporting the weight of the transmission, withdraw it in a straight line from the engine. Do not allow the weight of the transmission to hang upon the clutch shaft while the shaft is engaged in the driven plate, or the clutch mechanism may be damaged.
3   Reconnection is a reversal of separation but if the clutch has been disturbed, the driven plate must be centralized first as described in Chapter 5.

9 Engine/automatic transmission – separation and reconnection

1   Repeat paragraph 1 of Section 8.
2   Unbolt and remove the cover plate from the lower front face of the torque converter housing.
3   Mark the relative position of the flexplate to the torque converter and then unbolt the flexplate from the torque converter. To bring each bolt into view so that it can be unscrewed, the engine crankshaft will have to be turned by applying a wrench to the crankshaft pulley bolt. If the spark plugs are first removed, the job will be made easier.
4   Disconnect the detent (downshift) rod or cable, then extract the

bolts which hold the torque converter housing to the engine.

5   Support the weight of the transmission and withdraw it in a straight line. As the transmission starts to move, pry the torque converter rearwards. This will prevent loss of fluid and keep the torque converter in engagement with the oil pump.

6   Once the transmission has been withdrawn, use a tool similar to the one described in Chapter 6 to keep the torque converter in the fully rearward position.

7   Reconnection is a reversal of separation. Remember to align the flexplate marks with those made on the torque converter.

10 Engine dismantling – general

1   It is best to mount the engine on a dismantling stand but if one is not available, then stand the engine on a strong bench so as to be at a comfortable working height.

2   During the dismantling process the greatest care should be taken to keep the exposed parts free from dirt. As an aid to achieving this, it is a sound scheme to thoroughly clean down the outside of the engine, removing all traces of oil and congealed dirt.

3   Use kerosene or a water-soluble grease solvent. The latter compound will make the job much easier, as, after the solvent has been applied and allowed to stand for a time, a vigorous jet of water will wash off the solvent and all the grease and filth. If the dirt is thick and deeply embedded, work the solvent into it with a wire brush.

4   Finally wipe down the exterior of the engine with a rag and only then, when it is quite clean should the dismantling process begin. As the engine is stripped, clean each part in a bath of kerosene or gasoline.

5   Never immerse parts which have internal oilways (such as the crankshaft) in kerosene but wipe them carefully with a gasoline soaked rag. Probe the oilways with a length of wire and if an air line is available, blow the oilways through to clean them.

6   Re-use of old engine gaskets is false economy and can give rise to oil and water leaks, if nothing worse. To avoid the possibility of trouble after the engine has been reassembled, **always** use new gaskets throughout.

7   Do not throw the old gaskets away as it sometimes happens that an immediate replacement cannot be found and the old gasket is then very useful as a template. Hang up the old gaskets as they are removed on a suitable hook or nail.

8   Wherever possible, install nuts, bolts and washers finger-tight from wherever they were removed. This helps avoid later loss and muddle. If they cannot be installed then lay them out in such a fashion that it is clear from where they came.

9   It is recommended that if a major overhaul is being carried out that all the ancillary components such as the emission control equipment (see Chapter 3), the fuel pump, distributor and alternator, together with the water pump, are first removed from the engine as described in the appropriate Chapters of this Manual.

6.20 Rear mounting crossmember

PART 2 – IN-LINE ENGINES

11 Cylinder head – removal

1   If the engine is in position in the vehicle, disconnect the battery, drain the cooling system and disconnect all hoses, controls and wires from the cylinder head.

2   Remove the manifold assembly complete with carburetor.

3   Extract the bolts from the rocker cover and then remove the cover. If the cover is stuck tight tap the front end of the cover with a rubber mallet.

4   Unscrew each of the rocker arm nuts in sequence and remove the rocker arm ball, rocker arm and pushrod. Keep the components together. The best way to do this is to sub-divide a box or tray with the divisions numbered 1 to 12, number 1 being at the front end of the engine.

5   Disconnect the radiator upper hose.

6   Disconnect the ground strap from the cylinder head.

7   Unscrew the cylinder head bolts and lift the cylinder head from the block. If it is stuck tight, tap it sharply with a heavy hammer but use a block of hardwood as an insulator.

8   Remove and discard the cylinder head gasket.

12 Cylinder head – dismantling

1   Using a suitable valve spring compressor, compress each spring in turn to permit the locks to be removed. Release the compressor and remove the spring cap or rotator, shield (where applicable), spring and damper, then remove the oil seals and spring shims.

2   Remove the valves and place them in the box in their proper sequence with their associated pushrods etc (see previous Section).

3   Unscrew and remove each spark plug.

13 Crankshaft – torsional damper – removal

1   If the engine is still in position in the vehicle then drain the cooling system, remove the radiator and drivebelts.

2   Unscrew and remove the bolts which secure the crankshaft pulley. Pull off the crankshaft pulley.

3   The torsional damper should now be removed using the special tool J-23523 or a three legged puller engaged in the cut-outs of the damper (Fig. 1.14).

4   If it is a problem to prevent the crankshaft turning when the pulley bolts are being unscrewed, jam the flywheel starter ring gear with a large screwdriver or cold chisel inserted either through the bellhousing cover plate aperture or through the hole left when the starter is removed.

14 Timing gear and camshaft – removal

1   Remove the crankshaft torsional damper as described in the preceding Section.

2   Unscrew and remove the two screws which hold the oil pan to the timing cover.

3   Unscrew and remove the screws which hold the timing cover to the front face of the engine.

4   If the oil pan is still in position, then the oil pan front flange gasket should be cut-through flush (on both sides) with the cylinder block. If the oil pan has been removed or is going to be removed, then the oil pan gasket can be destroyed by pulling the timing cover forward.

5   Remove the timing cover and gasket.

6   Drive out and discard the cover oil seal.

7   Unbolt and remove the pushrod covers from the side of the engine and extract the valve lifters. Keep them in their original order together with the other valve components in the sub-divided box.

8   Make sure that the fuel pump was removed at an earlier stage (see Section 10) and then turn the crankshaft until the timing marks on the timing gears are in alignment.

9   By inserting a socket wrench through the holes in the larger gearwheel, the camshaft thrust plate bolts can now be unscrewed.

10 Pull the camshaft and gear from the engine out of the front of the block. Take care not to damage the camshaft bearings as the lobes of

the cams pass through them.
11 If the camshaft gear must be removed, then a press will be required and in consequence this job should be left to your dealer.

15 Oil pan and pump – removal

1   If the engine is in position in the vehicle, disconnect the battery, drain the engine oil, remove the starter motor, and flywheel housing cover plate. Disconnect the engine front mountings and raise the engine using a hoist or with a jack placed under the crankshaft torsional damper.
2   Unscrew and remove the oil pan bolts and remove the oil pan.
3   Unscrew and remove the two flange mounting bolts from the oil pump.
4   Unscrew and remove the bolt which secures the pick-up pipe in position and then withdraw the oil pump and pipe complete with filter screen.

16 Piston/connecting rod assemblies – removal

1   If the engine is still in position in the vehicle, remove the cylinder head, oil pan and oil pump as described in earlier Sections of this Chapter.

2   Feel round the tops of the cylinder bores. If a distinct wear ridge can be felt, then this must be carefully scraped away before any attempt is made to push the pistons out of the top of the block.
3   Check that each connecting rod big-end bearing cap is numbered 1 to 6 from the front of the engine with a corresponding number on the connecting rod at an adjacent point. If these numbers are not visible, dot punch both caps and rods. Note also to which side the numbers face. Although the notch in the piston crown faces the front of the engine and so will determine which way round the connecting rod is located, this may not be very helpful if new components are fitted or if the piston is removed from the connecting rod before marking it.
4   Unscrew and remove the nuts from the connecting rod caps, and remove the caps. If the original shell bearings are to be used again, make sure that they are kept with their respective caps by taping them together.
5   Using the wooden handle of a hammer, tap the piston/connecting rod assemblies out of the top of the cylinder block. As each assembly is removed, clean the piston crown and check that it bears the correct cylinder sequence number. If not, mark it unless the pistons are not to be removed from their connecting rods or if new pistons are to be fitted.
6   To remove all six pistons, the crankshaft will have to be rotated in order to bring some of the cap nuts into a suitable position for removal.
7   If the shell bearings are to be used again, retain the rod bearings

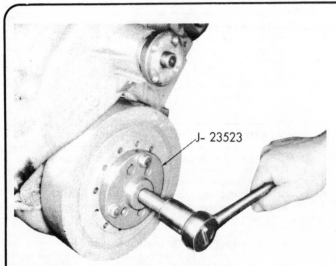
Fig. 1.14 Using special tool to remove torsional damper

Fig. 1.16 Timing gear marks (6-cylinder engine)

Fig. 1.15 Cutting through tabs on oil pan front seal

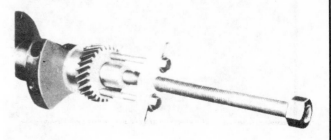
Fig. 1.17 Removing crankshaft sprocket gear

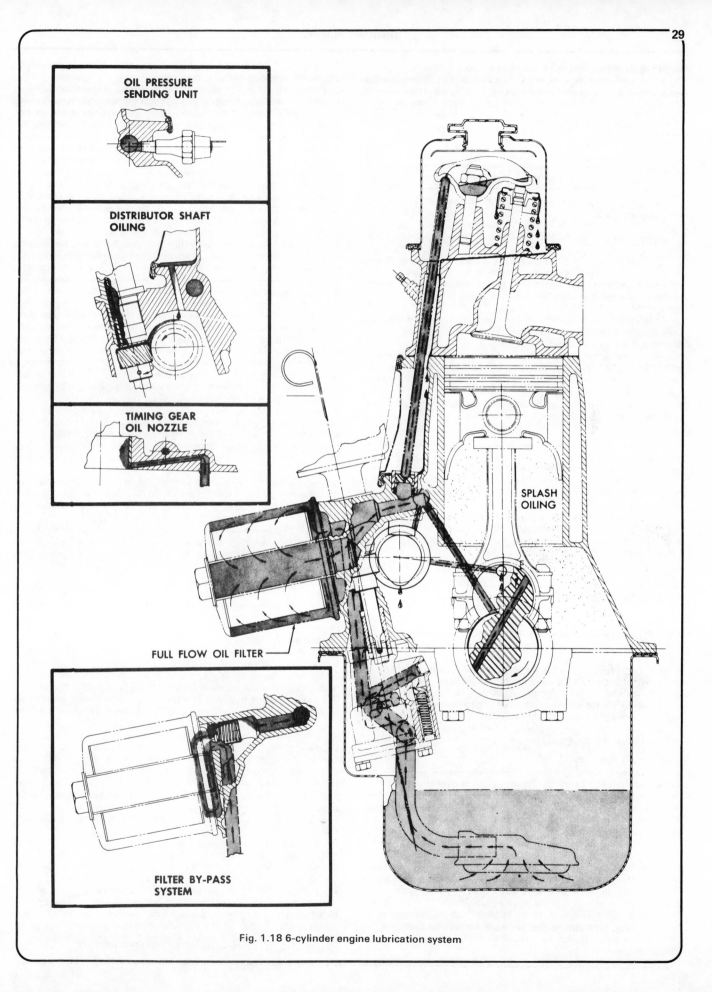

OIL PRESSURE
SENDING UNIT

DISTRIBUTOR SHAFT
OILING

TIMING GEAR
OIL NOZZLE

FULL FLOW OIL FILTER

FILTER BY-PASS
SYSTEM

SPLASH
OILING

Fig. 1.18 6-cylinder engine lubrication system

with their respective rods in a similar way to those for the caps.

8   Piston rings can be removed by slipping two or three old feeler blades behind the top ring and removing it using a twisting motion. The feeler blades will prevent the lower rings dropping into the higher empty grooves from which the rings have already been removed.

9   The piston pins are an interference fit in the connecting rods and removal should be left to your dealer (see Section 22).

17 Crankshaft and main bearings – removal

1   With the connecting rod/piston assemblies removed as described in the preceding Section, remove the clutch by unbolting the clutch pressure plate cover and extracting the driven plate.

2   Unbolt and remove the flywheel (or flexplate, automatic transmission).

3   Check that the main bearing caps are numbered in sequence from the front of the engine and also that they indicate which way round they are fitted by a directional arrow. If such markings are indistinct, re-mark the caps and their adjacent crankshaft webs with dots by using a punch.

4   Unbolt each main bearing cap and remove it, keeping the bearing shell together with its cap if the shells are to be used again.

5   Lift the crankshaft from the crankcase.

6   Extract the half shells from the crankcase, keeping them identified in respect of position if they are to be used again. The shell bearings used on No. 7 main bearing position incorporate thrust flanges to control crankshaft endfloat.

7   If necessary, the gear can be drawn off the front end of the crankshaft with a suitable puller (Fig. 1.17).

18 Lubrication system

1   Engine lubrication is provided by a gear-type oil pump which is driven by an extension of the distributor shaft which itself is driven by a helical gear on the camshaft.

2   Full pressure lubrication is provided through a full-flow filter. The main oil gallery supplies oil through drilled passages to the camshaft and crankshaft bearings, also to the hydraulic type valve lifters. The rocker arms are fed through hollow pushrods.

19 Examination and renovation – general

1   With the engine completely stripped, clean every component (except the cylinder bores) in kerosene and dry off. Make sure that all oilways are then thoroughly cleaned out to remove all trace of kerosene.

2   Pay particular attention to the engine block. Scrape off old pieces of gasket or jointing compound, probe the oilways and waterways, examine the casting for cracks, and check the freeze plugs for security.

3   **Never clean the cylinder bores with gasoline or kerosene but use hot water and detergent and when dry, apply clean engine oil.**

4   The individual components should be carefully checked for wear or distortion, as described in the following Sections.

20 Crankshaft and bearings – examination and renovation

1   Examine the crankpin and main journal surfaces for scoring, scratches or corrosion. If evident, then the crankshaft will have to be reground professionally.

2   Using a micrometer, test each journal and crankpin at several different points for ovality. If this is found to be more than 0.001 inch then the crankshaft must be reground. Undersize bearings are available as listed in Specifications to suit the recommended reground diameter, but normally your Chevrolet dealer will supply the correct matching bearings with the reconditioned crankshaft.

3   After a high mileage, the main bearings and the connecting rod bearings may have worn to give an excessive running clearance. The correct running clearance for the different journals is given in the Specifications.

    The clearance is best checked using a proprietary product such as

'Plastigage', having refitted the original bearings and caps and tightened the cap bolts to the torque settings specified in the Specifications. **Never attempt to correct excessive running clearance by filing the caps. Always fit new shell bearings,** having first checked the crankshaft journals and crankpins for ovality and to establish whether their diameters are of standard or reground sizes. Do not turn the crankshaft while the 'Plastigage' material is in position.

4   Checking the connecting rod bearings is carried out in a similar manner to that described for the main bearings. The correct running clearance is given in the Specifications.

5   The crankshaft endplay should be checked by forcing the crankshaft to the extreme front position, then using a feeler gauge at the front end of the rear main bearing. Refer to the Specifications for the permissible clearance (Fig. 1.19).

6   The connecting rod side-clearance should be measured with a feeler gauge between the connecting rod caps. If the side clearance is outside the specified tolerance, renew the rod assembly (Fig. 1.20).

21 Cylinder block – examination and renovation

1   The cylinder bores must be examined for taper, ovality, scoring and scratches. Start by carefully examining the top of the bores. If they are worn, a ridge will be found on the thrust side. The bottom of the ridge marks the upper limit of piston ring travel and the thickness of the ridge will be a guide to the amount of bore wear.

2   Another indication of cylinder bore wear will be evident before engine dismantling takes place by the emission of blue smoke from the exhaust and the frequent need for topping-up the engine oil.

3   Using an internal type dial gauge, measure each bore at three different points in both the thrust and axial directions. Carry out this operation near the top of the bore and then near the bottom of the bore. From the readings obtained, establish the out-of-round which must not exceed 0.002 inch, and the taper which must not exceed 0.005 inch.

4   Where the cylinder bores are worn beyond the permitted tolerance then they must be honed or bored to the next oversize. This is a specialist operation and must be carried out in a properly equipped workshop.

5   New pistons are available in standard and oversizes as listed in the Specifications Section and they will be supplied to match the new bore diameters of the cylinder block. Keep each piston identified in respect of its cylinder. The maximum permissible piston to bore clearance is given in the Specifications.

22 Pistons, piston pins and rings – servicing

Note: *Refer to Section 26 for decarbonising.*

1   Each ring should be sprung open only just sufficiently to permit it to ride over the lands of the piston body.

2   Once a ring is out of its groove, it is helpful to cut three $\frac{1}{4}$ inch wide strips of tin and slip them under the ring at equidistant points.

3   Using a twisting motion this method of removal will prevent the ring dropping into an empty groove as it is being removed from the piston.

4   If the old pistons are to be re-installed, carefully remove the piston rings and then thoroughly clean them. Take particular care to clean out the piston ring grooves. At the same time do not scratch the aluminum in any way. If new rings are to be installed to the old pistons then the top ring should be stepped so as to clear the ridge left in the cylinder bore, above the previous top ring. If a normal but oversize new ring is used, it will hit the ridge and brake, because the new ring will not have worn in the same way as the old, which will have worn in unison with the ridge.

5   Both compression rings are marked to indicate their top surfaces and the upper compression ring is chromium plated or treated with a molybdenum compound. The oil control ring is of three section construction.

6   Before installing the compression rings, insert each one in turn, into its respective cylinder bore. Push the ring squarely down the bore to a position about $\frac{1}{4}$ inch below its normal upper travel limit. Now measure the end gap with a feeler blade and compare the gap with that given in the Specifications. Carefully grind the endfaces of the rings if necessary to adjust the gap.

7   Now check the fit of the piston rings in their grooves, removing

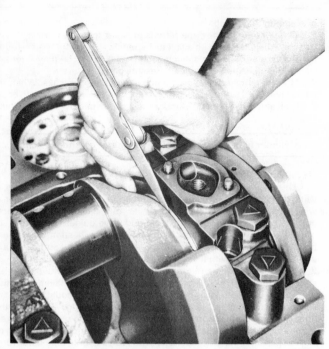

Fig. 1.19 Checking crankshaft endfloat

Fig. 1.20 Checking connecting rod side clearance

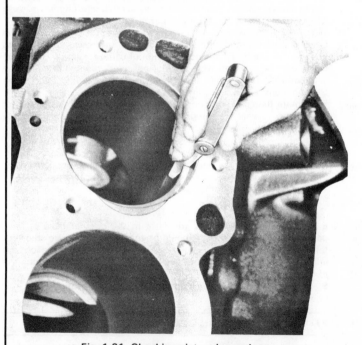

Fig. 1.21. Checking piston ring end gap

Fig. 1.22. Checking piston ring groove clearance

ENGINE FRONT

Fig. 1.23 Piston ring end gap installation diagram (6-cylinder)

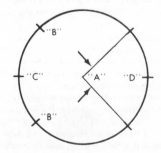

A   Ring spacer gap (oil control)
B   Ring rail gaps (oil control)
C   2nd compression
D   Top compression

any burrs which might cause them to stick.

8   Using a feeler blade, check the ring to groove clearance and compare the clearances with those given in the Specifications.

9   Refitting piston rings to the piston is a reversal of the removal method but ensure that the end-gaps of the rings are positioned as indicated to prevent gas blow-by (Fig. 1.23).

10 The piston pins are a press fit and are only available as matched sets together with the pistons.

11 In order to remove a piston from the connecting rod, an arbor press will be required and this is usually a job best left to your Chevrolet dealer. The relationship of the piston to connecting rod is very important.

23 Camshaft and bearings – examination and renovation

1   Check all the cam lobes for wear, chipping and scoring.

2   Check the teeth of the cam gearwheel for worn or chipped teeth.

3   Where any fault shows up, the camshaft will have to be renewed. Removal of the gearwheel is explained in Section 14.

4   If the camshaft bearings are worn, renewal is best left to your dealer although they can be removed and new ones installed using a long bolt, nut, washer and distance pieces to draw the bearings out of, or into, their crankcase seats.

5   When drawing new bearings into position, make sure that the oil hole in the bearing is in alignment with the one in the crankcase. The plug at the rear of the camshaft must be removed from the cylinder block in order to renew the camshaft bearings. Install a new plug on completion, flush with the rear face of the cylinder block.

24 Oil pump – overhaul

Note: *Oil pump gears and the body are not serviced separately. If wear or damage is evident on the gears or body, the complete pump assembly must be renewed.*

1   Remove the pump cover retaining screws and the pump cover. Index mark the gearteeth to permit reassembly in the same position.

2   Remove the idler gear, drivegear and shaft from the body.

3   Remove the pressure regulator valve retaining pinn th regulator valve and the related parts.

4   If necessary, the pick-up screen and pipe assembly can be extracted from the pump body.

5   Wash all the parts in kerosene or gasoline, and thoroughly dry them. Inspect the body for cracks, wear or other damage. Similarly inspect the gears.

6   Check the drivegear shaft for looseness in the pump body, and the inside of the pump cover for wear that would permit oil leakage past the ends of the gears.

7   Inspect the pick-up screen and pipe assembly for damage to the screen, pipe or relief grommet.

8   Apply a gasket sealant to the end of the pipe (pick-up screen and pipe assembly) and tap it into the pump body taking care that no damage occurs. If the original press-fit cannot be obtained a new assembly must be used to prevent air leaks and loss of pressure. Make sure that the final setting of the filter screen is parallel to the bottom face of the oil pan.

9   Install the pressure regulator valve and related parts.

10 Install the drivegear and shaft in the pump body, followed by the idler gear, with the smooth side towards the pump cover opening. Lubricate the parts with engine oil.

11 Install the cover and tighten the screws to the specified torque.

12 Turn the driveshaft to ensure that the pump operates freely.

25 Oil filter – renewal

1   *On some earlier type engines,* the oil filter may be the separate disposable internal element type.

2   To renew this type of filter element, unscrew the through-bolt and draw the filter body downward. Be prepared for some loss of engine oil.

3   Discard the internal element and wipe out the interior of the casing. Install the new rubber sealing ring and washers supplied with the new element.

4   Refit the components in the reverse order to removal but do not overtighten the through bolt.

5   *On all other engines,* the filter is of the disposable cartridge type. Unscrew the old filter with a suitable wrench.

6   Apply grease to the sealing rubber gasket on the new filter and screw it into position using hand pressure only.

7   Run the engine for a few minutes and check for leaks. When the oil has had time to settle after the engine has been switched off, check the level and top-up to make-up for the oil absorbed by the new filter.

26 Cylinder head – decarbonising, examination and servicing

Decarbonising

1   This can be carried out with the engine either in or out of the car. With the cylinder head off, carefully remove with a blunt scraper or wire brush all traces of carbon deposits from the combustion spaces and the ports. The valve head stems and valve guides should also be freed from any carbon deposits. Wash the combustion spaces and ports down with gasoline and scrape the cylinder head surface free of any foreign matter with the side of a steel rule, or a similar article.

2   Clean the pistons and top of the cylinder bores. If the pistons are still in the block then it is essential that great care is taken to ensure that no carbon gets into the cylinder bores as this could scratch the cylinder walls or cause damage to the piston and rings. To ensure this does not happen, first turn the crankshaft so that two of the pistons are at the top of their bores. Stuff rag into the other bores or seal them off with paper and masking tape. The waterways should also be covered with small pieces of masking tape to prevent particles of carbon entering the cooling system and damaging the water pump.

3   Press a little grease into the gap between the cylinder walls and the two pistons which are to be worked on.

4   With a blunt scraper carefully scrape away the carbon from the piston crown, taking great care not to scratch the aluminum. Also scrape away the carbon from the surrounding lip of the cylinder wall. When all carbon has been removed, scrape away the grease which will now be contaminated with carbon particles, taking care not to press any into the bores. To assist prevention of carbon build-up the piston crown can be polished with a metal polishing compound but on no account allow this to seep down the cylinder bore or it will congeal in the ring grooves and cause the rings to seize.

5   Rotate the crankshaft until the next two pistons are at the top of their bores. Repeat the foregoing operation until all six cylinders are decarbonised.

Examination

6   Inspect the cylinder head for cracks in the exhaust ports and combustion chambers, or external cracks into the water chambers.

7   Inspect the rocker arm studs for wear and damage.

Servicing

8   If the rocker arm studs are loose in the cylinder head or have damaged threads, then they should be renewed by oversize studs but this will require reaming the holes to accept them and this is a job best left to your dealer. It is important that the correct interference fit is obtained for the new studs.

9   Refer to the next two Sections for details of valve renovation.

27 Valves and valve seats – examination and renovation

1   Examine the heads of the valves for pitting and burning, especially the heads of the exhaust valves. The valve seatings should be examined at the same time. If the pitting on valve and seat is very slight the marks can be removed by grinding the seats and valves together with coarse, and then fine, valve grinding paste.

2   Valve grinding is carried out as follows: Smear a trace of coarse carborundum paste on the seat face and apply a suction grinder tool to the valve head. With a semi-rotary motion, grind the valve head to its seat, lifting the valve occasionally to redistribute the grinding paste. When a dull matt even surface finish is produced on both the valve seat and the valve, wipe off the paste and repeat the process with fine carborundum paste, lifting and turning the valve to redistribute the paste as before. A light spring placed under the valve head will greatly ease this operation. When a smooth unbroken ring of light grey matt finish is produced, on both valve and valve seat faces, the grinding

operation is completed.

3   Where the valve or seat shows signs of bad pitting or burning, then the valve should be refaced by your dealer and the seat recut. If the refacing of the valve will reduce the edge of the valve head to less than that given in the Specifications, renew the valve.

4   Scrape away all carbon from the valve head and the valve stem. Carefully clean away every trace of grinding compound, taking great care to leave none in the ports or in the valve guides. Clean the valves and valve seats with a kerosene soaked rag then with a clean rag, and finally, if an air line is available, blow the valves, valve guides and valve ports clean.

28 Valve guides and springs – examination and renovation

1   Thoroughly clean out each valve guide and then insert the appropriate valve. Using a dial gauge test the movement of the valve (at 90° to the centerline of the cylinder head) making sure that the valve is held from its seat by about $\frac{1}{16}$ inch.

2   If the stem clearance exceeds that given in the Specifications it will be necessary to ream the valve guide and install oversize valve stems. Check the availability with your Chevrolet dealer or engine repair specialist for this servicing operation.

3   Each valve spring and damper should be compared with the specified free-length and renewed if it is shorter. In any event it is recommended that new springs and dampers are installed if the engine has covered more than 30 000 miles since they were new.

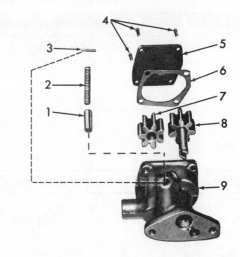

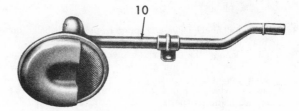

Fig. 1.25. Exploded view of the oil pump (6-cylinder)

1 Pressure regulating valve	6 Cover gasket
2 Spring	7 Idler gear
3 Retaining pin	8 Drive gear and shaft
4 Screws	9 Pump body
5 Oil pump cover	10 Pick-up screen and pipe.

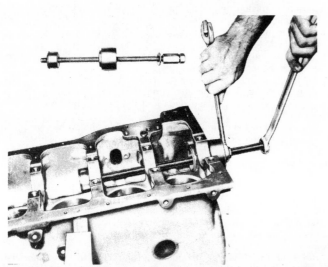

Fig. 1.24 Renewing camshaft bearings

Fig. 1.26 Disposable internal element type oil filter

Fig. 1.27. Disposable cartridge type oil filter

29 Flywheel (or flexplate) and starter ring gear – examination

1   The starter ring gear is attached to the outer edge of the flywheel (manual transmission) or the flexplate (automatic transmission). If the gear teeth are chipped or broken, renew the flywheel or flexplate complete.
2   Examine the driven plate contact surface of the flywheel. If deep scoring or tiny cracks are visible (due to overheating), then renew the flywheel.
3   If the flexplate bolt holes appear elongated then renew the flexplate.

30 Valve lifters – dismantling, cleaning and reassembly

1   The valve lifters are the hydraulic type and are designed to reduce engine valve noise and to obviate the need for precise valve clearance adjustment.
2   To disassemble, hold down the plunger with a pushrod and remove the rod seat retainer with a small screwdriver.
3   Remove the pushrod seat and metering valve.
4   Remove the plunger, ball check valve assembly and plunger spring.
5   Remove the ball check valve and spring by prying the ball retainer loose from the plunger with the blade of a small screwdriver.
6   Thoroughly clean all the parts and inspect for wear or damage. If any parts are unserviceable the complete lifter must be renewed. Where wear is present, also inspect the mating surfaces (eg; the camshaft lobe, cylinder block lifter bore, pushrod end) and renew/repair the appropriate parts.
7   To assemble, place the check ball on the small hole in the bottom of the plunger. Insert the spring on the seat in the ball retainer then place the retainer over the ball so that the spring rests on the ball (Fig. 1.29).
8   Carefully press the retainer into position in the plunger with the blade of a small screwdriver.
9   Place the plunger spring over the ball retainer and slide the lifter body over the spring and plunger, aligning the oil feed holes in plunger and lifter body.
10 Fill the assembly with SAE 10 oil then insert the end of a $\frac{1}{8}$ inch drift pin into the plunger and press down solid to align the oil feed holes in the lifter body and plunger assembly. Do not force or attempt to pump the plunger.
11 Insert a $\frac{1}{16}$ inch drift pin through both oil holes to hold the plunger down against the lifter spring tension.
12 Remove the $\frac{1}{8}$ inch pin and refill the lifter with SAE 10 oil.
13 Install the metering valve and pushrod seat.
14 Install the pushrod seat retainer, press down on the pushrod seat and extract the $\frac{1}{16}$ inch drift-pin from the oil holes.
15 The lifter is now assembled, charged with oil and ready for use.
16 Before installing the lifters coat their bottom surfaces with Molykote or similar anti-friction compound.

31 Engine reassembly – general

1   To ensure maximum life with minimum trouble from a rebuilt engine, not only must everything be correctly assembled, but everything must be spotlessly clean, all the oilways must be clear, locking washers and spring washers must always be installed where indicated, and all bearing and other working surfaces must be thoroughly lubricated during assembly.
2   Before assembly begins, renew any bolts or studs the threads of which are in any way damaged.
3   Apart from your normal tools, a supply of clean rag, an oil can filled with engine oil, a supply of assorted spring washers, a set of new gaskets, and a torque wrench, should be collected together.

32 Crankshaft, main bearings, pistons/connecting rods and flywheel (or flexplate) – reassembly and installation

1   If the gear was removed from the front end of the crankshaft, tap the new one into position using a piece of tubing as a drift.
2   Install the rear oil seal half sections into the grooves in the crankcase and in the rear bearing cap. Position the lip of the seal towards the front of the engine. If the seal has two lips, install so that the lip and helix are towards the front of the engine.
3   Insert the shell bearings into the crankcase recesses and the main bearing caps. If the original shells are being used, make sure that they are returned to their original positions. Note that the flanged (thrust control) shells are located at No. 7 main bearing position.
4   Oil the bearing shells liberally and lower the crankshaft carefully into position.
5   Apply a little sealant to the end surfaces of the crankcase oil seal section and then install the main bearing caps in their correct sequence with their directional arrows pointing towards the front of the engine.
6   Tighten all the main bearing cap bolts to the specified torque with the exception of the rear (No. 7) one. The bolts for this cap should only be tightened to 10 lbf ft at this stage.
7   Now tap the crankshaft first rearward and then fully forward to line up the rear bearing and crankshaft thrust surfaces. Now tighten all main bearing cap bolts to the specified torque.
8   The crankshaft endfloat will probably already have been checked but if not, do it now as described in Section 20.
9   With the pistons assembled to the connecting rods and fitted with their piston rings as described in Section 22, they should now be installed into the cylinder block. Set the block on its side for this operation.
10 Locate the shell bearings in the connecting rod and cap recesses. If the original shells are being used, see that they are returned to their original locations.
11 Lightly coat the cylinder bores, pistons and rings with engine oil; also apply some to the surfaces of the bearing shells.
12 Check that the piston ring end gaps are correctly positioned as described in Section 22.
13 Apply a piston ring clamp to the first piston and then insert the connecting rod into its correct bore (from which it was removed or if new components are being used, into which the piston was selectively matched). Make sure that the front-facing notch on the top of the piston is facing forward and that the base of the piston is standing square on the top of the cylinder block.
14 Place the end of a wooden hammer handle against the top of the piston and strike the head of the hammer with the hand. This will send the piston with compressed rings into the bore. Remove the clamp (Fig. 1.32).
15 Push the piston carefully down until the big-end of the connecting rod can be engaged with its crankpin on the crankshaft. Install the correct cap with its shell bearing, making sure that it is the right way round with the cap sequence number adjacent to the number on the connecting rod.
16 Screw on and tighten the connecting rod nuts to the specified torque.
17 Repeat the operations on the remaining piston/connecting rod assemblies. The crankshaft will probably need to be turned periodically to enable the various connecting rods to be engaged with their crankpins.
18 Install the flywheel (manual transmission) to the crankshaft mounting flange so that its locating dowel engages correctly. Screw in the bolts and tighten to the specified torque. To prevent the flywheel turning while the bolts are tightened, jam the crankshaft web.
19 When installing the flexplate (automatic transmission), make sure that the torque converter mounting pads on the flexplate are towards the transmission.

33 Oil pump and oil pan – installation

1   Install the oil pump into the crankcase using a new gasket. Tighten the screws to the specified torque.
2   Insert and tighten the oil pick-up tube screw.
3   Thoroughly clean all the crankcase and oil pan mating surfaces and stick new side gaskets into position on the crankcase flanges.
4   Fit a new gasket onto the rear main bearing cap.
5   Offer up the oil pan and tighten all bolts in diagonal sequence to the specified torque.

34 Timing gear and camshaft – installation

1   Oil the camshaft bearing and then pass the camshaft complete

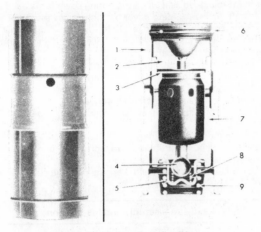

Fig. 1.28 Hydraulic valve lifter

1 Body
2 Pushrod seat
3 Metering valve
4 Check ball
5 Check ball retainer
6 Pushrod seat retainer
7 Plunger
8 Check ball spring
9 Plunger spring

Fig. 1.29 Installing check ball valve in lifter

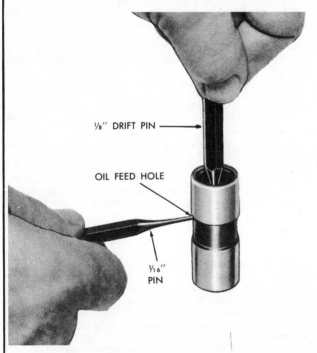

⅛″ DRIFT PIN

OIL FEED HOLE

1/16″ PIN

Fig. 1.30 Assembling valve lifter

APPLY SEALANT TO SHADED AREAS ONLY

Fig. 1.31. Crankshaft rear oil seal: sealant application points

Fig. 1.32. Installing a piston/connecting rod assembly

Fig. 1.33. Oil pan front seal modification when refitting timing cover without removal of oil pan

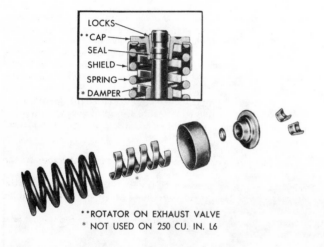

Fig. 1.34 Valve spring detail (6-cylinder engines)

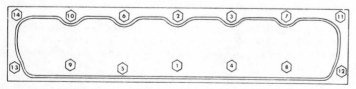

Fig. 1.35 Cylinder head bolt tightening sequence (6-cylinder)

with gearwheel into the crankcase.

2   Turn the crankshaft (by means of a wrench on one of the flywheel bolts) until the timing marks on the crankshaft and camshaft gears are in alignment and on an imaginary line drawn through the centers of the crankshaft and camshaft. The camshaft will have to be pulled partly out, turned and re-inserted to achieve this.

3   Fit the camshaft thrust plate. Screw in the plate retaining bolts through the holes in the camshaft gear and tighten to specified torque.

4   Fit a new oil seal to the timing cover so that the open end of the seal faces inward. Support the timing cover so that it is not bent when the seal is tapped into position.

5   Engage a new strip seal at the lower edge of the timing cover so that the tips go into the holes provided in the cover.

6   *If the timing cover was removed without disturbing the oil pan* (see Section 14) then a new section must now be cut from a gasket set and located on the front ends of the oil pan flanges. Also in this case, place a bead of silicone jointing compound at either side of the

joint to make a good seal when the timing cover is installed (Fig. 1.33).

7   Install the front timing cover but only insert the cover screws and oil pan-to-cover screws finger tight until the crankshaft torsional damper has been installed; this will have the effect of centralising the cover round the crankshaft.

8   Install the torsional damper to the front end of the crankshaft using a piece of tubing as a drift, but take care that the damper assembly does not separate by using too much force. Drive it home until it bottoms against the crankshaft gear.

9   Tighten the timing cover bolts and front two oil pan-to-timing cover bolts.

10   Bolt on the drivebelt pulley.

11   Lubricate the valve lifters and insert them into position with the engine standing upright on its oil pan.

12   Using new gaskets install the engine pushrod side covers.

35 Cylinder head – reassembly and installation

1   Insert the first valve into the seat into which it was ground. Oil the valve stem.

2   Fit the valve spring shim, valve spring, damper (not on 250 cu in engines) valve shield, cap and rotator (exhaust valves only) (Fig. 1.34).

3   Using the valve spring compressor, compress the spring, install the oil seal into the lower groove in the valve stem and then install the valve locks. Release the compressor gently so that the locks engage positively in the upper groove in the valve stem.

4   Repeat the operations on all the remaining valves making sure that they are fitted into their correct valve seats.

5   Thoroughly clean the mating surfaces of the head and block, and clean out the bolt holes.

6   Lay a new gasket on top of the block so that the gasket bead is uppermost.

7   Lower the cylinder head into position over the dowel pins and onto the gasket.

8   Screw in the cylinder head bolts finger tight and then tighten them fully to the specified torque wrench settings, in stages and in the sequence shown (Fig. 1.35).

9   Install the pushrods in their original sequence making sure that they engage in the lifter sockets.

10   Install the rocker arms, bolts and nuts. Tighten the rocker arm nuts until any lash in the pushrod (up and down movement) is eliminated.

11   The valves must be finally adjusted as described in Section 37 either now or when the engine has been installed in the vehicle.

36 Engine ancillary components – installation

1   Install the distributor, clutch, fuel pump, alternator and water pump as described in the appropriate Chapters of this manual.

2   The manifolds and carburetor can also be fitted at this time or if preferred delayed until the engine is installed.

37 Valve adjustment

1   The valves should be adjusted after major overhaul, or whenever the cylinder head bolts have been tightened, after head removal and installation.

2   Mark the distributor body with a piece of chalk at the positions opposite number 1 and number 6 plug wire entries to the distributor cap.

3   Remove the distributor cap and put it to one side.

4   Turn the crankshaft until the rotor in the distributor is in alignment with the No. 1 chalk mark.

5   Adjust the following valves counting from the front of the engine:

Inlet valves 2 – 3 – 7
Exhaust valves 1 – 5 – 9

6   Back off the rocker adjuster nut until lash can be felt at the pushrod and then tighten the nut until all lash disappears. Now turn the adjuster nut one full turn.

7   Turn the crankshaft until the distributor rotor is in alignment with the No. 6 chalk mark.

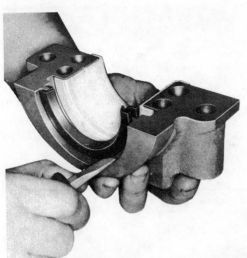

Fig. 1.36 Removing main bearing cap oil seal

Fig. 1.37 Removing crankshaft rear oil seal (engine in vehicle)

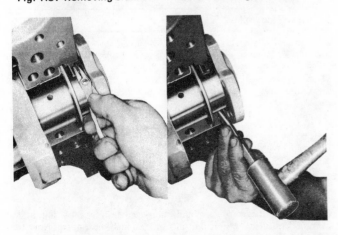

Fig. 1.38 Removing crankshaft rear upper main bearing (engine in vehicle)

8   Adjust the following valves again counting from the front of the engine:

   Inlet valves 6 – 10 – 11
   Exhaust valves 4 – 8 – 12

9   Install the rocker cover using a new gasket if necessary.
10   Install the distributor cap.

38 Engine-to-transmission reconnection, and engine installation

1   Refer to the relevant earlier Sections of this Chapter.

39 Engine start-up after major repair or overhaul

1   Refill the cooling system (refer to Chapter 2).
2   Refill the crankcase with the correct grade and quantity of engine oil. If a new camshaft or valve lifters have been installed, an additive containing EP lube, such as EOS, should be added to the crankcase oil for the break-in period.
3   Make a final check to ensure that all cables and pipes have been connected, and that no tools or rags have been left in the engine compartment.
4   Start the engine and check for water and oil leaks. **Note:** *The engine may not start readily since there may be condensation inside; also it may take a little while for the fuel pump to deliver fuel to the carburetor.*
5   Check that the instruments are indicating satisfactory readings.
6   Run the engine until normal operating temperature is reached.
7   Check the carburetor and emission control settings, as described in Chapter 3.
8   Check the ignition timing (Chapter 4).
9   Top-up the engine oil level to make up for the oil absorbed by the new filter element.
10   Run the vehicle for between 500 and 1000 miles and with the engine cold, check the torque settings of all engine nuts and bolts, particularly the cylinder head bolts.
11   Re-check the valve adjustment after having tightened the cylinder head bolts.

40 Oil seals – renewal with engine in vehicle

1   *The timing cover oil seal* can be renewed after first removing the crankshaft pulley and torsional damper.
2   Pry out the defective seal and drive in a new one.
3   Install the damper and pulley.
4   *The crankshaft rear oil seals* may be removed if the oil pan and oil pump are first removed and the rear main bearing cap withdrawn.
5   Pry out the cap section of the seal with a small screwdriver and insert the new one.
6   The upper section of the seal can be removed if it is first tapped round with a small punch until its end can be gripped with a pair of pliers (Fig. 1.37).
7   Insert the new upper seal section (well oiled) by pressing it into position with the lip towards the front of the engine. Turning the crankshaft at the same time as the seal is pressed will help to locate it.
8   Apply a little sealant to the end faces of the seals before bolting up the main bearing cap and tightening to the specified torque.
9   Install the oil pump and oil pan, and refill with engine oil.

41 Main bearings – renewal with engine in vehicle

1   Renewal of the crankshaft main bearing shells can be carried out in the following way without having to remove the engine from the vehicle. However the need for new bearings will usually be the result of lack of oil or general overall wear and the reason for renewal should first be established; also, whether the crankshaft itself and other engine internal components require attention at the same time. It is no good fitting new bearing shells to a worn crankshaft.
2   Remove the oil pan, the oil pump and the spark plugs.
3   Unbolt and remove No. 1 main bearing cap and remove the shell

bearing.

4   To remove the upper shell, insert a cotter pin into the oil hole in the crankshaft journal. Turn the crankshaft in a clockwise direction and the head of the cotter pin will roll the shell out of its recess in the crankcase.

5   Installation of the new upper shell can be carried out using the same method to roll it into position.

6   Install the new shell into the bearing cap and tighten the bolts to the specified torque.

7   Repeat the foregoing operations on all other main bearings except the rear one. As the journal at this position has no oil hole, tap out the flanged upper shell bearing with a small punch until the opposite end can be gripped with a pair of pliers as described for the oil seal in the preceding Section.

8   Install the new shell in similar manner.

9   Install the oil pump and oil pan, and refill with oil.

42 Engine front and rear mountings – renewal with engine in vehicle

1   The front mountings can be renewed if the engine is supported under the oil pan with a jack and a block of wood as an insulator. Do not raise the engine any more than is necessary or damage to the engine controls, hoses or wires may result.

2   The engine rear mountings can be renewed if the transmission is supported on a jack and the crossmember removed.

PART 3 – V8 ENGINES

43 Cylinder heads – removal

Note: *If the engine has been removed, ignore those operations, in the following paragraphs, which have already been carried out.*

Inlet manifold

1   Drain the radiator and remove the carburetor air cleaner.

2   Disconnect the battery cables, upper radiator and heater hose at the manifold, the accelerator linkage at the pedal, the fuel line at the carburetor, the coil and temperature sender switch wires, the power brake hose, the distributor spark advance hose and the appropriate emission control and crankcase ventilation hoses.

3   Remove the distributor cap and mark the distributor body and rotor position (where applicable). Remove the distributor clamp and distributor, then position the cap rearwards, clear of the manifold.

4   Remove the Delcotron upper bracket, and the coil and its bracket.

5   Remove the manifold to head attaching bolts, and lift off the manifold complete with carburetor.

6   Remove the carburetor (and choke tube assembly, where applicable), the water outlet and thermostat, heater hose adapter, choke coil and EGR valve, if the manifold is to be renewed.

Exhaust manifold

7   Remove the air injection reactor (AIR) air manifold and tubes (refer to Chapter 3), if considered necessary.

8   Remove the battery ground cable and the air cleaner pre-heater air stove.

9   Remove the manifold-to-exhaust flange nuts, then lower the pipe assembly. Hang it from the frame to prevent undue loading.

10   Remove the end mounting bolts followed by the center ones and lift the manifold away from the engine (photo).

Head assembly

11   If the engine is still in position, remove the appropriate crankcase ventilation hoses.

12   Disconnect the wiring harness from the clips on the rocker covers remove the cover retaining screws and lift off the covers.

13   If the engine is installed, drain the coolant from the cylinder block (refer to Chapter 2).

14   Working on each valve in turn, loosen the rocker arm nut until the rocker can be pivoted, then remove the pushrod and valve lifter. Place the pushrods and valve lifters in a rack so that they may be installed in the same location during engine assembly (photos).

15   Remove the valve rocker arm nuts, balls and rocker arms.

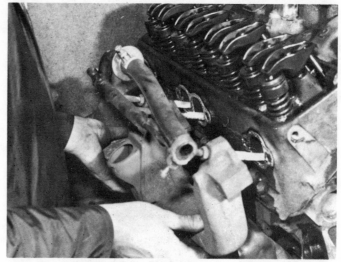
43.10 Removing exhaust manifold (V8)

43.14A Removing a pushrod (V8)

43.14B Removing a valve lifter (V8)

16 Unscrew the cylinder head bolts, one turn at a time and remove them.

17 With the aid of an assistant lift the cylinder heads from the block. If they are stuck, do not attempt to lever them off, but tap upwards using a block of wood and a hammer at each end. Place the heads on a clean workbench for further dismantling.

44 Cylinder head – dismantling

1 Using a suitable valve spring compressor, compress each spring in turn to permit the locks to be removed. Release the compressor and remove the spring cap or rotator, shield (where applicable), spring and damper, then remove the oil seals and spring shims (Fig. 1.39).

2 Remove the valves and place them in a rack in their proper sequence with their associated pushrods etc.

3 Unscrew and remove each spark plug.

45 Oil pan and oil pump – removal

If the engine is still in position in the vehicle, carry out the following preliminary work (paragraph 1 through 4).

1 Disconnect the battery. Remove the fan shroud, disconnect the exhaust pipes or crossover pipes. Drain the engine oil and, where

automatic transmission is fitted, remove the converter housing underpan and splash shield. Remove the starter motor.

2 Turn the crankshaft until the timing mark on the torsional damper at the front end of the crankshaft is at the 6 o'clock position.

3 Remove both front engine mount through-bolts.

4 Using suitable jacks and wooden blocks positioned beneath the torsional damper, raise the engine until 3 inch wooden spacers can be inserted at the engine mounts. Lower the engine onto the 3 inch spacers.

5 On all models remove the oil pan retaining bolts and the oil pan. If stuck, tap it sharply with a soft-faced mallet or cut around the joint with a thin sharp knife. Do not pry against the crankcase or irreparable distortion may occur.

6 Where applicable, remove the oil pan baffle.

7 Remove the oil pump and screen assembly, and the extension shaft (photo).

46 Timing chain, sprockets and camshaft – removal

If the engine is still in the vehicle, remove the drive belts, fan and pulley. Remove the fan shroud, drain the cooling system, and remove the radiator and the grille. Remove the cylinder heads, valve gear and pushrods.

1 Remove the accessory drive pulley, then remove the torsional

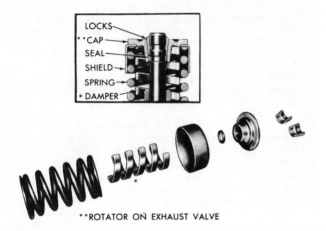
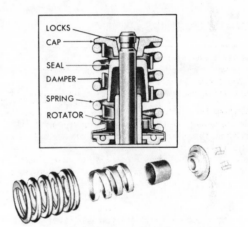

Fig. 1.39. Valve spring detail (V8 engine) (A) small V8 (B) large V8

45.7 Removing oil pump and screen (V8)

46.1 Crankshaft pulley (V8)

46.2 Removing crankshaft torsional damper (V8)

Fig. 1.40 Cutting tabs on oil pan front seal (oil pan not to be removed)

Fig. 1.41. Withdrawing camshaft

damper retaining bolt (photo).
2   Using a suitable extractor, draw off the torsional damper (photo).
3   Remove the water pump (refer to Chapter 2).
4   *Small V8:* Unscrew the crankcase front cover attaching bolts, then remove the cover.
5   *'Large' or Mk IV V8:* Remove the timing cover screws and pull the cover slightly forward to enable the front seal of the oil pan to be cut either side of the cylinder block (this operation is only required if the oil pan is still in position and not intended to be removed) (Fig. 1.40).
6   Turn the crankshaft until the timing marks on the crankshaft and camshaft sprockets are in alignment.
7   Remove the camshaft sprocket bolts, pull off the sprocket and remove the timing chain.
8   The crankshaft sprocket can be removed if essential, using a suitable puller.
9   Before removing the camshaft, withdraw the fuel pump pushrod and the valve lifters. Keep the latter in strict original order.
10   Withdraw the camshaft taking great care not to damage the camshaft bearings as the lobes pass through them.

47 Pistons, connecting rods and bearings – removal

1   Initially remove the cylinder heads, oil pan and oil pump, as described previously in this Chapter.
2   Ensure that identification marks are present on each connecting rod and bearing cap to enable them to be installed in their original positions. If no marks are present small punch indentations will be satisfactory (left-bank – 1, 3, 5, 7; right-bank – 2, 4, 6, 8).
3   Turn the crankshaft so that the relevant piston is at the lowest point of its stroke. Place a piece of rag on top of the piston and then carefully remove the wear ridge from the top of the cylinder bore. Remove the rag and the metal scrapings.
4   Turn the crankshaft so that one piston is at the top of its stroke.
5   Remove the connecting rod bearing cap, push a piece of rubber or plastic tubing onto each of the connecting rod studs to prevent them scratching the soft cylinder bores as the rods are removed.
6   Push the piston/connecting rod assembly out of the top of the cylinder block.
7   Repeat the operations on the remaining seven cylinders turning the crankshaft as necessary, to gain access to the connecting rod cap bolts and to bring the piston to the bottom or top of its stroke as required.

48 Flywheel (or flexplate) – removal

1   To remove either component, simply unbolt it from the crankshaft rear flange.
2   If the flywheel must be removed while the engine is still in position in the vehicle, the transmission must be withdrawn as described in Chapter 6.

49 Crankshaft and main bearings – removal

1   The crankshaft can be removed only after the engine has been removed from the vehicle and completely dismantled as described in the earlier Sections of this Chapter.
2   Check that the main bearing caps are marked in respect of their location in the crankcase (and their orientation), as carried out for the connecting rod bearing caps.
3   Unbolt the main bearing caps, (keeping their shell bearings together with their respective caps if they are to be used again).
4   Lift the crankshaft from the crankcase, with help from an assistant.
5   If the upper half shell bearings are to be removed, and it is intended to use them again, keep them identified with (but not interchanged with) their respective lower half shell bearings.
6   Remove the two halves of the crankshaft rear oil seal.

50 Lubrication system

1   The lubrication system for the engine is very similar to that described for in-line engines in Section 18 but the different pressure circuit should be observed from the illustrations (Figs. 1.42 and 1.43).

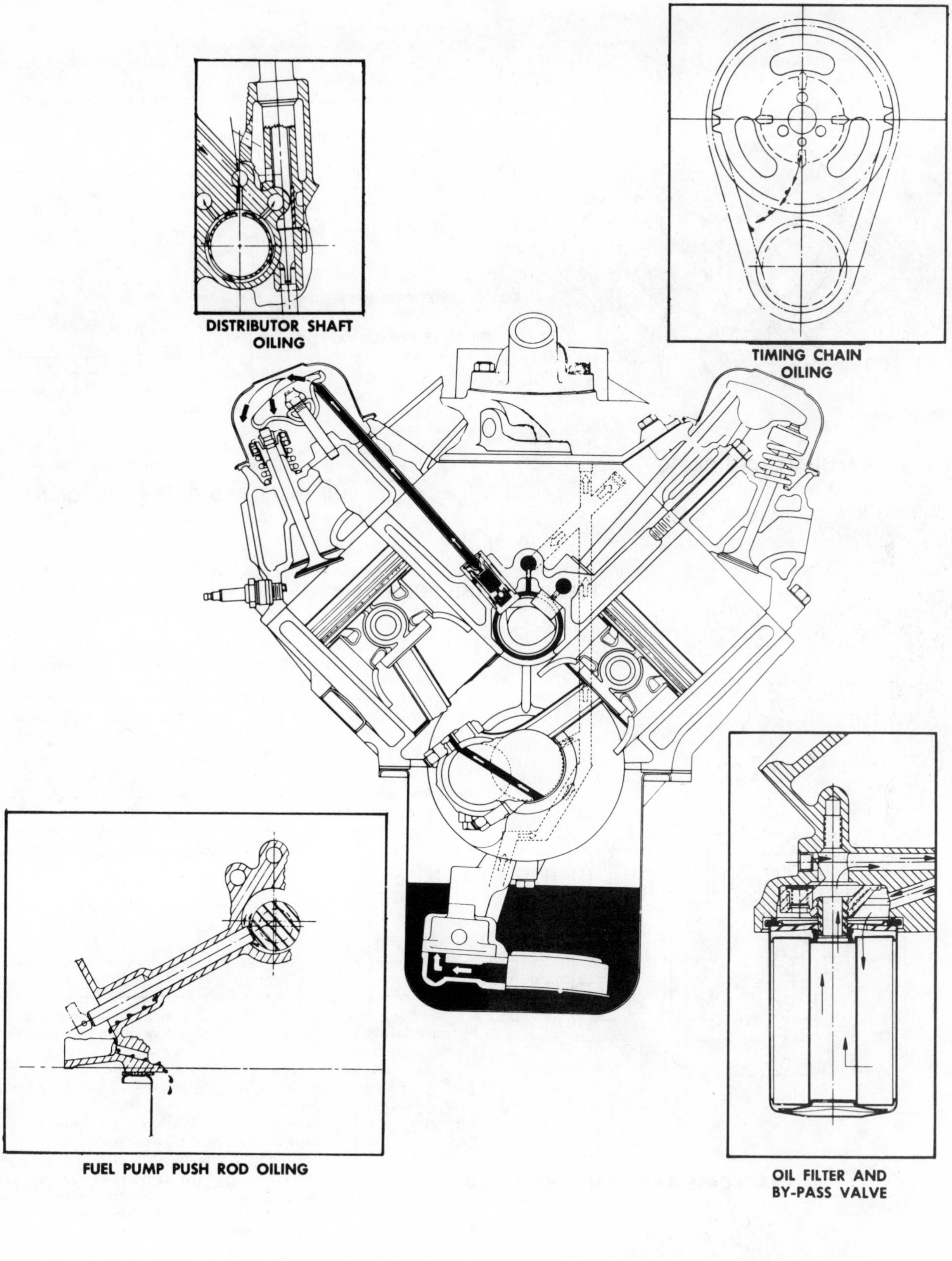

DISTRIBUTOR SHAFT
OILING

TIMING CHAIN
OILING

FUEL PUMP PUSH ROD OILING

OIL FILTER AND
BY-PASS VALVE

Fig. 1.42 Engine lubrication system (small V8 engine)

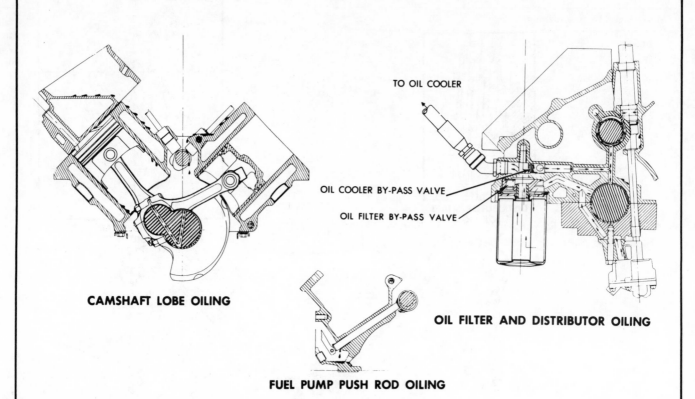

CAMSHAFT LOBE OILING

TO OIL COOLER

OIL COOLER BY-PASS VALVE

OIL FILTER BY-PASS VALVE

OIL FILTER AND DISTRIBUTOR OILING

FUEL PUMP PUSH ROD OILING

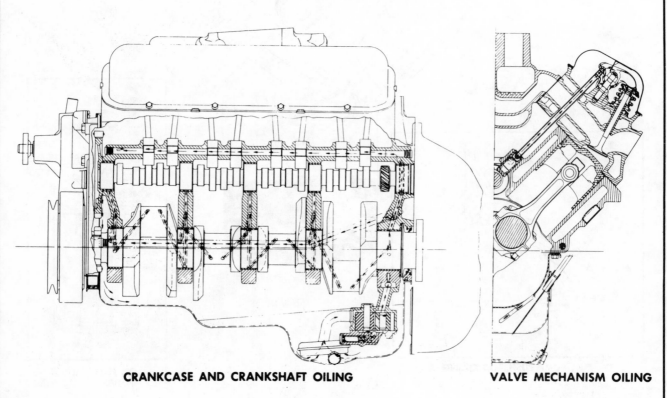

CRANKCASE AND CRANKSHAFT OILING

VALVE MECHANISM OILING

Fig. 1.43. Engine lubrication system (large V8 engines)

51 Examination and renovation

1   The operations for the V8 type engines are essentially the same as for the in-line engines, and reference should be made to Part 2 of this Chapter, Sections 19 to 29.

2   The following differences should however be noted and refer only to the V8 Section of the Specifications.

Crankshaft and main bearings

3   There are only five main bearings.

Piston rings

4   The piston ring end gaps should be 'staggered' as shown in the diagram (Fig. 1.44).

Oil pump

5   Note the different construction of the V8 oil pumps, otherwise overhaul procedure is as for in-line engines (Figs. 1.45 through 1.48).

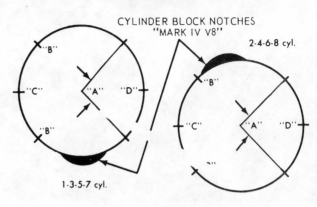

Fig. 1.44 Piston ring end gap installation diagram (V8 engines)

A   Ring spacer gap (oil control)
B   Ring rail gaps (oil control)
C   2nd compression
D   Top compression

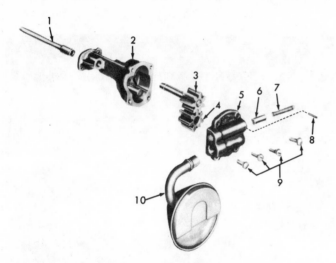

Fig. 1.45 Exploded view of oil pump (small V8)

1	Shaft extension	6	Pressure regulator valve
2	Pump body	7	Spring
3	Drive gear and shaft	8	Retaining pin
4	Idler gear	9	Screws
5	Pump cover	10	Pick-up screen and pipe

Fig. 1.46 Exploded view of large (Mk VI) V8 oil pump

1	Shaft extension	7	Pump cover
2	Shaft coupling	8	Pressure regulator valve
3	Pump body	9	Spring
4	Drive gear and shaft	10	Washer
5	Idler gear	11	Retaining pin
6	Pick-up screen and pipe	12	Screws

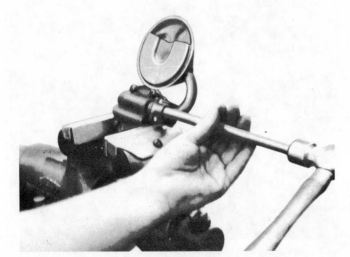

Fig. 1.47 Installing oil pump pick-up (small V8)

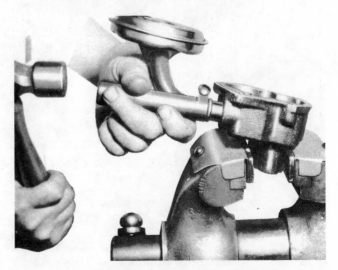

Fig. 1.48 Installing oil pump pick-up (large V8)

53.3A Main bearing shell in crankcase (V8)

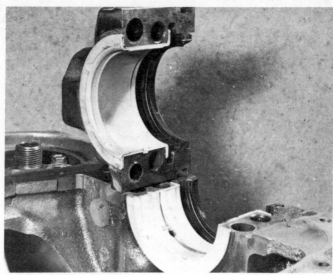

53.3B Rear main bearing shells showing thrust flanges (V8)

53.4 Oiling crankshaft journals (V8)

53.6 Installing a main bearing cap (V8)

53.7A Tapping the crankshaft to the rear prior to checking endfloat (V8)

53.7B Tightening a main bearing cap bolt using a torque wrench (V8)

Cylinder heads

6   On Mark IV V8 cylinder heads inspect the pushrod guides for wear and damage.

7   On Mark IV V8 and some high performance small V8 heads the pushrod guides are retained by nuts on the rocker arm studs. These studs can be unscrewed for renewal of the guides. When assembling, coat the stud with a gasket sealant and torque tighten.

8   On small V8 engines the studs are pressed in, but replacement is considered a specialist operation involving the reaming of the stud holes 0.003 or 0.013 inch oversize, the new studs being lubricated with hypoid axle oil and pressed in to their original depth.

52 Engine reassembly – general

Refer to Section 31 of Part 2.

53 Crankshaft and main bearings – installation

1   Install the rear main bearing oil seal in the cylinder block and rear main bearing cap grooves, with the seal lip towards the front of the engine (where a seal has two lips, the lip with the helix is towards the front of the engine).

2   Lubricate the seal lips with engine oil.

3   Install the main bearing shells in the cylinder block and main bearing caps and lubricate the bearing surface with engine oil (photos). The rear shells incorporate the thrust flanges.

4   With the aid of an assistant, install the crankshaft, taking care not to damage the bearing surfaces. Lubricate the crankshaft journals with engine oil (photo).

5   Apply a thin coat of a brush-on sealant to the block rear seal end faces and corresponding surfaces of the cap. Do not allow the sealant to contact the crankshaft or seal.

6   Install the main bearing caps in their correct positions, arrows towards the front of the engine (photo).

7   Torque-tighten the main bearing caps with the exception of the rear cap bolts. Tighten these to 10/12 lbf ft, then tap the end of the crankshaft rearwards then forwards with a hammer interposed with a block of wood to align the rear main bearing thrust faces. Retorque all the bearing caps to the specified value (photos).

54 Pistons and connecting rods – installation

1   Check that the piston ring gaps are as described in Section 16, also that the piston is correctly aligned to the connecting rod. Apply engine oil to the cylinder bores.

2   Install a piston ring compressor over the piston rings which should have been well lubricated.

54.3 Installing a connecting rod bearing cap shell

54.5 Piston ring compressor installed

54.6A Installing connecting rod cap (V8)

54.6B Connecting rod and cap sequence number (V8)

55.1 Alignment of flywheel dowel hole (V8)

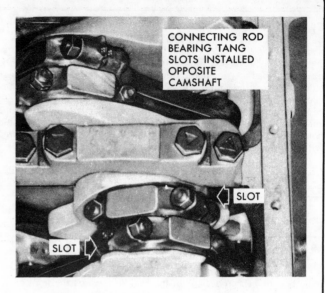

CONNECTING ROD BEARING TANG SLOTS INSTALLED OPPOSITE CAMSHAFT

SLOT

SLOT

Fig. 1.49 Connecting rods correctly installed in V8 engine

Fig. 1.50 Installing timing chain and camshaft sprocket

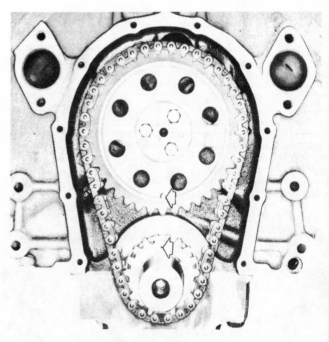

Fig. 1.51 Timing marks (V8 engine)

3   Install pieces of plastic or rubber tube to the threads of the connecting rod bolts. Install and lubricate the bearing shells (photo).
4   Insert the connecting rod/piston assembly into its respective bore, ensuring that it is the correct way round (connecting rod tang slot towards camshaft).
5   With the base of the base of the piston ring compressor resting on the top face of the cylinder block, tap the assembly into the bore using the wooden handle of a hammer (photo).
6   Carefully guide the connecting rod to engage with the crankpin and install the bearing cap so that the numbers on the rod and cap are adjacent (photos).
7   Tighten the cap bolts to the specified torque.
8   Repeat the operations on the remaining pistons. The crankshaft will have to be rotated to facilitate connection of the connecting rods and bearing caps.

55   Flywheel (flexplate) – installation

1   Install the flywheel with the dowel hole aligned with the dowel hole in the crankshaft. On vehicles with automatic transmission, the converter attaching pads and flange collar should face towards the transmission (photo).
2   Torque-tighten the attaching bolts. A clean wooden block wedged between the crankshaft and cylinder block will prevent rotation while the bolts are being tightened.
3   Where this operation is being carried out with the engine installed, install the clutch, clutch housing and manual transmission, or the automatic transmission (refer to Chapters 5 and 6).

56   Camshaft, timing chain and sprockets – installation

1   Install two $\frac{5}{16}$ inch – 18 x 4 inch bolts in the camshaft bolt holes, to act as holding points, then lubricate the journals with engine oil.
2   Carefully install the camshaft, taking care to feed the journals and cams through the bearings to prevent damage. When the camshaft is fully home, remove the two $\frac{5}{16}$ inch bolts.
3   Place the timing chain on the camshaft sprocket then align the marks on the camshaft and crankshaft sprockets. Connect the chain to the crankshaft sprocket, align the camshaft dowel with the dowel hole

in the sprocket and install the sprocket on the camshaft (Fig. 1.51).
4   Draw the sprocket onto the camshaft using the attaching bolts. Do not drive the sprocket on, or the rear plug may be loosened. Torque tighten the sprocket attaching bolts.
5   Lubricate the timing chain with engine oil.
6   If not already carried out, pry out the old seal from the front of the front cover using a screwdriver.
7   Ensure that the seal housing is clean then install a new seal so that the open end is towards the inside of the cover. The seal must be carefully pressed in with the cover supported and care must be taken to prevent damage to the seal lips.
8   Smear the front cover oil seal lips with engine oil.

Small V8

9   Ensure that the block and crankcase front cover are clean.
10   Use a sharp knife to remove any oil pan gasket material protruding at the oil pan to engine block junction.
11   Apply a $\frac{1}{8}$ inch bead of silicone rubber sealer (Chevrolet part No. 1051435 – or equivalent) to the joint formed at the oil pan and block, as well as the front lip of the oil pan (Fig. 1.52).
12   Coat the cover gasket with a non-setting sealant, position it on the cover then loosely install the cover. First install the top four bolts loosely then install two $\frac{1}{4}$ inch – 20 x $\frac{1}{2}$ inch screws at the lower cover holes. Apply a bead of the silicone sealer on the bottom of the cover then install the cover, tightening the screws alternately and evenly whilst using a suitable tool to align the dowel pins.
13   Remove the two $\frac{1}{4}$ inch – 20 x $\frac{1}{2}$ inch screws and install the remaining cover screws.

Mark IV V8

14   Ensure that the block and crankcase front cover are clean.
15   Cut the tabs from the new oil pan front seal, using a sharp knife.
16   Install the seal to the front cover, pressing the lips into the holes provided in the cover.
17   Coat the gasket with a non-setting sealant and position it on the cover.
18   Apply a $\frac{1}{8}$ inch bead of silicone rubber sealer (Chevrolet part No. 1051435 – or equivalent) to the joint formed at the oil pan and block.
19   Install the cover attaching screws and torque tighten the specified value (Fig. 1.53).

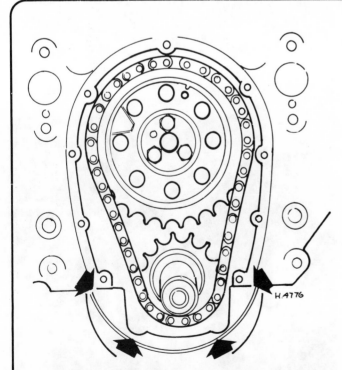

Fig. 1.52 Timing cover sealant application points (small V8)

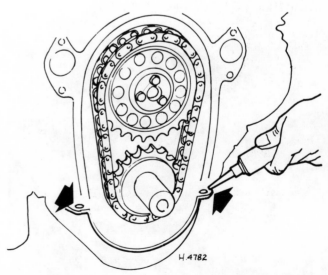

Fig. 1.53 Timing cover sealant application points (large V8)

56.20 Installing crankshaft torsional damper (V8)

58.2A Intake valve shield and cap (V8)

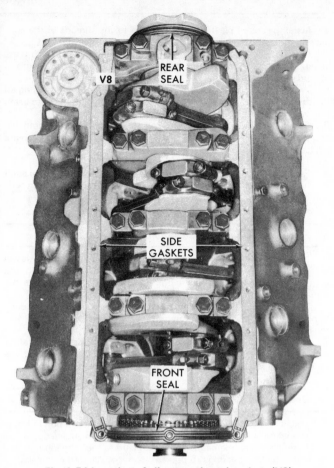
Fig. 1.54 Location of oil pan seals and gaskets (V8)

REAR SEAL

V8

SIDE GASKETS

FRONT SEAL

58.2B Exhaust valve shield and rotator (V8)

58.3 Compressing a valve spring (V8)

All engines
20 Coat the front cover seal area of the torsional damper with engine oil, place the damper in position, then use a suitable bolt and spacers to draw the damper into position. Install and torque tighten the damper retaining bolt. Take care that the damper is not damaged during this operation (photo).
21 Install the accessory drive pulley.
22 Install the valve lifters.
Note: *Where a new camshaft or valve lifters are being fitted, the cam lobes must be coated with 'Molykote' or an equivalent anti-scuffing compound.*
23 Install the fuel pump pushrod.

57 Oil pump and oil pan – installation

1 Assemble the pump and extension shaft to the rear main bearing cap. Align the slot at the top end of the extension shaft with the drive tang on the lower end of the distributor shaft, if the distributor is installed.
2 Install the pump to the rear bearing cap bolt and torque tighten the bolts. Where applicable install the oil baffle.
3 Use a non-setting gasket sealant and install the oil pan sealing side gaskets on the cylinder block. Apply the sealant at the intersection of the side gaskets and end seals.
4 Install the oil pan rear seal in the groove in the rear main bearing cap, with the ends butting the side gaskets (Fig. 1.54).
5 Install the oil pan and tighten the bolts to the specified torque. Some of the bolts have clips bolted under them to support wiring harness, hoses etc.

58 Cylinder head – reassembly

1 Apply engine oil to the stem of No. 1 valve and insert it in its correct guide.

Small V8
2 Set the valve spring shim, spring, damper, valve shield and cap (inlet valve) or rotator (exhaust valve) in place (photos).
3 Using a suitable valve spring compressor, compress the spring and install the oil seal in the lower groove of the valve stem, ensuring that it is seated squarely (photo).
4 Insert the valve locks and release the spring compressor, ensuring that the locks seat properly in the stem upper groove.

Mark IV V8
5 Install the valve spring shim on the valve spring seat and then install a new valve stem oil seal over the valve and valve guide.
6 Set the valve spring, damper and valve cap in place, then use a suitable compressor to compress the spring.
7 Insert the valve locks and release the spring compressor, ensuring that the locks seat properly in the stem groove.

All versions
8 Install the remaining valves in their correct positions following the same procedure.
9 Using a soft-faced mallet, tap the end of each valve stem sharply to settle the valve components, then measure the installed height of the valve spring. To do this, use a narrow scale passed down beside the spring to rest on the valve spring seat. Now measure the height of the upper surface of the spring and compare the measurement with that given in the Specifications. If the specified height is exceeded, install a valve spring seat shim of approximately $\frac{1}{16}$ inch thickness. At no time should the spring installed height be less than that specified.

59 Cylinder head – installation

Head assembly
1 Scrupulously clean the mating surfaces of the head and block, and the cylinder head bolt threads.
2 Where a steel gasket is used, coat both sides thinly and evenly with a non-setting gasket sealant. Where a steel/asbestos composition gasket is used, no gasket sealant is permitted.

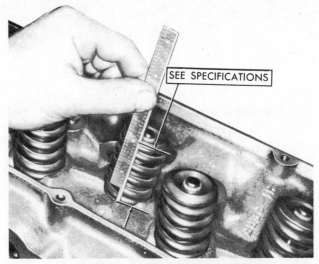
Fig. 1.55 Checking valve spring installed height

59.3 A cylinder head gasket in position (V8)

59.4 Installing a cylinder head (V8)

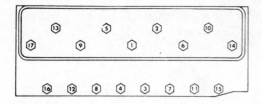

Fig. 1.56 Cylinder head bolt tightening sequence (small V8)

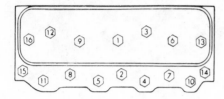

Fig. 1.57 Cylinder head bolt tightening sequence (large V8)

Fig. 1.58 Adjusting valve lash

3   Place the gasket over the dowel pins with the bead upwards (photo).
4   Guide the cylinder head into position over the dowel pins and gasket (photo).
5   Apply gasket sealant to the bolt threads and install them finger-tight. Tighten them progressively in the sequence shown (Figs. 1.56 and 1.57), to the specified torque.
6   Install the pushrods in their original positions.
7   Install the valve rocker arms, rocker arm balls and nuts, and tighten the rocker arm nuts until all endplay has *just* been taken up. Do not install the rocker cover. **Note**: *Where new rocker arms and balls are being used, the contact surfaces should be coated with 'Molykote'*

or an equivalent anti-scuffing compound.

Exhaust manifold
8   Clean the mating surfaces of the manifold and head, then install the manifold in position with the center bolts, using new gaskets. Where applicable, at this stage, it may be found easier to install the spark plug heat shields (photos).
9   Install the end bolts then lightly tighten all the bolts.
10 Torque-tighten the two center bolts to the specified value, then torque-tighten the four end bolts. Refer also to Chapter 3.

Intake manifold
11 Thoroughly clean the gasket and sealing surfaces of the manifold, cylinder heads and block.
12 Install the manifold end seals on the block and the side gaskets on the cylinder heads. Use a gasket sealant around the water passages.
13 Install the manifold and carburretor, and torque-tighten the bolts to the specified value. Note the spark plug lead clips . Refer also to Chapter 3.

60 Engine ancillary components – installation

1   If not already done, install the distributor, clutch, fuel pump, alter-nator and water pump; also the emission control equipment.

61 Valve adjustment

1   The valves must be finally adjusted as described in the following paragraphs either at this stage or when the engine has been installed in the vehicle.
2   The valves should be adjusted after major overhaul or whenever the cylinder head bolts have been tightened after cylinder head removal and refitting.
3   If valve adjustment is being carried out at a normal service interval with the engine in the vehicle then remove the air cleaner, the rocker cover (PCV) ventilation hoses, the wiring harness clips and then unbolt and remove the rocker covers (photo).
4   Rotate the crankshaft until the mark on the torsional damper aligns with the center or O-marking on the timing indicator. If No. 1 cylinder valves are moving, the engine is in No. 6 cylinder firing posi-tion and the crankshaft must be rotated 360°. If No. 1 cylinder valves are not moving, the piston is at top-dead-centre (TDC) which is correct.
5   Back-off the rocker arm stud adjusting nut on each intake and exhaust valves in turn, until there is play in the pushrod; tighten the nut to *just* eliminate play then rotate the nut one complete turn (Fig. 1.58).
6   With the engine in this position the following valves can be adjusted counting from the front of each cylinder bank:

    Left-hand cylinder bank (cylinders No. 1 – 3 – 5 – 7)
    Right-hand cylinder bank (cylinders No. 2 – 4 – 6 – 8)
    Inlet valves of cylinders 1 – 2 – 5 – 7
    Exhaust valves of cylinders 1 – 3 – 4 – 8

7   Rotate the crankshaft through 360° so that the mark on the torsional damper is once more in alignment (No. 6 piston at TDC) and adjust the following valves:

    Inlet valves of cylinders 3 – 4 – 6 – 8
    Exhaust valves of cylinder 2 – 5 – 6 – 7

8   Clean the gasket surfaces of the cylinder head and rocker arm cover with gasoline and wipe dry with a lint-free cloth.
9   Using a new gasket, install the rocker arm cover and torque-tighten the bolts to the specifed value. Note the spark plug lead clips (photos).
10 Where applicable, connect the crankcase ventilation hoses and the electrical wiring harness at the rocker arm cover clips. Install the air cleaner.

62 Engine-to-transmission reconnection, and engine installation

1   Refer to the earlier Sections of this Chapter.

63 Engine start-up after major repair or overhaul

1   Repeat the operations described for in-line engines in Section 39.

64 Oil seals – renewal with engine in vehicle

1   The operations are as described in Section 40.

65 Main bearings – renewal with engine in vehicle

1   The operations are as described in Section 41.

66 Engine front and rear mountings – renewal with engine in vehicle

1   The operations are as described in Section 42.

59.8A Exhaust manifold gasket in position (V8)

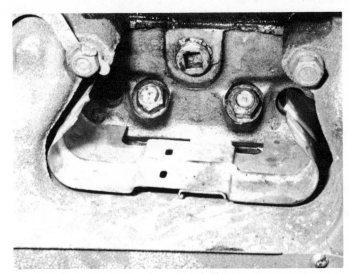

59.8B Spark plug heat shield in position (V8)

61.3 PCV hose attachment to a V8 cylinder head

61.9A Spark plug head clips on V8 rocker cover

61.9B Spark plug lead clips on V8 rocker cover

PART 4 – FAULT DIAGNOSIS

67   Fault diagnosis – engine

Symptom	Reason/s
Engine fails to start	Discharged battery
	Loose battery connection
	Disconnection or broken ignition leads
	Moisture on spark plugs, distributor or leads
	Incorrect spark plug gap
	Dirt or water in carburetor jets
	Empty fuel tank
	Faulty fuel pump
	Faulty starter motor
	Transmission park or neutral switch inoperative
	Faulty carburetor choke mechanism
	Distributor internal fault
Engine idles erratically	Air leak at intake manifold
	Leaking cylinder head gasket
	Worn timing sprockets
	Worn camshaft lobes
	Overheating
	Choked PCV valve
	Faulty fuel pump
	Leaking EGR valve (emission control)
Engine misses at idling speed	Incorrect spark plug gap
	Uneven compression between cylinders
	Faulty coil or condenser
	Faulty contact points (where applicable)
	Poor connections or condition of ignition leads
	Dirt in carburetor jets
	Incorrectly adjusted carburetor
	Worn distributor cam
	Air leak at carburetor flange gasket
	Faulty ignition advance mechanism
	Sticking valves
	Incorrect valve lash
	Low cylinder compression
	Leaking EGR valve (emission control)
Engine misses throughout speed range	Dirt or water in carburetor or fuel lines
	Incorrect ignition timing
	Contact points incorrectly gapped (where applicable)
	Worn distributor
	Faulty coil or condenser
	Spark plug gaps incorrect
	Weak valve springs
	Overheating
	Leaking EGR valve (emission control)
Engine stalls	Incorrectly adjusted carburetor
	Dirt or water in fuel
	Ignition system incorrectly adjusted
	Sticking choke mechanism
	Faulty spark plugs or incorrectly gapped
	Faulty coil or condenser
	Incorrect contact points gap (where applicable)
	Exhaust system clogged
	Distributor advance inoperative
	Air leak at intake manifold
	Air leak at carburetor mounting flange
	Incorrect valve lash
	Sticking valve
	Overheating
	Low compression
	Poor electrical connections on ignition system
	Leaking EGR valve (emission control)
Engine lacks power	Incorrect ignition timing

Faulty coil or condenser
Worn distributor
Dirt in carburetor
Spark plugs incorrectly gapped
Incorrectly adjusted carburetor
Faulty fuel pump
Weak valve springs
Sticking valve
Incorrect valve timing
Incorrect valve lash
Blown cylinder head gasket
Low compression
Brakes dragging
Clutch slipping
Overheating
Transmission regulator valve sticking
(Hydra-Matic automatic transmission)

Note: *In addition to the foregoing, reference should also be made to the fault finding chart for emission control equipment which is to be found at the end of Chapter 3. Such a fault can have an immediate effect upon engine performance.*

Chapter 2 Cooling system

Contents

Specifications

System type	Thermo-syphon, pressurized with belt-driven water pump
Radiator pressure cap rating	15 lbf/in²
Thermostat rating	195° F (91°C)

Coolant capacity

230 cu in engine	13 US qts
250 cu in engine	
Manual transmission	15 US qts
Automatic transmission	15.2 US qts
292 cu in engine	14.8 US qts
305, 307 and 350 cu in (V8) engines	
Manual transmission	17.9 US qts
Automatic transmission	17.7 US qts
400 cu in (V8) engine	
Manual transmission	18.2 US qts
Automatic transmission	19.9 US qts

Torque wrench settings	**lbf ft**
Thermostat housing cover bolts	30
Water pump bolts	
6-cylinder engine	5
V8 engine	30
Temperature sender unit	20
Radiator drain plug	15
Radiator upper retainer-to-tie bar	20

1 General description

1 The cooler system is the pressurized type and includes a crossflow radiator, a thermostat, and a water pump driven by a belt from the crankshaft pulley.
2 The radiator cooling fan is mounted on the front of the water pump and, on later models, incorporates an automatic clutch which disengages the fan at high roadspeeds when the ram effect of the cooling air is sufficient. On some models, a fan shroud is mounted on the rear face of the radiator.
3 The system is pressurized by means of a spring loaded radiator filler cap which prevents premature boiling by increasing the boiling point of the coolant. If the coolant temperature goes above this increased boiling point, the extra pressure in the system forces the radiator cap internal spring loaded valve off its seat and exposes the overflow pipe down which displaced coolant escapes (Fig 2.1).
4 It is important to check that the radiator cap is in good condition and that the spring behind the sealing washer has not weakened or corroded. Most service stations have a machine for testing that the cap operates at the specified pressure.
5 On all later vehicles, a coolant recovery system is provided. This consists of a plastic reservoir into which the coolant which normally escapes down the overflow pipe is retained. When the engine cools and the coolant contracts, coolant is drawn back into the radiator and thus maintains the system at full capacity. This is a continuous process and provided the level in the reservoir is correctly maintained, no topping-up of the radiator or cooling system will be necessary.
6 The cooling system functions in the following manner. Cold water in the right-hand side of the radiator circulates up the lower radiator

hose to the water pump where it is pushed round the water passages in the cylinder block, helping to keep the cylinder bores and pistons cool. The water then travels up into the cylinder head and circulates around the combustion chambers and valve seats absorbing more heat and then travels out of the cylinder head past the open thermostat into the upper radiator hoses on the left-hand side of the cross-flow type radiator.

7   The coolant travels across the radiator where it is rapidly cooled by the in-rush of cold air through the radiator core. The air flow is created by both the engine fan and the ram effect of the forward motion of the vehicle. The coolant, now cooled, reaches the right-hand side of the radiator where the cycle is repeated.

8   When the engine is cold the thermostat (a valve which opens and closes according to the temperature of the water) restricts the circulation of the water to the engine. Only when the correct minimum operating temperature has been reached, does the thermostat begin to open, allowing water to return to the radiator.

9   On some models, with automatic transmission, a fluid cooler is built into the radiator.

2   Coolant level – vehicles without expansion reservoir

1   The level of coolant in the radiator should be maintained at one inch below the bottom of the filler neck. Carry out this check when the engine and coolant are cold. If the engine is hot and the radiator cap must be removed, cover it with a cloth before unscrewing it *slowly*.

3   Coolant level – vehicles with expansion reservoir

1   The level of coolant in the expansion reservoir should be maintained between the 'FULL' and 'ADD' marks on the see-through plastic. Any checking and topping-up should be carried out with the engine and cooling system at normal operating temperature. If the engine is hot and the radiator cap must be removed, cover it with a cloth before unscrewing it *slowly*.

4   Cooling system – draining, flushing and refilling

1   Every two years or 24 000 miles (whichever occurs first) the cooling system should be drained, flushed and refilled.

2   Remove the radiator pressure cap and place the heater control to the full heat position.

3   Unscrew the radiator drain valve (where applicable).

4   On vehicles without a drain valve, disconnect the radiator bottom hose.

5   Place a cold water hose in the radiator filler neck and flush the system until the water runs clear.

6   On systems with an expansion reservoir, disconnect the overflow pipe, and remove the reservoir and flush it out with clean water.

7   In severe cases of contamination or clogging of the radiator, remove the radiator as described in Section 6 and reverse-flush it. This is simply inserting the cold water pressure hose in the bottom radiator outlet to eject water from the top outlet, which is against the normal direction of flow.

8   Where the coolant is regularly drained and the system refilled with the correct antifreeze/inhibitor mixture there should be no need to employ chemical cleaners or descalers, but if the system has been neglected then use a branded cleaning agent in accordance with the manufacturer's instructions.

9   Close the radiator drain valve and reconnect the radiator lower hose and expansion reservoir.

10   *On vehicles without an expansion reservoir:* refill the system through the radiator filler cap until the level is one inch below the filler neck.

11   *On vehicles with an expansion reservoir:* fill the radiator to the base of the filler neck and then add more coolant to the expansion reservoir so that it reaches the 'FULL' mark. Install the reservoir cap but not the radiator cap. Run the engine until normal operating temperature is reached and, with the engine idling, add coolant up to the bottom of the radiator filler neck then install the radiator cap.

12   Always refill the system with a mixture as described in the next Section.

13   Periodically, brush away bugs and dirt from the front of the

Fig. 2.1 Sectional views of the radiator pressure cap in alternative operational modes

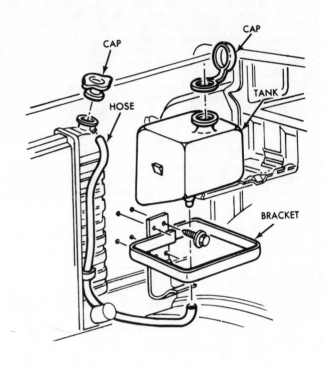

Fig. 2.2 Typical coolant expansion reservoir layout

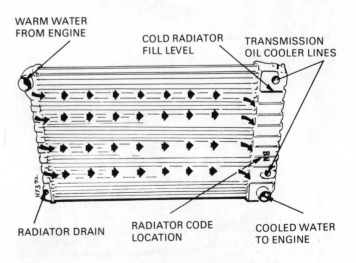

Fig. 2.3 Typical crossflow radiator

radiator to prevent restriction of the cooling air flow.

5 Antifreeze and corrosion inhibiting mixtures

1   It is recommended that the system is filled with an antifreeze mixture where climatic conditions warrant its use. The cooling system should be drained, flushed and refilled every alternate Fall. The use of antifreeze solutions for periods of longer than two years is likely to cause damage and encourage the formation of rust and scale due to the corrosion inhibitors gradually loosing their efficiency. If the use of antifreeze mixture is not necessary because of favourable climatic conditions, never use ordinary water but always fill the system with a corrosion inhibiting mixture of recommended brand to protect the aluminium contents of the engine.
2   Before adding antifreeze to the system, check all hose connections and check the tightness of the cylinder head bolts as such solutions are searching. The cooling system should be drained and refilled with clean water as previously explained, before adding antifreeze.
3   The quantity of antifreeze which should be used for various levels of protection is given in the table below, expressed as a percentage of the system capacity.

Antifreeze volume	Protection to	Safe pump circulation
25%	−26°C (−15°F)	−12°C (10°F)
30%	−33°C (−28°F)	−16°C (−3°F)
35%	−39°C (−38°F)	−20°C (−4°F)

4   Where the cooling system contains an antifreeze or corrosion inhibiting solution any topping-up should be done with a solution made up in similar proportions to the original in order to avoid dilution.

6 Radiator – removal, inspection and installation

1   Drain the cooling system as described in Section 4.
2   Disconnect the upper and lower radiator hoses. If an automatic transmission fluid cooler is fitted, disconnect the fluid pipes from the radiator and plug them.
3   On vehicles equipped with an expansion reservoir, disconnect the overflow pipe.
4   Unscrew the radiator mountings and remove the radiator from the engine compartment taking care not to damage the matrix with the fan blades.

5   Do not allow antifreeze solution to spill onto the bodywork during removal of the radiator or damage may result.
6   Radiator repair is best left to a specialist but minor leaks may be temporarily sealed with a proprietary sealant.
7   Renew any hose clips which have rusted or corroded, then install the radiator by reversing the removal process.
8   Check the automatic transmission fluid level (if a fluid cooler is fitted).

7 Thermostat – removal, testing and installation

1   Drain off enough coolant (about 3 quarts) from the radiator so that the coolant level is below the thermostat housing joint face.
2   Disconnect the radiator upper hose from the thermostat housing which is located at the forward end of the cylinder head.
3   Unscrew and remove the thermostat housing cover bolts, pull off the cover and peel away the gasket.
4   Lift out the thermostat. If it is stuck in its seat, cut round it with a sharp pointed knife to release it (Fig 2.4).
5   To test the thermostat, suspend it in a container of water and heat the water until the thermostat opens. By immersing a thermometer in the water, check the opening temperature of the thermostat and if this varies considerably from the figure stamped on it, install a new one. Always renew the thermostat if it is stuck open or if one of incorrect rating (see Specifications) has been installed by a previous owner. The installation of a thermostat of incorrect rating will cause either over-heating or cool-running of the engine, slow warm-up and an inefficient interior heater.
6   Installation is a reversal of removal, but use new gaskets.

8 Thermostatically controlled fan clutch – description, removal and installation

1   The automatic fan clutch is disengaged when the engine is cold or at high engine speeds when the silicone fluid within the clutch is contained in the reservoir section.
2   Engagement of the clutch is dependent upon two factors: (i) the engine speed and (ii) the engine temperature and its effect on the bimetallic coil within the fan assembly.
3   As the engine temperature rises, the bimetallic coil actuates a shaft which in turn uncovers an aperture in the pump plate to permit silicone fluid to flow from the reservoir to the working chamber of the clutch. The higher the temperature, the greater the opening and the flow.
4   When sufficient fluid has entered the grooves in the clutch body and plate, the clutch becomes fully engaged.
5   When the engine temperature drops as a result of the cooling action of the fan, the apertures in the pump plate are covered again and the speed of the fan decreases as the clutch begins to partially disengage or 'slip'.
6   Continuous noisy operation, looseness leading to vibration, or

Fig. 2.4 Removing thermostat

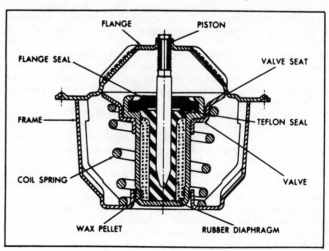

Fig. 2.5 Sectional view of thermostat

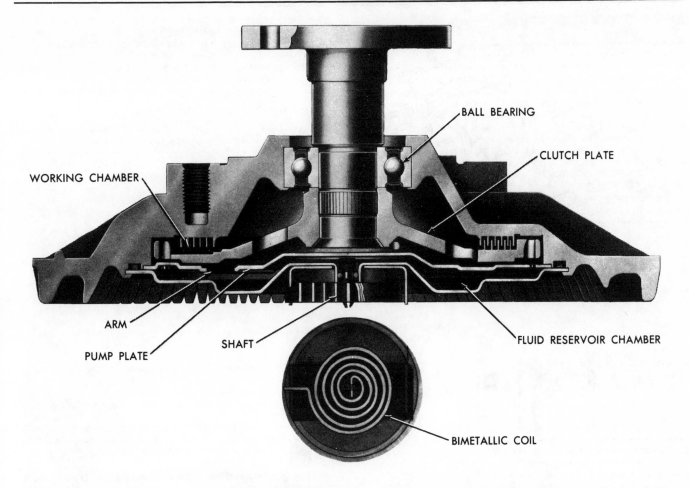

Fig. 2.6 Sectional view of viscous-type automatic fan clutch

evidence of silicone fluid leaks can only be rectified by renewal of the complete fan/clutch unit.

7   To remove the fan, loosen the alternator mounting and adjustment link bolts, push the alternator in towards the engine and slip the drivebelt from the water pump pulley.

8   Unbolt the fan and remove it and the drive pulley.

9   Installation is a reversal of removal but adjust the drivebelt as described in the next Section.

9   Drivebelts – adjustment and renewal

1   At the intervals specified in 'Routine Maintenance' check the tension of all drivebelts. Where the pulley centers are between 13 and 16 inches apart, the drivebelt tension should be adjusted to give a deflection of $\frac{1}{2}$inch at the mid-point of the belt when it is pressed firmly with the thumb.

2   If the pulley centers are between 7 and 10 inches apart, then the deflection should be $\frac{1}{4}$inch.

3   To adjust a belt, release the alternator (or pump) mounting bolts and the adjuster link bolts, and pry the alternator (or pump) away from the engine, until the belt appears tight. Hold the alternator (or pump) in the position while the adjustor link bolt is tightened. Check the belt deflection and if correct; tighten the remaining mounting bolts.

4   Periodically inspect the belts for fraying or cuts. If evident, renew them. To do this, slacken all the alternator (or pump) mounting and adjustor link bolts, and push the alternator (or pump) in towards the engine as far as it will go. Slip the belt off the pulleys. Never attempt to remove or install a drivebelt by prying it over the pulley flanges without first having released the alternator (or other driven components such as the air pump, power steering pump or air conditioning pump) mountings.

5   Adjust the tension of the new drivebelt as described in earlier paragraphs of this Section.

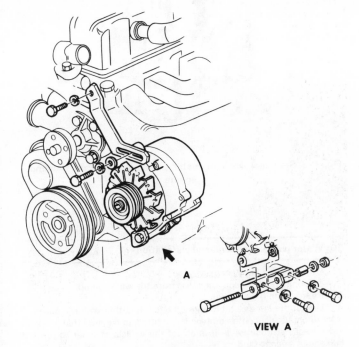

Fig. 2.7 Alternator mounting arrangement on 6-cylinder in-line engine

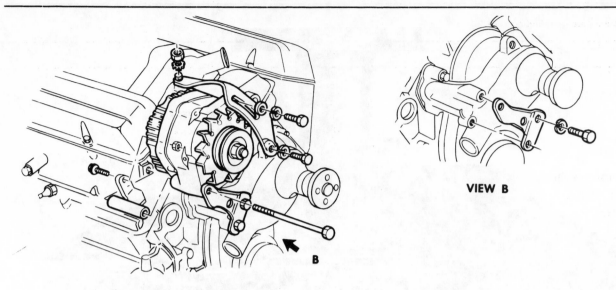

Fig. 2.8 Alternator mounting arrangement on V8 engines

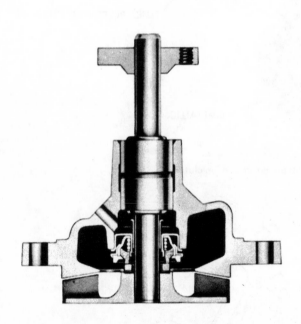

Fig. 2.9 Sectional view of water pump installed on 6-cylinder engine

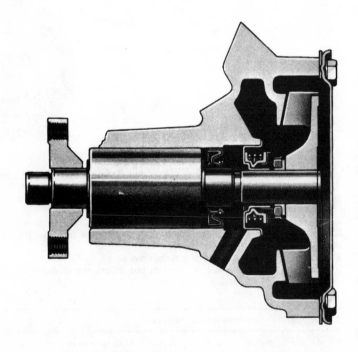

Fig. 2.10 Sectional view of water pump installed on V8 engines

10 Water pump – removal and installation

1   Drain the cooling system.
2   Disconnect all the coolant hoses from the water pump.
3   Remove the fan drivebelt.
4   Unbolt the fan assembly and remove it together with the pulley. If a thermostatically controlled type fan is fitted, make sure that it is kept in its in-car attitude while it is out of the vehicle in order to prevent leakage of silicone fluid.
5   Unbolt the water pump from the cylinder block and remove it. On in-line engines, pull the pump straight out of the block in order to avoid damage to the water pump impeller.
6   Peel away the old gasket and clean the face of the cylinder block.
7   If the water pump is faulty or worn, it should be renewed complete as overhaul of the original pump is not recommended and spare parts are not available.
8   Installation of the new pump is a reversal of removal, but use a new flange gasket smeared both sides with jointing compound.

11 Coolant temperature gage and sender unit

1   If the engine coolant temperature gage fails to give a reading, first check the security of the connecting leads between the sender unit and gage terminals. If these are in order, the only satisfactory check is by substitution of new units.
2   To remove the sender unit, the engine cooling system will first have to be drained.
3   To remove the gage, refer to Chapter 10.

12 Fault diagnosis – cooling system

Symptom	Reason/s
Overheating	Low coolant level
	Faulty radiator pressure cap
	Thermostat stuck shut
	Drivebelt slipping or incorrectly tensioned
	Clogged radiator matrix
	Incorrect engine timing
	Corroded system
Cool running	Incorrect type thermostat
Slow warm up	Thermostat stuck open
Coolant loss	Faulty radiator pressure cap
	Split hose
	Leaking water pump-to-block joint
	Leaking freeze plug
	Blown cylinder head gasket
Corrosion in system	Air being drawn in through loose hose clips
	Exhaust gas leakage into coolant due to leaking cylinder head or manifold gaskets

Chapter 3 Fuel and emission control systems

Refer to Chapter 13 for specifications and information applicable to 1979 through 1985 models.

Contents

Specifications

System type . . . . Rear mounted fuel tank, mechanically operated fuel pump with 1, 2 or 4 barrel downdraft carburetor
Emission control on all later vehicles

Fuel tank capacity
1968 thru 1972 . . . . 24.5 US gal or 22.0 US gal with anti-overfill device
1973 . . . . 21.0 US gal
1974 . . . . 21.0 US gal (optional 30 US gal)
1975 thru 1976 . . . . 21.0 US gal (optional 36 US gal)
1977 . . . . 22.0 US gal
1978 . . . . 22.0 US gal (optional 33 US gal)

Fuel pump
Type . . . . Sealed, operated from engine camshaft. Pressure 4.5 to 5.0 lbf/in^2

Air cleaner . . . . Disposable paper element or oil bath type. All later models have automatic temperature controlled type.

Fuel filter . . . . Disposable paper element type located in carburetor fuel inlet

Carburetor application (All units are of Rochester manufacture)

| | In-line engines | | | V8 engines | | |
	230 cu in	250 cu in	292 cu in	307 cu in	350 cu in	400 cu in
1968 thru 1970	M	M	M	2G	–	–
1971 thru 1972	–	M	–	2GV	4MV	–

1973 thru 1974	–	MV	MV	2GV	4MV	–
1975 thru 1976	–	1MV	1MV	–	2GC or 4MV or M4MC	4MV
1977 thru 1978	–	1ME	1ME	–	4MV or M4MC	M4MC

Idle speed settings

In the following table 'High' indicates initial setting of curb idle speed and 'Low' indicates final setting of curb idle speed

	230 cu in		250 cu in		292 cu in		307 cu in		350 cu in		400 cu in	
	High	Low	High	Low	High	Low	High	Low	High	Low	High	Low
1968 thru 1970 (without emission control)												
MT	550	530	550	530	550	530	550	530	–	–	–	–
AT	500	480	500	480	500	480	500	530	–	–	–	–
(with emission control)												
MT	700	680	700	680	700	680	700	680	–	–	–	–
AT	500	480	500	480	600	580	–	–	–	–	–	–
1971												
MT	–	–	800	750	600	550	800*	700* 450†	775	770	–	–
AT‡	–	–	630	600	550* 400†	500*	630*	600* 450†	630	600	–	–
1972												
MT (G10)	–	–	800	700	–	–	1000	900	1000	900	–	–
(G20 – 30)	–	–	775	700	–	–	700	600	–	–	–	–
AT‡ (G10)	–	–	630	600	–	–	650	600	–	–	–	–
(G20 – 30)	–	–	775	700	–	–	700	600	630	600	–	–
1973												
MT (G10)	–	–	750	700	775	700	950	900	920	900	–	–
G20 – 30)	–	–	775	700	675	600	700	600	750	600	–	–
AT‡ (G10)	–	–	630	600	775	700	630	600	620	600	–	–
§ (G20 – 30)	–	–	775	700	675	600	700	–	750	600	–	–
1974 thru 1975									Dual barrel			
MT	–	–	850* lean drop 950/850	450†	600 lean drop 700/600	450	–	–	900* lean drop 1000/900	500†	–	–
AT‡	–	–	600 lean drop 650/600	450	–	–	–	–	600 lean drop 650/600	500	–	–
1976												
MT (Fed)	–	–	900 lean drop 1075/900	425	600 lean drop 700/600	450	–	–	800 lean drop 900/800	–	–	–
MT (Cal)	–	–	1000 lean drop 1150/1000	425	600 lean drop 700/600	450	–	–	800 lean drop 900/800	–	–	–
AT‡ (Fed)	–	–	550 lean drop 575/550	425	1000 lean drop 700/600	450	–	–	600 lean drop 650/600	–	700 lean drop 770/700	–
AT‡ (Cal)	–	–	1000 lean drop 630/600	425	600 lean drop 700/600	450	–	–	600 lean drop 650/600	–	700 lean drop 770/700	–
1977 thru 1978 MT (Fed)												
(G10)	–	–	750	425	–	–	–	–	800	700	–	–
(G20 – 30)	–	–	600	450	600	450	–	–	875	700	770	700
MT (Cal)												
(G10)	–	–	850	425	–	–	–	–	–	–	–	–
(G20 – 30)	–	–	–	–	–	–	–	–	800	700	–	–
AT‡ (G10)	–	–	550 with A/C 600	425	–	–	–	–	550	500 solenoid screw 650	–	–

AT‡ (G20 – 30)   –   –   600   450   600   450   –   –   –   –   –   –

Note: *Solenoid energized*
   † *Solenoid disconnected*
   ‡ *In drive*
   § *In Neutral*
   MT – Manual transmission
   AT – Automatic transmission
   A/C – Air conditioning
   Fed – Federal
   Cal – California

Maximum CO levels for vehicles equipped with emission control carburetors

G10 models (light duty emission)
   250 cu in engine 0.3%
   350 cu in engine (2-barrel carburetor) 0.5%
   350 cu in engine (4-barrel carburetor) 0.5%
G20 and G30 models (heavy duty emission)
   250 cu in engine 2.0%
   292 cu in engine 0.3%
   350 cu in engine (4 barrel carburetor) 0.5%
   400 cu in engine 0.5%

Carburetor adjustment data
All dimensions are in inches. For procedure, refer to text

Rochester M 1968 thru 1970

Float level	Dashpot	Metering rod	Choke rod	Fast idle (rpm)
$\frac{9}{32}$	$\frac{1}{16}$ to $\frac{3}{32}$ Plunger to throttle lever	0.140	0.150	2400

Rochester 2G Series

	Float level	Float drop	Accelerator pump	Choke rod	Choke vacuum break	Choke unloader	Fast idle (rpm)
Rochester 2G 1968 thru 1970	$\frac{3}{4}$	$1\frac{3}{4}$	$1\frac{1}{8}$		N/A (Manual choke)		2100
Rochester 2GV 1971	$\frac{23}{32}$	$1\frac{3}{4}$	$1\frac{3}{8}$	0.60	0.140	0.215	2200 to 2400
1972	$\frac{21}{32}$	$1\frac{9}{32}$	$1\frac{5}{16}$	0.075	0.110	0.210	2200
1973	$\frac{21}{32}$ except No. 7043108 $\frac{25}{32}$	$1\frac{9}{32}$	$1\frac{5}{16}$ except No. 7043108 $\frac{7}{16}$	0.150 except No.7043108 0.200	0.080 except No.7043108 0.250	0.215 except No.7043108 0.250	2400 on high step of cam
1974 thru 1975	$\frac{19}{32}$	$1\frac{9}{32}$	$1\frac{9}{32}$ except Nos. 7044114 7044124 $1\frac{3}{16}$	0.200 except Nos. 7044114 7044124 0.130	0.140 except Nos. 7044114 7044124 0.325	0.250 except Nos. 7044114 7044124 0.325	1600
Rochester 2GC 1976	$\frac{21}{32}$	$1\frac{9}{32}$	$1\frac{11}{16}$	0.260	0.130	0.325	2000

Rochester MV series

	Float level	Choke rod	Choke vacuum break	Choke unloader	Metering rod	Fast idle (rpm)
1970 thru 1971	$\frac{1}{4}$	0.190 (1970) 0.180 (1971)	0.230 (1970) 0.260 (1971)	0.350	0.070	2400
1972	$\frac{1}{4}$	0.180	0.260	0.500	0.070	2400
1973	$\frac{1}{4}$	0.375	0.430	0.600	0.070	2400
1974 thru 1975 Carburetor No. 7044021	0.295	0.275	0.350	0.500	0.080	
7044022	0.295	0.245	0.300	0.500	0.080	1800 to

7044321	0.295	0.300	0.375	0.500	0.080	2400 on high
7044025	$\frac{1}{4}$	0.245	0.300	0.521	0.070	of cam
7044026	$\frac{1}{4}$	0.275	0.350	0.521	0.070	

Rochester 1M Series

	Float level	Choke rod	Choke vacuum break		Choke unloader	Metering rod	Fast idle (rpm)
Rochester 1MV			Primary	Auxiliary			

1976

Carburetor No.	Float level	Choke rod	Choke vacuum break Primary	Auxiliary	Choke unloader	Metering rod	Fast idle (rpm)
17056002 17056003 17056004	$\frac{11}{32}$	0.130 except No. 17056003 0.145	0.165 except No. 17056 003 0.180	0.265	0.335	0.080	2100
17056006 17056007 17056008 17056009	$\frac{1}{4}$	0.130 except No. 17056008 and 17056009 0.150	0.165 except No. 17056 008 17056 009 0.190	–	0.275	0.070	2100
17056302 17056303	$\frac{11}{32}$	0.155 0.180	0.190 0.225	–	0.325	0.080	2100
17056308 17056309	$\frac{1}{4}$	0.150	0.190	–	0.295	0.070	2100

Rochester 1ME
1977 thru 1978   *For data refer to relevant text describing adjustment*

Rochester 4MV Series

	Float level	Accelerator pump	Choke rod	Choke vacuum break	Choke unloader	Air valve dashpot	Air valve wind–up	Fast idle (rpm)
1971	$\frac{1}{4}$	$\frac{5}{16}$	0.100	0.245	0.450	0.020	–	1500 MT 1800 AT
1972	$\frac{3}{16}$	$\frac{3}{8}$	0.100	0.215	0.450	0.020	–	1350 MT 1500 AT set on second step of cam
1973 7043202 7043203 7043210 7043211	$\frac{7}{32}$	$\frac{13}{32}$	0.403	0.215	0.450	0.020	$\frac{1}{2}$	As 1972
7043208 7043215	$\frac{5}{16}$	$\frac{13}{32}$	0.430	0.215	0.450	0.020	$\frac{1}{2}$	
7043200 7043216 7043207 7043507	$\frac{1}{4}$	$\frac{13}{32}$	0.430	0.250 except No. 7043507 0.275	0.450	0.020	$\frac{11}{16}$	1300 MT G10 models (High step of cam) 1600 MT G20–30 models (High step of cam) 1600 AT (High step of cam)
1974 thru 1975 7044202 7044502 7044203 7044503 7044218	$\frac{1}{4}$	$\frac{13}{32}$	0.430	0.230	0.450	0.020	$\frac{7}{8}$	1600 on high step of cam

Part number	Float level	Accelerator pump rod	Choke coil cover	Choke rod (fast idle cam)	Air valve dashpot	Front vacuum break	Air valve spring wind-up	Choke unloader	Fast idle (rpm)
7044518									
7044219									
7044519									
7044213 7044513	$\frac{11}{32}$	$\frac{13}{32}$	0.430	0.215	0.450	0.020	$\frac{7}{8}$		1600 on high step of cam
7044223 7044227 7044212 7044217 7044500 7044520	0.657	$\frac{13}{32}$	0.430	0.230 except No. 7044500 0.250	0.450	0.020	$\frac{7}{16}$		1600 on high step of cam
7044224 7044214 7044514 7044215 7044515 7044216 7044516	$\frac{11}{32}$	$\frac{13}{32}$	0.430	0.215	0.450	0.020	$\frac{7}{8}$		1600 on high step of cam

1976 thru 1978

Part number	Float level	Accelerator pump rod	Choke coil cover	Choke rod (fast idle cam)	Air valve dashpot	Front vacuum break	Air valve spring wind-up	Choke unloader	Fast idle (rpm)
7045213	$\frac{11}{32}$	$\frac{9}{32}$	0.290	0.145	0.295	0.015	$\frac{7}{8}$		1600
7045214				0.145			$\frac{7}{8}$		
7045215				0.145			$\frac{7}{8}$		
7045216				0.145			$\frac{7}{8}$		
7045225				0.138			$\frac{3}{4}$		
7045229				0.138			$\frac{3}{4}$		
7045583				0.155			$\frac{7}{8}$		
7045584				0.155			$\frac{7}{8}$		
7045585				0.155			$\frac{7}{8}$		
7045586				0.155			$\frac{7}{8}$		
7045588				0.155			$\frac{3}{4}$		
7045589				0.155			$\frac{3}{4}$		
17056212				0.155			$\frac{7}{16}$		
17056217				0.155			$\frac{7}{16}$		

Rochester M4 MC Series

Part number	Float level	Accelerator pump rod	Choke coil cover	Choke rod (fast idle cam)	Air valve dashpot	Front vacuum break	Air valve spring wind-up	Choke unloader	Fast idle (rpm)
1976									
17056208 17056209 17056218 17056219 17056508 17056509	$\frac{5}{16}$	$\frac{9}{32}$	0.120	0.325	0.015	0.185	$\frac{7}{8}$	0.325	1600
17056512 17056517	$\frac{7}{16}$	$\frac{9}{32}$	0.120	0.325	0.015	0.185	$\frac{7}{8}$	0.275	1600
17056518 17056519	$\frac{5}{16}$	$\frac{9}{32}$	0.120	0.325	0.015	0.185	$\frac{7}{8}$	0.325	1600

1977 thru 1978 *For carburetor adjustment data refer to appropriate sections in text*

Torque wrench settings   lbf ft

Exhaust manifold bolts	20
Inlet manifold bolts	20
Inlet-to-exhaust manifold bolts	30

1 General description

1   The fuel system on all models comprises a rear-mounted fuel tank, a mechanically-operated fuel pump, a carburetor and an air cleaner.
2   The carburetor may be of single, dual or four barrel type, depending upon the engine capacity and the date of production of the vehicle.

3   All models are equipped with some form of emission control equipment, but the later the date of the vehicle so the more complex and sophisticated will the carburetor and the emission control system become.
4   On very late models, a catalytic converter is fitted (see Section 30).

2 Fuel tank filler cap – location and type

1 On vehicles built up until 1970 the gas cap is of the vented type located directly on the left rear body panel.
2 On later models, the cap is located under a hinged flap in a rather higher location and is a non-vented type used in conjunction with a fuel evaporative control system
3 Use only fuel of the octane rating specified on your particular vehicle decal. Where a catalytic converter is incorporated in the exhaust system, only unloaded fuel must be used.

3 Air cleaner – servicing

Non-temperature-controlled type (paper element)
1 At the intervals specified in Routine Maintenance, unscrew the wing nut on top of the air cleaner cover then remove the cover.
2 Remove the filter element and discard it, then wipe out the interior of the casing, insert a new element and install the cover.

Non-temperature-controlled type (oil bath)
3 With this type of air cleaner, release the clamp screw at the base of the reservoir and lift the cleaner assembly from the carburetor.
4 Remove the wing nut and then take off the cover and element.
5 Release the clamp screw and remove the air intake horn from the carburetor, then loosen the stud wing nut to allow removal of the reservoir.
6 Drain the oil from the reservoir and clean all components in a suitable solvent.
7 Reassemble and install, fill the reservoir with SAE 50 engine oil when operating in above freezing temperatures, or SAE 20 below freezing.

Temperature-controlled (thermostatic) air cleaner (TAC)
8 If a plain paper filter element is used, renew it as described in paragraphs 1 and 2 of this Section.
9 If a Polywrap element is used, then remove the Polywrap band from the paper element and discard the element. If the band is in good undamaged condition, rinse it clean in kerosene and squeeze dry. Now dip the band in clean engine oil and gently squeeze out the excess. Install the band to a new paper element and reassemble.
10 Any malfunction in the temperature-controlled air cleaner should first be checked out by starting the engine (**COLD**) and observing the position of the deflector flap valve using a mirror to look up the intake nozzle of the cleaner. This should be closed to cold air but open to warm air. Conversely, once the engine has warmed up, the flap valve should be open to cold air and closed to warm. Both tests are carried out with the engine idling.
11 The vacuum unit can be removed from the air cleaner by drilling

Fig. 3.1 Typical air cleaner (non-temperature-controlled)

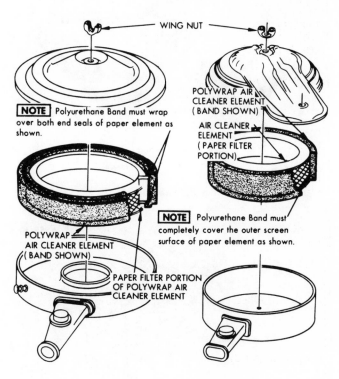

NOTE Polyurethane Band must wrap over both end seals of paper element as shown.

POLYWRAP AIR CLEANER ELEMENT (BAND SHOWN)

POLYWRAP AIR CLEANER ELEMENT (BAND SHOWN)

WING NUT

POLYWRAP AIR CLEANER ELEMENT (BAND SHOWN)

AIR CLEANER ELEMENT (PAPER FILTER PORTION)

NOTE Polyurethane Band must completely cover the outer screen surface of paper element as shown.

PAPER FILTER PORTION OF POLYWRAP AIR CLEANER ELEMENT

Fig. 3.2 Polywrap type element installation diagram

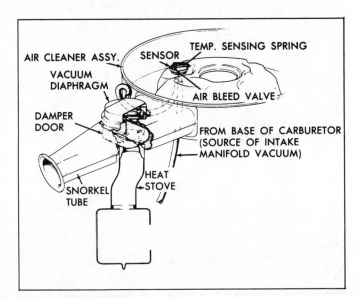

AIR CLEANER ASSY.
SENSOR
TEMP. SENSING SPRING
VACUUM DIAPHRAGM
AIR BLEED VALVE
DAMPER DOOR
FROM BASE OF CARBURETOR (SOURCE OF INTAKE MANIFOLD VACUUM)
HEAT STOVE
SNORKEL TUBE

Fig. 3.3 Temperature-controlled type air cleaner

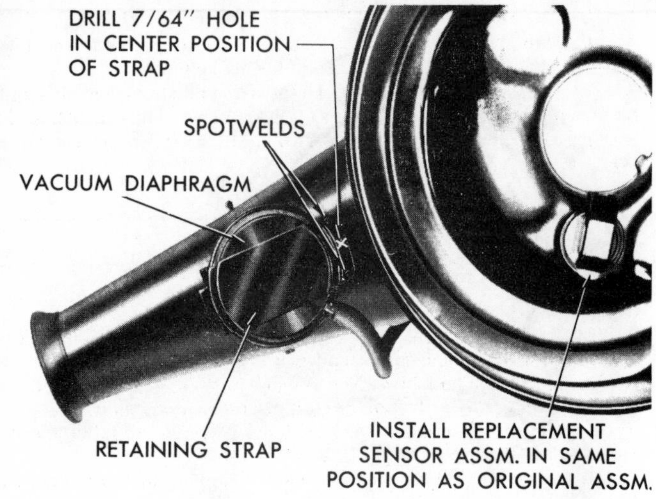

DRILL 7/64" HOLE
IN CENTER POSITION
OF STRAP

SPOTWELDS

VACUUM DIAPHRAGM

RETAINING STRAP

INSTALL REPLACEMENT
SENSOR ASSM. IN SAME
POSITION AS ORIGINAL ASSM.

Fig. 3.4 Vacuum diaphragm attachment to temperature-controlled
type air cleaner

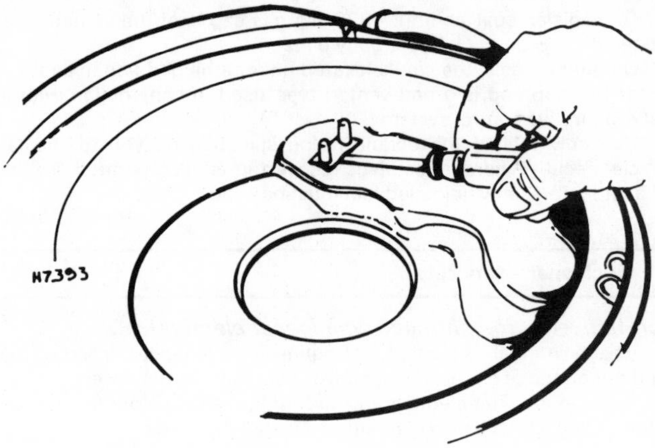

H7393

Fig. 3.5 Removing sensor unit (temperature-controlled air cleaner)

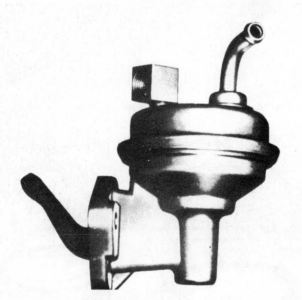

Fig. 3.6 Fuel pump

FUEL PIPE
ASSEMBLY

SPARK CONTROL
PIPE

CLIP

FUEL
PUMP
ASSEMBLY

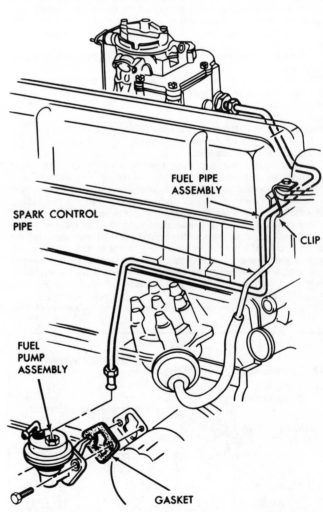

GASKET

Fig. 3.7 Fuel pump attachment to in-line engine

PIPE ASSEMBLY

PIPE ASSEMBLY

ROD

GASKET

PLATE

GASKET

PUMP

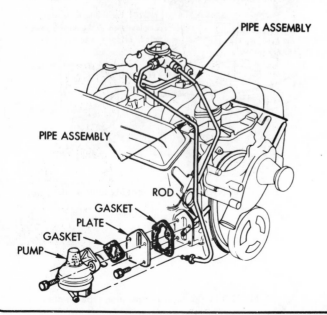

 Fig. 3.8 Fuel pump attachment to V8 engine

out the two spotwelds to remove the retaining strap. The new vacuum unit repair pack will contain the necessary sheet metal screws to hold the retaining strap in position when reassembling.
12 The sensor can be removed by prying up the tabs on the sensor retaining clip (Fig. 3.5).

4 Fuel pump – description, testing, removal and installation

1 The fuel pump is a sealed type and is actuated from the engine camshaft. On in-line engines the pump rocker arm bears directly on an eccentric cam on the camshaft while on V8 engines, a push-rod is used between the camshaft and the pump rocker.
2 No servicing can be carried out as the unit is sealed but if the pump is suspected of being faulty, carry out the following test.
3 Verify that gas is in the fuel tank. Disconnect the primary wire which runs between the coil and the distributor to prevent the engine firing when the starter is actuated.
4 Disconnect the fuel inlet pipe from the carburetor and place its open end in a container.
5 Operate the starter and check that well-defined spurts of fuel are seen being ejected from the open end of the pipe. If so, the pump is operating correctly; if not, renew the pump as described in the following paragraphs.
6 Disconnect the fuel inlet and outlet pipes from the pump.
7 Unscrew and remove the pump mounting bolts, then withdraw the pump and gasket.
8 Installation is a reversal of removal; use a new flange gasket and apply sealer to the mounting bolt threads.
9 On some fuel pumps fitted to very late models, the pump incorporates a metering outlet for a vapor return system

5 Fuel filters – renewal

1 All vehicles except the very earliest models have a disposable type filter element incorporated in the fuel inlet union on the carburetor (photo).
2 At the specified intervals, unscrew the fuel pipe from the filter body and then unscrew the filter body from the carburetor.
3 Withdraw the filter element, together with the spring and gasket. If a paper element is installed, discard it and install a new one (Fig. 3.9).

4 If a porous bronze element is installed blow through it to see if it is still clear. If it is, it may be installed for further service.
5 *On very early vehicles*, the fuel filter is of a bowl type which should be unscrewed to obtain access to the disposable element. Make sure that the sealing ring is in good order before the filter bowl is screwed up.

6 Fuel tank – removal and installation

Early vehicles
1 The fuel tank is mounted behind the rear axle between the frame side rails. It is held in place by two metal straps (Fig. 3.10.)
2 To remove the tank, first drain any fuel into a suitable container.
3 Disconnect the leads from the fuel contents sender unit.
4 Unclamp the filler neck and the vent tube hoses and then disconnect the fuel outlet pipe from the tank.
5 Never be tempted to weld or solder a leaking fuel tank yourself. Leave it to the professionals as the tank will need steaming-out for some time before it is safe to work on.

5.1 Carburetor fuel filter

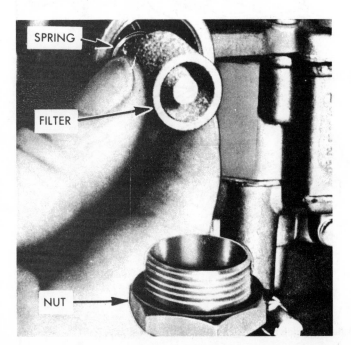

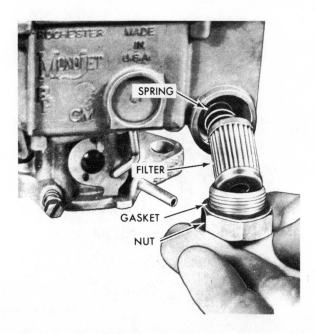

Fig. 3.9 Removing a fuel filter element (A) Porous bronze (B) Paper

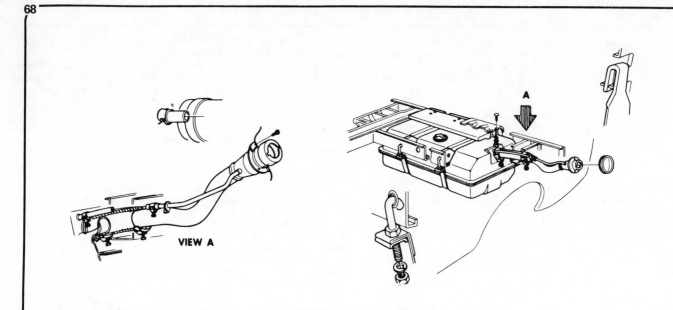

Fig. 3.10 Fuel tank (early models)

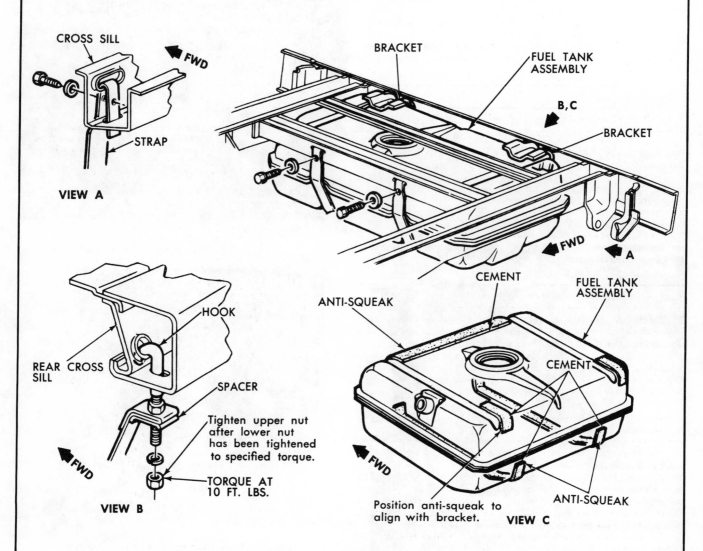

CROSS SILL

FWD

STRAP

VIEW A

BRACKET

FUEL TANK ASSEMBLY

B,C

BRACKET

FWD

A

CEMENT

HOOK

REAR CROSS SILL

SPACER

Tighten upper nut after lower nut has been tightened to specified torque.

FWD

TORQUE AT 10 FT. LBS.

VIEW B

ANTI-SQUEAK

FUEL TANK ASSEMBLY

CEMENT

FWD

ANTI-SQUEAK

Position anti-squeak to align with bracket.

VIEW C

Fig. 3.11 Fuel tank (later models)

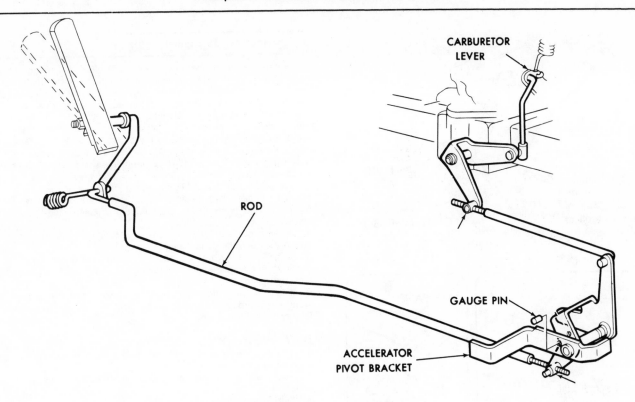

Fig. 3.12 Rod-type accelerator linkage

Later vehicles

6   Later models have a fuel tank of different design using a non-vented fuel filler cap (Fig. 3.11).

7   In addition, nearly all vehicles have an evaporative emission control system to control the escape of fuel vapor to atmosphere (see Section 27).

8   Removal of the fuel tank is very similar to that described in the earlier part of this Section except that additional pipe work must be disconnected from the tank before removal.

9   Nearly all later models have a flow-and-return line running between the tank and fuel pump

10   Installation of the fuel tank on all models is a reversal of removal but make sure that the anti-vibration strips are in position and that they are in good condition.

---

7   Fuel tank (contents level) unit – removal and installation

1   These units are generally very reliable but, in the event of a fault developing, first check all the connecting wires and have the fuel gage checked out. If these are in order, renew the tank unit.

2   To remove the unit, it will have to be rotated to release it from its retaining collar cut-outs. Two screwdrivers used as levers to turn the unit in a counterclockwise direction will usually do the job.

3   Always use a new sealing washer when installing the unit.

---

8   Accelerator linkage

1   The accelerator linkage on early models is a rod type while on later vehicles a cable control is used.

2   *To adjust the rod type linkage,* have an assistant hold the throttle lever on the carburetor wide open and then adjust the swivels so that the accelerator pedal is $\frac{1}{4}$ inch from the floor. A hole is provided in the levers to facilitate the adjustment of the swivels on the rods. Insert a $\frac{3}{16}$ inch diameter gage pin through the holes (Fig. 3.12).

3   *On later cable operated layouts,* no adjustment is provided for. Failure to obtain full throttle when the accelerator is depressed to within $\frac{1}{4}$ inch of the floor can therefore only be due to bent or damaged components.

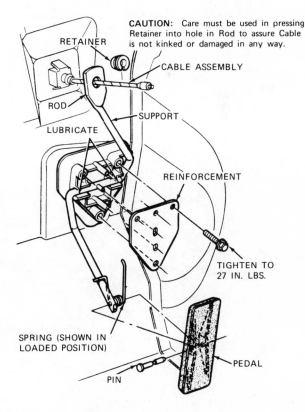

Fig. 3.13 Typical accelerator pedal arrangement

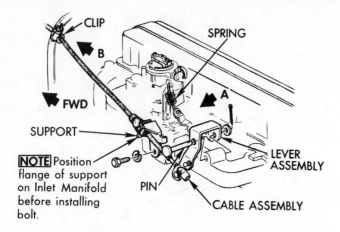

NOTE Position flange of support on Inlet Manifold before installing bolt.

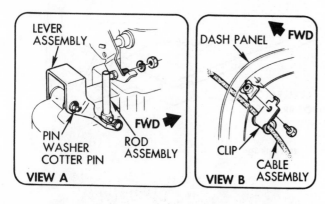

Fig. 3.14 Typical accelerator cable connection to carburetor on in-line engine

9 Carburetors – description

1   Reference should be made to the Specifications for the general application of the different types of carburetor installed during the production run of vehicles covered by this Manual. It is emphasized that the information given is not intended to identify a particular carburetor with a specific vehicle and the actual carburetor fitted to your engine should be checked out by recording the number stamped on the unit and checking it with you partsman. It is very important not to use an incorrect unit, or to modify the jets or internal components by substituting parts with different manufacturers' part numbers from those originally used.

2   Between 1968 and 1970, some carburetors have manually-operated chokes, otherwise all units have automatic chokes, either stove (hot air) heated from the manifold or electrically heated (IME carburetor).

3   Depending on engine capacity, the carburetor may be of single, dual or four barrel downdraft type.

4   Overhaul of a worn carburetor is not difficult, but always obtain a repair kit in advance which will contain all the necessary gaskets and renewable items.

5   If a carburetor has seen considerable use and is obviously well worn, it will probably be more economical to replace it with a new or factory reconditioned unit.

The Rochester MV Series carburetor

6   This is a single bore downdraft unit using a triple venturi with a plain tube nozzle.

7   Fuel metering is controlled by a main well air bleed and a fixed orifice jet.

8   During acceleration and at high engine speeds, a power enrichment system maintains top performance. On later model vehicles, an automatic choke system is incorporated which operates by means of an exhaust heated coil; a throttle closing solenoid (controlled through the ignition switch) is used to ensure that the throttle valve closes fully after the ignition is switched off to prevent running-on.

The Rochester 2G Series carburetor

9   This is a dual barrel, side bowl design.

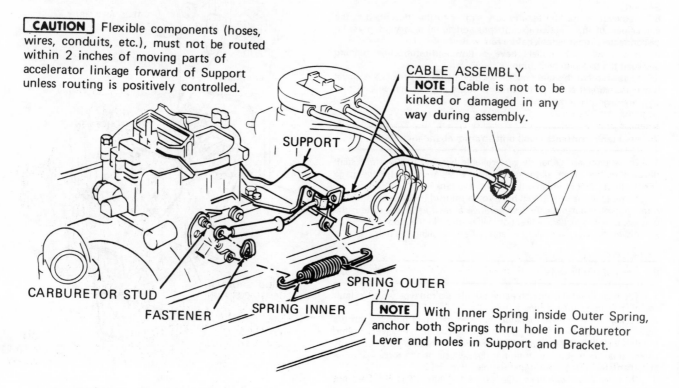

CAUTION Flexible components (hoses, wires, conduits, etc.), must not be routed within 2 inches of moving parts of accelerator linkage forward of Support unless routing is positively controlled.

CABLE ASSEMBLY
NOTE Cable is not to be kinked or damaged in any way during assembly.

NOTE With Inner Spring inside Outer Spring, anchor both Springs thru hole in Carburetor Lever and holes in Support and Bracket.

Fig. 3.15 Typical accelerator cable connection carburetor on V8 engine

10 The units fitted to manual and automatic transmission vehicles are similar but vary in calibration.

11 The main metering jets are of a fixed type, calibration being accomplished through a system of air bleeds.

12 A power enrichment valve assembly is incorporated, by which power mixtures are controlled by air velocity past the boost venturi according to engine demands.

13 On later model vehicles, an electrically-operated throttle closing solenoid (controlled through the ignition switch) is used to ensure that the throttle valve closes fully after the ignition is switched off, to prevent running-on.

14 The choke is automatic and is operated by an exhaust manifold heated coil.

The Rochester 4MV (Quadrajet) carburetor

15 This is a downdraft two stage unit. The primary side used a triple venturi system. The secondary side has two large bores and one metering system which supplements the primary main metering system and reclaims fuel from a common float chamber.

The Rochester M4MC (Quadrajet) carburetor

16 This is also a downdraft two stage unit and is very similar to the 4MV unit.

---

10 Carburetor – (Rochester M and MV) – on-vehicle adjustments

Idle adjustment (1968 through 1972)

1 Run the engine to normal operating temperature, make sure that the choke valve plate is fully open and have the air cleaner in position. If air-conditioning is installed, switch it on during adjustment.

2 Make sure that the ignition settings are corrrect.

3 Adjust the idle speed screw until the engine idles at the level specified in the Specifications according to engine capacity. A tachometer should be connected to the engine to check this.

4 Now turn the mixture screw in or out to achieve the fastest, smoothest idling speed.

5 Now screw the mixture screw in to obtain the specified decrease in the idling speed (lean drop) as shown in the Specifications.

6 Switch off the engine.

Idle adjustment (1973 on)

7 With the engine running and the solenoid lead connected, rotate the complete solenoid body to set the curb idle. This should be in accordance with the information provided on the individual vehicle sticker but a guide is given in the Specifications.

8 The solenoid should be energized and the air-conditioner (if installed) switch off.

9 Now set the low idle by first disconnecting the lead from the solenoid and then inserting a $\frac{1}{8}$ inch Allen key into the end of the solenoid and turning it until the engine speed is as specified on the individual vehicle sticker. A guide is given in the Specifications.

10 Reconnect the lead to the solenoid and switch off the engine.

NOTE: *These operations do not include altering the setting of the mixture screw which is pre-set during production. However, to improve the quality of the idling, the mixture screw may be turned within the limits of its cap stops. To correct grossly incorrect mixture or if the caps have been broken off during major overhaul, reset the screw by one of the methods described in Section 15 for two barrel carburetors.*

Manual choke adjustment

11 Remove the air cleaner, then push the choke control knob fully in and then withdraw it $\frac{1}{8}$ inch.

12 Release the choke cable clamp at the carburetor and adjust the position of the cable in the clamp until the choke valve plate is fully open.

13 Tighten the cable clamp screw then check direction of the cable when the knob is pulled and pushed. Install the air cleaner.

Automatic choke adjustment

14 Remove the air cleaner and disconnect the choke rod from the choke lever.

15 Hold the choke valve plate closed with one hand and with the other pull the choke rod downward against its top. The top of the

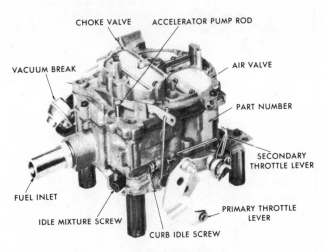

Fig. 3.16 Rochester 4MV carburetor

Fig. 3.17 Rochester M4MC carburetor

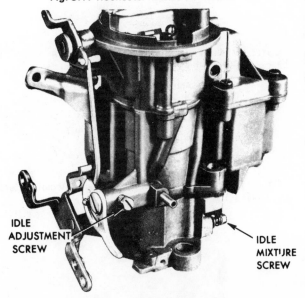

Fig. 3.18 Rochester M carburetor

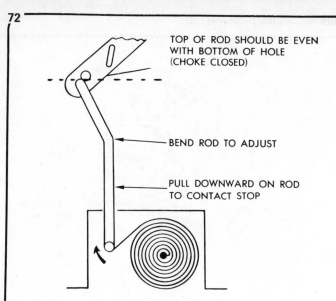

TOP OF ROD SHOULD BE EVEN WITH BOTTOM OF HOLE (CHOKE CLOSED)

BEND ROD TO ADJUST

PULL DOWNWARD ON ROD TO CONTACT STOP

Fig. 3.19 Automatic choke adjustment diagram (M and MV carburetors)

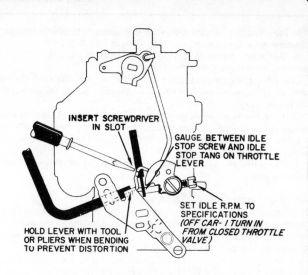

INSERT SCREWDRIVER IN SLOT

GAUGE BETWEEN IDLE STOP SCREW AND IDLE STOP TANG ON THROTTLE LEVER

SET IDLE R.P.M. TO SPECIFICATIONS (OFF CAR- I TURN IN FROM CLOSED THROTTLE VALVE)

HOLD LEVER WITH TOOL OR PLIERS WHEN BENDING TO PREVENT DISTORTION

Fig. 3.20 Fast idle adjustment diagram (M and MV carburetors)

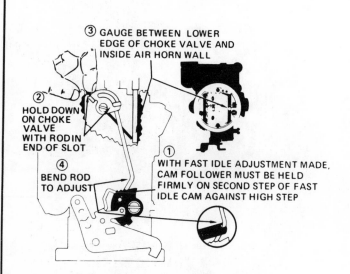

③ GAUGE BETWEEN LOWER EDGE OF CHOKE VALVE AND INSIDE AIR HORN WALL

② HOLD DOWN ON CHOKE VALVE WITH ROD IN END OF SLOT

④ BEND ROD TO ADJUST

① WITH FAST IDLE ADJUSTMENT MADE, CAM FOLLOWER MUST BE HELD FIRMLY ON SECOND STEP OF FAST IDLE CAM AGAINST HIGH STEP

NOTE: MANUAL CHOKE MODELS WITH SMOOTH CONTOUR CAM.

USE THE SAME PROCEDURE AS ABOVE EXCEPT FOR STEP (1). AS THERE ARE NO STEPS ON MANUAL CHOKE CAM, THE INDEX LINE ON SIDE OF CAM SHOULD BE LINED UP WITH CONTACT POINT OF THE FAST IDLE CAM FOLLOWER TANG.

Fig. 3.21 Fast idle cam adjustment (M and MV carburetors)

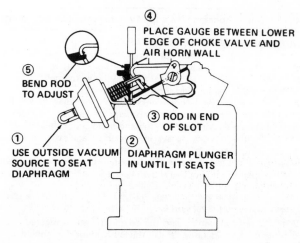

④ PLACE GAUGE BETWEEN LOWER EDGE OF CHOKE VALVE AND AIR HORN WALL

⑤ BEND ROD TO ADJUST

③ ROD IN END OF SLOT

① USE OUTSIDE VACUUM SOURCE TO SEAT DIAPHRAGM

② DIAPHRAGM PLUNGER IN UNTIL IT SEATS

Fig. 3.22 Vacuum break adjustment (M and MV carburetors)

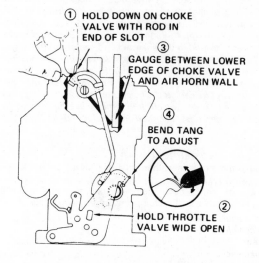

① HOLD DOWN ON CHOKE VALVE WITH ROD IN END OF SLOT

③ GAUGE BETWEEN LOWER EDGE OF CHOKE VALVE AND AIR HORN WALL

④ BEND TANG TO ADJUST

② HOLD THROTTLE VALVE WIDE OPEN

Fig. 3.23 Choke unloader adjustment (M and MV carburetors)

choke rod should now be level with the bottom of the hole in the choke lever. If necessary, bend the rod to achieve this (Fig. 3.19).
16 Reconnect the rod and install the air cleaner.

Fast idle speed adjustment
17 Make sure that the idle speed is correctly set according to the Specifications.
18 *With manual choke carburetors,* turn the fast idle cam to its highest position.
19 *With automatic choke models,* set the cam follower on the highest stop of the cam (Fig. 3.20).
20 Bend the cam follower as necessary so that it will give a fast idle in accordance with that listed in the Specifications.

Fast idle cam (choke rod) adjustment
21 With the fast idle speed adjustment correctly made, set the cam follower on the second step of the fast idle cam (Fig. 3.21).
22 Hold the choke valve plate down. This should position the choke rod in the bottom end of the slot.
23 Insert a twist drill of suitable diameter between the lower edge of the choke valve plate and the air horn wall. The diameter of the twist drill should match the gap for this setting shown in the Specifications according to carburetor type.
24 Bend the choke rod as necessary to adjust the gap.

Vacuum break adjustment
25 Seat the vacuum diaphragm. This can be done by using a hand-operated pump attached to a length of flexible pipe and when the diaphragm is seated, clamp the pipe to maintain the vacuum conditions.
26 Push the diaphragm plunger in if necessary until it too seats.
27 Insert a twist drill of suitable diameter (see the Specifications) using it as a gage between the lower edge of the choke valve plate and the air horn wall (Fig. 3.22).
28 Bend the connecting rod as necessary to alter the gap to conform to that specified.

Choke unloader
29 Press down on the choke valve plate. The choke rod should be in the end of the slot under this setting (Fig. 3.23).
30 Move the throttle lever to hold the throttle valve plate wide open.
31 Insert a twist drill of suitable diameter (see the Specifications) between the lower edge of choke valve plate and the air horn wall to measure the gap. If it differs from that specified, bend the tang on the throttle lever.

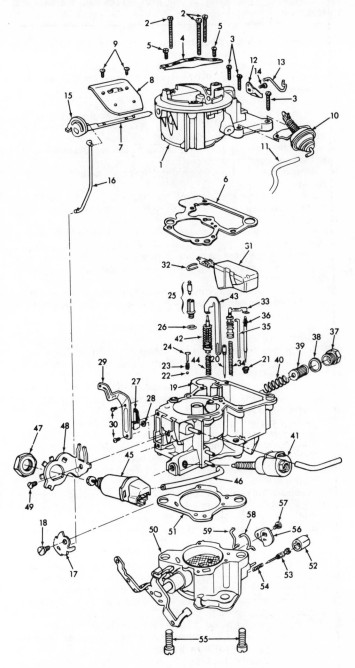

Fig. 3.24 Exploded view of M/MV carburetor

1 Air horn	16 Choke rod	30 Screw	45 Vacuum advance solenoid
2 Screws	17 Fast idle cam	31 Float	46 Vacuum tube
3 Screws	18 Cam screw	32 Float pivot pin	47 Valve nut
4 Air cleaner bracket	19 Float bowl	33 Power piston	48 Valve bracket
5 Screw	20 Idle tube	34 Spring	49 Screw
6 Gasket	21 Main metering jet	35 Power piston rod	50 Throttle body
7 Choke shaft and lever	22 Pump discharge ball	36 Metering rod and spring	51 Gasket
8 Choke valve plate	23 Spring	37 Filter nut	52 Limiter cap
9 Screw	24 Pump discharge guide	38 Gasket	53 Idle mixture screw
10 Choke vacuum break unit	25 Fuel inlet needle valve and seat	39 Fuel filter element	54 Spring
11 Vacuum break hose	26 Gasket	40 Spring	55 Throttle body screws
12 Lever	27 Idle compensator	41 Idle stop solenoid	56 Lever
13 Link	28 Gasket	42 Pump	57 Lever screw
14 Screw	29 Cover	43 Pump actuating lever	58 Link
15 Choke lever		44 Pump return spring	59 Link

11 Carburetor (Rochester M and MV) – removal, overhaul and installation

1   Disconnect the fuel pipes, the accelerator and choke controls, and the vacuum pipe from the carburetor.
2   Remove the air cleaner and disconnect the solenoid wires.
3   Unscrew and remove the mounting nuts, and lift the carburetor from the intake manifold.
4   Remove the flange gasket and discard it.
5   Clean away all external dirt from the carburetor.
6   Some carburetors will not incorporate an idle stop solenoid; instructions for its removal should be ignored on these models.
7   Disconnect the lead from the idle stop solenoid and unscrew the solenoid body from the carburetor.
8   Remove the fast idle cam from the float bowl by unscrewing the securing screw.
9   Remove the fast idle cam from the choke rod and the choke rod from the choke upper lever. Do not try to remove the choke upper lever from its shaft.
10 Remove the three long, and the three short, air horn-to-float bowl screws.
11 Remove the air horn, at the same time disconnecting the vacuum hose from the air horn casting and the choke diaphragm stem linkage from the choke lever.
12 Peel the air horn to float bowl gasket from its location and then extract the float assembly from the float bowl. Remove the pivot pin from the float arm.
13 Remove the fuel inlet needle, seat and gasket.
14 Remove the fuel inlet nut and gasket, the filter element and spring.
15 Using a long-nosed pliers, remove the pump discharge guide.
16 Invert the float bowl, and extract the pump spring and ball. Also remove the idle tube and power valve.
17 Remove the accelerator pump plunger by detaching the actuating lever from the throttle shaft, and disconnecting the actuating link and pump lever from the plunger shaft.
18 Extract the return spring from the accelerator pump well.
19 Remove the main metering jet from the bottom of the float bowl.
20 Invert the carburetor bowl and remove the screws which secure the throttle body to it. Remove the throttle body and gasket.
21 Do not dismantle the throttle valve but check that the shaft screws are securely staked.
22 Thoroughly clean the carburetor and components in a solvent or clean fuel, and dry with compressed air. Do not probe the jets or passages with wire but clear them with compressed air only.
23 Reassembly is a reversal of dismantling but the float level must be checked and adjusted in the following manner.
    Press down on the float arm above the fuel inlet needle valve and then measure the distance between the top surface of the float and the surface of the float bowl rim (gasket removed). The measurement should be as specified; if otherwise, bend the float arm as necessary. The float level adjustment may be carried out without removing the carburetor from the vehicle (Fig. 3.25).
24 When installing the air horn, tighten the securing bolts evenly.
25 When the carburetor is completely assembled, check all the settings and adjustments described in Section 10.

12 Carburetor (Rochester 1MV) – on-vehicle adjustments

Idle speed adjustment

1   Run the engine to normal operating temperature. Leave the air cleaner in position. If air conditioning is fitted, switch it off (G10 models) or on (G20-30 models).
2   Connect a tachometer to the engine in accordance with the manufacturer's instructions.
3   On G10 models, disconnect and plug the carburetor and PCV hoses at the vapor canister.
4   On G20 and heavier models, disconnect the fuel tank hose from the vapor canister.
5   Set manual transmission in Neutral; set automatic transmission in Drive (G10 models) or Neutral (G20 – 30 models).
6   With the engine running, turn the idle stop solenoid (energized) in or out as necessary to set the specified curb (higher) idle speed (Fig. 3.27).

7   Now de-energize the idle stop solenoid by pulling off its electrical connector; if the air conditioning is switched on, switch it off.
8   Turn the hexagonal screw at the end of the solenoid body to set the low (initial) idle speed to the specified figure (see Specifications).
9   Check the fast idle adjustment as described later in this Section, switch off the engine and remove the tachometer. Reconnect all the hoses.

Idle mixture adjustment

10 The idle mixture screw is fitted with a limiter cap. Normally, this screw should only be turned to the limit of its cap stop which is one turn clockwise (leaner) to improve the idle quality.
11 If after major overhaul or if the cap has been broken, set the mixture screw as described but then fit a new cap so that future adjustment will be limited to one turn clockwise (leaner).
12 Repeat the operations described in paragraphs 1 to 5.
13 Turn the mixture screw as necessary to achieve maximum idle speed.
14 Now set the idle speed to the curb (higher) speed as specified by turning the solenoid in or out.
15 Next turn the idle mixture screw clockwise (leaner) until the idle speed is at the lower specified level (lean drop method).
16 Switch off the engine, reconnect all hoses and remove the tachometer.

Fast idle adjustment

17 Verify that the low and high (curb) idle speeds are correct.
18 With the engine at normal operating temperature, the air cleaner is position and the choke fully open, disconnect the EGR signal line and plug it. Switch the air conditioning off.
19 Connect a tachometer to the engine in accordance with the manufacturer's instructions.
20 Disconnect the vacuum advance hose from the distributor. Plug the hose if the vehicle is equipped with transmission controlled spark advance.
21 Start the engine and with the transmission in Neutral, set the fast idle cam follower so that its tang is on the high step of the cam.
22 Bend the tang as necessary to achieve the specified fast idle setting.

Fast idle cam adjustment

23 Repeat the operations described in Section 10, paragraph 17 through 20.

Choke coil rod adjustment (G10 models)

24 Disconnect the upper end of the choke coil rod from the choke valve plate (Fig. 3.29).
25 Close the choke valve plate with the hand.
26 Push up on the choke coil rod to the limit of its travel.
27 The bottom of the rod should now be level with the top of the lever. If it is not, bend the rod.

Choke coil rod adjustment (G20 – 30 models)

28 Repeat the operations described in Section 10, paragraph 14 through 16.

Primary vacuum break adjustment

29 Set the cam follower on the highest step of the fast idle cam (Fig. 3.30).
30 Seal the purge bleed hole in the vacuum break endcover with masking tape.
31 Using a suction pump, apply vacuum to the primary vacuum break diaphragm until the plunger is fully seated.
32 Push the choke coil rod upwards to the end of its slot.
33 Check the gap between the upper edge of the choke valve plate and the air horn wall. Use a twist drill of suitable diameter to measure this. If the gap is not to specification, bend the vacuum break rod. Remember to remove the tape on completion.

Auxiliary vacuum break adjustment (G10 models)

34 Set the cam follower on the highest step of the fast idle cam (Fig. 3.31).
35 Using a suction pump, apply vacuum to the auxiliary vacuum break diaphragm until the plunger is fully seated.
36 Now check the gap between the upper edge of the choke valve plate and the air horn wall. Use a twist drill of suitable diameter for

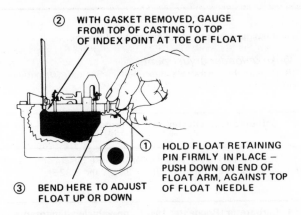

② WITH GASKET REMOVED, GAUGE FROM TOP OF CASTING TO TOP OF INDEX POINT AT TOE OF FLOAT

① HOLD FLOAT RETAINING PIN FIRMLY IN PLACE – PUSH DOWN ON END OF FLOAT ARM, AGAINST TOP OF FLOAT NEEDLE

③ BEND HERE TO ADJUST FLOAT UP OR DOWN

Fig. 3.25 Float level adjustment diagram (M and MV)

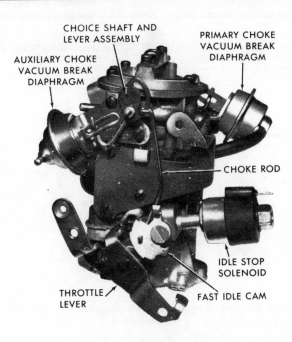

CHOICE SHAFT AND LEVER ASSEMBLY

AUXILIARY CHOKE VACUUM BREAK DIAPHRAGM

PRIMARY CHOKE VACUUM BREAK DIAPHRAGM

CHOKE ROD

IDLE STOP SOLENOID

THROTTLE LEVER

FAST IDLE CAM

Fig. 3.26 Rochester 1MV carburetor

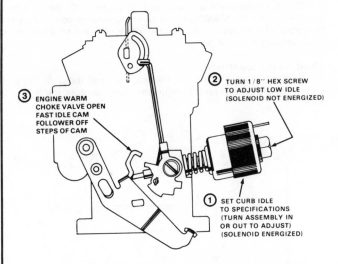

③ ENGINE WARM CHOKE VALVE OPEN FAST IDLE CAM FOLLOWER OFF STEPS OF CAM

② TURN 1/8″ HEX SCREW TO ADJUST LOW IDLE (SOLENOID NOT ENERGIZED)

① SET CURB IDLE TO SPECIFICATIONS (TURN ASSEMBLY IN OR OUT TO ADJUST) (SOLENOID ENERGIZED)

Fig. 3.27 Idle speed adjustment diagram (1MV carburetor)

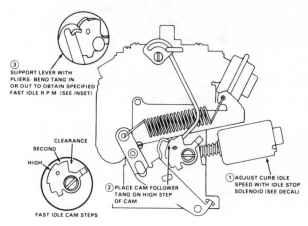

③ SUPPORT LEVER WITH PLIERS. BEND TANG IN OR OUT TO OBTAIN SPECIFIED FAST IDLE R.P.M. (SEE INSET)

CLEARANCE
SECOND
HIGH

② PLACE CAM FOLLOWER TANG ON HIGH STEP OF CAM

① ADJUST CURB IDLE SPEED WITH IDLE STOP SOLENOID (SEE DECAL)

FAST IDLE CAM STEPS

Fig. 3.28 Fast idle adjustment diagram (1MV carburetor)

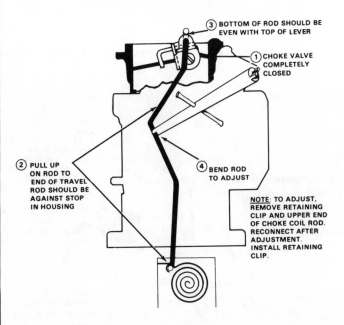

③ BOTTOM OF ROD SHOULD BE EVEN WITH TOP OF LEVER

① CHOKE VALVE COMPLETELY CLOSED

② PULL UP ON ROD TO END OF TRAVEL ROD SHOULD BE AGAINST STOP IN HOUSING

④ BEND ROD TO ADJUST

NOTE: TO ADJUST, REMOVE RETAINING CLIP AND UPPER END OF CHOKE COIL ROD. RECONNECT AFTER ADJUSTMENT. INSTALL RETAINING CLIP.

Fig. 3.29 Choke coil rod adjustment diagram (1MV carburetor on G10 vehicle)

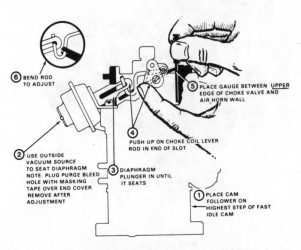

⑥ BEND ROD TO ADJUST

⑤ PLACE GAUGE BETWEEN UPPER EDGE OF CHOKE VALVE AND AIR HORN WALL

④ PUSH UP ON CHOKE COIL LEVER ROD IN END OF SLOT

② USE OUTSIDE VACUUM SOURCE TO SEAT DIAPHRAGM NOTE: PLUG PURGE BLEED HOLE WITH MASKING TAPE OVER END COVER. REMOVE AFTER ADJUSTMENT

③ DIAPHRAGM PLUNGER IN UNTIL IT SEATS

① PLACE CAM FOLLOWER ON HIGHEST STEP OF FAST IDLE CAM

Fig. 3.30 Primary vacuum break adjustment (1MV carburetor)

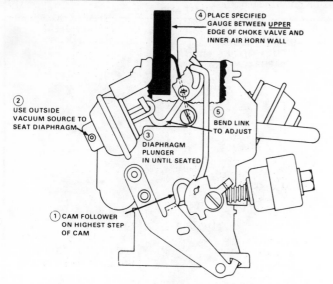

Fig. 3.31 Auxiliary vacuum break adjustment (1MV carburetor on G10 vehicles)

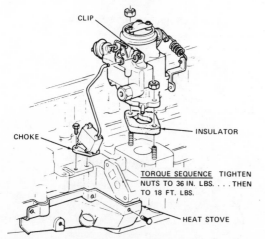

Fig. 3.32A View of 1MV carburetor attachment to intake manifold

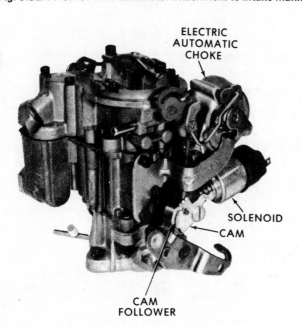

Fig. 3.33 Rochester 1ME carburetor

this.

37　If the gap is not to specification, bend the link.

Choke unloader adjustment

38　Repeat the operations described in Section 10, paragraphs 29 through 31.

13　Carburetor (Rochester 1MV) – removal, overhaul and installation

1　The operations are very similar to those described in Section 11 for the M and MV carburetors (Figs. 3.32A and 3.32B).

14　Carburetor (Rochester 1ME) – on-vehicle adjustments

Idling adjustment

1　The operations are as described in Section 20, paragraphs 1 through 11 for the M4MC carburetor except that of course only one mixture control screw is used and the idle speeds are set by means of the solenoid (Figs. 3.34 and 3.35).

Float level adjustment

2　Push down on the end of the float arm and measure from the surface of the carburetor casting to the index point on the float (Fig. 3.35).

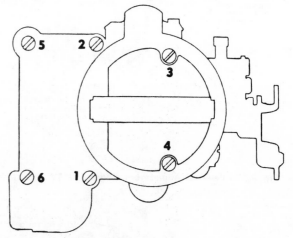

Fig. 3.32B Air horn screw tightening sequence diagram (1MV carburetor)

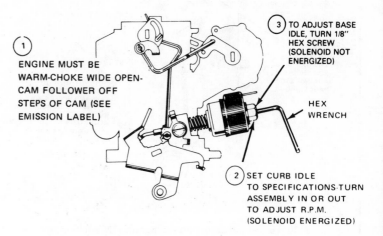

Fig. 3.34 Idle speed adjustment diagram (1ME carburetor)

3   If the measurement is not as specified, bend the float arm.

Vehicle   **Float measurement**
G10 models $\frac{3}{8}$ inch
G20 – 30 models $\frac{5}{16}$ inch

Fast idle adjustment

4   Set the curb idle speed with the idle stop solenoid.
5   Set the cam follower tang on the high step of the cam (Fig. 3.36).
6   Support the lever with pliers and bend the tang to obtain the specified idling speed.

Vehicle
G10 models   2100 rpm in Neutral
G20 – 30 models   2400 rpm in Neutral

Choke coil lever adjustment

7   Set the cam follower on the highest step of the fast idle cam (Fig. 3.37).
8   Hold the choke valve plate completely closed.
9   A gage of 0.120 inch diameter must now pass through the hole in the lever and into the hole in the casting. If this is not so, bend the link.

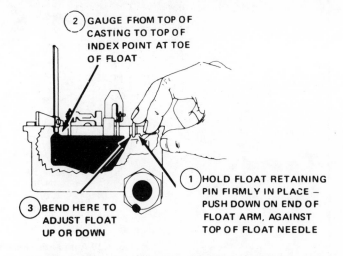

Fig. 3.35 Float level adjustment diagram (1ME carburetor)

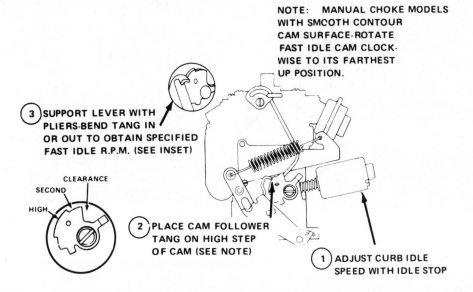

Fig. 3.36 Fast idle adjustment diagram (1ME carburetor)

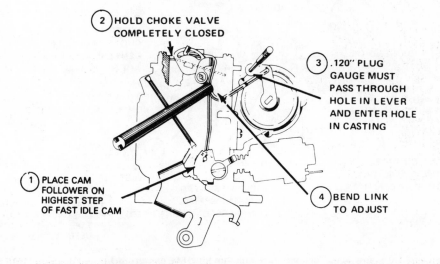

Fig. 3.37 Choke coil lever adjustment (1ME carburetor)

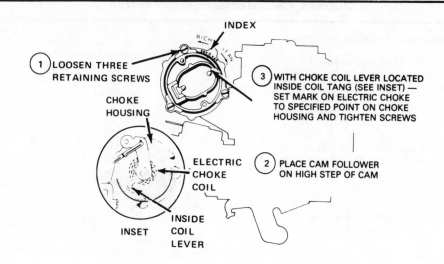

Fig. 3.38 Automatic choke adjustment (1ME carburetor)

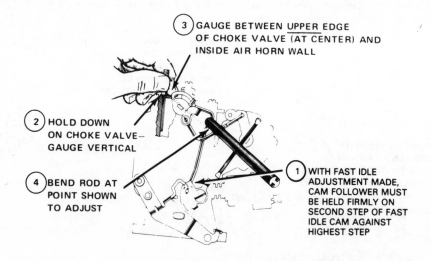

Fig. 3.39 Choke rod (fast idle cam) adjustment diagram (1ME carburetor)

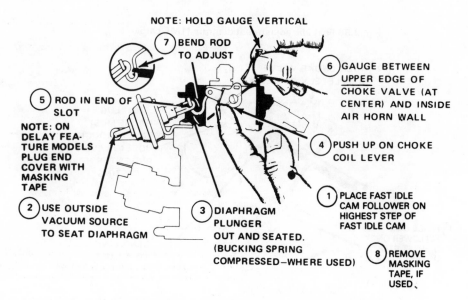

Fig. 3.40 Vacuum break adjustment (1ME carburetor)

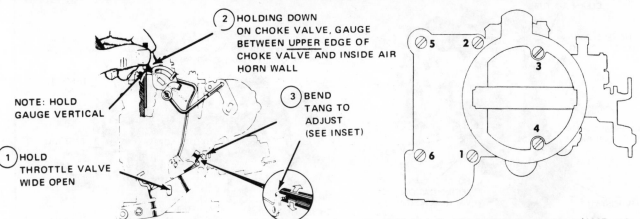

Fig. 3.41 Choke unloader adjustment (1ME carburetor)

Fig. 3.42 Air horn screw tightening sequence(1ME carburetor)

Automatic choke adjustment

10 Release the three screws which secure the choke housing (Fig. 3.38).

11 Place the cam follower on the high step of the cam.

12 Set the index (datum) marks in alignment and then retighten the screws.

Choke rod (fast idle cam adjustment)

13 Check that the fast idle speed is correct and then set the cam follower on the second step of the fast idle cam against the highest step (Fig. 3.39).

14 Depress the choke valve plate and then check the gap between the upper edge of the plate and the air horn.

15 If this is not to specification, bend the rod.

Carburetor no.	Gap
17057001	0.125 inch
17057303	
17057005	
17057002	0.110 inch
17057004	
17057302	
17057010	
17057006	0.150 inch
17057007	
17057008	
17057009	
17057308	
17057309	

Vacuum break adjustment

16 Place the cam follower on the highest step of the fast idle cam.

17 Use a suction pump and apply vacuum to seat the diaphragm.

18 Push the choke coil lever upwards and then check the gap between the upper edge of the choke valve plate and the air horn (Fig. 3.40).

19 Bend the link rod to adjust the gap if it does not conform to specification.

Carburetor no.	Gap
17057001	0.150 inch
17057303	
17057002	0.135 inch
17057004	
17057302	
17057005	0.180 inch
17057006	
17057007	
17057008	
17057009	

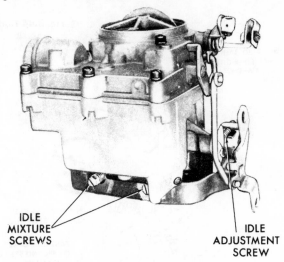

Fig. 3.43 Rochester 2G carburetor

17057308
17057309

Choke unloader adjustment

20 Hold the throttle valve plate wide open and then depress the choke valve plate.

21 Measure the gap between the upper edge of the choke valve plate and the air horn (Fig. 3.41).

22 Where this is not as specified, bend the tang.

Vehicle	Gap
G10 models	0.325 inch
G20 – 30 models	0.275 inch

15 Carburetor (Rochester 1ME) – removal, overhaul and installation

1 Refer to Section 11 and carry out the operations described. Remember to disconnect the wire from the solenoid and the choke coil.

2 When installing the air horn, tighten the screws in the sequence shown (Fig. 3.42).

16 Carburetor (Rochester 2G series) – on-vehicle adjustments

Idle adjustment (1968 through 1972)

1 The operations are similar to those described in Section 10, paragraphs 1 through 6, for single barrel carburetors except that the

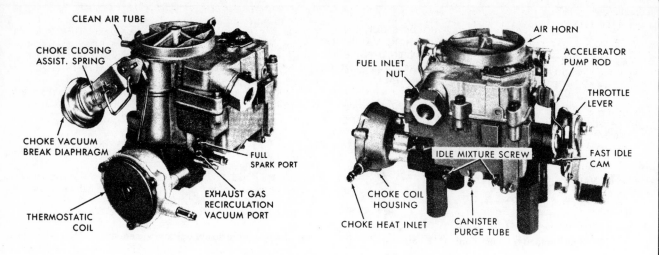

Fig. 3.44 Rochester 2GC carburetor

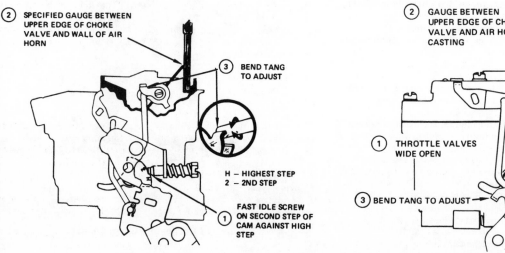

Fig. 3.45 Choke rod adjustment diagram (2GV carburetor)

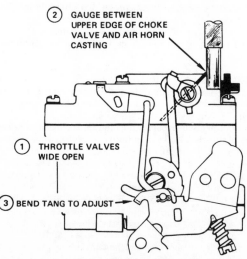

Fig. 3.46 Choke unloader adjustment diagram (2GV carburetor)

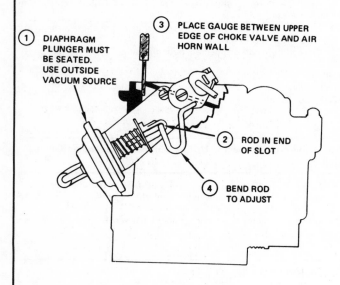

Fig. 3.47 Vacuum break adjustment diagram (2GV carburetor)

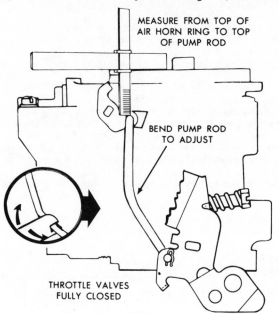

Fig. 3.48 Accelerator pump rod adjustment diagram (2GV carburetor)

dual barrel unit has two mixture screws. These should both be adjusted in turn to achieve the best idling quality (Fig. 3.43).

Idle adjustment (1973 on)

2 The mixture screws on these carburetors are fitted with limiter caps. Do not break off the caps but adjust to specification (lean drop method) only to the limits of the cap stops (Fig. 3.44).
3 Where an idle stop solenoid is fitted, run the engine to normal operating temperature and ensure that the air cleaner is in position and that the air conditioning system is off.
4 Disconnect the hose from the fuel tank nozzle on top of the carbon canister.
5 Disconnect and plug the vacuum pipe to the distributor.
6 With the engine running (manual transmission in Neutral, automatic transmission in 'D') disconnect the electrical lead from the carburetor solenoid.
7 Turn the throttle idle speed screw until the engine idle speed is as specified in the Specifications.
8 Reconnect the lead to the solenoid, open the throttle momentarily and then set the specified curb idle speed by adjusting the screw on the solenoid.
9 Reconnect the vacuum pipe and carbon canister hose, and switch off the engine.
10 In the event of the carburetor having been dismantled to such an extent that the mixture screw limiter caps have had to be removed or, if after checks of all other engine tune-up specifications the idle mixture is suspect, carry out the following operations in order to maintain the exhaust emission levels set by the vehicle manufacturer.

(a) Lean drop method

11 Disconnect the hose from the FUEL TANK nozzle on the carbon canister.
12 Disconnect the plug and distributor vacuum pipe.
13 Run the engine to normal operating temperature and make sure that the air cleaner is in position and the conditioner (if applicable) is off.
14 On vehicles with automatic transmission, place the selector in 'D'.
15 On vehicles with manual transmission disconnect the electrical lead from the carburetor idle stop solenoid.
16 Break off the tab on the limiter cap of the idle mixture screws if not already done.
17 Adjust the idle stop solenoid so that the engine speed is as specified (see Specifications). This is the initial idle speed.
18 Unscrew the idle mixture screws (equally) until the idle speed reaches its highest point and any further movement of the screws would cause it to decrease.
19 Readjust the idle stop solenoid if necessary to bring the engine speed back to that previously set.
20 Now screw in the mixture screws until the final curb idle speed is set according to the type of transmission, and is as shown in the Specifications.
21 Reconnect all disconnected components and switch off the engine.
Note: *The rev/min settings shown in this Section are known as 'Lean drop idle mixture' settings and should be compared with those used on the individual vehicle sticker. Where the sticker figures differ from those given in this description then the sticker figures should be used.*

(b) CO meter method

22 This method can be employed if a reliable CO meter can be obtained.
23 Carry out the operations already described in paragraphs 11 through 16 of this Section.
24 Connect the CO meter to the exhaust tail pipe.
25 Set the initial idle speed according to the specification by adjustment of the idle stop solenoid (if automatic tranmission is fitted, place selector in 'D').
26 If the engine idles smoothly and the CO level does not exceed 0.5% no further adjustment is necessary.
27 Where the CO level exceeds that specified, turn the idle mixture screws clockwise until the idle CO level is acceptable. Readjust the curb idle speed if necessary to bring the idling speed down to that specified.

Choke rod adjustment

28 Turn the idle stop screw in until it just touches the bottom step of

the fast idle cam, then screw it in exactly one full turn.
29 Position the fast idle screw so that it is on the second step of the fast idle cam against the shoulder of the high stem (Fig. 3.45).
30 Hold the choke valve plate towards the closed position (using a rubber band to keep it in place) and check the gap between the upper edge of the choke valve plate and the inside wall of the air horn. Use a twist drill of appropriate diameter to check.
31 The gap should be in accordance with the Specifications; if otherwise, bend the tang to correct.

Choke unloader adjustment

32 Hold the throttle valve plates in the fully open position.
33 Hold the choke valve plate towards the closed position using a rubber band to keep it in place.
34 Check the gap between the upper edge of the choke valve plate and the inside wall of the air horn. The gap should be as shown in the Specifications (Fig. 3.46).
35 Bend the tang on the throttle lever to adjust the gap.

Vacuum break adjustment

36 Remove the air cleaner. With temperature controlled air cleaners, plug the sensor vacuum take-off port (Fig. 3.47).
37 Apply vacuum to the vacuum break diaphragm until the plunger is fully seated. A hand-operated pump will be suitable to generate vacuum pressure.
38 Push the choke valve towards the closed position, then measure the gap between the lower edge of the choke valve plate and the air horn wall. Use a twist drill to check this gap.
39 The gap should be in accordance with that shown in the Specifications. If it is not, bend the vacuum break rod.

Accelerator pump rod adjustment

40 Unscrew the idle speed screw.
41 Close both throttle valve plates completely and measure from the top surface of the air horn ring to the tip of the pump rod.
42 This measurement should be as shown in the the Specifications. Bend the rod as required to obtain the setting (Fig. 3.48).

Choke coil rod adjustment

43 Hold the choke valve plate fully open and then with the thermostatic coil rod disconnected from the upper lever, push down on the rod to the end of its travel.
44 The bottom of the rod should now be level with the bottom of the elongated hole in the lever. If this is not so, bend the lever by inserting a screwdriver blade in its slot (Fig. 3.49).

---

17 Carburetor (Rochester 2G Series) – removal, overhaul and installation

1 Refer to Section 11, paragraphs 1 through 5 for the removal procedure.
2 Remove the accelerator pump rod retaining clip at the throttle lever end, and remove the rod from the throttle lever and pump upper lever.

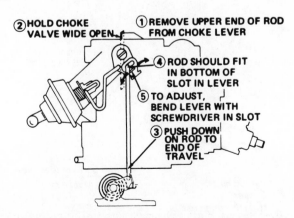

Fig. 3.49 Choke coil rod adjustment diagram (2GV carburetor)

3   Remove the cam which secures the fast idle cam and rotate the choke rod so that the tang on the end of the choke rod aligns with the groove in the choke lever. Remove the cam and the rod from the lever.
4   Disconnect the choke vacuum diaphragm hose.
5   Remove the fuel inlet filter assembly.
6   Remove the thermostatic coil lever from the end of the choke shaft.
7   Remove the vacuum break diaphragm from the air horn.
8   Remove the air horn from the float bowl (eight screws).

9   Invert the air horn and remove the float assembly.
10   Remove the fuel inlet needle valve; unscrew the valve seat and remove the gasket. Do not remove the fuel inlet baffle from the air horn as it is staked in position.
11   Remove the accelerator pump assembly by releasing the screw on the pump inner arm. Retain the plastic washer which is located between the pump outer lever and the air horn casting. The pump assembly should be removed from the pump inner lever by first rotating and then withdrawing the end of the pump plunger shaft from the

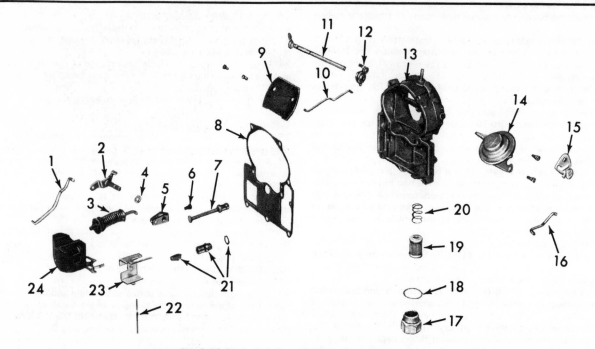

Fig. 3.50 Exploded view of 2G carburetor air horn

1 Pump rod	7 Power piston	13 Air horn	20 Spring
2 Pump outer lever	8 Gasket	14 Vacuum diaphragm	21 Fuel inlet needle valve
3 Accelerator pump	9 Choke valve plate	15 Choke lever	and seat
4 Washer	10 Choke rod	16 Diaphragm link	22 Float pivot pin
5 Pump inner lever	11 Choke shaft	17 Fuel inlet nut	23 Splash shield
6 Lever retainer	12 Choke kick lever	18 Gasket	24 Float
		19 Fuel filter	

Fig. 3.51 Exploded view of 2G carburetor bowl and throttle body

1 Venturi cluster	5 Main jets	9 Idle speed screw	13 Accelerator pump spring
2 Gasket	6 Bowl assembly	10 Brake rod	14 Pump discharge check
3 Hot idle compensator	7 Gasket	11 Idle mixture screw	assembly
4 Power valve	8 Throttle body	12 Fast idle cam	

hole in the pump inner arm.

12 Dismantle (if necessary) the accelerator pump plunger by compressing the spring and removing the retainer.

13 Peel off the air horn-to-float bowl gasket.

14 Do not remove the choke valve plate from its shaft unless it is essential, as the securing screws are staked and must be filed flush before they can be removed.

15 From the bottom of the float bowl, remove the two main metering jets and power enrichment valve assembly.

16 Remove the venturi cluster (three screws), the gasket and the main well inserts. Note that the cluster center screw has a fiber sealing gasket.

17 With a pair of long nosed pliers, extract the pump discharge spring retainer. Invert the float bowl and shake out the spring and check ball (Fig. 3.52).

18 Invert the carburetor bowl and remove the two throttle-to-float bowl screws. Remove the throttle body and gasket.

19 Do not break the idle mixture screw limiter cap as the needle is preset in production.

20 Do not dismantle the throttle valve plates from their shafts.

21 Thoroughly clean the carburetor and components in a solvent or clean fuel, and dry with compressed air. Do not probe the jets or passages with wire but clear them with compressed air only.

22 Reassembly is a reversal of dismantling but the float adjustment must be checked in the following manner. Invert the air horn and temporarily locate its gasket in position. Now measure the distance between the surface of the gasket and the seam of the float. Check this against the measurement shown in the Specifications; if necessary bend the float arm to adjust (Fig. 3.53).

23 Now hold the air horn in its normal attitude so that the float hangs freely. Measure the distance from the lowest point on the float to the surface of the gasket. This again should be as specified; if otherwise, bend the float tang (Fig. 3.54).

24 When installing the air horn, tighten the securing screws in the sequence shown (Fig. 3.55).

25 When reassembly is complete, carry out all the checks and adjustments shown in the preceding Section.

18 Carburetor (Rochester 4MV) – on-vehicle adjustments

Idle adjustment

1 The procedure is very similar to that described for the 2G Series carburetor. Refer to Section 16, paragraphs 2 through 27.

Fast idle adjustment

2 Set the transmission in Neutral and the fast idle lever on the high step of the fast idle cam (Fig. 3.56).

3 Make sure that the engine is at normal operating temperature with the choke valve plate fully open.

4 On vehicles equipped with manual transmission, disconnect the vacuum advance pipe.

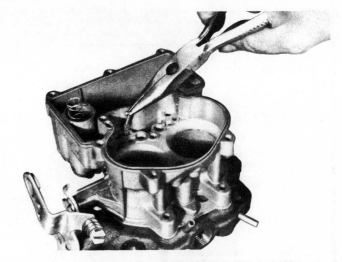

Fig. 3.52 Extracting pump discharge spring retainer (2G Series carburetor)

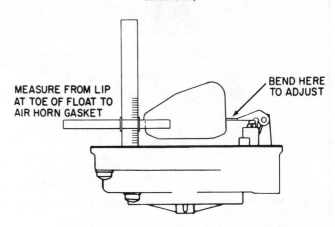

MEASURE FROM LIP AT TOE OF FLOAT TO AIR HORN GASKET

BEND HERE TO ADJUST

Fig. 3.53 Float level adjustment (air horn inverted) – 2G carburetor

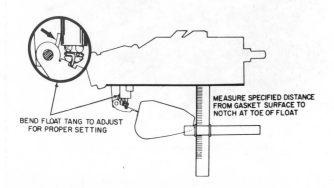

BEND FLOAT TANG TO ADJUST FOR PROPER SETTING

MEASURE SPECIFIED DISTANCE FROM GASKET SURFACE TO NOTCH AT TOE OF FLOAT

Fig. 3.54 Float drop adjustment (air horn normal attitude) – 2G carburetor

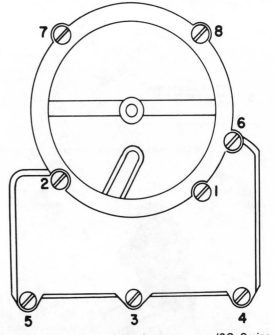

Fig. 3.55 Air horn screw tightening sequence (2G Series carburetor)

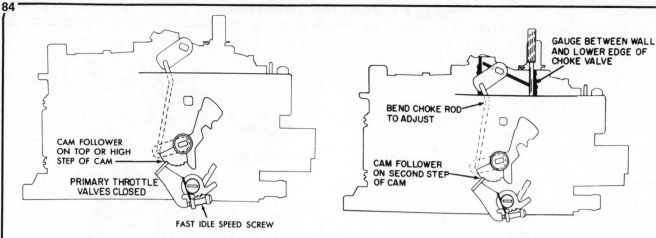

Fig. 3.56 Fast idle adjustment diagram (4MV carburetor)

Fig. 3.57 Choke rod (fast idle cam) adjustment (4MV carburetor)

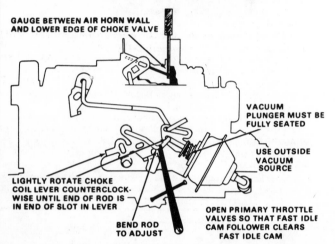

Fig. 3.58 Choke vacuum break adjustment diagram (4MV carburetor)

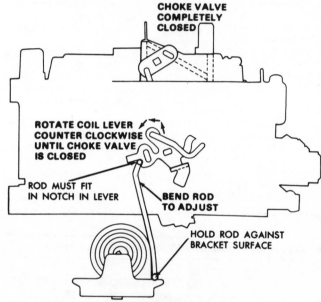

Fig. 3.59 Choke coil rod adjustment diagram (4MV carburetor)

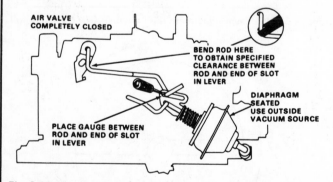

Fig. 3.60 Air valve dashpot adjustment diagram (4MV carburetor)

Fig. 3.61 Rochester 4MV carburetor

Fig. 3.62 Exploded view of the air horn (4MV carburetor)

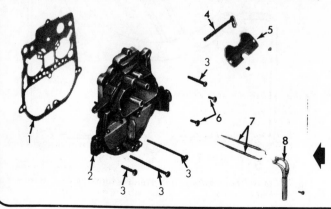

1 Gasket
2 Air horn
3 Air horn screws
4 Choke shaft and lever
5 Choke valve plate
6 Screws
7 Secondary metering rod
8 Metering rod hanger

5   Adjust the fast idle speed to that specified by turning the fast idle screw in or out as necessary. A tachometer will have to be connected to the engine in accordance with the manufacturers' instructions to perform this adjustment correctly.

Choke rod (fast idle cam) – adjustment

6   Set the cam follower on the second step of the fast idle cam and against the high step. Rotate the choke valve towards the closed position by turning the external choke lever counterclockwise. Use a twist drill as a gage and measure the gap between the lower edge of the choke valve plate (lever end) and air horn wall. This must be as specified; if otherwise, bend the choke rod (Fig. 3.57).

Choke vacuum break adjustment

7   Using an external vacuum source (hand pump) seat the choke vacuum break diaphragm.
8   Open the throttle valve plate slightly so that the cam follower will clear the steps of the fast idle cam. Now rotate the vacuum break lever counterclockwise and use a rubber band to hold it in position (Fig. 3.58).
9   Make sure that the end of the vacuum break rod is in the outer slot of the diaphragm plunger.
10   Measure the gap between the lower edge of the choke valve plate and the inside of the air horn wall. Use a twist drill of suitable diameter as a gage. If the gap is not as shown in the Specifications, bend the link rod.

Choke coil rod adjustment

11   Hold the choke valve plate closed by turning the choke coil lever counterclockwise.
12   Disconnect the thermostatic coil rod and remove the coil cover, then push the coil rod downward so that the rod contacts the surface of the bracket.
13   Check that the coil rod fits in the notch in the choke lever. If it does not, bend the rod (Fig. 3.59).

Air valve dashpot adjustment

14   Using an external vacuum source (such as a suction hand pump) completely seat the choke vacuum break diaphragm.
15   With the diaphragm seated and the air valve fully closed, measure the distance between the end of the slot in the vacuum break plunger lever and the air valve. If this does not conform to the figure given in the Specifications, bend the link rod as shown (Fig. 3.60).

19 Carburetor (Rochester 4MV) – removal, overhaul and installation

1   Remove the carburetor as described in Section 11, paragraph 1 through 5.
2   Do not immerse the idle stop solenoid in solvent to clean it.
3   Unscrew and remove the larger screw from the bracket which supports the idle stop solenoid.
4   Disconnect the choke rod by removing the clip from its upper end and withdrawing it from the lower lever.
5   Remove the roll pin from the pump lever pivot.
6   Remove the pump lever from the air horn.
7   Unscrew and remove the air horn fixing screws noting that two of the screws are located next to the primary venturi.
8   Extract the small screw from the top of the secondary metering rod hanger. Remove the hanger and rods as an assembly.
9   Lift the air horn directly upwards leaving the gasket in position. Do not bend or remove the air bleed or accelerator wall tubes as these are pressed into the carburetor casting.
10   It is not recommended that further dismantling of the air horn is carried out. In cases of extreme wear, a repair kit is available which includes all the components for renewing the air valve/shaft.
11   To dismantle the float bowl, extract the pump plunger from the pump well.
12   Remove the air horn gasket from the dowels on the secondary side of the bowl, remove the gasket from around the power piston and

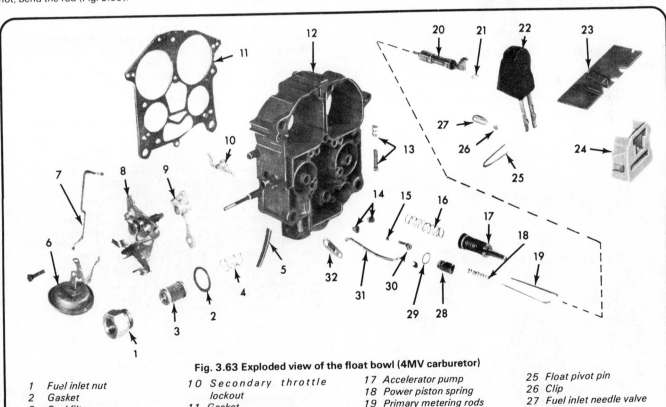

Fig. 3.63 Exploded view of the float bowl (4MV carburetor)

1 Fuel inlet nut	10 Secondary throttle lockout	17 Accelerator pump	25 Float pivot pin
2 Gasket	11 Gasket	18 Power piston spring	26 Clip
3 Fuel filter	12 Float bowl	19 Primary metering rods	27 Fuel inlet needle valve
4 Spring	13 Idle speed screw	20 Power piston	28 Fuel inlet valve seat
5 Vacuum brake hose	14 Primary jets	21 Metering rod retainer	29 Gasket
6 Vacuum diaphragm	15 Pump discharge ball	22 Float	30 Discharge ball retainer
7 Air valve dashpot	16 Pump return spring	23 Secondary air baffle	31 Choke rod
8 Choke control bracket		24 Float bowl insert	32 Choke lever
9 Fast idle cam			

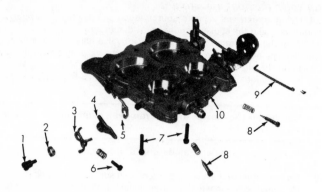

Fig. 3.64 Exploded view of the throttle body (4MV carburetor)

1	Screw	6	Fast idle screw
2	Spring	7	Screws
3	Fast idle adjusting lever	8	Idle mixture screw
4	Fast idle cam lever	9	Accelerator pump rod
5	Choke unloader lever	10	Throttle body

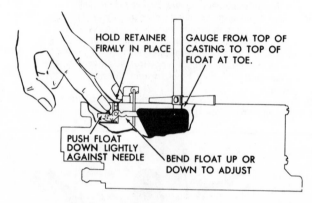

Fig. 3.65 Float level adjustment diagram (4MV carburetor)

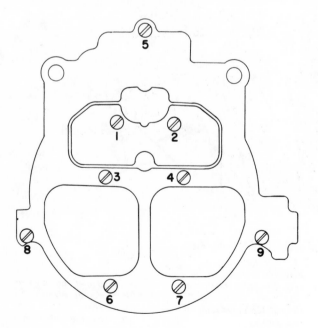

Fig. 3.66 Air horn screw tightening sequence diagram (4MV carburetor)

primary metering rods. Remove the pump return spring.

13 Remove the plastic insert from above the fuel inlet needle valve.

14 Remove the power piston by depressing the piston and releasing it. Extract the spring from the well.

15 Remove the metering rods from the power piston by disconnecting the tension springs and rotating the rods.

16 Remove the float by sliding the pin towards the pump well. Once the pin has been withdrawn, slide the float towards the front of the bowl to disengage the needle pull clip.

17 Remove the fuel inlet needle and seat using a wide blade screwdriver for the latter. Remove the gasket and discard.

18 Remove the primary metering jets but not the secondary metering discs.

19 Remove the pump discharge check ball retainer and ball.

20 Remove the baffle from the secondary side of the bowl.

21 Extract the retaining screw from the choke assembly on the side of the float bowl and remove the assembly.

22 Remove the secondary locknut lever from the cast boss on the bowl.

23 Remove the fast idle cam from the choke assembly.

24 Remove the intermediate choke rod and actuating lever from inside the float bowl well.

25 Remove the fuel inlet filter assembly.

26 Remove the throttle body by extracting the securing screws. Remove the gasket.

27 If the throttle body must be dismantled, do not break the idle mixture screw caps unless absolutely essential, in which case they will have to be renewed after reassembly when the idling speed has been adjusted by the lean drop or CO meter method as described in Section 16.

28 Remove the pump rod from the throttle lever by twisting it out of the primary lever.

29 No further dismantling of the throttle body should be carried out.

30 Clean all components, and renew any which are worn. Obtain a repair kit which will contain all the new gaskets and other renewable items.

31 Reassembly is a reversal of dismantling but observe the points, in the following paragraphs.

32 If a new throttle body has been obtained, carefully screw the idle mixture screws fully in and back them off four complete turns as an initial setting just to get the engine started.

33 When the float assembly has been installed, check the float adjustment in the following way. Using an adjustable T-scale, measure from the top surface of the carburetor casting (no gasket fitted) to a position $\frac{3}{16}$ inch back from the highest point of the float. Compare the measurement with that shown in the Specifications, and adjust if necessary by bending the float arm. Float level adjustment may also be carried out without removing the carburetor from the vehicle (Fig. 3.65).

34 If the choke valve plate was removed make sure that on reassembly the two securing screws are lightly staked.

35 Tighten the air horn retaining screws in the sequence shown (Fig. 3.66).

36 When installing the secondary metering rods, make sure that their upper ends pass through the hanger holes and are towards each other.

37 Installation is a reversal of removal; use a new gasket and then carry out the checks and adjustments described in Section 18.

20 Carburetor (Rochester M4MC) – on-vehicle adjustments

Idling adjustments

1 Remove the air cleaner for access to the carburetor but keep the vacuum hoses connected. Disconnect the remaining hose from the air cleaner and plug them (Fig. 3.69)

2 Have the engine at normal operating temperature with the choke fully off and the air conditioning system (where installed) off. The ignition timing must be correct.

3 Connect an accurate tachometer to the engine in accordance with the maker's instructions.

4 Remove the limiter caps from the idle mixture screws. Screw in the screws until they seat lightly, then unscrew them equally until the engine will just run.

5 Set the transmission in 'D' (G10 models with automatic transmission or 'Neutral' (G20 and 30 models with automatic transmission, or

manual transmission models).

6 Back off each mixture screw equally $\frac{1}{8}$ turn at a time until the maximum engine speed is obtained. Now turn the idle speed screw until the initial idle speed as shown in the Specifications is obtained.

7 Repeat the adjustment to make quite sure that the maximum idle speed was obtained when unscrewing the mixture screws.

8 Now turn each of the idle mixture screws in $\frac{1}{8}$ turn at a time until the idle speed is as shown for lean drop in the Specifications.

9 Check that the speed shown in the Specifications is the same as is shown on the particular vehicle Emission Control Label. If not, readjust to conform with the figure on the label.

10 Reconnect the vacuum hoses, install the air cleaner and switch off the engine.

11 Install new cap screws so that a future adjustment of one turn clockwise (leaner) can be obtained.

Pump rod adjustment

12 With the fast idle cam follower off the steps of the fast idle cam, back out the idle speed screw until the throttle valves are completely closed in the bore. Make sure that the secondary actuating rod is not restricting movement; bend the secondary closing tang if necessary then readjust it after pump adjustment (Fig. 3.70).

Fig. 3.67 Installing secondary metering rods (4MV carburetor)

13 Place the pump rod in the specified hole in the lever. All carburetors except 17057586, 17057588 use a $\frac{9}{32}$ inch gage, rod in the inner hole. Carburetors 17057586, 17057588 use a $\frac{9}{32}$ inch gage, rod in the outer hole.

14 Measure from the top of the choke valve wall (next to the vent stack) to the top of the pump stem.

15 If necessary, adjust to obtain the specified dimension by bending the lever whilst supporting it with a screwdriver.

16 Adjust the idle speed.

Fast idle adjustment

17 Set transmission in Park (automatic) or Neutral (manual).

Fig. 3.68 Rochester M4MC carburetor

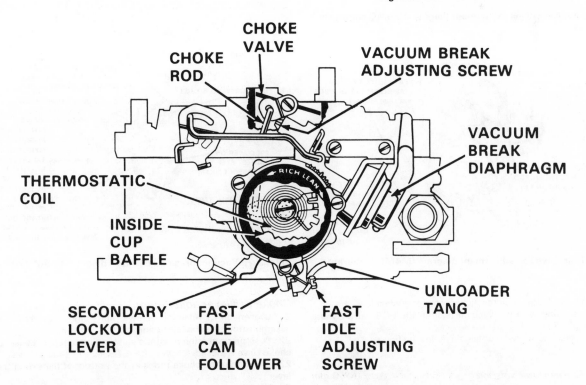

Fig. 3.69 Choke system (M4MC carburetor)

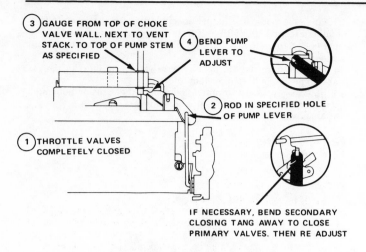

Fig. 3.70 Pump rod adjustment diagram (M4MC carburetor)

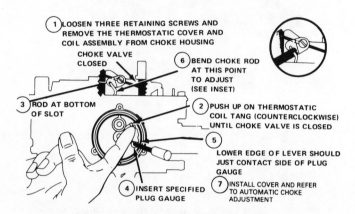

Fig. 3.72 Choke coil lever adjustment diagram (M4MC carburetor)

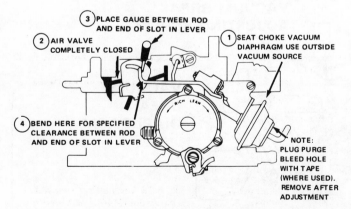

Fig. 3.74 Air valve rod adjustment diagram (M4MC carburetor)

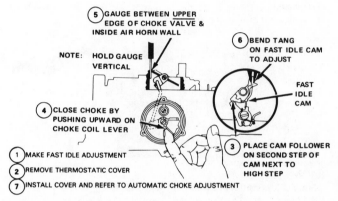

Fig. 3.71 Fast idle adjustment diagram (M4MC carburetor)

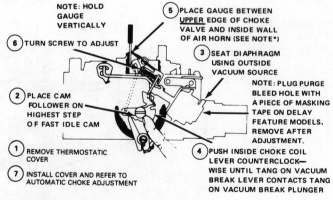

Fig. 3.73 Choke rod (fast idle cam) adjustment diagram (M4MC carburetor)

Fig. 3.75 Vacuum break adjustment diagram (M4MC carburetor)

18 Hold the cam follower on the highest step of the fast idle cam.
19 Disconnect and plug the vacuum hose at the EGR valve (where installed) (Fig. 3.71).
20 Turn the fast idle screw to obtain the following figures.

Vehicle

G10 models, manual transmission	1300 rpm
G10 models, automatic transmission	1600 rpm
G20 – 30 models, all transmissions	1600 rpm

Choke coil lever adjustment
21 Loosen the 3 retaining screws, and remove the cover and coil assembly from the choke housing.
22 Push up on the thermostatic coil tang (counterclockwise) until the choke valve is closed.
23 Check that the choke rod is at the bottom of the slot in the choke lever.
24 Insert a plug gage (a drill shank is suitable) of the specified size in the hole in the choke housing.

25 The lower edge of the choke coil lever should just contact the side of the plug gage.
26 If necessary, bend the choke rod at the point shown to adjust (Fig. 3.72).

Choke rod (fast idle cam) adjustment
27 Turn the fast idle screw in until it contacts the fast idle cam follower lever, then turn in 3 full turns more. Remove the coil cover.
28 Place the lever on the second step of the fast idle cam against the rise of the high step.
29 Push upwards on the choke coil lever inside the housing to close the choke valve.
30 Measure between the upper edge of the choke valve and the air horn wall using a twist drill of suitable diameter to do this (Fig. 3.73).
31 If necessary, bend the tang on the fast idle cam to adjust, but ensure that the tang lies against the cam before bending. The correct gap is as follows:

Vehicle	
G10 models	0.325 inch
G20 models	0.285 inch

32 Recheck the fast idle adjustment.

Air valve rod adjustment
33 Using an external source of suction, seat the choke vacuum break diaphragm.
34 Ensure that the air valves are completely closed then measure between the air valve dashpot and the end of the slot in the air valve lever. The gap should be 0.015 inch (Fig. 3.74).
35 Bend the air valve dashpot rod at the point shown, if adjustment is necessary.

Vacuum break adjustment
36 Remove the thermostatic coil cover.
37 Place the cam follower on the highest step of the fast idle cam.
38 Using a suction pump, seat the vacuum diaphragm
39 Push the inner choke coil lever counterclockwise, until the tang on the vacuum break lever contacts the tang on the vacuum break plunger (Fig. 3.75).
40 Check the gap between the upper edge of the choke valve plate and the inside wall of the air horn. Use a twist drill of suitable diameter to do this.
41 Turn the adjuster screw to achieve the correct gap.
42 Install the cover and check the automatic choke adjustment (paragraph 43 through 46).

Carburetor no.	Gap
17057202	0.160 inch
17057204	
17057218	
17057222	
17057219	0.165 inch
17057502	
17057503	
17057504	
17057512	
17057517	
17057518	
17057519	
17057522	
17057582	0.180 inch
17057584	
17057586	
17057588	

Automatic choke coil adjustment
43 Place the cam follower on the highest point of the cam (Fig. 3.76).
44 Loosen the three retaining screws and rotate the coil cover until the choke valve plate just closes.
45 Align the mark on the cover with the specified point on the housing according to the carburetor type.

Carburetor no.	Housing mark
17057503	1 notch lean
17057519	
17057202	2 notches lean
17057204	
17057218	
17057222	
17057502	
17057504	
17057518	
17057518	
17057522	
17057582	
17057584	
17057586	
17057588	
17057209	3 notches lean
17057219	
17057512	Center mark
17057517	

46 Tighten the cover screws.

Choke unloader adjustment
47 Make sure that the automatic choke housing cover is set to the specified position (paragraphs 43 through 46).

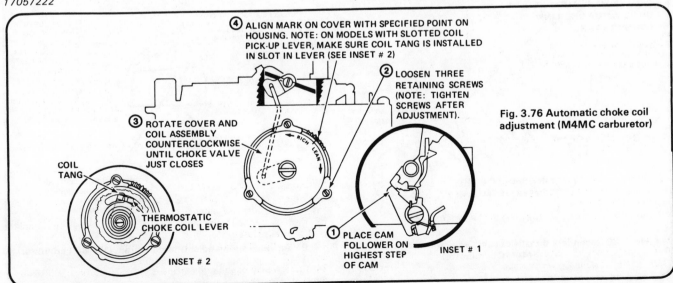
Fig. 3.76 Automatic choke coil adjustment (M4MC carburetor)

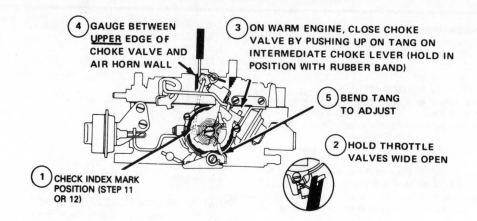

④ GAUGE BETWEEN UPPER EDGE OF CHOKE VALVE AND AIR HORN WALL

③ ON WARM ENGINE, CLOSE CHOKE VALVE BY PUSHING UP ON TANG ON INTERMEDIATE CHOKE LEVER (HOLD IN POSITION WITH RUBBER BAND)

⑤ BEND TANG TO ADJUST

② HOLD THROTTLE VALVES WIDE OPEN

① CHECK INDEX MARK POSITION (STEP 11 OR 12)

Fig. 3.77 Choke unloader adjustment (M4MC carburetor)

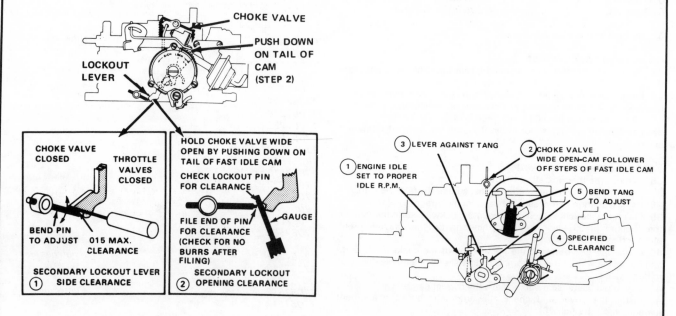

CHOKE VALVE

PUSH DOWN ON TAIL OF CAM (STEP 2)

LOCKOUT LEVER

CHOKE VALVE CLOSED

THROTTLE VALVES CLOSED

BEND PIN TO ADJUST   .015 MAX. CLEARANCE

SECONDARY LOCKOUT LEVER ① SIDE CLEARANCE

HOLD CHOKE VALVE WIDE OPEN BY PUSHING DOWN ON TAIL OF FAST IDLE CAM

CHECK LOCKOUT PIN FOR CLEARANCE

FILE END OF PIN FOR CLEARANCE (CHECK FOR NO BURRS AFTER FILING)

GAUGE

SECONDARY LOCKOUT ② OPENING CLEARANCE

Fig. 3.78 Secondary throttle lockout adjustment diagram (M4MC carburetor)

③ LEVER AGAINST TANG

② CHOKE VALVE WIDE OPEN—CAM FOLLOWER OFF STEPS OF FAST IDLE CAM

① ENGINE IDLE SET TO PROPER IDLE R.P.M.

⑤ BEND TANG TO ADJUST

④ SPECIFIED CLEARANCE

Fig. 3.79 Secondary throttle closing adjustment diagram (M4MC carburetor)

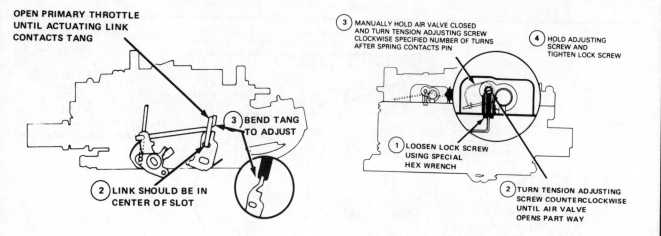

OPEN PRIMARY THROTTLE UNTIL ACTUATING LINK CONTACTS TANG

③ BEND TANG TO ADJUST

② LINK SHOULD BE IN CENTER OF SLOT

③ MANUALLY HOLD AIR VALVE CLOSED AND TURN TENSION ADJUSTING SCREW CLOCKWISE SPECIFIED NUMBER OF TURNS AFTER SPRING CONTACTS PIN

④ HOLD ADJUSTING SCREW AND TIGHTEN LOCK SCREW

① LOOSEN LOCK SCREW USING SPECIAL HEX WRENCH

② TURN TENSION ADJUSTING SCREW COUNTERCLOCKWISE UNTIL AIR VALVE OPENS PART WAY

Fig. 3.80 Secondary throttle opening adjustment diagram (M4MC carburetor)

Fig. 3.81 Air valve spring adjustment diagram (M4MC carburetor)

48 Hold the throttle valve plates wide open.

49 Close the choke valve plate by pushing up on the tang of the intermediate choke lever (Fig. 3.77).

50 Check the gap between the upper edge of the choke valve plate and the air horn inner wall. Use a twist drill of suitable diameter as a gage.

51 Bend the tang if necessary to adjust.

Carburetor no.	Gap
17057221	0.325 inch
17057209	
17057512	0.240 inch
17057517	
All other carburetors	0.280 inch

Secondary throttle lockout adjustment

Lockout lever clearance

52 Hold the choke valves and secondary lockout valves closed then measure the clearance between the lockout pin and lockout lever.

53 If adjustment is necessary, bend the lockout pin to obtain the specified clearance (Fig. 3.78).

Opening clearance

54 Push down on the tail of the fast idle cam to hold the choke wide open.

55 Hold the secondary throttle valve partly open then measure between the end of the lockout pin and the toe of the lockout lever.

56 If adjustment is necessary, file the end of the lockout pin, but ensure that no burrs remain afterwards.

Secondary closing adjustment

57 Adjust the engine idle speed, as described previously in this Chapter.

58 Hold the choke valve wide open with the cam follower lever off the steps of the fast idle cam (Fig. 3.79).

59 Measure the clearance between the slot in the secondary throttle valve pick-up lever and the secondary actuating rod.

60 If adjustment is necessary, bend the secondary closing tang on the primary throttle lever to obtain a clearance of 0.020 inch.

Secondary opening adjustment

61 Lightly open the primary throttle lever until the link just contacts the tang on the secondary lever. (Fig. 3.80).

62 Bend the tang on the secondary lever, if necessary, to position the link in the center of the secondary lever slot.

Air valve spring adjustment

63 Using a suitable hexagonal wrench loosen the lock screw then turn the tension adjusting screw counterclockwise until the air valve is partly open.

64 Hold the air valve closed then turn the tension adjusting screw clockwise the specified number of turns after the spring contacts the pin (Fig. 3.81).

65 Tighten the lockscrew.

---

21 Carburetor (Rochester M4MC) — removal, overhaul and installation

1 Remove the air cleaner and gasket.

2 Disconnect the wire from the solenoid, where applicable.

3 Disconnect the fuel pipes and vacuum hoses from the carburetor.

4 Disconnect the air hose (hot air choke).

5 Disconnect the accelerator linkage.

6 If the vehicle is equipped with automatic transmission, disconnect the down shift cable.

7 If equipped with cruise control, disconnect the linkage.

8 Unbolt the carburetor and remove it from the intake manifold. Remove the gaskets and insulator.

9 If the carburetor has an idle stop solenoid, remove the bracket retaining screws, and lift away the solenoid, remove the bracket retaining screws, and lift away the solenoid and bracket assembly.

10 Remove the upper choke lever from the end of the choke shaft (1 screw) then rotate the lever to remove it, to disengage it from the choke rod.

11 Remove the choke rod from the lower lever inside the float bowl by holding the lever outwards with a small screwdriver and twisting the rod counterclockwise.

12 Remove the vacuum hose from the choke vacuum break unit.

13 Remove the small screw at the top of the metering rod hanger, and remove the secondary metering rods and hanger.

14 Using a suitable drift, drive the small pump lever pivot roll pin inwards to permit removal of the lever.

15 Remove 2 long screws, 5 short screws and 2 countersunk head screws to detach the float bowl. Remove the secondary air baffle deflector (where applicable) from beneath the 2 center air horn screws (Fig. 3.84).

16 Remove the float bowl but leave the gasket in position at this stage. Do not attempt to remove the small tubes protruding from the air horn.

Fig. 3.82 Removing secondary metering rods (M4MC carburetor)

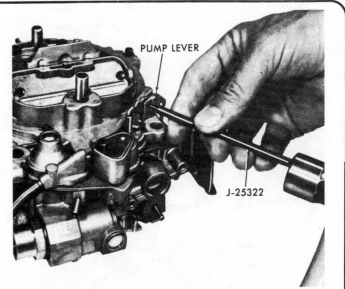

Fig. 3.83 Removing pump lever (M4MC carburetor)

Fig. 3.84 Air horn retaining screws (M4MC carburetor)

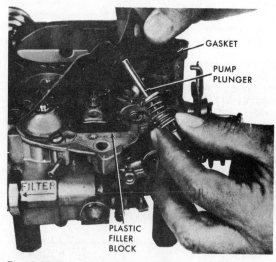

GASKET

PUMP
PLUNGER

FILTER

PLASTIC
FILLER
BLOCK

Fig. 3.85 Removing air horn gasket and pump plunger
(M4MC carburetor)

FILTER

Fig. 3.86 Removing power piston and metering rods
(M4MC carburetor)

17 Remove the vacuum break bracket screws and lift off the unit. Detach the air valve dashpot rod from the diaphragm assembly and the air valve lever.

18 If considered necessary, remove the staked choke valve attaching screws then remove the choke valve and shaft from the air horn. Do not remove the air valve and the air valve shaft. The air valve closing spring or center plastic cam can be renewed by following the instructions in the appropriate repair kit.

19 Remove the air horn gasket from the float bowl taking care not to distort the springs holding the main metering rods.

20 Remove the pump plunger and pump return spring from the pump well.

21 Depress the power piston stem and allow it to snap free, withdrawing the metering rods with it. Remove the power piston spring from the well.

22 Taking care to prevent distortion, remove the metering rods from the power piston by disconnecting the tension springs then rotating the rods.

23 Remove the plastic filler block over the float valve, then remove the float assembly and needle by pulling up on the pin. Remove the needle seat and gasket.

24 Remove the 2 cover screws and carefully lift out the metering rod from the float bowl.

25 Remove the primary main metering jets.

26 Remove the pump discharge check ball retainer and the ball.

27 Remove the vacuum break hose and the bracket retaining screws. Remove the vacuum break rod from the slot in the plunger head.

28 Press down on the fast idle cam and remove the vacuum break rod. Move the end of the rod away from the float bowl, then disengage the rod from the hole in the intermediate lever.

29 Remove the choke cover attaching screws and retainers. Pull off the cover and remove the gasket.

30 Remove the choke housing assembly from the float bowl by removing the retaining screw and washer.

31 Remove the secondary throttle valve lockout lever from the float bowl.

32 Remove the lower choke lever by inverting the float bowl.

33 Remove the plastic tube seal from the choke housing.

34 If it is necessary to remove the intermediate choke shaft from the choke housing, remove the coil lever retaining screw and withdraw the lever. Slide out the shaft and (if necessary) remove the fast idle cam.

35 Remove the fuel inlet filter nut, gasket and filter from the float bowl.

36 If necessary, remove the pump well fill slot baffle and the secondary air baffle.

37 Remove the throttle body attaching screws and lift off the float bowl. Remove the insulator gasket.

38 Remove the pump rod from the lever on the throttle body.

39 If it is essential to remove the idle mixture needles, pry out the plastic limiter caps then count the number of turns to bottom the needles and fit replacement in exactly the same position. New limiter caps should be fitted after running adjustments have been made.

40 Clean all metal parts in a suitable cold solvent. Do not immerse rubber parts, plastic parts, pump plungers, or vacuum breaks. If the choke housing is to be immersed, remove the cup seal from inside the choke housing shaft hole. If the bowl is to be immersed remove the cup seal from the plastic insert; do not attempt to remove the plastic insert. Do not probe the jets, but blow through with clean, dry compressed air. Examine all fixed and moving parts for cracks, distortion, wear and other damage; replace as necessary. Discard all gaskets and the fuel inlet filter.

41 Assembly is essentially the reverse of the dismantling procedure but the following points should be noted.

  a) If new idle mixture screws were used, and the original setting was not noted, install the screws finger-tight to seat them, then back off 4 full turns.
  b) The lip on the plastic insert cup seal (on the side of the float bowl) faces outwards.
  c) The lip on the inside choke housing shaft hole cup seal faces inwards towards the housing.
  d) When installing the assembled choke body, install the choke rod lever into the cavity in the float bowl. Install the plastic tube seal into the housing cavity before installing the housing. Ensure that the intermediate choke shaft engages into the lower choke lever. The choke coil is installed at the last stage

of assembly.

e) *Where applicable the notches on the secondary float bowl air baffle are towards the top, and the top edge of the baffle must be flush with the bowl casting.*

f) *To adjust the float, hold the retainer firmly in place and push down lightly against the needle. Measure from the top of the float bowl casting (air horn gasket removed) to a point on the top of the float $\frac{3}{16}$ inch back from the toe. Bend the float arm to obtain the specified dimension.*

Carburetor no.	Float dimension (casting to float)
17057202	$\frac{15}{32}$ inch
17057204	
17057502	
17057582	
17057584	
17057503	
17057504	
17057209	$\frac{7}{16}$ inch
17057218	
17057222	
17057518	
17057522	
17057586	
17057588	
17057219	
17057519	
17057512	
17057517	
17056212	$\frac{3}{8}$ inch
17057221	
17056217	
17057213	$\frac{11}{32}$ inch
17057215	
17057216	
17057525	
17057514	
17057529	
17057229	
7045583	
7045585	
7045586	

42 On completion of reassembly, carry out the adjustments described in the preceding Section.

22 Emission control system – general description

1 These are devices for controlling the emission of fumes and noxious gases from the engine, the exhaust pipe and the fuel tank.
2 All vehicles are equipped with a crankcase ventilation system, but the number and complexity of the additional control systems depends upon the vehicle model and date of production.
3 The following list gives a guide to the type of emission control equipment which may be encountered on vehicles of different production periods.

All vehicles
Positive Crankcase Ventilation (PCV)
Air Injection Reactor System (AIR)

1971 to 1975
Transmission Controlled Spark System (TCS)
Exhaust Gas Recirculation System (EGR)
Evaporation Control System (ECS)

1976 onward
Exhaust Gas Recirculation System (EGR)
Catalytic Converter (refer to Section 30)

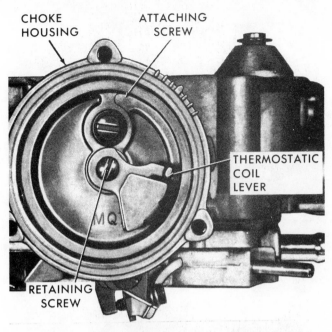

Fig. 3.87 Removing the choke housing (M4MC carburetor)

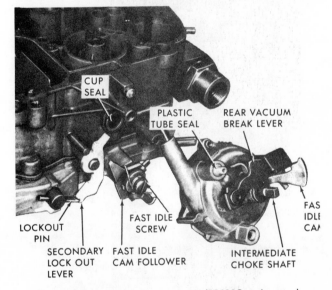

Fig. 3.88 Choke housing assembly (M4MC carburetor)

Fig. 3.89 Float adjustment diagram (M4MC carburetor)

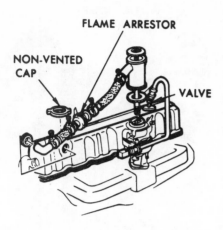

Fig. 3.90 Typical PCV installation on in-line engine

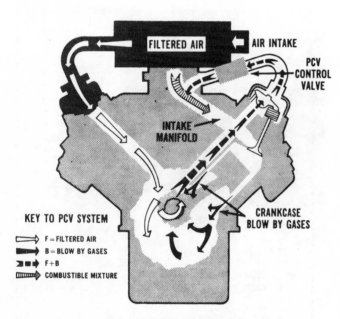

KEY TO PCV SYSTEM

⇨ F = FILTERED AIR
➧ B = BLOW BY GASES
⫸ F + B
▭▭▭ COMBUSTIBLE MIXTURE

Fig. 3.91 PCV system on V8 engine

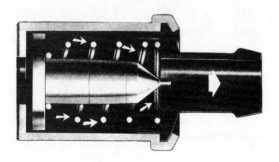

Fig. 3.92 Cut-away view of PCV valve

Early Fuel Evaporation System (EFE)
Throttle Return Control (TRC)

4   Also providing a contributory factor to the general reduction in the level of fume emission, the calibration of carburetors and the modification of ignition settings over the years to enable the engine to run on ever leaner mixtures must be taken into account. These developments are often referred to as the Controlled Combustion System (CCS) and include the carburetor, distributor, spark plugs, thermostatically controlled air cleaner and automatic choke. These components must always be maintained in first class condition as an essential basic requirement for 'clean' engine operation.

23 Positive Crankcase Ventilation (PCV) – description and maintenance

1   The PCV system is designed to draw fumes from the engine crankcase by means of manifold vacuum and to burn them in the combustion chambers during the normal process of engine operation.
2   These fumes or vapors collect in the crankcase as a result of 'blow-by' past the piston rings. This may be due to high combustion chamber pressures, increased piston ring-to-groove clearance or misalignment of the piston ring end gaps. The volume of vapors and gases will increase with engine wear.
3   As the gases are drawn out of the crankcase, fresh air is drawn in from the clean air side of the air cleaner.
4   Components of the system include a control valve and connecting hoses.
5   Regularly check the hoses for splits, and renew as necessary.
6   At the specified intervals, remove the control valve and clean it thoroughly in kerosene.
7   Renew the valve at the mileages indicated in Routine Maintenance.

24 Air Injection Reactor (AIR) System – description and maintenance

1   The system comprises a belt-driven air injection pump and the necessary valves and connecting hoses to provide a controlled supply of air to the area of the exhaust valves, where it dilutes the exhaust gases and helps to burn the unburned portion of the exhaust gases in the exhaust system.
2   The diverter valve is actuated by a sharp increase in manifold vacuum and under these conditions, the valve shuts off the injected air to prevent backfiring during this period of richer mixture.
3   On engine overrun, the air generated by the air pump is expelled to atmosphere through the diverter valve and muffler. At high engine speeds, excess air pressure is released through the pressure relief valve of the diverter valve.

Drivebelt - renewal and adjustment
4   Loosen the air injection pump mounting bolt and adjustment bracket then move the pump to permit the belt to be removed.
5   Install the new drivebelt and adjust the tension so that there is approximately $\frac{1}{2}$ inch free play in the longest run of the belt, then tighten the adjustment bracket and mounting bracket bolts.

Pump filter - renewal
6   Compress the pump drivebelt to prevent the pulley turning then loosen the pulley bolts.
7   Remove the drivebelt and the pulley.
8   Where applicable, pry loose the filter fan outer disc. Pull off the filter with pliers, taking care that no debris enters the air intake hole. (Fig. 3.96).
9   Carefully, and evenly, draw the new filter onto the pump using the pulley and pulley bolts. The filter must slip squarely into the housing; a slight interference is normal and it may initially squeal when running until the sealing lip has worn in.
10 The remainder of the installation is the reverse of the removal procedure.

Air manifold, hose and tube
11 Periodically inspect all the connections, pipes and hoses for deterioration and for loose connections.
12 Leakage on the pressure side may be detected by brushing or

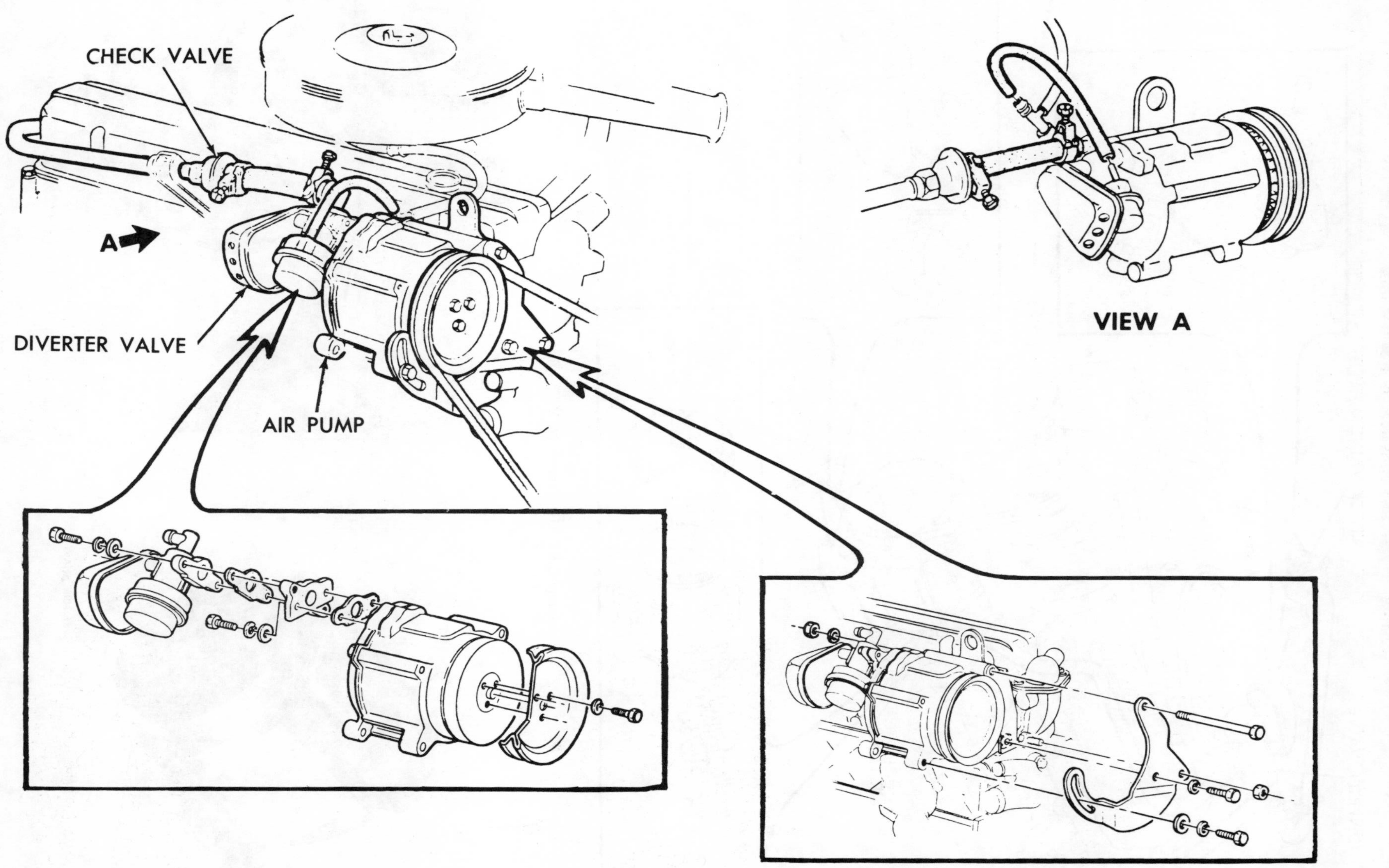

VIEW A

CHECK VALVE

DIVERTER VALVE

AIR PUMP

A

Fig. 3.93 AIR system on in-line engine

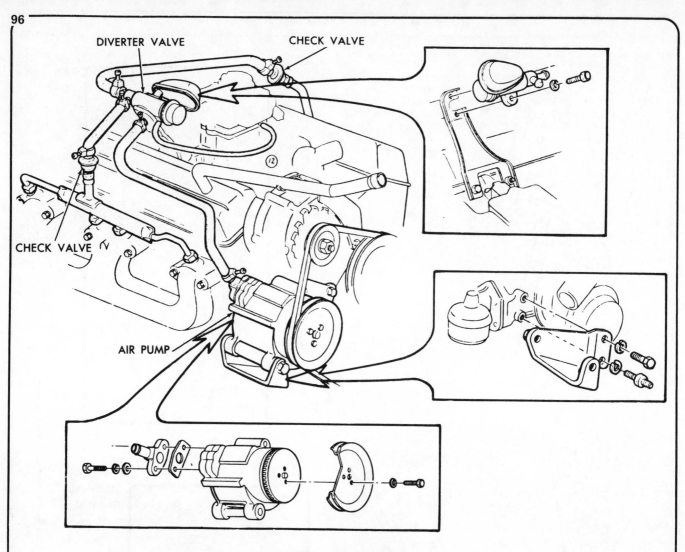

Fig. 3.94 AIR System on V8 engine

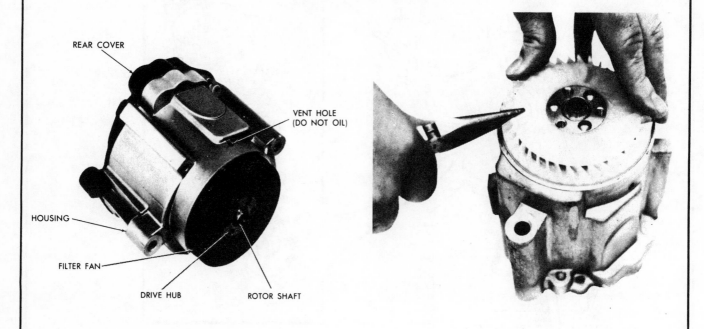

Fig. 3.95 Air injection pump

Fig. 3.96 Removing Air Injection Pump filter

pouring a soap-and-water solution around the joints and connections with the engine running.

13 Renewal of hoses and tubes is a straightforward but only Chevrolet approved parts are permitted. Anti-seize compound should be used on air manifold and exhaust manifold screw threads.

Check valve

14 To test the operation of the check valve, it should be possible to blow through it (by mouth)) towards the manifold, but not be possible to suck through it.

15 The check valve can be unscrewed from the manifold when renewal is required.

Diverter valve

16 Check the condition of all the lines and connections.

17 To check the operation, disconnect the signal line at the valve and check that suction can be felt when the engine is running. Under normal operating conditions and the engine idling, no air should be escaping through the muffler; when the throttle is manually opened, then quickly closed, an air blast lasting at least one second should be discharged through the muffler. A defective valve must be renewed.

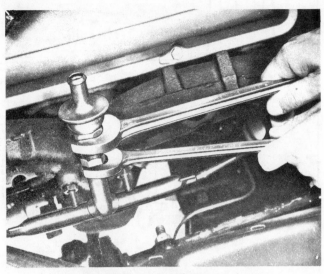

Fig. 3.97 Removing AIR check valve

Fig. 3.98 Checking for vacuum signal at AIR system diverter valve

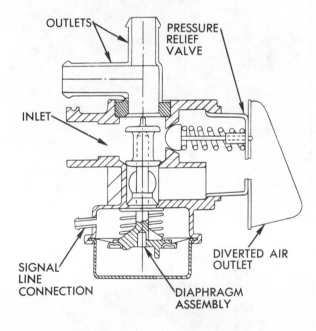

Fig. 3.99 Sectional view of diverter valve (early AIR system)

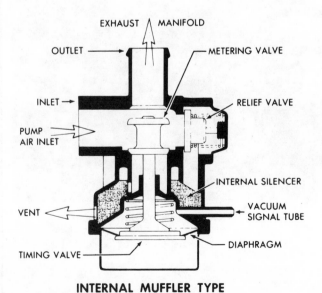

INTERNAL MUFFLER TYPE

Fig. 3.100 Sectional view of diverter valve (later AIR system)

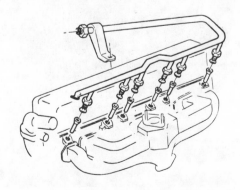

Fig. 3.101 Air Injection tubes on in-line engine

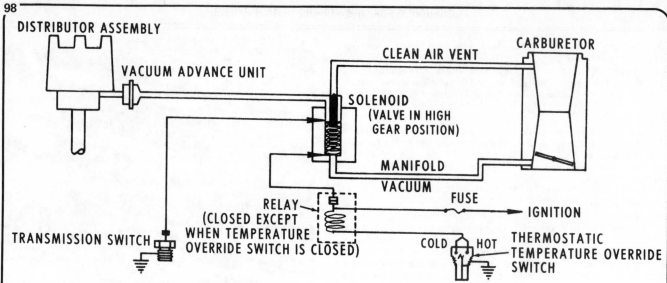

DISTRIBUTOR ASSEMBLY

VACUUM ADVANCE UNIT

CLEAN AIR VENT

CARBURETOR

SOLENOID
(VALVE IN HIGH
GEAR POSITION)

MANIFOLD
VACUUM

FUSE

IGNITION

RELAY
(CLOSED EXCEPT
WHEN TEMPERATURE
OVERRIDE SWITCH IS CLOSED)

TRANSMISSION SWITCH

COLD   HOT

THERMOSTATIC
TEMPERATURE OVERRIDE
SWITCH

Fig. 3.102 Layout (diagrammatic) of TCS system

Fig. 3.103 Location of TCS transmission switch (manual)

Fig. 3.104 Location of TCS transmission switch (automatic)

CEC SOLENOID

IDLE STOP SOLENOID

Fig. 3.105 Idle stop and vacuum advance cut-off solenoid on in-line engine

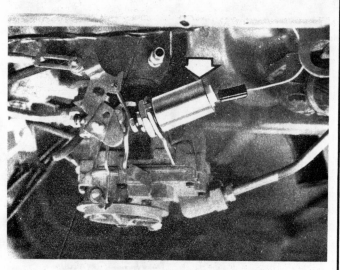

Fig. 3.106 Idle stop solenoid on V8 engine

Air injection tubes

18 No periodic inspection is required, but when exhaust manifolds are removed any carbon build-up in the tubes should be removed with a wire brush. Warped or burned tubes must be renewed.

19 To remove the tubes, clamp the manifold in a vise, clean away as much carbon as possible and work the tubes out of the manifold using penetrating oil.

Air injection pump

20 To check the pump operation, accelerate the engine to approximately 1500 rpm and check that airflow from the hose(s) increases.

21 The pump can be removed by disconnecting the hoses, removing the pulley, then removing the pump mounting bolts.

22 Installation is the reverse of removal, following which the belt tension must be adjusted.

25 Transmission Controlled Spark (TCS) System – description and maintenance

1 This system is installed on most models equipped with either an in-line or V8 engine. Its purpose is to reduce the emission of noxious exhaust gases by eliminating ignition vacuum advance when the vehicle is operating in low forward gears.

2 Vacuum advance is controlled by a solenoid-operated switch which is actuated by a transmission switch. When the switch is in operation, the vacuum normally applied to the distributor is vented to atmosphere and its advance characteristic is obtained solely by the mechanical counter weights.

3 A thermostatically controlled coolant temperature switch is wired into the solenoid circuit to prevent vacuum cut-off to the distributor at engine temperatures below 93°F.

4 In order to compensate for the retarded spark, and possibly engine run-on (dieseling) when the engine is switched off, an idle stop solenoid is provided on many carburetors to permit the throttle valve to close further than the normally (slightly open) idling position of the valve plate.

5 Maintenance consists of occasionally checking the security of the electrical connections and the vacuum pipes. In the event of malfunction of the system, refer to Section 33 and renew the faulty component as necessary.

26 Exhaust Gas Recirculation (EGR) System – description and maintenance

1 This system is designed to reduce the emissions of nitrogen oxides from the exhaust pipe. Formation of this pollutant occurs during the period of highest temperature during the combustion cycle.

2 To accomplish a reduction in these toxic products, a small quantity of inert gas is introduced into the combustion process.

Fig. 3.107 Vacuum advance cut-off solenoid on V8 engine

Fig. 3.109 TCS System oil temperature switch on V8 engine

Fig. 3.108 TCS System coolant temperature switch on in-line engine

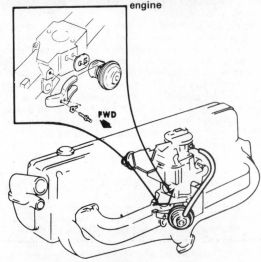

Fig. 3.110 EGR valve (early in-line engines)

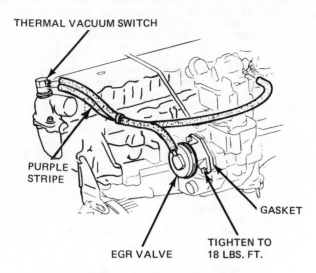

Fig. 3.111 EGR valve (later in-line engines)

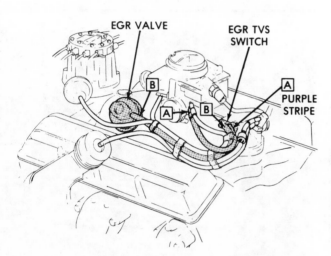

Fig. 3.113 EGR valve (later V8 engine)

Fig. 3.112 EGR valve (early V8 engines)

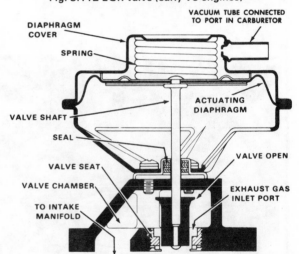

Fig. 3.114 Sectional view of EGR valve

3   A U-connection between the exhaust and intake manifolds is used for the purpose and the continuous supply of exhaust gas is tapped as the source of inert gas.

4   A vacuum-controlled EGR combined shut off and metering valve controls the flow of exhaust (inert) gas according to engine operating conditions. The system is ineffective at coolant temperatures below 100°f which are monitored by a Thermal Vacuum Switch (TVS).

5   At the intervals specified in Routine Maintenance the EGR valve should be removed and its base cleaned with a wire brush. The valve seat should be cleaned using an abrasive type spark plug cleaning machine, with the valve in both open and closed positions. Finally apply compressed air to remove all traces of abrasive material.

6   Other maintenance consists of checking the security and condition of the hoses in the system.

27 Evaporation Control System (ECS) – description and maintenance

1   The system is designed to minimize the escape of fuel vapor from the fuel tank and carburetor bowl to atmosphere.

2   The vapor is retained in a canister filled with carbon. The canister is purged by manifold vacuum (when the engine is operating) and the vapor is burned in the combustion chambers.

3   Check the connecting hoses of the system regularly both with

respect to condition and security of connections.

4   At the intervals specified in Routine Maintenance the carbo canister filter must be renewed. To do this, raise the vehicle, note th installed position of the hoses, disconnect them, loosen the caniste retaining clamps and remove the canister (photo).

5   Remove the old filter and install the new one on to the lower en of the canister.

6   The canister incorporates a purge valve which can be renewed necessary by first disconnecting the hoses from the valve and the prying off the cap.

7   Remove the cap, diaphragm, spring retainer and spring.

28 Early Fuel Evaporation (EFE) System – description an maintenance

1   This system improves cold engine warm-up and driveability k routing hot exhaust gases under the base of the carburetor whic results in better atomization of fuel and reduced exhaust emission.

2   The system consists of a vacuum controlled actuator which linked to a stainless steel exhaust heat valve and a method of control ing the vacuum source.

3   On in-line engines the vacuum is controlled according to c temperature while on V8 engines the vacuum is controlled by coolant temperature switch.

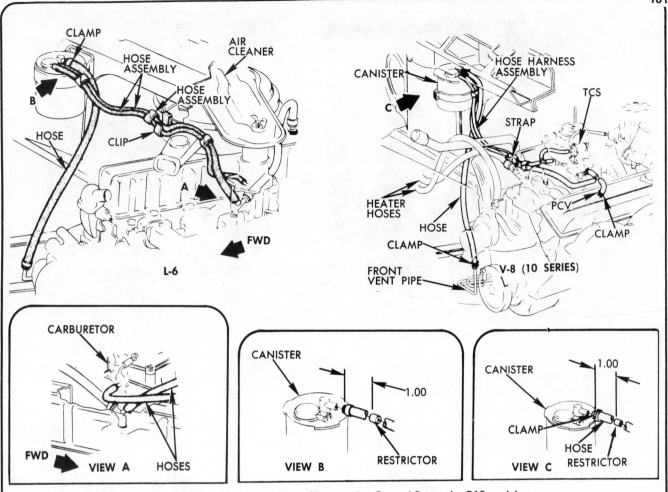

Fig. 3.115 Carbon canister hoses (Evaporation Control System) – G10 models

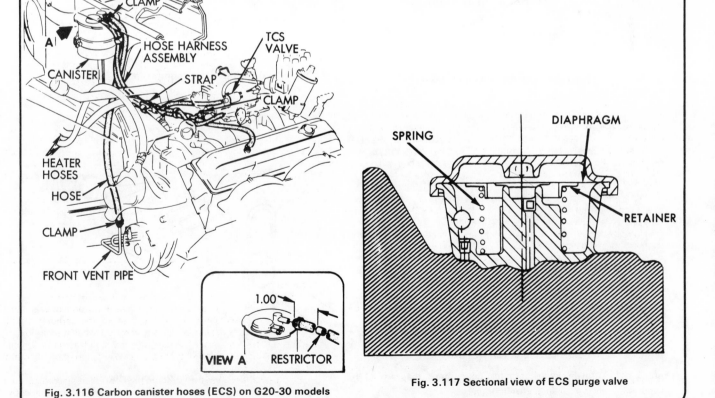

Fig. 3.116 Carbon canister hoses (ECS) on G20-30 models

Fig. 3.117 Sectional view of ECS purge valve

27.4 Carbon canister (ECS)

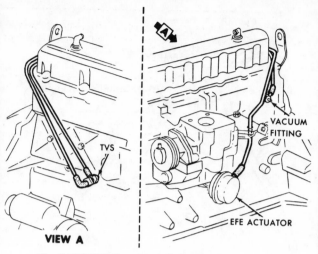

VIEW A

Fig. 3.118 EFE System on in-line engine

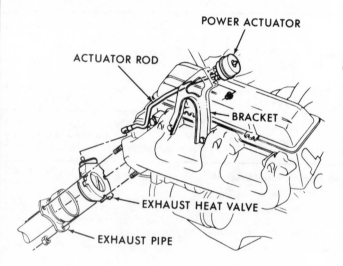

Fig. 3.119 EFE System on V8 engines

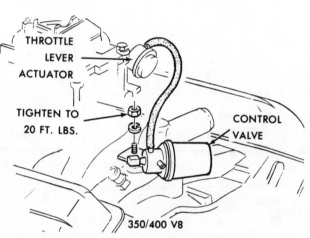

350/400 V8

Fig. 3.120 Throttle return control valve

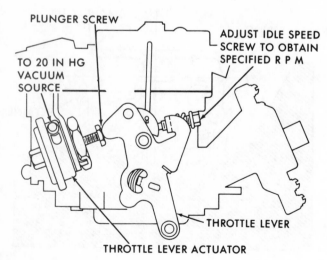

Fig. 3.121 Throttle lever actuator adjustment diagram (TRC system)

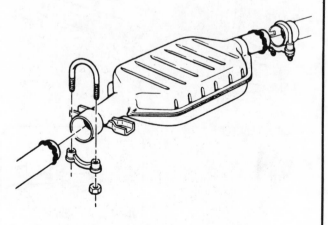

Fig. 3.122 Catalytic converter

4   Maintenance consists of inspecting all hoses for security of connection and for splits. Move the exhaust valve by hand. If it is stiff to operate or seized, free it with special GM heat valve lubricant.

29 Throttle Return Control (TRC) System – description and maintenance

1   This system is used on V8 engined G20 and 30 vehicles operating in California. Its purpose is to open the throttle lever slightly when coasting to reduce the emission of hydrocarbons.
2   Periodically check the security of the vacuum hose and the adjustment of the actuator.
3   To check the actuator valve, disconnect the hose from the valve and connect the valve to an external vacuum source such as a suction pump.
4   Have the engine at normal operating temperature, idling with the transmission in Neutral or Park.
5   Apply a vacuum of 20 in Hg to the actuator and then manually open the throttle slightly and let it close again against the actuator plunger. Record the engine rpm which should be approximately 1500 rpm. If it is not, turn the screw on the plunger and repeat the check (Fig. 3.121).

30 Catalytic Converter – description, removal and installation

1   This device is fitted into the exhaust system on G10 vehicles. It reduces hydrocarbon and carbon monoxide pollutants in the exhaust gas stream as it passes over the catalytic material contained in the converter casing.
2   It should be remembered that the fuel for use in vehicles equipped with a catalytic converter must be of unleaded type only.
3   The converter can be removed by unbolting the clamp at its front and rear, then cutting through the pipe sealant and withdrawing the exhaust pipes from it.
4   If the catalyst beads must be removed, have your dealer carry out this work as it requires the use of special equipment and tools.
5   Installation is a reversal of removal.

31 Manifolds and exhaust system

1   The intake and exhaust manifolds are located in the left side of the engine on six cylinder-in-line units.
2   On 250 cu in engines the intake manifold is in one section while on 292 cu in engines the manifold is of a two-section design. The exhaust manifold is of a four-port type.
3   On V8 engines, the intake manifold is a cast iron double level design and incorporates an EGL port. It is located between the two cylinder banks.
4   A cast iron exhaust manifold is located on each side of the engine to serve each of the banks of four cylinders.
5   Removal of all manifolds is a matter of disconnecting the carburetor, emission control and vacuum connections, then unbolting the assemblies.
6   Always use new gaskets on installation and tighten all nuts and bolts to the specified torque wrench settings, and in the sequence specified (V8). (Fig. 3.124).
7   When any one section of the exhaust system needs renewal it often follows that the whole lot is best renewed.
8   It is most important when fitting exhausts that the twists and contours are carefully followed and that each connecting joint overlaps the correct distance. Any stresses or strain imparted, in order to force the system to fit the hanger rubbers, will result in early fractures and failures.
9   When fitting a new part or a complete system it is well worth removing ALL the system from the vehicle and cleaning up all the joints so that they assemble together easily. The time spent struggling with obstinate joints whilst flat on your back under the vehicle is eliminated and the likelihood of distorting or even breaking a section is greatly reduced. Do not waste a lot of time trying to undo rusted and corroded clamps and bolts. Cut them off. New ones will be required anyway if they are that bad.

32 Manifold heat control valve – description and servicing

1   On earlier models, a manifold heat control valve is installed. The purpose of the valve is to deflect hot exhaust gases onto the underside of the intake manifold during warm up to improve the atomization of the fuel (Figs. 3.126 and 3.127).
2   As the engine warms up, the valve which is controlled by a bimetallic spring is rotated to allow normal passage to the exhaust gases.
3   Periodically attempt to move the valve by holding the counterweight. If it is stiff or siezed, apply special GM solvent or gently tap the end of the valve shaft to free it.

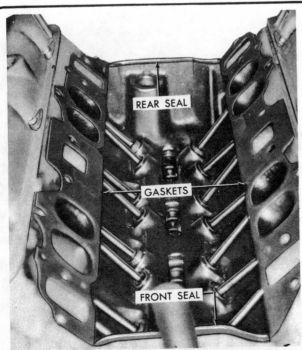

Fig. 3.123 Intake manifold seals and gaskets (V8 engines)

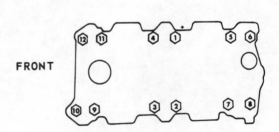

FRONT

Fig. 3.124 Intake manifold attachment bolts (V8 engines)

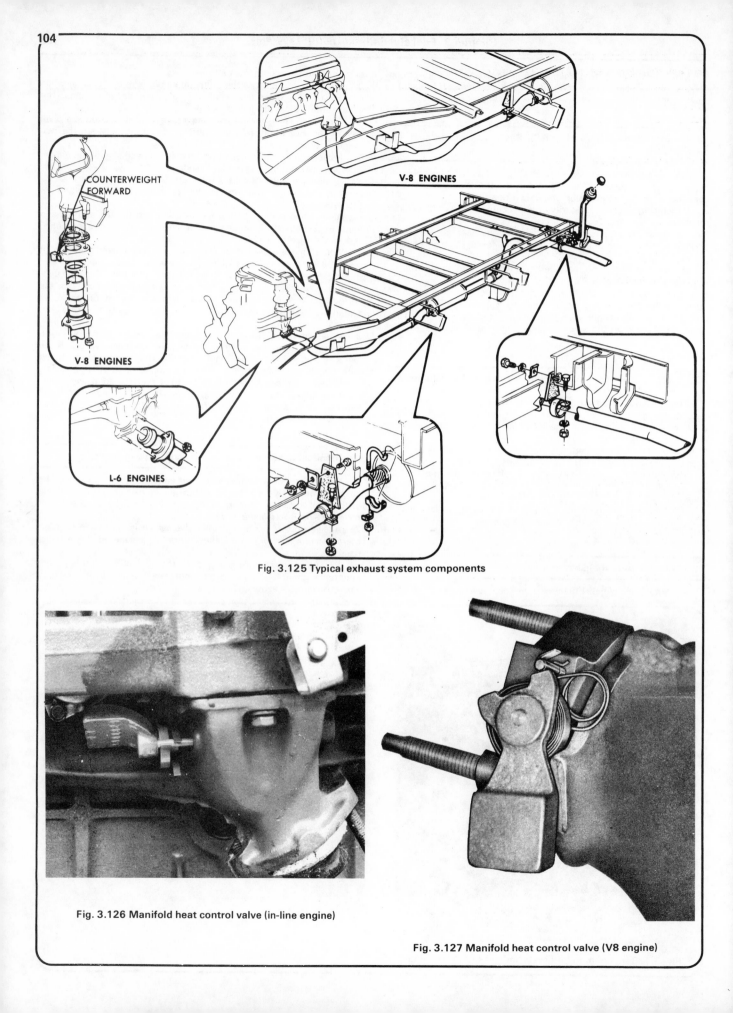

COUNTERWEIGHT
FORWARD

V-8 ENGINES

V-8 ENGINES

L-6 ENGINES

Fig. 3.125 Typical exhaust system components

Fig. 3.126 Manifold heat control valve (in-line engine)

Fig. 3.127 Manifold heat control valve (V8 engine)

33 Fault diagnosis – fuel and emission control systems

Symptom	Reason/s
Fuel system	
Excesive fuel consumption*	Air cleaner choked
	Leaks in fuel tank, carburetor or fuel lines
	Fuel level in float chamber too high
	Mixture too rich
	Incorrect valve clearances
	Dragging brakes
	Tires underinflated

May also be caused by an ignition fault

Symptom	Reason/s
Insufficient fuel delivery or lean mixture	Clogged fuel filter
	Stuck carburetor inlet needle valve
	Faulty fuel pump
	Leaking fuel pipe unions
	Leaking inlet manifold gasket
	Leaking carburetor mounting flange gasket
	Incorrect carburetor adjustment
PCV system	
Escaping fumes from engine	Clogged PCV valve
	Split or collapsed hoses
Fuel evaporative emission control system (ECS)	
Fuel odor and/or rough running engine	Choked carbon canister
	Stuck filler cap valve
	Collapsed or split hoses
Transmission controlled spark (TCS) system	
Idle speed too low or too high or dieseling	Faulty idle stop solenoid
Poor high gear performance	Blown fuse
Excessive fuel consumption	Loose connections or broken leads
Backfire on deceleration	Faulty coolant temperature switch
Difficult cold start	Faulty transmission switch
	Faulty vacuum advance solenoid
Air injection reactor (AIR) system	
Fume emission from exhaust pipe	Slack air pump drive belt
	Split or broken hoses
	Clogged pump air filter
	Defective air pump
	Leaking pressure relief valve
Exhaust gas recirculation (EGR) system	
Rough idling	Faulty or dirty EGR valve
	Broken valve diaphragm spring
	Disconnected or split vacuum hose
	Split valve diaphragm
	Leaking valve gasket

Chapter 4 Ignition system

Refer to Chapter 13 for specifications and information applicable to 1979 through 1985 models

Contents

Specifications

System type . . . . 12V, battery and coil
1967 thru 1974 . . . . Mechanical breaker type distributor
1975 on . . . . Electronic type distributor

Firing order
6-cylinder 1-5-3-6-2-4
V8 1-8-4-3-6-5-7-2

Mechanical contact breaker type distributor
Rotation . . . . Clockwise
Points gap . . . . 0.016 in (new points 0.019 in)
Dwell angle
6-cylinder . . . . 31 to 34°
V8 . . . . 29 to 31°
Condenser . . . . 0.18 to 0.23 microfarad

Distributor data

Check also with vehicle decal. The timing figures should be used in conjunction with the specified idling speeds: see Chapter 3.

	6-cylinder engine			V8 engines		
	230 cu in	250 cu in	292 cu in	307 cu in	350 cu in	400 cu in
1968		Without emission control			Without emission control	
	4° BTDC	4° BTDC	–	2° BTDC	–	–
		With emission control			With emission control	
	TDC Manual	TDC Manual	–	2° BTDC	–	–
	4° BTDC Auto	4° BTDC Auto	–			
1969		Without emission control			Without emission control	
	4° BTDC	4° BTDC	–	2° BTDC	–	–
		With emission control			With emission control	
	TDC Manual	TDC Manual	–	2° BTDC	–	–
	4° BTDC Auto	4° BTDC Auto	–	–	–	–
1970	–	TDC Manual	–	2° BTDC	TDC Manual	–
	–	4° BTDC Auto	–	–	4° BTDC Auto	–
1971	–	TDC Manual	–	2° BTDC	TDC Manual	–
	–	4° BTDC Manual	–	–	4° BTDC Auto	–
1972	–	4° BTDC	–	4° BTDC Manual	4° BTDC Manual	–
				8° BTDC Auto	8° BTDC Auto	
1973	–	6° BTDC	–	4° BTDC Manual	8° BTDC Manual	–
				8° BTDC Auto	12° BTDC Auto	–

Year						
1974	–	8° BTDC	–	–	2-barrel carburetor TDC Manual 8° BTDC Auto	–
					4-barrel carburetor 8° BTDC Manual 12° BTDC Auto	–
					California 4° BTDC Manual 8° BTDC Auto	–
1975	–	10° BTDC	8° BTDC	–	Light duty 6° BTDC	4° BTDC
					Heavy duty 8° BTDC	California 2° BTDC
					California 2° BTDC	
1976	–	10° BTDC California 6° BTDC Manual 10° BTDC Auto	8° BTDC	–	2-barrel carburetor 2° BTDC Manual 6° BTDC Auto 4-barrel carburetor 8° BTDC California 6° BTDC	4° BTDC
1977 – 78	–	8° BTDC Manual 12° BTDC Auto California 6° BTDC Manual 10° BTDC Auto	8° BTDC	–	2-barrel carburetor 8° BTDC (except California) 6° BTDC (California) 4-barrel carburetor 8° BTDC (except California) 2° BTDC (California)	4° BTDC California 2° BTDC

Spark plugs

Year	Engine	Original Plug	Gap	Alternative (colder) plug
1968	6-cylinder V8	AC 46N AC 45	0.035 inch	AC 44N AC 44
1969	6-cylinder V8	R 46N R 44	0.035 inch	R 44N CR 43
1970	6-cylinder V8 (307) V8 (350)	R 46T R 45 R 44	0.035 inch	R 44T R 44 R 43
1971	6-cylinder V8 (307) V8 (350)	R 46TS R 45TS R 44TS	0.035 inch	R 44T R 44 R 43
1972 1973 1974	6-cylinder V8	R 46T R 44T	0.035 inch	R 45T R 43T
1975	6-cylinder (250) 6-cylinder (292) V8	R 46TX R 44TX R 44TX	0.060 inch	–
1976 1977 1978	6-cyl (250) 6-cyl (292) V8 (350-2) V8 (350 and 400-4)	R 46TS R 44T R 45TS R 44TS	0.035 inch 0.045 inch except California (350-4) 0.060 inch	– –

Torque wrench settings

	lbf ft
Distributor clamp	20
Spark plugs ($\frac{5}{8}$ inch)	15
Spark plugs ($\frac{13}{16}$ inch)	25

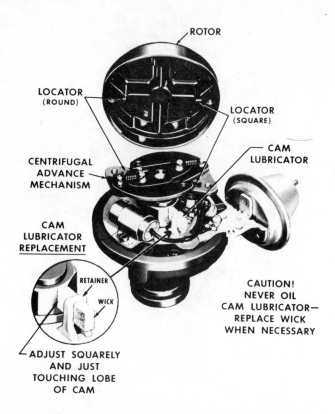

Fig. 4.1. Distributor (mechanical contact breaker type)

ROTOR

LOCATOR (ROUND)

LOCATOR (SQUARE)

CAM LUBRICATOR

CENTRIFUGAL ADVANCE MECHANISM

CAM LUBRICATOR REPLACEMENT

RETAINER

WICK

ADJUST SQUARELY AND JUST TOUCHING LOBE OF CAM

CAUTION! NEVER OIL CAM LUBRICATOR— REPLACE WICK WHEN NECESSARY

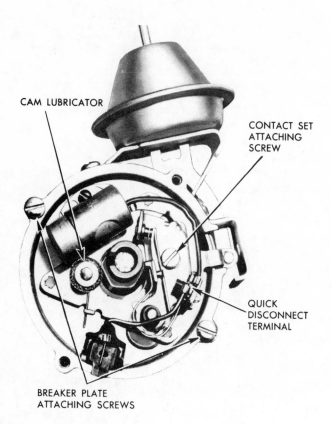

Fig. 4.2. Distributor contact breaker plate

CAM LUBRICATOR

CONTACT SET ATTACHING SCREW

QUICK DISCONNECT TERMINAL

BREAKER PLATE ATTACHING SCREWS

1 General description

1   In order that the engine can run correctly it is necessary for an electrical spark to ignite the fuel/air mixture in the combustion chamber at exactly the right moment in relation to engine speed and load. The ignition system is based on feeding low tension (LT) voltage from the battery to the coil where it is converted to high tension (HT) voltage. The high tension voltage is powerful enough to jump the spark plug gap in the cylinders many times a second under high compression pressures, providing that the system is in good condition and that all adjustments are correct.

2   The ignition system is divided into two circuits: the low tension circuit and the high tension circuit.

3   The low tension (sometimes known as the primary) circuit consists of the battery lead to the control box, lead to the ignition switch, lead from the ignition switch to the low tension or primary coil windings (+ terminal), and the lead from the low tension coil windings (− terminal) to the contact breaker points and condenser in the distributor.

4   The high tension circuit consists of the high tension or secondary coil windings, the heavy ignition lead from the center of the coil to the center of the distributor cap, the rotor arm, and the spark plug leads and spark plugs.

5   The system functions in the following manner. Low tension voltage is changed in the coil into high tension voltage by the opening and closing of the contact breaker points in the low tension circuit. High tension voltage is then fed via the carbon brush in the center of the distributor cap to the rotor arm of the distributor cap, and each time it comes in line with one of the four metal segments in the cap, which are connected to the spark plug leads, the opening and closing of the contact breaker points causes the high tension voltage to build up, jump the gap from the rotor arm to the appropriate metal segment and so via the spark plug lead to the spark plug, where it finally jumps the spark plug before going to earth.

6   The ignition advance is controlled both mechanically and by a vacuum operated system. The mechanical governor mechanism comprises two lead weights, which move out from the distributor shaft as the engine speed rises due to centrifugal force. As they move outwards they rotate the cam relative to the distributor shaft, and so advance the spark. The weights are held in position by two light springs and it is the tension of the springs which is largely responsible for correct spark advancements.

7   The vacuum control consists of a diaphragm, one side of which is connected via a small bore tube to the carburetor, and the other side to the contact breaker plate. Depression in the intake manifold and carburetor, which varies with engine and throttle opening, causes the diaphragm to move, so moving the contact breaker plate, and advancing or retarding the spark.

8   On vehicles built through 1974, a mechanical contact breaker type ignition was used but after this date, an electronic system was substituted. With this later system, a magnetic pick-up assembly is located inside the distributor. The assembly comprises a permanent magnet, a pole piece and a pick-up coil. When the teeth of the timer core which rotate inside the pole piece line up with the teeth on the pole piece, an induced voltage in the pick-up coil signals the electronic module to open the coil primary circuit. The primary current then decreases and a high voltage is induced in the ignition coil secondary winding which then passes through the rotor and leads to fire the spark plugs.

9   The distributor used with the breakerless system differs between the 6-cylinder and V8 engines. With 6-cylinder engines, the ignition coil is mounted separately but with V8 engines, the coil is mounted in compact form within the distributor cap.

10 The capacitor which is mounted in the electronic type distributor is solely for radio interference suppression purposes.

2 Mechanical type breaker points (6-cylinder engine) – adjustment

1   To adjust the contact points to the specified gap, first release the distributor cap hold-down screws and lift off the cap. Clean the cap inside and out with a dry cloth. It is unlikely that the four segments will be badly burned or scored but if they are, then the cap will have to be renewed.

2   Inspect the carbon brush contact located in the top of the cap - see that it is unbroken and stands proud of the plastic surface.

3   Check the contact spring on the top of the rotor arm. It must be clean and have adequate tension to ensure good contact,

4   Remove the rotor arm and the dust cover (where installed).

5   Gently pry the contact breaker points open to examine the condition of their faces. If they are rough, pitted of dirty, it will be necessary to remove them for resurfacing, or for replacement points to be installed.

6   Presuming the points are satisfactory, or that they have been cleaned and installed, measure the gap between the points by turning the engine over until the heel of the breaker arm is on the highest point of the cam.

7   If the original contact points are being retained in use, the gap should be 0.016 inch. If new points have been fitted then the gap should be 0.019 inch, as the heel of the contact breaker arm wears down rapidly in the initial stages of use.

8   If the gap varies from this amount slacken the contact plate securing screw.

9   Adjust the contact gap by inserting a screwdriver in the notched hole in the breaker plate. Turn clockwise to increase and counterclockwise to decrease the gap. When the gap is correct tighten the securing screw and check the gap again. Install the dust cover, rotor and distributor cap.

10   Always make sure that the faces of the contact points are in perfect alignment; if necessary, bend the fixed contact support.

11   On modern engines, setting the distributor contact points gap must be regarded as the initial setting. For optimum engine performance, the cam (or dwell) angle should be checked as described in Section 4.

Fig. 4.3. Adjusting contact breaker points gap

3   Mechanical type breaker points (6-cylinder engine) – renewal

1   Release the distributor cap hold-down screws, then remove the cap, the rotor and the dust cover (where installed).

2   Disconnect the primary circuit and condenser wires from the contact assembly terminal clip.

3   Unscrew and remove the contact assembly securing screws, and lift the assembly from the baseplate.

4   Inspect the faces of the contact points. If they are only lightly burned or pitted then they may be ground square on an oilstone or by rubbing a carborundum strip between them. Where the points are found to be severely burned or pitted, then they must be renewed and at the same time the cause of the erosion of the points established. This is most likely to be due to a faulty condenser, poor ground connections from the battery negative lead to body ground or the engine to ground strap. Remove the connecting bolts at these points, scrape the surface free from rust and corrosion and tighten the bolts using a star-type lockwasher.

5   Clean away any oil or dirt from the baseplate and install the new contact assembly, making sure that it engages in its positioning hole, then insert the securing screw, tightening it only a little more than finger tight.

6   Reconnect the primary circuit and condenser wires.

7   Set the points gap as described in the preceding Section.

8   Take the opportunity to rotate the cam lubricator through 180° in order to present a new face to the cam. Alternatively, if the lubricator is well worn, renew it.

9   Install the dust cover, rotor and cap.

10   Check the dwell angle (Section 4) and the ignition timing (Section 10).

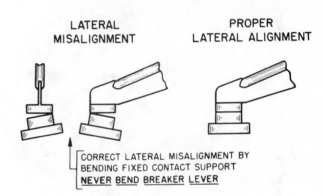

Fig. 4.4. Contact breaker points alignment diagram

4   Dwell angle – checking and adjusting

1   The dwell angle is the number of degrees through which the distributor cam turns during the period between the closure and opening of the contact breaker points. It can only be checked with a dwell meter. The correct dwell angle is given in Specifications. If the angle is too large, increase the points gap; if too small, reduce the points gap.

5   Mechanical type breaker points (V8 engine) – renewal and adjustment

1   Release the distributor cap. To do this, insert a screwdriver in the

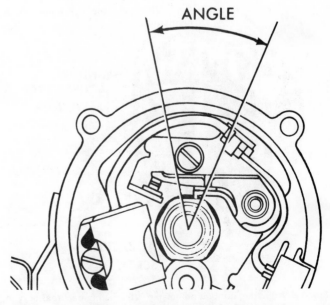

Fig. 4.5. Dwell angle diagram (6-cylinder shown)

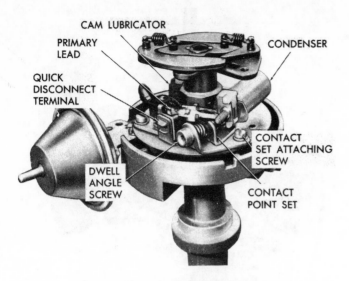

Fig. 4.6. Distributor details (V8 mechanical contact breaker type)

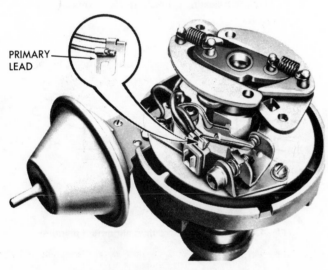

Fig. 4.7. Lead arrangement (V8 mechanical breaker type distributor)

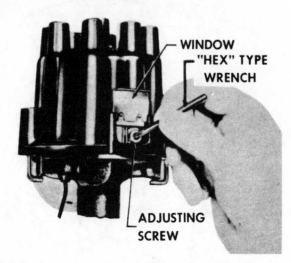

Fig. 4.8. Adjusting contact points gap (V8 mechanical breaker type distributor)

slot of the latch, depress and rotate $\frac{1}{4}$ turn in either direction.
2   Extract the rotor screws and remove the rotor.
3   Slacken the retaining screws and slide the contact set from the breaker plate.
4   Disconnect the primary lead from the insulated terminal.
5   The new contact set is supplied complete with condenser and should be refitted by reversing the removal process. Make sure that the primary lead is connected to the terminal exactly as shown (Fig 4.7).
6   Turn the cam lubricator through 180° to present a new face to the cam. If it is very worn, renew it.
7   Install the rotor and distributor cap, then check the dwell angle (also see Section 4). This is the only adjustment required to this type of distributor contact set.
8   To adjust the dwell angle, have the engine idling to normal operating temperature with a dwell meter connected in accordance with the maker's instructions.
9   Raise the window on the side of the distributor and insert a hexagonal wrench (Allen key) to engage with the joints adjusting screw sockets. Now turn the screw until the dwell angle is in accordance with the figure given in the Specifications.
10   Check the ignition timing (see Section 10).

6   Condenser – testing, removal and installation

1   The condenser ensures that with the contact breaker points open, the sparking between them is not excessive to cause severe pitting. The condenser is fitted in parallel and its failure will automatically cause failure of the ignition system as the points will be prevented from interrupting the low tension circuit.
2   Testing for an unservicable condenser may be carried out by switching on the ignition and separating the contact points by hand. If this action is accompanied by a blue flash then condenser failure is indicated. Difficult starting, misfiring of engine after several miles running or badly pitted points are other indications of a faulty condenser.
3   The surest test is by substitution of a new unit.
4   To renew the condenser, on 6-cylinder engines, release the distributor cap hold-down screws and remove the cap.
5   Remove the rotor.
6   Disconnect the condenser lead from the contact points quick release terminal.
7   Remove the condenser securing screw, lift the condenser from the breaker plate and wipe any oil from the plate.
8   Installation of the condenser is a reversal of removal.
9   Renewal of the condenser on V8 engines can only be achieved by renewal of the complete contact assembly.

7   Distributor (mechanical breaker type) – removal and installation

1   Release the distributor cap hold-down screws and remove the distributor cap. Disconnect the vacuum pipe.
2   Disconnect the primary (LT) lead from the coil terminal.
3   If the crankshaft is not to be rotated while the distributor is out, scribe a mark on the outside of the distributor housing to coincide with the center line of the rotor arm (segment end).
4   Remove the distributor hold-down bolt and clamp, and after noting the relative position of the distributor vacuum unit to the engine, withdraw the distributor.
5   *If the crankshaft has not been rotated* during the period when the distributor was removed from the engine, turn the rotor of the distributor about $\frac{1}{8}$ turn in a clockwise direction past the mark made on the distributor housing prior to removal.
6   Push the distributor into its recess in the cylinder head so that the vacuum unit is in the same relative position as it was before removal (line drawn from cap attaching screw through the vacuum unit 30° to center line of crankshaft; 75° from a line drawn through both cap screws). As the distributor driven gear meshes with the camshaft drivegear the rotor will turn and align with the mark made on the distributor housing (Fig. 4.9).
7   *If the crankshaft has been rotated* during the period when the distributor was removed from the engine, remove No. 1 spark plug and with a finger placed over the plug hole turn the crankshaft until com-

pression can be felt being generated in No. 1 cylinder (piston on firing stroke). Continue to turn the crankshaft until the timing notch on the crankshaft pulley is in alignment with the specified timing mark of the timing tab (photo).

8 Hold the distributor above its cylinder head recess so that the vacuum unit points towards the front of the engine and the punch mark on the distributor drive gear is in line with No. 1 distributor cap terminal. Now turn the distributor body ⅛ turn in a counterclockwise direction and push the distributor into mesh with the camshaft drive gear. If correctly installed, a line drawn from the cap attaching screw through the vacuum unit will be at 30° to the center line of the crankshaft (75° from a line drawn through both cap screws).

9 Install the distributor clamp and hold-down bolt and before finally tightening, turn the distributor body so that the contact points are just opening.

10 Attach the primary lead, the spark plug leads (in their correct order) and connect the vacuum pipe.

11 Check (and adjust if necessary) the ignition timing as described in Section 10.

8 Distributor (6-cylinder mechanical breaker type) – overhaul

1 With the distributor removed from the engine, pull off the rotor and dust cover (where installed).

2 Unscrew the securing screws from the vacuum control assembly and detach it from the distributor body.

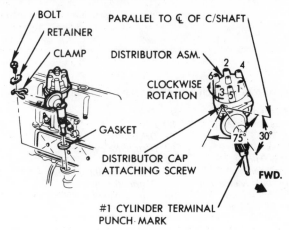

Fig. 4.9. Distributor installation diagram (6-cylinder engine)

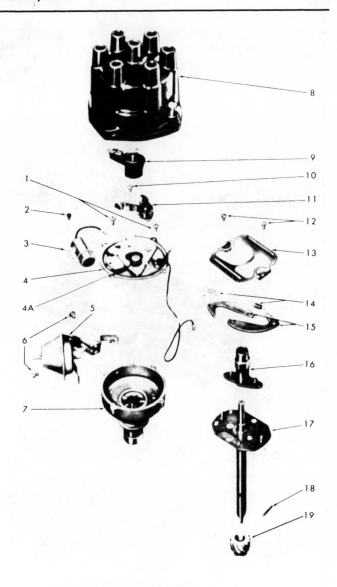

Fig. 4.10. Exploded view of 6-cylinder engine mechanical type distributor

1 Screws
2 Condenser retaining screws
3 Condenser
4 Breaker plate
4A Cam lubricator
5 Vacuum control assembly
6 Screws
7 Distributor body
8 Cap
9 Rotor
10 Contact points assembly screw
11 Contact set
12 Counterweight cover screws
13 Counterweight cover
14 Counterweight springs
15 Counterweight
16 Cam
17 Distributor shaft
18 Roll pin
19 Drive gear

7.7 Typical engine ignition timing marks

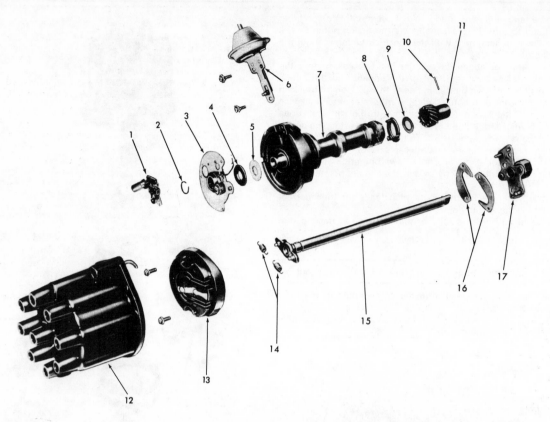

Fig. 4.11. Exploded view of V8 engine mechanical type distributor

1	Contact points/ condenser assembly	9	Shim
2	Circlip	10	Pin
3	Breaker plate	11	Drive gear
4	Felt washer	12	Distributor cap
5	Plastic seal	13	Rotor
6	Vacuum advance unit	14	Counterweight springs
7	Distributor body	15	Distributor shaft
8	Tanged washer	16	Counterweights
		17	Cam

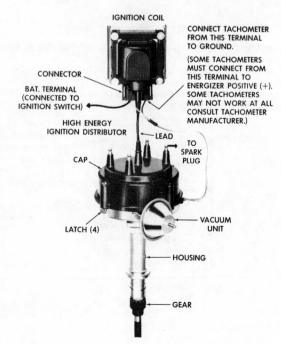

Fig. 4.12. Electronic type distributor (6-cylinder)

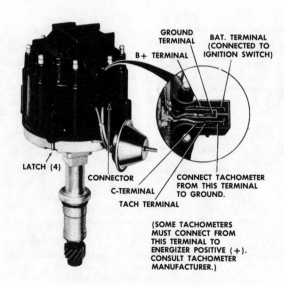

Fig. 4.13. Electronic type distributor (V8)

3   Disconnect the primary circuit and condenser leads from the quick release terminal.
4   Extract the securing screw, and remove the contact set and the condenser.
5   Unscrew and remove the screws which hold the breaker plate in position and then remove the plate.
6   Drive out the roll pin which retains the driven gear to the distributor shaft. Slide the gear from the shaft.
7   Slide the cam/shaft assembly from the distributor body.
8   Remove the cover from the counterweights, and the stop plate screws. Remove the weights, springs and cam assembly.
9   Clean and inspect all components, and renew any that are worn.
10 Commence reassembly by applying grease to the top end of the shaft, then attach the counterweights to their pivot pins; engage the springs and locate the weight cover and the stop plate.
11 Oil the distributor shaft and push it into the distributor body.
12 Install the driven gear and insert the roll pin.
13 Install the breaker plate, condenser and contact set.
14 Connect the vacuum control assembly and then install the dust cover, rotor and cap.
15 The points gap and dwell angle should be adjusted as described earlier in this Chapter once the distributor has been installed on the engine.

9 Distributor (V8 mechanical breaker type) – overhaul

1   With the distributor removed from the engine, pull off the rotor.
2   Remove the counterweights and their springs.
3   Drive out the roll pin which retains the driven gear to the distributor shaft. Slide the gear and spacers from the shaft.
4   Slide the distributor shaft from the body.
5   Extract the screws and remove the advance vacuum unit from the distributor body.
6   Remove the spring retainer and the breaker plate assembly, then detach the contact points and the condenser from the breaker plate. Extract the felt washer and the plastic seal which are located beneath the breaker plate.
7   Clean and inspect all components, and renew any that are worn.
8   Commence reassembly by packing the lubricating cavity in the distributor body with grease, then press in a new plastic seal and install the felt washer.
9   Install the advance vacuum unit, the breaker plate and the spring retainer on the upper bushing.
10 Lubricate and install the counterweights and springs.
11 Install the distributor shaft, washers and drivegear. Press in a new roll pin.
12 Install the contact point/condenser assembly and connect the primary circuit lead.
13 Install the rotor.
14 The dwell angle should be adjusted as described earlier in this Chapter once the distributor has been installed on the engine.

10 Ignition timing (mechanical breaker type distributor)

1   Whenever the contact points have been renewed, the distributor removed and installed, or a change made to a fuel of different anti-knock (octane) rating, the ignition timing must be checked and if necessary adjusted.
2   Disconnect the vacuum hose from the distributor and plug the hose with a rod of suitable diameter.
3   Connect a timing light in accordance with the manufacturer's instructions. Generally, a high voltage type source light should be connected between the spark plug and a terminal of the disconnected high tension lead. An external source light is usually connected by attaching the red leads to the battery positive terminal and the black leads to ground. A single lead is provided for connection to No. 1 spark plug HT lead.
4   Clean and rub chalk on the crankshaft pulley timing notch, also the tab of the timing pointer in accordance with the specified number of degrees shown in the Specifications or on the vehicle tune-up decal, according to engine type.
5   Take care that the leads of the timing light are well clear of the fan and then start the engine.
6   Point the timing light at the timing marks and they will appear

stationary. If the marks are in alignment then the timing is correct but, if they are out of alignment, loosen the distributor locknut and turn the distributor one way or the other until the timing marks coincide. Re-tighten the locknut, switch off the engine and remove the timing light. Reconnect the distributor vacuum pipe.
7   It should be noted that each peak on the timing pointer plate represents an increment of 2 degrees, the word 'BEFORE' indicates advance and 'AFTER' retard.

11 Electronic type distributor – maintenance and precautions

1   No routine maintenance is required. The failure of any component within the unit should be rectified by renewal of the part concerned.
2   The following precautions should be observed when operating on engines fitted with this type of ignition system:

(i)   Always connect a timing light in parallel using an adaptor at the distributor No. 1 terminal.
(ii) When connecting a tachometer for tuning purposes, note that there is a 'TACH' terminal in the distributor cap. The tachometer should be connected between the terminal and ground or battery (energizer) positive terminal according to the manufacturer's instructions.
(iii) Do not pull off the spark plug leads while the engine is running.

12 Electronic type distributor – removal and installation

1   Disconnect the wiring harness connectors which are located at the side of the distributor cap.
2   Remove the distributor cap and place it to one side.
3   Disconnect the vacuum advance hose from the distributor.
4   Scribe alignment marks on the engine to indicate the setting of the rotor and the distributor body in relation to the engine.
5   Unscrew and remove the distributor hold-down nut and clamp.
6   Lift the distributor from the engine.
7   To install the distributor refer to Section 7 and repeat the appropriate operations, but using the alignment marks made on the engine for reference points.
8   Install the distributor cap so that the tab in its base is engaged in the notch in the body. Secure the cap with the four latches.
9   Reconnect the wiring plug.
10 Check and adjust the ignition timing as described in the next Section.

13 Ignition timing (electronic distributor)

1   The procedure is similar to that described in Section 10 but remember to connect the timing light as described in Section 11, paragraph 2 (ii).
2   Refer to the Specifications or vehicle tune-up decal for initial timing figures according to engine type.

14 Distributor (electronic type) – dismantling and reassembly

1   With the distributor removed from the engine, unscrew the two securing screws and pull off the rotor.
2   Remove the springs, counterweight retainer and the counterweights.
3   Extract the two screws which hold the module to the distributor body. Move the module to permit disconnection of the connector from the 'B' and 'C' terminals.
4   Disconnect the leads from the 'W' and 'G' terminals of the module.
5   Drive the roll pin from the drivegear (Fig. 4.17).
6   Remove the gear, the shim and the washer from the distributor shaft.
7   Withdraw the shaft from the distributor housing and extract the washer from the upper end of the housing.
8   Remove the lock ring and the top of the housing and withdraw the pole piece, plate and felt washer.
9   The vacuum advance unit can be removed after extracting the two securing screws.
10 Remove the capacitor (one screw) and remove the wiring harness.
11 Inspect all components and renew as necessary. If the shaft bush-

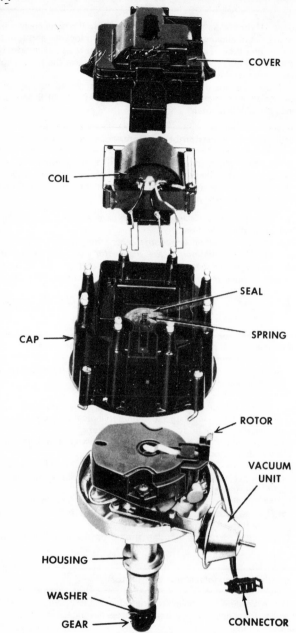

COVER

COIL

SEAL

SPRING

CAP

ROTOR

VACUUM UNIT

HOUSING

WASHER

GEAR

CONNECTOR

Fig. 4.14. Exploded view of electronic type distributor (V8)

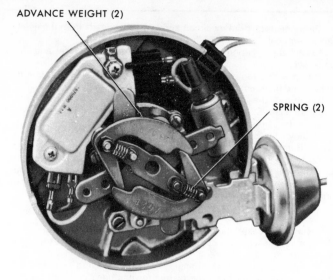

ADVANCE WEIGHT (2)

SPRING (2)

Fig. 4.15. Centrifugal advance mechanism (electronic type distributor)

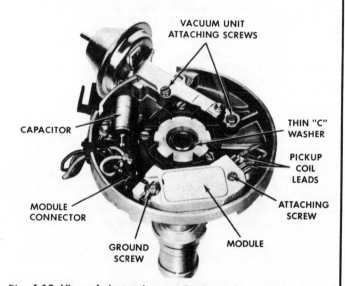

VACUUM UNIT ATTACHING SCREWS

THIN "C" WASHER

PICKUP COIL LEADS

ATTACHING SCREW

CAPACITOR

MODULE CONNECTOR

GROUND SCREW

MODULE

Fig. 4.16. View of electronic type distributor (centrifugal advance mechanism removed)

Fig. 4.17. Removing drive gear roll pin (electronic type distributor)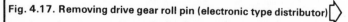

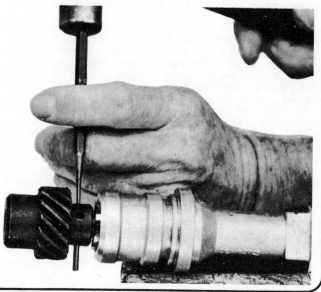

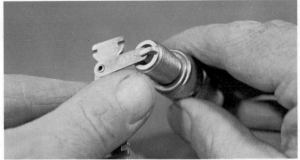

Measuring plug gap. A feeler gauge of the correct size (see ignition system specifications) should have a slight 'drag' when slid between the electrodes. Adjust gap if necessary

Adjusting plug gap. The plug gap is adjusted by bending the ground electrode inwards, or outwards, as necessary until the correct clearance is obtained. Note the use of the correct tool

Normal. Gray brown deposits, lightly coated core nose. Gap increasing by around 0.001 in (0.025 mm) per 1000 miles (1600 km). Plugs ideally suited to engine, and engine in good condition

Carbon fouling. Dry, black, sooty deposits. Will cause weak spark and eventually misfire. Fault: over-rich fuel mixture. Check: carburetor mixture settings, float level and jet sizes; choke operation and cleanliness of air filter. Plugs can be re-used after cleaning

Oil fouling. Wet, oily deposits. Will cause weak spark and eventually misfire. Fault: worn bores/piston rings or valve guides; sometimes occurs (temporarily) during running-in period. Plugs can be re-used after thorough cleaning

Overheating. Electrodes have glazed appearance, core nose very white – few deposits. Fault: plug overheating. Check: plug value, ignition timing, fuel octane rating (too low) and fuel mixture (too weak). Discard plugs and cure fault immediately

Electrode damage. Electrodes burned away; core nose has burned, glazed appearance. Fault: pre-ignition. Check: as for 'Overheating' but may be more severe. Discard plugs and remedy fault before piston or valve damage occurs

Split core nose (may appear initially as a crack). Damage is self-evident, but cracks will only show after cleaning. Fault: pre-ignition or wrong gap-setting technique. Check: ignition timing, cooling system, fuel octane rating (too low) and fuel mixture (too weak). Discard plugs, rectify fault immediately

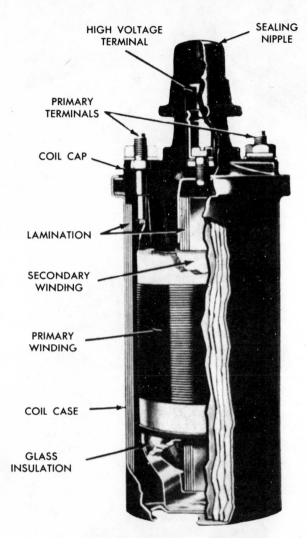

HIGH VOLTAGE TERMINAL

SEALING NIPPLE

PRIMARY TERMINALS

COIL CAP

LAMINATION

SECONDARY WINDING

PRIMARY WINDING

COIL CASE

GLASS INSULATION

Fig. 4.18. Ignition coil (mechanical breaker type distributor)

ings in the distributor body are worn, renew the body complete.

12 Commence reassembly by installing the vacuum advance unit.

13 Install the felt washer on top of the lubricant reservoir on the distributor body.

14 Apply two or three drops of engine oil to the felt wick, then install pole piece and plate assembly over the upper bushing and vacuum advance unit.

15 Install the lock ring.

16 Install the distributor shaft with rotor into the distributor body.

17 On V8 engine distributors, install the tanged washer, shim and drivegear to the distributor shaft.

18 On 6-cylinder engine distributors, install the drive gear; no washer or shims are required.

19 Set the drive gear on the shaft so that the alignment mark on the gear is in line with the contact end of the rotor. Install a new roll pin.

20 Install the capacitor to the distributor body and insert one securing screw, finger-tight.

21 Fit the connector to the 'B' and 'C' terminals of the module so that the tab is uppermost.

22 Special silicone grease (available from your dealer) must now be applied to the metal mounting surface of the module to ensure adequate cooling during operation. Secure the module with two screws.

23 Position the wiring harness so that the grommet engages in the notch in the distributor body.

24 Connect the leads (PINK) to the capacitor stud and (BLACK) to the capacitor mounting screw.

25 Connect the wires from the pick-up coil to terminals 'G' and 'W' of the module.

26 Fit the centrifugal weights, the weight retainer (dimple downward), and the springs.

27 Fit the rotor and the two securing screws. Make sure that the notch on the side of the rotor is engaged with the tab on the counterweight baseplate.

15 Ignition coil (used with mechanical breaker distributor)

1 Secondary (or high tension) current should be negative at the spark plug terminals. To ensure this is so, check that the primary (LT) connections to the coil terminals are correctly made.

2 The primary lead from the distributor must connect with the negative (-) terminal on the coil. An incorrect connection can cause as much as 60% loss of spark efficiency and although the engine will run, rough idling and misfiring at speed will occur.

3 The only test for a faulty coil which can readily be carried out by the home mechanic is by substitution of a new unit.

4 The ignition coil is mounted on the right side of the cylinder block.

16 Ignition coil (used with electronic type distributor)

1 *On 6-cylinder engined vehicles* equipped with electronic ignition, the coil is mounted as an individual component on the side of the engine in a similar way to the coil with conventional ignition systems.

2 *On V8 engined vehicles,* the coil is built into the distributor cap. The coil can be removed after first extracting the screws which hold the coil cover in position and then removing the coil mounting screws.

3 Installing the coil to the cap is a reversal of removal but make sure that the wiring is as follows:

    Side cap connector - ground wire (black) in center.

    Brown next to vacuum advance unit.

    Pink opposite vacuum advance unit.

4 When inserting the coil mounting screws, make sure that the ground wire is located under one of them.

17 Spark plugs and high tension leads

1 Correct functioning of the spark plugs is vital for the highest performance and engine efficiency. The spark plugs installed as standard equipment cannot be improved upon. Some types have built-in resistors for interference suppression.

2 At intervals of 5000 miles, remove the spark plugs, clean and re-gap them to the specified clearance. Cleaning can be carried out using a wire brush but taking the plugs to a service station to be sandblasted is to be preferred.

3 The spark plug gap is of considerable importance as, if it is too large or too small, the size of the spark and its efficiency will be seriously impaired. To set it, measure the gap with a feeler gage, and then bend open, or close, the outer plug electrode until the correct gap is achieved. The center electrode should never be bent as this may crack the insulation and cause plug failure, if nothing worse.

4 The condition and appearance of the spark plugs will tell much about the condition and tune of the engine.

5 If the insulator nose of the spark plug is clean and white, with no deposits, this is indicative of a weak mixture, or too hot a plug (a hot plug transfers heat away from the electrode slowly - a cold plug transfers it away quickly).

6 If the tip and insulator nose is covered with hard black looking deposits, then this is indicative that the mixture is too rich. Should the plug be black and oily, then it is likely that the engine is fairly worn, as well as the mixture being too rich.

7 If the insulator nose is covered with light tan to grayish brown deposits, then the mixture is correct and it is likely that the engine is in good condition.

8 If there are any traces of long brown tapering stains on the outside of the white portion of the plug, then the plug will have to be renewed, as this shows that there is a faulty joint between the plug body and the insulator, and compression is being allowed to leak away.

9 Every 12 000 miles, the spark plugs should be renewed.

10 Always tighten a spark plug to the specified torque – no tighter.

11 Wipe the spark plug leads occasionally with a kerosene soaked rag and always connect them in the correct order.

12 The leads are of special carbon cored type and in the event of a terminal becoming detached, renew the lead complete as a repair is not possible.

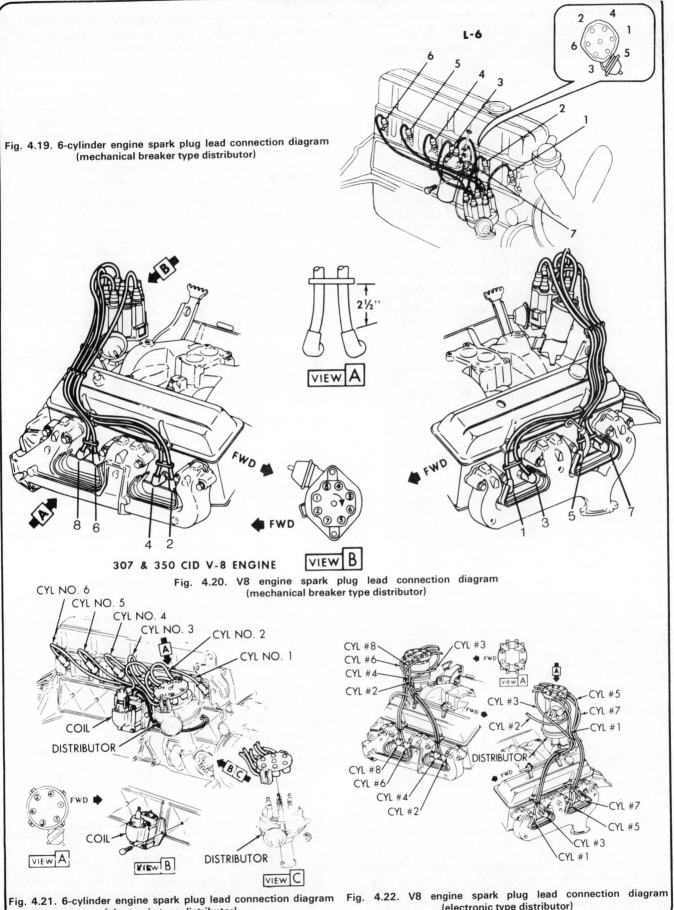

L-6

Fig. 4.19. 6-cylinder engine spark plug lead connection diagram (mechanical breaker type distributor)

2½''

VIEW A

FWD

FWD

307 & 350 CID V-8 ENGINE

VIEW B

Fig. 4.20. V8 engine spark plug lead connection diagram (mechanical breaker type distributor)

8 6

4 2

FWD

FWD

1 3 5 7

CYL NO. 6
CYL NO. 5
CYL NO. 4
CYL NO. 3
CYL NO. 2
A
CYL NO. 1

COIL
DISTRIBUTOR

A
B C

FWD

VIEW A
COIL
VIEW B
DISTRIBUTOR
VIEW C

CYL #8
CYL #6
CYL #4
CYL #2

FWD

VIEW A

CYL #3

CYL #2

CYL #3
CYL #5
CYL #7
CYL #1

DISTRIBUTOR

FWD

CYL #8
CYL #6
CYL #4
CYL #2

CYL #7
CYL #5
CYL #3
CYL #1

Fig. 4.21. 6-cylinder engine spark plug lead connection diagram (electronic type distributor)

Fig. 4.22. V8 engine spark plug lead connection diagram (electronic type distributor)

18 Fault diagnosis (mechanical contact breaker type ignition)

Engine fails to start

1 If the engine fails to start and the vehicle was running normally when it was last used, first check there is fuel in the fuel tank. If the engine turns over normally then the fault may be in either the high or low tension circuits. First check the HT circuit. **Note:** *If the battery is known to be fully charged, the ignition light comes on, and the starter motor fails to turn the engine, check the tightness of the leads on the battery terminal and also the secureness of the ground lead to its connection to the body. It is quite common for the leads to have worked loose, even if they look and feel secure. If one of the battery terminal posts gets very hot when trying to work the starter motor this is a sure indication of a faulty connection to that terminal.*

2 One of the commonest reasons for bad starting is wet and damp spark plugs leads and distributor. Remove the distributor cap. If condensation is visible internally, dry the cap with a rag and also wipe over the leads. Replace the cap.

3 If the engine still fails to start, check that current is reaching the plugs by disconnecting each plug in turn at the spark plug end, and hold the end of the cable about 3/16th inch away from the cylinder block. Spin the engine on the starter motor.

4 Sparking between the end of the cable and the block should be fairly strong with a regular blue streak (Hold the lead with a dry cloth or rubber glove to avoid electric shocks). If current is reaching the plugs, then remove them and clean and regap them. The engine should now start.

5 If there is no spark at the plug leads, take off the HT lead from the center of the distributor cap and hold it to the block as before. Spin the engine on the starter once more. A rapid succession of blue sparks between the end of the lead and the block indicate that the coil is in order and that the distributor cap is cracked, the rotor arm faulty, or the carbon brush in the top of the distributor cap is not making good contact with the spring on the rotor arm. Possibly the points are in bad condition. Clean and reset them as described in this Chapter.

6 If there are no sparks from the end of the lead from the coil, check the connections at the coil end of the lead. If it is in order start checking the low tension circuit.

7 Use a 12V voltmeter or a 12V bulb and two lengths of wire. With the ignition switch on and the points open, test between the low tension wire to the coil (it is marked +) and ground. No reading indicates a break in the supply from the ignition switch. Check the connections at the switch to see if any are loose. Reconnect them and the engine should run. A reading shows a faulty coil or condenser, or broken lead between the coil and the distributor.

8 Take the condenser wire off the points assembly and with the points open, test between the moving points and ground. If there now is a reading, then the fault is in the condenser. Install a new one and the fault is cleared.

9 With no reading from the moving point to ground take a reading between ground and the (−) terminal of the coil. A reading here shows a broken wire which will need to be renewed between the coil and distributor. No reading confirms that the coil has failed and must be renewed, after which the engine will run once more. Remember to reconnect the condenser wire to the points assembly. For these tests it is sufficient to separate the points with a piece of dry paper while testing with the points open.

Engine misfires

10 If the engine misfires regularly, run it at a fast idling speed. Pull off each of the plug caps in turn and listen to the note of the engine. Hold the plug cap in a dry cloth or with a rubber glove as additional protection against a shock from the HT supply.

11 No difference in engine running will be noticed when the lead from the defective circuit is removed. Removing the lead from one of the good cylinders will accentuate the misfire.

12 Remove the plug lead from the end of the defective plug, and hold it about 3/16 inch away from the block. Restart the engine. If the sparking is fairly strong and regular, the fault must lie in the spark plug.

13 The plug may be loose, the insulation may be cracked, or the points may have burnt away giving too wide a gap for the spark to jump. Worse still, one of the points may have broken off. Either renew the plug, or clean it, reset the gap, and then test it.

14 If there is no spark at end of the plug lead, or if it is weak and intermittent, check the ignition lead from the distributor to the plug. If the insulation is cracked or perished, renew the lead. Check the connections at the distributor cap.

15 If there is still no spark, examine the distributor cap for tracking. This can be recognised by a very thin black line running between two or more electrodes or between an electrode and some other part of the distributor. These lines are paths which now conduct electricity acorss the cap thus letting it run to ground. The only answer is a new distributor cap.

16 Apart from the ignition timing being incorrect, other causes of misfiring have already been dealt with under the section dealing with the failure of the engine to start. To recap - these are that:

   a) the coil may be faulty giving an intermittent misfire;
   b) there may be a damaged wire or a loose connection in the low tension circuit;
   c) the condenser may be short circuiting;
   d) there may be a mechanical fault in the distributor (broken driving spindle or contact breaker spring).

17 If the ignition timing is too far retarded, it should be noted that the engine will tend to overheat, and there will be a quite noticeable drop in power. If the engine is overheating and the power is down and the ignition timing is correct, then the carburetor should be checked, as it is likely that this is where the fault lies.

19 Fault diagnosis (electronic ignition – 6-cylinder engines)

Carry out the following operations in the sequence given, testing the engine starting or running capability between each step.

Engine cranks but will not start

1 Connect a test lamp between the battery lead terminal of the coil and ground, then switch on the ignition. If the lamp lights the ignition circuit is alright so check for a fuel blockage or fouled plugs. *If the lamp does not light*, check for loose connections at the coil or ignition switch (Fig. 4.23).

2 Remove the distributor cap, and check for cracks, moisture, etc.

3 Disconnect the wiring connector from coil, and substitute an ohmmeter (Fig. 4.24). If the reading is above 1 ohm (x1 scale) renew the coil. If the reading is 0 to1 ohm (x1 scale) proceed to Paragraph 4.

4 Reconnect the ohmmeter to the coil leads as shown (Fig. 4.25). If the reading is less than 6000 ohms or more than 30 000 ohms, renew the coil. If the reading is between 6000 and 30 000 ohms reconnect the ohmmeter as shown (Fig. 4.26) and proceed to Paragraph 5.

5 If the reading is less than infinity, renew the coil. If the reading is infinity (x1000 scale) proceed to Paragraph 6.

6 Remove the green and white leads from the module and connect the ohmmeter between ground and either lead. If the reading is less than infinity (x1000 scale) renew the pick-up assembly. If the reading is infinity proceed to Paragraph 7.

7 Reconnect the ohmmeter across the module green and white leads. If the reading is between 500 and 1500 ohms, renew the module. If the reading is not within the 500 to 1500 ohm range, renew the pick-up assembly.

Engine runs roughtly or cuts out

8 Check the spark plug condition and leads.
9 Remove the distributor cap and check for cracks or moisture.
10 Repeat Paragraph 4.
11 Repeat Paragraph 6.
12 Repeat Paragraph 7.

20 Fault diagnosis (electronic ignition - V8 engines)

Carry out the following operations in the sequence given, testing the engine starting or running capability between each step.

Engine cranks but will not start

1 Connect a test lamp between ground and the battery lead terminal on the distributor. Switch on the ignition. *If the lamp lights*, the ignition circuit is all right so check for a fuel blockage or fouled plugs. *If the lamp does not light*, check for loose connections at the distributor or

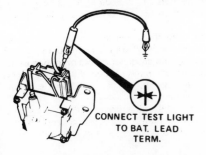

Fig. 4.23. Fault diagnosis test connections (Section 19/1)

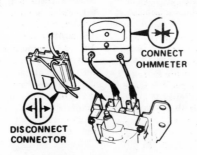

Fig. 4.24. Fault diagnosis test connections (Section 19/3)

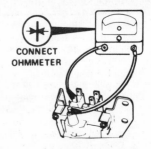

Fig. 4.25. Fault diagnosis test connections (Section 19/4)

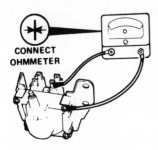

Fig. 4.26. Fault diagnosis test connections (Section 19/4)

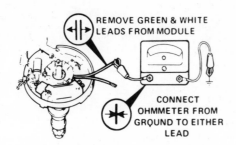

Fig. 4.27. Fault diagnosis test connections (Section 19/6)

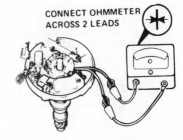

Fig. 4.28. Fault diagnosis test connections (Section 19/7)

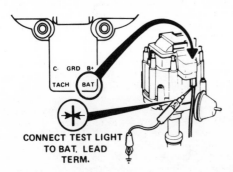

Fig. 4.29. Fault diagnosis test connections (Section 20/1)

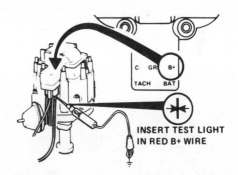

Fig. 4.30. Fault diagnosis test connections (Section 20/2)

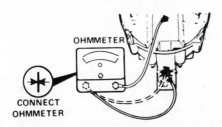

Fig. 4.31. Fault diagnosis test connections (Section 20/3)

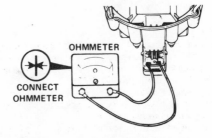

Fig. 4.32. Fault diagnosis test connections (Section 20/4)

ignition switch (Fig. 4.29).

2   Insert the test lamp probe in the red B+ wire on the side of the distributor. *If the lamp does not light*, check for a broken lead. *If the lamp lights*, remove the distributor cap assembly and check for cracks or moisture. If the engine still does not start, proceed to Paragraph 3.

3   Connect an ohmmeter as shown. If the reading is above 1 ohm (x1 scale) renew the coil. If the reading is between 0 and 1 ohm (x1 scale), proceed to Paragraph 4 (Fig. 4.31).

4   Reconnect the ohmmeter as shown, noting that the readings should be observed with the lower lead in the alternative position. If both readings show infinity, renew the coil. If both readings are between 6000 and 30 000 ohms, proceed to Paragraph 5 (Fig. 4.32).

5   Repeat Paragraph 6 in Section 19.

6   Repeat Paragraph 7 in Section 19.

Engine runs roughly or cuts out

7   Check the spark plug condition and leads.

8   Remove the distributor cap and check for cracks or moisture.

9   Repeat Paragraph 4.

10   Repeat Paragraph 6 of Section 19.

11   Repeat Paragraph 7 of Section 19.

Chapter 5 Clutch

Contents

Specifications

Type .... Single dry plate; diaphragm spring with in-line engines, coil springs with V8 engines
Mechanical actuation

Free movement
At fork lever .... $\frac{3}{16}$ to $\frac{1}{4}$ inch
At pedal
    Early, rigid front axle .... $\frac{3}{4}$ to 1 inch
    Later .... 1 to $1\frac{1}{2}$ inches

Throwout bearing .... Grease sealed, ball

Driven plate diameter
In-line engines .... 10 inch
V8 engines .... 11 inch
Late models, heavy duty option .... 12 inch

Torque wrench settings **lbf ft**
Clutch cover bolts to flywheel 18
Fork lever pivot ballstud 25
Flywheel housing to engine bolts 25

1 General description

1   All clutches incorporate a single dry plate but on vehicles with a six cylinder engine, the pressure plate is of the diaphragm spring type whereas one of coil spring design is used in conjunction with V8 engines (Fig. 5.1).

2   On all models, the clutch operating linkage is of a mechanical (rod) design.

2 Clutch – adjustment and maintenance

1   In order to be able to fully disengage the clutch to shift gears and also to ensure that the clutch is fully engaged after the drive is taken up, the clutch pedal free movement must be checked and adjusted if necessary, at the intervals specified in Routine Maintenance at the front of this Manual.

2   On early models with a rigid front axle the pedal free movement should be between $\frac{3}{4}$ and 1 inch. Where it is outside these limits, alter the effective length of the pushrod by releasing and turning the jam nuts as necessary (Fig. 5.2A).

3   To check the free movement on later models which have independent front suspension and pendant pedal, first disconnect the return spring from the clutch release fork.

4   Release the jam nut (A) and unscrew it towards the end of the threaded pushrod (Fig. 5.2B).

5   Now press the rod so that the clutch release fork can be felt to move the throwout bearing against the fingers of the pressure plate.

6   Now measure the distance between the face of the adjuster nut (B) and the swivel. This should be between $\frac{3}{16}$ and $\frac{1}{4}$ inch. If necessary, turn the adjuster nut to achieve this.

7   When the adjustment is correct, tighten the jam nut without moving the position of the adjuster nut, and attach the return spring.

8   If the adjustment has been carried out correctly, the free movement at the pedal pad should be between 1 and $1\frac{1}{2}$ inches.

9   At the specified intervals, lubricate the clutch linkage cross-shaft and swivel, and apply some grease to the return spring and threads of

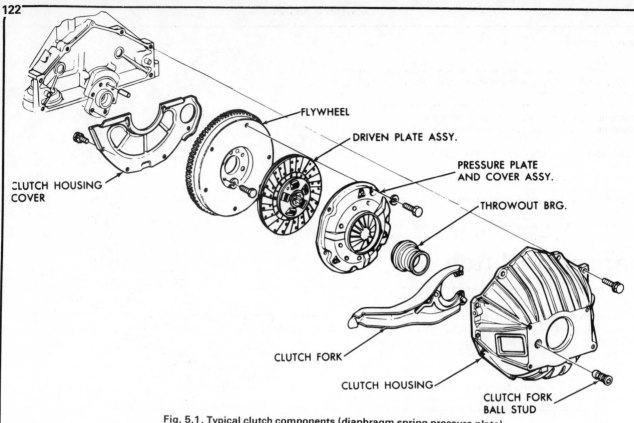

FLYWHEEL

DRIVEN PLATE ASSY.

PRESSURE PLATE
AND COVER ASSY.

THROWOUT BRG.

CLUTCH HOUSING
COVER

CLUTCH FORK

CLUTCH HOUSING

CLUTCH FORK
BALL STUD

Fig. 5.1. Typical clutch components (diaphragm spring pressure plate)

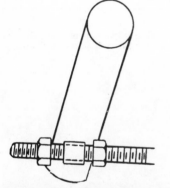

Fig. 5.2A. Clutch operating rod adjustment diagram (early models)

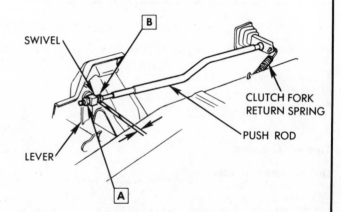

B

SWIVEL

CLUTCH FORK
RETURN SPRING

PUSH ROD

LEVER

A

Fig. 5.2B. Clutch operating rod adjustment diagram (later models)

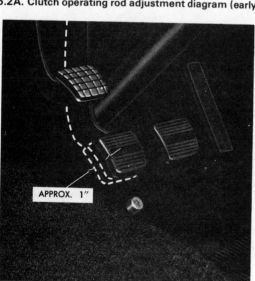

APPROX. 1"

Fig. 5.3. Clutch pedal free movement diagram

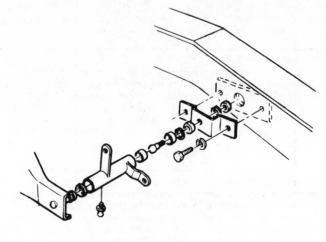

Fig. 5.4. Clutch linkage cross-shaft (later models)

the control rod.

3 Clutch cross-shaft (later models with pendant pedal) – removal and installation

1   Disconnect the clutch release fork return spring.
2   Disconnect the operating rod (pedal to cross-shaft) from the cross-shaft.
3   Disconnect the operating rod (release fork to cross-shaft) from the release fork.
4   Loosen the cross-shaft ball stud nut and then slide the ball stud from the slot in the bracket.
5   Pull the cross-shaft from the ballstud at the engine end, and remove it.
6   Installation is a reversal of removal but apply grease to the ball-studs first and, when installation is complete, adjust the pedal free movement.

4 Clutch pedal – removal and installation

Early models with rigid front axle
1   Disconnect the upper pedal from the lower one by unscrewing and removing the nut, seal and spacer.
2   Remove the pedal return spring, the pedal retainer, bolt, washers and nut from the inboard side of the frame rail.
3   Withdraw the pedal assembly.
4   Renew any worn sleeve bushings and install.
5   Lubricate the sleeve and bushings, then adjust the push-rod to provide the correct pedal free movement (see Section 2).

Later models with independent front suspension
6   Apply the parking brake pedal firmly.
7   Disconnect the wires from the neutral start switch (if installed) on the pedal arm.
8   Unbolt and remove the pushrod lever from the pivot shaft of the

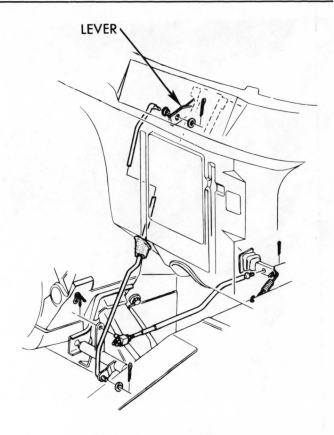

Fig. 5.5. Clutch control rods (later models)

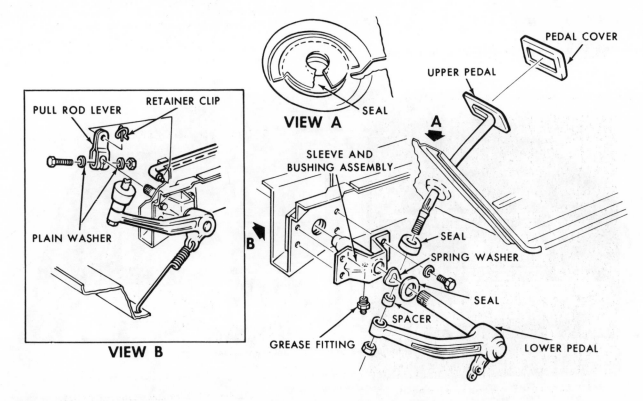

Fig. 5.6A. Clutch pedal detail (early models)

5.3 Dismantling the clutch

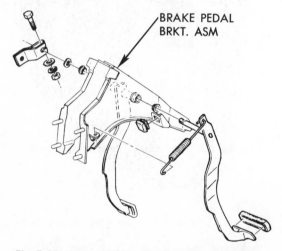

Fig. 5.6B. Foot pedals and bracket (later models)

clutch pedal.

9   Hold the clutch pedal pad in one hand and slide the pedal sideways until it clears the pedal stop, then let the return spring pull the pedal upwards until the spring loses its tension and can be unhooked.

10   The clutch pedal can now be removed from the bracket.

11   If the pedal shaft bushes are worn, renew them.

12   Installation is a reversal of removal, but apply grease to the shaft and bushes, and tighten the pedal arm lever pinch bolt to the specified torque.

13   Adjust the pedal free movement on completion.

5   Clutch – removal

1   Access to the clutch assembly and to the clutch throwout mechanism may be gained in one of two ways:

    (i) by removing the transmission leaving the engine in position in the vehicle (see Chapter 6).
    (ii) by removing the engine/transmission as one unit (at the time of major overhaul), and then separating the engine from the transmission as described in Chapter 1.

Obviously, unless the engine needs overhaul, the simpler method is to remove the transmission.

2   With the clutch now exposed, mark the relative position of the clutch pressure plate to the flywheel so that it can be installed in its original position. If a new pressure plate is to be fitted then the 'X' on the new plate cover should be aligned with the 'X' on the flywheel.

3   Unscrew each of the cover bolts a turn at a time until the spring tension in the assembly is relieved and the cover can be withdrawn. Catch the driven plate as it falls from the face of the flywheel (photo).

6   Clutch – inspection and renovation

1   It is not practical to dismantle the pressure plate assembly and the term 'dismantling' is usually used for simply fitting a new clutch driven plate.

2   If a new clutch disc is being fitted it is false economy not to renew the throwout bearing at the same time. This will preclude having to renew it at a later date when wear on the clutch linings is still very small.

3   The type of pressure plate assembly differs according to the type of engine fitted. With in-line engines, a diaphragm spring clutch is

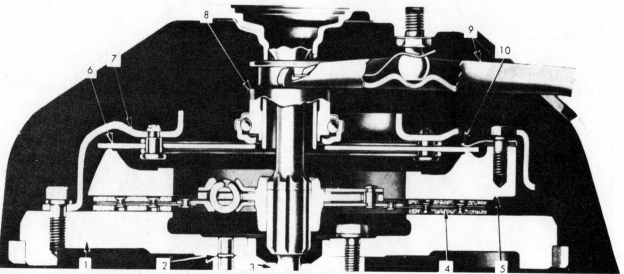

Fig. 5.7. Sectional view of typical diaphragm spring clutch

1 Flywheel	*5 Pressure plate*	*8 Throw out bearing*
2 Dowel	*6 Diaphragm spring*	*9 Fork*
3 Pilot bushing	*7 Cover*	*10 Retracting spring*
4 Driven plate		

used, whereas with V8 engines, a coil spring unit is used.

4   If the pressure plate assembly requires renewal an exchange unit must be purchased. This will have been accurately set up and balanced to very fine limits.

5   Examine the clutch plate friction linings for wear and loose rivets, and the disc for rim distortion, cracks, broken hub springs, and worn splines. The surface of the friction linings may be highly glazed, but as long as the clutch material pattern can be clearly seen this is satisfactory. Compare the amount of lining wear with a new clutch disc. If worn, the driven plate must be renewed.

6   Check the machined faces of the flywheel and the pressure plate. If either are grooved or have a multitude of cracks, they should be renewed.

7   If the pressure plate is cracked or split it is essential that an exchange unit is installed; also if the pressure of the diaphragm or coil springs is suspect.

8   Check the throwout bearing for smoothness of operation. There should be no harshness or slackness in it. It should spin reasonably freely bearing in mind it has been pre-packed with grease.

7   Clutch throwout bearing – renewal

1   From within the flywheel housing, remove the clutch fork by prying it from its ball mounting.

2   Pull the throwout bearing from the clutch fork.

3   If the ball stud is worn, it may be removed by unbolting it (photo).

4   The clutch fork retainer may be removed by prying it from the fork with a small screwdriver.

5   Apply some high melting point grease to the clutch fork pivot ball seat, then snap the fork on to the ball stud. If a new retainer was fitted to the fork, make sure that its higher side is away from the ball socket with its open end horizontal.

6   Pack the recess in the throwout bearing collar with graphite grease and also apply a smear to the groove (Fig. 5.10).

7   Install the throwout bearing on the fork.

8   Clutch – installing and centralising

1   It is important that no oil or grease gets on the clutch plate friction linings, or the pressure plate and flywheel faces. It is advisable to replace the clutch with clean hands and to wipe down the pressure plate and flywheel faces with a clean dry rag before assembly begins.

2   Place the driven plate against the flywheel, making sure that the projecting torsion spring hub is *away* from the flywheel and the longer splined boss is *towards* the flywheel.

3   Install the clutch cover assembly so that the marks made on dismantling are in alignment. Tighten the bolts only finger-tight so that the driven plate is gripped but can still be slid sideways.

7.3 Clutch fork ball stud locknut

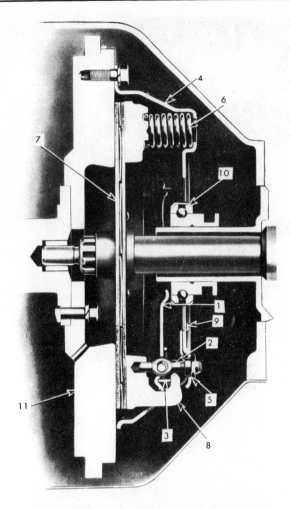

Fig. 5.8. Sectional view of typical coil spring clutch

1	Release lever	7 Driven plate
2	Eyebolt	8 Pressure plate
3	Strut	9 Anti-rattle spring
4	Cover	10 Throwout bearing
5	Nut	11 Flywheel
6	Pressure spring	

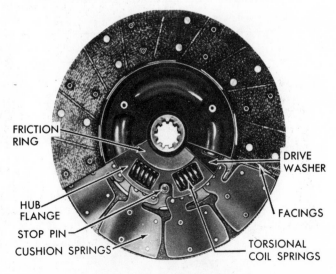

Fig. 5.9. Typical driven plate

8.5 Centralising clutch driven plate

8.9 Tightening a clutch cover bolt

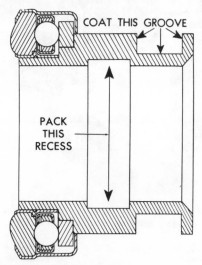

Fig. 5.10. Grease application diagram for clutch throwout bearing collar

4   The clutch plate must now be centralised so that when the engine and transmission are mated, the gearbox input shaft splines will pass through the splines in the center of the driven plate hub.

5   Centralisation can be carried out quite easily by inserting a round bar or long screwdriver through the hole in the center of the clutch, so that end of the bar rests in the small hole in the end of the crankshaft containing the input shaft pilot bush. Ideally an old clutch drive gear should be used (photo).

6   Using the input shaft bearing bush as a fulcrum, moving the bar sideways or up and down will move the clutch plate in whichever direction is necessary to achieve centralisation.

7   Centralisation is easily judged by removing the bar and viewing the driven plate hub in relation to the hole in the center of the clutch cover plate diaphragm spring. When the hub appears exactly in the center of the hole all is correct. Alternatively, the input shaft will fit the bush and center of the clutch hub exactly, obviating the need for visual alignment.

8   Tighten the clutch bolts firmly in a diagonal sequence to ensure that the cover plate is pulled down evenly and without distortion to the flange.

9   Finally progressively tighten, in a diagonal sequence, the clutch cover bolts to the specified torque (photo).

10   Install the transmission to the engine and adjust the clutch (Chapters 6 and 5).

9   Fault diagnosis – clutch

Symptom	Reason/s
Judder when taking drive	Loose engine mountings
	Worn or oil-contaminated driven plate friction linings
	Worn splines on driven plate hub or input shaft
	Worn crankshaft spigot bush
Clutch slip	Damaged or distorted pressure plate assembly
	Driven plate linings worn or oil contaminated
	No free movement at pedal
Noise on depressing clutch pedal	Dry, worn or damaged clutch release bearing
	Excessive play in first motion shaft splines
Noise as clutch pedal is released	Distorted driven plate
	Broken or weak driven plate hub cushion coil springs
	Distorted or worn input shaft
	Release bearing loose on throwout collar
Difficulty in disengaging clutch for gearchange	Driven plate hub splines rusted on shaft
	Excessive pedal free movement

Chapter 6 Transmission

Refer to Chapter 13 for specifications and information applicable to 1979 through 1985 models

Contents

Specifications

Manual transmission

Type .... Synchromesh on all forward gears

Make
1968 thru 1970 .... Warner 4-speed T10
1970 thru 1978 .... Saginaw 3-speed or Muncie 3-speed

Oil capacities
Warner 4-speed .... 6·0 US pints
Saginaw 3-speed .... 3·2 US pints
Muncie 3-speed .... 4·6 US pints

Automatic transmission

Make
1968 thru 1970 .... POW-R-FLO 218 (Powerglide) 2-speed
1971 thru 1976 .... Turbo Hydra-matic 350 3-speed
1977 on .... CBC 350 3-speed

Fluid capacity
Powerglide
  Refill .... 4·0 US pints
  From dry .... 16·0 US pints
Turbo Hydra-matic 350
  Refill .... 5·0 US pints
  From dry .... 20·0 US pints
CBC 350
  Refill .... 5·0 US pints
  From dry .... 20·0 US pints

Torque wrench settings   lbf ft
Warner 4-speed
Front bearing retainer bolts 20
Side cover bolts 20
Extension housing bolts 40
Shift lever-to-shifter shaft 20
Filler plug 25

Case-to-flywheel housing	55
Crossmember-to-frame	55
Rear mounting bolts-to-transmission	40

Saginaw/Muncie 3-speed

Front bearing retainer bolts	15
Side cover bolts	15
Extension housing bolts	45
Shift lever-to-shifter shaft bolts	25
Filler plug	18
Case-to-flywheel housing	75
Crossmember-to-frame nuts	25
Rear mounting bolts-to-transmission	50
Crossmember-to-mounting bolts	40
Drain plug (Muncie)	30

Automatic transmission

Transmission-to-engine bolts	35
Oil pan bolts	8
Rear extension housing-to-case bolts	25
Low band adjuster locknut	15
Converter-to-flexplate bolts	35
Oil cooler pipe unions	10
Oil pan drain plug	20
Vacuum modulator-to-case	15

PART 1 – MANUAL TRANSMISSION

1 General description

1   Vehicles built in 1968 and 1969 are equipped with 4-speed Warner transmission.
2   All later vehicles are fitted with a 3-speed Saginaw or Muncie transmission.
3   The gearshift on all models is steering column mounted with rod linkage to the side of the transmission casing. Warner 4-speed units have a cable operated reverse gear selector.

2 Maintenance

1   At the intervals specified in Routine Maintenance, check the oil level in the transmission. To do this, clean away external dirt from the combined filler/level plug on the side of the transmission case, and unscrew and remove the plug.
2   With the vehicle standing on level ground, the oil level should be at the bottom of the filler plug hole.
3   If it is not, top it up with the specified type of lubricant. Allow any excess oil to run from the filler plug hole before screwing in the plug.
4   Apply a few drops of oil to the gearshift linkage friction points.

3 Gearshift linkage (4-speed Warner) – adjustment

1   If faulty gearshifting occurs or if the components of the steering column shift mechanism have been dismantled and reassembled, adjust the linkage in the following way.
2   Disconnect the control rods from the levers on the transmission.
3   Disconnect the reverse shift cable from the reverse lever on the transmission.
4   Position the shift levers at the transmission case in Neutral.
5   Remove the engine splash shield and insert a suitable guide pin (see Fig. 6.1) through the upper control shaft bracket into the cut-outs in the shift levers and into the holes provided at the base of the control shaft.
6   Now adjust the position of the swivel on each control rod and the reverse shift cable so they can be connected to the levers without any necessity to exert force on the rods or levers to provide alignment.
7   Reconnect the control rods and the cable.
8   Remove the guide pin and install the splash shield.
9   Check the gearshift operation at the steering column hand control lever.

4 Gearshift linkage (3-speed) – adjustment

1   Set both the shifter levers on the transmission case in Neutral.
2   Disconnect the control rods from the levers on the steering column tube (photo).
3   Set the levers on the steering column tube to the neutral position and insert a guide pin (between $\frac{3}{16}$ and $\frac{7}{32}$ inch diameter) through the holes in the levers so that the hand control lever is retained in the Neutral position.
4   Connect the control rods to the column tube levers by adjusting the clamps to ensure that the levers are not displaced from their Neutral positions.
5   Remove the guide pin then check all gearshift positions.

5 On-vehicle repairs (4-speed Warner)

Rear extension housing oil seal – renewal
1   A leaking rear extension housing oil seal may be renewed without

4.2 Steering column linkage (3-speed)

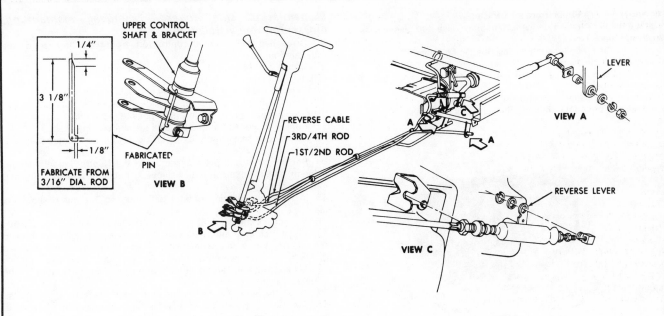

Fig. 6.1 Linkage used with Warner 4–speed transmission

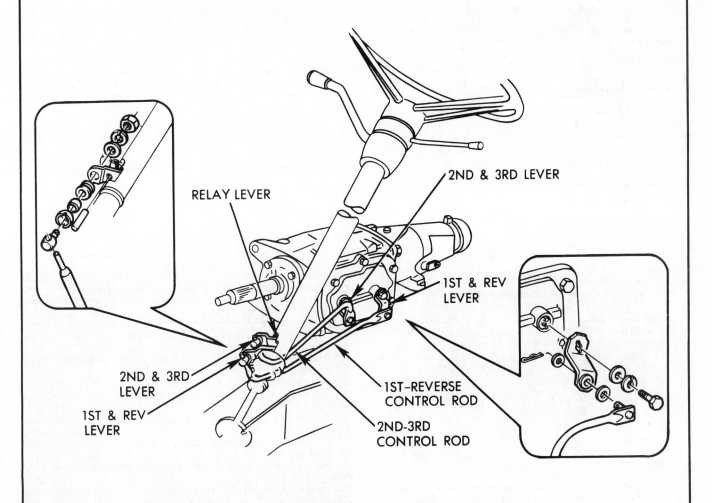

Fig. 6.2 Gearshift used with 3-speed transmission

removing the transmission from the vehicle.

2   Place the vehicle over an inspection pit or raise it to give access to the transmission.

3   Remove the propeller shaft as described in Chapter 7.

4   Pry the defective seal from the extension housing.

5   Apply grease to the lips of the new seal, and drive it carefully and squarely into position.

6   Install the propeller shaft and lower the vehicle.

7   Check and top up the transmission lubricant if necessary.

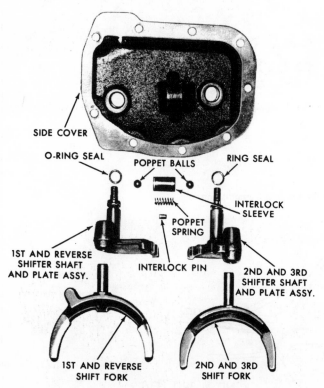

SIDE COVER

O-RING SEAL   POPPET BALLS   RING SEAL

INTERLOCK SLEEVE

POPPET SPRING

1ST AND REVERSE SHIFTER SHAFT AND PLATE ASSY.

INTERLOCK PIN

2ND AND 3RD SHIFTER SHAFT AND PLATE ASSY.

1ST AND REVERSE SHIFT FORK

2ND AND 3RD SHIFT FORK

Fig. 6.3 Components of the side cover (Warner 4-speed T10)

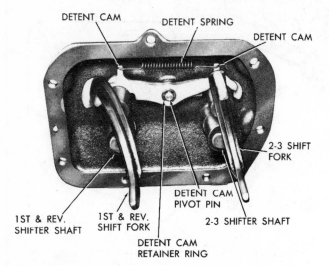

DETENT CAM   DETENT SPRING   DETENT CAM

2-3 SHIFT FORK

DETENT CAM PIVOT PIN

1ST & REV. SHIFTER SHAFT

1ST & REV. SHIFT FORK

2-3 SHIFTER SHAFT

DETENT CAM RETAINER RING

Fig. 6.4 Transmission side cover (3-speed Saginaw)

Transmission side cover – removal, dismantling, reassembly and installation

8   Disconnect the gearshift control rods from the shift levers on the transmission.

9   Unbolt and remove the side cover, allowing the oil to drain into a suitable container (Fig. 6.3).

10   Remove the shift forks and outer shift levers from the shafts.

11   Gently tap the shafts from the side cover and extract the poppet balls, the poppet spring, the interlock pin and the interlock sleeve.

12   Renew all worn components; also the shaft O-ring seals.

13   Commence reassembly by installing 1st/reverse shifter shaft and plate.

14   Set the shaft and plate assembly in the Neutral (middle detent) position, and install the interlock sleeve, poppet ball, poppet spring and interlock pin.

15   Install the remaining poppet ball and 2nd/3rd shifter shaft and plate.

16   Now check the clearance between the end of the interlock sleeve and the shifter shaft and plate cams when one plate is in Neutral and the other one is in gear. The clearance should be between 0.002 and 0.008 inch. If the clearance is incorrect, four alternative size interlock sleeves are available, and a suitable one should be substituted for the original sleeve.

17   Install the outer shift levers and then install the forks to the shafts.

18   The 1st/reverse shift fork offset should be toward the bottom of the transmission case.

19   Set the gears in Neutral and install the side cover. Use a new gasket, and tighten the securing bolts to the specified torque.

20   Reconnect the gearshift control rods.

21   Refill the transmission with the correct grade of lubricant up to the level of the filler plug hole.

22   Check the operation of the gearshift hand control lever and adjust if necessary as described earlier in this Chapter.

6   On-vehicle repairs (3-speed transmission)

Rear extension housing oil seal – renewal

1   The operations are similar to those described in the preceding Section.

Speedometer driven gear – removal and installation

2   Disconnect the speedometer cable, and then unbolt and remove the lockplate.

3   Insert a screwdriver into the groove in the driven gear, and pry the assembly from the transmission.

4   Extract the O-ring from the groove in the driven gear fitting.

5   Install a new O-ring. Installation is a reversal of removal, but make sure that the slot in the fitting is toward the lockplate boss.

6   Install the lockplate and bolt, and connect the cable.

7   Transmission side cover – removal, dismantling, reassembly and installation

1   Disconnect the gearshift control rods from the levers on the transmission.

2   Disconnect the wiring from the back-up lamp and the TCS switch (where installed).

3   Set the levers on the transmission to the Neutral position.

4   Unbolt and remove the side cover, and allow the oil to drain into a suitable container.

5   Remove the outer shifter levers and then withdraw the shift forks from the shafts.

6   Remove the shifter shafts from the side cover and then pry out the shaft oil seals.

7   Remove the detent cam spring and pivot retainer C-ring. Withdraw both detent cams.

8   Renew components as necessary, and then commence reassembly.

9   With the tang of the detent spring projecting over the 2nd and 3rd shifter shaft cover opening, install the 1st/reverse detent cam onto its pivot pin.

10   With the tang of the detent spring projecting over the 1st/reverse shifter shaft hole in the side cover, install the 2nd/3rd detent cam.

11 Install the detent cam retaining C-ring to the pivot shaft and hook the spring into the detent cam notches.

12 Carefully install both shifter shaft assemblies into the side cover taking care not to damage the O-ring seals. Raise the detent cam to allow the forks to seat fully.

13 Install the outer shifter levers, washers, lockwashers and bolts.

14 Set the shifter levers into Neutral and then install the side cover taking care to engage the shift forks with their respective synchroniser sliding sleeves.

15 Tighten the side cover bolts to the specified torque, and reconnect the gearshift control rods.

16 Reconnect the wires to the TCS back-up lamp switches.

17 Refill the transmission to its correct level with the specified type of lubricant.

8 Transmission – removal and installation

1 Place the vehicle over an inspection pit or raise it sufficiently high that the flywheel housing can pass beneath the vehicle as the

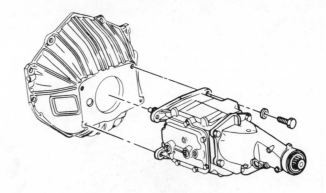

Fig. 6.5 Typical transmission case attachment to flywheel housing

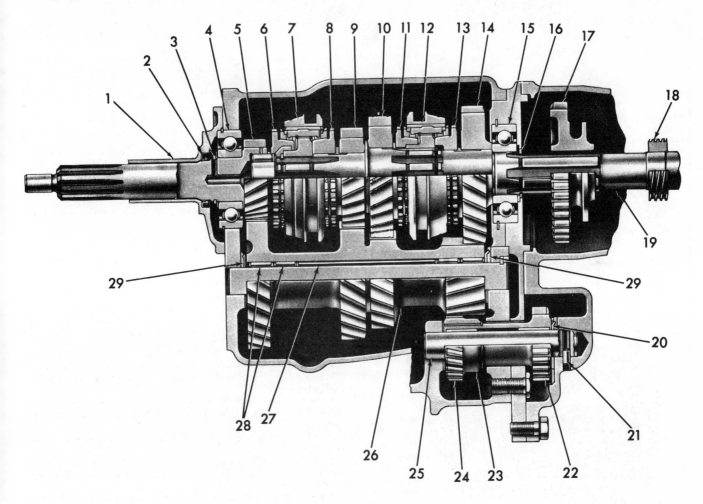

Fig. 6.6 Sectional view of 4-speed Warner transmission

1 Clutch gear bearing retainer	9 3rd speed gear	16 Snap-ring and washer	23 Spacer
2 Oil seal	10 2nd speed gear	17 Reverse gear	24 Front idler gear
3 Snap-ring and washer	11 2nd speed synchronizer ring	18 Speedometer gear	25 Reverse idler shaft
4 Front bearing	12 1st/2nd speed synchronizer	19 Mainshaft	26 Countergear
5 Clutch gear	13 1st speed synchronizer ring	20 Thrust washer	27 Countergear sleeve
6 4th speed synchronizer ring	14 1st speed gear	21 Idler shaft roll pin	28 Countergear bearing rollers
7 3rd/4th speed synchronizer	15 Rear mainshaft bearing	22 Rear idler gear	29 Thrust washers
8 3rd speed synchronizer ring			

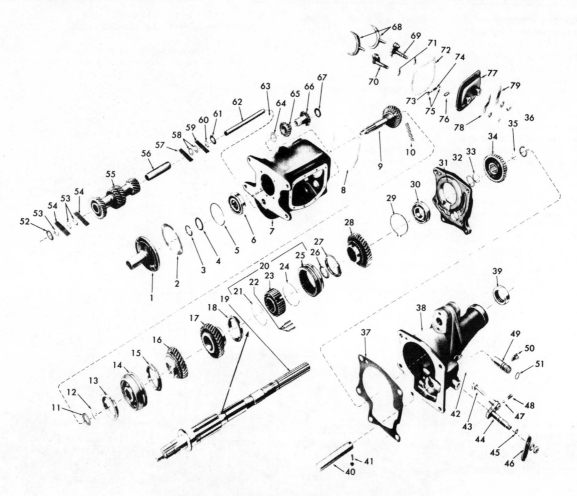

Fig. 6.7 Exploded view of 4-speed Warner transmission

1 Front bearing retainer	29 Rear bearing snap-ring	54 Needle rollers
2 Gasket	30 Rear bearing	55 Countergear
3 Snap-ring	31 Rear bearing retainer	56 Spacer
4 Spacer	32 Washer	57 Needle rollers
5 Bearing snap-ring	33 Snap-ring	58 Spacer
6 Front bearing	34 Reverse gear	59 Needle rollers
7 Transmission case	35 Speedometer drive gear	60 Spacer
8 Rear bearing retainer	36 Snap-ring	61 Washer with tang
9 Clutch drive gear	37 Gasket	62 Countershaft
10 Needle rollers	38 Rear extension housing	63 Woodruff key
11 Washer	39 Oil seal	64 Reverse idler front thrust washer
12 Snap-ring	40 Reverse idler shaft	65 Reverse idler gear (front)
13 4th speed gear synchronizer ring	41 Reverse idler shaft lock pin and welch plug	66 Reverse idler gear (rear)
14 3rd/4th speed synchronizer	42 Reverse shifter shaft lock pin	67 Thrust washer with tang
15 3rd speed synchronizer ring	43 Reverse shift fork	68 Shift forks
16 3rd speed gear	44 Reverse shifter shaft and detent plate	69 1st/2nd gear shifter shaft and detent plate
17 2nd speed gear	45 Reverse shifter shaft O-ring	70 3rd/4th gear shifter shaft and detent plate
18 2nd speed synchronizer ring	46 Reverse shifter lever	71 O-ring seals
19 Mainshaft	47 Reverse shifter shaft detent ball	72 Gasket
20 1st/2nd speed synchronizer	48 Detent spring	73 Interlock pin
21 Synchronizer key spring	49 Speedometer driven gear	74 Poppet spring
22 Synchronizer keys	50 Retainer and bolt	75 Detent balls
23 Synchronizer hub	51 O-ring	76 Interlock sleeve
24 Key spring	52 Washer with tang	77 Side cover
25 1st/2nd synchronizer sleeve	53 Spacer	78 3rd/4th speed shifter lever
26 Snap-ring		79 1st/2nd speed shift lever
27 1st speed gear synchronizer ring		
28 1st gear		

transmission is withdrawn.

2 Drain the transmission. If a drain plug is not fitted, remove the side cover as described earlier in this Chapter.

3 Disconnect the speedometer cable, the wire from the back-up lamp switch and the wire from the TCS (Emission Control) switch, if installed.

4 Disconnect the gearshift control rods from the levers on the side of the transmission.

5 Disconnect the parking brake lever, rods and cables as necessary to prevent obstruction to the transmission.

6 Remove the propeller shaft as described in Chapter 7.

7 Support the transmission on a trolley jack and then remove the rear mounting crossmember.

8 Unbolt and remove the underpan from the flywheel housing, then unscrew and remove the transmission-to-flywheel housing bolts.

9 Support the engine with a second jack and then pull the transmission towards the rear of the vehicle to separate it from the engine. Do not allow the weight of the engine to hang upon the clutch shaft while the latter is engaged in the driven plate. It may be necessary to lower both jacks simultaneously to obtain the necessary clearance to withdraw the transmission.

10 Once the transmission is free, lower the trolley jack and remove the unit from under the vehicle.

11 Installation is a reversal of removal but if the clutch mechanism has been disturbed (after removal of the flywheel housing from the engine) then the clutch driven plate must be centralised as described in Chapter 5 before the transmission is installed. Install the crossmember so that the tapered surface is towards the rear of the vehicle.

12 When installation is complete, adjust the clutch pedal free movement as described in Chapter 5.

13 Refill the transmission with the correct grade and quantity of lubricant.

9 Transmission (4-speed Warner) – dismantling and reassembly

1 Remove the transmission as described in the preceding Section and clean away all external dirt.

2 Shift the transmission into 2nd gear, and then remove the side cover and gasket.

3 Remove the front bearing, retainer and gasket.

4 Unscrew and remove the back-up switch from the transmission.

5 Drive the lock pin from the reverse shifter lever boss, then pull the shifter partially out to disengage the reverse shift fork from reverse gear.

6 Unbolt and remove the rear extension. If necessary, tap the exten-

sion housing off with a soft-faced mallet.

7 Extract the reverse idler gear from the rear of the transmission case.

8 Shift the transmission into 3rd gear to lock the mainshaft and then extract the snap-ring from the rear splines of the mainshaft.

9 Remove the speedometer drive gear from the mainshaft using a suitable puller, followed by the reverse gear.

10 Unscrew the self-locking bolt which holds the rear bearing retainer to the transmission case.

11 Extract the retainer alignment pin with a pair of self-locking grips.

12 Rotate the rear bearing retainer until the countergear shaft lines up with the reverse idler shaft hole in the retainer.

13 Drive the countershaft out of the rear of the transmission casing, letting the countergear rest in the bottom of the casing.

14 Now slide 3rd/4th synchro sleeve forward on its hub, and remove the mainshaft and rear bearing retainer from the casing. Extract the 4th gear synchro ring from the casing if it fell off during removal of the mainshaft, also any loose clutch gear roller bearings.

15 Remove the front reverse idler gear and thrust washer from the transmission casing.

16 Remove the clutch gear shaft snap-ring (not the snap-ring on the

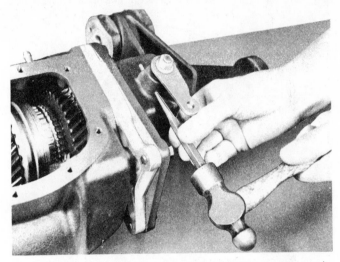

Fig. 6.8 Removing reverse shift shaft lock pin (4-speed Warner)

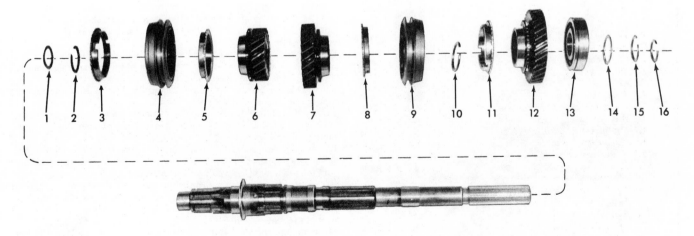

Fig. 6.9 Exploded view of the mainshaft (4-speed Warner)

1 Washer	*7 2nd speed gear*	*12 Reverse gear*
2 Snap-ring	*8 2nd speed synchronizer ring*	*13 Rear bearing*
3 4th speed synchronizer ring	*9 1st/2nd speed synchronizer*	*14 Washer*
4 3rd/4th synchronizer sleeve	*sleeve*	*15 Snap-ring*
5 3rd speed synchronizer ring	*10 Snap-ring*	*16 Snap-ring*
6 3rd speed gear	*11 1st speed synchronizer ring*	*17 Mainshaft*

Fig. 6.10 Removing mainshaft front snap-ring (4-speed Warner)

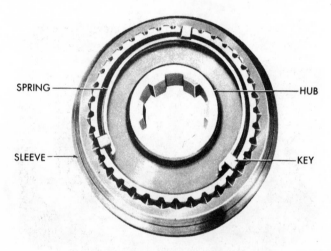

Fig. 6.11 Synchronizer unit (4-speed Warner)

SPRING

HUB

SLEEVE

KEY

Fig. 6.12 Removing reverse idler shaft retaining pin (4-speed Warner)

outside of the bearing).

17 Press the clutch gear out of the front bearing into the case.

18 Working inside the transmission casing, tap out the front main bearing and snap-ring.

19 Remove the countergear and thrust washers from the transmission casing.

20 If the mainshaft must be dismantled, first remove the front snap-ring. Slide 3rd/4th synchronizer unit, 3rd speed gear and the synchronizing ring from the mainshaft.

21 Spread the rear bearing retainer snap-ring and slide the retainer from the mainshaft.

22 Extract the mainshaft rear snap-ring and spacer and then, either using a press or bearing extractor, remove the rear bearing and 1st gear from the mainshaft.

23 Remove 1st/2nd synchronizer unit snap-ring and then slide the clutch assembly and 2nd speed gear from the mainshaft.

24 With the transmission dismantled, inspect all components for wear and renew as necessary. If there has been a history of noisy gearshifts or if the synchronizer can be easily beaten by rapid gearshifts, renew the synchronizer unit. If the original synchronizer unit is being dismantled, mark the relative position of hub and sleeve before dismantling (Fig. 6.11).

25 At the time of major overhaul it is recommended that all the oil seals and O-rings are renewed.

26 The reverse idler shaft can be removed for renewal if required by using a small punch to drive the plug and retaining pin into the shaft until the shaft can be pulled from the rear extension.

27 When installing the new shaft, install a new pin and plug.

28 Commence reassembly by installing the roller spacer into the countergear.

29 Stick 20 rollers into each end of the countergear, using heavy grease to retain them. Insert two spacers 0·050 inch thick then 20 more rollers and one spacer 0·050 inch thick into each end of the gear.

30 A dummy countershaft such as a piece of rod of suitable diameter should now be passed carefully through the countergear to retain the rollers in position.

31 Set the transmission casing on its side so that the side cover opening is uppermost.

32 Using thick grease, stick the thrust washers for the countergear into the casing. Make sure that the tangs of the thrust washers are located in the casing notches.

33 Carefully lower the countergear complete with dummy countershaft into the bottom of the casing.

34 Lubricate and then push the countershaft through the countergear (supported by one hand) to displace the dummy shaft. Make sure that the rollers are not displaced nor the thrust washers. Before the countershaft is pushed finally home, turn the shaft to align the Woodruff key slots, although the key should not be inserted yet.

35 The countergear endplay must now be checked using a dial indicator or feeler blades. If the play exceeds 0·025 inch, renew the thrust washers.

36 Once the endplay has been checked, withdraw the countershaft and let the countergear rest on the bottom of the transmission casing until the mainshaft has been installed.

37 To reassemble the mainshaft, install the 2nd gear (hub to rear of shaft) to the rear end of the shaft.

38 Install 1st/2nd synchronizer unit (sleeve taper toward the rear), together with a synchronizer ring on each side so that the keyways align with the keys.

39 Install a new snap-ring to the groove in the mainshaft at the rear of the synchronizer hub. The snap-ring should be the thickest possible from the range of selective thicknesses available.

40 Install 1st speed gear (hub toward the front of the mainshaft) and then supporting the inner race, press the rear bearing onto the mainshaft so that the snap-ring groove on the bearing is nearer the front of the transmission.

41 Install the spacer and the thickest snap-ring which will fit into the groove on the mainshaft behind the rear bearing.

42 Install 3rd speed gear (hub towards the front of the mainshaft) and the 3rd speed synchronizer ring (notches toward the front of the mainshaft).

43 Install 3rd/4th speed synchronizer unit so that the taper is toward the front. Make sure that the keys in the hub correspond with the notches in the 3rd speed gear synchronizing ring.

44 Install the thickest snap-ring which will fit into the groove in the mainshaft in front of 3rd/4th synchronizer unit.

45 Install the rear bearing retainer over the end of the mainshaft. Spread the snap-ring in the plate so that it engages round the rear bearing.

46 Install reverse gear (shift collar nearer rear end of the mainshaft).

47 Press the speedometer drive gear onto the mainshaft, so positioning the gear to obtain a dimension of $4\frac{1}{2}$ in from the center of the gear to the surface of the rear bearing retainer (Fig. 6.15).

48 Locate the front main bearing (complete with outer snap-ring) in the transmission casing, and tap the bearing into position so that the snap-ring is nearer the front of the casing.

49 Press the clutch gear into the bearing from the inside of the casing. Install the washer and the front bearing snap-ring to the shaft. Select the thickest snap-ring available which will fit in the groove.

50 Install front reverse idler gear (teeth facing front of the transmission), and the thrust washer.

51 Using heavy grease, install the clutch gear pilot needle bearings into the recess in the clutch gear.

52 Stick a new gasket to the rear face of the transmission casing, then pass the mainshaft into the casing from the rear and at the same time remembering to install 4th speed synchronizer ring and washer onto the front end of the mainshaft. Make sure that the notches on the ring correspond with the keys in the synchronizer unit.

53 With the mainshaft installed into the casing, turn the rear bearing retainer until the reverse collar shaft hole lines up with the countershaft case opening.

54 Carefully lift the countergear which has been lying in the bottom of the casing and then install the countershaft complete with Woodruff key. Make sure that the countergear needle rollers and thrust washers are not displaced as the countershaft is installed. Make sure that the Woodruff key engages correctly in its cutout and that the end of the countershaft is flush with the transmission casing.

55 Align the rear bearing retainer, and install the locating pin and locking bolt. Tighten the bolt to the specified torque.

56 Install the rear reverse idler gear, engaging its splines with the gear within the casing.

57 Locate a new gasket on the rear face of the bearing retainer.

58 Install the thrust washer in position on the reverse idler shaft with the tang on the washer in the notch of the idle thrust face of the extension.

59 Using a screwdriver, move the two synchronizer units to the Neutral position.

60 Pull the reverse selector rod partially out of the extension housing then rotate it to bring the reverse shift fork as far forward in the extension housing as possible.

61 Now offer the extension housing to the mainshaft, at the same time pushing on the selector rod to engage the shift fork with the reverse gear shift collar. Once the fork has engaged, rotate the selector rod to move the reverse gear to the rear, allowing the extension housing to locate tight against the main transmission casing.

62 Install the extension housing bolts and tighten to the specified torque wrench settings.

63 Install a new gasket on the front bearing retainer and screw in the bolts to the specified torque.

64 Install the side cover after reference to Section 5.

10 Transmission (3-speed Saginaw) – dismantling and reassembly

1 Remove the side cover assembly (refer to Section 7).

2 Remove the drivegear bearing retainer and gasket.

3 Remove the drivegear bearing stem snap-ring, then pull out the gear until a large screwdriver can be used to lever the drivegear bearing from its location.

4 Remove the speedometer driven gear from the rear extension, then remove the extension retaining bolts.

5 Remove the reverse idler shaft E-ring.

6 Withdraw the drivegear, mainshaft and extension assembly together through the rear casing.

7 From the mainshaft, detach the drivegear, needle bearings and synchronizer ring.

8 Expand the snap-ring in the rear extension which retains the rear bearing and then withdraw the rear extension.

9 Using a dummy shaft drive the countershaft (complete with Woodruff key) out of the rear of the transmission case. Carefully remove the dummy shaft and extract the countergear, bearings and

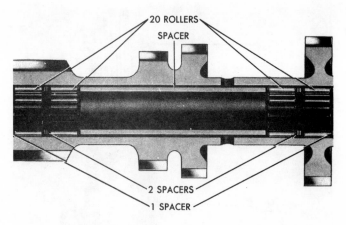

Fig. 6.13 Sectional view of countergear (4-speed Warner)

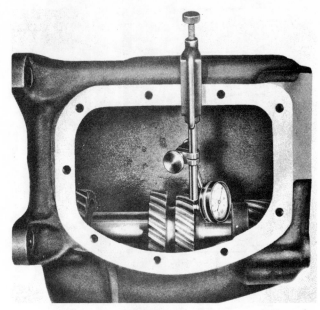

Fig. 6.14 Checking countergear end-play (4-speed Warner)

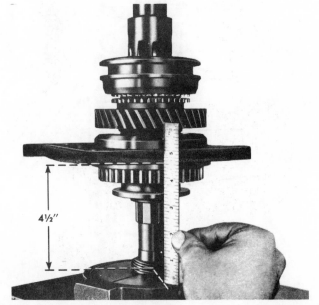

Fig. 6.15 Checking installation of speedometer drivegear (4-speed Warner)

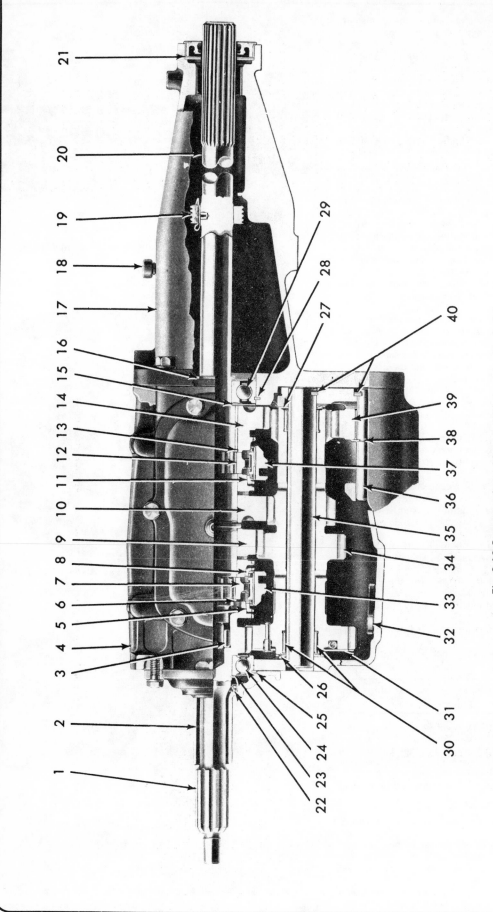

Fig. 6.16 Cutaway view of 3-speed Saginaw transmission

1 Clutch gear
2 Bearing retainer
3 Pilot needle roller bearing
4 Case
5 3rd speed blocker ring
6 Snap-ring
7 2nd/3rd synchronizer hub
8 2nd speed blocker ring
9 2nd speed gear
10 1st speed gear

11 1st speed blocker ring
12 1st speed synchronizer hub
13 Snap-ring
14 Reverse gear
15 Reverse gear thrust and spring
   washers
16 Snap-ring
17 Rear extension housing
18 Vent

19 Speedometer drive gear and
   clip
20 Mainshaft
21 Oil seal
22 Oil seal retainer
23 Snap-ring
24 Clutch gear bearing
25 Snap-ring
26 Countergear front thrust

   washer
27 Countergear rear thrust
   washer
28 Snap-ring
29 Rear bearing
30 Countergear needle roller
   bearings
31 Anti-lash plate
32 Magnet

33 2nd/3rd synchronizer sleeve
34 Countergear
35 Countershaft
36 Reverse idler shaft
37 1st speed synchronizer sleeve
38 E-ring
39 Reverse idler gear
40 Thrust washer
41 Woodruff key

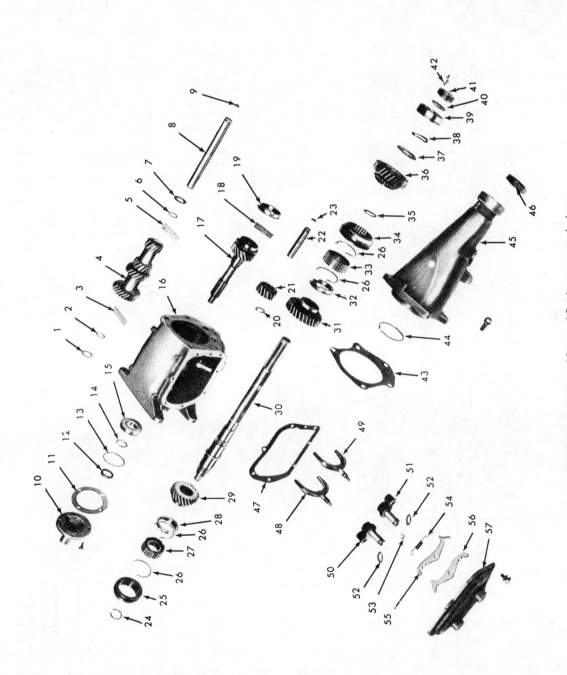

1 Countergear front thrust washer
2 Washer
3 Needle bearings
4 Countergear
5 Needle bearings
6 Washer
7 Rear thrust washer
8 Countershaft
9 Woodruff key
10 Bearing retainer
11 Gasket
12 Oil seal
13 Snap-ring
14 Snap-ring
15 Clutch gear housing
16 Case
17 Clutch gear
18 Pilot bearing needle rollers
19 3rd speed blocker ring
20 E-ring
21 Reverse idler gear
22 Reverse idler shaft
23 Woodruff key
24 Snap-ring
25 2nd/3rd synchronizer sleeve
26 Synchronizer key spring
27 Synchronizer hub
28 2nd speed blocker ring
29 2nd speed gear
30 Mainshaft
31 1st speed gear
32 1st speed blocker ring
33 1st/2nd speed synchronizer hub
34 1st/2nd synchronizer sleeve
35 Snap-ring
36 Reverse gear
37 Thrust washer
38 Wave washer
39 Rear bearing
40 Snap-ring
41 Speedometer drivegear
42 Clip
43 Gasket
44 Snap-ring
45 Extension housing
46 Oil seal
47 Gasket
48 2nd/3rd shift fork
49 1st/reverse shift fork
50 2nd/3rd shifter shaft
51 1st/reverse shifter shaft
52 O-ring seal
53 E-ring
54 Spring
55 2nd/3rd detent cam
56 1st/reverse detent cam
57 Side cover

Fig. 6.17 Exploded view of 3-speed Saginaw transmission

Fig. 6.18 Extracting rear bearing snap-ring (3-speed Saginaw)

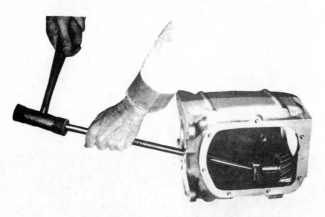

Fig. 6.19 Removing reverse idler shaft (3-speed Saginaw)

thrust washers from the interior of the transmission case.

10 Drive the reverse idler shaft out of the rear of the transmission case using a long drift (Fig. 6.19).

11 The mainshaft should only be dismantled if a press or bearing puller is available, otherwise take the assembly to your Chevrolet dealer.

12 Remove the 2nd/3rd synchro hub snap-ring from the mainshaft. Do not mix up the synchro unit components; although identical, the components of each unit are matched in production (photo).

13 Remove the synchro unit, 2nd speed blocker ring and 2nd speed gear from the front end of the mainshaft (photo).

14 Depress the speedometer drivegear retaining clip and remove the gear from the mainshaft (photo).

15 Remove the rear bearing snap-ring from its mainshaft groove.

16 Support the reverse gear and press the mainshaft out of the rear bearing and snap-ring from the rear end of the mainshaft.

17 Remove 1st/reverse synchro hub snap-ring from the mainshaft and remove the synchro unit.

18 Remove the 1st speed blocker ring and 1st speed gear from the rear end of the mainshaft.

19 Clean all components in kerosene and dry throughly. Check for wear or chipped teeth. If there has been a history of noisy gearshifts or the synchro facility could easily be 'beaten', then renew the appropriate synchro unit.

20 Extract the oil seal from the rear end of the rear extension and drive in a new one with a tubular drift.

21 Clean the transmission case inside and out and check for cracks, particularly round the bolt holes.

22 Extract the drivegear bearing retainer seal and drive in a new one.

23 Commence rebuilding the transmission by first reassembling the mainshaft. Install 2nd speed gear so that the rear face of the gear butts against the flange on the mainshaft.

24 Install the blocker ring, followed by the 2nd/3rd synchro assembly (shift fork groove nearer rear end of the mainshaft). Make sure that the notches of the blocker ring align with the keys of the synchro assembly.

25 Install the snap-ring which retains the synchro hub to the mainshaft.

26 To the rear end of the mainshaft, install the 1st speed gear, followed by the blocker ring.

27 Install the 1st/reverse synchro unit (shift fork groove nearer the front end of the mainshaft), again making sure that the notches of the blocker ring align with the keys of the synchro unit.

28 Install the snap-ring, reverse gear, reverse gear thrust washer and spring washer.

Fig. 6.20 Mainshaft (3-speed Saginaw)

5 Snap-ring	10 1st speed gear	16 Wave washer
6 2nd/3rd speed synchronizer assembly	11 1st speed blocker ring	17 Rear bearing
	12 1st speed synchronizer	18 Snap-ring
7 2nd speed blocker ring	13 Snap-ring	19 Speedometer drive gear and clip
8 2nd speed gear	14 Reverse gear	
9 Mainshaft dividing shoulder	15 Reverse gear thrust washer	20 Mainshaft

29 Install the mainshaft rear ball bearing with the outer snap-ring groove nearer the front of the shaft.
30 Install the rear bearing shaft snap-ring.
31 Install the speedometer drivegear and retaining clip.
32 Insert a dummy shaft through the countergear and stick the roller bearings (27 at each end), needle retainer washers and the transmission case thrust washers in position using thick grease. Note that the tangs on the thrust washers are away from the gear faces (photos).
Note: *If no dummy shaft is available, carefully stick the roller bearings in place, but when installing the shaft (paragraph 34), take care that they are not dislodged.*
33 Install reverse idler gear and shaft with its Woodruff key from the rear of the transmission case. Do not install the idler shaft E-ring at this time (photo).
34 Install the countergear assembly from the rear of the transmission

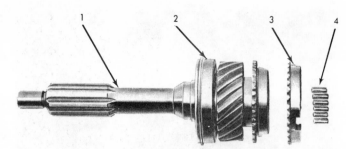

Fig. 6.21 Clutch gear (3-speed Saginaw)

1 Clutch gear
2 Clutch gear bearing retainer
3 3rd speed blocker ring
4 Pilot bearing rollers

10.12 Removing 2nd/3rd synchro snap-ring (3 speed Saginaw)

10.13 Removing 2nd speed blocker ring and 2nd gear (3-speed Saginaw)

10.14 Speedometer drivegear retaining clip (3-speed Saginaw)

10.15 Extracting mainshaft rear bearing snap-ring (3-speed Saginaw)

10.32A Installing countergear rollers using a dummy shaft

10.32B Countergear rollers retained in postion with grease

10.32C Countershaft needle roller retainer and anti-lash plate (only used on certain models) in position (3-speed Saginaw)

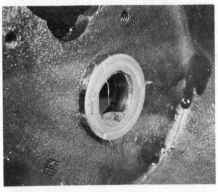

10.32D Countergear thrust washer attached to case with grease

10.33 Reverse idler gear and shaft (3-speed Saginaw)

10.34 Installing countershaft (3-speed Saginaw)

10.35A Mainshaft rear bearing snap-ring ready for installing

10.35B Expanding the mainshaft rear bearing snap-ring

10.36 Needle rollers in position in clutch drivegear (3-speed Saginaw)

10.38 Assembling rear extension with mainshaft and clutch drivegear to case (3-speed Saginaw)

10.40 Clutch drivegear bearing outer snap-ring (3-speed Saginaw)

10.41 Fitting clutch drive bearing shaft snap-ring (3-speed Saginaw)

10.42 Installing bearing retainer and gasket (3-speed Saginaw)

case and then insert the countershaft so that it picks up the roller bearings and the thrust washers, and at the same time displaces the dummy shaft. The countershaft should be inserted so that its slot is at its rear end when installed (photo).

35 Expand the snap-ring in the rear extension and locate the extension over the rear end of the mainshaft and onto the rear bearing. Make sure that the snap-ring seats in the rear bearing groove (photos).

36 Insert the mainshaft pilot bearings (14 of them) into the clutch gear cavity and then assemble the 3rd speed blocker ring onto the clutch drive gear (photo).

37 Locate the clutch drivegear, pilot bearings and 3rd speed blocker ring over the front of the mainshaft. Do not install the drivegear bearing at this time; also make sure that the notches in the blocker ring align with the keys in the 2nd/3rd synchro unit.

38 Stick a new gasket (using grease) to the rear face of the transmission case and then from the rear, insert the combined clutch drive gear, mainshaft and rear extension. Make sure that the 2nd/3rd synchro sleeve is pushed fully forward so that the clutch drivegear

engages with the countergear anti-lash plate (photo).

39 Install the rear extension-to-transmission case bolts.

40 Install the outer snap-ring to the clutch drivegear bearing and install the bearing over the drivegear into the front of the transmission case (photo).

41 Install the clutch drivegear bearing shaft snap-ring (photo).

42 Install the clutch drivegear bearing retainer and its gasket making sure that the oil return hole is at the bottom (photo).

43 Now install the reverse idler gear E-ring to the shaft.

44 With the synchronizer sleeves in the Neutral positions, install the side cover, gasket and fork assembly (Section 6). Torque-tighten all the bolts.

45 Install the speedometer driven gear in the rear extension.

11 Transmission (3-speed Muncie) – dismantling and reassembly

1   Remove the side cover as described in Section 7 (Fig. 6.22).

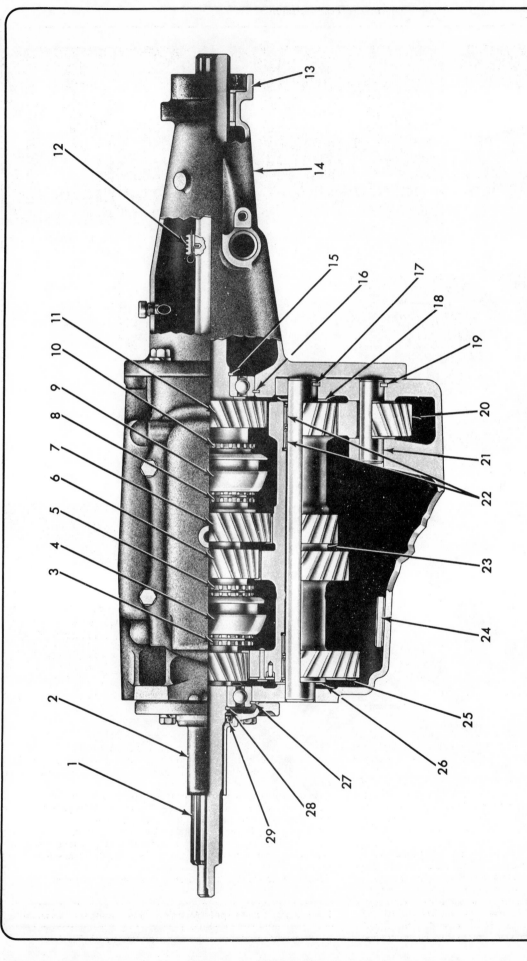

Fig. 6.22 Cutaway view of the 3-speed Muncie transmission

1 Clutch gear
2 Clutch gear bearing retainer
3 3rd speed synchronizer ring
4 2nd/3rd speed synchronizer
5 2nd speed synchronizer ring
6 2nd speed gear

7 1st speed gear
8 1st speed synchronizer ring
9 1st/reverse synchronizer
10 Reverse synchronizer ring
11 Reverse gear
12 Speedometer drivegear and

   clip
13 Oil seal
14 Rear extension housing
15 Snap-ring
16 Snap-ring
17 Woodruff key

18 Thrust washer
19 Woodruff key
20 Reverse idler gear
21 Reverse idler shaft
22 Countershaft needle rollers
23 Countergear

24 Magnet
25 Anti-lash plate
26 Thrust washer
27 Clutch gear bearing
28 Snap-ring
29 Oil seal

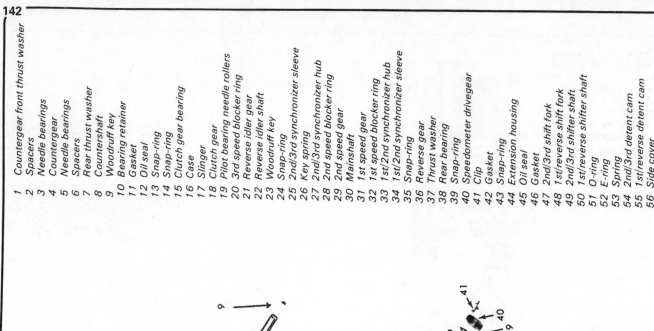

1 Countergear front thrust washer
2 Spacers
3 Needle bearings
4 Countergear
5 Needle bearings
6 Spacers
7 Rear thrust washer
8 Countershaft
9 Woodruff key
10 Bearing retainer
11 Gasket
12 Oil seal
13 Snap-ring
14 Snap-ring
15 Clutch gear bearing
16 Case
17 Slinger
18 Clutch gear
19 Pilot bearing needle rollers
20 3rd speed blocker ring
21 Reverse idler gear
22 Reverse idler shaft
23 Woodruff key
24 Snap-ring
25 2nd/3rd synchronizer sleeve
26 Key spring
27 2nd/3rd synchronizer hub
28 2nd speed blocker ring
29 2nd speed gear
30 Mainshaft
31 1st speed gear
32 1st speed blocker ring
33 1st/2nd synchronizer hub
34 1st/2nd synchronizer sleeve
35 Snap-ring
36 Reverse gear
37 Thrust washer
38 Rear bearing
39 Snap-ring
40 Speedometer drivegear
41 Clip
42 Gasket
43 Snap-ring
44 Extension housing
45 Oil seal
46 Gasket
47 2nd/3rd shift fork
48 1st/reverse shift fork
49 2nd/3rd shifter shaft
50 1st/reverse shifter shaft
51 O-ring
52 E-ring
53 Spring
54 2nd/3rd detent cam
55 1st/reverse detent cam
56 Side cover

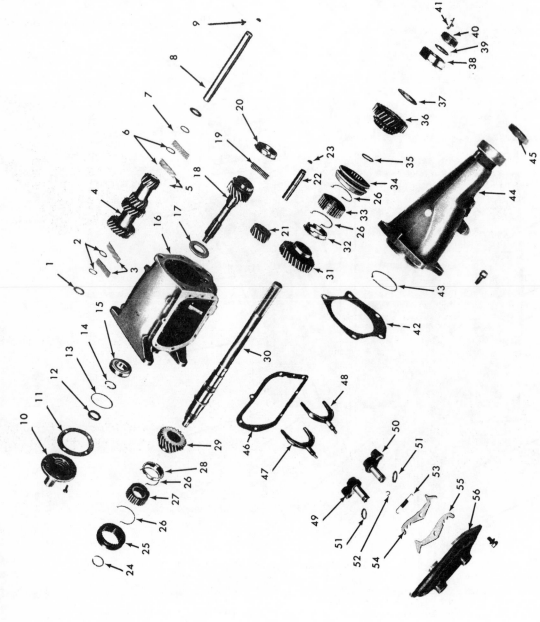

Fig. 6.23 Exploded view of 3-speed Muncie transmission

2   Remove the drivegear bearing retainer and gasket.
3   Remove the drivegear bearing stem snap-ring then pull out the gear until a large screwdriver can be used to lever the drivegear bearing from its location.
4   Remove the speedometer driven gear from the rear extension, then remove the extension retaining bolts.
5   Rotate the extension to the left until the groove in the extension housing flange aligns with the reverse idler shaft then, using a suitable drift, drive out the reverse idler shaft from the case. Remove the drivegear, mainshaft and extension assembly through the rear opening, and remove the reverse idler from the case. Remove the drivegear and mainshaft pilot bearings from the mainshaft.
6   Remove the snap-ring which retains the mainshaft rear bearing in the extension, then tap gently on the end of the mainshaft to separate it from the extension.
7   Using a suitable drift, drive out the countergear shaft and Woodruff key from the case.
8   To disassemble the mainshaft, a press or suitable bearing puller will be required. If not available, your GM dealer is best equipped to carry out this operation.
9   First, depress the speedometer gear retaining clip to permit removal of the gear.
10 Remove the rear bearing snap-ring then press the reverse gear, thrust washer and rear bearing from the shaft.
11 Remove the 1st/reverse sliding clutch hub snap-ring from the mainshaft.
12 Press on the rear of the mainshaft to remove the clutch assembly, blocker ring and 1st gear.
13 Remove the 2nd/3rd sliding clutch hub snap-ring then press on the front of the mainshaft to remove the clutch assembly, 2nd speed blocker ring and second gear.
14 Carry out the operations described in paragraphs 19 through 22 of Section 10.
15 Commence rebuilding the transmission by first reassembling the mainshaft. Hold the shaft vertically, front upwards, then install the 2nd gear (clutch teeth upwards) to butt the face against the mainshaft flange.
16 Install a blocking ring (teeth downwards) over the synchronizing surface of the 2nd gear.
17 Install the 2nd/3rd synchronizer assembly with the fork slot downwards, pressing it onto the mainshaft splines until it bottoms. Ensure that the notches in the blocker ring align with the keys in the synchronizer assembly.
18 Install the snap-ring to retain the assembled parts.
19 Invert the mainshaft and install the 1st gear (clutch teeth upwards) to butt the face against the mainshaft flange.
20 Install a blocking ring (teeth downwards) over the synchronizing surface of the 1st gear.
21 Install the 1st/reverse synchronizer assembly with the fork slot upwards, pressing it onto the mainshaft splines until it bottoms.

Fig. 6.24 Removing reverse idler shaft (3-speed Muncie)

Fig. 6.25 Extracting rear bearing outer snap-ring (3-speed Muncie)

Fig. 6.26 Mainshaft (3-speed Muncie)

6 Snap-ring	14 Snap-ring
7 2nd/3rd synchronizer	15 Reverse gear
8 2nd speed blocker ring	16 Thrust washer
9 2nd speed gear	17 Rear bearing
10 Mainshaft dividing shoulder	18 Snap-ring
11 1st speed gear	19 Speedometer drivegear
12 1st speed blocker ring	20 Mainshaft
13 1st speed synchronizer	

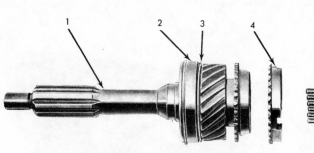

Fig. 6.27 Clutch gear (3-speed Muncie)

1   *Drivegear*
2   *Drivegear bearing*
3   *Oil slinger*
4   *Blocker ring (3rd)*
5   *Pilot bearings*

Ensure that the notches in the blocker ring align with the keys in the synchronizer assembly.
22 Install the snap-ring to retain the assembled parts.
23 Install the reverse gear (clutch teeth downwards) and steel thrust washer, aligning the flats.
24 Install the rear bearing with the groove downwards. Press it onto the mainshaft and install the snap-ring.
25 Install the speedometer driving gear and clip.

26 Load a double row of 29 roller bearings and the thrust washers in the countergear, using heavy grease to hold them in place.
27 Insert the countergear through the rear opening of the case, with a tanged thrust washer (tang away from gear) at each end. Install the shaft and Woodruff key from the rear end of the case.
28 Position the reverse idler gear, without its shaft, in the case.
29 Install the snap-ring in the extension, then assemble the extension over the rear of the mainshaft and onto the rear bearing. Seat the snap-ring in the bearing groove.
30 Load the mainshaft pilot bearings (16 of them), into the drive gear cavity, using heavy grease to hold them in place. Assemble the 3rd gear blocking ring onto the drivegear clutching surface, teeth towards the gear.
31 Feed the drivegear, pilot bearings and 3rd gear blocking ring over the front of the mainshaft assembly. Ensure that the notches in the ring align with the keys in the 2nd/3rd synchronizer assembly.
32 Position the extension to case gasket on the extension, retaining it with grease, then assemble the clutch drivegear, mainshaft and extension to the case. Don't forget to place the oil slinger onto the clutch gear before installing.
33 Rotate the extension and install the reverse idler shaft and Woodruff key.
34 Apply a non-setting gasket sealant to the extension retaining bolts, then install them.
35 Install the front bearing and snap-ring, and install to the clutch gear. Install the clutch gear snap-ring.
36 Install the bearing retainer (oil return hole lowermost) and gasket to the case. Use a non-setting sealant on the bolts.
37 Shift the synchronizer sleeves to Neutral and install the cover, gasket and fork assemblies (refer to Section 7). Ensure that the forks align with their synchronizer sleeve grooves.
38 Tighten all the bolts to the specified torque.

12 Fault diagnosis – manual transmission

Symptom	Reason/s
Stiff hand control lever	Linkage out of adjustment
	Lack of lubrication
	Wear in linkage components
Gear clash on shift	Linkage out of adjustment
	Worn synchronizer units
Slipping out of top gear	Transmission case-to-flywheel housing bolts loose
	Binding linkage
	Damaged mainshaft pilot bearing
	Drivegear retainer broken or loose
Noisy operation (all gears)	Insufficient oil
	Worn countergear bearings
	Worn countergear anti-lash plate
	Worn or damaged mainshaft bearings
	Worn or damaged gearwheels
Noisy operation (top gear)	Damaged maindrive gear bearing
	Damaged mainshaft bearing
	Damaged top gear synchronizer gears
Noisy operation (intermediate gears)	Worn constant mesh gears
	Worn synchronizer unit
	Worn countergear bearings
Noisy operation (reverse gear)	Worn idler or bush
	Worn or damaged mainshaft reverse gear
	Worn or damaged reverse countergear
Noisy operation (in neutral, engine running)	Worn or loose mainshaft pilot bearing
	Worn countergear anti-lash plate
	Worn countergear bearings
	Damaged maindrive gear bearing
Excessive backlash in all gears	Worn countergear bearings
	Excessive end-play in countergear

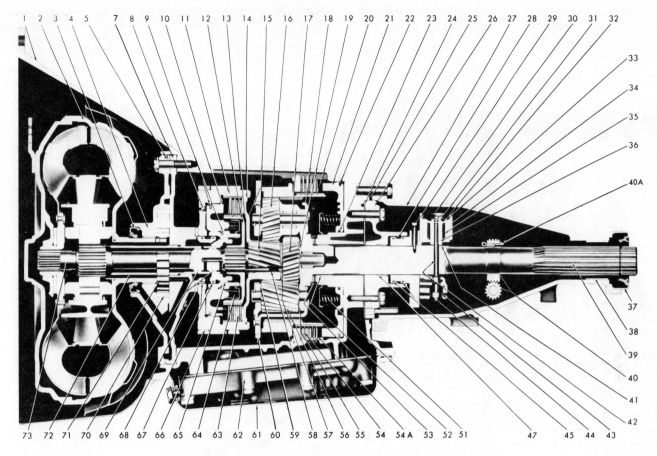

Fig. 6.28 Cutaway view of Powerglide 2-speed automatic transmission

1 Transmission case	20 Ring gear	40 Speedometer drive and driven gear	55 Pinion thrust washer
2 Converter	21 Reverse piston		56 Planet long pinion
3 Oil pump seal assembly	22 Reverse piston outer seal	40a Speedometer driven gear retaining clip	57 Low sun gear needle thrust bearing
4 Oil pump body	23 Reverse piston inner seal	41 Governor shaft urethane washer	58 Low sun gear bushing (splined)
5 Oil pump body square ring seal	24 Governor support gasket		
	25 Extension seat ring	42 Governor shaft	59 Pinion thrust washer
7 Oil pump cover	26 Governor support	43 Governor valve	60 Parking lock gear
8 Clutch relief valve ball	27 Extension	44 Governor valve retaining clip	61 Transmission oil pan
9 Clutch piston inner and outer seal	28 Governor hub		62 Valve body
	29 Governor hub drive screw	45 Governor hub seal rings	63 High clutch pack
10 Clutch piston	30 Governor body	47 Governor support bushing	64 Clutch piston return spring retainer and retainer ring
11 Clutch drum	31 Governor shaft retainer clip		
12 Clutch hub		51 Reverse piston return springs, retainer and retainer ring	65 Clutch drum bushing
13 Clutch hub thrust washer	32 Governor outer weight retainer ring		66 Low brake band
	33 Governor inner weight retainer ring	52 Transmission rear case bushing	67 High clutch seal rings
14 Clutch flange retainer ring			68 Clutch drum thrust washer (selective)
15 Low sun gear and clutch flange assembly	34 Governor outer weight	53 Output shaft thrust bearing	
	35 Governor spring		69 Turbine shaft seal rings
16 Planet short pinion	36 Governor inner weight	54 Reverse clutch pack	70 Oil pump driven gear
17 Planet input sun gear	37 Extension rear oil seal	54a Reverse clutch cushion spring (waved)	71 Oil pump drive gear
18 Planet carrier	38 Extension rear bushing		72 Stator shaft
19 Planet input sun gear thrust washer	39 Output shaft		73 Input shaft

PART 2 – AUTOMATIC TRANSMISSION

13 General description

1   Fully automatic transmissions have been optionally available throughout the production run of the range of vehicles covered by this manual.

2   Early models were fitted with POW-R-FLO 218, known later as the Powerglide. This is a two-speed transmission which changes speed depending on load and throttle position. A 'kickdown' facility is provided for immediate change to low speed for rapid acceleration.

3   Later models are equipped with a Turbo Hydra-matic transmission which is a three-speed unit. The type of Turbo Hydra-matic unit used in a particular vehicle varies according to date of production but all transmissions are essentially the same even though those used from 1977 are designated CBC 350 units.

4   Automatic transmissions comprise a 3-element hydrokinetic torque converter coupling capable of torque multiplication in an infinitely variable ratio between approximately 2 : 1 and 1 : 1, and a

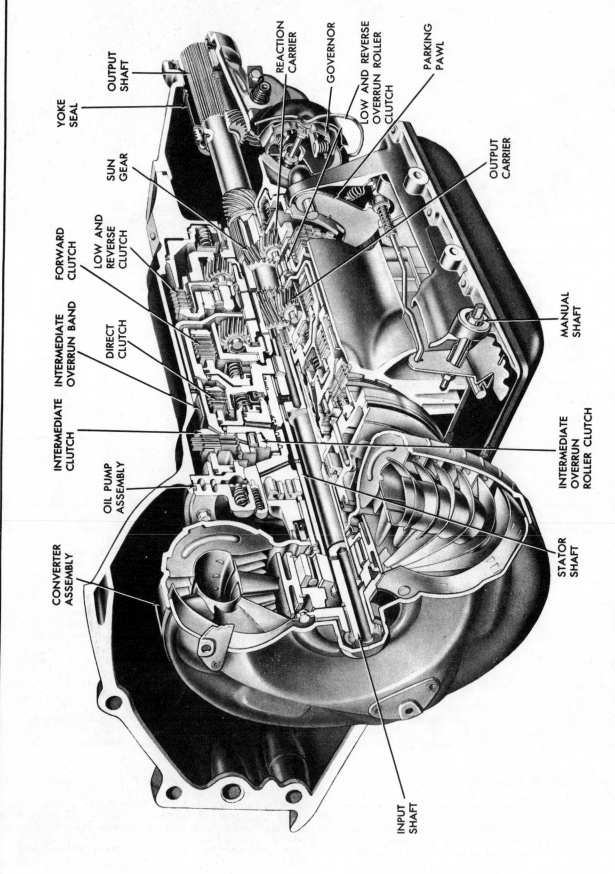

OUTPUT SHAFT

YOKE SEAL

REACTION CARRIER

GOVERNOR

LOW AND REVERSE OVERRUN ROLLER CLUTCH

PARKING PAWL

SUN GEAR

OUTPUT CARRIER

FORWARD CLUTCH

LOW AND REVERSE CLUTCH

INTERMEDIATE OVERRUN BAND

DIRECT CLUTCH

MANUAL SHAFT

INTERMEDIATE CLUTCH

OIL PUMP ASSEMBLY

INTERMEDIATE OVERRUN ROLLER CLUTCH

CONVERTER ASSEMBLY

STATOR SHAFT

INPUT SHAFT

Fig. 6.29 Cutaway view of Turbo Hydra-matic 350 automatic transmission (designated CBC 350 transmission from 1977)

torque/speed responsive, hydraulically operated, epicyclic gearbox.

5 In view of the need for special tools and equipment to carry out overhaul and repair operations to any of these automatic transmission units, the information in this Chapter is restricted to maintenance and adjustment procedures; also included are the removal and installation of the transmission, which will enable the home mechanic to install a new or rebuilt unit which, after a high mileage, is probably the most economical method of repair when a fault develops.

14 Fluid level checking and fluid changing

1 Drive the vehicle for a minimum distance of 15 miles to ensure that the transmission oil is at normal operating temperature.
2 Park the vehicle on a level surface, place the selector lever in Neutral (Powerglide) or Park (Turbo Hydra-matic), apply the parking brake fully and let the engine idle.
3 Withdraw the dipstick (located at right rear of the engine compartment), wipe it clean and re-insert it (photo).
4 Withdraw the dipstick for the second time and check the oil level. If necessary, pour in fluid (into the dipstick guide tube) of the correct grade to bring it up to the Full mark.
5 Every 24 000 miles change the oil in the transmission unit. Should the vehicle be operating under severe conditions such as hauling a trailer or stop/start delivery operations then halve the oil change frequency to 12 000 miles.
6 Run the engine for a minute or two with the selector lever in Neutral.
7 Remove the oil pan drain plug and catch the oil in a suitable container (if no drain plug is fitted it will be necessary to remove the oil pan. When this is done, the filter screen should be cleaned also). **Note:** *On some Turbo Hydra-matic transmissions it will be necessary to support the engine and remove the crossmember support to permit removal of the oil pan.*
8 Install the drain plug, then remove the dipstick and into the dipstick guide tube pour two quarts of transmission oil of the specified grade ($2\frac{1}{2}$ quarts for Turbo Hydra-matic).
9 Run the vehicle until the transmission is at normal operating temperature and then check and adjust the oil level, as described earlier in this Section.

15 Powerglide (2-speed) – on-vehicle adjustments

Low band adjustment
1 This adjustment should normally be carried out at the time of the first oil change and thereafter only when a fault in performance indicates it to be necessary (see Fault diagnosis).
2 Raise the vehicle to provide access to the transmission.
3 Place the selector lever in the Neutral position.
4 Remove the protective cap from the transmission adjusting screw.
5 Release and unscrew the adjusting screw locknut one quarter turn and hold it in this position with a wrench (Fig. 6.31).
6 Using the special tool (J–21848) or a torque wrench and adaptor, tighten the adjusting screw to 70 lbf in, then back off the screw **an exact number of turns** as follows:

   a) *for a low band which has been in operation for less than 6000 miles – 3 complete turns.*
   b) *for a low band which has been in operation for more than 6000 miles – 4 complete turns.*

7 Tighten the adjusting screw locknut to the specified torque.

Throttle valve adjustment
8 No provision is made for adjustment in conjunction with fluid pressures, therefore any adjustment will be on a trial-and-error basis. The adjustment will only be required if the shift points are considerably outside those specified below.
9 To vary the pressure, release the jam nut one full turn while holding the end of the screw against rotation with an Allen key. This will have the effect of raising the fluid pressure by 3 lbf/in², which in turn will alter the full throttle upshift point by between 2 and 3 mph (Fig. 6.32).
10 If the jam nut is tightened by one turn, then the pressure will be

14.3 Withdrawing fluid dipstick from transmission

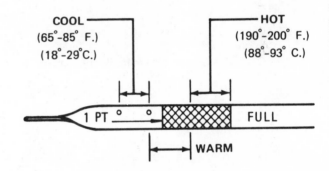

NOTE: **DO NOT OVERFILL.** IT TAKES ONLY ONE PINT TO RAISE LEVEL FROM ADD TO FULL WITH A HOT TRANSMISSION.

Fig. 6.30 Marking on automatic transmission dipstick

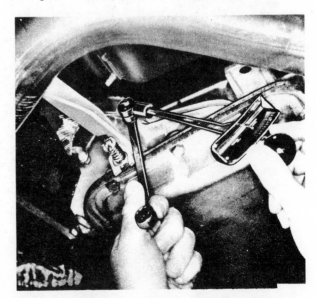

Fig. 6.31 Adjusting Powerglide low band

148

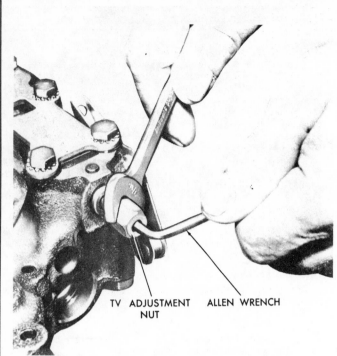

Fig. 6.32 Adjusting Powerglide throttle valve

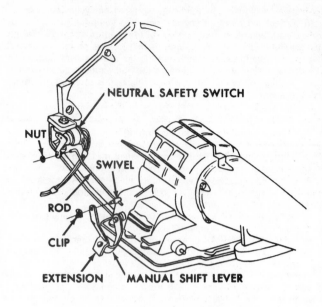

Fig. 6.33 Powerglide neutral safety switch

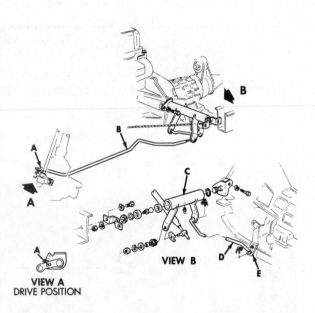

Fig. 6.34 Powerglide shift linkage

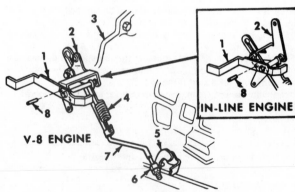

Fig. 6.35 Throttle valve linkage on Powerglide Transmission

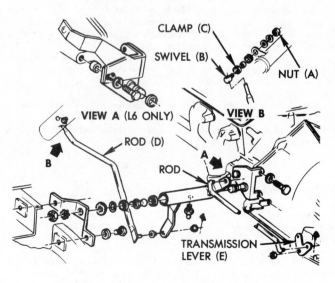

Fig. 6.36 Turbo Hydra-matic column shift linkage

lowered by 3 lbf/in^2.

	Upshift range	Downshift range
Closed throttle	11–16 mph	10 – 15 mph
Throttle touching detent	36–46 mph	20–36 mph
Throttle at full detent	44–51 mph	40–48 mph

Neutral safety switch adjustment

11 To check the operation of the switch, pull the high tension (secondary) wire from the center of the distributor cap.
12 Set the parking brake fully, and place the speed shift lever in Drive.
13 Turn the starter switch to the Start position. The starter motor should not operate. If it does, adjust the switch as described in the following paragraph.
14 Release the switch mounting bracket clamp screw, and move the control rod swivel to the point where the starter motor will only operate when the speed shift lever is in Neutral or Park (Fig. 6.33).
15 Reconnect the distributor wire.

Shift linkage adjustment (Fig. 6.34).

16 Set the shift lever (E) on the side of the transmission to Drive. To do this, disconnect the control rod (D) from the lever and turn the lever fully counterclockwise then turn the lever clockwise one detent.
17 Adjust the swivel on the control rod (B) so that with the hand control lever in Drive, the rod (D) can be reconnected to the lever (E) without any side force having to be used on the lever to allow perfect engagement.
18 Re-adjust the selector indicator needle and the neutral safety switch, if necessary.

Throttle valve linkage adjustment (Fig. 6.35).

19 Rotate the lever (5) until it is up against its stop.
20 Now insert a $\frac{3}{16}$ inch diameter guide pin into the hole in the lever (2) and bracket (1). If the holes in these components are not in perfect alignment, adjust the length of the rod (7) by means of the swivel locknuts (6).

16 Turbo Hydra-matic 350 – on-vehicle adjustments

Speed shift linkage adjustment (Fig. 6.36).

1 To check for correct linkage adjustment, lift the hand control lever towards the steering wheel and select Drive by the action of the transmission detent. Do not be guided by the indicator needle, as this may be out of adjustment.
2 Release the hand control lever and check that Low cannot be selected unless the lever is lifted.
3 Finally lift the hand control lever towards the steering wheel and let the action of the transmission detent set the lever in Neutral.
4 Release the selector lever and check that Reverse cannot be selected unless the lever is first lifted. A correctly adjusted linkage will prevent the hand control lever from moving beyond the Neutral and the Drive detents unless the control lever is first lifted to pass over the mechanical stop.
5 Where adjustment is required, release the nut (A) on the steering column so that the swivel (B) and clamp (C) move freely on the rod (D).
6 Set the lever (E) on the side of the transmission to Neutral. To do this, move the lever counterclockwise to the L1 detent and then clockwise three detents to Neutral.
7 Set the hand control lever in Neutral and then tighten nut (A).
8 If necessary, adjust the indicator needle and the neutral safety switch.

Detent cable adjustment (Fig. 6.37).

9 Disengage the cable snap lock and then manually open the carburetor lever to the full throttle position.
10 Now push the snap lock downwards until its upper surface is flush with the cable conduit.

Neutral start switch adjustment

11 Disconnect the control rod from the switch lever.
12 Align the hole in the lever with the corresponding one in the

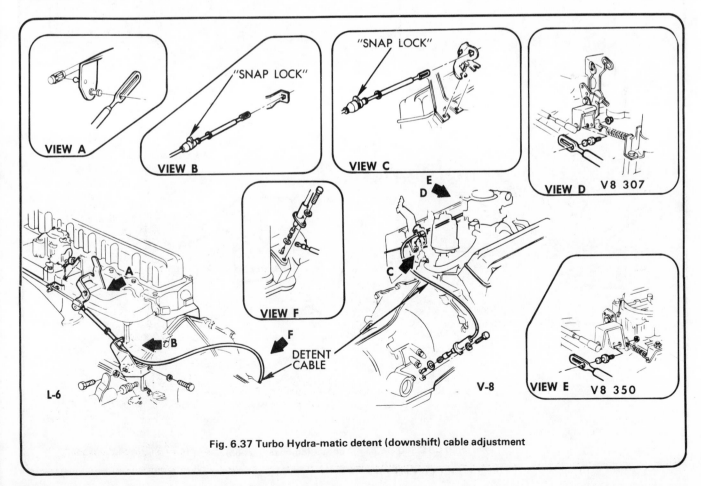

Fig. 6.37 Turbo Hydra-matic detent (downshift) cable adjustment

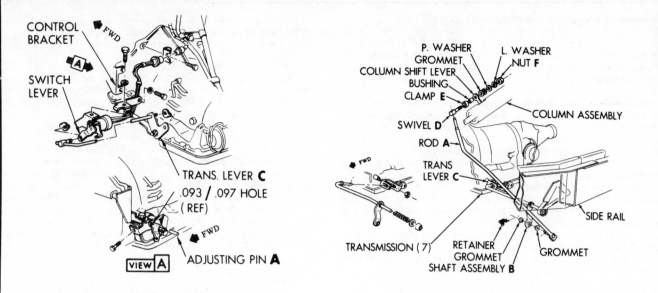

Fig. 6.38 Turbo Hydra-matic neutral start switch

Fig. 6.39 CBC 350 (1977 on) column shift linkage

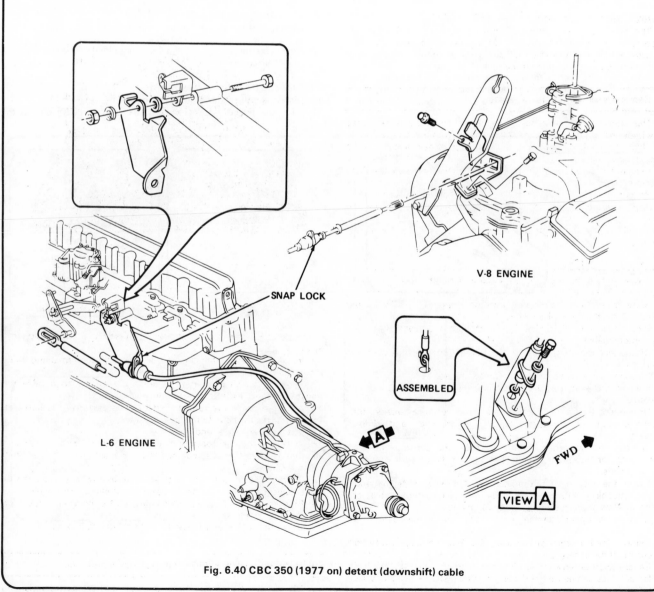

Fig. 6.40 CBC 350 (1977 on) detent (downshift) cable

switch. Use a guide pin (0·095 in diameter) to do this.
13 Set the lever on the side of the transmission to Neutral as described in paragraph 6.
14 Adjust the swivel on the switch control rod so that the swivel will connect with the switch without any need for side force to be applied. Install the securing clip.

17 CBC 350 automatic transmission – on-vehicle adjustment

Speed shift linkage adjustment (Fig. 6.39).
1   Set the transmission lever (C) in Neutral. To do this, turn the lever counterclockwise to L1 and then clockwise three detent positions.
2   Set the hand control lever to Neutral.
3   Attach the control rod (A), without its swivel, to the shaft (B). Re-attach the swivel (D) and clamp (E) onto the rod (A), then connect the swivel loosely to the column lever.
4   Hold the column lever hard against the Neutral stop on the side nearer Park. Tighten the swivel nut (F).
5   If necessary, adjust the indicator needle and the neutral start switch.

Detent (downshift) cable adjustment (Fig. 6.40).
6   The adjustment is similar to that described in Section 16, .pargraphs 9 and 10, but note the differences in components.

Neutral start switch adjustment (Fig. 6.41).
7   The operations are similar to those described in Section 16, paragraphs 11 through 14, except that the switch has elongated bolt holes to provide the necessary adjustment, the control rods being of fixed length without adjustable swivels.

18 Rear extension oil seal – renewal

1   This operation is similar for all transmissions and can be carried out without having to remove the transmission from the vehicle.
2   Place the vehicle over a pit, or jack it up to gain access to the transmission.
3   Disconnect the propeller shaft from the transmission as described in Chapter 7.
4   Pry out the defective seal using a screwdriver or chisel as a lever.
5   Apply jointing compound to the outer edge of the new seal and drive it into position using a piece of tubing as a drift.
6   Install the propeller shaft and check the fluid level in the transmission unit.

19 Powerglide transmission – removal and installation

1   Raise the vehicle or place it over an inspection pit for access beneath. Drain the transmission oil.
2   Disconnect the oil cooler lines, vacuum modulator line, and speedometer cable.
3   Disconnect the throttle valve and manual control rods from the transmission.
4   Disconnect the propeller shaft (refer to Chapter 7).
5   Support the weight of the transmission using a suitable jack and insulators.
6   Disconnect the rear mount on the transmission extension, then disconnect the transmission support crossmember and slide it rearward.
7   Remove the converter underpan, scribe the converter/flexplate relationship for assembly, then remove the flexplate-to-converter attaching bolts.
8   Lower the rear of the transmission slightly so that the upper housing attaching bolts can be reached using a suitable socket and extension. Now support the engine on another jack.
9   Remove the upper attaching bolts first, then the remainder of the bolts.
10 Remove the transmission rearward and downward, and away from the engine. If necessary, pry it free from the flexplate. Keep the rear of the transmission downward at all times or the front of the converter will fall out. This can be retained using a holding strap – see Fig. 6.42.
11 When installing, remove the converter holding strap, keep the rear

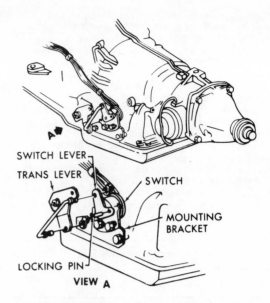

Fig. 6.41 CBC 350 (1977 on) neutral start switch

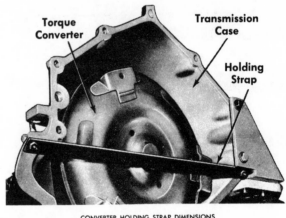

Fig. 6.42 Torque converter retaining strap in position

of the transmission slightly downward then raise the transmission into place.
12 Install the upper attaching bolt, followed by the remaining bolts; torque-tighten to the specified value.
13 Remove the support from beneath the engine then raise the transmission into its installed position.
14 Align the scribe marks and install the converter to the flexplate. Torque-tighten the bolts to the specified value.
15 Install the converter underpan.
16 Install the support crossmember to the transmission and frame.
17 Remove the lifting equipment then connect the propeller shaft (refer to Chapter 7).
18 Connect the manual and throttle valve control lever rods, the oil cooler lines, vacuum modulator line and speedometer drive cable.
19 Refill the transmission (Section 14), check for proper operation and examine for leaks.
20 Lower the vehicle and check the transmission fluid level.

20 Turbo Hydra-matic 350 – removal and installation

1   Disconnect the battery ground cable and release the parking

brake.

2   Raise the vehicle on a hoist or place it over an inspection pit.

3   Disconnect the speedometer cable, detent cable, electrical leads, modulator vacuum line and oil cooler pipes, as appropriate.

4   Disconnect the shift control linkage and remove the propeller shaft (Chapter 7).

5   Support the transmission with a suitable jack, and disconnect the rear mount from the frame crossmember.

6   Remove the two bolts at each end of the crossmember then remove the crossmember.

7   Remove the converter underpan.

8   Remove the converter-to-flexplate bolts then lower the transmission until the jack is barely supporting it.

9   Remove the transmission-to-engine mounting bolts and remove the oil filler tube at the transmission.

10 Raise the transmission to its normal position, support the engine with the jack and slide the transmission rearward from the engine.

Keep the rear of the transmission downward so that the converter does not fall off.

11 Installation is the reverse of the removal procedure, but additionally ensure that the weld nuts on the converter are flush with the flexplate, and that the converter rotates freely in this position. Tighten all bolts finger-tight before torque-tightening to the specified value.

12 Refill the transmission and check the adjustment of the shift linkage, detent cable and neutral start switch.

21 CBC 350 automatic transmission – removal and installation

1   The operations are very similar to those described for the Turbo Hydra-matic in the preceding Section.

2   On certain models, the catalytic converter will have to be removed before there is sufficient room to withdraw the transmission.

22 Fault diagnosis – automatic transmission

Symptom	Reason/s
Powerglide	
No drive in any selector position	Low oil level Clogged oil filter screen Internal fault
Engine races as drive taken up but lack of acceleration	Low oil level Incorrect band adjustment Internal fault
Engine races on upshift	Low oil level Incorrect band adjustment Obstructed vacuum modulator line Clogged oil filter screen

No upshift at all	Low band not releasing due to:
	    Stuck throttle valve
	    Incorrectly adjusted manual valve lever
	    Internal fault

No downshift	Internal fault
Harsh (jerky) upshift	Incorrect carburetor-to-transmission throttle valve rod adjustment Incorrect band adjustment Leaking vacuum modulator line Leaking vacuum modulator diaphragm Internal fault
Harsh (jerky) downshift	High engine idle speed Incorrect band adjustment Faulty downshift valve
No drive in reverse	Incorrect linkage adjustment Internal fault
Incorrect shift points	Incorrect carburetor-to-transmission linkage adjustment Incorrect throttle valve adjustment
Excessive creep in Drive range	Engine idle speed too high
Creep in neutral	Incorrect linkage adjustment Low band not releasing
Turbo Hydra-matic	
No drive in Drive range	Low oil level Incorrect linkage adjustment
1 to 2 shift on full throttle only	Detent valve cable incorrectly set Detent valve sticking Leak in vacuum line Internal fault

No upshift from 1 to 2	Detent cable binding
	Incorrectly adjusted intermediate band
	Internal fault
No upshift from 2 to 3	Internal fault
Moves off in second speed	Intermediate band adjustment too tight
Drive in neutral	Incorrectly adjusted linkage
No drive in reverse	Low fluid level
	Incorrectly adjusted linkage
	Internal fault
Slip in all ranges and upshifts	Low oil level
	Incorrectly adjusted intermediate band
	Internal fault
No engine braking	Incorrectly adjusted intermediate band
	Internal fault
No part throttle downshift	Detent valve cable broken or incorrectly adjusted
No full throttle downshift	Detent valve cable broken or incorrectly adjusted
Shift points too high or too low	Fault in vacuum line
	Faulty vacuum modulator assembly
Won't hold in 'P'	Incorrectly adjusted linkage
	Internal fault in parking pawl mechanism

CBC 350

No drive in Drive range	Low fluid level
	Fluid leaks
	Faulty vacuum modulator
	Incorrect linkage adjustment
	Internal fault
1 to 2 shift on full throttle only	Faulty detent valve
	Incorrect detent valve linkage adjustment
	Leaking vacuum circuit
	Internal fault
No 1 to 2 upshift	Detent (downshift) cable binding
	Internal fault
No 2 to 3 upshift	Internal fault
Moves off in second speed	Internal fault
Drives in neutral	Incorrectly adjusted linkage
	Internal fault
No drive in reverse, or slips	Low fluid level
	Incorrectly adjusted linkage
	Internal fault
Slips in all ranges	Low fluid level
	Internal fault
No engine braking	Internal fault
No part throttle downshift	Detent valve linkage binding or broken
	Internal fault
No full throttle downshift	Detent linkage not adjusted correctly
	Internal fault
Shift points incorrect	Fault in vacuum circuit
	Detent linkage stuck full open
	Internal fault
Won't hold in Park	Incorrectly adjusted linkage
	Internal damaged

Chapter 7 Propeller shaft

Contents

Specifications

Type . . . .   Tubular, one or two-section with slipjoint, and universal joints
Two-section shaft has center support bearing

Torque wrench settings
U-bolt-to-rear axle flange

	lbf ft
G35 models	20
Other models	15
Strap bolts-to-rear axle flange	15
Center bearing bracket bolts	25

1 General description

1 The propeller shaft is of tubular construction and may be of a one or two-section type according to the wheelbase of the vehicle.
2 All shafts have needle bearing type universal joints. Single-section shafts have a splined sliding sleeve at the front and connecting to the output shaft of the transmission while two-section shafts have a central slip joint. The purpose of these devices is to accommodate by retraction or extension, the variable shaft length caused by the movement of the rear axle as the rear suspension deflects.
3 Where a two-section shaft is used, the shaft is supported near its forward end on a ball bearing which is flexibly mounted in a bracket attached to the frame crossmember.
4 Some universal joints can be lubricated but other types are grease sealed for life.
5 The attachment of the rear end of the propeller shaft to the rear axle pinion flange may be by U-bolt or bolted strap, according to its date of production and model.
6 The propeller shaft is finely balanced during manufacture and it is recommended that an exchange unit is obtained rather than dismantling the universal joints when wear is evident. However, this is not always possible and provided care is taken to mark each individual yoke in relation to the one opposite then the balance will usually be maintained. Do not drop the assembly during servicing operations.

2 Lubrication

1 On early vehicles, the universal joints at the center bearing are fitted with grease nipples. Apply the grease gun as specified in Routine Maintenance at the beginning of this Manual.
2 All models having two-section propeller shafts have a grease nipple on the slip joint. Lubricate this also as specified.
3 On single-section shafts, the splined sliding section at the front is automatically lubricated by oil from the transmission.

3 Propeller shaft – correcting out-of-balance

1 Vibration not caused by worn universal joints may be due to mud or underbody sealing compound adhering to the shaft. Check this and remove it, where applicable.
2 Some improvement may be experienced if the attachment of the rear end of the shaft is moved through 180° and then reconnected to the rear axle drive pinion flange.
3 It is important that the relative position of the propeller shaft to this flange is maintained, therefore always make alignment marks on the shaft and flange before removing the shaft.
4 In difficult cases of out of balance condition, try a worm drive clip round each section of the shaft in sequence, with the worm moved to different positions until road tests prove that the trouble has been eliminated.

4 Universal joints – testing for wear

1 Wear in the needle roller bearings is characterized by vibration in the transmission, 'clonks' on taking up the drive, and in extreme cases lack of lubrication, metallic squeaking and ultimately grating and shrieking sounds as the bearings break up.
2 It is easy to check if the needle roller bearings are worn with the propeller shaft in position, by trying to turn the shaft with one hand, the other hand holding the rear axle flange when the rear universal joint is being checked, and the front half coupling when the front universal joint is being checked. Any movement between the propeller shaft and the front half couplings, and round the rear half couplings, is indicative of considerable wear.
3 If wear is evident, either fit a new propeller shaft assembly complete or renew the universal joints as described later in this Section.

Fig. 7.1 Center support bearing detail (two-section propeller shaft)

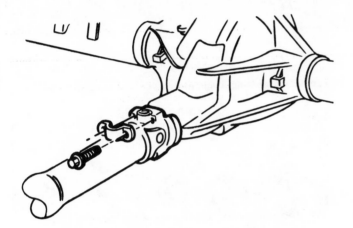

Fig. 7.2 Propelier shaft attached by strap to rear axle flange

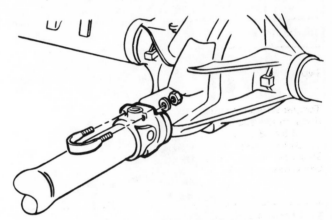

Fig. 7.3 Propeller shaft attached by U-bolt to rear axle flange

4   A final test for wear is to attempt to lift the shaft and note any movement between the yokes of the joints.

5   Propeller shaft – removal and installation

1   Place the vehicle over an inspection pit or raise the rear end on stands.
2   Mark the relationship of the shaft to the rear axle companion flange.
3   Unbolt the rear connnecting U-bolt or straps, whichever type of fixing is used. It is advisable to tape the universal joint bearing cups to the trunnions to prevent displacement of cups or needle rollers.
4   On vehicles which have a two-section shaft, unscrew and remove the bolts from the center bearing bracket (photo).
5   Push the shaft slightly forward to disengage it from the rear axle, and then lower the shaft and withdraw it from the transmission.
6   *To install a single-section propeller shaft*, simply reverse the removal operations.
7   *To install a two-section propeller shaft on all other vehicles*, slide the front part of the shaft into the transmission and bolt the center bearing bracket to the crossmember.
8   Slide the grease cap and gasket onto the rear splines, then rotate the shaft so that the front universal joint trunnion is in a vertical attitude.
9   Support the rear section of the shaft and align the universal joint

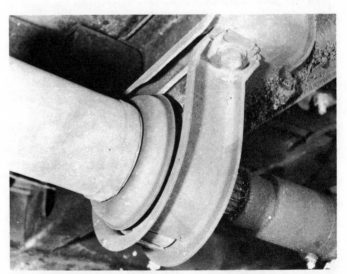

5.4 Center support bearing on two-section propeller shaft

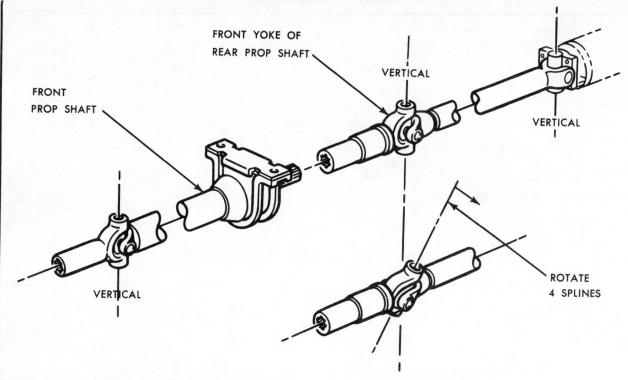

FRONT YOKE OF
REAR PROP SHAFT

VERTICAL

VERTICAL

FRONT
PROP SHAFT

VERTICAL

ROTATE
4 SPLINES

Fig. 7.4 Two-section propeller shaft installation (phasing) diagram

Fig. 7.5 Cutaway view of two-section propeller shaft center bearing

Fig. 7.6 Universal joint components (outer snap-ring type)

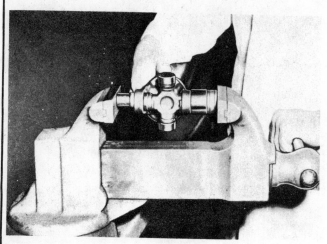

Fig. 7.7 Removing a universal joint bearing cup (outer snap-ring type)

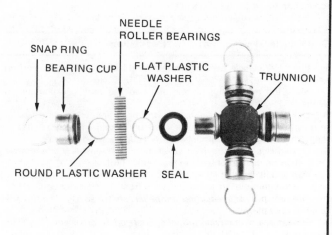

NEEDLE
ROLLER BEARINGS

SNAP RING

BEARING CUP

FLAT PLASTIC
WASHER

TRUNNION

ROUND PLASTIC WASHER

SEAL

Fig. 7.8 Universal joint components (inner snap-ring type)

trunnions in the same vertical attitude as the front one.

10 Now rotate the rear section of the shaft four splines (90°) in an anti-clockwise direction (facing front of vehicle) and connect the rear shaft to the front shaft. This alignment operation is known as 'phasing' (Fig. 7.4).

11 Connect the rear of the shaft to the rear axle flange, then tighten the grease cap on the slip joint.

6 Center support bearing – dismantling and reassembly

1   With the propeller shaft removed from the vehicle and the shaft sections separated at the center bearing, remove the bearing dust shield.

2   Remove the strap which retains the rubber cushion to the bearing support bracket.

3   Separate the cushion, bracket and bearing.

4   Pull the bearing assembly from the propeller shaft.

5   Renew any worn components and then commence reassembly. If the inner deflector was removed, install it to the shaft and stake it at two opposite points to ensure that it is a tight fit.

6   Pack the space between the inner dust deflector and the bearing with lithium base grease.

7   Carefully tap the bearing and slinger assembly onto the propeller shaft journal until the components are tight against the shoulder on the shaft. Use a suitable piece of tubing to do this, taking care not to damage the shaft splines.

8   Install the dust shield (small diameter first) and press it up against the outer slinger.

9   Install the bearing rubber cushion, bracket and strap.

7 Universal joints – overhaul

Outer snap-ring type

1   With the propeller shaft removed, mark the location of the joint yokes in relation to each other.

2   Extract the snap-rings from the ends of the bearing cups.

3   Using socket wrenches or pieces of pipe of suitable diameter, use a vise to press on the end of one cup and so displace the opposite one into the larger socket wrench or pipe. The bearing cup will not be fully ejected and it should be gripped in the jaws of the vise and twisted completely out of the yoke.

4   Remove the first bearing cup by pressing the trunnion in the opposite direction, then repeat the operations on the other two cups.

5   Clean the yoke and inspect for damage or cracks.

6   Obtain the appropriate repair kit which will include, trunnion, cups, needle rollers, seals, washers and snap-rings.

7   Before commencing reassembly, pack the reservoirs in the ends of the trunnion with grease and work some into the needle bearings taking care not to displace them from their location around the inside of the bearing cups.

8   Position the trunnion in the yoke, partially install one cup into the yoke and insert the trunnion a little way into it. Partially install the opposite cup, center the trunnion then, using the vise, press both cups into position using socket wrenches of diameter slightly less then that of the bearing cups. Make sure that the needle bearings are not displaced and trapped during this operation.

9   Fit the snap-rings.

10   Align the shaft yokes and install the other two bearing cups in the same way.

Injected plastic (inner snap-ring) type

11   This type of universal joint will be found on late model vehicles. Repair can be carried out after destroying the production line plastic retainers and fitting conventional snap-ring type repair kits.

12   Support the joint yoke in a press so that using a suitable forked pressing tool, pressure can be applied to two 'eyes' of the yoke to eject a bearing cup partially into a socket wrench of adequate diameter.

13   Repeat on all the cups and then twist the cups out of the yokes with a vise.

14   Clean away all trace of the plastic bearing cup retainers. This can be facilitated by probing through the plastic injection holes.

15   Obtain the appropriate repair kit which will include one pre-lubricated trunnion assembly, bearing cups, seals, and other components as shown (Fig. 7.8).

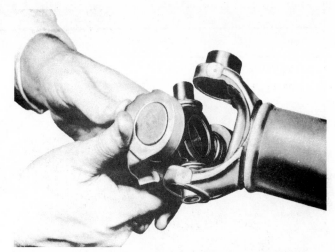

Fig. 7.9 Fitting trunnion to yoke (inner snap-ring type joint)

Fig. 7.10 Fitting snap-ring to universal joint

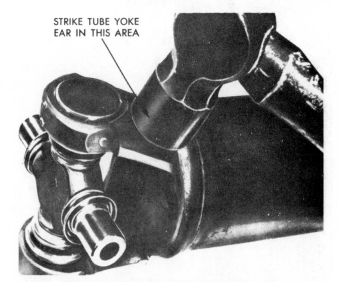

STRIKE TUBE YOKE EAR IN THIS AREA

Fig. 7.11 Easing universal joint bearing cups

16   Assemble the universal joint as described in paragraphs 8 ,9 and 10 of this Section. Note that the snap-rings are installed on the inside of the yokes on this type of joint.

17   When reassembly is complete, if the joint is stiff to move, apply some hammer blows to the yoke which will free the bearing cups from the snap-rings (Fig. 7.11)

8   Fault diagnosis – Propeller shaft

Symptom	Reason/s
Vibration	Wear in sliding sleeve splines
	Loose U-bolts on rear universal joint
	Worn universal joint bearings
	Out of balance driveshaft
	Distorted driveshaft or incorrect 'phasing' (Section 5)
Knock or 'clunk' when taking up drive or shifting gear	Loose U-bolts on rear universal joint
	Worn universal joint bearings
	Worn driven pinion splines causing looseness in companion flange
	Excessive backlash in differential gears (see Chapter 8)

Chapter 8 Rear axle

Contents

Specifications

Type and Make

Series G10 - 20 (GE/GS 1500 - 2500)	Semi-floating hypoid
Series G30 (GE/GS 3500)	Fully-floating hypoid

General Specifications

	Ring gear diameter	Make	Lubricant capacity	Standard Ratio	Optional Ratios
G10, G20 GE/GS 1500–2500 models	$8\frac{1}{2}$ inch	Salisbury or Dana	4.25 US pints	3.42	2.73, 2.76, 3.07, 3.08, 3.73
	$8\frac{7}{8}$ inch	Salisbury or Dana	3.5 US pints	3.40	
G30 GE/GS 3500 models	$9\frac{3}{4}$ inch	Dana	6.0 US pints	4.10	3.73, 4.56
	$10\frac{1}{2}$ inch	Dana	7.2 US pints		
	$10\frac{1}{2}$ inch	Chevrolet	5.4 US pints		

The ratios given may vary over the years of production; consult the individual vehicle decal or rear axle plate for positive identification

Torque wrench settings

	lbf ft
Differential rear cover bolts	
Semi-floating axle	23
Dana fully-floating axle	35
Chevrolet fully-floating axle	18
Oil filler plug	
$10\frac{1}{2}$ in Dana	10
All other axles	18
Axleshaft-to-hub bolts (fully-floating axle)	90
Axleshaft bearing adjusting nut (fully-floating axle)	
Stage 1	50
Stage 2 (after release)	35 then unscrew $\frac{1}{4}$ turn
Axleshaft bearing locknut (fully-floating axle)	65

1 General description

1   The rear axle may be one of three types and makes, depending upon the vehicle model and date of production.

2   The Salisbury or Dana axle installed on lighter duty vehicles is of the semi-floating fabricated type, consisting of a cast carrier into which the axle casing tubes are welded.

3   The differential assembly is a hypoid pinion and ring gear design incorporating two pinions.

4   On heavier duty vehicles, a Dana or Chevrolet axle is installed which is a fully-floating type. This type of construction permits easy removal of the axle shafts without having to unload the vehicle or to jack up the axle.

5   Due to the need for special tools and equipment, it is recommended that operations on the rear axle are limited to those described in this Chapter. Where repair or overhaul is required, remove the rear axle assembly and take it to a specialist company, or exchange it for a new or reconditioned unit. It is becoming increasingly rare to be able to obtain individual rear axle components for local repair work as it is generally recognised that dismantling and rebuilding this unit is an 'in plant' job.

6   Always make sure that a rear axle unit is changed for one of identical type and reduction ratio. The identification number is located

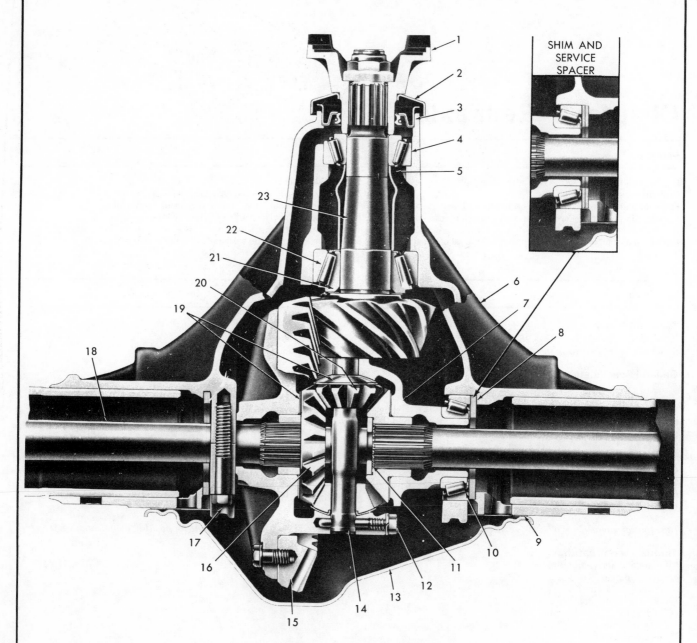

Fig. 8.1 Cutaway view of semi-floating type rear axle

1 Pinion companion flange	7 Differential case	13 Rear cover	19 Thrust washer
2 Dust deflector	8 Shim and spacer	14 Pinion pin	20 Differential pinions
3 Pinion oil seal	9 Rear cover gasket	15 Ring gear	21 Shim
4 Pinion front bearing	10 Differential bearing	16 Side gear	22 Pinion rear bearing
5 Collapsible spacer	11 C-locking ring	17 Bearing cap	23 Drive pinion
6 Differential carrier	12 Pinion shaft lock bolt	18 Axleshaft	

SHIM AND SERVICE SPACER

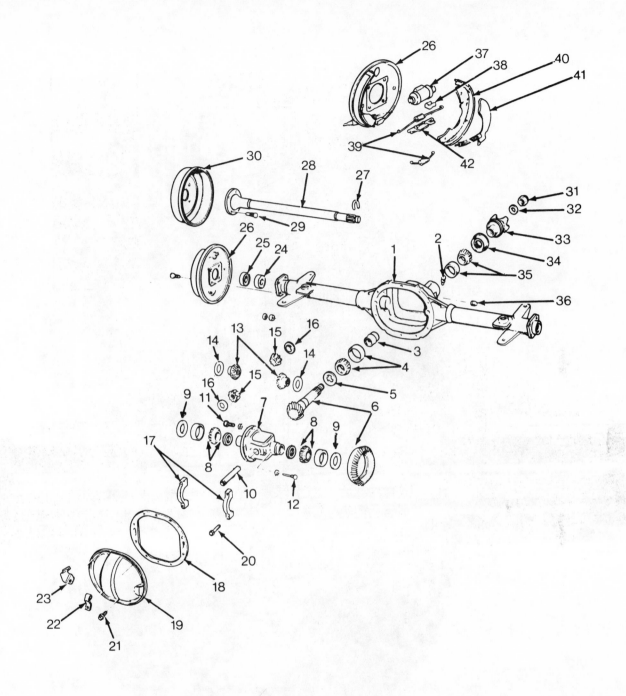

Fig. 8.2 Exploded view of typical semi-floating type rear axle

1 Axle casing	12 Pinion shaft lock screw	22 Clip	32 Thrust washer
2 Breather	13 Side gear	23 Bracket	33 Companion flange
3 Collapsible spacer	14 Thrust washer	24 Axleshaft bearing	34 Oil seal
4 Pinion rear bushing	15 Pinion wheel	25 Oil seal	35 Pinion front bearing
5 Thrust washer	16 Thrust washer	26 Brake backing plate	36 Filter plug
6 Drive pinion and ring gear	17 Bearing caps	27 C-retainer	37 Wheel cylinder
7 Differential case	18 Gasket	28 Axleshaft	38 Clip
8 Differential bearing	19 Cover	29 Wheel stud	39 Shoe springs
9 Shim	20 Bearing cap bolt	30 Brake drum	40 Brake shoe
10 Pinion shaft	21 Cover bolt	31 Pinion self-locking nut	41 Parking brake lever
11 Case-to-ring gear bolt			42 Strut

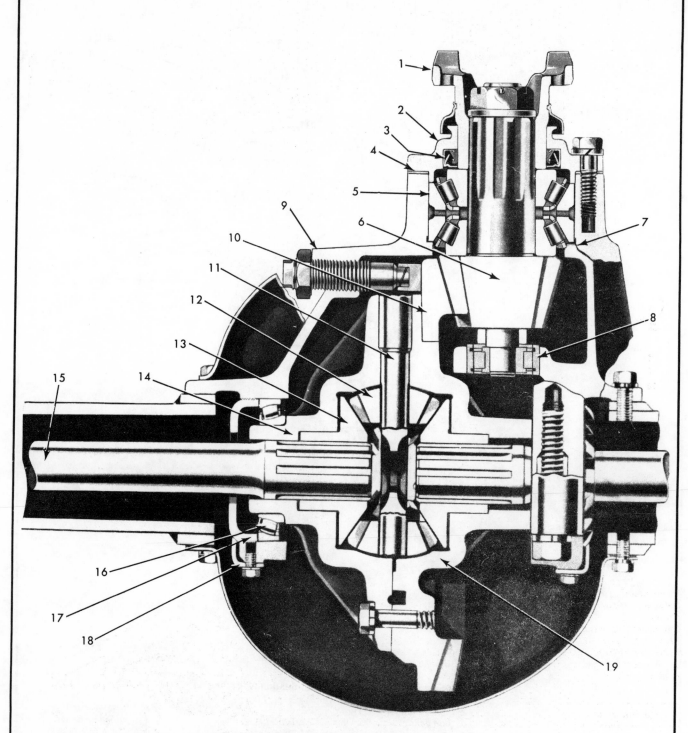

Fig. 8.3 Cut-away view of fully-floating type rear axle

1   Companion flange
2   Pinion bearing and oil seal
     retainer
3   Oil seal
4   Gasket
5   Pinion front bearing
6   Drive pinion
7   Shim

8   Pinion rear bearing
9   Ring gear thrust pad
10 Ring gear
11 Pinion pin
12 Pinion gear
13 Side gear
14 Left half of differential
      case

15 Axleshaft
16 Differential bearing
17 Differential bearing
      adjusting nut
18 Adjusting nut lockplate
19 Right half of differential
      case

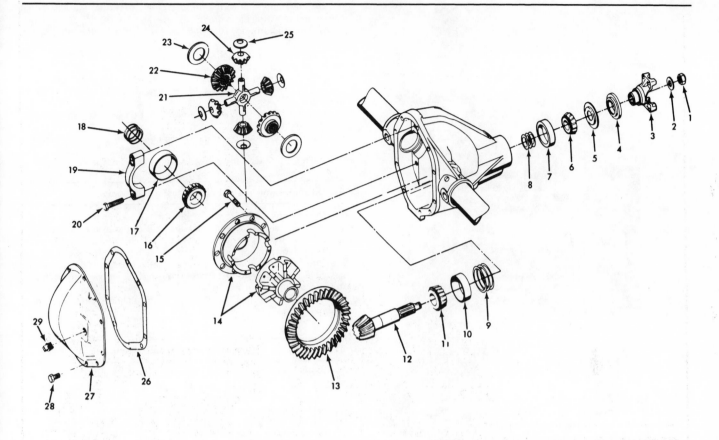

Fig. 8.4 Exploded view of typical fully-floating rear axle

1	Pinion nut	9	Pinion depth setting shims	16	Differential side bearing
2	Washer	10	Rear bearing track	17	Side bearing track
3	Companion flange	11	Pinion rear bearing	18	Side bearing adjusting shims
4	Oil seal	12	Drive pinion	19	Bearing cap
5	Oil slinger	13	Ring gear	20	Bearing cap bolt
6	Pinion front bearing	14	Differential case	21	Differential cross
7	Front bearing track	15	Ring gear bolt	22	Side gear
8	Bearing pre-load shims				

23	Washer
24	Pinion gear
25	Washer
26	Gasket
27	Cover
28	Cover bolt
29	Filler/level plug

in the following position:
Salisbury: bottom flange of carrier housing or front upper surface of carrier.
Dana: rear face of right axle tube.
Chevrolet: (G10 and 1500 Series) front face of right axle tube, (G20/30 and 2500/3500 Series) upper face of right axle tube.
7   On some models, a limited slip differential unit is fitted as an option.

2 Maintenance

1   On semi-floating rear axles, check its oil level at the mileages recommended in Routine Maintenance and top up if necessary to the level of the filler plug hole.
2   On fully-floating rear axles, check the oil level as just described, and also drain and refill the axle at the specified intervals. If no drain plug is installed, remove the rear cover plate.
3   Periodically, check the tightness of the axle cover bolts and the suspension attachments to the axle casing.

3 Semi-floating type axleshafts – removal and installation

1   Raise the rear of the vehicle and support securely.
2   Remove the roadwheel and the brake drum.

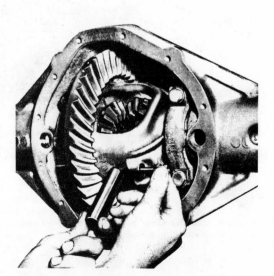

Fig. 8.5 Removing differential pinion pin and lockscrew from semi-floating type axle

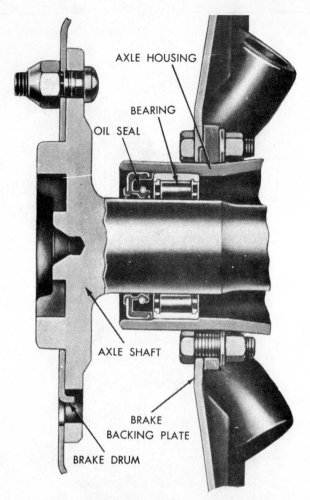

Fig. 8.6 Cutaway view of axleshaft bearing and seal (semi-floating type axle)

Fig. 8.7 Using a slide hammer to extract an axleshaft bearing (semi-floating type rear axle)

3 Unscrew and remove the pressed steel cover from the differential carrier and allow the oil to drain into a suitable container.

4 Unscrew and remove the lock screw from the differential pinion pin (Fig. 8.5).

5 Push the outer (flanged) end of the axleshaft inwards and remove the C-lock ring from the inner end of the shaft.

6 Withdraw the axleshaft taking care not to damage the oil seal in the end of the axle housing as the splined end of the axleshaft passes through it.

7 Installation is a reversal of removal, but tighten the lock screw to the specified torque.

8 Always use a new cover gasket and tighten the cover bolts to the specified torque.

9 Refill the unit with the correct quantity and grade of lubricant.

4 Oil seal (semi-floating type axleshaft) – renewal

1 Remove the axleshaft as described in the preceding Section.

2 Pry out the old oil seal from the end of the axle casing using a large screwdriver or the inner end of the axleshaft itself, as a lever.

3 Apply high melting point grease to the oil seal recess and tap the seal into position so that the lips are facing inwards and the metal face is visible from the end of the axle housing. When correctly installed, the face of the oil seal should be flush with the end of the axle casing.

4 Installation of the axleshaft is as described in the preceding Section.

5 Bearing (semi-floating type axleshaft) – renewal

1 Remove the axleshaft (Section 3) and the oil seal (Section 4).

2 A bearing extractor will now be required, or a tool made up which will engage behind the bearing.

3 Attach a slide hammer and extract the bearing from the axle casing.

4 Clean out the bearing recess and drive in the new bearing using a piece of tubing **applied against the outer bearing track.** Make sure that the bearing is tapped in to the full depth of its recess, and that the numbers on the bearing are visible from the outer end of the axle casing.

5 Discard the old oil seal and install a new one, then install the axleshaft.

6 On some very early models, the bearings are pressed onto the axleshaft itself. Have your dealer remove these as they are very tight and before removal, a retaining collar must be cut away.

6 Pinion oil seal (semi-floating type axle) – renewal

1 Raise the rear axle and support it on axlestands so that the roadwheels are clear of the ground. Remove the brake drums and roadwheels.

2 Disconnect the driveshaft from the rear axle drive pinion as described in Chapter 7 and tie it to the body sideframe.

3 Using a torque wrench check the torque required to rotate the pinion and record this for use later. If a torque wrench is not available, use a spring balance with a length of cord wound round the pinion companion flange.

4 Scribe or dot punch alignment marks on the pinion stem, nut and flange so that they can be installed in the same relative position.

5 Count the number of threads visible between the end of the nut and the end of the pinion stem, and record for later use.

6 A suitable tool must now be used to hold the pinion flange quite still while the self-locking pinion nut is removed. This can easily be made by drilling two holes at the end of a length of flat steel bar and bolting it to the flange.

7 Unscrew and remove the pinion nut.

8 Withdraw the companion flange. If this is tight, use a two or three legged extractor engaged behind the flange. On no account attempt to lever behind the deflector or to hammer on the end of the pinion stem.

9 Pry out the old seal and discard it.

10 Tap the new oil seal into position making sure that it enters the housing squarely and to its full depth.

11 Align the mating marks made before dismantling and install the companion flange. If necessary, use a piece of tubing as a spacer and

screw on the pinion nut to force the flange fully home on the stem. **On no account attempt to hammer the flange home.**

12 Smear jointing compound on the ends of the splines which are visible in the center of the companion flange so that any oil seepage will be sealed in.

13 Install the thrustwasher and nut but tighten the nut carefully so that the original number of threads is exposed.

14 Now measure the torque required to rotate the pinion and tighten the nut fractionally until the figure compares with that recorded before dismantling. In order to compensate for the drag of the new oil seal, the nut should be further tightened so that the rotational torque of the pinion exceeds that recorded before dismantling by between 1 and 5 lbf in.

15 Install the driveshaft, brake drum, roadwheel and lower the vehicle.

NOTE: *With this type of axle having a collapsible spacer, it is most important that the pinion nut is not overtightened. Backing off the nut will not rectify the situation and the only remedy is to remove the front bearing assembly, extract the collapsible spacer and install a new one, then repeat the adjustment operations.*

7 Semi-floating type axle assembly – removal and installation

1 Raise the rear of the vehicle and support it securely on stands or blocks placed under the bodyframe side members. Remove the roadwheels.

2 Position a jack under the rear axle differential carrier.

3 Disconnect the propeller shaft from the rear axle companion flange. Push the shaft to one side and tie it up out of the way to the bodyframe.

4 Disconnect the shock absorber lower mountings.

5 Disconnect the axle vent hose from the connector on the axle casing and tie it to one side.

6 Disconnect the hydraulic brake flexible hose from the axle casing and plug the open pipes.

7 Remove the brake drums.

8 Disconnect the parking brake cables from the actuating levers and at the backplate (see Chapter 9).

9 Disconnect the rear spring U-bolts; remove the spacers and clamp plates.

10 Lower the jack under the differential and then remove the rear axle assembly from under the vehicle.

11 Installation is a reversal of removal, but tighten the spring U-bolts to the specified torque after the weight of the vehicle is again on the roadwheels.

12 Bleed the brake hydraulic circuit as described in Chapter 9.

8 Fully-floating type axleshafts – removal and installation

1 Unscrew and remove the bolts which attach the axleshaft flange to the hub. There is no need to remove the roadwheel or jack-up the car. In the illustration, the roadwheel has been removed in the interest of clarity (Fig. 8.11).

2 Tap the flange with a soft-faced hammer to loosen the shaft and then grip the rib of the face of the flange with a pair of self-locking grips; twist the shaft slightly in both directions and then withdraw it

Fig. 8.8 Installing axleshaft bearing and oil seal (semi-floating type rear axle)

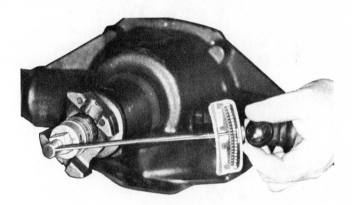

Fig. 8.9 Measuring drive pinion bearing torque (pre-load)

Fig. 8.10 Rear axle pinion nut and companion flange alignment marks

Fig. 8.11 Remoivng an axleshaft flange bolt (fully-floating rear axle)

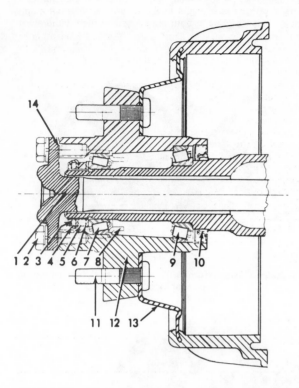

Fig. 8.12 Sectional view of fully-floating type rear axle hub

1	Axleshaft	8	Snap-ring
2	Shaft-to-hub bolt	9	Hub inner bearing
3	Locknut	10	Oil seal
4	Locknut retaining plate	11	Roadwheel stud
5	Adjusting nut	12	Hub assembly
6	Thrust washer	13	Drum
7	Hub outer bearing	14	Gasket

Fig. 8.13 Extracting hub outer bearing snap-ring (fully-floating rear axle

Fig. 8.14 Adjusting hub bearings (fully-floating type rear axle)

from the axle tube.

3   Installation is a reversal of removal but hold the axleshaft level in order to engage the splines at its inner end with those in the differential side gear. Always use a new gasket on the flange and keep both the flange and hub mating surfaces free from grease or oil.

9   Hub/drum assembly (fully-floating axle) – removal and installation

1   Remove the axleshaft as described in the preceding Section.
2   Jack-up the axle and remove the roadwheel.
3   Release the tang of locknut retainer, and unscrew and remove the locknut from the axletube.
4   Release the tang of the retainer from the adjusting nut and remove the retainer.
5   Unscrew and remove the adjusting nut.
6   Remove the thrust washer.
7   Pull the hub/drum assembly straight off the end of the axle tube. On some axles, the drum can be removed separately after extracting the countersunk retaining screws.
8   Remove the oil seal and discard it.
9   To further dismantle the hub, drive out the inner bearing, track and oil seal using a long drift.
10   Extract the outer bearing snap-ring and drive out the outer bearing and its track.
11   On axles where the brake drum is not secured independently by screws, the drum can be detached from the hub if necessary by pressing out the roadwheel studs. When reassembling this type of hub and drum make sure that the drain holes are in alignment and then apply an even coating of jointing compound to the hub oil deflector contact surface before locating the deflector to the drum.

12 Commence installation of the hub/drum assembly by first packing the bearings with the specified lubricant and also smearing it on the hub-to-axle tube contact surfaces.

13 Offer the hub/drum assembly to the axle tube, taking care not to damage the oil seal.

14 Fit the thrust washer so that the internal tang engages in the groove on the axle tube.

15 Screw on the adjusting nut.

16 Before adjusting the hub bearings, make sure that the brakes are not dragging then install the roadwheel.

17 Keep the roadwheel turning and tighten the adjuster nut to a torque wrench setting of 50 lbf ft, then back-off the nut and retighten to 35 lbf ft; finally back off the nut $\frac{1}{4}$ turn.

18 If this adjustment has been correctly carried out, the end play will be between 0.001 and 0.010 inch, or if the tire is gripped top and bottom and the wheel pulled back and forth, there will be an almost imperceptible movement between brake drum and brake backplate, and the roadwheel will turn freely.

19 Install the tanged retainer; install the locknut and tighten to 65 lbf ft. Bend over the long tang of the retainer.

20 Install the axleshaft and lower the vehicle to the ground.

10 Pinion oil seal (fully-floating type axle) – renewal

1 Disconnect the propeller shaft from the rear axle companion flange (see Chapter 7).

2 Refer to Figs. 8.3 and 8.10, and scribe a line down the pinion stem, the pinion nut and the companion flange.

3 A suitable tool must now be used to hold the pinion flange quite still while the self-locking pinion nut is removed. This can easily be made by drilling two holes at the end of a length of flat steel bar and bolting it to the flange.

4 Extract the split pin from the slotted pin nut. Unscrew the nut and remove the companion flange.

5 Unscrew and remove the bolts which secure the oil seal retainer to the differential carrier.

6 Pry out the deflective oil seal and tap in the new one. Fill the space between the seal lips with high melting point grease.

7 Install the retainer and the companion flange.

8 Install the washer and slotted nut, tightening the nut only until the scribed marks made before dismantling are in alignment.

9 Insert a new split pin and then re-connect the propeller shaft.

11 Fully-floating type axle assembly – removal and installation

1 The operations are similar to those described in Section 7 of this Chapter.

12 Fault diagnosis – rear axle

Symptom	Reason/s
Vibration	Worn axle shaft bearing
	Loose U-bolts (propeller shaft to companion flange)
	Tires require balancing
	Propeller shaft out of balance
Noise on turns	Worn differential gear
Noise on drive or coasting *	Worn or incorrectly adjusted ring and pinion gear
'Clunk' on acceleration or deceleration	Worn differential gear cross-shaft
	Worn propeller shaft
	Loose flange U-bolts
Positraction type axle	
Chatter on turn	Incorrect lubricant in differential
	Brake cones worn
	Coil springs weak

It must be appreciated that tire noise, wear in the rear suspension bushes, and worn or loose shock absorber mountings can all mislead the mechanic into thinking that components of the rear axle are the source of the trouble.

Chapter 9 Braking system

Contents

Specifications

Type

Thru 1970	Four wheel hydraulic, dual circuit, vacuum booster except on small engine models
	Parking brake mechanical to rear wheels
1971 up	Four wheel hydraulic, dual circuit, vacuum booster or hydraulically operated Hydro-boost. Disc front, drum rear, parking brake mechanical to rear wheels

Disc brakes

Disc thickness	1.28 or 1.53 inch, according to vehicle model
Disc diameter	11.86, 12.50 or 14.50 inch, according to model

Drum brakes

Width	2.0, 2.50, 2.75 or 3.50 inch according to model
Internal diameter	11.0, 11.15, or 13.0 inch according to model

Torque wrench settings

	lbf ft
Master cylinder mounting nuts	25
Booster mounting nuts	25
Combination (pressure regularity) valve mounting nuts-to-bracket ...	17
Combination valve bracket-to-body	25
Caliper mounting bolts	35
Front brake hose-to-caliper	22
Brake pedal pivot nut	28
Parking brake equaliser jam nuts	18
Master cylinder reservoir-to-cylinder mounting bolts (Bendix)	12 to 15
Caliper support key locking screw (Bendix)	12 to 18

1 General description

1   The braking system is of four wheel, dual circuit hydraulic type on all models.

2   Vehicles built through 1970 have four wheel drum brakes, while later models have front discs and rear drums.

3   On the earlier models, the parking brake is operated by a hand control while on later vehicles, a foot pedal is used.

4   Only the vehicles with the smallest engines are not equipped with a brake booster system; all other models have such assistance as standard. On all models except some of the latest long wheelbase versions the booster is of the vacuum servo type. On these heavier duty vehicles, the booster operates in conjunction with the power steering system and operates hydraulically. Generally, the braking equipment on vehicles with manually-operated brakes or with vacuum servo boosters is of Delco manufacture while the equipment used with hydro-boosters is of Bendix make.

5   The drum brakes are of duo-servo, single anchor pin type which means that they are self-energizing when the vehicle is in motion either forwards or in reverse.

6   The disc brakes incorporate a single piston sliding caliper.

7   All later models incorporate a pressure regulating 'combination' valve which is located adjacent to the master cylinder. The purpose of this device is to meter the hydraulic pressure during heavy brake applications so that the front brakes are not applied in advance of the rear ones while the latter are overcoming the restriction of the shoe return springs. This makes for even braking on both front and rear axles.

8   An additional function of the valve is to sense pressure failure in either hydraulic circuit and to indicate this by illuminating a warning lamp.

2   Maintenance and adjustment

1   The most important task with the braking system is to maintain the fluid level in the master cylinder at the indicated level. Only use clean hydraulic fluid of the specified type for this purpose.

2   At the intervals specified in Routine Maintenance at the beginning of this manual, check the wear in the disc pads and shoe linings. Refer to Sections 3, 4, 6 and 7.

3   Also at the specified intervals, check for hydraulic fluid leaks at all pipe unions and hydraulic components; also check the condition of the flexible and rigid pipes of the system as described in Section 15.

4   None of the brakes installed requires adjustment. Disc calipers are self-adjusting, drum brakes incorporate automatic adjusters which are actuated when the foot brake is applied when the vehicle is in forward or reverse motion, and the parking brake is adjusted automatically at the same time as the rear shoes.

3   Front drum brakes – shoe inspection and renewal

1   Raise the front of the vehicle and remove the roadwheels.

2   Extract the drum securing screws and pull off the drum. If the drum cannot be withdrawn due to the shoe having worn a channel in the drum interior, the automatic adjuster will have to be released. To do this, knock out the oval shaped blanking plate in the web of the brake drum and insert a screwdriver to release the adjuster sprocket until the drum can be withdrawn clear of the shoes. Retrieve the blanking plate from the interior of the drum and discard it.

3   On no account depress the brake pedal while the drum is removed.

4   Inspect the thickness of the linings. With riveted linings, if the friction material is worn down to, or nearly down to, the rivets, renew the shoes as an axle set. With bonded linings, if there is only a thickness of $\frac{1}{16}$ inch of the friction material left, renew the shoes.

Fig. 9.1 Typical brake drum. Knockout panel (arrowed)

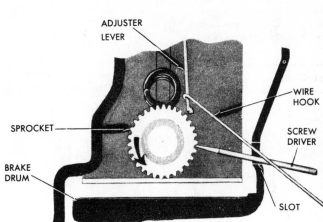

Fig. 9.2 Turning the shoe adjuster wheel with a screwdriver

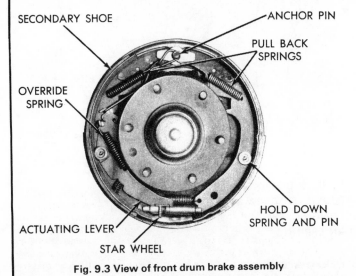

Fig. 9.3 View of front drum brake assembly

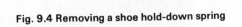

Fig. 9.4 Removing a shoe hold-down spring

Fig. 9.5 Removing actuating lever assembly

5   *If the friction linings are in good condition*, brush away all dust from the shoes and drum interior, *taking care not to inhale it*, then install the drum.

6   If the automatic adjuster sprocket was turned, during dismantling, rotate it in the opposite direction until the drum locks, then back it off until the drum is free to turn without drag.

7   *If the shoes are to be removed*, disconnect the shoe return springs.

8   Remove the shoe hold-down springs. To do this, grip the dished cup with a pair of pliers, depress it and turn it through 90°. Release it and remove, cup, spring and pin.

9   Remove the actuating lever assembly. It is not recommended that the assembly is dismantled.

10   Remove the shoes noting carefully which way round they are installed with reference to the greater portions of shoe web not covered by lining material.

11   Remove the star wheel adjuster, clean and lubricate it, and set it to its fully retracted position.

12   Install the new shoes in the same relative positions as the old ones, keeping them free from oil and grease. Make sure that the star wheel adjuster is attached so that the wheel is nearer the secondary shoe. The star wheel adjusters are left-hand and right-hand; do not mix them up if both front brakes are being dismantled at the same time. Make sure that the tension spring just above the adjuster is installed so as not to interfere with the star wheel.

13   Engage the upper ends of the shoes with the wheel cylinder and with the anchor pin. Use a pair of needle nosed pliers to connect the hold-down springs.

14   Install the actuator and the anchor plate and install the wire link. Connect the actuator spring.

15   Pry the brake shoes away from the brake backplate just enough to be able to apply a smear of recommended brake grease to the rubbing surfaces on the backplate.

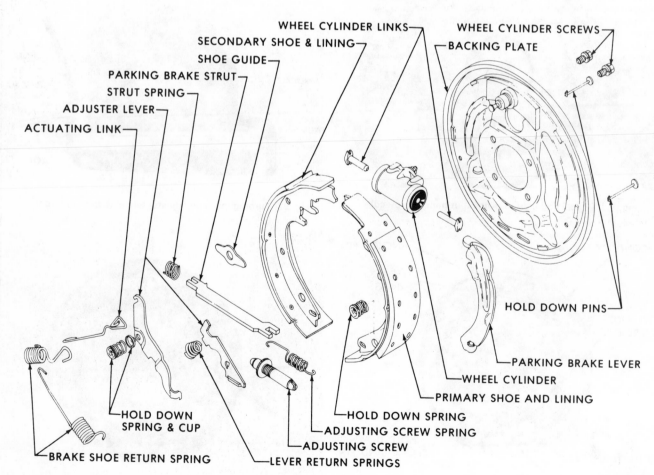

Fig. 9.6 Exploded view of typical rear drum brake

16 Turn the adjuster wheel until the shoes have been expanded to the point where the drum will only just pass over them into position.
17 Install the drum and the securing screws.
18 Make sure that the opposite brake drum is in position and then apply the footbrake hard several times.
19 Now check that the drum in which the new shoes have been installed can be turned with only an imperceptible drag. If the drum drags, release the star wheel until it is free.
20 Repeat all the foregoing operations on the opposite front wheel, then install the roadwheels and lower the vehicle.

4   Rear drum brake shoes — inspection and renewal

1   The operations are very similar to those described in the preceding Section but observe the following differences (photos).

(a) On vehicles with fully-floating rear axles and composite hub/drum assemblies, the axleshafts will first have to be removed before the hub/drums can be withdrawn, as described in Chapter 8.
(b) Once the shoe return springs and the hold-down spring have been removed, spread the shoes to clear the wheel cylinder connecting links and detach the parking brake strut and spring. Disconnect the cable from the parking brake lever.

5   Drum brake wheel cylinder — removal, overhaul and installation

1   The need for wheel cylinder overhaul will usually arise if leakage of hydraulic fluid is evident from the assembly. However, renewal of the cup seals is recommended in any event at 50 000 mile intervals.
2   Jack-up the vehicle securely and remove the roadwheel, brake drum and brake shoes as previously described.
3   Tape over the vents in the master cylinder reservoir cover to create a partial vacuum in the hydraulic circuit which is to be disconnected and so will prevent undue loss of fluid.
4   Pull out the wheel cylinder links (pushrods) from the wheel cylinder and remove the rubber boots (Fig. 9.7).
5   The piston assemblies will now be ejected under the pressure of the internal coil spring.
6   At this point, examine the interior of the cylinder (a small mirror is useful for this). If there is any sign of scoring, or 'bright' wear areas are visible, then the cylinder must be renewed complete. To do this, disconnect the hydraulic line and unbolt the cylinder from the backplate.
7   Where the components are in good condition, remove the cup seals from the spring expanders. Discard the seals. Obtain the appropriate repair kit which will contain all the renewable items.
8   Wash all the internal parts in clean hydraulic fluid or denatured alcohol. *Never use mineral oil, solvents or kerosene when cleaning*

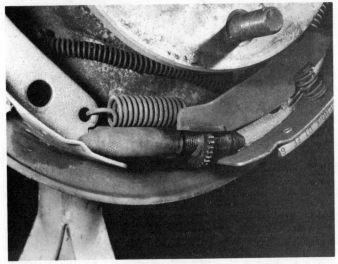
4.1A Lower part of rear drum brake assembly

4.1B Upper part of rear drum brake assembly

4.1C Rear brake shoe hold-down spring cup and parking brake cable

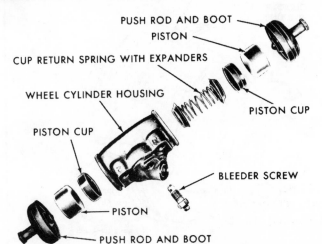

PUSH ROD AND BOOT
PISTON
CUP RETURN SPRING WITH EXPANDERS
WHEEL CYLINDER HOUSING
PISTON CUP
PISTON CUP
PISTON
BLEEDER SCREW
PUSH ROD AND BOOT

Fig. 9.7 Exploded view of typical rear drum brake wheel cylinder

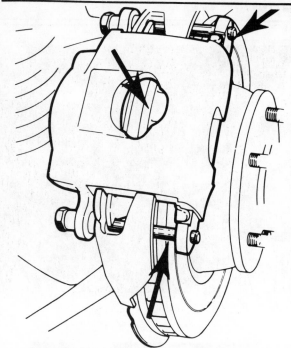

Fig. 9.8 Disc brake pad (Delco) inspection points

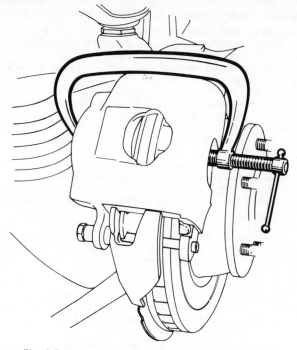

Fig. 9.9 Using a clamp to move caliper piston (Delco)

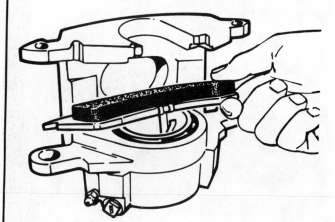

Fig. 9.10 Attaching disc brake pad shoe support spring (Delco)

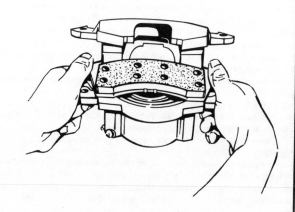

Fig. 9.11 Installing disc brake inboard pad (Delco)

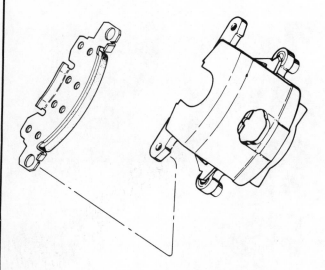

Fig. 9.12 Installing disc brake outboard pad (Delco)

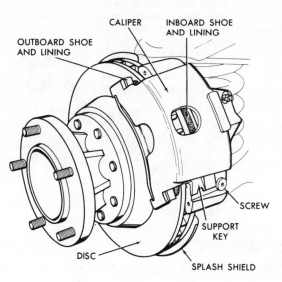

CALIPER
INBOARD SHOE AND LINING
OUTBOARD SHOE AND LINING
SCREW
SUPPORT KEY
DISC
SPLASH SHIELD

Fig. 9.13 Bendix type disc brake

components of the brake hydraulic system.

9   Using the fingers only, manipulate the new cup seals into position of the spring expanders.

10   Dip the cup seals in clean hydraulic fluid, and insert the spring and seals into the cylinder.

11   Install the pistons, pushrods and boots.

12   Install the shoes and the drum, then bleed the appropriate hydraulic circuit as described in Section 16. Don't forget to remove the tape from the master cylinder vents before bleeding.

6   Front disc brake pads (Delco type) – inspection and renewal

1   At the intervals specified in Routine Maintenance or whenever the roadwheels are removed, check the wear of the friction material on the disc pads.

2   To do this, jack-up the car and remove the roadwheel.

3   Check both ends of the outboard shoe by looking in at each end of the caliper. Then look down through the inspection hole in the caliper to check the inboard shoe. If the friction material has worn down to, or nearly down to, the rivets at either end of the pad, then the pads should be renewed as an axle set (Fig. 9.8).

4   Syphon off some of the hydraulic fluid from the front compartment of the master cylinder. An old hydrometer or syringe is useful for this, which is necessary to accommodate the rise in fluid level when the caliper piston is depressed.

5   A 7 inch clamp will now be required, located as shown, with the non-adjustable side resting against the backing plate of the outboard pad. Tighten the clamp to move the caliper so that the piston can be depressed to the bottom of its bore (Fig.9.9).

6   Remove the clamp and observe that the disc pads are now backed-off from the disc.

7   Unscrew and remove the two mounting bolts (photo).

8   Lift the caliper from the disc and remove the inboard shoe (photo).

9   Dislodge the outboard shoe and then tie the caliper to the front suspension arm with a piece of wire to prevent strain on the hydraulic flexible hose.

10   Extract the pad support spring from the cavity in the piston.

11   Remove the sleeves from the inboard ears of the calipers and then extract the rubber bushings from all four caliper ears.

12   Clean away all dirt and obtain new sleeves and rubber bushings. If the caliper mounting bolts are corroded, renew these as well (photo).

13   Commence reassembly by installing the new rubber bushings followed by the new sleeves. Make sure that the sleeves are installed with the end nearest the pads flush with the machined surface of the caliper ear.

14   Insert the shoe support spring so that the single tang end of the spring is over the notch in the center of the edge of the pad. Now press the two tangs at the end of the inboard shoe spring over the bottom edge of the pad (Fig.9.10).

15   Position the inboard pad complete with spring into the caliper so that the wear indicator is towards the rear of the caliper.

16   Position the outboard pad in the caliper so that the tab at the bottom of the pad is engaged in the cutout in the caliper.

17   Hold the caliper in position over the disc and screw the mounting bolts through the sleeves in the inboard ears and the mounting bracket. Pass the bolts through the outboard holes and tighten them to the specified torque wrench setting.

18   Use self-locking grips to clinch the upper ears of outboard pad flat against caliper housing.

19   Apply the foot brake pedal several times to position the pads against the disc and then top up the master cylinder reservoir with clean fluid which has been stored in an airtight container and has remained unshaken for the previous 24 hours.

20   Renew the disc pads on the opposite front brake.

7   Front disc brake pads (Bendix type) – inspection and renewal

1   Carry out the operations described in paragraphs 1 through 4 of Section 6.

2   Using a clamp, move the caliper so that the piston is depressed to the bottom of its bore.

3   Using a brass drift, drive out the caliper support key and spring.

4   Lift the caliper from the disc and tie it up to the suspension arm so that the hydraulic flexible hose is not strained.

6.7 Removing Delco type caliper mounting bolt

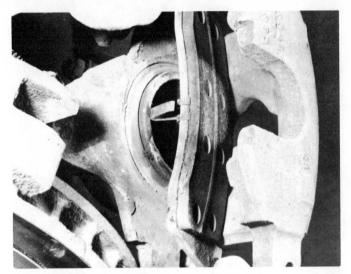

6.8 Removing Delco type caliper

6.12 Delco type caliper mounting bolt

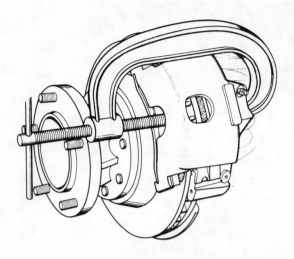

Fig. 9.14 Using a clamp to move caliper piston (Bendix)

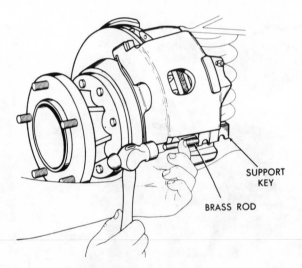

Fig. 9.15 Removing caliper support key (Bendix)

SUPPORT KEY

BRASS ROD

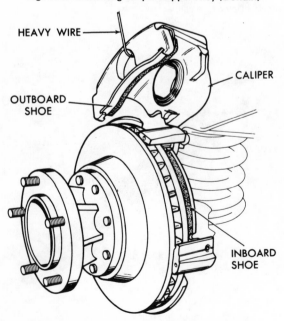

HEAVY WIRE

OUTBOARD SHOE

CALIPER

INBOARD SHOE

Fig. 9.16 Removing caliper from disc (Bendix)

5   Remove the inboard pad (its ends rest in the steering knuckle). Discard the pad clip.

6   Remove the outboard pad from the caliper.

NOTE: *If the original pads are to be re-installed, mark them so that they can be installed in their original position.*

7   If the friction material is worn down to, or nearly down to, the rivet heads, renew the disc pads as an axle set.

8   Wipe or brush away all dirt, taking care not to inhale any of the dust.

9   Smear Silicone grease on the sliding surfaces of the caliper and install a new inboard pad clip, making sure that the loop of the spring is away from the disc.

10   Install the inboard pad into the groove in the steering knuckle, and the outboard pad into the caliper.

11   Position the caliper over the disc making sure that the flexible hydraulic hose is not twisted.

12   Tap the support key and spring into position, and screw in the lock bolt, tightening to the specified torque wrench setting. Make sure that the boss on the bolt engages with the cutout in the key.

13   Apply the brake pedal several times to position the pads against the disc and then top up the fluid reservoir on the master cylinder using fluid which has been stored in an airtight container and has remained unshaken for the preceding 24 hours.

14   Repeat the operations on the opposite front brake.

8   Disc caliper (Delco) – overhaul

1   Carry out the operations described in Section 6 to the point where the caliper is removed from the disc. Tape over the master cylinder reservoir vents.

2   Mark the relative position of the flexible hose union to the caliper, then unscrew and remove the bolt which secures the hose union to the caliper. Retain the bolt and the two copper sealing washers (one fitted each side of the union block). Cap the open end of the hose with plastic sheet and tape to prevent the entry of dirt.

3   With the caliper removed, clean away all external dirt.

4   Place a pad of rag in the caliper to insulate the piston when it is ejected. To remove the piston, apply air from a tire pump to the fluid entry hole. Only gentle air pressure is required; a foot or hand operated pump is adequate.

5   At this point, with the piston removed, inspect the surfaces of the piston and cylinder. If there is any sign of scoring or 'bright' wear areas then the caliper must be renewed complete.

6   If the components are in good condition, discard the piston seal and dust excluding boot, and obtain a repair kit which will contain all the renewable items.

7   Wash the piston and cylinder bore in clean hydraulic fluid or denatured alcohol - nothing else.

8   Manipulate the new piston seal into its groove in the cylinder using the fingers only to do this.

9   Engage the new dust excluding boot with the groove in the end of the piston; dip the piston in hydraulic fluid and insert it squarely into the cylinder. Depress the piston to the bottom of the cylinder bore.

10   Seat the boot in the caliper counterbore using a suitable piece of tubing.

11   Connect the flexible hose to the caliper making sure that the copper gaskets are in position, and align the union fitting with the marks made before dismantling to ensure that the hose will not rub or twist.

12   Install the caliper as described in Section 6, then bleed the front hydraulic circuit (see Section 16).

9   Disc caliper (Bendix) – overhaul

1   Refer to Section 7 and carry out the operations to the point where the caliper is removed from the disc. Tape over the master cylinder reservoir vents.

2   Mark the relative position of the flexible hose union to the caliper, then unscrew and remove the bolt which secures the hose union to the caliper. Retain the bolt and the two copper sealing washers (one fitted each side of union block). Cap the open end of the hose with plastic sheet and tape to prevent the entry of dirt.

3   With the caliper removed, clean away all external dirt.

4   The overhaul operations are now as described in the preceding

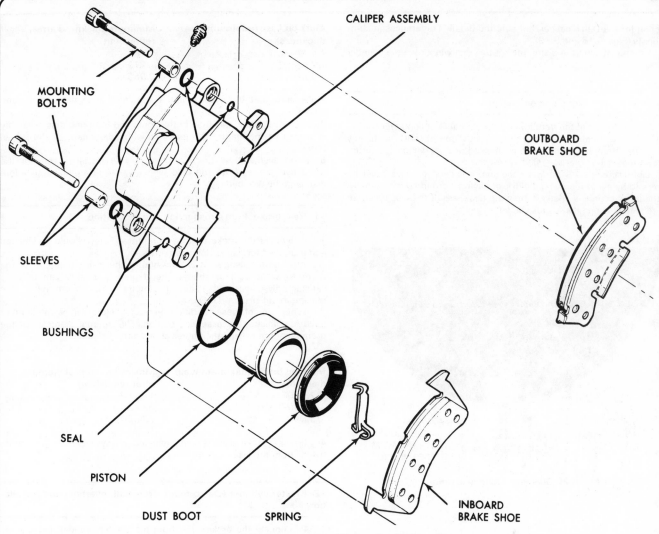

Fig. 9.17 Components of Delco disc brake caliper

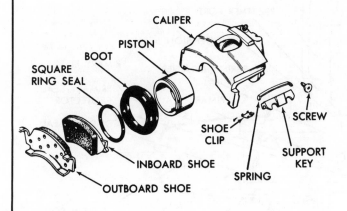

Fig. 9.18 Components of Bendix disc brake caliper

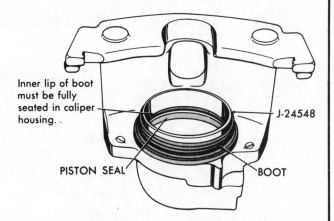

Fig. 9.19 Bendix disc caliper boot installation diagram

section for the Delco caliper, but note the detailed differences in components (Figs. 9.18 and 9.19).
5   When installing the piston push it only halfway down the cylinder bore.

10 Brake disc – inspection and repair

1   The condition of the front brake discs is vital to braking efficiency.
2   The disc should run true with a run-out limit of 0.005 inch. Any distortion can only satisfactorily be checked using a dial gauge. If run-out is greater than that specified, renew the disc.
3   Light scoring is a normal condition, but deep grooves must be removed by either renewing the disc or having it ground professionally. If the latter course is adopted, then the thickness of the disc must not be reduced beyond the figures shown.

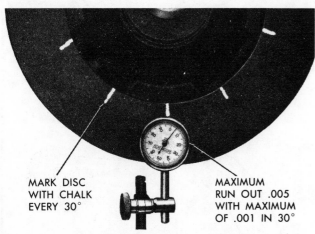

MARK DISC
WITH CHALK
EVERY 30°

MAXIMUM
RUN OUT .005
WITH MAXIMUM
OF .001 IN 30°

Fig. 9.20 Checking brake disc runout

Mark on Disc (minimum wear thickness)	Minimum thickness after refinishing
1.480	1.465
1.230	1.215
0.980	0.965

Make sure that both sides of the ventilated type disc are ground equally.
4   Removal and installation of the combined front hub/disc assembly is described in Chapter 11 together with adjustment of the wheel bearing.
5   Whenever a new disc/hub assembly is installed, remove the protective grease from the disc with a gasoline soaked rag before installing the disc pads.

11 Rear brake drum – inspection and renovation

1   Whenever the brake drums are removed, they should be cleaned and examined for cracks and deep grooves.
2   After high mileages, it is possible for the inside diameter of the drum to wear oval in shape. The degree of ovality can only be satisfactorily measured using an internal type micrometer. The maximum out-of-round is 0.006 inch.
3   Where any of these conditions are found, either renew the drum or have it refinished by a service station. The internal diameter of the drum must not exceed the figures shown after finishing.

Mark on drum (maximum wear diameter)	Maximum internal diameter after refinishing
11.090	11.060
12.090	12.060
13.090	13.060

4   If a new brake drum is being installed, always clean off the protective oil from the inside before installing it.

12 Master cylinder (Delco type) – removal, overhaul and installation

1   Disconnect the brake pipes from the master cylinder and cap the ends of the pipes to prevent entry of dirt.

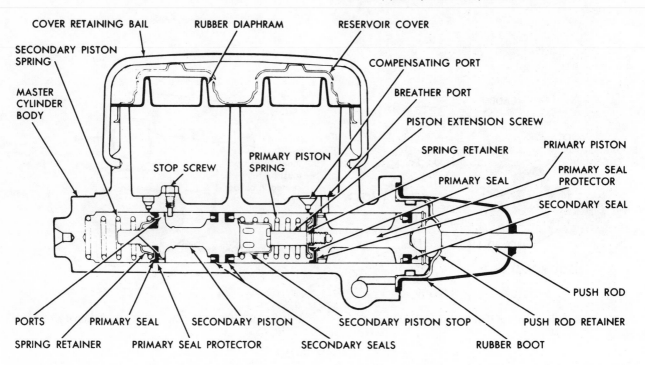

COVER RETAINING BAIL   RUBBER DIAPHRAM   RESERVOIR COVER

SECONDARY PISTON
SPRING

MASTER
CYLINDER
BODY

COMPENSATING PORT

BREATHER PORT

PISTON EXTENSION SCREW

STOP SCREW   PRIMARY PISTON
SPRING

SPRING RETAINER   PRIMARY PISTON

PRIMARY SEAL
PROTECTOR

PRIMARY SEAL

SECONDARY SEAL

PUSH ROD

PORTS   PRIMARY SEAL   SECONDARY PISTON   SECONDARY PISTON STOP   PUSH ROD RETAINER

SPRING RETAINER   PRIMARY SEAL PROTECTOR   SECONDARY SEALS   RUBBER BOOT

Fig. 9.21 Sectional view of Delco type master cylinder

2   *On vehicles without power assistance*, disconnect the brake pedal from the master cylinder pushrod.

3   Unbolt the master cylinder from the engine compartment rear firewall or the power booster, as applicable. As the master cylinder is removed, take care not to drip hydraulic fluid onto the paintwork or it will act as an effective paint stripper!

4   Clean away all external dirt and remove the reservoir cover. Pour out the hydraulic fluid and discard it.

5   Depress the pushrod (manual brakes), or use a rod to depress the primary piston (power brakes), to eject the hydraulic fluid from the master cylinder.

6   *On manual-type master cylinders*, pull the dust excluding boot away to expose the pushrod retainer. Bend up the tab on the retainer to release it (Fig. 9.21).

7   Inspect the bottom of the front fluid reservoir. If a stop bolt is visible, unscrew and remove it.

8   Secure the master cylinder in a vise fitted with jaw protectors and then extract the snap-ring from the end of the cylinder.

9   Extract the primary piston, and the secondary piston and spring. The latter can be ejected by applying air pressure at the front fluid outlet.

10 Examine the surfaces of the cylinder bore and the secondary piston. If there is evidence of scoring or 'bright' wear areas, renew the master cylinder complete.

11 If the components are in good condition, wash in clean hydraulic fluid. Discard all rubber components and the primary piston complete. The repair kit will contain all necessary replacements including a new (completely assembled) primary piston.

12 Install new seals in the grooves of the secondary piston using the fingers only to manipulate them into position. The front seal must have its lip towards the pointed end of the piston and make sure that the seal protector is in position. The seal which has the smallest internal diameter is the front seal.

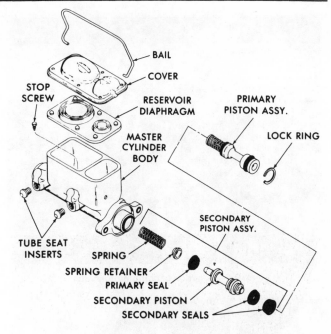

Fig. 9.22 Exploded view of Delco type master cylinder

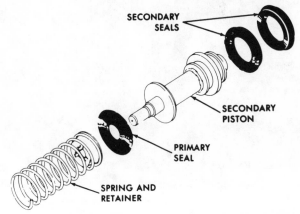

Fig. 9.23 Delco master cylinder secondary piston seal fitting diagram

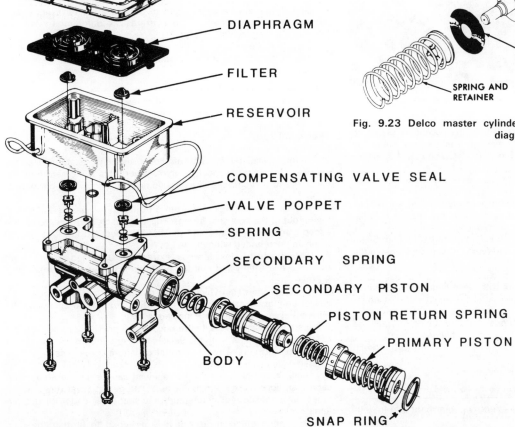

Fig. 9.24 Exploded view of Bendix type master cylinder

Fig. 9.25 Location of combination valve

14.1 Alternative type combination (pressure regulating) valve with bleed nipple

13 The second seal should be installed on the secondary piston so that its lips face the pointed end of the piston. The third seal should be installed in the rear groove of the secondary piston so that its lips face the flat end of the piston.
14 Apply clean hydraulic fluid to the cylinder bores and to the piston assemblies.
15 Install the secondary piston spring over the pointed end of the secondary piston and insert the assembly into the master cylinder bore. Take care not to trap or distort the seal lips.
16 Insert the primary piston and pushrod (complete with retainer) into the master cylinder bore. Exert pressure on the pushrod and install the snap-ring. Fit the stop bolt.
17 Install the rubber boot (manual brakes).
18 Fill the master cylinder reservoirs with clean hydraulic fluid which has been stored in an airtight container and has remained unshaken for at least 24 hours.
19 Depress the primary piston two or three times using the pushrod (manual brakes) or a thin rod until the cylinder is filled with fluid.
20 Install the master cylinder and connect the pushrod to the brake pedal (manual brakes only).
21 Bleed the system as described in Section 16.

13 Master cylinder (Bendix type) – removal, overhaul and installation

1   Remove the master cylinder from the booster unit as described in

the preceding Section (Fig. 9.24).
2   Tip out the fluid from the reservoirs.
3   Unscrew and remove the four bolts which secure the body to the reservoir.
4   Remove the small O-ring and the two compensating valve seals from the recesses on the underside of the reservoir. Do not remove the two small filters unless they are damaged and require renewal.
5   Depress the primary piston with a thin rod, then remove the compensating valve poppets and springs.
6   Extract the snap-ring from the end of the master cylinder and pull out the piston assemblies.
7   Inspect the surfaces of the pistons and cylinder bore for scoring or 'bright' wear areas. If these are evident, renew the master cylinder complete.
8   If the components are in good condition, renew the seals or obtain completely assembled new piston assemblies.
9   Clean all parts in hydraulic fluid or denatured alcohol - nothing else!
10 Install the secondary spring (shorter one) into the open end of the secondary piston actuator then install the piston return spring onto the projection at the rear of the secondary piston.
11 Insert the secondary piston assembly (actuator end first) into the master cylinder and depress it fully.
12 Dip the primary piston into hydraulic fluid and insert this (actuator end first) into the master cylinder.
13 Depress the pistons with a thin rod so that the snap-ring can be installed.
14 Install the compensating valve seals and the O-ring into the reservoir recesses.
15 Hold the pistons depressed and install the compensating valve springs and poppets, then secure the reservoir, tightening the bolts to specified torque.
16 Install the master cylinder to the booster and bleed the system as described in Section 16.

14 Pressure regulating combination valve – testing, removal and installation

1   This device is located adjacent to the brake master cylinder and incorporates the dual hydraulic circuit pressure differential valve and the warning lamp switch (photo).
2   Any fault developing in the assembly can only be rectified by renewal. Bleed the hydraulic system after installing the new component.

15 Hydraulic lines – inspection and renewal

1   Periodically, examine all hydraulic brake lines, both rigid and flexible, for rusting, chafing and general deterioration. Also check the security of the unions.
2   Before disconnecting any of the hoses or pipes, tape over the vents in the master cylinder reservoir cover. This will create a partial vacuum and prevent loss of hydraulic fluid at the point of disconnection.
3   To disconnect a rigid line from a flexible hose, unscrew the connector out of the hose end fittings. These connectors are located at the support brackets. Always hold the flexible hose end fitting quite still using an open-ended wrench.
4   To remove the flexible hose, extract the U-shaped retainer from the hose end fitting and pull the hose from the support bracket (Fig. 9.26.)
5   Unscrew the bolts which secure the end of the flexible hose to a caliper unit, or unscrew the hose end fitting from the connector on the differential carrier as the case may be.
6   Installation is a reversal of removal, but if possible use new copper gaskets in conjunction with the flexible hose end fittings and always let the flexible hose take up its natural curvature; never secure it in a twisted or kinked position.
7   Rigid lines which need to be renewed can be purchased at most service stations. Take the old pipe as a pattern and make sure that the pipes have the correct connectors and that their ends are double-flared.
8   The spring steel shield which is designed to protect the rigid hydraulic lines must be installed after a new length of line has been inserted in the circuit.

16 Hydraulic system – bleeding

1   Whenever the hydraulic system is disconnected (to remove or install a component) air will enter the fluid lines and bleeding must be carried out. This is not a routine operation and if air enters the system without any repair operations having been carried out, then the cause must be sought and the fault rectified.

2   When applying the foot brake pedal, if the first application causes the pedal to go down further than usual but an immediate second or third application (pumping) reduces the pedal travel and improves the braking effect, this is a sure sign that there is air in the system.

3   Use only clean hydraulic fluid (which has remained unshaken for 24 hours and has been stored in an airtight container) for topping-up the master cylinder reservoirs during the following operations. Make sure that the reservoirs are kept topped-up during the whole of the bleeding operations otherwise air will be drawn into the system and the whole sequence of bleeding will have to be repeated.

4   If a vacuum servo booster is installed, depress the brake pedal several times to destroy the vacuum.

5   The brakes should be bled in the following order - right rear, left rear, right front, left front. If only one hydraulic circuit has been 'broken' then this circuit only need be bled but where the master cylinder or pressure differential valve has been removed and installed then obviously the complete system will require bleeding.

6   Push a length of plastic or rubber hose onto the bleeder valve of the first brake which is to be bled.

7   Immerse the open end of the hose in a jar containing sufficient hydraulic fluid to keep the end of the hose well covered.

8   Unscrew the bleeder valve one quarter-turn and have an assistant depress the brake pedal to the full limit of its travel.

9   Gently retighten the bleed valve and have the brake pedal return to its stop with the foot of the assistant completely removed.

10   Again release the bleeder valve and repeat the operation. Air will be seen being expelled from the open end of the hose beneath the fluid in the jar. Carry out the process until no further air bubbles appear and finally tighten the bleeder valve when the pedal is fully depressed.

11   Remove the bleed hose and transfer it to the next brake, but before repeating the bleeding operations, check and top-up the fluid level in the master cylinder reservoir. Use clean fluid, not that which has been bled from the system which must (later) be discarded.

12   Repeat the operations on the remaining brakes in sequence.

13   Finally top-up both the master cylinder reservoirs to within $\frac{1}{4}$ inch of the top.

14   Never allow hydraulic fluid to come in contact with the paintwork of the vehicle as it acts as a paint stripper.

17 Hydro-boost (steering) system – bleeding

1   On vehicles equipped with a brake booster which is operated in conjunction with the power steering system, the bleeding of *the brake hydraulic system* is carried out as described in the preceding Section. *The steering hydraulic booster system* however, should be bled in the following way whenever lack of power assistance indicates the need for it.

2   If the power steering fluid has foamed due to low fluid level, first park the vehicle with the reservoir cap removed until the foam has cleared.

3   Raise the front of the vehicle until the roadwheels are clear.

4   Top up the power steering reservoir with specified fluid. Leave the reservoir cap off.

5   Disconnect the primary lead from the coil negative terminal and then crank the engine on the starter motor (connect separate, temporary jumper leads if necessary) for five second intervals, topping up the power steering reservoir between cranking.

6   When the reservoir will accept no more fluid, reconnect the primary lead and start the engine. Depress the brake pedal several times while turning the steering from stop to stop.

7   Switch off the engine and depress the brake pedal four or five times. Top up the reservoir.

8   Repeat the operations described in paragraphs 6 and 7.

9   Install the reservoir cap and switch off the engine, and lower the vehicle to the ground.

10 **CAUTION - DO NOT CONFUSE THE HYDRO-BOOST CIRCUIT WITH THE BRAKE HYDRAULIC CIRCUITS. DIFFERENT FLUIDS MUST BE USED IN EACH.**

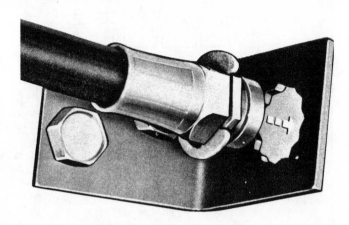

Fig. 9.26 Flexible hose attachment to support bracket

Fig. 9.27 Typical flexible hose connection to caliper

Fig. 9.28 Bleeding a front brake

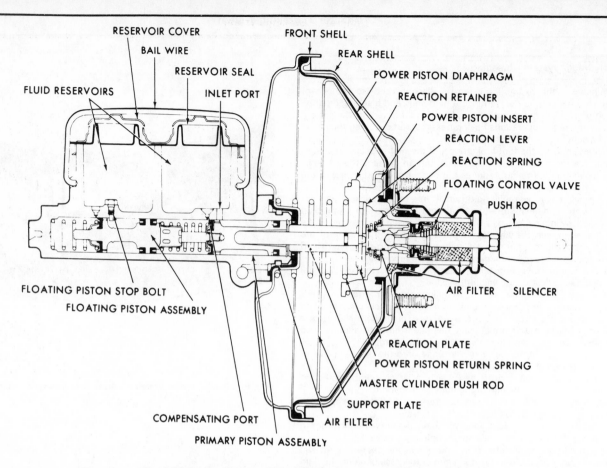

RESERVOIR COVER
BAIL WIRE
RESERVOIR SEAL
INLET PORT
FLUID RESERVOIRS
FRONT SHELL
REAR SHELL
POWER PISTON DIAPHRAGM
REACTION RETAINER
POWER PISTON INSERT
REACTION LEVER
REACTION SPRING
FLOATING CONTROL VALVE
PUSH ROD
AIR FILTER
SILENCER
AIR VALVE
REACTION PLATE
POWER PISTON RETURN SPRING
MASTER CYLINDER PUSH ROD
SUPPORT PLATE
AIR FILTER
FLOATING PISTON STOP BOLT
FLOATING PISTON ASSEMBLY
COMPENSATING PORT
PRIMARY PISTON ASSEMBLY

Fig. 9.29 Sectional view of booster and master cylinder in released mode

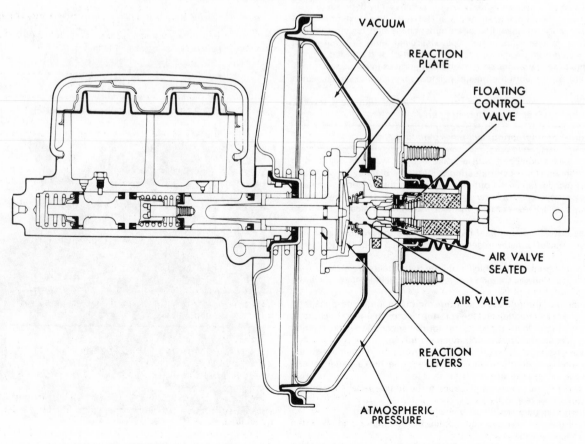

VACUUM
REACTION PLATE
FLOATING CONTROL VALVE
AIR VALVE SEATED
AIR VALVE
REACTION LEVERS
ATMOSPHERIC PRESSURE

Fig. 9.30 Sectional view of booster and master cylinder in brakes applied mode

18 Vacuum booster unit – description and maintenance

1   The vacuum servo unit is installed into the brake hydraulic circuit in series with the master cylinder, to provide assistance to the driver when the brake pedal is depressed. This reduces the effort required by the driver to operate the brakes under all braking conditions.

2   The unit operates by vacuum obtained from the induction manifold and comprises basically a booster diaphragm and non-return valve. The servo unit and hydraulic master cylinder are connected together so that the servo unit piston rod acts as the master cylinder pushrod. The driver's braking effort is transmitted through another pushrod to the servo piston and its built-in control system. The servo unit piston does not fit tightly into the cylinder, but has a strong diaphragm to keep its edges in constant contact with the cylinder wall, so assuring an air tight seal between the two parts. The forward chamber is held under vacuum conditions created in the inlet manifold of the engine and, during periods when the brake pedal is not in use, the controls open a passage to the rear chamber so placing it under vacuum conditions as well. When the brake pedal is depressed, the vacuum passage to the rear chamber is cut off and the chamber opened to atmospheric pressure. The consequent rush of air pushes the servo piston forward in the vacuum chamber and operates the main pushrod to the master cylinder.

3   The controls are designed so that assistance is given under all conditions and, when the brakes are not required, vacuum in the rear chamber is established when the brake pedal is released. All air from the atmosphere entering the rear chamber is passed through a small air filter.

4   Under normal operating conditions the vacuum servo unit is very reliable and does not require overhaul except at very high mileages. In this case it is far better to obtain a service exchange unit , rather than repair the original unit.

5   On some early models, two remotely-sited booster units are installed. These boosters have air intake filters positioned at the end of intake pipes.

6   Periodically inspect the tightness of the mounting bolts; also the condition of the vacuum hose and tightness of the clips.

7   At the intervals specified in Routine Maintenance renew the air filter which is located under the dust excluding boot at the rear of the unit on single-type firewall-mounted boosters, or under the vehicle at the ends of the intake pipes on the dual remotely-sited type. If the filter element is not contaminated with oil or grease, it can be satisfactorily cleaned in soap and water, dried and used again.

19 Vacuum booster unit – removal and installation

1   Provided that the hydraulic pipes connected to the master cylinder have sufficient flexibility, there is no need to disconnect them; the master cylinder can simply be unbolted from the front face of the booster end and pulled gently forward.

2   On some models, the pipes do not have enough flexibility and they will have to be disconnected before the master cylinder can be removed.

3   Disconnect the vacuum hose from the check valve on the front face of the booster.

4   Disconnect the pushrod from the brake pedal by extracting the spring clip and clevis pin.

5   Working inside the vehicle, unscrew and remove the four mounting nuts and lift the unit from the vehicle.

6   Installation is a reversal of removal, but if the hydraulic pipes to the master cylinder were disconnected, remember to bleed the system.

20 Hydro-boost unit – removal and installation

1   With the engine switched off, depress and release the brake pedal several times to discharge all pressure from the accumulator. Unbolt the master cylinder from the booster and pull it gently forward without straining the hydraulic pipes.

2   Disconnect the booster pushrod from the booster bracket pivot lever and disconnect the hydraulic lines from the booster unit. Plug all openings.

3   Remove the booster support braces and then remove the support bracket and the booster itself.

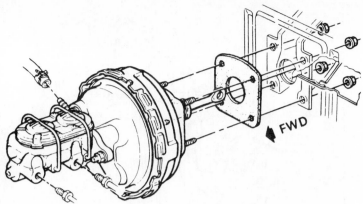

Fig. 9.31 Typical booster/master cylinder mounting

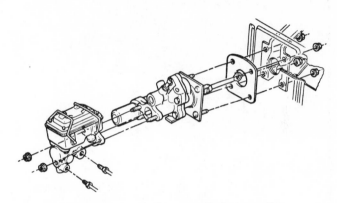

Fig. 9.32 Hydro-boost/master cylinder mounting

4   Installation is a reversal of removal, but bleed the steering hydraulic system as described in Section 17.

21 Parking brake (early models) – adjustment

1   The parking brake on early models (through 1970) is of the hand-lever type and, as with all other models, it is normally self-adjusting. Supplementary adjustment may be required in the event of excessive travel of the hand control occurring due to cable stretch or wear in the linkage and also after fitting new components.

2   To adjust, fully release the control and then pull it on two notches.

3   Jack-up the rear of the vehicle until the roadwheels are clear of the ground.

4   Loosen the locknuts on the cable equaliser and adjust until, when the rear wheels are turned, a slight drag can be felt of the shoes on the drums.

5   Fully release the hand control and check that the rear wheels now turn without any drag.

6   Fully tighten the equaliser locknuts.

22 Parking brake hand control and cables (early models) – removal and installation

1   Fully release the hand control.

2   Disconnect the front cable from the equaliser by removing the locknut at the rear end of the cable.

3   Pull up the control lever until the ball end of the cable can be slipped out of the lever.

4   Unscrew and remove the two screws which attach the lever to the engine compartment wall; also the single nut which secures the lever to the floor.

5   To remove the rear cables, fully release the hand control lever and then remove the equaliser locknut and the front cable connecting clevis so that all tension is removed from the rear cables.

6   Disconnect the rear cable clevis from the equaliser.

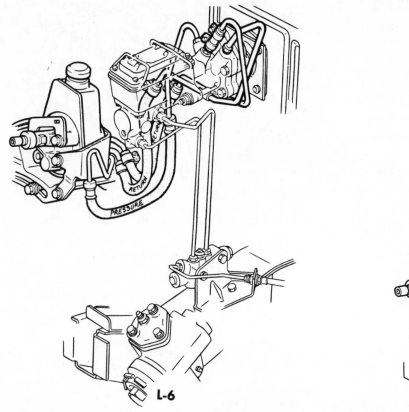
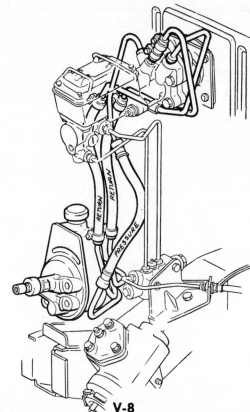

Fig. 9.33 Typical fluid hose routing between power steering pump and hydro-boost unit

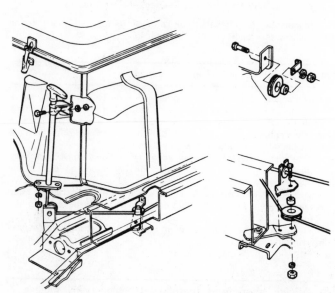

Fig. 9.34 Early model hand control type parking brake

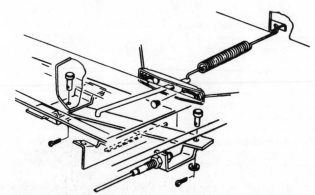

Fig. 9.35 Parking brake equalizer and linkage (early models)

23 Parking brake (later models) – adjustment

1   The parking brake on all later models is of the foot pedal operated type and it is normally self-adjusting through the automatic adjusters in the rear brake drums. However, supplementary adjustment may be needed in the event of cable stretch, wear in the linkage or after installation of new components (photo).

2   Raise the rear of the vehicle until the roadwheels are clear of the ground. Fully release the parking brake pedal by pulling on the release lever.

3   Apply the parking brake carefully over four notches of its ratchet.

4   Loosen the locknut on the cable equaliser and then tighten the adjuster nut until when the rear roadwheels are turned, a slight drag is felt.

5   Fully release the parking brake pedal and check that there is no longer any drag when the roadwheels are turned.

7   Extract the U-shaped retainer from the rear cable bracket on the bodyframe. Pull the cable from the bracket.

8   Remove the rear brake drum and shoes as described in Chapter 9.

9   Disconnect the end of the parking brake cable from the parking brake actuating lever.

10   Compress the fingers which hold the cable conduit into position in the brake backplate and pull out the cable assembly.

11   Installation of all components is a reversal of removal but adjust the cables as described in Section 21.

6   Tighten the equaliser locknut and lower the vehicle to the ground.

24 Parking brake pedal and cables – removal and installation

1   Fully release the brake pedal.
2   Remove the pedal mounting nuts and bolts, and lower the assembly.
3   Slip the ball at the end of the cable out of the clevis on the parking brake pedal.
4   To remove the front cable, remove the adjusting nut from the equaliser and then extract the clip from the rear section of the front cable and from the lever arm. Disconnect the cable.
5   To remove the center cable, again remove the adjusting nut at the equaliser. Unhook the connector at each end of the cable and disengage the hooks and the guides (photo).
6   To remove the rear cable, remove the rear brake drum as described in Chapter 8 then loosen the adjusting nut at the equaliser. Disengage the rear cable at the connector and from the brake shoe operating lever. Compress the conduit fingers and withdraw the cable assembly from the brake backplate.
7   Installation of all components is a reversal of removal but adjust the parking brake on completion, as described in Section 23.

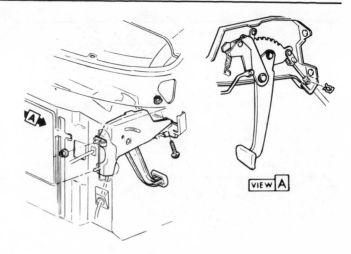

Fig. 9.36 Foot-operated parking brake

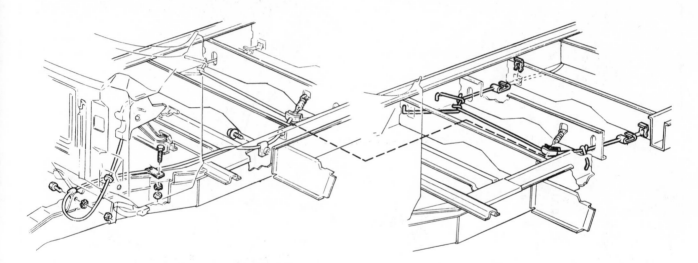

Fig. 9.37 Foot-operated parking brake cable routing

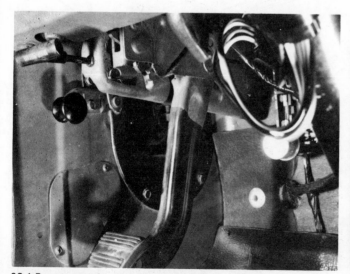

23.1 Foot-operated type parking brake and release lever

24.5 Parking brake equalizer and cable

25 Brake pedal – removal and installation

1   On later vehicles with manual transmission, the clutch and brake pedals operate on a common pivot shaft and reference should be made to Chapter 5.

2   On vehicles equipped with automatic transmission the brake pedal is removable after unscrewing the nut on the end of the pivot bolt and disconnecting the pushrod.

3   The brake pedal pushrod should not normally require adjustment but where new components have been installed, check that there is the slightest ($\frac{1}{16}$ in) amount of free movement at the pedal before normal pedal pressure is applied. If necessary, release the locknut and turn the pushrod to alter its effective length.

4   On early models, the brake pedal connects with linkage which is located below the floor pan.

26 Stop lamp switch – adjustment

1   The brake stop lamp switch is mounted on the brake pedal support bracket.

2   The position of the switch should be adjusted by screwing it in or out so that the stop lamps are actuated (ignition On) after the pedal has been depressed $\frac{1}{2}$ inch.

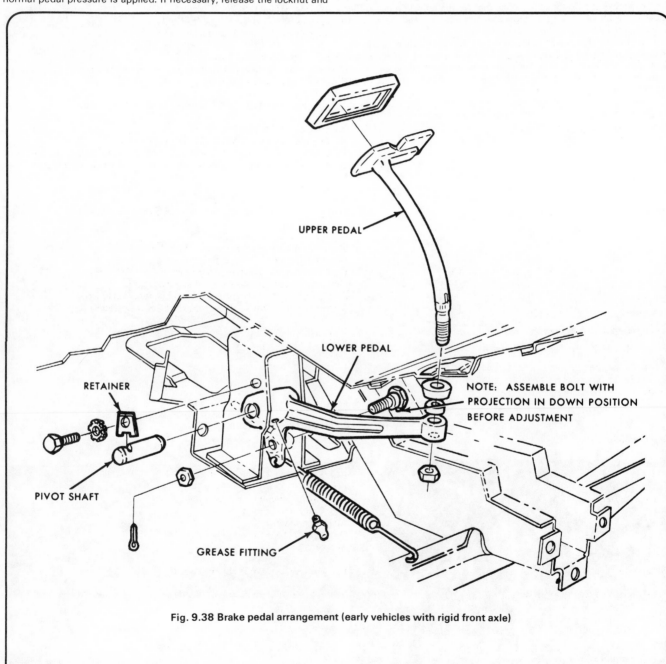

Fig. 9.38 Brake pedal arrangement (early vehicles with rigid front axle)

27 Fault diagnosis – braking system

Symptom	Reason/s
Pedal travels almost to floor before brakes operate	Brake fluid level too low Caliper or wheel cylinder leaking Master cylinder leaking (bubbles in master cylinder fluid) Brake flexible hose leaking Brake line fractured Brake system unions loose Rear automatic adjusters seized
Brake pedal feels springy	New linings not yet bedded in Brake discs or drums badly worn or cracked Master cylinder securing nuts loose
Brake pedal feels spongy and soggy	Caliper or wheel cylinder leaking Master cylinder leaking (bubbles in master cylinder reservoir) Brake pipe or flexible hose leaking Union in brake system loose Air in hydraulic system
Excessive effort required to brake vehicle	Pad or shoe linings badly worn New pads or shoes recently fitted - not yet bedded in Harder linings fitted than standard causing increase in pedal pressure Linings and brake drums contaminated with oil, grease or hydraulic fluid Servo unit inoperative or faulty
Brakes uneven and pulling to one side	Linings and discs ordrums contaminated with oil, grease or hydraulic fluid Tire pressures unequal Radial ply tire installed at one end of the vehicle only Brake caliper loose Brake pads or shoes installed incorrectly Different types of linings installed at each wheel Anchorages for front suspension or rear suspension loose Brake discs or drums badly worn, cracked or distorted
Brakes tend to bind, drag or lock-on	Air in hydraulic system Wheel cylinders seized Parking cables too tight

Particular to Hydro-boost systems

Symptom	Reason/s
Excessive effort required to brake vehicle	Slack or broken power steering pump drivebelt Low fluid level in power steering pump Hydraulic lines leaking or routed incorrectly
Slow pedal return	Internal fault
Brakes grab	Internal fault Dirty power steering fluid
Brake pedal vibrates	Slipping power steering pump belt Low fluid level in pump Air in steering fluid Dirty power steering fluid Internal fault
Pump noisy on application of brakes	Low fluid level in power steering pump
Pedal depresses on starting engine	Restriction in hydraulic lines to booster

Chapter 10 Electrical system

Refer to Chapter 13 for specifications and information applicable to 1979 through 1985 models

Contents

Specifications

System type . . . . 12V negative ground, with alternator, battery and pre-engaged starter motor

Battery
Type . . . . Lead acid
Capacity (minutes with 25 amp reserve) . . . . Between 60 and 80, depending on engine size

Generator
Type . . . . Delcotron alternator
Field current (at 12V and 80°F/27°C) . . . . 4 to 4·5 amps
Cold output (@ 5000 rpm) . . . . Between 33 and 76 amps, depending on engine size

Starter motor
Voltage 9
Free-running current . . . . Between 50 to 95 amps, depending upon starter model
Speed . . . . Between 5500 and 10 500 rpm, depending upon starter model

Fuses *(typical – see individual fuse block)*

Circuit protected	Fuse rating (amps)
Heater, air conditioning	25
Idle stop solenoid, Cruise master, turn signal	10
Cigar lighter, interior lamp, spot lamp	15
Fuel gauge, brake warning, temperature warning, generator warning, oil pressure warning lamps	3
Stop lamp, hazard lamps	15
Back-up lamp, radio	15
Instrument cluster, heater dial lamp, windshield wiper, switch lamps	3
Rear license plate, parking, side marker, tail lamps	15
Windshield wiper motor	25

Circuit breakers
Headlamp, parking lamp circuit 15

Fusible links
Circuits protected .... Ignition
Horn
Headlamp hi-beam indicator

Bulbs

Lamp	Bulb number	Power (CP)
Interior	211 – 2	12
Instrument and warning	168	3
Parking and turn signal	1157	3 – 32
Tail/stop	1157	3 – 32
Rear license plate	67	4 CP
Headlamp	6014	60/50W
Back-up lamp	1156	32
Radio dial	1893	2
Heater control or air conditioning	1895	2
Transmission control with tilt steering wheel	1445	0·7
Cruise control	53	1
Windshield wiper switch	161	1

Windshield wiper
Type .... Two-speed
Crank arm speed (no load)
   Low .... 35 rpm
   High .... 60 rpm
Current draw .... 5·5 amps (max)

Windshield washer
Pressure .... 11 to 15 lbf/in^2
Coil resistance .... 20 ohms

Cruise master
Solenoid resistance .... 5 ohms
Solenoid wire resistance .... 40 ohms
Operational test speed .... 60 mph

1 General description

1 The electrical system is a 12 volt negative ground type.
2 Power for the ignition system, the lighting equipment and all the electrical accessories is supplied by a lead/acid battery which is charged by a belt-driven alternator.
3 The starter motor is a pre-engaged type.
4 The standard of electrical specification varies with the vehicle model and all vehicles will not therefore be equipped with all the items described in this Chapter.
5 Although repair procedures and methods are described in this Chapter, in view of the long life of the major electrical components, it is recommended that when a fault does develop, consideration should be given to exchanging the unit for a factory reconditioned assembly rather than renew individual components of a well worn unit.

2 Battery – removal and installation

1 The battery is located within the engine compartment and is accessible after raising the hood.
2 To remove the battery, first disconnect the negative cable from the battery terminal followed by the positive one.
3 Release the battery hold-down clamp and bolt, and lift the battery from its tray, taking care not to spill electrolyte on the vehicle paintwork.
4 Installation is a reversal of removal. Make sure that the positive lead is connected first, followed by the negative one.

3 Battery – maintenance

1 Carry out the regular weekly maintenance described in the Routine Maintenance Section at the front of this manual. This includes topping-up the cells if necessary with distilled water, and checking the security of the battery terminals. Never inspect the electrolyte level with a naked flame, or smoke while doing it; an explosion could result. Many different types of filler devices are used on batteries including some with flame arrestors. Consult your driver's manual for the precise method of topping-up.
2 Clean the top of the battery, removing all dirt and moisture.
3 As well as keeping the terminals clean and covered with petroleum jelly, the top of the battery, and especially the top of the cells, should be kept clean and dry. This helps prevent corrosion and ensures that the battery does not become partially discharged by leakage through dampness and dirt.
4 Once every three months, remove the battery and inspect the battery securing bolts, the battery clamp plate, tray and battery leads for corrosion (white fluffy deposits on the metal which are brittle to touch). If any corrosion is found, clean off the deposits with ammonia and paint over the clean metal with an anti-rust/anti-acid paint.
5 At the same time inspect the battery case for cracks. If a crack is found, clean and plug it with one of the proprietary compounds marketed for this purpose. If leakage through the crack has been excessive then it will be necessary to refill the appropriate cell with fresh electrolyte. Cracks can be caused to the top of the battery case by pouring in water in the middle of winter *after* instead of *before* a run. This gives the water no chance to mix with the electrolyte and so the former freezes and splits the battery case.
6 If topping-up the battery becomes excessive and the case has been inspected for cracks that could cause leakage, but none are found, the battery is being over-charged and the alternator will have to be tested and if necessary the regulator renewed.
7 If a battery fails to hold its charge or is in a discharged state for no obvious reason (low mileage, defective alternator), it is normal practice to take it for testing to your dealer and to accept his advice with regard to a new battery. However, where a hydrometer is available, the test can be carried out by the home mechanic.
   First measure its specific gravity with the hydrometer to determine the state of charge and condition of the electrolyte. There should be very little variation between the different cells and if a variation in

excess of 0·025 is present it will be due to either:

     a) *Loss of electrolyte from the battery at some time caused by spillage or a leak, resulting in a drop in the specific gravity of the electrolyte when the deficiency was replaced with distilled water instead of fresh electrolyte.*

     b) *An internal short circuit caused by buckling of the plates or a similar malady pointing to the likelihood of total battery failure in the near future.*

8   The specific gravity of the electrolyte at the temperature of 80°F (26·7°C) will be approximately 1·270 for a fully charged battery. For every 10°F (5·5°C) that the electrolyte temperature is above that stated, add 0·004 to the specific gravity or subtract 0·004 if the temperature is below that stated.

9   A specific gravity reading of 1·240 with an electrolyte temperature of 80°F (26·7°C) indicates a half-charged battery.

4 Battery – electrolyte replenishment

1   Where tests by a hydrometer or a voltmeter indicate that electrolyte has been lost from a cell at some time, the deficiency should be made good by your service station. The mixing and handling of sulphuric acid is dangerous and such work should be left to battery specialists.

2   Remember the need for the addition of acid to a battery at any time after its initial filling is very rare. Acid does not evaporate, only the water content of the electrolyte does.

5 Battery – charging

1   In winter time when heavy demand is placed upon the battery, such as when starting from cold, and much electrical equipment is continually in use, it is a good idea to occasionally have the battery fully charged from an external source at the rate of 3·5 to 4 amps.

2   Continue to charge the battery at this rate until no further rise in specific gravity is noted over a four hour period.

3   Alternatively, a trickle charger charging at the rate of 1·5 amps can be safely used overnight.

4   Specially rapid 'boost' charges which are claimed to restore the power of the battery in 1 to 2 hours are most dangerous as they can cause serious damage to the battery plates.

6 Alternator – maintenance and special precautions

1   All models are fitted with a Delcotron type alternator, the output of which varies according to vehicle type and engine capacity. Alternators used through 1972 have an externally mounted voltage regulator while later versions have an integral regulator (Fig. 10.1).

2   Maintenance consists of occasionally wiping away any dirt or oil which may have collected on the unit.

3   Check the tension of the driving belt at the intervals specified in Routine Maintenance adjusting if necessary as described in Chapter 2, Section 9.

4   No lubrication is required as the bearings are grease-sealed for the life of the unit.

5   Take extreme care when making circuit connections to a vehicle fitted with an alternator and observe the following. When making connections to the alternator from a battery always match correct polarity. Before using electric-arc welding equipment to repair any part of the vehicle, disconnect the connector from the alternator and disconnect the positive battery terminal. Never start the car with a battery charger connected. Always disconnect both battery leads before using a mains charger. If boosting from another battery, always connect in parallel using heavy cable. It is not recommended that testing of an alternator should be undertaken at home due to the testing equipment required and the possibility of damage occurring during testing. It is best left to automotive electrical specialists.

    Before having the alternator tested, check that the cause of low battery charge is not due to a slipping drive belt, a defective battery, loose connections or too low a mileage to charge the battery effectively.

7 Alternator – removal and installation

1   Disconnect both leads from the battery terminals.

2   Disconnect the leads from the rear face of the alternator, marking them first to ensure correct installation.

3   Loosen the alternator mounting and adjuster link bolts, push the unit in toward the engine as far as possible, and slip off the drivebelt.

4   Installation is a reversal of removal; adjust the drivebelt tension as described in Chapter 2, Section 9. **Note:** *New alternators are not usually supplied with pulleys. The old one should therefore be removed if a new unit is to be purchased. To do this, hold the alternator shaft still with an Allen wrench while the pulley nut is unscrewed.*

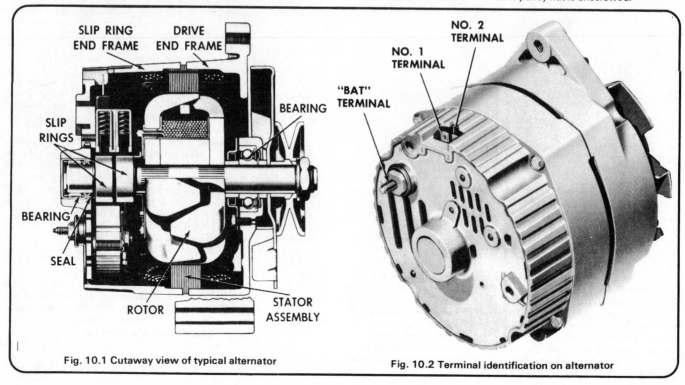

Fig. 10.1 Cutaway view of typical alternator

Fig. 10.2 Terminal identification on alternator

OHMMETER
(CHECK FOR SHORTS AND OPENS)

Fig. 10.3 Checking alternator rotor field windings

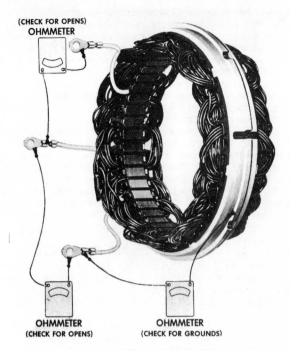

Fig. 10.4 Checking alternator stator

8   Alternator – overhaul

1   Remove the alternator and pulley as described in the preceding Section.

2   Secure the alternator in the jaws of a vise, applying the pressure to the mounting flange.

3   Remove the four through-bolts, and separate the slip-ring, end frame and stator assembly from the drive-end and rotor assembly. Use a screwdriver to lever them apart and mark the relative position of the end frames to facilitate reassembly.

4   Remove the stator lead securing nuts and separate the stator from the end frame. At this stage, the following checks may be carried out without the need for further dismantling.

5   *To check the rotor field windings:* connect a 110 volt test lamp or an ohmmeter (1 to $1\frac{1}{2}$ volt test cell) between the slip rings. If the lamp fails to light or the ohmmeter readings are high (on the lowest range) then there is an open-circuit in the windings (Fig. 10.3).

6   Now check the windings for short-circuits by connecting a 12 volt battery and an ammeter in series with the two slip rings. If the ammeter indicates a reading above 4 to 4·5 amps, then the windings are shorted.

7   *To check the stator:* connect a 110 volt test lamp or an ohmmeter between any one of the stator leads and the stator frame. If the test lamp lights, or if the ohmmeter reading is low, the windings are grounded. If the lamp fails to light or the ohmmeter has a high reading when connected between each pair of stator leads in succession, then the windings are open. Short-circuits in the stator windings are difficult to detect without special equipment but if there are signs on them of discoloration by heat, this is a good indication of such faults (Fig. 10.4).

8   *To check the diode trio for a grounded brush lead:* connect an ohmmeter between the brush lead clip and the end-frame. Note the reading and then reverse the ohmmeter connections and again note the reading. If they are both zero, the brush lead clip is probably grounded due to a missing insulating washer or sleeve. Where this is not the fault, renew the regulator (Fig. 10.5).

9   *To check the condition of the diode trio:* remove the screw which secures it to the brush holder assembly and withdraw the diode trio from the end-frame. Connect an ohmmeter between the larger, single connector and one of the three smaller connectors. Note the reading and then reverse the ohmmeter leads between the two connectors. If the diode trio is in good condition, one high and one low reading will have been indicated during the tests. If both readings are almost the same, renew the diode trio. Repeat the test between the single connector and each of the remaining smaller connectors in succession (Fig. 10.6).

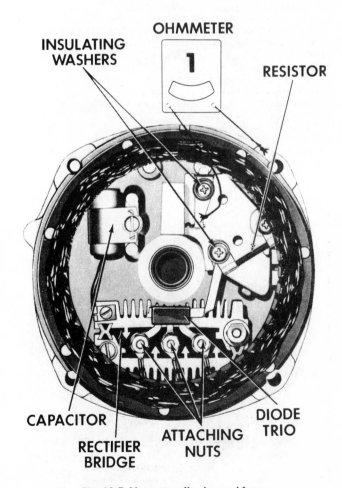

INSULATING WASHERS   **OHMMETER**   **RESISTOR**

CAPACITOR   **RECTIFIER BRIDGE**   **ATTACHING NUTS**   **DIODE TRIO**

Fig. 10.5 Alternator slip-ring end frame

10 *To check the rectifier bridge:* connect an ohmmeter between the grounded heat sink and one of its three terminals. Now reverse the ohmmeter connections and if the two readings are the same, renew the rectifier bridge. Take two readings in a similar way between the heat sink and the remaining terminals in succession. A rectifier bridge in good condition will show three high and three low readings when the tests just described are carried out.

11 Continue dismantling, by removing the rectifier bridge securing screw and the BAT terminal screw. Disconnect the capacitor lead and remove the rectifer bridge from the end-frame.

12 Unscrew the two securing screws and remove the brush holder and regulator. Carefully retain the insulating sleeves and washers.

13 Remove the capacitor (one screw) from the end-frame.

14 If the slip ring end-frame bearing is dry or noisy when rotated, it must be renewed (not greased). Greasing will not extend its service life. Press out the old bearing and discard the oil seal. Press in the new bearing, squarely, until the bearing is flush with the outside of the end-frame. Install a new oil seal. During these operations, support the end-frame adequately to prevent cracking or distorting the frame.

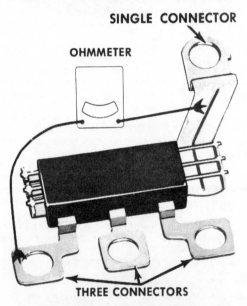

SINGLE CONNECTOR

OHMMETER

THREE CONNECTORS

Fig. 10.6 Checking alternator diode trio

15 Now insert a $\frac{5}{16}$ inch Allen wrench into the socket in the centre of the shaft at the drive pulley end. Using this to prevent the shaft from rotating, unscrew the pulley retaining nut and remove the washer, pulley, fan and the spacer.

16 Remove the rotor and spacers from the drive end-frame.

17 If the bearing in the drive end-frame is dry or noisy it must be renewed. Do not grease it in the hope that this will extend its life. Access to the bearing is obtained after removing the retainer plate bolts and separating the plate/seal assembly. Press the bearing out using a piece of tube applied to the inner race and press the new one in by applying the tube to the outer race. Make sure that the slinger is correctly located and recommended grease is applied to the bearing before installation.

18 With the alternator completely dismantled, wipe all components clean (do not use solvent on the stator or rotor windings), and examine for wear or damage. Renew the components as necessary.

19 If the slip rings are dirty they should be cleaned by spinning the rotor and holding a piece of 400 grain (maximum coarseness) abrasive paper against them. This method will avoid the creation of flat spots on the rings. If the rings are badly scored, out-of-round or otherwise damaged, the complete rotor assembly must be renewed.

20 Check the brushes for wear. If they are worn halfway or more in length, renew them. Renew the springs only if they appear weak or are distorted.

21 Reassembly is a reversal of dismantling but observe the following points:

   a) *Tighten the pulley nut to a torque of between 40 and 50 lbf ft. Take great care to position the insulating washers and sleeves correctly on the brush clip screws.*
   b) *Clean the brush contact surfaces before installing the slip ring end-frame and hold the brushes up in their holders by passing a thin rod through the opening in the slip ring end-frame to permit the brushes to pass over the slip rings.*
   c) *Finally make sure that the marks on the slip ring and drive end-frame (which were made before dismantling) are in alignment.*

---

9 Voltage regulator (through 1972) – removal and installation

1 The voltage regulator is normally very reliable but any indication of battery overcharging or lack of charge which could be attributable to the regulator should be checked out by your dealer.

2 Three adjustments are possible, two mechanical (points opening and airgap), and voltage adjustment. In view of the precise nature of the work and the need for special equipment, it is recommended that the work is carried out by your dealer with the regulator still in position in the vehicle.

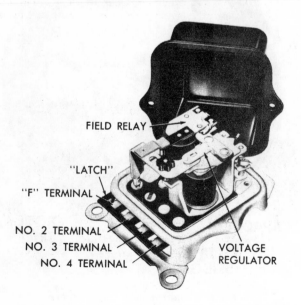

FIELD RELAY

"LATCH"

"F" TERMINAL

NO. 2 TERMINAL
NO. 3 TERMINAL
NO. 4 TERMINAL

VOLTAGE REGULATOR

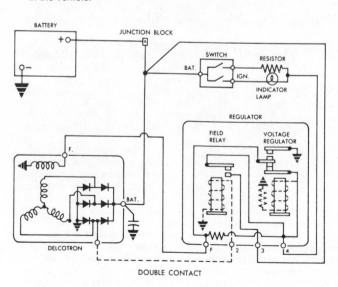

Fig. 10.7 Voltage regulator and circuit

3   If the unit is diagnosed faulty and incapable of adjustment, it should be exchanged for a new unit which will have been pre-set in production.
4   To remove the voltage regulator, simply disconnect the battery, disconnect the wiring from the regulator and extract the mounting screws.
5   Installation is a reversal of removal.

10 Starter motor – general description

The starter motor incorporates a solenoid mounted on top of the starter motor body. When the ignition switch is operated, the solenoid moves the starter drive pinion, through the medium of the shift lever, into engagement with the flywheel starter ring gear. As the solenoid reaches the end of its stroke and with the pinion by now fully engaged with the flywheel ring gear, the fixed and moving contacts close and energize the starter motor to rotate the engine.

11 Starter motor – testing in vehicle

1   If the starter motor does not rotate at all when the switch is operated, check that the speed selector lever is in N or P (automatic transmission) and that the front seat belts are connected (starter interlock system) and also that the clutch pedal is depressed (manual transmission).
2   Check that the battery is well charged and all cables, both at the battery and starter solenoid terminals, are secure.
3   If the motor can be heard spinning but the engine is not being cranked, then the over-running clutch in the starter motor is slipping and the assembly must be removed from the engine and dismantled.
4   If when the switch is actuated, the starter motor does not operate at all but the solenoid plunger can be heard to move with a loud 'click' then the fault lies in the main solenoid contacts or the starter motor itself.
5   If the solenoid plunger cannot be heard to move when the switch is actuated then the solenoid itself is defective or the solenoid circuit is open.
6   To check out the solenoid, connect a jumper lead between the battery positive terminal and the terminal on the solenoid to which the purple cable is attached. If the starter motor now operates, the solenoid is OK and the fault must lie in the ignition or neutral start switches, or in their interconnecting wiring.
7   If the starter motor still does not operate, remove the starter/solenoid assembly for dismantling, testing and repair.
8   If the starter motor cranks the engine at an abnormally slow speed, first ensure that the battery is fully charged and all terminal connections are tight; also that the engine oil is not too thick a grade and that the resistance is not due to a mechanical fault within the power unit.
9   Run the engine until normal operating temperature is attained, disconnect the coil-to-distributor LT wire so that the engine will not fire during cranking.
10 Connect a voltmeter positive lead to the starter motor terminal of the solenoid and then connect the negative lead to ground.
11 Actuate the ignition switch and take the voltmeter reading as soon as a steady figure is indicated. Do not allow the starter motor to turn for more than 30 seconds at a time. A reading of 9 volts, or more, with the starter motor turning at normal cranking speed proves it to be in good condition. If the reading is 9 volts, or more, but the cranking speed is slow, then the motor is faulty. If the reading is less than 9 volts and the cranking speed is slow, the solenoid contacts are probably at fault and should be renewed.

12 Starter motor – removal and installation

1   Disconnect the ground cable from the battery.
2   Disconnect all the leads from the solenoid terminals. Temporarily install the terminal nuts to their respective terminals as they are of differing threads and if mixed up may damage the threads of the terminal posts when an attempt is made to screw them on.
3   Loosen the starter motor front bracket and then remove the two mounting bolts.
4   Remove the front bracket bolt, then rotate the bracket so that the

starter motor can be withdrawn by lowering its front end.
5   Installation is a reversal of removal but tighten the mounting bolts first to the specified torque, then tighten the front bracket bolt and nut.

13 Starter motor – dismantling and component testing

1   Disconnect the starter motor field coil connectors from the solenoid terminals.
2   Unscrew and remove the through bolts.
3   Remove the commutator end-frame, field frame assembly and the armature from the drive housing.
4   Slide the two-section thrust collar off the end of the armature shaft and then using a piece of suitable tube drive the stop/retainer up the armature shaft to expose the snap-ring.
5   Extract the snap-ring from its shaft groove and then slide the stop/retainer and over-running clutch assembly from the armature shaft.
6   Dismantle the brush components from the field frame.
7   Release the V-shaped springs from the brush holder supports.
8   Remove the brush holder support pin and then lift the complete brush assembly upwards.
9   Disconnect the leads from the brushes if they are worn down to half their original length and they are to be renewed.
10 The starter motor is now completely dismantled except for the field coils. If these are found to be defective during the tests described later in this Section removal of the pole shoe screws is best left to a service station having the necessary pressure driver.
11 Clean all components and renew any obviously worn components. **On no account attempt to undercut the insulation between the commutator segments on starter motors having the molded type commutators.** On commutators of conventional type, the insulation should be undercut (below the level of the segments) by $\frac{1}{32}$ inch. Use an old hacksaw blade to do this and make sure that the undercut is the full width of the insulation and the groove is quite square at the bottom. When the undercutting is completed, brush away all dirt and dust.

Clean the commutator by spinning it while a piece of number '00' sandpaper is wrapped round it. On no account use any other type of abrasive material for this work.

If necessary, because the commutator is in such bad shape, it may be turned down in a lathe to provide a new surface. Make sure to undercut the insulation when the turning is completed.
12 *To test the armature for ground:* use a lamp-type circuit tester. Place one lead on the armature core or shaft and the other on a segment of the commutator. If the lamp lights then the armature is grounded and must be renewed (Fig. 10.8).
13 *To test the field coils for open circuit:* place one test probe on the insulated brush and the other on the field connector bar. If the lamp

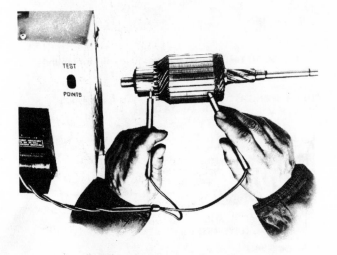

Fig. 10.8 Checking starter motor armature for ground

Fig. 10.9 Testing starter motor field coils for open-circuit

Fig. 10.10 Testing starter motor field coils for ground

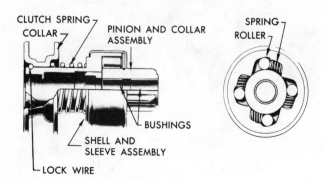

Fig. 10.11 Starter motor over-running clutch

does not light, the coils are open and must be renewed (Fig. 10.9).
14 *To test the field coils for ground:* place one test probe on the connector bar and the other on the grounded brush. If the lamp lights then the field coils are grounded (Fig. 10.10).
15 The over-running clutch cannot be repaired and if faulty, it must be renewed as a complete assembly.

14 Starter motor – reassembly and adjustment

1   Install the brush assembly to the field frame as follows:
2   Install the brushes to their holders.
3   Assemble the insulated and grounded brush holders together with the V-spring and then locate the unit on its support pin.
4   Push the holders and spring to the bottom of the support and then rotate the spring to engage the V in the support slot.
5   Connect the ground wire to the grounded brush and the field lead wire to the insulated brush.
6   Repeat the operations for the second set of brushes.
7   Smear silicone oil onto the drive end of the armature shaft and then slide the clutch assembly (pinion to the front) onto the shaft.
8   Slide the pinion stop/retainer onto the shaft so that its open end is facing away from the pinion.
9   Stand the armature vertically on a piece of wood and then position the snap-ring on the end of the shaft. Using a hammer and a piece of hardwood, drive the snap-ring onto the shaft (Fig. 10.12).
10 Slide the snap-ring down the shaft until it drops into its groove.
11 Install the thrust collar on the shaft so that the shoulder is next to the snap-ring. Using two pairs of pliers, squeeze the thrust collar and stop/retainer together until the snap-ring fully enters the retainer.
12 Lubricate the drive housing bush with silicone oil and after ensuring that the thrust collar is in position against the snap-ring, slide the armature and clutch assembly into the drive housing so that at the same time, the shift lever engages with the clutch.
13 Position the field frame over the armature and apply sealing compound between the frame and the solenoid case.
14 Position the field frame against the drive housing taking care not to damage the brushes.
15 Lubricate the bush in the commutator end-frame using silicone oil; place the leather brake washer on the armature shaft and then slide the commutator end-frame onto the shaft.
16 Reconnect the field coil connectors to the MOTOR terminal of the solenoid.
17 Now check the pinion clearance. To do this, connect a 6 volt battery between the solenoid S terminal and ground and at the same time fix a heavy connecting cable between the MOTOR terminal and ground (to prevent any possibility of the starter motor rotating). As the solenoid is energized it will push the pinion forward into its normal cranking position and retain it there. With the fingers, push the pinion away from the stop/retainer in order to eliminate any slack and then check the clearance between the face of the pinion and the face of the stop/retainer using a feeler gauge. The clearance should be between 0·010 and 0·140 inch to ensure correct engagement of the pinion with the flywheel (or driveplate - automatic transmission) ring-gear. If the clearance is incorrect, the starter will have to be dismantled again and any worn or distorted components renewed, no adjustment being provided for (Figs. 10.14 and 10.15).

15 Starter motor solenoid – removal, repair and installation

1   Disconnect the connector strap from the solenoid MOTOR terminal.
2   Remove the two screws which secure the solenoid housing to the end-frame assembly.
3   Twist the solenoid in a clockwise direction to disengage the flange key and then withdraw the solenoid.
4   Remove the nuts and washers from the solenoid terminals and then unscrew the two solenoid end-cover retaining screws and washers and pull off the end-cover.
5   Unscrew the nut and washer from the battery terminal on the end-cover and remove the terminal.
6   Remove the resistor bypass terminal and contactor.
7   Remove the motor connector strap terminal and solder a new terminal in position.
8   Use a new battery terminal and install it to the end-cover. Install

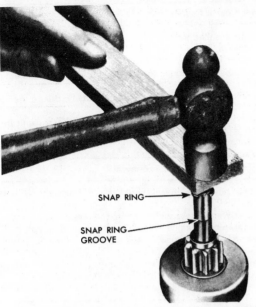

Fig. 10.12 Forcing starter motor shaft snap-ring into position

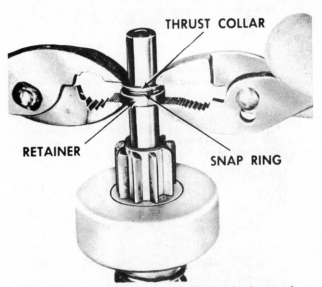

Fig. 10.13 Forcing starter motor shaft snap-ring into retainer

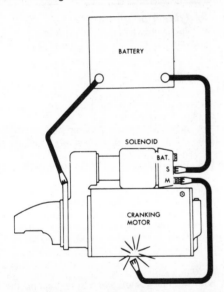

Fig. 10.14 Starter motor pinion clearance checking diagram

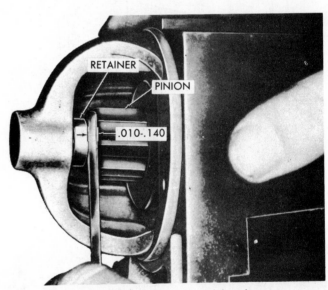

Fig. 10.15 Checking starter motor pinion clearance

the bypass terminal and contactor.

9   Install the end-cover and the remaining terminal nuts.

10 Install the solenoid to the starter motor by first checking that the return spring is in position on the plunger and then insert the solenoid body into the drive housing and turn the body counterclockwise to engage the flange key.

11 Install the two solenoid securing screws and connect the MOTOR connector strap.

16 Circuit breakers, fuses and fusible links

1   The electrical circuits are protected by a combination of fuses, circuit breakers and fusible thermal links.

2   The headlamps are protected by a circuit breaker incorporated in the light switch. An overload will cause the lamps to go on and off intermittently. Should this happen, have all circuits checked immediately.

3   The fuses are grouped together in a block just beneath the dash on the driver's side, and this block also incorporates the direction indicator flasher unit on most models.

4   The fuse arrangement differs slightly according to vehicle model

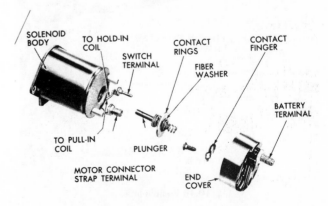

Fig. 10.16 Exploded view of starter motor solenoid

and date of production but the circuits protected are plainly marked at each fuse.

5   The fuse elements are visible through their glass capsules and if they have 'blown' this can be easily checked. Replace a fuse with one of the same rating and if it melts for the second time immediately, check out the cause (usually a short-circuit in the wiring), before renewing it again.

6   Fusible links are incorporated in certain sections of the wiring harness. These links are color-coded and are of smaller gage wire than the circuit wire which it protects although, due to the insulation used to protect the link, it may appear to be of heavier gauge than the circuit wire.

7   Links are normally used in the harness to the starter solenoid BAT terminal, the alternator warning lamp and field circuit and the headlamp hi-beam indicator circuits.

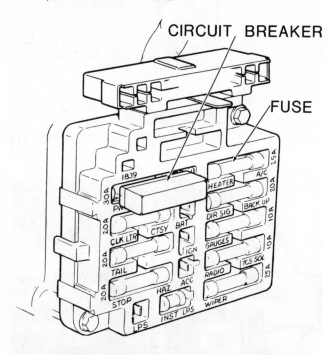

Fig. 10.17 Typical fuse block and circuit breaker

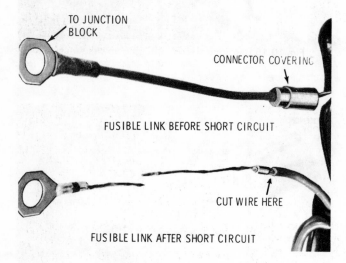

Fig. 10.18 Fusible link

17 Direction indicator flasher unit

1   The flasher unit is plugged into the fuse block or, on some models, located adjacent to it.

2   If the direction indicators cease to work or operate very rapidly, first check the bulbs in the indicator lamps and then the connecting wiring (photo).

3   Complete failure of the lamps in the circuit may be due to the fuse having 'blown'.

4   If everything else seems to be in order, pull the flasher unit from the fuse block and install a new one.

18 Headlamp sealed beam unit – renewal

1   Unscrew the headlamp bezel screws and remove the bezel (photo).

2   Remove the (lower) screws which secure the retaining ring. Do not disturb the headlamp beam adjustment (upper) screws (photos).

3   Pull the sealed beam unit forward and disconnect the plug from its rear (photo).

4   Installation is a reversal of removal, but make sure that the number molded into the face of the lens is at the top.

19 Bulbs – renewal

Front parking and direction indicator lamp

1   Extract the retaining screws and remove the lens.

2   Remove the defective bulb, then install the new one followed by the lamp lens.

Front side marker lamp

3   If the left lamp is being worked on, the hood will first have to be raised and then the bulb holder twisted 90° counterclockwise and removed from the rear of the lamp (photo).

4   Access to the bulb holder on the right lamp is obtainable only after first extracting the lamp retaining screws and pulling the lamp assembly outward (photo).

5   Renew the bulb, then reverse the removal operations.

Rear side marker lamp

6   The bulb can be renewed after extracting the lamp securing screws as described for the right front marker lamp.

7   Where the vehicle is not equipped with any interior trim, then the bulb holder can be twisted from the lamp body as described for the left front marker lamp (photo).

Rear lamp cluster

8   Access to both the bulbs is obtained by extracting the four lens screws (photo).

9   The bulbs for the tail, stop, back-up or direction signal facility can then be renewed as necessary (photo).

Rear license plate lamp

10   Unscrew the two screws which hold the lamp assembly to the license plate frame. Remove the lens and renew the bulb.

Instrument panel bulbs

11   The indicator and illumination bulbs can be renewed by reaching up under the instrument panel and turning the bulb holder counterclockwise (photo).

12   Pull the bulb straight out of the holder, insert the new bulb, and press it well in to lock it in position.

13   Install the holder to the instrument panel making sure that its lugs engage in the notches and then turn the holder clockwise to lock it in position.

20 Headlamp beams – adjustment

1   It is recommended that the headlamp beams are adjusted by your dealer using special equipment.

2   In an emergency, the position of the adjustment screws should be

17.1 Typical fuse block showing direction indicator flasher unit

18.1 Removing a headlamp bezel

18.2A Headlamp sealed beam unit retaining ring screw (upper) and horizontal aim adjustment screw (lower)

18.2B Removing a sealed beam retaining ring

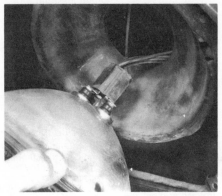

18.3 Sealed beam unit connecting plug

19.1 Removing a parking lamp lens

19.3 Removing a left front side marker lamp bulb holder

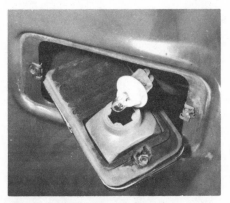

19.4 Right front side marker lamp

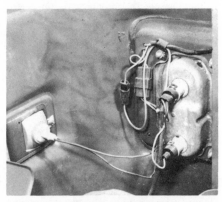

19.7 Rear side marker lamp and rear lamp cluster

19.8 Rear lamp cluster lens

19.9 Rear lamp bulbs (lens removed)

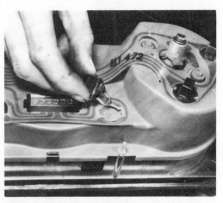

19.11 Removing an instrument panel bulb

observed as shown, in order that a temporary adjustment can be carried out (Fig. 10.19).

21 Switch – removal and installation

Lighting switch
1   Disconnect the battery ground cable.
2   Reach up behind the instrument panel and depress the switch shaft retaining plunger and then remove the switch knob shaft.
3   From the front of the instrument panel, unscrew and remove the switch retaining nut.
4   Push the switch from the instrument panel and disconnect the plug from the switch terminals.
5   Install the switch by reversing the removal operations but make sure that the grounding ring is installed on the switch.

Headlamp dimmer switch
6   Peel back the left upper corner of the floor mat and unscrew the two screws which hold the switch to the floor pan.
7   Disconnect the plug from the switch terminals.
8   Installation is a reversal of removal.

Neutral start/back-up lamp switch (automatic transmission)
9   Raise the vehicle on a hoist, jacks or axle stands so that the transmission is accessible.
10 Disconnect the wires from the switch terminals.
11 Remove the switch mounting bolts and remove the switch.
12 Install the new switch to its mounting bracket and then align the hole in the lever (B) with the one in the switch. Use a guide pin (A) for this (Fig. 10.21).
13 Loosen the swivel on the speed selector control rod and set the lever (C) on the side of the transmission in the Neutral mode. To do this, move lever (C) counterclockwise to L1 detent and then move it three detents in a clockwise direction.
14 Set the speed selector hand control in Neutral.
15 Set the position of the swivel so that it will enter the holes in the levers freely and then push it into position and secure it with its clip.
16 Lower the vehicle and check for correct operation of the switch with the ignition switched on.

Column-mounted back-up lamp switch (manual transmission)
17 Disconnect the battery ground cable.
18 Disconnect the switch wiring harness multi-pin connector.
19 Remove the switch mounting screws and remove the switch.
20 Installation is a reversal of removal.

Transmission mounted back-up lamp switch (manual transmission)
21 Working under the vehicle, disconnect the leads from the switch.
22 Remove the switch from the transmission.
23 Install the switch by reversing the removal operations.

Windshield washer/wiper switch
24 Disconnect the battery ground cable.
25 Reach up behind the left side of the instrument panel and pull the connector plug from the rear of the switch, then remove the mounting screws which secure the bezel and the ground wires to the switch.
26 Installation is a reversal of removal.

Ignition switch
27 Disconnect the battery ground cable.
28 Remove the lock cylinder by setting the key to the ACC position, then inserting a piece of stiff wire into the small hole in the cylinder face. Depress the plunger with the wire and turn the key counterclockwise until the lock cylinder can be removed.
29 Remove the metal nut from the ignition switch and then pull the switch out from behind the instrument panel.
30 Pry the tangs from the theft resistant connector and then snap the connector into place on the new switch.
31 Installation is a reversal of removal but position the grounding ring first and then screw on the nut.
32 The lock cylinder is inserted with its key in position.

Steering column switches
33 Removal of these switches is described in Chapter 11 in conjunction with the steering column.

22 Instrument cluster – removal and installation

1   Disconnect the battery negative (ground) cable.
2   Reach up behind the instrument panel and disconnect the speedometer cable from the speedometer head. This is done by depressing the retaining spring clip and pulling the cable clear (photo).
3   *On early models,* disconnect all the wiring harness multi-pin plugs

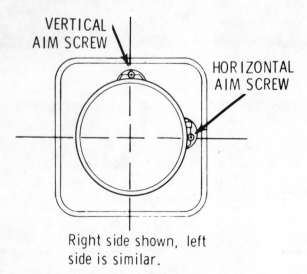

Fig. 10.19 Typical headlamp adjustment screws

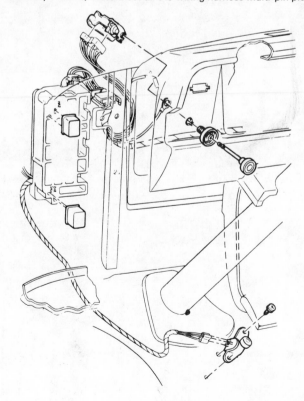

Fig. 10.20 Lighting and headlamp dimmer switches

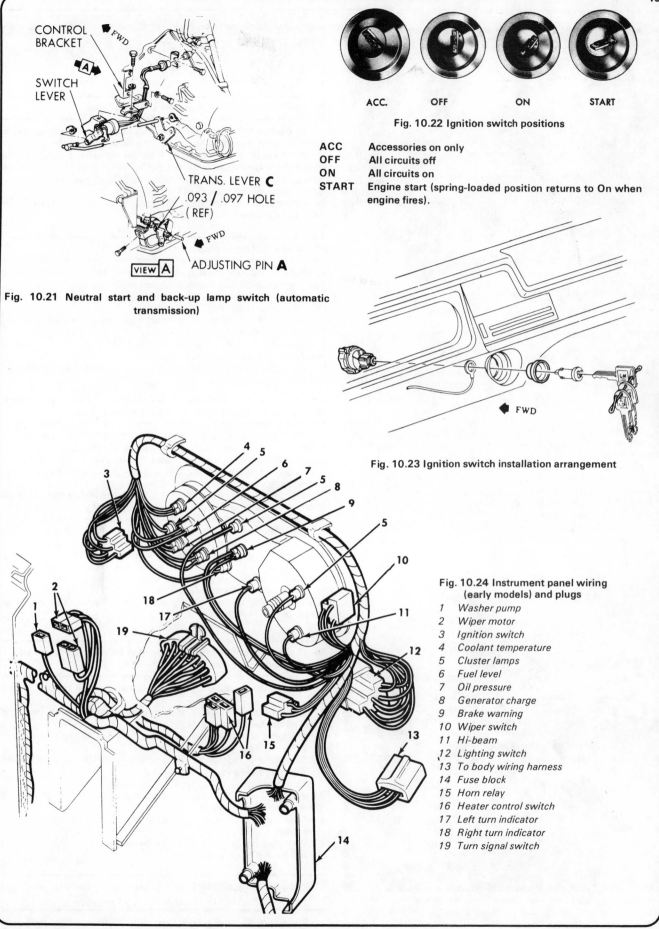

CONTROL BRACKET

SWITCH LEVER

FWD

A

TRANS. LEVER **C**

.093 / .097 HOLE (REF)

FWD

VIEW **A**   ADJUSTING PIN **A**

Fig. 10.21 Neutral start and back-up lamp switch (automatic transmission)

| ACC. | OFF | ON | START |

Fig. 10.22 Ignition switch positions

ACC   Accessories on only
OFF   All circuits off
ON   All circuits on
START Engine start (spring-loaded position returns to On when engine fires).

FWD

Fig. 10.23 Ignition switch installation arrangement

Fig. 10.24 Instrument panel wiring
(early models) and plugs

1   Washer pump
2   Wiper motor
3   Ignition switch
4   Coolant temperature
5   Cluster lamps
6   Fuel level
7   Oil pressure
8   Generator charge
9   Brake warning
10 Wiper switch
11 Hi-beam
12 Lighting switch
13 To body wiring harness
14 Fuse block
15 Horn relay
16 Heater control switch
17 Left turn indicator
18 Right turn indicator
19 Turn signal switch

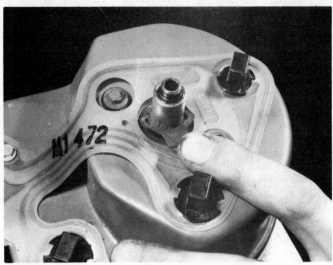

22.2 Speedometer cable retaining clip

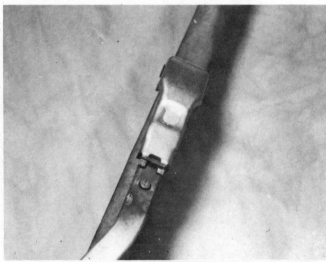

24.3 Windshield wiper blade attachment to arm

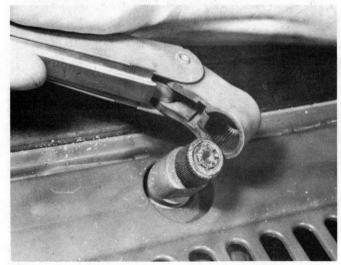

25.3 Windshield wiper arm removal from driving spindle

and then unscrew the two instrument cluster mounting nuts and withdraw the cluster.

4   *On later models,* having a laminated (printed) circuit there is only one wiring harness multi-pin plug to be disconnected.

5   Installation is a reversal of removal.

23 Speedometer cable – removal and installation

1   To remove the speedometer inner cable (core), disconnect it from the speedometer head as described in the preceding Section.

2   If the cable is unbroken, pull it out of the outer conduit. If it is broken then pull the upper section out and then disconnect the lower end of the conduit from the transmission and pull the remaining section out from the bottom end.

3   Before installing the inner cable, apply multi-purpose grease to the lower three quarters of its length.

24 Windshield wiper blades – renewal

1   At two yearly intervals or whenever the blades fail to clean the glass satisfactorily, they should be renewed.

2   Pull the blade/arm away from the glass so that it locks in position away from the windshield.

3   Depress the blade-to-arm connector so that the blade holder can be slid from the wiper arm and over the retaining stud (photo).

4   Either obtain a new holder/blade assembly complete or remove the flexible blade and install a new one.

5   Install the blade assembly to the arm by reversing the removal operation.

25 Windshield wiper arm – removal and installation

1   Make sure that the wiper arms are in the self-parked position, the motor having been switched off in the low speed mode.

2   Note carefully the position of the wiper arm in relation to the windshield lower reveal molding. It should be approximately two inches above the molding.

3   Using a suitable hooked tool or a small screwdriver, pull aside the small spring tang which holds the wiper arm to the splined transmission shaft and at the same time pull the arm from the shaft (photo).

4   Installation is a reversal of removal but do not push the arm fully home on the shaft until the alignment of the arm has been checked. If necessary, the arm can be pulled off again and turned through one or two serrations of the shaft to correct the alignment without the necessity of pulling aside the spring tang.

5   Finally, press the arm fully home on its shaft and then wet the windshield glass and operate the motor on low speed to ensure that the arc of travel is correct.

26 Windshield wiper motor, pump and linkage (early models) – removal and installation

1   *To remove the wiper motor,* first disconnect the battery ground cable.

2   Disconnect all the electrical connections and hoses from the wiper/pump assembly.

3   Slacken the nuts which secure the drive link to the wiper motor crankarm and disengage the balljoint.

4   Remove the motor mounting screws and lift the motor/pump assembly from the vehicle.

5   *To remove the linkage,* first lift off the wiper arms.

6   Working inside the vehicle, remove the radio (if installed); also the heater distributor and outlet duct.

7   Disconnect the two screws which attach each of the wiper arm pivot shafts.

8   Withdraw the linkage from under the dash.

9   Installation is a reversal of removal.

27 Windshield wiper motor and linkage (later models) – removal and installation

1   Make sure that the wipers have been switched off by the wiper

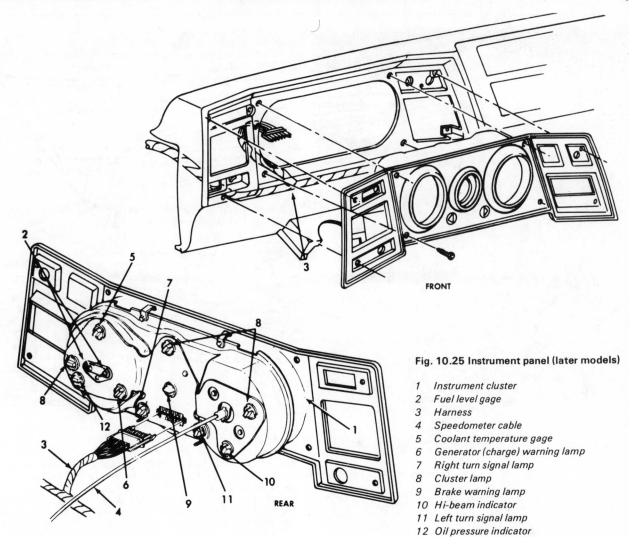

FRONT

REAR

Fig. 10.25 Instrument panel (later models)

1 Instrument cluster
2 Fuel level gage
3 Harness
4 Speedometer cable
5 Coolant temperature gage
6 Generator (charge) warning lamp
7 Right turn signal lamp
8 Cluster lamp
9 Brake warning lamp
10 Hi-beam indicator
11 Left turn signal lamp
12 Oil pressure indicator

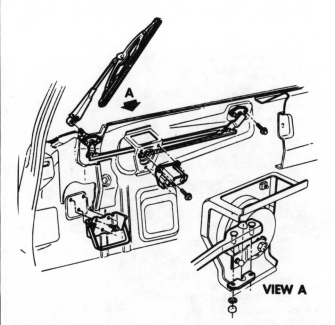

VIEW A

Fig. 10.26 Wiper motor and linkage (early type) location

Fig. 10.27 Removing heater duct (early models)

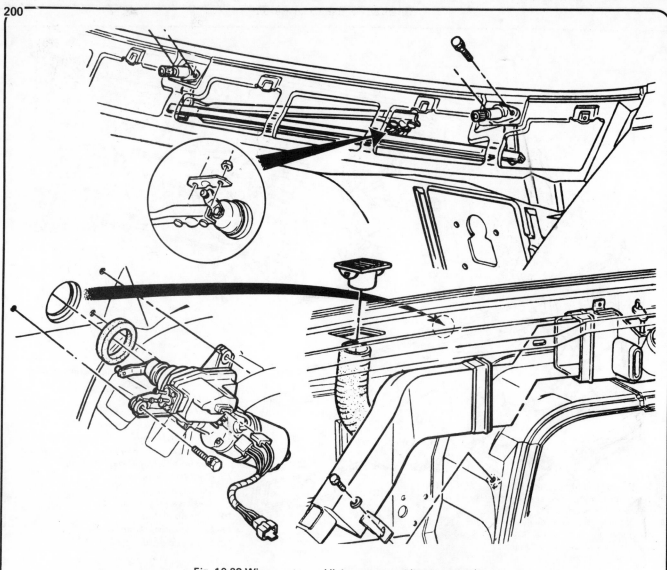

Fig. 10.28 Wiper motor and linkage removal (later models)

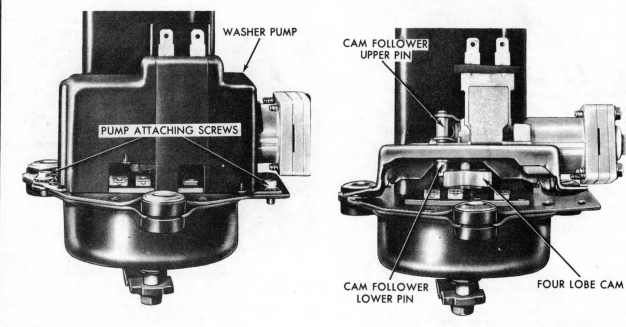

WASHER PUMP

PUMP ATTACHING SCREWS

CAM FOLLOWER
UPPER PIN

CAM FOLLOWER
LOWER PIN

FOUR LOBE CAM

Fig. 10.29 Washer pump attachment to wiper motor (early
models)

Fig. 10.30 Washer pump drive cam (early models)

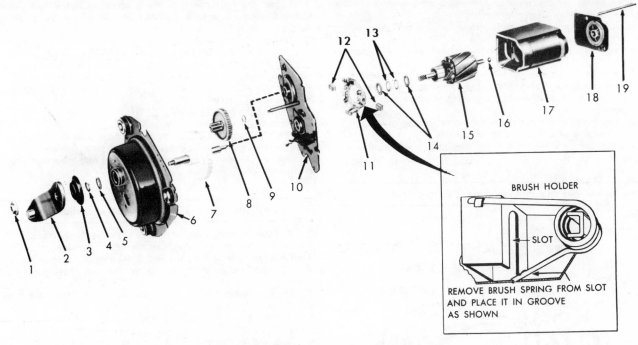

Fig. 10.31 Exploded view of early type wiper motor

1	Nut	6	Gearbox cover
2	Crank arm	7	Output gear/shaft
3	Seal cap	8	Intermediate gear
4	Retaining cap	9	Wave washer
5	Washer	10	Gearbox housing

11	Brush plate	16	Thrust plug
12	Brushes	17	Field frame
13	Wave washers	18	End plate
14	Flat washers	19	Tie-bolts
15	Armature		

motor control switch and that they are in their parked position.

2   Open the hood and disconnect the battery ground cable.

3   Remove the wiper arms.

4   Remove the screws which secure the cowl panel and lift it off.

5   Unscrew the nuts which hold the linkage to the motor crank arm and separate the linkage from the arm.

6   Disconnect the leads from the motor.

7   Remove the left defroster outlet from the flexible hose and push the hose aside for access to the wiper motor mounting screws.

8   Extract the single screw from the left heater duct and slip the duct from the engine cover shroud.

9   Remove the windshield washer hoses from the washer pump, taking care not to damage the floor covering with spilt washer fluid.

10 Remove the three screws which secure the wiper motor to the cowl and withdraw the wiper motor from under the dash.

11 Installation is a reversal of removal but make sure that the motor is in the PARK position first.

28 Wiper motor (early models) – overhaul and adjustment

1   With the motor/pump removed (see Section 26), first unscrew the two washer pump mounting screws and lift the pump from the motor.

2   Remove the washer pump drive cam, using two screwdrivers as levers.

3   Remove the crank arm retaining nut after clamping the crank arm in a vise.

4   Withdraw the crank arm, seal cap, retaining ring and end-float washers.

5   Drill out the gearbox cover retaining rivets and remove the cover.

6   Remove the output gear and shaft, and then slide the intermediate gear and pinion from the shaft.

7   If essential, the terminal board and park switch can be removed after drilling out the rivets.

8   Unscrew and remove the motor through-bolts and disengage the motor from the mounting plate.

9   Relieve the brush spring tension and slide the armature and the end-plate from the motor frame, noting the thrust plug located between the armature and the end-plate.

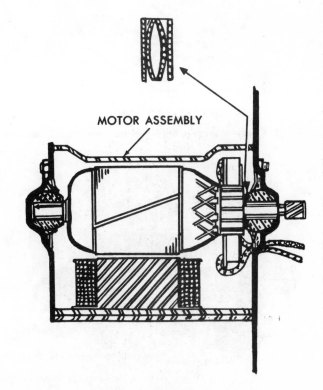

Fig. 10.32 Wiper motor armature shaft end-float washers – installation diagram (early models)

10 Obtain a repair kit which will contain the necessary nuts and bolts to replace the rivets which were drilled out.
11 Inspect all components and renew any which are worn, particularly the brushes.
12 Reassembly is a reversal of dismantling but observe the following:

   a) *Pack the seal cap with waterproof grease before reassembly.*
   b) *Lubricate the armature shaft bushings with light machine oil.*
   c) *Ensure the armature shaft end-float washers are correctly positioned.*
   d) *Temporarily reconnect the wiper motor and then switch it on and off so that it stops in its Parked position.*
   e) *Install the crank arm so that the positioning marks are in alignment (Fig. 10.33).*

29 Windshield washer pump (early models) – overhaul

1 Remove the pump as described in the preceding Section.
2 Remove the pump cover.

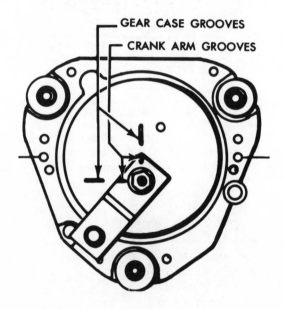

GEAR CASE GROOVES
CRANK ARM GROOVES

Fig. 10.33 Wiper motor crank arm alignment marks (early models)

3 Extract the ratchet dog retaining screw. Hold the spring-loaded solenoid plunger in position and then lift the solenoid assembly from the pump frame.
4 Disconnect the ratchet pawl spring. Remove the pawl retaining ring and slide the ratchet pawl from the cam follower shaft.
5 Move the ratchet wheel spring out of the shaft groove and slide the ratchet wheel from the shaft.
6 Pull the pump housing from the frame until the grooves in the housing clear the frame.
7 Remove the actuator plate.
8 Remove the valve assembly.
9 Mark the pipe assembly mounting baseplate in relation to the valve body so that it can be installed in its original position.
10 Renew all worn components and reassemble by reversing the dismantling operations.

30 Wiper motor (later models) – overhaul and adjustment

1 Remove the motor/washer pump as described in Section 27.
2 Remove the washer pump from the wiper assembly.
3 *To remove the park switch and terminal board,* remove the screw which retains the park switch, remove the spacer and unsolder the leads.
4 *The gear assembly* can be withdrawn after removing the nut and crank arm.
5 Remove the seal cap, the C-ring, washer, end-float washers and outer spacer.
6 Slide the gear assembly out of the housing and remove the inner spacer washer.
7 *To dismantle the wiper motor,* first scribe a line along the side of the casing and the end cap to ensure correct reassembly.
8 Unscrew the two through-bolts.
9 Ease the casing and field assembly/armature apart, at the same time feeding the exposed wiring leads through the rubber grommet.
10 Unsolder the lead from the contact breaker.
11 Carefully straighten the four tabs which secure the brush plate to the field coil retainers.
12 Grip the brush holders and lift them off the mounting tabs to clear the commutator on the armature.
13 Remove the armature from the casing. The thrust ball can be removed from the end of the shaft if required, using a magnet.
14 The casing and field assembly is supplied only as a complete assembly. If the assembly is to be renewed, cut the solid black plastic insulation and leads (black with pink stripe) near the terminal board where they can be spliced to the new assembly.
15 Renew any worn components and reassemble by reversing the dismantling operations. Adjust the armature end-float using the screw

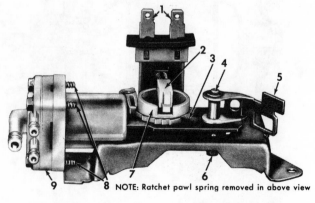

NOTE: Ratchet pawl spring removed in above view

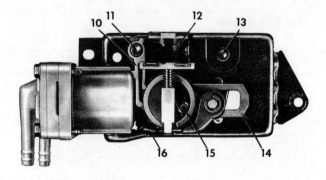

Fig. 10.34 Windshield washer pump (early models)

1	Terminals	5	Ratchet pawl
2	Solenoid plunger	6	Cam follower lower pin
3	Actuator plate tang	7	Ratchet wheel
4	Cam follower upper pin	8	Valve mounting screws

9	Valve assembly	13	Pivot pin
10	Ratchet dog	14	Piston actuator plate
11	Dog retaining screw	15	Ratchet wheel spring
12	Solenoid coil	16	Ratchet pawl spring

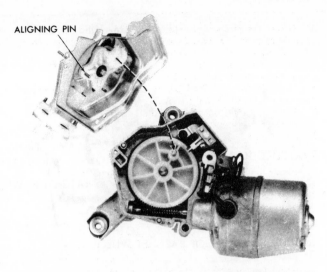

Fig. 10.35 Removing the washer pump from the wiper assembly

ALIGNING PIN

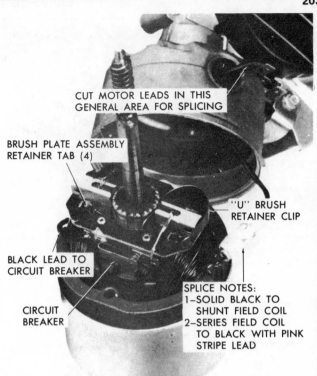

CUT MOTOR LEADS IN THIS GENERAL AREA FOR SPLICING

BRUSH PLATE ASSEMBLY RETAINER TAB (4)

"U" BRUSH RETAINER CLIP

BLACK LEAD TO CIRCUIT BREAKER

CIRCUIT BREAKER

SPLICE NOTES:
1–SOLID BLACK TO SHUNT FIELD COIL
2–SERIES FIELD COIL TO BLACK WITH PINK STRIPE LEAD

Fig. 10.36 Lead connecting details (later model wiper motor)

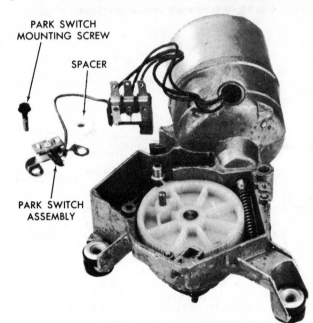

PARK SWITCH MOUNTING SCREW

SPACER

PARK SWITCH ASSEMBLY

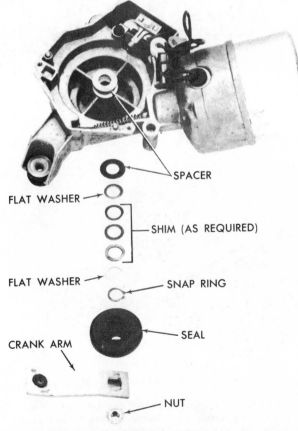

SPACER

FLAT WASHER

SHIM (AS REQUIRED)

FLAT WASHER

SNAP RING

SEAL

CRANK ARM

NUT

ARMATURE END PLAY ADJUSTING SCREW AND LOCKNUT

Fig. 10.37 Extracting gear assembly C-ring (later model wiper)

Fig. 10.38 Crank arm attachment (later type wiper motor)

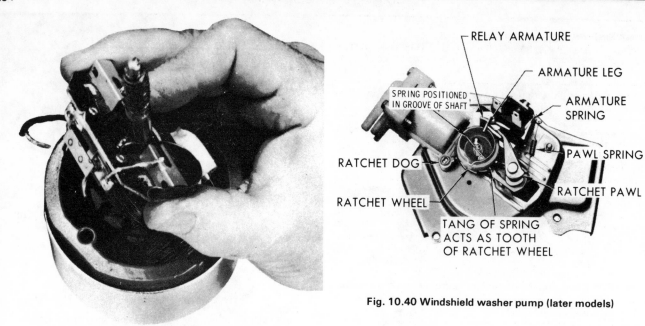

Fig. 10.39 Removing wiper motor brush holder (later models)

Fig. 10.40 Windshield washer pump (later models)

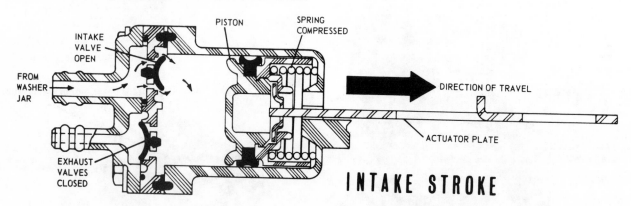

INTAKE STROKE

Fig. 10.41 Sectional view of later type washer pump

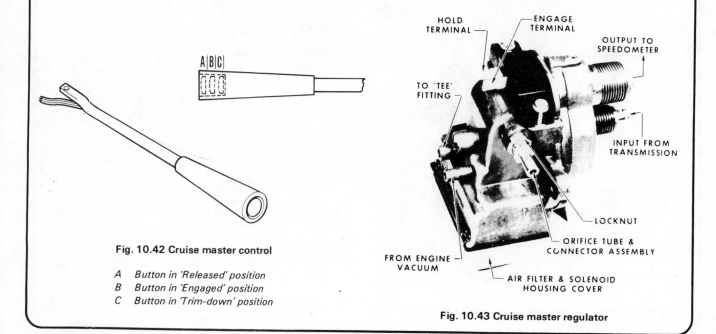

Fig. 10.42 Cruise master control

A   Button in 'Released' position
B   Button in 'Engaged' position
C   Button in 'Trim-down' position

Fig. 10.43 Cruise master regulator

and locknut, so that the screw is just finger-tight.
16 Adjust the gear assembly end-float using washers to obtain a clearance of 0·005 inch.

31 Washer pump (later models) – removal, overhaul and installation

1   The washer pump can be removed from the wiper motor independently without having to remove the complete assembly.
2   To do this, disconnect the battery ground cable, remove the left heater duct from the engine shroud.
3   Disconnect the washer hoses and electrical connections.
4   Extract the three screws which secure the washer pump to the wiper and remove the pump.
5   Once the pump has been removed, mark the position of the valve body to the pump and remove it (four screws).
6   Renew any worn components as necessary, and reassemble making sure that the valve plate gasket is correctly installed, and that the triple O-ring is installed between the valve and pipe assembly.
7   Installing the pump to the wiper is a reversal of removal.

32 Seat belts and warning system

1   Seat belts are provided at all passenger positions and on some models an inertia reel type belt is installed on the driver's seat.
2   Check the condition of the belts occasionally and renew any which appear cut or frayed.
3   Where customizing is carried out and includes the addition of more passenger seats, these too should be equipped with new seat belts. Make sure that the anchorage points are in accordance with the maker's specification.

33 Cruise master – description, adjustments and component renewal

1   This cruising speed control system is optionally available on certain models and allows the driver to maintain a constant highway speed without the necessity of continual adjustment of foot pressure on the accelerator pedal (Fig. 10.42).
2   The system employs a servo unit connected to the intake manifold, a speedometer cable-driven regulator and various switches.
3   An over-ride capability is built in.
4   Any malfunction in the performance of the system should first be checked out by inspecting the fuse, the security of the leads and terminals, and the vacuum pipes and connections.
5   The following adjustments should then be checked and if necessary altered to conform to those specified.
6   *The servo operating cable* which connects to the carburetor should be adjusted by means of the jam nuts at the cable bracket so that there is the minimum of slack in the cable.
7   *The regulator* can be adjusted by turning the orifice tube in or out (*never remove it as it cannot be re-installed*). If the vehicle cruises below the engagement speed, screw the orifice tube out. If the vehicle cruises above the engagement speed, screw the orifice tube in. Each $\frac{1}{4}$ turn of the orifice tube will change the cruise speed by about 1 mph. Tighten the locknut after each adjustment.
8   *The brake release switch* contacts must open when the brake pedal is depressed between 0·38 and 0·64 inch measured at the pedal pad.
9   The vacuum valve plunger must clear the pedal arm when the arm is moved $\frac{5}{16}$ inch measured at the switch.
10 *The column mounted engagement switch* is non-adjustable, and is renewable only as part of the complete turn signal lever assembly.
11 Faulty components should be renewed as complete assemblies after disconnecting electrical leads, vacuum hoses and control cables from them as necessary.

34 Radio and antenna

1   Radio equipment may be installed as a factory option or at a later date (aftermarket type).
2   The manufacturer's recommended locations for the receiver,

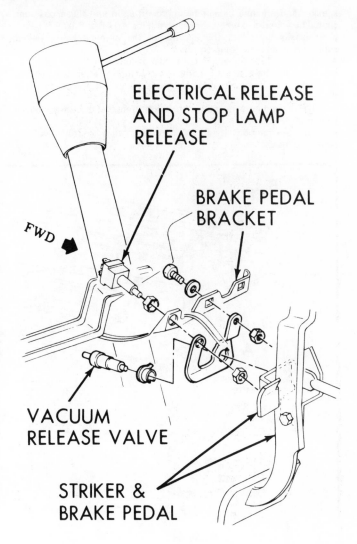

Fig. 10.44 Cruise control brake release switch attachment

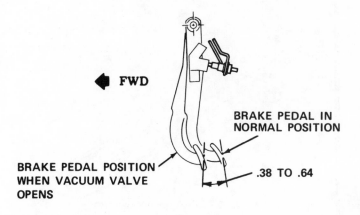

Fig. 10.45 Cruise control brake release switch adjustment diagram

speaker and antenna cannot be improved upon and these positions should be adhered to wherever possible (Figs. 10.46 and 10.47).

3   Occasionally check the security of the antenna leads, power supply wires and mounting bolts.

4   Check the fuse in the event of sudden failure.

5   Trimming the antenna is normally only required at time of installation but if new items of equipment are installed at any time, trim it in the following way.

6   Set the antenna to maximum height, remove the tuner control knob (right) and bezel.

7   Turn the ignition key to ACC and then turn the radio volume control to maximum.

8   Tune in to a weak station (near 1400 kHz) on the AM scale. Adjust the trimmer screw until maximum volume is obtained.

9   Refit the knob and bezel, then turn off the radio and ignition.

35 Radio equipment (factory installed) – removal and installation

Radio receiver

1   Disconnect the battery ground cable.

2   Remove the engine cover.

3   Remove the air cleaner from the carburetor.

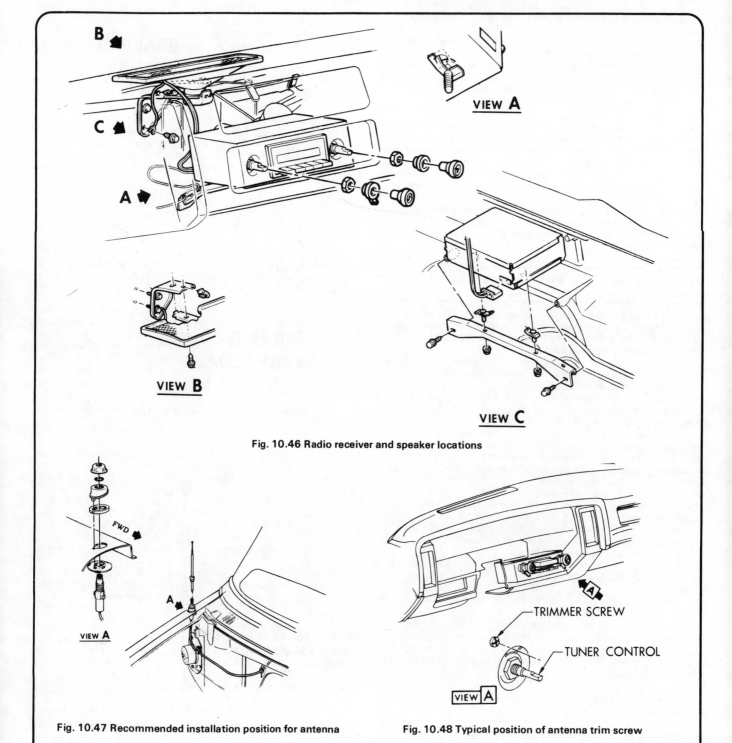

Fig. 10.46 Radio receiver and speaker locations

Fig. 10.47 Recommended installation position for antenna

Fig. 10.48 Typical position of antenna trim screw

4   Remove the air cleaner mounting stud from the carburetor throat and then cover the carburetor to prevent any objects dropping into it.
5   Remove the control knobs from the radio.
6   Remove the screw which holds the radio to its support bracket. Guide the radio forward and downward until the leads can be disconnected, then remove it completely.

Speaker

7   The speaker can only be removed after the radio receiver has been withdrawn.
8   Then extract the screw which holds the left heater duct to the engine cover and remove the duct.
9   Remove the mounting screws and remove the speaker through the engine cover aperture.

Antenna

10 Unscrew the mast securing nut. Prevent the antenna turning by using two wrenches.
11 Withdraw the assembly downwards noting the sequence of installing the seals and spacers.
12 If the assembly is to be completely removed, pull the antenna lead from the socket in the radio receiver.

36 Radios and tape players (aftermarket type) – installation (general)

A radio or tape player is an expensive item to buy, and will only give its best performance if installed correctly. It is useless to expect concert hall performance from a unit that is suspended from the dash-panel on string with its speaker resting on the back of the seat. If you do not wish to do the installation yourself there are many in-car entertainment specialists' who can do the job for you.

Make sure the unit purchased is of the same polarity as the vehicle (negative ground). Ensure that units with adjustable polarity are correctly set before commencing installation.

It is difficult to give specific information with regard to installing, as final positioning of the radio/tape player, speakers and antenna is entirely a matter of personal preference. However, the following paragraphs give guidelines to follow, which are relevant to all installations.

Radios

Most radios are a standardized size of 7 inches wide, by 2 inches deep – this ensures that they will go into the radio aperture provided in most vehicles.

Where no radio aperture is provided, the following points should be borne in mind before deciding exactly where to install the unit.

a) *The unit must be within easy reach of the driver wearing a seat belt.*
b) *The unit must not be mounted in close proximity to an electric tachometer, the ignition switch and its wiring, or the flasher unit and associated wiring.*
c) *The unit must be mounted within reach of the antenna lead, and in such a place that the antenna lead will not have to be routed near the components detailed in the preceding paragraph 'b'.*
d) *The unit should not be positioned in a place where it might cause injury to the car occupants in an accident; for instance, under the dashpanel above the driver's or passenger's legs.*
e) *The unit must be installed really securely.*

Some radios will have mounting brackets provided together with instructions: others will need to be installed using drilled and slotted metal strips, bent to form mounting brackets – these strips are available from most accessory stores. The unit must be properly grounded, by connecting a separate ground lead between the casing of the radio and the vehicle frame.

Use the radio manufacturer's instructions when wiring the radio into the vehicle's electrical system. If no instructions are available refer to the relevant wiring diagram to find the location of the radio 'feed' connection in the vehicle's wiring circuit. A 1–2 amp 'in-line' fuse must be fitted in the radio's 'feed' wire – a choke may also be necessary (see next Section).

The type of antenna used, and its installed position is a matter of personal preference. In general the taller the antenna, the better the reception. It is best to install a fully retractable antenna – especially, if a mechanical car-wash is used or if you live in an area where cars tend to be vandalized. In this respect electric antennae which are raised and lowered automatically switching the radio on or off are convenient, but are more likely to give trouble than the manual type.

When choosing a site for the antenna the following points should be considered:

a) *The antenna lead should be as short as possible – this means that the antenna should be mounted at the front of the vehicle.*
b) *The antenna must be mounted as far away from the distributor and HT leads as possible.*
c) *The part of the antenna which protrudes beneath the mounting point must not foul anything.*
d) *If possible the antenna should be positioned so that the coaxial lead does not have to be routed through the engine compartment.*
e) *The plane of the panel on which the antenna is mounted should not be so steeply angled that the antenna cannot be mounted vertically (in relation to the 'end-on' aspect of the vehicle). Most antennae have a small amount of adjustment available.*

Having decided on a mounting position, a relatively large hole will nave to be made in the panel. The exact size of the hole will depend upon the specific antenna being installed, although, generally, the hole required is of $\frac{3}{4}$ inch diameter. A 'tank-cutter' of the relevant diameter is the best tool to use for making the hole. This tool needs a small diameter pilot hole drilled through the panel, through which, the tool clamping bolt is inserted. When the hole has been made the raw edges should be de-burred with a file and then painted, to prevent corrosion.

Fit the antenna according to the manufacturer's instructions. If the antenna is very tall, or if it protrudes beneath the mounting panel for a considerable distance it is a good idea to install a stay between the antenna and the vehicle frame. This stay can be made from the slotted and drilled metal strips previously mentioned. The stay should be securely screwed or bolted in place. For best reception it is advisable to install a ground lead between the antenna body and the vehicle frame.

It will probably be necessary to drill one or two holes through bodywork panels in order to feed the antenna lead into the interior of the vehicle. Where this is the case ensure that the holes have rubber grommets to protect the cable, and to stop possible entry of water.

Positioning and installation of the speaker depends mainly on its type. Generally, the speaker is designed to go directly into the aperture already provided in the vehicle. Where this is the case, installing the speaker is just a matter of bolting in place. Take great care not to damage the speaker diaphragm whilst doing this. It is a good idea to place a 'gasket' between the speaker frame and the mounting panel in order to prevent vibration – some speakers will already have such a gasket.

When connecting a rear mounted speaker to the radio, the wires should be routed through the vehicle beneath the carpets or floor mats – preferably through the middle, or along the side of the floorpan, where they will not be trodden on. Make the relevant connections as directed by the radio manufacturer.

By now you will have several yards of additional wiring in the vehicle; use PVC tape to secure this wiring out of harm's way. Do not leave electrical leads dangling. Ensure that all new electrical connection are properly made (wires twisted together will not do) and completely secure.

The radio should now be working, but before you pack away your tools it will be necessary to 'trim' the radio to the antenna. Follow the radio manufacturer's instructions regarding this adjustment.

Tape players

Installation instructions for both cartridge and cassette stereo tape players are the same and in general the same rules apply as when installing a radio. Tape players are not usually prone to electrical interference like radio – although it can occur – so positioning is not so critical. If possible the player should be mounted on an 'even-keel'. Also, it must be possible for a driver wearing a seat belt to reach the unit in order to change, or turn over, tapes.

For the best results from speakers designed to be recessed into a panel, mount them so that the back of the speaker protrudes into an enclosed chamber within the vehicle (eg; door interiors).

To install recessed type speakers in the front doors first check that there is sufficient room to mount the speaker in each door without it

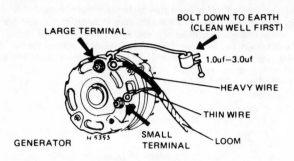

Fig. 10.49 Generator (alternator) noise suppression capacitor installation

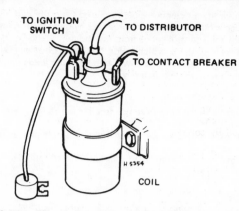

Fig. 10.50 Ignition noise suppression capacitor installation

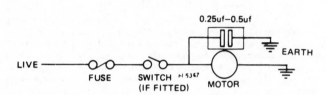

Fig. 10.51 Electric motor noise suppression capacitor installation

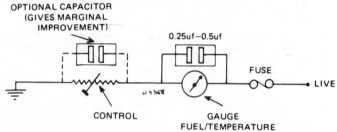

Fig. 10.52 Instrument noise suppression capacitor installation

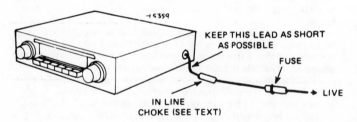

Fig. 10.53 Radio power feed line with in-line choke

fouling the latch or window winding mechanism. Hold the speaker against the skin of the door, and draw a line around the periphery of the speaker. With the speaker removed draw a second 'cutting' line, within the first, to allow enough room for the entry of the speaker back, but at the same time providing a broad seat for the speaker flange. When you are sure that the 'cutting-line' is correct, drill a series of holes around its periphery. Pass a hacksaw blade through one of the holes and then cut through the metal between the holes until the centre section of the panel falls out.

De-burr the edges of the hole and then paint the raw metal to prevent corrosion. Cut a corresponding hole in the door trim panel – ensuring that it will be completely covered by the speaker grille. Now drill a hole in the door edge and a corresponding hole in the door surround. These holes are to feed the speaker leads through – so use grommets. Pass the speaker leads through the door trim, door skin and out through the holes in the side of the door and door surround. Install the door trim panel and then secure the speaker to the door using self-tapping (sheet metal) screws. **Note:** *If the speaker has a shield to prevent water dripping on it, ensure that this shield is at the top.*

37 Radios and tape players – suppression of interference (general)

To eliminate buzzes, and other unwanted noises, costs very little and is not as difficult as sometimes thought. With a modicum of common sense and patience, and following the instructions in the following paragraphs, interference can be virtually eliminated (Reference should be made to Figs. 10.49 through 10.53).

The first cause for concern is the alternator. The noise this makes over the radio is like an electric mixer and the noise speeds up when you rev up (if you wish to prove the point, you can remove the fanbelt and try it). The remedy for this is simple; connect a 1.0 mfd – 3.0 mfd capacitor between ground, (probably the bolt that holds down the alternator base) and the *large* terminal on the alternator. This is most important, for if you connect it to the small terminal, you will probably damage the alternator permanently.

A second common cause of electrical interference is the ignition system. Here a 1.0 mfd capacitor must be connected between ground and the + terminal on the coil. This may stop the tick, tick, tick sound that comes over the speaker. Next comes the spark itself.

There are several ways of curing interference from the ignition HT system. One is to use carbon core HT leads and the more successful method is to use resistive spark plug caps of about 10 000 to 15 000 ohms resistance. If, due to lack of room, these cannot be used, an alternative is to use 'in-line' suppressors. If the interference is not too bad, you may get away with only one suppressor in the coil to distributor line. If the interference does continue (a 'clacking' noise) then 'doctor' all HT leads.

At this stage it is advisable to check that the radio is well grounded, also the antenna and to see that the antenna plug is pushed well into the set and that the radio is properly trimmed (see preceding Section). In addition, check that the wire which supplies the power to the set is as short as possible and does not wander all over the vehicle. At this stage it is a good idea to check that the fuse is of the correct rating. For most sets this will be about 1 to 2 amps.

At this point the more usual causes of interference have been suppressed. If the problem still exists, a look at the causes of interference may help to pinpoint the component generating the stray electrical discharges.

The radio picks up electromagnetic waves in the air; now some are transmitted and some, which we do not want, are made by the vehicle. The home-made signals are produced by stray electrical discharges floating around the vehicle. Common producers of these signals are electric motors, ie, the windshield wipers, electric screen washers, electric window winders, heater fan or an electric antenna if installed. Other sources of interference are electric fuel pumps, flashing turn signal and instruments. The remedy for these cases is shown for an electric motor whose interference is not too bad and for instrument suppression. Turn signals are not normally suppressed. In recent years, radio manufacturers have included in the feed wire to the radio, in addition to the fuse, an 'in-line' choke.

All the foregoing components are available from radio stores or accessory stores. If you have an electric clock fitted this should be suppressed by connecting a 0.5 mfd capacitor directly across it as shown.

If after all this, you are still experiencing radio interference, first assess how bad it is, for the human ear can filter out unobtrusive unwanted noises quite easily, but if you are still adamant about eradicating the noise, then continue.

As a first step, a few 'experts' seem to favour a screen between the radio and the engine. This is OK as far as it goes – literally! – for the whole set is screened anyway and if interference can get past that then a small piece of aluminum is not going to stop it.

A more sensible way of screening is to discover if interference is coming down the wires. First, take the live lead; interference can get between the set and the choke (hence the reason for keeping the wires short). One remedy here is to screen the wire and this is done by buying screened wire and using that. The speaker lead could be screened also to prevent 'pick-up' getting back to the radio – although this is unlikely.

Without doubt, the worst source of radio interference comes from the ignition HT leads, even if they have been suppressed. The ideal way of suppressing these is to slide screening tubes over the leads themselves. As this is impractical, we can place an aluminium shield over the majority of the lead areas. In a V8 engine this is relatively easy but for an in-line engine, the results are not particularly good.

Now for the really impossible cases, here are a few tips to try out. Where metal comes into contact with metal, an electrical disturbance is caused which is why good clean connections are essential. To remove interference due to overlapping or butting panels you must bridge the join with a wide braided earth strap (like that from the frame to the engine/transmission). The most common moving parts that could create noise and should be strapped are, in order of importance:

a) Muffler to frame.
b) Exhaust pipe to engine block and frame.
c) Air cleaner to frame.
d) Front and rear bumpers to frame.
e) Steering column to frame.
f) Hood lid to frame.

These faults are most pronounced when (1) the engine is idling, (2) laboring under load. Although the moving parts are already connected with nuts, bolts, etc, these do tend to rust and corrode, thus creating a high resistance interference source.

If you have a 'ragged' sounding pulse when mobile, this could be wheel or tire static. This can be cured by buying some anti-static powder and sprinkling it liberally inside the tires.

If the interference takes the shape of a high pitched screeching noise that changes its note when the car is in motion and only comes now and then, this could be related to the antenna, especially if it is of the telescopic or whip type. This source can be cured quite simply by pushing a small rubber ball on top of the antenna (yes, really!) as this breaks the electric field before it can form; but it would be much better to buy yourself a new antenna of a reputable brand. If, on the other hand, you are getting a loud rushing sound every time you brake, then this is brake static. This effect is most prominent on hot dry days and is cured only by installing a special kit, which is quite expensive.

In conclusion, it is pointed out that it is relatively easy, and therefore cheap, to eliminate 95 per cent of all noise, but to eliminate the final 5 per cent is time and money consuming. It is up to the individual to decide if it is worth it. Please remember also, that you cannot get concert performance out of a cheap radio.

38 Fault diagnosis – electrical system

Symptom	Reason/s
Starter motor fails to turn engine	Battery discharged
	Battery defective internally
	Battery terminal leads loose or ground lead not securely attached to body
	Loose or broken connections in starter motor circuit
	Starter motor switch or solenoid faulty
	Starter motor pinion jammed in mesh with flywheel ring gear
	Starter brushes badly worn, sticking or brush wires loose
	Commutator dirty, worn or burnt
	Starter motor armature faulty
	Field coils grounded
	Incorrect starting sequence (starter interlock system)
Starter motor turns engine very slowly	Battery in discharged condition
	Starter brushes badly worn, sticking or brush wires loose
	Loose wires in starter motor circuit
Starter motor operates without turning engine	Starter motor pinion sticking on sleeve
	Pinion or flywheel gear teeth broken or worn
	Over-running clutch sticking
Starter motor noisy or engagement excessively rough	Pinion or flywheel ring gear teeth broken or worn
	Starter motor retaining bolts loose
Starter motor remains in operation after ignition key released	Faulty ignition switch
	Faulty solenoid
Charging system indicator on with ignition switch off	Faulty alternator diode
Charging system indicator light on – engine speed above idling	Loose or broken drivebelt
	Shorted negative diode
	No output from alternator

Charge indicator light not on when ignition switched on but engine not running	Burned out bulb Field circuit open Lamp circuit open
Battery will not hold charge for more than a few days	Battery defective internally Electrolyte level too weak or too low Battery plates heavily sulphated
Horns will not operate or operate intermittently	Loose connections Defective switch Defective relay Defective horns
Horns blow continually	Faulty relay Relay wiring grounded Horn button stuck (grounded)
Lights do not come on	If engine not running, battery discharged Light bulb filament burnt out or bulbs broken Wire connection loose, disconnected or broken Light switch shorting or otherwise faulty
Lights come on but fade out	If engine not running battery discharged
Lights give very poor illumination	Lights not properly grounded Lamp glasses dirty Lamps badly out of adjustment
Lights work erratically – flashing on and off, especially over bumps	Battery terminals or ground connection loose Lights not grounded properly Contacts in light switch faulty Short in lighting circuit
Wiper motor fails to work	Blown fuse Wire connections loose, disconnected or broken Brushes badly worn Armature worn or faulty Field coils faulty
Wiper motor works very slowly and takes excessive current	Commutator dirty, greasy or burnt Armature bearings dirty or unaligned Armature badly worn or faulty
Wiper motor works slowly and takes little current	Brushes badly worn Commutator dirty, greasy or burnt Armature badly worn or faulty
Wiper motor works but wiper blades remain static	Wiper motor gearbox parts badly worn or teeth stripped

Wiring diagrams follow on pages 211 – 221

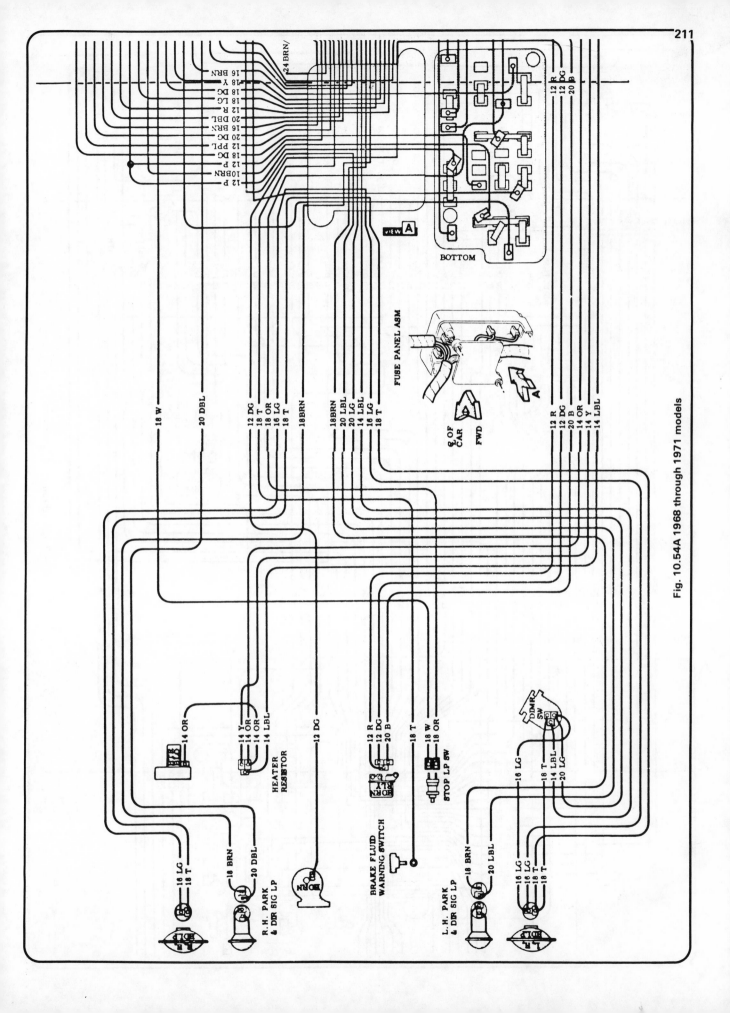

Fig. 10.54A 1968 through 1971 models

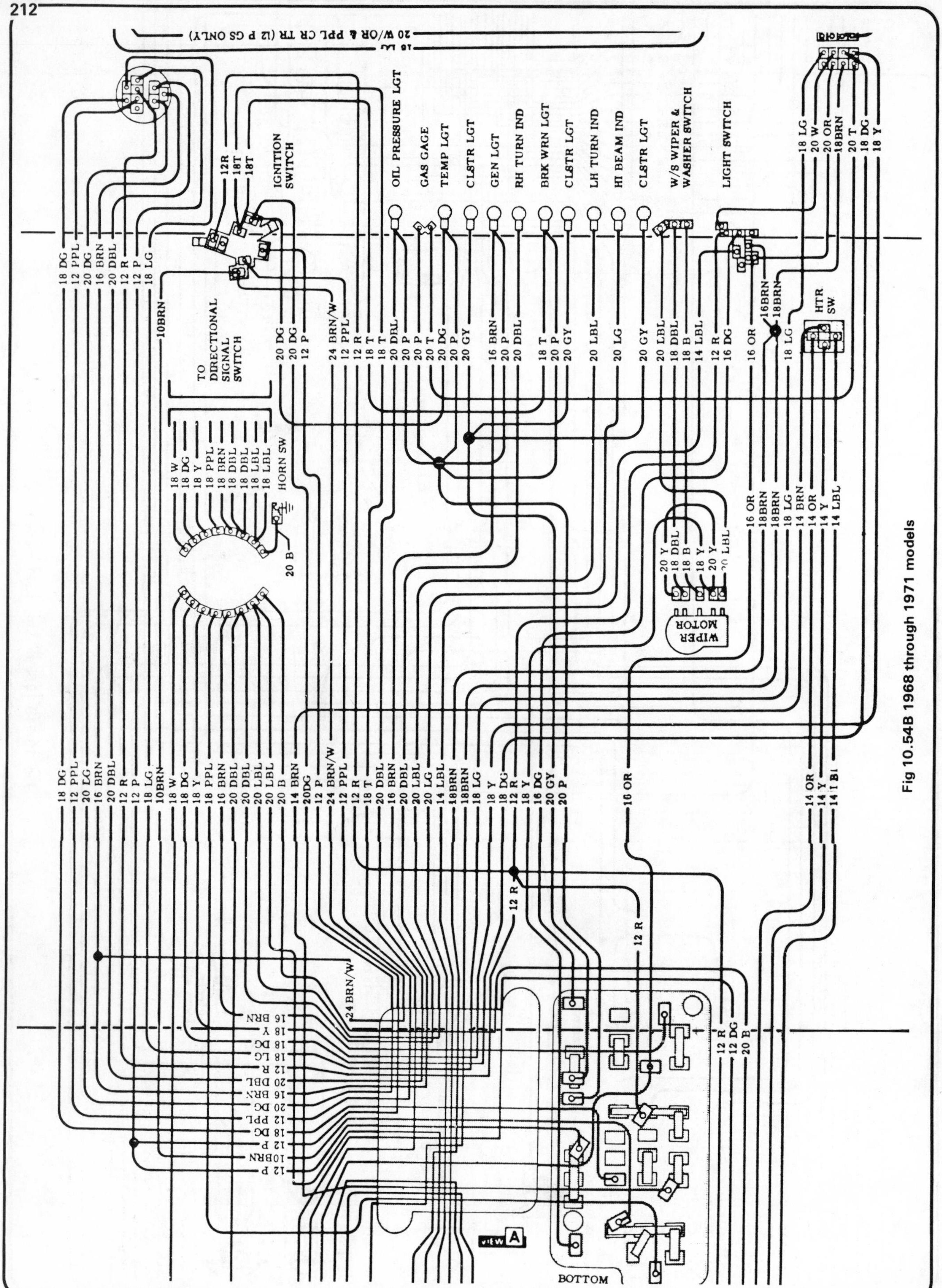

20 W/OR & PPL CR TR (12 P GS ONLY)
18 LG

IGNITION SWITCH

OIL PRESSURE LGT
GAS GAGE
TEMP LGT
CLSTR LGT
GEN LGT
RH TURN IND
BRK WRN LGT
CLSTR LGT
LH TURN IND
HI BEAM IND
CLSTR LGT
W/S WIPER & WASHER SWITCH
LIGHT SWITCH

18 LG
20 W
20 OR
18BRN
20 T
18 DG
18 Y

12R 18T 18T

18 DG
12 PPL
20 DG
16 BRN
20 DBL
12 R
12 P
18 LG

10BRN

TO DIRECTIONAL SIGNAL SWITCH

20 DG
20 DG
12 P

24 BRN/W
12 PPL
12 R
18 T
18 T
20 DBL
20 P
20 T
20 DG
20 P
20 GY
16 BRN
20 P
20 DBL
18 T
20 P
20 GY
20 LBL
20 LG
20 GY
20 LBL
18 DBL
18 B
14 LBL
12 R
16 DG
16 OR
16BRN
18BRN
18 LG

HTR. SW

18 W
18 DG
18 Y
18 PPL
18 BRN
18 DBL
18 DBL
18 LBL

HORN SW

20 B

16 OR
18BRN
18BRN
18 LG
14 BRN
14 OR
14 Y
14 LBL

20 Y
18 DBL
18 B
18 Y
20 Y
20 LBL

WIPER MOTOR

18 DG
12 PPL
20 LG
16 BRN
20 DBL
12 R
12 P
18 LG
10BRN
18 W
18 DG
18 Y
18 PPL
16 BRN
20 DBL
20 DBL
20 LBL
20 LG
14 LBL
18BRN
18BRN
18 LG
18 Y
18 DG
12 R
18 Y
16 DG
20 GY
20 P

24 BRN/W
12 P
12 PPL
12 R
18 T
20 DBL
16 BRN
20 DBL
20 LBL
14 LBL

10 OR

14 OR
14 Y
14 LBL

12 R

12 R

16 BRN
18 Y
18 DG
18 LG
12 R
20 DBL
16 BRN
20 DG
12 PPL
18 DG
12 P
10BRN
12 P

24 BRN/W

12 R
12 DG
20 B

VIEW A

BOTTOM

Fig 10.54B 1968 through 1971 models

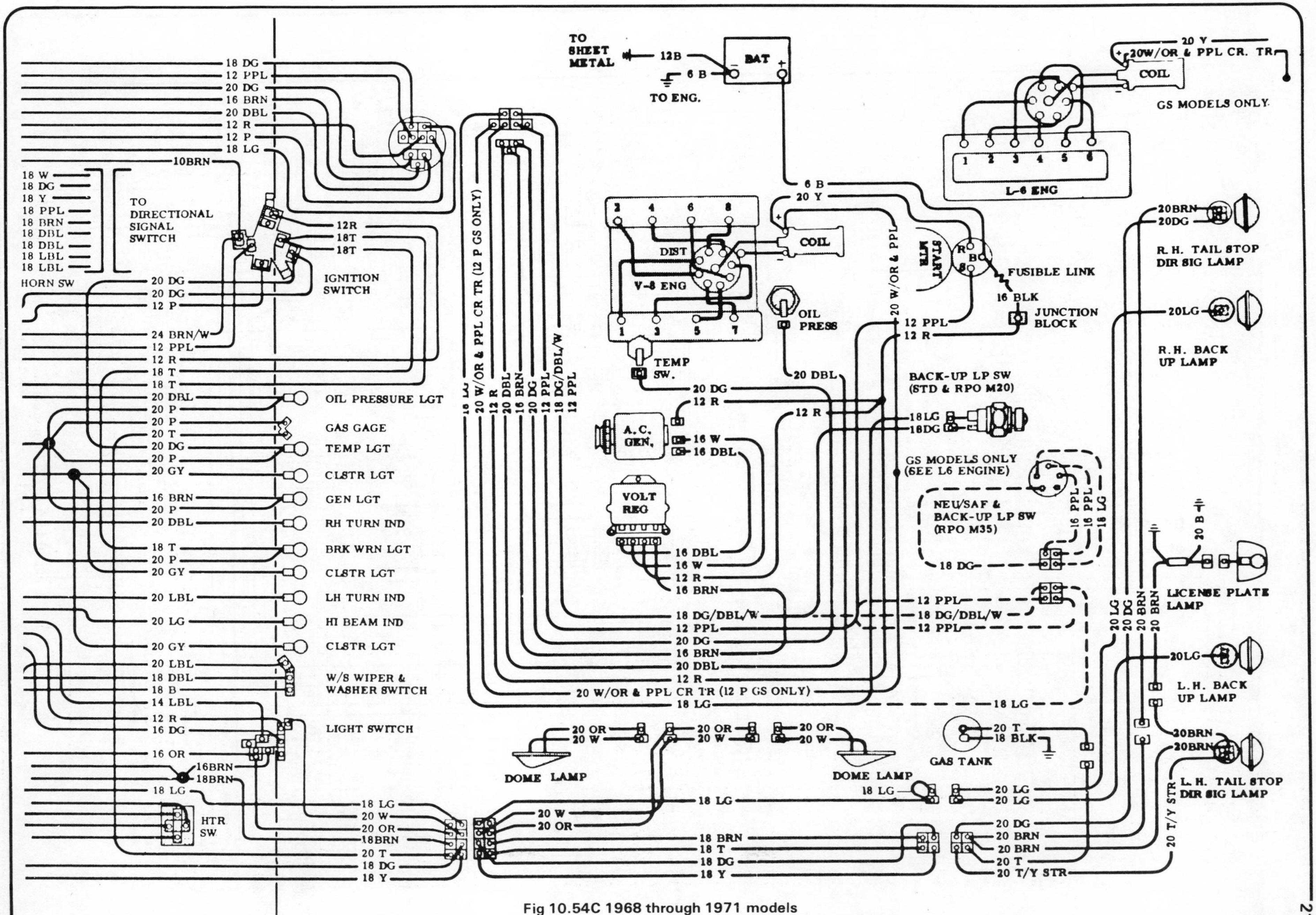

GS MODELS ONLY.

+20W/OR & PPL CR. TR.
+20 V

COIL

L-6 ENG

R.H. TAIL & STOP
DIR SIG LAMP
20BRN
20DG

R.H. BACK
UP LAMP
20LG

LICENSE PLATE
LAMP
20 B
20 BRN

L.H. BACK
UP LAMP
20LG

L.H. TAIL STOP
DIR SIG LAMP
20BRN
20BRN
20 T/Y STR

20 BRN
20 DG
20 LG

16 LG
16 PPL
16 PPL

18 DG

12 PPL
18 DG/DBL/W
12 PPL

20 LG
20 LG

20 DG
20 BRN
20 T
20 T/Y STR

FUSIBLE LINK
16 BLK
JUNCTION BLOCK

START MTR

12 PPL
12 R

BACK-UP LP SW
(STD & RPO M20)

NEU/SAF &
BACK-UP LP SW
(RPO M35)
(6EE L6 ENGINE)

GS MODELS ONLY

18 LG
18 BLK

GAS TANK

6 B
20 Y

COIL

OIL PRESS

20 DBL

12 R

20 W/OR & PPL

18 LG

DOME LAMP
18 LG

20 OR
20 W

BAT

12B
6 B

TO ENG.

DIST

V-8 ENG

TEMP SW.

20 DG
12 R

16 W
16 DBL

A.C. GEN.

VOLT REG

16 DBL
16 W
12 R
16 BRN

18 DG/DBL/W
12 PPL
20 DG
16 BRN
20 DBL

20 W/OR & PPL CR TR (12 P GS ONLY)
18 LG

20 OR
20 W

20 OR
20 W

18 LG

18 BRN
18 T
18 DG
18 Y

DOME LAMP

20 W
20 OR

TO SHEET METAL

12 PPL
18 DG/DBL/W
12 PPL
20 DG
16 BRN
20 DBL
12 R
20 W/OR & PPL CR TR (12 P GS ONLY)
18 LG

IGNITION SWITCH

18 DG
12 PPL
20 DG
16 BRN
20 DBL
12 R
12 P
18 LG

12R
18T
18T

TO DIRECTIONAL SIGNAL SWITCH

20 DG
12 P

24 BRN/W
12 PPL
12 R
18 T

OIL PRESSURE LGT
GAS GAGE
TEMP LGT
CLSTR LGT
GEN LGT
RH TURN IND
BRK WRN LGT
CLSTR LGT
LH TURN IND
HI BEAM IND
CLSTR LGT
W/S WIPER & WASHER SWITCH
LIGHT SWITCH

20 DRL
20 P
20 P
20 T
20 DG
20 P
20 GY
16 BRN
20 P
20 DBL
18 T
20 P
20 GY
20 LBL
20 LG
20 GY
20 LBL
18 DBL
18 B
14 LBL
12 R
16 DG

16 OR

18 LG
20 OR
20 BRN
20 T
18 DG
18 Y

16BRN
18BRN

HTR SW

HORN SW
18 W
18 DG
18 Y
18 PPL
18 BRN
18 DBL
18 DBL
18 LBL
18 LBL

10BRN

Fig 10.54C 1968 through 1971 models

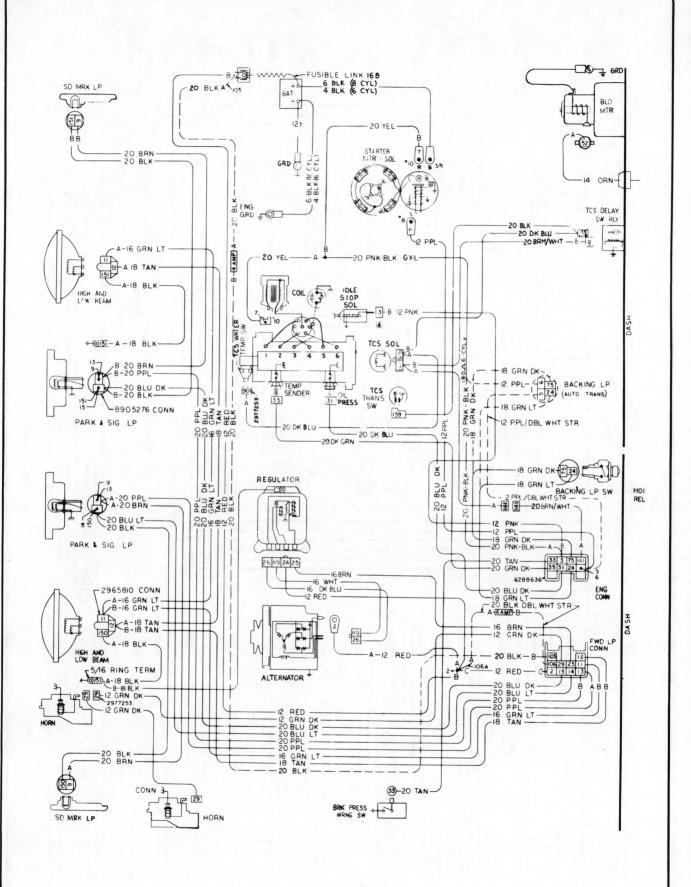

Fig 10.55A 1972/73 models

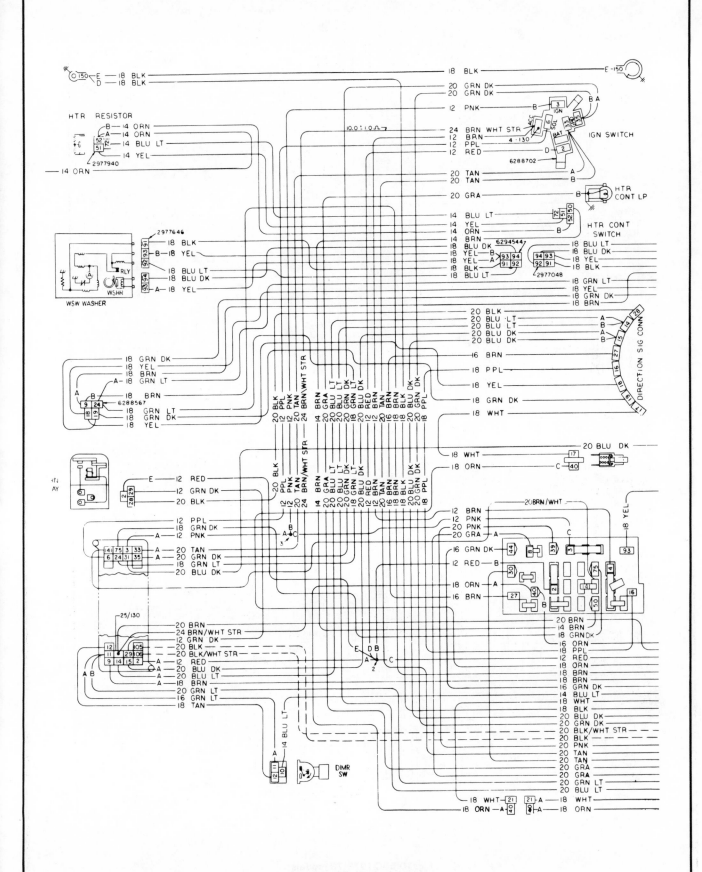

Fig. 10.55B 1972/73 models

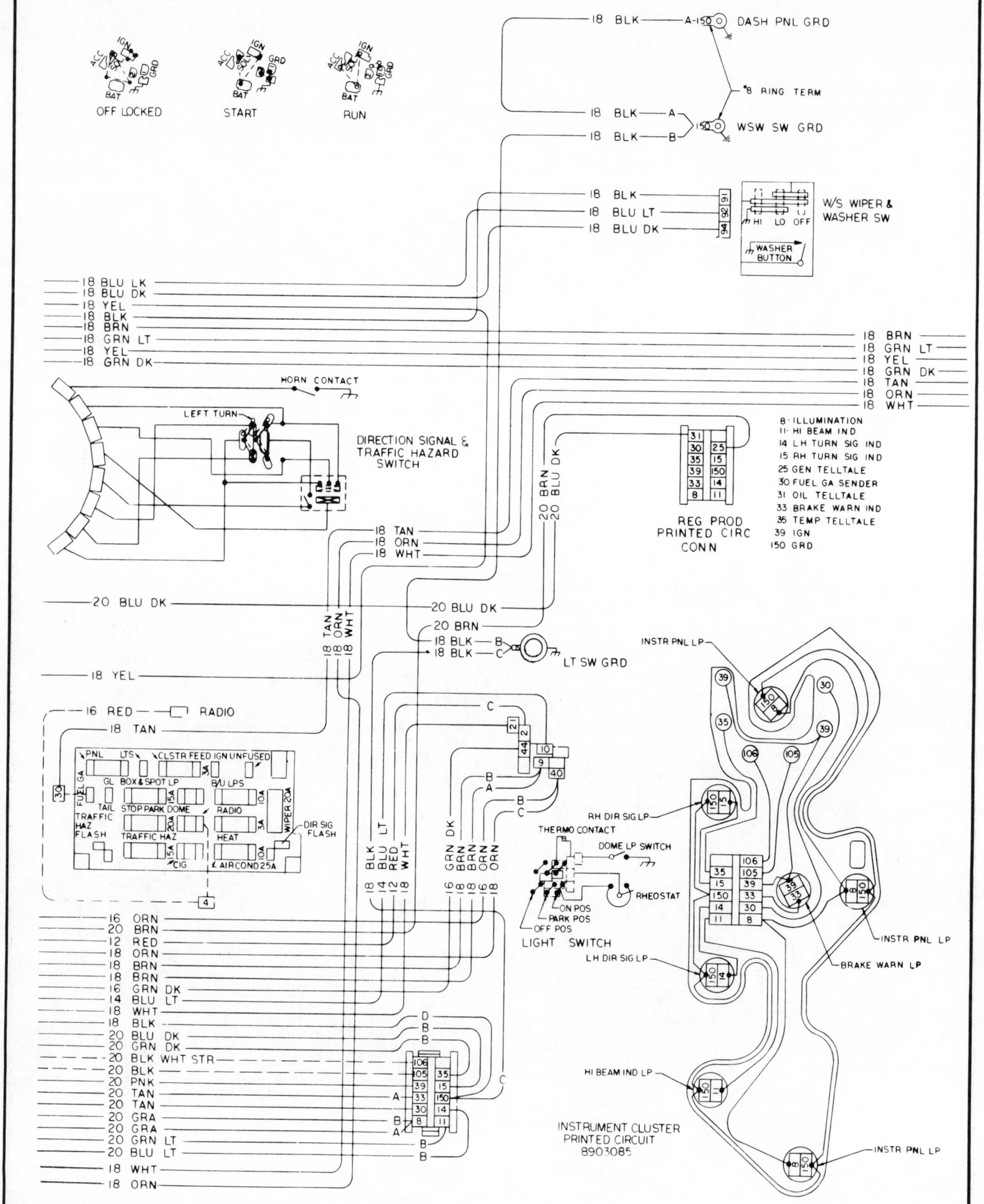

18 BLK — A-150 — DASH PNL GRD

*B RING TERM

18 BLK — A
18 BLK — B — 150 — WSW SW GRD

OFF LOCKED   START   RUN

ACC IGN SOL GRD BAT

18 BLK — 92 91
18 BLU LT — 93
18 BLU DK — 94

W/S WIPER & WASHER SW

HI LO OFF

WASHER BUTTON

18 BLU LK
18 BLU DK
18 YEL
18 BLK
18 BRN
18 GRN LT
18 YEL
18 GRN DK

18 BRN
18 GRN LT
18 YEL
18 GRN DK
18 TAN
18 ORN
18 WHT

HORN CONTACT

LEFT TURN

DIRECTION SIGNAL & TRAFFIC HAZARD SWITCH

20 BRN
20 BLU DK

31 30 25
30 35 15
35 39 150
39 33 14
33 8 11

REG PROD PRINTED CIRC CONN

8 - ILLUMINATION
11 - HI BEAM IND
14 - LH TURN SIG IND
15 - RH TURN SIG IND
25 - GEN TELLTALE
30 - FUEL GA SENDER
31 - OIL TELLTALE
33 - BRAKE WARN IND
35 - TEMP TELLTALE
39 - IGN
150 - GRD

18 TAN
18 ORN
18 WHT

18 TAN
18 ORN
18 WHT

20 BLU DK

20 BLU DK
20 BRN
18 BLK — B
18 BLK — C — LT SW GRD

18 YEL

16 RED — RADIO
18 TAN

30 FUEL GA

PNL LTS CLSTR FEED IGN UNFUSED
GL BOX & SPOT LP   B/U LPS
15A   20A
TAIL   STOP PARK DOME   RADIO
3A   3A
TRAFFIC HAZ FLASH   HEAT   10A
TRAFFIC HAZ   WIPER 20A
CIG   6A   AIRCOND 25A   DIR SIG FLASH

4

C
21 2
44 10
9 40
B
A
B
C

THERMO CONTACT
DOME LP SWITCH

ON POS
PARK POS
OFF POS
RHEOSTAT

LIGHT SWITCH

18 BLK
14 BLU
12 RED
18 WHT
LT

16 GRN DK
18 BRN
16 BRN
18 ORN

INSTR PNL LP

39   30
35   39
106   105

39
150

RH DIR SIG LP
106
35 105
15 39
150 33
14 30
8 11

INSTR PNL LP

BRAKE WARN LP

LH DIR SIG LP
150 14

16 ORN
20 BRN
12 RED
18 ORN
18 BRN
18 BRN
16 GRN DK
14 BLU LT
18 WHT
18 BLK
20 BLU DK
20 BLU DK
20 BLK WHT STR
20 BLK
20 PNK
20 TAN
20 TAN
20 GRA
20 GRA
20 GRN LT
20 BLU LT
18 WHT
18 ORN

D
B
B
106
105 35
39 15
33 150
30 14
8 11
A
B
A
B

HI BEAM IND LP

INSTRUMENT CLUSTER PRINTED CIRCUIT 8903085

INSTR PNL LP

Fig. 10.55C 1972/73 models

217

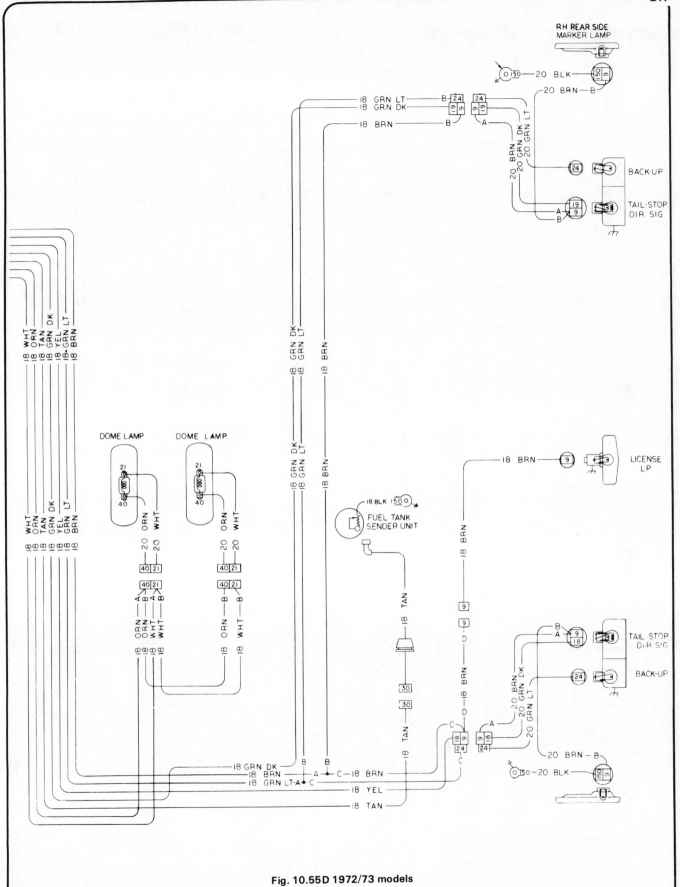

Fig. 10.55D 1972/73 models

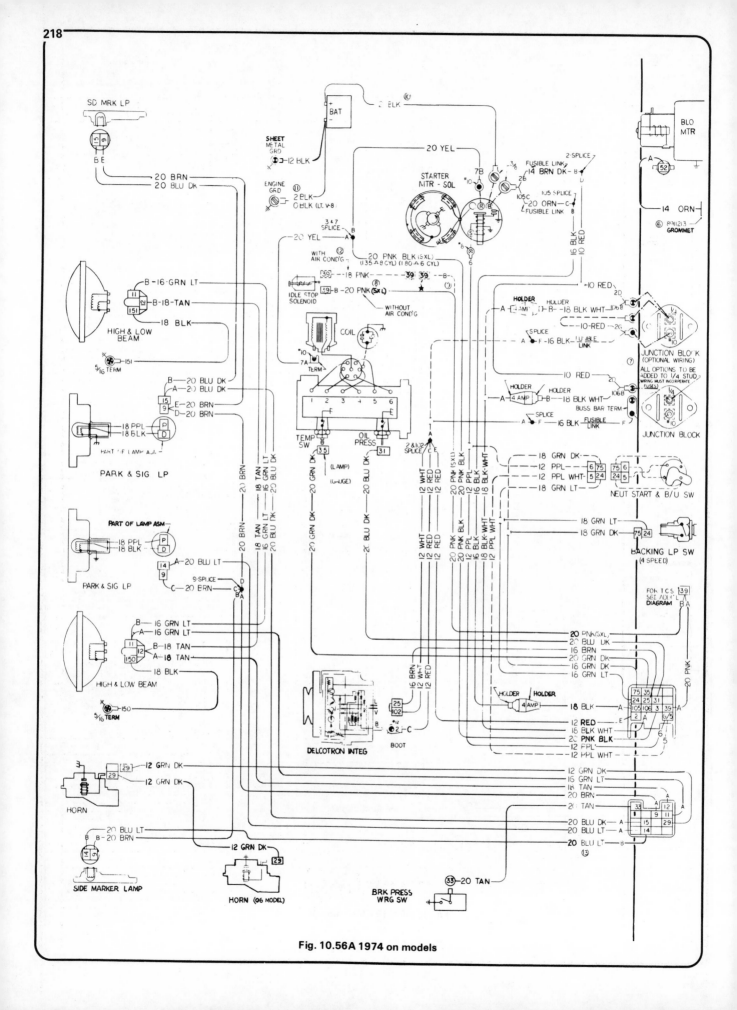

Fig. 10.56A 1974 on models

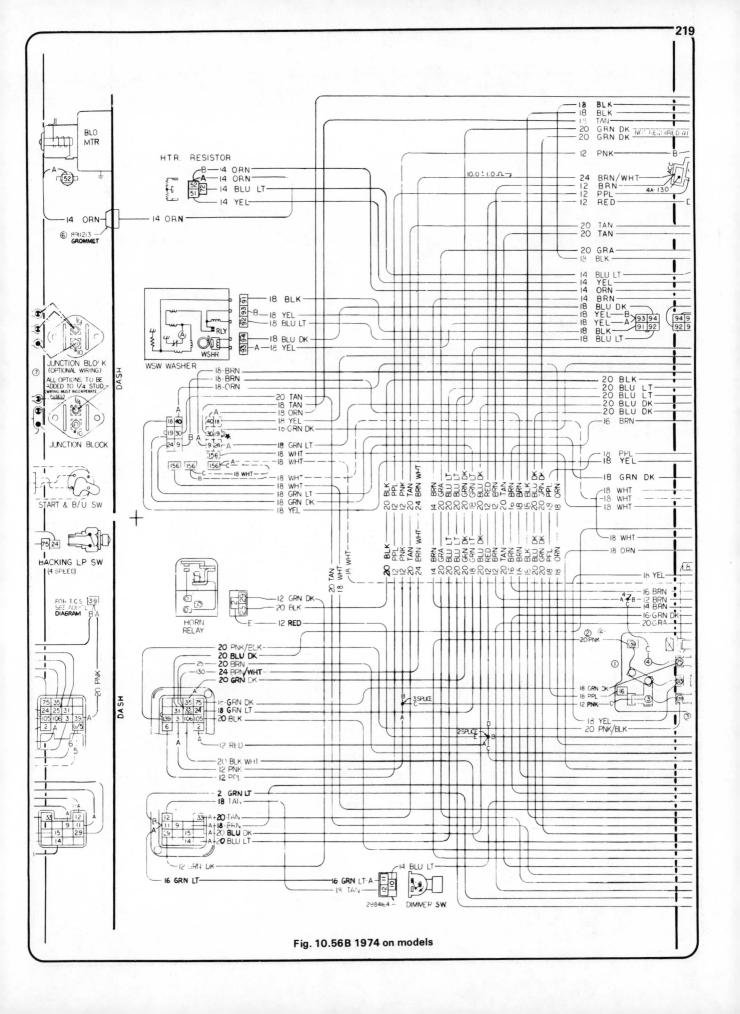

Fig. 10.56B 1974 on models

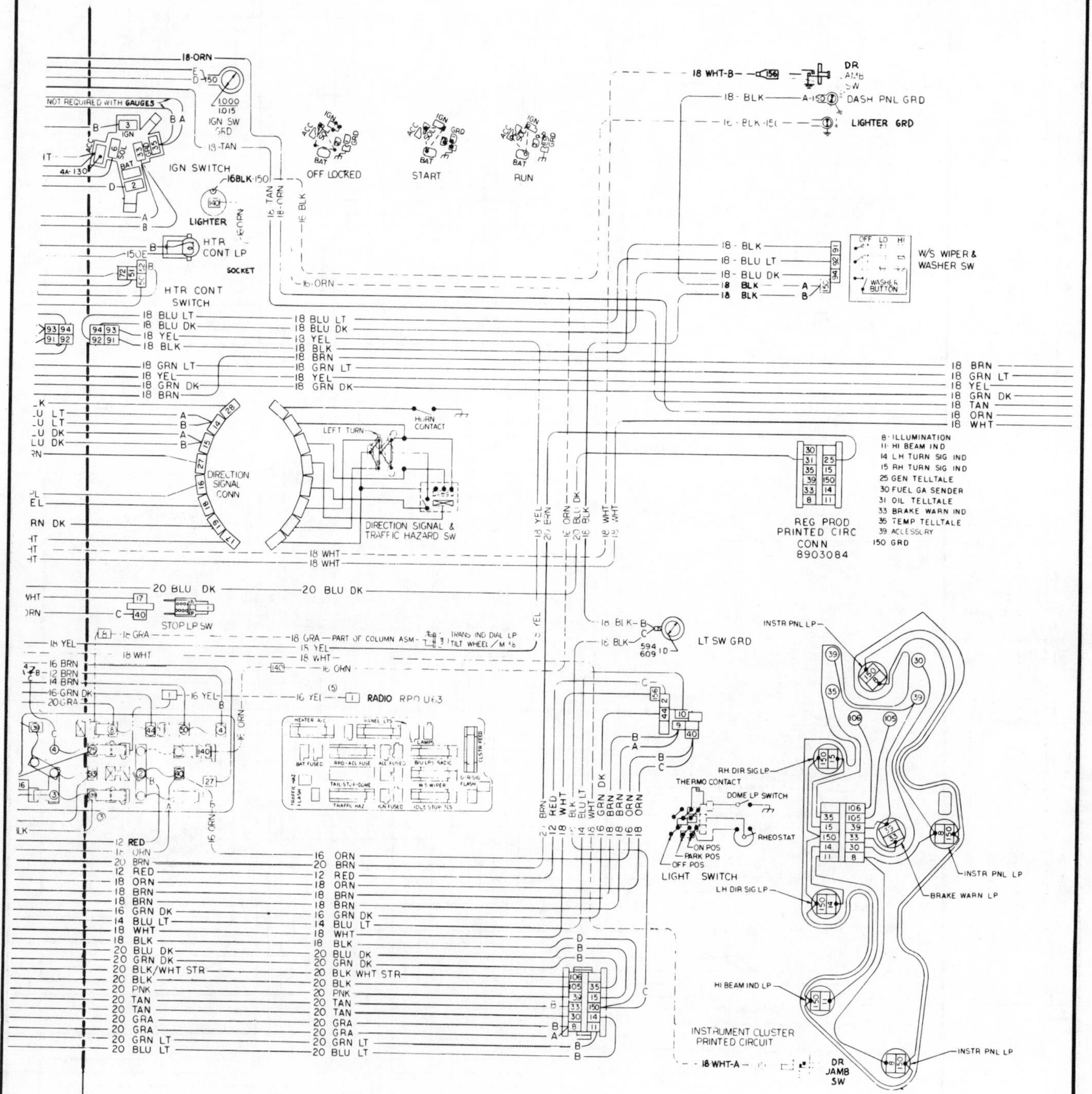

18-ORN

NOT REQUIRED WITH GAUGES

1000
1015
IGN SW
GRD

18-TAN

IGN SWITCH

16 BLK-150

IGN

LIGHTER

HTR CONT LP

SOCKET

HTR CONT SWITCH

18 WHT-B

18-BLK — A-150

16-BLK-151

DR AMB SW

DASH PNL GRD

LIGHTER GRD

OFF LOCKED   START   RUN

16-ORN

18-BLK
18-BLU LT
18-BLU DK
18 BLK   A
18 BLK   B

OFF LO HI

WASHER BUTTON

W/S WIPER & WASHER SW

18 BLU LT
18 BLU DK
18 YEL
18 BLK
18 GRN LT
18 YEL
18 GRN DK
18 BRN

18 BLU LT
18 BLU DK
18 YEL
18 BLK
18 BRN
18 GRN LT
18 YEL
18 GRN DK

18 BRN
18 GRN LT
18 YEL
18 TAN
18 ORN
18 WHT

DIRECTION SIGNAL CONN

LEFT TURN

HORN CONTACT

DIRECTION SIGNAL & TRAFFIC HAZARD SW

18 WHT
18 WHT

8 ILLUMINATION
11 HI BEAM IND
14 LH TURN SIG IND
15 RH TURN SIG IND
25 GEN TELLTALE
30 FUEL GA SENDER
31 OIL TELLTALE
33 BRAKE WARN IND
35 TEMP TELLTALE
39 ACCESSORY
150 GRD

REG PROD PRINTED CIRC CONN 8903084

20 BLU DK

20 BLU DK

STOP LP SW

18 GRA — PART OF COLUMN ASM

TRANS IND DIAL LP
TILT WHEEL / M46

18 YEL
18 WHT
16 ORN

16 YEL
16 YEL (5)

RADIO RPO U63

18 BLK-B
18 BLK   594 609 ID

LT SW GRD

INSTR PNL LP

HEATER A/C   PANEL LTS

BAT FUSED
RPO ACI FUSE
AIR FUSED
B-LPS SWTC

TAIL ST 4 DOME

TRAFFIC HAZ
IGN FUSED
IDLE STOP SOL

THERMO CONTACT

ON POS
PARK POS
OFF POS

LIGHT SWITCH

DOME LP SWITCH

RHEOSTAT

RH DIR SIG LP

LH DIR SIG LP

BRAKE WARN LP

INSTR PNL LP

HI BEAM IND LP

INSTRUMENT CLUSTER PRINTED CIRCUIT

18 WHT-A

DR JAMB SW

INSTR PNL LP

12 RED
18 ORN
20 BRN
12 RED
18 ORN
18 BRN
18 GRN DK
14 BLU LT
18 WHT
18 BLK
20 BLU DK
20 GRN DK
20 BLK/WHT STR
20 BLK
20 PNK
20 TAN
20 GRA
20 GRA
20 GRN LT
20 BLU LT

16 ORN
20 BRN
12 RED
18 ORN
18 BRN
16 GRN DK
14 BLU LT
18 WHT
18 BLK
20 BLU DK
20 GRN DK
20 BLK/WHT STR
20 BLK
20 PNK
20 TAN
20 GRA
20 GRA
20 GRN LT
20 BLU LT

Fig. 10.56C 1974 on models

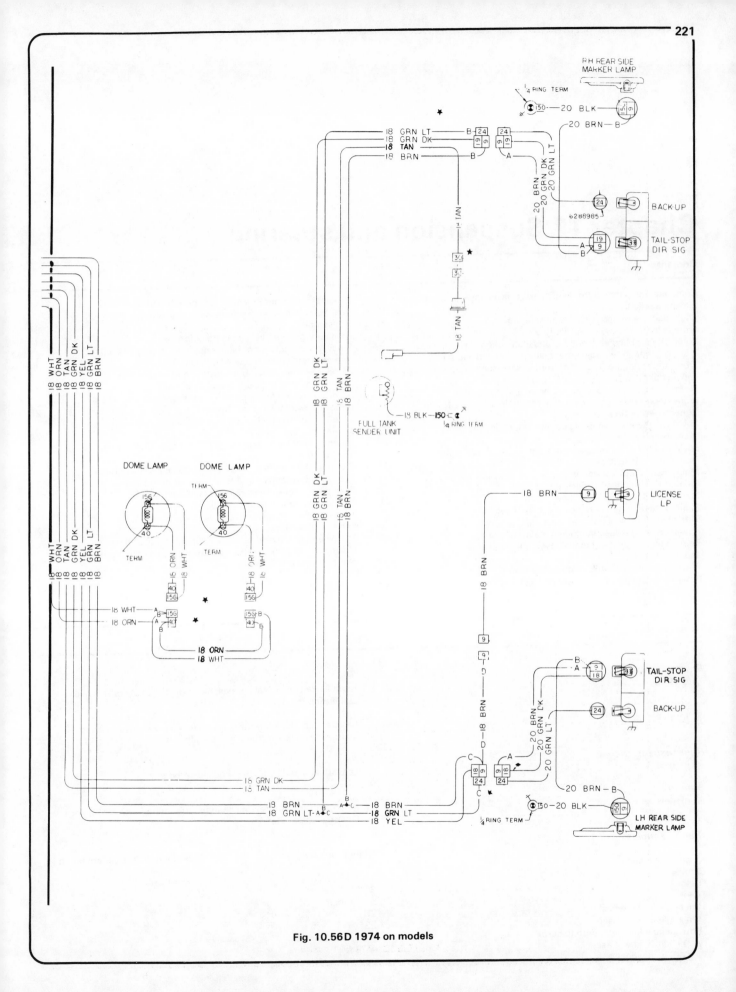

Fig. 10.56D 1974 on models

Chapter 11 Suspension and steering

Contents

Specifications

Front suspension

Thru 1970 .... Rigid I-beam axle, leaf springs, hydraulic shock absorbers and stabilizer bar

1971 on .... Independent with coil springs, upper and lower control arms, hydraulic shock absorbers and stabilizer bar

Rear suspension

All models .... Leaf springs and hydraulic shock absorbers

Steering

All models .... Recirculating ball; steering shaft incorporating flexible coupling
Optional power steering

Steering angles

	Rigid Front Axle	Independent front suspension
Kingpin inclination	$7\frac{1}{4}°$	-
Camber	$1° \pm \frac{1}{2}°$ positive	$\frac{1}{4}°$ positive
Castor	$3\frac{1}{4}°$	0 to 1°
Toe-in	$\frac{3}{32}$ to $\frac{3}{16}$ inch	$\frac{3}{16}$ inch
Turn angle (outer wheel)	20°	-
Turn angle (inner wheel)	23°	-
Turning circle (diameter curb to curb)		
110 inch wheelbase	41.8 ft	
125 inch wheelbase	46.6 ft	

Torque wrench settings

	lbf ft
Front suspension (Rigid axle)	
Stabilizer bar bracket	25
Stabilizer bar link	20
Kingpin bearing caps	3
Kingpin lock bolt	30
Shock absorber upper mounting	75
Shock absorber lower mounting	55
Spring U-bolt nuts	80
Spring front eye-bolt	75
Spring rear shackle bolts	50
Independent front suspension (G10 - 20 and GE/GS 1500 -	
2500 models)	
Lower control arm U-bolts	45
Upper control arm shaft nuts	70
Control arm flexible bushings	140
Upper swivel balljoint nut	50
Lower swivel balljoint nut	90
Crossmember-to-frame side rail	65
Crossmember-to-bottom rail	100
Stabilizer bar-to-control arm	25
Stabilizer bar-to-frame	25
Shock absorber upper and lower mountings	75
Independent front suspension (G30 and GE/GS 3500 models)	
Lower control arm U-bolt	85
Upper control arm shaft nuts	105
Upper swivel balljoint nut	90
Lower swivel balljoint nut	90
Crossmember-to-frame side rail	65
Crossmember-to-bottom rail	100
Crossmember brake support struts	60
Stabilizer bar-to-control arm	25
Stabilizer bar-to-frame	25
Shock absorber upper and lower mountings	75
Rear suspension (through 1970)	
Spring U-bolt nuts	125
Spring front eyebolt	65
Spring rear eyebolt	50
Shock absorber upper and lower mountings	75
Rear suspension (1971 on)	
Spring U-bolt nuts	
G10 - 20 and GE/GS 1500 - 2500	120
G30 and GE/GS 3500	150
Spring front eyebolt nut	90
Spring rear shackle bolt nuts	90
Shock absorber upper and lower mountings	75
Steering (mechanical)	
Steering gear side cover bolts	35
Steering wheel nut	40
Flexible coupling pinch bolt	30
Column lower clamp bolt	20
Tie-rod balljoint nut	
G10 - 20 GE/GS 1500 - 2500	25
G30 GE/GS 3500	105
Tie-rod clamp bolt	20
Idler arm mounting bolts	40
Pitman arm-to-relay rod nut	60
Idler arm-to-relay rod nut	60
Steering connecting rod nut	50
Pitman arm-to-shaft nut	140
Steering gear-to-frame bolts	100
Steering (power assisted)	
Overcenter adjuster screw locknut	35
Thrust bearing locknut	80
Pump mounting bolts	35
Flexible hose end fittings	35
Roadwheels	
G10 - 20, GE/GS 1500 - 2500	75 to 100

G30, GE/GS 3500
   Single wheels . . . .   90 to 120
   Dual wheels . . . .   110 to 140

1 General description

1   The front suspension on vehicles built through 1970 is of the
I-beam axle and leaf spring type. On all later models, independent
suspension is used with coil springs and unequal length control arms.
Telescopic hydraulic shock absorbers are used on all vehicles.
2   The rear suspension on all models is of the leaf spring type with
telescopic hydraulic shock absorbers.
3   The steering gear is of the recirculating ball type; later models
have a flexible coupling in the steering shaft.
4   Power steering is available as an option on certain models.

2 Maintenance and inspection

1   At the intervals specified in Routine Maintenance lubricate the
suspension and steering linkage joints. On early models with I-beam
rigid axles, there are a considerable number of lubrication points,
including those on the leaf spring shackles (see appropriate lubrication
chart).
2   The manual steering gear is filled with lubricant during production
and requires no topping up. However, make regular inspections to
check that lubricant is not leaking from the gaskets or seals of the
housing. If it is, renew the seals and then fill the housing with the

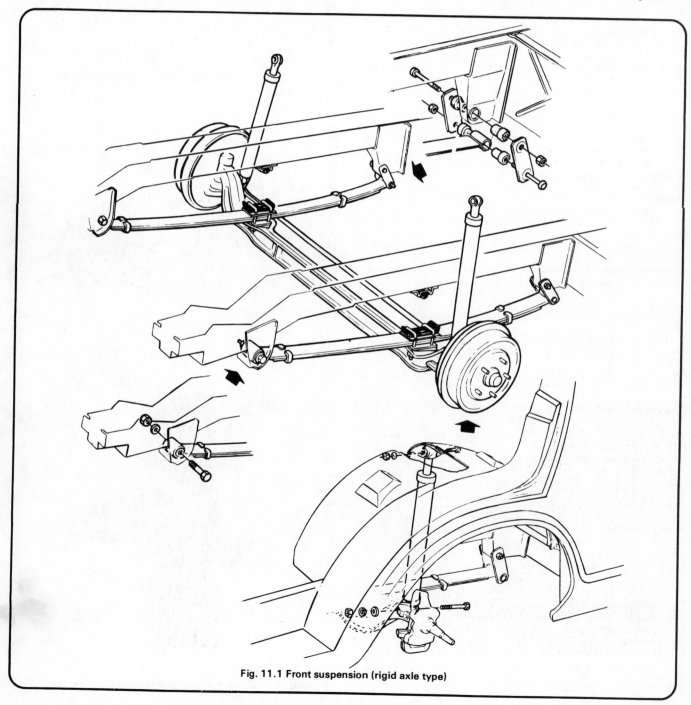

Fig. 11.1 Front suspension (rigid axle type)

specified lubricant only, after removing the side cover.

3   Check and top up the fluid in the power steering reservoir.

4   Clean and repack the hub bearings on the front wheels, and adjust. Have the front wheel alignment checked and also the steering angles (see Section 34).

5   By far the most important job is to regularly inspect all the steering components and suspension units for wear. Have an assistant to help by moving the steering wheel in both directions while you watch all the steering swivels and joints for slackness or movement caused by wear.

6   Check the suspension bushings for wear, and springs for cracks while the vehicle is bounced up and down.

7   Examine all dust excluding boots on the steering balljoints for splits.

8   Periodically check all nuts and bolts for correct torque on the complete steering and suspension system.

9   Routine checking of the shock absorbers and the tires should be carried out as described in Sections 4 and 36 of this Chapter.

3   Front hub bearings – adjustment, lubrication and overhaul

1   At the intervals specified in Routine Maintenance, jack up the front of the vehicle either under the rigid axle (through 1970) or the front crossmember (1971 on).

2   Grip the roadwheel, and push and pull the wheel in an attempt to rock it by gripping the top and bottom. If more than an almost imperceptible amount of movement is evident, then the bearings must be adjusted.

3   To adjust a bearing, tap off the dust cap from the end of the hub and pull out the cotter pin (photo).

4   Tighten the hub nut to a torque wrench setting of 15 lbf ft while turning the hub in both directions.

5   Unscrew the nut and then tighten it with the fingers only. Insert a new cotter pin. If the slot and hole are not in alignment, back off the nut slightly until they are.

6   Bend over the ends of the cotter pin neatly and install the dust cap.

7   If the adjustment has been correctly done, the endfloat of the hub will be between 0.001 and 0.005 inch.

8   If the bearings are to be re-packed with grease, remove the cotter pin as previously described and, if front drum brakes are fitted, unscrew and remove the hub nut and the thrust washer, and pull the hub/drum assembly straight off the steering knuckle spindle. Take care not to allow the outer roller bearing to drop to the ground as it is displaced (photo).

9   On vehicles with front disc brakes, the caliper will have to be removed as described in Chapter 9 before the hub/disc assembly can be removed.

10 With the hub removed, examine the area round the inner oil seal

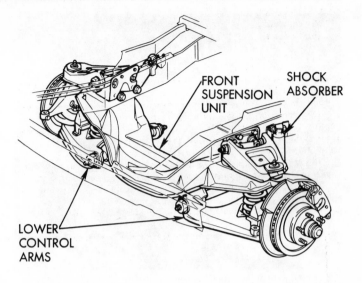

Fig. 11.2 Front suspension (independent type)

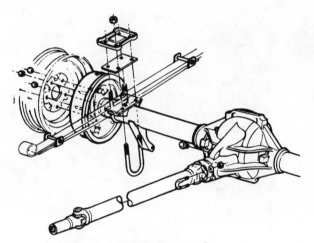

Fig. 11.3 Rear suspension

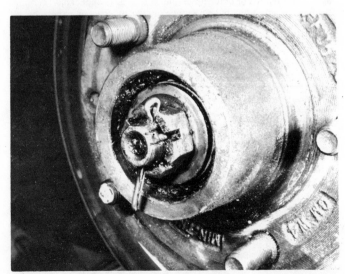

3.3 Front wheel hub nut and cotter pin

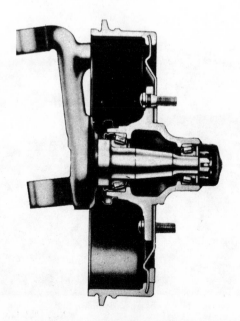

Fig. 11.4 Cutaway view of front hub (rigid axle type)

3.8 Front hub bearing thrust washer

3.10 Front hub oil seal

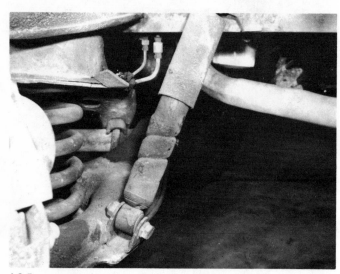

4.2 Front suspension shock absorber mounting

for evidence of grease leakage. If there is any sign of this then the oil seal must be renewed (photo).
11 If the oil seal is in good condition, wipe out all the old lubricant from the hub interior and bearings with a lint-free cloth, and re-pack with fresh grease of the specified type.
12 If the bearings are to be renewed because of excessive hub end-float which cannot be adjusted out, noise during rotation, or grooved or chipped rollers, first pry out the oil seal then extract the bearing inner races and drive out the bearing outer tracks. If both front hubs are being overhauled at the same time, do not mix the new bearing components but keep them in their cartons until required as they are manufactured as matched sets.
13 Install the new bearings and a new oil seal; lubricate and adjust as described earlier.

4 Shock absorbers – removal, testing and installation

1 Removal of a shock absorber should be carried out with the weight of the vehicle resting normally on its roadwheels. If this is not possible because of lack of access, raise the vehicle under the axles or suspension lower control arm so that the shock absorber is in its normal attitude, neither fully extended or retracted.
2 Disconnect the upper and lower mountings, and remove the unit (photo).
3 Inspect the shock absorber for signs of fluid leakage; if evident, renew the unit.
4 Examine the flexible mounting bushings. If these have worn oval or have hardened or deteriorated, renew them.
5 On shock absorbers having spirally-grooved bodies, secure the lower mounting eye in the jaws of a vise, and fully extend and compress the shock absorber at least six times. If the operation is noisy, jerky or offers no resistance in either direction then the unit must be renewed complete.
6 New spirally-grooved bodied shock absorbers are often stored in a horizontal position and they should be bled using the test method just described before installing.
7 Smooth-bodied shock absorbers incorporate a gas-filled cell which prevents aeration or foaming of the fluid. Any testing of this type of shock absorber should be carried out with the unit in an inverted position.
8 Installation is a reversal of removal, tightening the mounting nuts and bolts to the specified torque.

5 Front stabilizer bar – removal and installation

1 To remove the stabilizer bar, disconnect the bushings and support brackets which hold the bar to the chassis frame.
2 Disconnect the brackets which hold the bar to the suspension lower control arms or brackets on the axle ends as applicable.
3 Renew any worn bushings, and install by reversing the removal operations. Make sure that the slits in the flexible bushings at the frame attachment points are towards the front of the vehicle.

6 Front roadspring (rigid axle) – removal and installation

1 Raise the front of the vehicle and support the frame side-members on axle stands.
2 Support the axle so that the leaf springs are not under tension. Remove the roadwheel.
3 Unscrew and remove the nuts from the spring securing U-bolts.
4 Unscrew and remove the pivot bolts from the front and rear shackle spring eyes. Lift the spring from the vehicle.
5 Examine the spring eye bushings. Later types are of a flexible design while earlier versions have plain bushings with lubricators. Either type can be renewed by drawing out the old bushing using a long bolt, nut, washers and suitable tubular spacers. Install the new bushing in the same way.
6 Wire-brush the spring leaves and examine for cracks. If a leaf is broken, have the spring repaired by your dealer or obtain a new one complete.
7 To install the spring, locate it so that the head of the spring center bolt engages in the axle seat.
8 Install the U-bolts and nuts finger-tight.

9 Install the pivot bolts to the eyes, also finger-tight.
10 Install the roadwheel and then gently lower the vehicle and bounce it up and down several times to settle the suspension; then tighten all nuts to the specified torque.
11 Check the torque wrench settings again after 500 miles running.
12 Never lubricate flexible type spring eye bushings.
13 The spring leaves do not require regular lubrication, but an occasional spraying with de-rusting fluid or penetrating oil will help to keep them in good condition.

7 Front roadspring (independent suspension) – removal and installation

1 Raise the front of the vehicle under the crossmember so that the suspension control arms hang free. Remove the roadwheel.
2 Disconnect the shock absorber lower mounting.
3 Disconnect the stabilizer bar from the suspension lower control arm.
4 A suitable spring compressor will now be required to compress the spring so that its tension can be removed from the lower control arm. Do not use an unsuitable tool for this job as it can be a dangerous operation. Purchase or hire the correct equipment from your auto parts store.
5 Unscrew and remove the two U-bolts which secure the suspension lower control arm to the crossmember.
6 Lower the control arm until the spring in its compressed state can be removed.
7 If the original spring is to be re-installed, there is no need to remove the spring compressors. If a new spring is to be installed, carefully remove the compressors from the old spring and attach them to the new spring.
8 Installation is a reversal of removal but make sure that the alignment hole in the pivot cross-shaft of the lower control arm is engaged with the stud on the crossmember.

8 Front axle (rigid type) – overhaul

1 The steering knuckles and kingpins may be removed from the axle without the need for removing the axle itself from the vehicle.
2 Raise the front of the vehicle and support it securely. Remove the roadwheel and the hub/drum assembly (see Section 3).
3 Unbolt and remove the brake backplate from the steering knuckle.

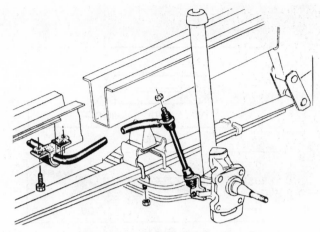

Fig. 11.5 Stabilizer bar mounting (rigid front axle)

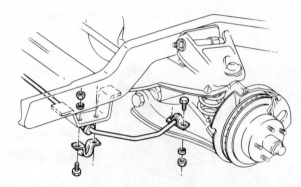

Fig. 11.6 Stabilizer bar mounting (independent front suspension)

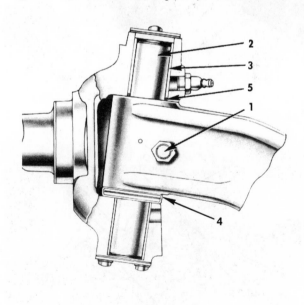

Fig. 11.8 Steering knuckle assembly (G20 Series and GE/GS 2500)

1 Lock pin	4 Thrust bearing or washers
2 Kingpin	5 Seal
3 Bushing	

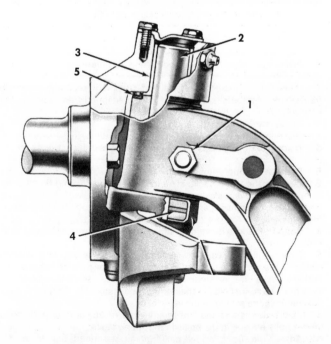

Fig. 11.7 Steering knuckle assembly (G10 Series and GE/GS 1500). For key see Fig. 11.8

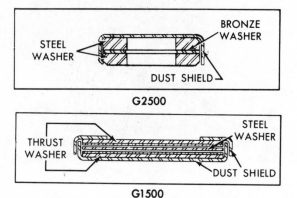

Fig. 11.9 Kingpin thrust washer installation

Fig. 11.10 Checking steering knuckle free play

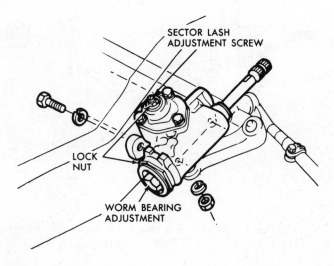

Fig. 11.11 Castor shim (rigid front axle)

Tie the plate and brake assembly out of the way to prevent strain on the brake hydraulic hoses.

4   Unbolt the steering arm then swing it and the tie-rod to one side.

5   Remove the dust caps from the top and bottom of the steering knuckle.

6   Unscrew the nut from the kingpin lock pin, and tap out the lock pin.

7   Tap the kingpin upwards until it can be removed, then take off the steering knuckle, the shim and the thrust bearing or washers.

8   If new kingpins and bushings are being installed, the Delrin split-type bushings can be removed by sliding them out of the steering knuckle bores.

9   Grease the outer surface of the new bushings and push them into position.

10 Install the O-ring seal into the upper bore in the knuckle joint below the upper bushing *except on G20 (GE/GS 2500) models where the seal is located on the axle.*

11 Commence reassembly by locating the steering knuckle on the end of the axle beam and then slide the thrust washer assembly between the lower face of the axle and the knuckle yoke.

12 Install the thrust washer assembly so that the marking on the dust shield is correctly placed (Fig. 11.9).

13 Lubricate the new kingpin and temporarily push it into position.

14 Take particular care when installing the steering knuckle on G20 (GE/GS 2500) models not to damage the kingpin upper seal. The knuckle must be seated over the seal before the lower thrust washer assembly is installed.

15 Place the jack under the steering knuckle and raise the jack just enough to take up the clearance between the knuckle yoke, the axle and the thrust bearings or washers. Now check the clearance between the upper face of the axle and the knuckle upper yoke. If the clearance exceeds 0.005 inch, add shims as necessary. On G20 (GE/GS 2500) models only, if the clearance exceeds 0.015 inch, add sufficient shims to reduce the clearance to between 0.003 and 0.008 inch (Fig. 11.10).

16 With any adjustment carried out and the kingpin finally pushed into position, make sure that the slot in the pin is in alignment with the lock pin hole in the axle.

17 Install the lock pin from the direction of the front of the vehicle.

18 Install dust caps with new gaskets.

19 Install the brake backplate assembly.

20 Install the steering arm and hub/drum assembly, adjusting the latter as described earlier in this Chapter.

21 Install the roadwheel and lower the vehicle.

22 Have the front wheel alignment checked at the earliest opportunity (see Section 34).

9   Front axle (rigid type) – removal and installation

1   Raise the front of the vehicle and support it securely under the frame side-members just behind the roadspring rear attachment brackets.

2   Remove the front roadwheels.

3   Disconnect the shock absorber lower mounting.

4   Disconnect the ends of the stabilizer bar from the brackets on the axle.

5   Remove the hub/drum assembly.

6   Remove the brake backplate and brake assembly, and tie it up out of the way to prevent strain on the hydraulic hose.

7   Using a balljoint separator, disconnect the tie-rods from the steering arms.

8   Support the axle beam on a jack and then disconnect the spring U-bolts.

9   Lower the jack carefully until the wedges which are located between the spring and the axle can be taped to the underside of the springs. These wedges are used to control castor (see Section 34) and they must be re-installed in their original positions (Fig. 11.11).

10 Remove the axle from the vehicle.

11 Installation is a reversal of removal but make sure that the spring center bolts engage in the holes in the spring seats.

12 Adjust the front wheel bearings as described earlier in this Chapter.

13 Have the front wheel alignment checked at the earliest opportunity (see Section 34).

10 Upper control arm (independent front suspension) – removal, overhaul and installation

1   Jack-up the front of the vehicle and support it under the crossmember.
2   Remove the roadwheel and then support the lower arm control arm with another jack.
3   Extract the cotter pin from the upper control arm ball stud, and unscrew the nut one turn.
4   The ball stud should now be released from the upper eye in the steering knuckle using a suitable balljoint separator or a heavy bolt and nut as shown in the illustration. The brake disc caliper will have to be removed to make room for the positioning of most tools (Fig. 11.12).
5   Remove the nut from the upper ball-stud and disconnect the balljoint from the steering knuckle.
6   With the upper control arm free, the pivot cross-shaft can now be unbolted from the crossmember. Take great care not to let the shims drop from their location between the cross-shaft and cross-member until their position and number have been established. These shims control the front wheel camber (see Section 34).
7   If the cross-shaft pivot bushings are worn, they can be renewed if the cross-shaft is first withdrawn using a suitable extractor; however, it is recommended that this work is left to your dealer.
8   The balljoint is spring-loaded to compensate for normal wear. However, when looseness in the joint indicates wear beyond the limit permissible, the balljoint should be renewed. To do this, drill out the rivets and remove the joint. The new balljoint kit will include the necessary nuts and bolts for installing.
9   Install the control arm by offering the crossshaft to the cross-member so that the special alignment washers have their convex and concave faces together.
10   Install the securing nuts but before tightening, insert the camber shims in their original positions. Tighten the nut at the thinner shim pack first.
11   Connect the ball stud to the steering knuckle, tighten to the specified torque and install a new cotter pin. If the cotter pin holes are not in alignment, tighten the nut further; never *back it off.*
12   Install the caliper and roadwheel and then lower the vehicle. Lubricate the new balljoint.

11 Lower control arm (independent front suspension) – removal, overhaul and installation

1   Raise the front of the vehicle and then remove the roadspring as described in Section 7.
2   Extract the cotter pin from the ballstud on the end of the control arm and unscrew the nut one complete turn.
3   Using the method described in the preceding Section, dislodge the ballstud from the steering knuckle lower eye.
4   Unscrew and remove the nut from the ballstud.
5   The inner cross-shaft will already have been disconnected for removal of the coil spring so that the control arm can now be removed from the vehicle.
6   The cross-shaft can be removed using a suitable extractor in order to renew the pivot bushes in the control arm. It is recommended that this work is left to your dealer.
7   The balljoint can be removed by pressing it out of the control arm. Distance pieces should be used in conjunction with a clamp for this job. (Fig. 11.13).
8   Installation is a reversal of removal but refer to Section 7 for details of coil spring installation. Tighten all nuts to the specified torque, and lubricate the new balljoint on completion.

12 Steering knuckle (independent front suspension) – removal and installation

1   Raise the front of the vehicle and support it securely on axle stands placed under the frame sidemembers.
2   Place additional jacks under the lower control arm so that the coil spring is compressed in its normal 'on the road' state.
3   Remove the roadwheel.
4   Remove the caliper (see Chapter 9).
5   Remove the disc splash shield after unscrewing the bolts.

Fig. 11.12 Method of disconnecting steering balljoints (independent front suspension)

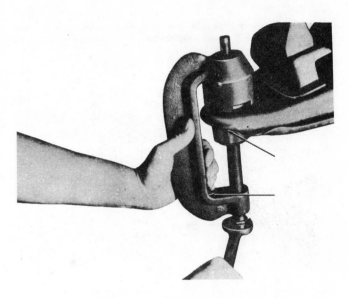

Fig. 11.13 Pressing a balljoint swivel from a suspension control arm (Tool arrowed)

10.6 Front suspension upper control arm

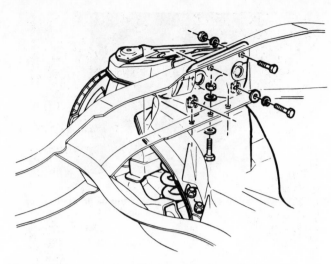

Fig. 11.14 Crossmember attachment to frame (independent front suspension)

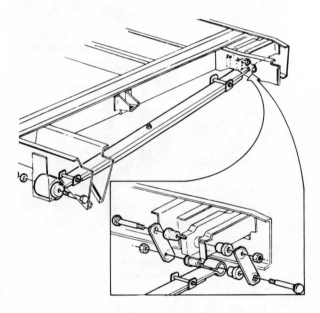

Fig. 11.15 Rear spring attachment (early models)

6   Disconnect the tie-rod balljoint from the eye of the steering arm on the knuckle.
7   Extract the cotter pins from the upper and lower ball studs, then release the studs from the eyes in the steering knuckle as described in Sections 10 and 11.
8   Remove the steering knuckle.
9   Installation is a reversal of removal; tighten all nuts to specified torque.

13 Complete independent front suspension assembly – removal and installation

1   Raise the front of the vehicle and support on stands placed under the frame sidemembers. Remove the roadwheels.
2   Disconnect the front shock absorber lower mounting.
3   Disconnect the idler arm and the Pitman arm from the steering linkage relay rod.
4   Support the engine under the oil pan and remove the front mounting center bolts.
5   Disconnect the brake hydraulic line from the tee-union on the crossmember.
6   Unscrew and remove the bolts which attach the crossmember to the frame side-members, supporting the crossmember on a trolley jack at the same time.
7   Lower the crossmember jack and withdraw the complete front axle assembly from the vehicle.
8   Overhaul may be carried out by removing the individual components as described in earlier Sections of this Chapter.
9   Installation is a reversal of removal but on completion, bleed the brake hydraulic circuit and have the front wheel alignment checked at the earliest opportunity.

14 Rear hubs (fully-floating rear axle) – dismantling and reassembly

1   Refer to Chapter 8, Section 9 for full information in connection with the rear axle assembly.

15 Rear spring – removal and installation

1   Raise the rear of the vehicle and place axle stands under the frame sidemembers.
2   Support the rear axle so that tension is removed from the road spring.
3   Disconnect the bolt which secures the shackle to the spring hanger.
4   Remove the bolt which secures the spring to the front hanger.
5   Remove the U-bolts and withdraw the spring plates.

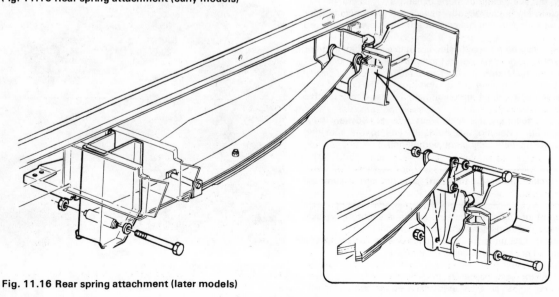

Fig. 11.16 Rear spring attachment (later models)

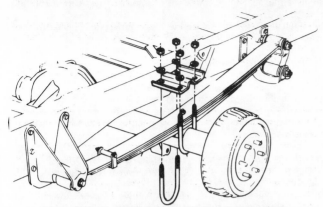

NOTE: "U" BOLTS MUST BE LOCATED AROUND THE AXLE TUBE SO THAT THE LEGS PASS THE SPRING SEAT WITHIN .060.

Fig. 11.17 Typical rear spring U-bolt attachment

6   Remove the springs.

7   New spring bushings can be installed using a bolt, nuts and suitable distance pieces to draw out the old ones and pull the new ones into position.

8   Wire-brush the spring leaves and inspect for cracks. If any are found, have a new leaf fitted by your dealer or obtain a new spring.

9   Installation is a reversal of removal; adjust the height of the axle and frame to align the spring eyes with hangers. Tighten the U-bolts nuts diagonally (Fig. 11.17).

10 Only on very early models do the spring bushings require lubrication, later vehicles have flexible type bushings.

11 The spring leaves are lubricated during manufacture and normally do not require further attention although occasionally spraying with rust preventative fluid or penetrating oil will help to keep them in good condition.

16 Tie-rod end balljoints – renewal

1   The most likely points of wear in the steering linkage are at the tie-rod balljoints which connect to the steering arms.

2   If wear is detected in a balljoint, extract the cotter pin from the ball-stud and then unscrew the nut a few turns.

3   Ideally, a balljoint separator or forked wedges should now be used to disconnect the tie-rod end from the steering arm eye. If this is not available place a heavy hammer against one side of the eye and then strike the opposite side with a lighter hammer. This will have the effect of momentarily distorting the eye so that the tapered ball stud drops free (Fig. 11.18).

4   Remove the ball-stud nut and disconnect the tie-rod end.

5   Now count the number of exposed threads at the point where the tie-rod end enters the tie-rod, and record this figure.

6   Release the clamp pinch-bolt, and unscrew and remove the tie-rod balljoint assembly.

7   If the inner balljoint (independent front suspension) is worn, this too should be removed from the relay rod in exactly the same way.

8   Clean and lubricate the threads in the tie-rod so that the new tie-rod balljoints can be screwed freely into position.

9   Screw the balljoint assembly into position so that the same number of threads is exposed as was originally recorded. If both balljoints were removed from the tie-rod (independent suspension), then an equal number of threads should be exposed with a differential not exceeding three threads.

10 Position the clamps as shown in the diagrams, and set the balljoints in their correct attitudes and reconnect their studs to the steering arm eye or relay rod as appropriate (Figs. 11.19 and 11.20).

11 Tighten the ball-stud nuts. If the cotter pin hole and slot are not in alignment, tighten the nut further, *never back it off*.

12 Before tightening the tie-rod clamp pinch-bolts, on vehicles having independent front suspension, make sure that the clamps are between the locating dimples, that the pinch-bolts are set at the specified

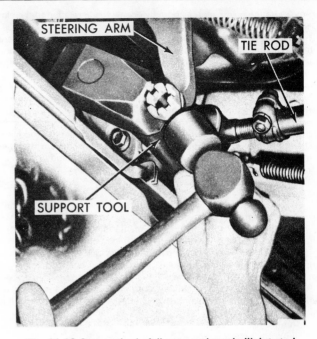

Fig. 11.18 One method of disconnecting a balljoint stud

STEERING ARM

TIE ROD

SUPPORT TOOL

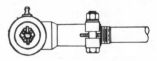

Fig. 11.19 Tie-rod clamp setting diagram (rigid axle)

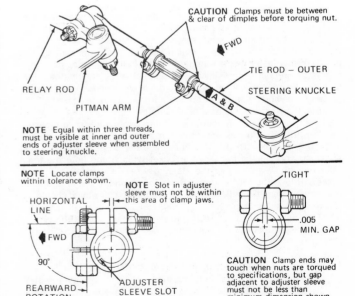

CAUTION Clamps must be between & clear of dimples before torquing nut.

FWD

TIE ROD – OUTER

STEERING KNUCKLE

A & B

RELAY ROD

PITMAN ARM

NOTE Equal within three threads, must be visible at inner and outer ends of adjuster sleeve when assembled to steering knuckle.

NOTE Locate clamps within tolerance shown.

NOTE Slot in adjuster sleeve must not be within this area of clamp jaws.

HORIZONTAL LINE

FWD

90°

REARWARD ROTATION

ADJUSTER SLEEVE SLOT

VIEW A

TIGHT

.005 MIN. GAP

CAUTION Clamp ends may touch when nuts are torqued to specifications, but gap adjacent to adjuster sleeve must not be less than minimum dimension shown.

VIEW B

Fig. 11.20 Tie-rod clamp setting diagram (independent front suspension)

attitude and the clamp slot is correctly positioned in relation to the slot in the sleeve.

13 Lubricate the tie-rods on completion and then have the front wheel alignment (toe-in) checked and adjusted as described in Section 34.

17 Relay rod and idler arm (independent front suspension) – removal, testing and installation

1 The relay rod can be removed after disconnecting the tie-rod inner balljoints from it and then disconnecting the relay rod from the idler arm and the Pitman arm. The disconnection of the ball-studs should be carried out as described in the preceding Section.

2 Wear in an idler arm assembly can be checked by the following method.

3 Raise the front of the vehicle so that the roadwheels hang free and are in the 'straight ahead' position.

4 Attach a spring scale to the end of the idler arm as near to the relay rod as possible and exert a pull of 25 lb first in one direction and then in the other while measuring the total distance that the end of the arm moves. This should not exceed $\frac{1}{8}$ inch in either direction, making a total movement of $\frac{1}{4}$ inch (Fig.11.22).

5 If the movement exceeds that specified, then the arm must be renewed as a complete assembly as its interior flexible component has deteriorated.

6 To remove the idler arm, disconnect it from the relay rod and then unbolt it from the frame (photo).

7 Installation is a reversal of removal, but have the front wheel alignment (toe-in) checked at the earliest opportunity (see Section 34).

18 Manual steering gear – adjustments

1 Several adjustments are possible to the manual steering gear. These are not to be considered routine but should be carried out only when slackness in the steering, or noise when travelling over rough terrain, indicates that the steering mechanism requires attention.

2 First check that the steering linkage is not worn and that all attachment bolts are secure.

Worm bearing adjustment

3 Disconnect the battery ground lead.

4 Raise the front of the vehicle and support securely.

5 Unscrew and remove the Pitman arm nut and washer.

6 Mark the relationship of the Pitman arm to the shaft and then, with a heavy duty extractor, remove the arm (Fig.11.24).

7 Loosen the adjuster screw locknut on the steering gear and then back off the adjuster screw $\frac{1}{4}$ turn.

8 Remove the horn button or shroud (see Section 19).

9 Turn the steering in one direction gently until it comes up against its stop. Now measure the number of turns to the opposite stop, then divide the number of turns by two in order that the steering can then be set to its center position. Mark the rim of the steering wheel with a piece of tape and count the number of turns as the tape passes a fixed point on the instrument panel.

10 The steering wheel must now be rotated through 90° to measure bearing drag. To do this, either attach a correctly calculated torque wrench and socket to the steering wheel nut or attach a cord and spring balance to the handle of a socket wrench and note the force (reading) required to move the steering wheel. If the latter is used, make sure that the cord is attached one inch from the center of the nut down the wrench handle as the thrust bearing pre-load should be between 6 and 11 lbf in.

11 Turn the adjuster screw as necessary and then repeat the turning check until pre-load is to specification, then tighten the adjuster screw locknut.

Pitman shaft lash adjustment (over-center pre-load)

12 Set the steering to the center position as described in paragraph 8.

13 Release the lash adjuster locknut and turn the adjuster screw clockwise until any backlash is eliminated. Retighten the locknut.

14 Check the turning torque as described in paragraph 10 taking the highest reading as the wheel passes through the center point. This should be between 5 and 11 lbf in *more* than the figure to which the worm bearing pre-load was finally set. If necessary release the locknut

and turn the adjuster screw until the correct over-centre torque is obtained.

15 Install the pitman arm, connect the battery and install the horn button.

Steering column lower bearing adjustment

16 Slacken the clamp at the lower end of the steering shaft.

17 Have an assistant apply reasonable hand pressure on the steering wheel in a downward direction and then set the position of the clamp as shown (Fig.11.26).

18 Tighten the clamp bolt to the specified torque without moving the position of the clamp.

Shift-tube adjustment (automatic transmission)

19 Set the steering column shift tube lever in the Neutral or Drive position.

20 Loosen the adjusting ring clamp screws and turn the shift tube adjusting ring to obtain between 0.33 and 0.36 inch clearance using a feeler gauge between the shift tube lever and the adjusting ring (Figs. 11.27 and 11.28).

21 When the adjustment is correct, tighten the clamp ring screws.

19 Steering wheel – removal and installation

1 Disconnect the battery ground cable.

2 Remove the horn button or shroud, cup, belleville spring and bushing.

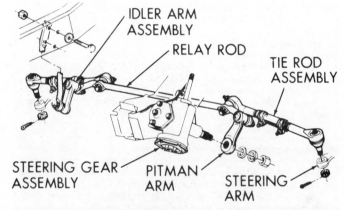

Fig. 11.21 Relay rod arrangement (independent front suspension)

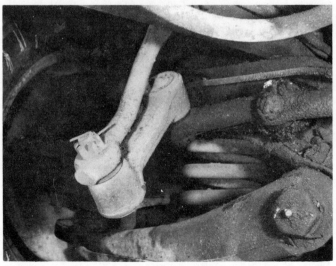

17.6 Steering idler arm (independent front suspension)

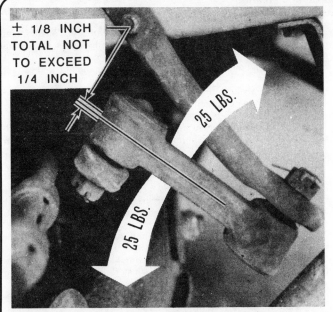

± 1/8 INCH
TOTAL NOT
TO EXCEED
1/4 INCH

25 LBS.

25 LBS.

Fig. 11.22 Steering idler checking diagram (independent front suspension)

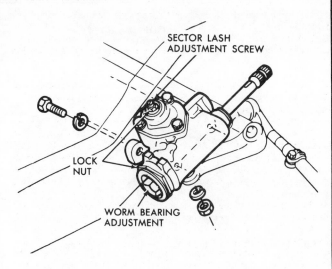

SECTOR LASH
ADJUSTMENT SCREW

LOCK
NUT

WORM BEARING
ADJUSTMENT

Fig. 11.23 Manual steering gear adjustment points

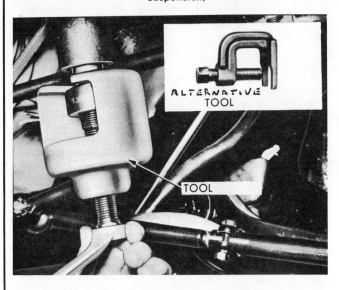

ALTERNATIVE
TOOL

TOOL

Fig. 11.24 Disconnecting a Pitman arm

Fig. 11.25 Checking worm bearing drag

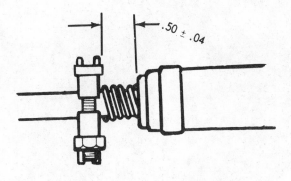

.50 ± .04

Fig. 11.26 Steering column lower bearing adjustment diagram

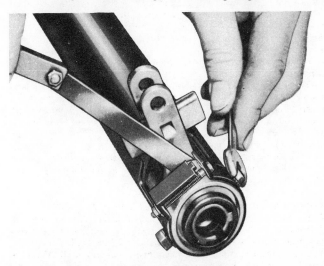

Fig. 11.27 Shift tube adjustment (3-speed manual transmission)

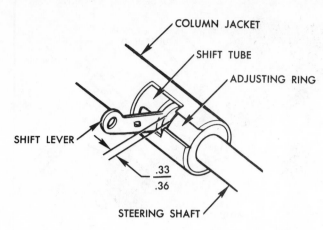

Fig. 11.28 Shift tube adjustment (automatic transmission)

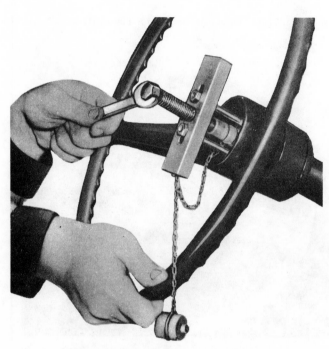

Fig. 11.29 Removing the steering wheel

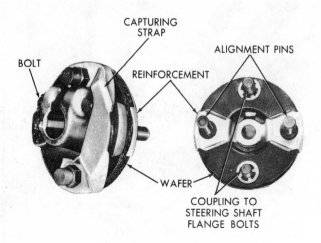

Fig. 11.30 Typical flexible steering coupling

3   Set the front roadwheels in the 'straight ahead' position and then mark the relationship of the steering wheel to the upper end of the shaft.

4   Unscrew and remove the steering wheel retaining nut, and extract the washer.

5   A suitable puller will now be required to remove the steering wheel from the shaft. Do not attempt to jar the wheel off by thumping it from the rear side as damage to the column may result.

6   Installation is a reversal of removal, but make sure that the turn signal switch is in the neutral position before pushing the wheel into place.

20 Steering shaft flexible coupling – removal and installation

1   On later vehicles which have this type of coupling, remove the nuts from the flange bolts.

2   Remove the coupling clamp pinch bolt. A 12 point socket wrench will be required for this.

3   Unscrew and remove the bolts which hold the steering box to the frame and then lower the steering box just far enough to be able to withdraw the coupling.

4   Installation is a reversal of removal but attach the coupling to the wormshaft so that the flat on the shaft is in alignment with the flat on the coupling. Push the coupling onto the wormshaft until the coupling reinforcement bottoms.

5   Make sure that a coupling-to-flange dimension of between 0.250 and 0.375 inch is maintained. The alignment pins should be centered in the flange slots.

21 Pitman shaft oil seal (manual steering) – renewal

1   A leaking Pitman shaft (sector shaft) oil seal can be renewed without having to remove or dismantle the steering gear.

2   Remove the Pitman arm as described in Section 18, paragraphs 5 and 6.

3   Center the steering gear by setting the front roadwheels in the 'straight ahead' position and then checking that the wormshaft flat is in the uppermost position.

4   Unbolt and remove the side cover from the steering box together with the Pitman shaft.

5   Pry the defective Pitman shaft oil seal from its seat and tap a new one into position.

6   Remove the lash adjuster screw locknut and then separate the side cover from the Pitman shaft by turning the lash adjuster screw clockwise and winding it out of the cover.

7   Install the Pitman shaft into the steering box so that the center tooth of the sector in the shaft enters the center tooth cutout of the ball nut.

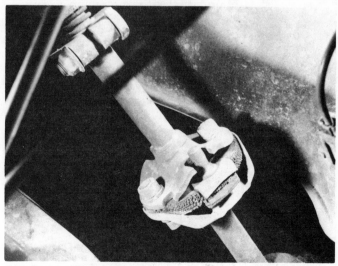

20.1 Steering shaft flexible coupling

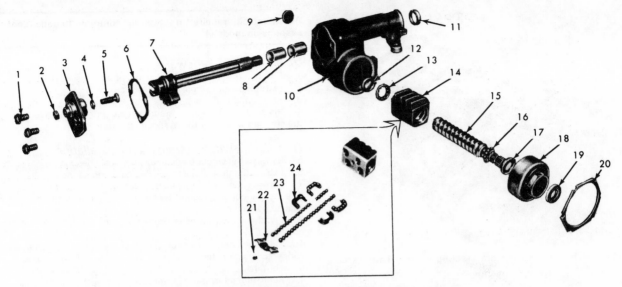

Fig. 11.31 Exploded view of the manual steering gear

1	Side cover screws	7	Pitman shaft	13	Lower bearing race	19	Seal
2	Lash adjuster locknut	8	Pitman shaft bushings	14	Ball nut	20	Locknut
3	Side cover and bushing	9	Expansion plug	15	Wormshaft	21	Clamp screw
4	Shim	10	Housing	16	Upper bearing race	22	Ball guide clamp
5	Adjuster screw	11	Oil seal	17	Upper bearing track	23	Balls
6	Gasket	12	Lower bearing track	18	Adjuster plug	24	Ball guides

8   Fill the steering gear with the specified type of lubricant and then locate a new side cover gasket in position.

9   Install the side cover onto the lash adjuster screw by passing a thin screwdriver through the hole in the side cover and turning the screw counterclockwise until it bottoms. Now turn the screw back $\frac{1}{4}$ turn.

10 Install the side cover.

11 Carry out the adjustment described in Section 18, paragraphs 2 to 15.

12 Install the Pitman arm.

22 Manual steering gear – removal and installation

Early models with rigid front axle

1   Raise the front of the vehicle and support it securely.

2   Remove the deflector and extension assembly.

3   Disconnect the Pitman arm having first marked its relative position on the sector shaft.

4   Disconnect the brake pedal from the lower brake control rods (see Chapter 9).

5   Disconnect the transmission shift linkage.

6   Remove the bolts which secure the steering gear to the frame.

7   Remove the brake pedal complete, then peel back the floor covering and remove the toe-pan cover plate.

8   Disconnect the steering column bracket.

9   Due to the fact that the steering assembly has no flexible coupling, and that it is cradle-mounted, the complete assembly must be withdrawn into the vehicle interior.

Later models with independent front suspension

10 Set the front roadwheels in the 'straight ahead' position.

11 Disconnect the steering shaft flexible coupling.

12 Mark the relationship of the Pitman arm to the Pitman shaft and then remove it using a heavy duty puller.

13 Unscrew and remove the steering gear mounting bolts and withdraw the gear downwards from the vehicle.

14 Installation of both types of gear is a reversal of removal.

Fig. 11.32 Typical steering gear mounting (rigid front axle)

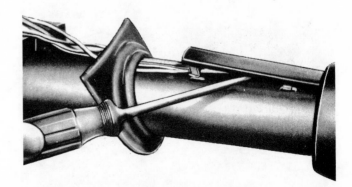

Fig. 11.33 Removing wiring harness protector from manual steering column (independent front suspension)

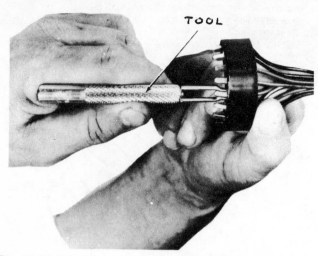

Fig. 11.34 Removing wires from steering column harness connector

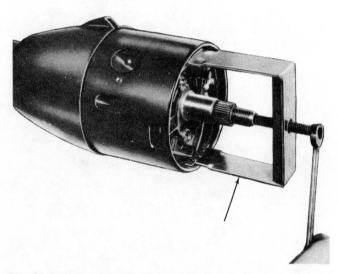

Fig. 11.35 Removing direction signal switch housing cover (tilt steering column) – puller arrowed

23 In-vehicle repairs to steering columns (independent front suspension models)

Upper bearing - renewal

1   Remove the steering wheel as previously described.
2   Extract the turn signal cancelling cam.
3   Pry out the upper bearing.
4   Install the components in the reverse order to removal and tighten the steering wheel nut to the specified torque.

Turn signal switch - removal and installation

5   Remove the steering wheel as previously described.
6   Extract the turn signal cancelling cam and spring.
7   Remove the column-to-instrument panel trim plate.
8   Disconnect the signal switch wiring harness at the half-moon shaped connector.
9   Pry the wiring harness protector from the slots in the steering column.
10 Mark the position of each wire and then push each one out of the connector using a tool similar to the one shown to depress the wire retainer tabs.
11 Remove the turn signal lever screw and withdraw the lever.
12 Depress the hazard warning lamp knob, then unscrew and remove the knob.
13 *If a Tilt column is installed* (see Section 26) unscrew and remove the tilt release lever. If the vehicle is equipped with automatic transmission, remove the speed selector position indicator dial screws and withdraw the dial, needle, cap and bulb from the housing cover. A small two-legged puller will now be required having outward pointing claws to pull off the turn signal housing cover. The turn signal switch can now be removed after extracting the three mounting screws and guiding the wiring harness through the opening in the shift lever housing.
14 Installation of the turn signal switch to both types of column is a reversal of removal.

24 Steering column (rigid front axle vehicles) – removal, overhaul and installation

1   Remove the complete steering gear as described in Section 22, paragraphs 1 to 9.
2   Remove the transmission lever housing from the steering gear mounting pad and then loosen the steering column and remove it after first noting its relationship to the gear.
3   Before dismantling the column, make sure that the necessary spare parts are available; otherwise a complete new or used column in good condition may be the best solution.

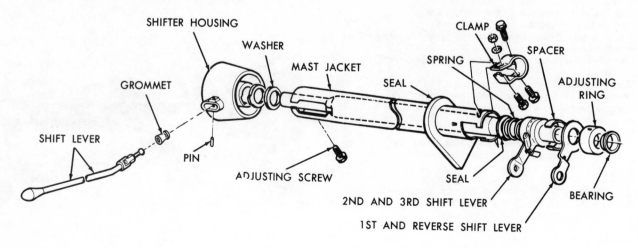

Fig. 11.36 Steering column jacket and shifter tube (rigid front axle) – Manual transmission

4   Remove the spacer and thrust washer from the shifter lever housing and then remove the housing.
5   Remove the bushing and bushing seat from the upper end of the column jacket.
6   Remove the bolt and screws from the adjusting ring clamp at the lower end of the column and then remove the clamp lower bearing and adjusting ring.
7   On 3-speed models, remove 1st and reverse shift lever and spacer.
8   On vehicles equipped with automatic transmission, extract the three screws from the selector plate clamp ring.
9   Tap the shift tube together with the lever out of the column jacket using a piece of wood.
10 Remove the felt seal from the shift tube.
11 Remove the firewall clamp oil seal and the dash panel seal from the column jacket.
12 Renew all worn components, then reassemble and adjust as described in Section 18, paragraphs 16 to 21.
13 Make sure that the column jacket is aligned with the steering gear by having the marks made before removal opposite each other.

25 Steering column (independent front suspension vehicles) – removal, overhaul and installation

1   Disconnect the battery ground cable.
2   *On column-shift models,* disconnect the transmission shift rods at the lower end of the column.
3   Disconnect the flexible coupling on the steering shaft.
4   Remove the clamp screws on the engine side of the firewall and slide the clamp downwards.
5   Working inside the vehicle, unbolt the toe-pan cover and slide both it and its seal up the column.
6   Remove the steering wheel as previously described in this Chapter.
7   Disconnect the turn signal wiring harness and, with automatic transmission, also the indicator conductor tube at the instrument panel.

8   Disconnect the column support bracket from the instrument panel.
9   Lower the column and withdraw it so that by rotating it, the shift levers clear the toe-pan opening.
10 To dismantle the column, slide the shaft out of the lower end of the column.
11 Remove the lower bearing pre-load spring and clamp from the shaft.
12 Remove the back-up lamp switch.
13 On steering column shift models, drive out the shift lever pivot pin and remove the lever.

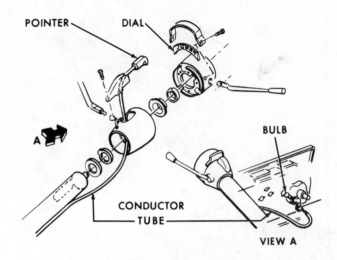

Fig. 11.37 Steering column jacket and shifter tube (independent front suspension) – Automatic transmission

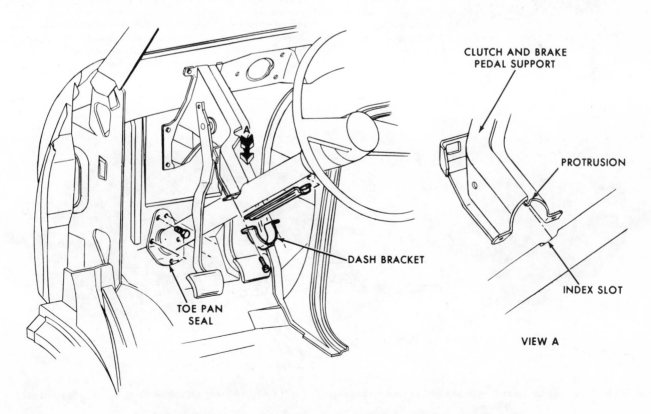

Fig. 11.38 Steering column installation details (independent front suspension)

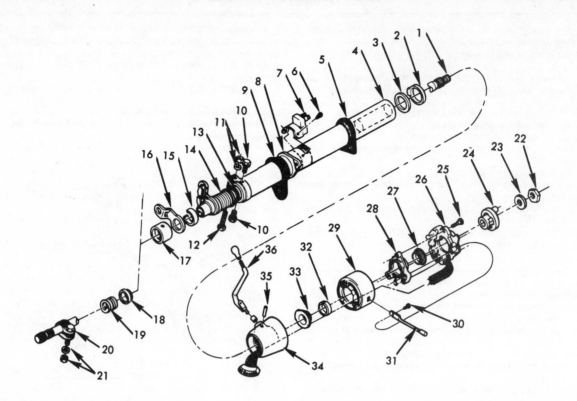

Fig. 11.39 Exploded view of steering column (independent front suspension)

1	Steering shaft	11	Nut and lockwasher
2	Shift housing bushing	12	Clamp bolt
3	Bushing seal	13	Shift tube felt washer
4	Column jacket	14	Shift tube assembly
5	Cover	15	Shift lever spacer
6	Screw	16	1st/reverse shift lever
7	Back-up lamp switch	17	Adjusting ring
8	Seal retainer	18	Lower bearing
9	Toe-pan seal	19	Bearing pre-load spring
10	Clamp screws		

20	Pre-load spring clamp	28	Switch contact support
21	Nut and lockwasher	29	Turn signal housing
22	Steering shaft nut	30	Screw
23	Lockwasher	31	Turn signal switch lever
24	Turn signal switch cancelling cam	32	Rubber ring
25	Screw	33	Plastic thrust washer
26	Turn signal switch	34	Shift lever housing
27	Upper bearing	35	Shift lever pin
		36	Shift lever

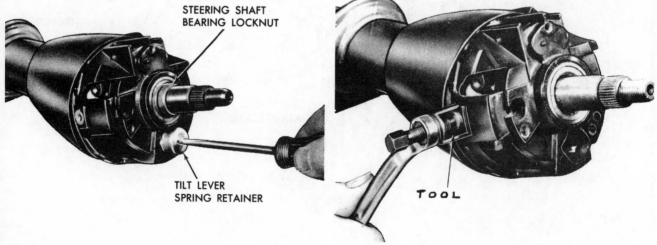

Fig. 11.40 Removing spring and retainer from tilt column bearing housing

Fig. 11.41 Removing tilt column bearing housing pivot pin

14 Remove the turn signal switch cancelling cam and switch lever.
15 Remove the column wiring harness cover.
16 Extract the turn signal switch screws, rotate the turn signal switch housing counterclockwise and remove it partially from the column. Once the plastic thrust washer and shift level housing have been removed then the turn signal switch housing can be fully withdrawn.
17 Press the steering shaft upper bearing from the switch contact support.
18 Remove the shift lever housing seat and bushing from the upper end of the column.
19 Remove the adjusting ring clamp followed by the ring and the lower bearing.
20 *With 3-speed steering column shift*, remove 1st/reverse shift lever and spacer. If the vehicle is equipped with automatic transmission, remove the selector plate clamping ring screws. Tap the shift tube out of the column with a piece of hardwood. Remove the felt seal from the shift tube.
21 Remove the firewall clamp, toe-pan seal and dash panel seals from the column jacket.
22 Renew all worn components and reassemble by reversing the dismantling operations. Carry out the necessary adjustments described in Section 18.
23 To install the column, first install plastic spacers onto the flexible coupling alignment pins, these items are available from your dealer.
24 Working inside the vehicle pass the lower end of the column through the hole in the toe-pan and connect the flexible coupling.
25 Engage the slot in the column jacket with the lug on the pedal support bracket.
26 Attach the column upper bracket but with the bolts only finger-tight.
27 Push the column downwards until the shaft flange bottoms on the plastic spacers of the coupling, then tighten the upper bracket bolts to the specified torque.
28 Pull out the plastic spacers using a hooked piece of wire. The coupling-to-flange clearance should be between 0.25 and 0.325 inch.

Re-adjust if necessary.
29 Re-connect the toe-pan cover and seal; connect the turn signal wiring harness, the conductor tube where applicable, the transmission linkage and the battery ground cable.
30 Install the steering wheel.

26 Tilt-type steering column bearing housing – removal and installation

1 The bearing housing on this type of column can be renewed without the need to remove the complete column assembly.
2 Disconnect the battery ground cable.
3 Remove the steering wheel as described earlier in this Chapter; also the turn signal switch.
4 *On column shift models,* drive out the shift lever pivot pin and remove the lever.
5 Using the tilt release lever, set the steering column in the fully UP position. Extract the tilt lever spring and retainer using a screwdriver. Insert the screwdriver into the slot and push it in about $\frac{3}{16}$ inch. Rotate it clockwise about $\frac{1}{8}$ of a turn until the retainer ears align with the grooves in the housing; then the spring and retainer can be withdrawn.
6 Remove the steering shaft bearing locknut and then extract the upper bearing race and track.
7 Remove the two bearing housing pivot pins. (Fig.11.4l).
8 Pull up the tilt release lever to disengage the lock shoes and remove the bearing housing.
9 Installation is a reversal of removal.

27 Tilt type steering column – removal, overhaul and installation

1 Removal of this type of column is very similar to the procedure described in Section 25 except that on vehicles equipped with

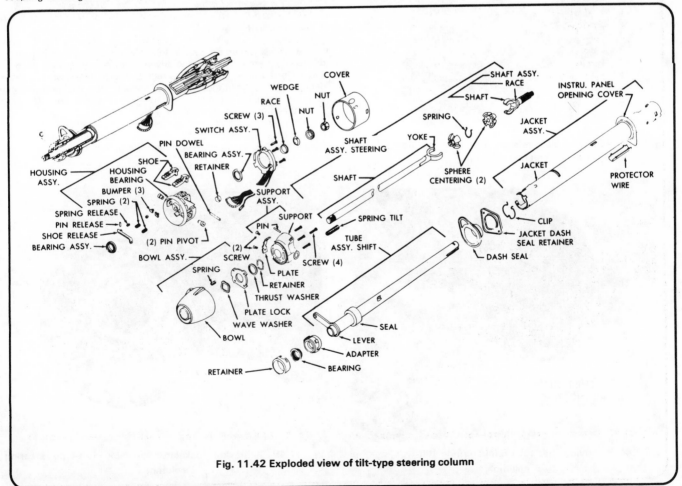

Fig. 11.42 Exploded view of tilt-type steering column

automatic transmission, disconnect the single wire at the fuse block and unclip it from the parking brake bracket.

2   With the complete column removed from the vehicle, withdraw the bearing housing as described in Section 26, paragraph 4, through 8.

3   Press the bearing from the housing.

4   Remove the tilt release lever.

5   Drive out the shoe release lever pivot pin and extract the lever spring and wedge.

6   Drive out the lock shoe pin, and remove the shoes and springs.

7   Withdraw the steering shaft through the upper end of the column.

8   If the shaft itself must be dismantled, turn the upper shaft through 90° in relation to the lower one and slide the upper shaft and centering spheres from the lower shaft.

9   Remove the four bearing housing support screws and withdraw the support.

10 *On column shift models,* remove the shift tube index plate (two screws).

11 Pry out the shift tube retaining ring and remove the thrust washer.

12 Remove the neutral or back-up lamp switch.

13 Remove the shift tube and the lockplate followed by the wave washer.

14 Remove the shift lever housing.

Fig. 11.43 Removing shoe release lever pivot pin from tilt-type steering column

15 *On column shift models,* remove the shift lever spring by winding it up with a pair of pliers.

16 Reassembly and installation are reversals of dismantling and removal; lubricate the bearings and then tighten the upper bearing locknut until all lash is removed then tighten between $\frac{1}{16}$ and $\frac{1}{8}$ of a turn further with the column in the 'straight ahead' position.

28 Manual steering gear – overhaul

1   It is recommended that a worn steering gear assembly is renewed complete rather than overhauling the original unit.

2   The removal and installation of the bushings and bearings require special equipment; the ball nut and wormshaft are supplied as a complete assembly so it will be realised that there is little to be saved by dismantling and reassembling the worn gear.

29 Power steering – description and maintenance

1   The power steering system operates on hydraulic pressure which is generated in a belt-driven pump. This pressure is available when the engine is running to assist in actuating the steering gear as the steering wheel is turned.

2   Any failure in the power-assist system is not dangerous as the normal manual steering capability will be retained although with noticeably greater effort being required to turn the wheel.

3   At the intervals specified in Routine Maintenance check the fluid level in the following way. Run the engine to normal operating temperature and then switch off. Remove the fluid reservoir cap and check that the fluid level is up to the HOT mark on the dipstick. Top up if necessary with the specified type of fluid only.

4   If a complete fluid change is called for, due to contamination or renewal of system components, carry out the following operations:

(i)   *Fill system with specified fluid to the COLD mark.*
(ii) *Bleed the power steering system as described in Section 30 of this Chapter.*

5   At regular intervals, check the tension of the steering pump drivebelt. Where the driving and driven pulley centers are between 13 and 16 inches apart, then the belt tension should be adjusted to give a deflection of $\frac{1}{2}$ inch at the midpoint of the belt when it is pressed firmly with the thumb. If the pulley centers are between 7 and 10 inches apart, then the deflection should be $\frac{1}{4}$ inch.

6   To adjust the belt tension, release the power steering pump mountings and pull the pump away from the engine. Do not pry against the fluid reservoir or filler neck. Re-tighten the bolts when the tension is correct.

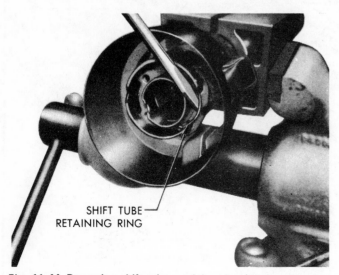

Fig. 11.44 Removing shift tube retaining ring (tilt-type steering column)

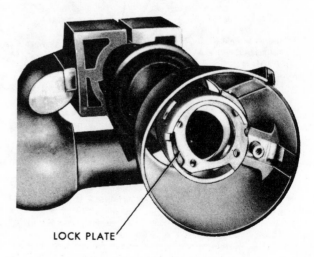

Fig. 11.45 Removing lockplate assembly (tilt-type steering column)

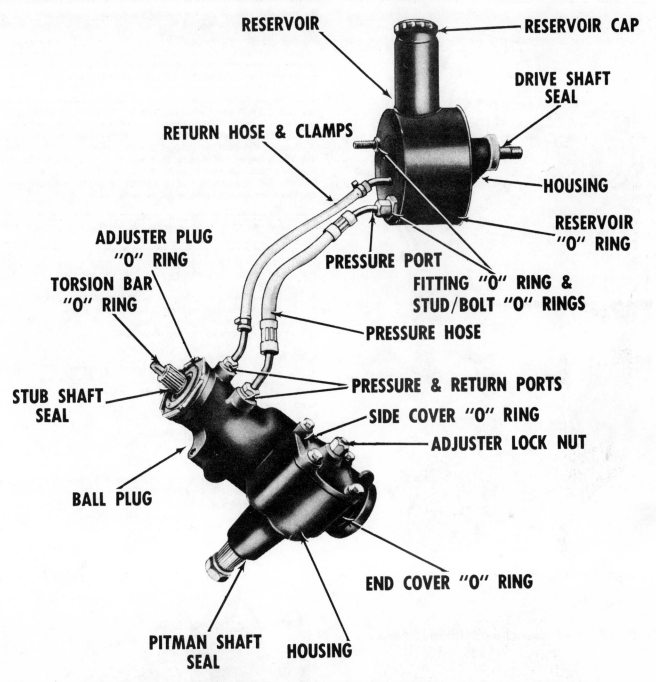

RESERVOIR

RESERVOIR CAP

DRIVE SHAFT SEAL

RETURN HOSE & CLAMPS

HOUSING

RESERVOIR "O" RING

ADJUSTER PLUG "O" RING

TORSION BAR "O" RING

PRESSURE PORT

FITTING "O" RING & STUD/BOLT "O" RINGS

PRESSURE HOSE

STUB SHAFT SEAL

PRESSURE & RETURN PORTS

SIDE COVER "O" RING

ADJUSTER LOCK NUT

BALL PLUG

END COVER "O" RING

PITMAN SHAFT SEAL

HOUSING

Fig. 11.46 Typical power steering pump and gear

30 Power steering hydraulic system – bleeding

1   Reference should also be made to Chapter 9, Section 17 for details of bleeding the brake assist hydro-boost system which relies on the power steering hydraulic system.

2   Turn the steering to full left lock and fill the system to the COLD mark on the dipstick in the pump fluid reservoir. Raise the front roadwheels.

3   Start the engine and run it at a fast idle. Recheck the fluid level and add if necessary to bring it to the COLD mark.

4   Now bleed the system by turning the wheels from stop to stop but only contact the stops very lightly and gently. Aerated fluid will be obvious by its light tan or red appearance. Maintain the fluid level in the reservoir.

5   Turn the roadwheels to the center position and continue to run the engine for two or three minutes then switch off.

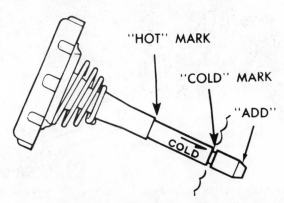

"HOT" MARK

"COLD" MARK

"ADD"

COLD

Fig. 11.47 Power steering fluid reservoir cap and dipstick

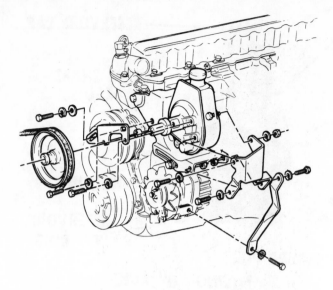

Fig. 11.48 Power steering pump attachment (six cylinder engines)

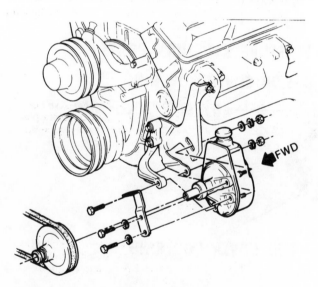

Fig. 11.49 Power steering pump attachment (V8 engine)

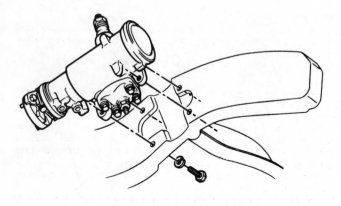

Fig. 11.50 Typical power steering gear mounting arrangement

6   Run the vehicle on the road to check for normal power-assist operation and then when the fluid is at normal operating temperature, check and top up to the HOT mark.

31 Power steering pump – removal and installation

1   Disconnect the fluid hoses from the power steering pump and tie them up in the raised position to prevent loss of fluid. Cap or tape the open ends to prevent loss of fluid.
2   Catch the fluid as it draws from the pump.
3   Loosen the pump-to-bracket mounting nuts, push the pump in toward the engine and remove the drivebelt.
4   Unbolt and remove the pump from the vehicle.
5   Installation is a reversal of removal but adjust the drivebelt tension and bleed the system as described in Sections 29 and 30.

32 Power steering gear – removal, overhaul, adjustment and installation

1   Disconnect the flexible hoses from the steering gear. Tie them up in a raised position to prevent loss of fluid and cap their open ends to stop entry of dirt.
2   Tape over the holes in the gear case to prevent entry of dirt.
3   Disconnect the steering shaft flexible coupling.
4   Mark the relationship of the Pitman arm to the Pitman shaft and then remove the arm using a heavy duty puller.
5   Unscrew and remove the bolts which hold the steering gear to the frame and remove the gear.
6   If the gear is faulty or worn, it should be replaced with a new or factory reconditioned unit. Do not dismantle the original unit.
7   Slight malfunctions in the operation of the gear may be due to the need for adjustment, and the following should be checked and any necessary adjustment carried out as described.

Thrust bearing adjustment
8   Drain the fluid from the gear by rotating the stub shaft fully in both directions several times.
9   Relieve the staking and unscrew the adjuster plug locknut.
10 Screw the adjuster plug fully in until it and the thrust bearing are bottomed. A torque of 20 lbf ft should be sufficient to achieve this,

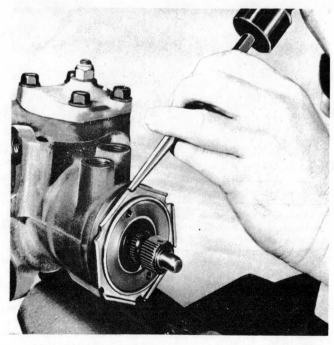

Fig. 11.51 Releasing thrust bearing locknut (power steering gear)

Fig. 11.52 Removing thrust bearing locknut (power steering gear)

Fig. 11.53 Marking power steering housing for thrust bearing adjustment

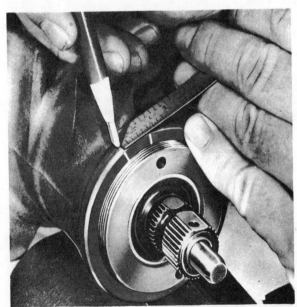

Fig. 11.54 Making second mark for power steering thrust bearing adjustment

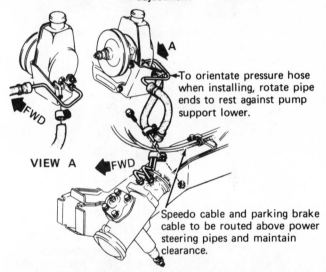

To orientate pressure hose when installing, rotate pipe ends to rest against pump support lower.

VIEW A

Speedo cable and parking brake cable to be routed above power steering pipes and maintain clearance.

Fig. 11.55 Power steering hydraulic pipes (six cylinder engines)

using a suitable pin wrench.

11 Make a mark on the housing opposite one of the pin wrench holes. Now measure back in a counterclockwise direction $\frac{1}{2}$ inch and make a second mark on the housing (Fig. 11.54).

12 Now turn the adjuster plug counterclockwise until the hole opposite the first mark is in alignment with the second mark.

13 Without moving the position of the adjuster plug, screw on and stake the locknut.

Pitman shaft lash adjuster (over-center preload)

14 For procedure, refer to Section 18, paragraph 12 through 15.

15 Installation is a reversal of removal but when connecting the flexible coupling make sure that the pinch bolt passes through the undercut in the steering shaft.

16 Make sure that the coupling alignment pins are centered in the

slots in the steering shaft flange. Special plastic screws are available from your dealer for this job but if used they must be removed before tightening the coupling bolts to the specified torque.

17 Bleed the system as described in Section 30.

33 Power steering pipes – removal and installation

1 It is most important that the hoses and pipelines of the power steering hydraulic system are inspected regularly and renewed immediately if there are signs of leakage or if the hoses or pipes are damaged, corroded or have deteriorated in any way.

2 Always mark the position of the hoses or pipes so that they can be reconnected correctly.

3 On vehicles with a Hydro-boost brake servo system, refer also to Chapter 9 for the routing of the hoses on this system.

4 Always bleed the steering hydraulic systems once the new components have been installed.

34 Steering angles and front wheel alignment

1   Accurate front wheel alignment is essential for good steering and slow tire wear. Before considering the steering angle, check that the tires are correctly inflated, that the front wheels are not buckled, the hub bearings are not worn or incorrectly adjusted and that the steering linkage is in good order, without slackness or wear at the joints.

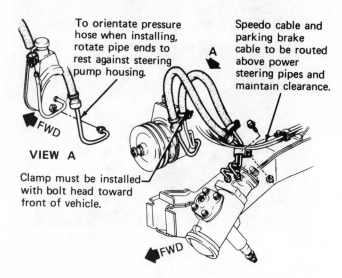

To orientate pressure hose when installing, rotate pipe ends to rest against steering pump housing.

Speedo cable and parking brake cable to be routed above power steering pipes and maintain clearance.

VIEW A

Clamp must be installed with bolt head toward front of vehicle.

Fig. 11.56 Power steering hydraulic pipes (V8 engines)

2   Wheel alignment consists of three factors:
   Camber is the angle at which the front wheels are set from the vertical when viewed from the front of the vehicle. Positive camber is the amount (in degrees) that the wheels are tilted outwards at the top from the vertical.
   Castor is the angle between the steering axis and a vertical line when viewed from each side of the vehicle. Positive castor is when the steering axis is inclined rearwards.
   Steering axis inclination is the angle, when viewed from the front of the vehicle, between the vertical and an imaginary line drawn between the upper and lower suspension arm swivels.
3   Steering angles are set in production and do not normally require adjustment unless new components have been installed. Adjustment of the camber and castor angles is best left to your dealer as it requires the use of very accurate equipment. For those who have access to such equipment, the means of adjusting these angles is as follows:

Vehicles with rigid front axles
4   *The castor angle* is altered by the use of wedges inserted between the leaf springs and the upper surface of the axle beam (see Fig.11.57).
5   *The camber angle* is set in production and is not adjustable. If incorrect, this must be due to wear or collision damage.

Vehicles with independent front suspension
6   *The castor and camber angles* are altered by varying the number of shims installed between the pivot cross-shaft of the suspension upper control arm and the frame crossmember.

Front wheel alignment
7   The front wheels on all models should be set to provide a 'toe-in' characteristic.
8   To check the front wheel alignment, place the vehicle on level ground with tires correctly inflated and the front roadwheels in the 'straight ahead' position.

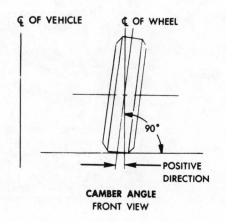

CAMBER ANGLE
FRONT VIEW

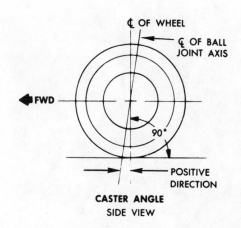

CASTER ANGLE
SIDE VIEW

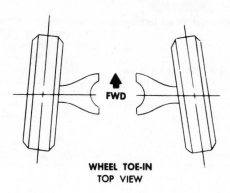

WHEEL TOE-IN
TOP VIEW

Fig. 11.57 Steering angle diagrams

9   If the tie-rod ends have been renewed, turn the single piece type tie-rod (rigid axle) until the roadwheels are parallel. With two section track rods (independent suspension), turn each one so that they are of equal length between the balljoint centers, and the roadwheels are parallel. This can best be checked by laying a length of steel rod or wood along the side of the vehicle. When it touches all four sidewalls of the front and rear tires, then the front wheels will be approximately parallel with each other.

10   Obtain or make a tracking gage. One can be easily made from tubing, cranked to clear the oil pan and transmission housing having a nut and setscrew at one end.

11   Using the gage, measure the distance between the two inner wheel rims at hub height at the rear of the wheels.

12   Rotate the roadwheels through 180° by pushing or pulling the vehicle and again using the gage, measure the distance at hub height between the two inner wheel rims at the front of the roadwheels. This last measurement should be less than the first by the amount given in Specifications according to vehicle type. This represents the correct toe-in.

13   Where this is not the case, release the tie-rod clamp and *with rigid axle vehicles,* rotate the single piece rod in the required direction until on repeating the checking operations, the toe-in is correct. *On vehicles with independent front suspension,* the two outer tie-rods should be rotated in opposite directions by exactly similar amounts in order to maintain them at equal length which is necessary to ensure the correct steering turning angles.

14   Set the tie-rod ends and tighten the clamps in accordance with the recommendation given in Section 16 of this Chapter.

35 Steering stop screw (rigid axle) – adjustment

1   The steering stop screws should be set on a gage to give a wheel turning angle in each direction at full lock of $35\frac{1}{2} \pm \frac{1}{2}°$.

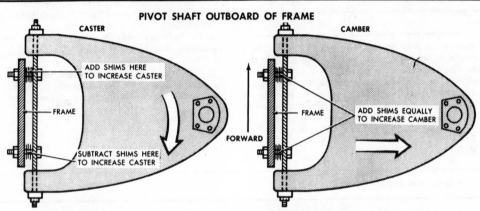
Fig. 11.58 Castor/camber adjustment diagram (independent front suspension)

Fig.11.59 Castor/camber shims (independent front suspension)

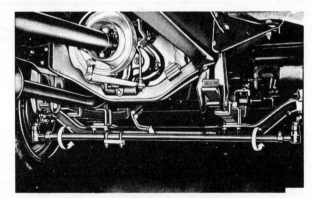
Fig. 11.60 Tie-rod (rigid front axle)

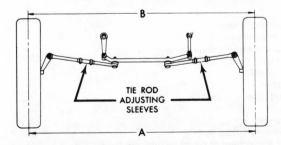
Fig. 11.61 Tie-rod (independent front suspension)

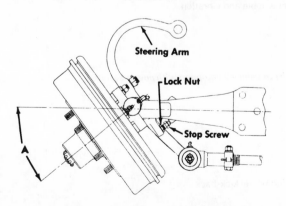
Fig. 11.62 Steering stop screw (rigid front axle)

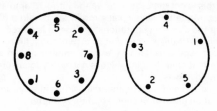

Fig. 11.63 Dual rear roadwheel nut tightening sequence

2   Where such a gage is not available, set the screws so that at full lock there is a clearance between the tire sidewall and the chassis frame of $\frac{5}{8}$ inch with the weight of the vehicle on the roadwheels.

36 Wheels and tires

1   Whenever the roadwheels are removed it is a good idea to clean the insides of the wheels to remove accumulations of mud and in the case of the front ones, disc pad dust.
2   Check the condition of the wheel for rust and repaint if necessary.
3   Examine the wheel stud holes. If these are tending to become elongated or the dished recesses in which the nuts seat have worn or become overcompressed, then the wheel will have to be renewed.
4   With a roadwheel removed, pick out any embedded flints from the tread and check for splits in the sidewalls or damage to the tire carcass generally.
5   Where the depth of tread pattern is $\frac{1}{16}$ in or less, the tire must be renewed.
6   Rotation of the roadwheels to even out wear is a worthwhile idea if the wheels have been balanced off the vehicle. Include the spare wheel in the rotational pattern.

With radial tires it is recommended that the wheels are moved between front and rear on the same side of the vehicle only.
7   If the wheels have been balanced on the vehicle then they cannot be moved round the vehicle as the balance of wheel, tire and hub willl be upset. In fact their exact stud fitting positions must be marked before removing a wheel so that it can be returned to its original 'in balance' state.
8   It is recommended that wheels are re-balanced halfway through the life of the tire, to compensate for the loss of tread rubber due to wear.
9   Finally, always keep the tire (including the spare) inflated to the recommended pressures and always reinstall the dust caps on the valves. Tire pressures are best checked first thing in the morning when they are cold.
10 On vehicles with dual rear wheels, the following installation sequence should be observed.

(i)   Install the inner and outer wheels and clamp ring on the rear of the wheel then the clamp ring on the front, making sure that the pins on the clamp ring face outboard.
(ii)   Screw on the nuts finger-tight.
(iii) Tighten the nuts to specified torque in the sequence shown in the diagram (Fig. 11.63).

37 Fault diagnosis – suspension and steering

Symptom	Reason/s
General faults	
Steering unstable, vehicle wanders or floats at speed	Uneven tire pressures
	Worn shock absorbers
	Worn tie-rod balljoints
	Incorrect steering angles
	Steering gear worn, or requires adjustment to eliminate free play
	Suspension attachment points out of alignment
	Loose U-bolts (rigid axle)
	Worn control arm swivels (independent suspension)
Stiff and heavy steering	Lack of lubrication
	Low tire pressures
	Incorrect front wheel alignment
	Lack of power assistance (where applicable)
	Incorrect steering angles
	Steering gear adjusted too tightly
	Misaligned steering column
Wheel wobble and vibration	Loose wheel nuts
	Wheels out of balance
	Worn control arm swivels (independent suspension)
	Worn hub bearings
	Excessive free play in steering gear
Special to vehicles equipped with power steering	
Noisy operation	Loose pump drivebelt
	Loose pump pulley nut
	Worn pump internal components
	Incorrect over-center adjustment
	Low fluid level
	Air in system
	Restricted pipes or hoses
Steering wheel kick-back	Air in system
	Excessive over-center lash
	Incorrect adjustment of thrust bearing pre-load
	Loose flexible coupling
	Worn steering linkage

Steering wheel jerks during parking

Low fluid level
Loose pump drivebelt
Worn pump giving low pressure

Lack of assistance when turning steering wheel

Worn pump giving low pressure
Loose pump drivebelt
Low fluid level
Worn steering gear internal components

Chapter 12 Bodywork and fittings

Contents

Specifications

Dimensions	Overall length	Overall height	Overall width	Wheelbase
1968 thru 1970	168·3 inches	77·28 inches	72·74 inches	90·0 inches
	LWB version	LWB version	LWB version	LWB version
	188·9 inches	79·1 inches	74·4 inches	108·0 inches
1971 on	176·9 inches	82·3 inches	79·9 inches	110·0 inches
	LWB version			LWB version
	200·9 inches			125·0 inches
				Dual rear wheel
				cutaway
				146·0 inches

Heater

Voltage	13·5V
Current	7·1A max.
Fan speed	2850 to 3250 rpm.

Auxiliary heater

Voltage	13·5V
Current	9·6A max.
Fan speed	2700 rpm.

Air conditioning

Blower voltage	12·0V
Current	13·7A max.
Fan speed	3400 rpm.

System capacity

Floor system	3 lb 4 oz of Refrigerant 12
Overhead system	5 lb 4 oz of Refrigerant 12

Torque wrench settings

	lbf ft
General	
Air conditioner compressor mounting bolts	22
Door hinge bolts	30
Door lock striker screws	45
Door lock-to-door frame screws	20
Rear door hinge bolts	30
Sliding side door	
Lower front roller support-to-door	24
Support-to-roller bracket	24
Roller-to-roller bracket	20
Upper front roller bracket	24
Roller-to-bracket	20
Upper left door hinge	25
Roller-to-hinge	20
Striker-to-body screws	20
Rear striker bolt	45

1 General description

1 The models covered in this manual are of all-steel construction and of the forward control design.
2 The frame side-rails, cross sills and outriggers are part of the underbody assembly which is a welded unit.
3 The front end radiator support and fenders are welded together as an integral part of the body.
4 Various styles, sizes, capacities and wheelbases are available and many of the basic vans are particularly suitable to customizing.
5 A 'cut away' van is also produced for custom bodywork to be fitted by the customer.

2 Maintenance – bodywork and underframe

1 The condition of your vehicle's bodywork is of considerable importance as it is on this that the second hand value will mainly depend. It is much more difficult to repair neglected bodywork than to renew mechanical assemblies. The hidden portions of the body, such as the fender arches, the underframe and the engine compartment are equally important, although obviously not requiring such frequent attention as the immediately visible paintwork.
2 Once a year or every 12 000 mile it is a sound scheme to visit your local dealer and have the underside of the body steam cleaned. All traces of dirt and oil will be removed and the underside can then be inspected carefully for rust, damaged hydraulic pipes, frayed electrical wiring and similar maladies. The front suspension should be greased on completion of this job.
3 At the same time, clean the engine and the engine compartment either using a steam cleaner or a water-soluble cleaner.
4 The fender arches should be given particular attention as undersealing can easily come away here and stones and dirt thrown up from the roadwheels can soon cause the paint to chip and flake, and so allow rust to set in. If rust is found, clean down to the bare metal and apply an anti-rust paint.
5 The bodywork should be washed once a week or when dirty. Thoroughly wet the vehicle to soften the dirt and then wash down with a soft sponge and plenty of clean water. If the surplus dirt is not washed off very gently, in time it will wear down paint.
6 Spots of tar or bitumen coating thrown up from the road surfaces are best removed with a cloth soaked in gasoline.
7 Once every six months, give the bodywork and chromium trim a thoroughly good wax polish. If a chromium cleaner is used to remove rust on any of the vehicle's plated parts remember that the cleaner also removes part of the chromium, so use it sparingly.

3 Maintenance – upholstery and carpets

1 Remove the carpets or mats and thoroughly vacuum clean the interior of the vehicle every three months or more frequently if necessary.
2 Beat out the carpets and vacuum clean them if they are very dirty. If the upholstery is soiled apply an upholstery cleaner with a damp sponge and wipe off with a clean dry cloth.

4 Bodywork repairs – minor damage

See photo sequences on pages 254 and 255

Repair of minor scratches in the vehicle's bodywork

If the scratch is very superficial, and does not penetrate to the metal of the bodywork, repair is very simple. Lightly rub the area of the scratch with a paintwork renovator or a very fine cutting paste, to remove loose paint from the scratch and to clear the surrounding bodywork of wax polish. Rinse the area with clean water.

Apply touch-up paint to the scratch using a thin paint brush; continue to apply thin layers of paint until the surface of the paint in the scratch is level with the surrounding paintwork. Allow the new paint at least two weeks to harden, then blend it into the surrounding paintwork by rubbing the paintwork in the scratch area with a paintwork renovator or a very fine cutting paste. Finally apply wax polish.

An alternative to painting over the scratch is to use a paint transfer. Use the same preparation for the affected area, then simply pick a patch of a suitable size to cover the scratch completely. Hold the patch against the scratch and burnish its backing paper; the patch will adhere to the paintwork, freeing itself from the backing paper at the same time. Polish the affected area to blend the patch into the surrounding paintwork.

Where a scratch has penetrated right through to the metal of the bodywork, causing the metal to rust, a different repair technique is required. Remove any loose rust from the bottom of the scratch with a penknife, then apply rust inhibiting paint to prevent the formation of rust in the future. Using a rubber or nylon applicator, fill the scratch with bodystopper paste. If required, this paste can be mixed with cellulose thinners to provide a very thin paste which is ideal for filling narrow scratches. Before the stopper paste in the scratch hardens, wrap a piece of smooth cotton rag around the tip of a finger. Dip the finger in cellulose thinners and then quickly sweep it across the surface of the stopper paste in the scratch; this will ensure that the surface of the stopper paste is slightly hollowed. The scratch can now be painted over as described earlier in this Section.

Repair of dents in the vehicle's bodywork

When deep denting of the vehicle's bodywork has taken place, the first task is to pull the dent out, until the affected bodywork almost attains its original shape. There is little point in trying to restore the original shape completely, as the metal in the damaged area will have stretched on impact and cannot be reshaped fully to its original contour. It is better to bring the level of the dent up to a point which is about $\frac{1}{8}$ inch below the level of the surrounding bodywork. In cases where the dent is very shallow anyway, it is not worth trying to pull it out at all.

If the underside of the dent is accessible, it can be hammered out gently from behind, using a mallet with a wooden or plastic head. Whilst doing this, hold a suitable block of wood firmly against the outside of the dent. This block will absorb the impact from the hammer blows and thus prevent a large area of bodywork from being 'belled-out'.

Should the dent be in a section of the bodywork which has double skin or some other factor making it inaccessible from behind, a different technique is called for. Drill several small holes through the metal inside the dent area – particularly in the deeper sections. Then screw long self-tapping sheet metal screws into the holes just sufficiently for them to gain a good 'key' in the metal. Now the dent can be pulled out by pulling on the protruding heads of the screws with a pair of pliers.

The next stage of the repair is the removal of the paint from the damaged area, and from an inch or so of the surrounding 'sound' bodywork. This is accomplished most easily by using a wire brush or abrasive pad on a power drill, although it can be done just as effectively by hand using sheets of abrasive paper. To complete the preparations for filling, score the surface of the bare metal with a screwdriver or the tang of a file, or alternatively, drill small holes in the affected area. This will provide a really good 'key' for the filler paste.

To complete the repair see the Section on filling and respraying.

Repair of rust holes or gashes in the vehicle's bodywork

Remove all paint from the affected area and from an inch or so of the surrounding 'sound' bodywork, using an abrasive pad or a wire brush on a power drill. If these are not available a few sheets of abrasive paper will do the job just as effectively. With the paint removed you will be able to gage the severity of the corrosion and therefore decide whether to replace the whole panel (if this is possible) or to repair the affected area. Replacement body panels are not as expensive as most people think and it is often quicker and more satisfactory to install a new panel than to attempt to repair large areas of corrosion.

Remove all fittings from the affected area except those which will act as a guide to the original shape of the damaged bodywork (eg; headlamp shells etc). Then, using tin snips or a hacksaw blade, remove all loose metal and any other metal badly affected by corrosion. Hammer the edges of the hole inwards in order to create a slight depression for the filler paste.

Wire-brush the affected area to remove the powdery rust from the surface of the remaining metal. Paint the affected area with rust inhibiting paint; if the back of the rusted area is accessible treat this also.

Before filling can take place it will be necessary to block the hole in some way. This can be achieved by the use of one of the following materials: Zinc gauze, Aluminum tape or Polyurethane foam.

Zinc gauze is probably the best material to use for a large hole. Cut a piece to the approximate size and shape of the hole to be filled, then position it in the hole so that its edges are below the level of the surrounding bodywork. It can be retained in position by several blobs of filler paste around its periphery.

Aluminum tape should be used for small or very narrow holes. Pull a piece off the roll and trim it to the approximate size and shape required, then pull off the backing paper (if used) and stick the tape over the hole; it can be overlapped if the thickness of one piece is insufficient. Burnish down the edges of the tape with the handle of a screwdriver or similar, to ensure that the tape is securely attached to the metal underneath.

Polyurethane foam is best used where the hole is situated in a section of bodywork of complex shape, backed by a small box section (eg; where the rocker panel meets the rear fender arch – most vehicles). The usual mixing procedure for this foam is as follows: Put equal amounts of fluid from each of the two cans provided in the kit, into one container. Stir until the mixture begins to thicken, then quickly pour this mixture into the hole, and hold a piece of cardboard over the larger apertures. Almost immediately the polyurethane will begin to expand, gushing out of any small holes left unblocked. When the foam hardens it can be cut back to just below the level of the surrounding bodywork with a hacksaw blade.

Having blocked off the hole the affected area must now be filled and sprayed – see Section on bodywork filling and respraying.

Bodywork repairs – filling and respraying

Before using this Section, see the Sections on dent, deep scratch, rust hole and gash repairs.

Many types of bodyfiller are available, but generally speaking those proprietary kits which contain a tin of filler paste and a tube of resin hardener are best for this type of repair. A wide, flexible plastic or nylon applicator will be found invaluable for imparting a smooth and well contoured finish to the surface of the filler.

Mix up a little filler on a clean piece of card or board – use the hardener sparingly (follow the maker's instructions on the pack) otherwise the filler will set very rapidly.

Using the applicator, apply the filler paste to the prepared area; draw the applicator across the surface of the filler to achieve the correct contour and to level the filler surface. As soon as a contour that approximates the correct one is achieved, stop working the paste – if you carry on too long the paste will become sticky and begin to 'pick-up' on the applicator.

Continue to add thin layers of filler paste at twenty-minute intervals until the level of the filler is just 'proud' of the surrounding bodywork.

Once the filler has hardened, excess can be removed using a Surform plane or Dreadnought file. From then on, progressively finer grades of abrasive paper should be used, starting with a 40 grade 'wet-and-dry' paper. Always wrap the abrasive paper around a flat rubber, cork, or wooden block – otherwise the surface of the filler will not be completely flat. During the smoothing of the filler surface the 'wet-and-dry' paper should be periodically rinsed in water – this will ensure that a very smooth finish is imparted to the filler at the final stage.

At this stage the 'dent' should be surrounded by a ring of bare metal, which in turn should be encircled by the finely 'feathered' edge of the good paintwork. Rinse the repair area with clean water, until all of the dust produced by the rubbing-down operation is gone.

Spray the whole repair area with a light coat of grey primer; this will show up any imperfections in the surface of the filler. Repair these imperfections with fresh filler paste or bodystopper, and once more smooth the surface with abrasive paper. If bodystopper is used, it can be mixed with cellulose thinners to form a really thin paste which is ideal for filling small holes. Repeat this spray and repair procedure until you are satisfied that the surface of the filler, and the feathered edge of the paintwork are perfect. Clean the repair area with clean water and allow to dry fully.

The repair area is now ready for spraying. Paint spraying must be carried out in a warm, dry, windless and dust free atmosphere. This condition can be created artificially if you have access to a large indoor working area, but if you are forced to work in the open, you will have to pick your day very carefully. If you are working indoors, dousing the floor in the work area with water will 'lay' the dust which would otherwise be in the atmosphere. If the repair area is confined to one body panel, mask off the surrounding panels; this will help to minimise the effects of a slight mis-match in paint colours. Bodywork fittings (eg: chrome strips, door handles etc) will also need to be masked off. Use genuine masking tape and several thicknesses of newspaper for the masking operations.

Before commencing to spray, agitate the aerosol can thoroughly, then spray a test area (an old tin, or similar) until the technique is mastered. Cover the repair area with a thick coat of primer; the thickness should be built up using several thin layers of paint rather than one thick one. Using 400 grade 'wet-and-dry' paper, rub down the surface of the primer until it is really smooth. While doing this, the work area should be thoroughly doused with water, and the wet-and-dry paper periodically rinsed in water. Allow to dry before spraying on more paint.

Spray on the top coat, again building up the thickness by using several thin layers of paint. Start spraying in the centre of the repair area and then using a circular motion, work outwards until the whole repair area and about 2 inches of the surrounding original paintwork is covered. Remove all masking material 10 to 15 minutes after spraying on the final coat of paint. Allow the new paint at least 2 weeks to harden fully; then, using a paintwork renovator or a very fine cutting paste, blend the edges of the new paint into the existing paintwork. Finally, apply wax polish.

5 Bodywork repairs – major damage

1   Because the body is built on the unitized principle and is integral with the underframe, major damage must be repaired by competent mechanics with the necessary welding and hydraulic straightening equipment.

2   If the damage has been serious it is vital that the body is checked for correct alignment as otherwise the handling of the vehicle will suffer and many other faults – such as excessive tire wear, and wear in the transmission and steering – may occur.

3   There is a special body jig which most large body repair shops have and to ensure that all is correct it is important that this jig be used for all major repair work.

6   Maintenance – hinges and locks

Once every 3000 miles or 3 months the door and hood hinges and locks should be given a few drops of oil from an oil can. The door striker plates can be given a thin smear of grease to reduce wear and to ensure free movement.

7   Windshield and fixed glass – removal and installation

1   It is recommended that removal and installation of the windshield is left to specialists but for those who are determined to do the work themselves, the following operations should be followed.
2   Where the windshield is to be removed intact (laminated type) then an assistant will be required. First release the rubber surround from the bodywork by running a blunt, small screwdriver around and under the rubber weatherstrip both inside and outside the vehicle. This operation will break the adhesive of the sealer originally used. Take care not to damage the paintwork or catch the rubber surround with the screwdriver. Remove the windshield wiper arms and interior mirror, and place a protective cover on the hood.
3   Have your assistant push the inner lip of the rubber surround off the flange of the windshield body aperture. Commence pushing the glass at one of the upper corners. Once the rubber surround starts to peel off the flange, the screen may be forced gently outwards by careful hand pressure. The second person should support and remove the glass complete with rubber surround and bright trim as it comes out.
4   Remove the bright trim from the rubber surround.
5   Before installing a windshield, ensure that the rubber surround is completely free from old sealant and glass fragments, and has not hardened or cracked. Install the rubber surround to the glass, and apply a bead of suitable sealant between the glass outer edge and the rubber.
6   Cut a piece of strong cord greater in length than the periphery of the glass, and insert it into the body flange locating channel of the rubber surround (Fig. 12.1).
7   Apply a thin bead of sealant to the face of the rubber channel which will eventually mate with the body.
8   Offer the windshield to the body aperture and pass the ends of the cord, previously installed and located at bottom center, into the vehicle interior.
9   Press the windshield into place, at the same time have an assistant pull the cords to engage the lip of the rubber channel over the body flange.
10   Remove any excess sealant with a kerosene soaked cloth and, install the bright trim.
11   Removal and installation of the rear window glass is carried out in an identical manner but (where applicable) disconnect the leads to the heating element in the glass.

8   Door trim panel – removal and installation

1   Extract the screws which hold the armrest to the door (photo).
2   Remove the door interior handles by pressing the trim plates inward and extracting the securing clips (later models) or by unscrewing the set-screw (early models) (photos).
3   Remove the screws from the trim panel and withdraw the panel. Peel away the waterproof seal (photo).
4   Installation is a reversal of removal.

9   Door ventilator – removal and installation

1   With the door glass fully down, remove the trim panel as described in the preceding Section.

8.1 Removing armrest screws

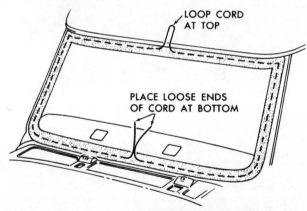

Fig. 12.1 Method of installing windshield

8.2A Removing door interior handle

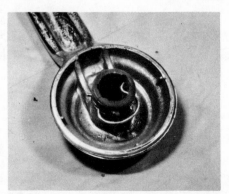

8.2B Door interior handle showing securing clip

8.3 Removing a door trim panel screw

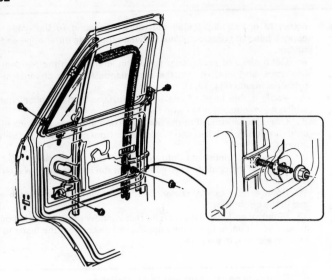

Fig. 12.2 Door ventilator assembly

Fig. 12.3 Removing door ventilator

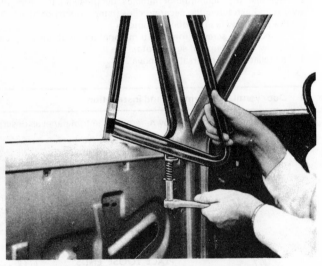

Fig. 12.4 Adjusting door ventilator swivel tension

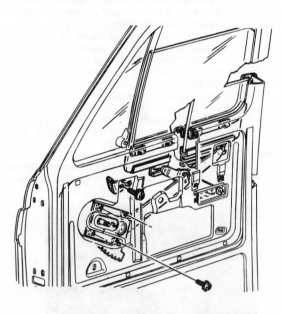

Fig. 12.5 Door window regulator mechanism

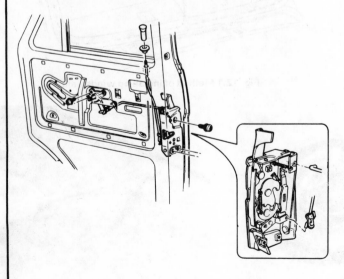

Fig. 12.6 Door lock assembly and securing screws

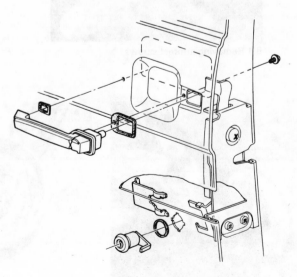

Fig. 12.7 Door exterior handle and lock cylinder

2 Extract the screws from the window glass run rear channel.
3 Slide the door glass away from the ventilator in a rearward direction.
4 Extract the three screws from the upper front edge of the door frame, then turn the ventilator assembly through 90° and withdraw it.
5 If the glass is to be renewed, pull it and its seal from the channel. Clean the channel thoroughly and install a new seal two inches longer than necessary.
6 Pinch the excess seal together while the glass is pushed into the frame.
7 One side of the seal is soapstoned and this is the side which should contact the metal channel (previously smeared with ordinary engine oil).
8 Installation is a reversal of removal but the tension of the ventilator pivot should be adjusted on all models by turning the nut below the pivot spring. Lock the nut on completion by bending down the tabs.

10 Door glass – removal and installation

1 Lower the door glass fully, then remove the door interior trim pad as described in Section 8.
2 Remove the ventilator assembly as described in Section 9.
3 Slide the door glass forward until the front roller is in line with the notch in the sash channel. Disengage the roller from the channel (photo).
4 Push the glass in a forward direction and tilt the front of the window up until the rear roller is disengaged.
5 Hold the glass in a level attitude and withdraw it from the door.
6 Installation is a reversal of removal.

11 Door window regulator – removal and installation

1 With the door glass fully up, remove the door trim panel as described in Section 8.
2 Extract the screws which hold the regulator assembly to the door inner panel.
3 Push the regulator out of the opening in the door but, while supporting it at the rear, slide it to the notches in the carrier channel and finally withdraw it completely.
4 Installation is a reversal of removal, but lubricate the regulator gears on installation.

12 Door lock – removal and installation

1 Raise the window fully and remove the trim panel as described in Section 8.
2 Remove the remote control knob from the door sill.
3 Working outside the door, extract the screws which hold the lock to the door edge. Lower the lock assembly carefully.
4 Extract the screws which hold the remote control assembly.
5 Remove the screws which secure the glass run guide channel.
6 Remove the lock, push button rod and remote control rod as an assembly from the door cavity.
7 If the door exterior handle or lock cylinder must be removed, unscrew the handle retaining screws and slide out the lock cylinder retaining clip (Fig. 12.7).
8 Installation is a reversal of removal.

13 Front door – removal and installation

1 Open the door to its fullest extent and support it on jacks or stands. Use pads of rag to prevent damage to the door paintwork.
2 Mark the position of the hinge plates on the door edge and then unscrew the bolts and lift the door from the hinges.
3 If the hinges must be removed from the body pillar, *on early models* a special cranked wrench will be required to reach the bolts. *On later vehicles* the bolts are accessible after removing the cover from the pillar.
4 Install the door, aligning the hinge plates with the marks made before removal. If new components are being used, the door can be adjusted in any direction to make it flush with the adjacent body

10.3 View of door glass regulator struts

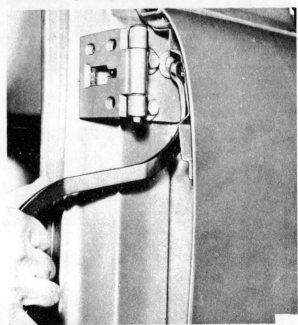

Fig. 12.8 Unscrewing a door hinge bolt (early models)

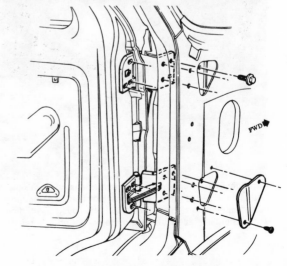

Fig. 12.9 Door hinges (later models)

This photo sequence illustrates the repair of a dent and damaged paintwork. The procedure for the repair of a hole is similar. Refer to the text for more complete instructions

After removing any adjacent body trim, hammer the dent out. The damaged area should then be made slightly concave

Use coarse sandpaper or a sanding disc on a drill motor to remove all paint from the damaged area. Feather the sanded area into the edges of the surrounding paint, using progressively finer grades of sandpaper

The damaged area should be treated with rust remover prior to application of the body filler. In the case of a rust hole, all rusted sheet metal should be cut away

Carefully follow manufacturer's instructions when mixing the body filler so as to have the longest possible working time during application. Rust holes should be covered with fiberglass screen held in place with dabs of body filler prior to repair

Apply the filler with a flexible applicator in thin layers at 20 minute intervals. Use an applicator such as a wood spatula for confined areas. The filler should protrude slightly above the surrounding area

Shape the filler with a surform-type plane. Then, use water and progressively finer grades of sandpaper and a sanding block to wet-sand the area until it is smooth. Feather the edges of the repair area into the surrounding paint.

Use spray or brush applied primer to cover the entire repair area so that slight imperfections in the surface will be filled in. Prime at least one inch into the area surrounding the repair. Be careful of over-spray when using spray-type primer

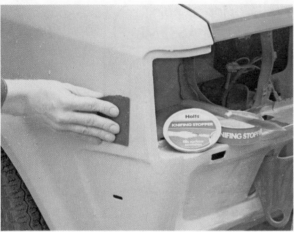

Wet-sand the primer with fine (approximately 400 grade) sandpaper until the area is smooth to the touch and blended into the surrounding paint. Use filler paste on minor imperfections

After the filler paste has dried, use rubbing compound to ensure that the surface of the primer is smooth. Prior to painting, the surface should be wiped down with a tack rag or lint-free cloth soaked in lacquer thinner

Choose a dry, warm, breeze-free area in which to paint and make sure that adjacent areas are protected from over-spray. Shake the spray paint can thoroughly and apply the top coat to the repair area, building it up by applying several coats, working from the center

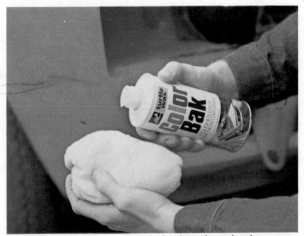

After allowing at least two weeks for the paint to harden, use fine rubbing compound to blend the area into the original paint. Wax can now be applied

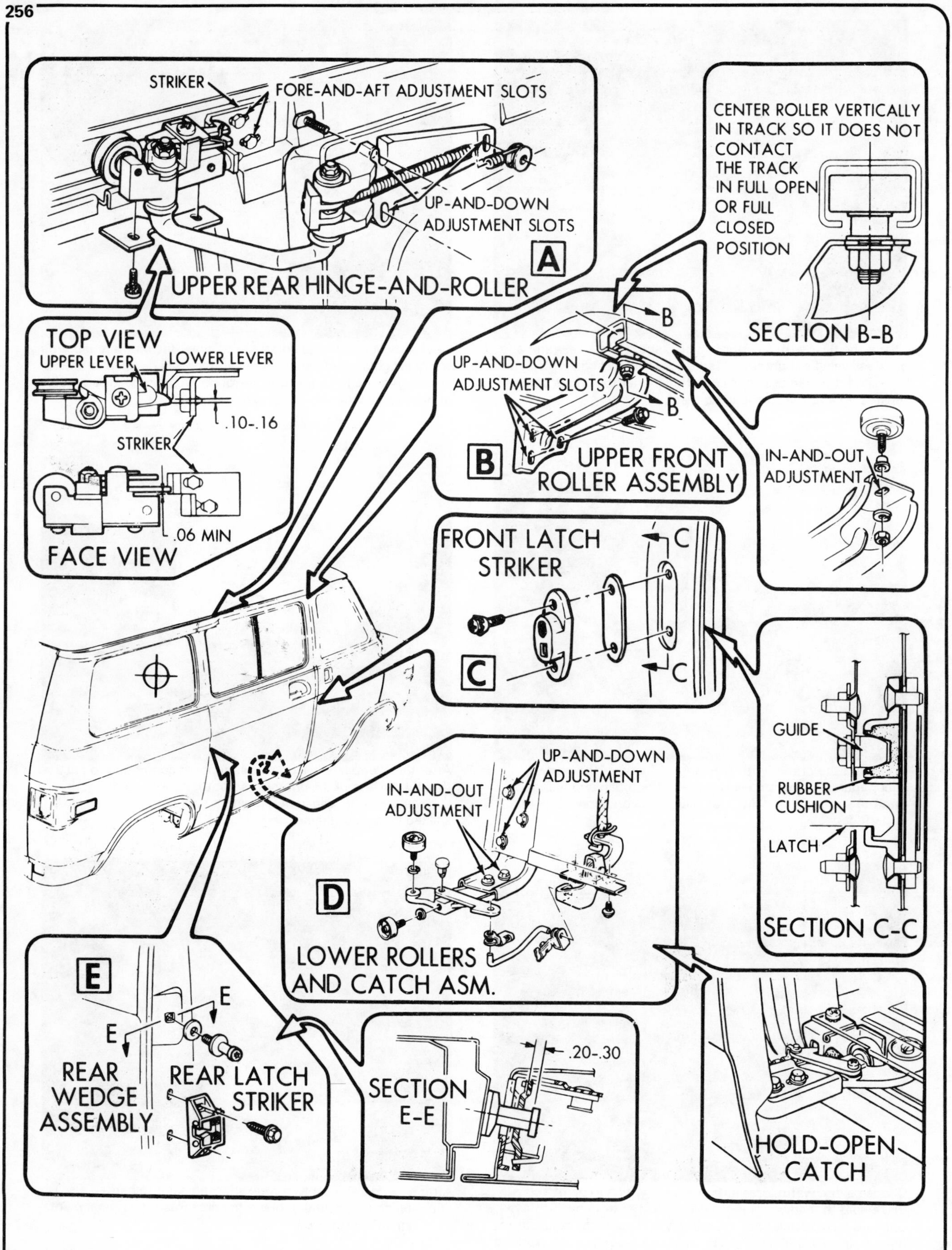

STRIKER

FORE-AND-AFT ADJUSTMENT SLOTS

UP-AND-DOWN ADJUSTMENT SLOTS

A

UPPER REAR HINGE-AND-ROLLER

CENTER ROLLER VERTICALLY IN TRACK SO IT DOES NOT CONTACT THE TRACK IN FULL OPEN OR FULL CLOSED POSITION

SECTION B-B

TOP VIEW

UPPER LEVER LOWER LEVER

STRIKER

.10-.16

.06 MIN

FACE VIEW

UP-AND-DOWN ADJUSTMENT SLOTS

B

B

B **UPPER FRONT ROLLER ASSEMBLY**

IN-AND-OUT ADJUSTMENT

FRONT LATCH STRIKER

C

C

C

GUIDE

RUBBER CUSHION

LATCH

SECTION C-C

IN-AND-OUT ADJUSTMENT

UP-AND-DOWN ADJUSTMENT

D

LOWER ROLLERS AND CATCH ASM.

E

E

E

E

REAR WEDGE ASSEMBLY

REAR LATCH STRIKER

SECTION E-E

.20-.30

HOLD-OPEN CATCH

Fig. 12.10 Sliding side door adjustment diagrams

panels, and for alignment by loosening the hinge bolts and moving the door within the limits of the hinge bolt holes which are drilled oversize.

5   The lock striker should be adjusted by moving its position on the door pillar so that the striker is in the center of the lock entry. If it is incorrectly positioned, strain will be placed on the door hinges.

14 Sliding side door – removal, installation and adjustment

1   The weight of the sliding side door is supported by the upper rear hinge and roller assembly and by the lower front catch and roller assembly.

2   To remove the door, unscrew and remove the bolts from these components.

3   Installation is the reverse of removal, but adjustments to the sliding door are critical and should be carried out in the following way.

4   *To adjust the door up or down,* partially open the door and loosen the front latch striker on the pillar.

5   Remove the rear upper hinge cover and release the hinge to door bolts.

6   Loosen the rear lock striker and door wedge assembly.

7   Align the rear edge of the door up or down then tighten the upper rear hinge to door bolts.

8   Loosen the upper front roller bracket-to-door bolts, partially close the door and align the front edge of the door up or down by loosening the front lower hinge-to-door bolts. Tighten the bolts.

9   Position the upper front roller in the center of its track then tighten the roller bracket to the door.

10   Adjust the front and rear strikers and the rear anti-vibration wedge. To do this, loosen the front latch striker screws and then slide the door towards the striker. The guide on the door just above the latch must fit snugly within the rubber-lined opening on the striker.

11   Make sure that the latch engages fully; use shims behind it if necessary.

12   To adjust the rear striker, first release it and then loosen the rear wedge assembly.

13   Center the striker vertically to the door striker opening.

14   Adjust the striker laterally to be level with the outer panel-to-body surface.

15   Grease the striker and then push the door until the rear lock contacts the striker sufficiently to make an impression on the grease.

16   Open the door and measure the distance between the rear of the striker head and the impression. This should be between 0·20 and 0·30 inch.

17   To adjust the rear anti-vibration wedge, release the screws which hold it to the body pillar then close the door (fully latched).

18   Center the wedge assembly and scribe a line round it.

19   Open the door and move the wedge $\frac{3}{16}$ inch (Fig. 12.12).

20   *To adjust the door in and out,* loosen the front latch striker.

21   Loosen the upper front roller from its bracket.

22   Loosen the lower front roller bracket-to-arm bolts. Adjust the door in and out as required, then re-tighten the bolts.

23   Adjust the door hold-open catch bracket by loosening the screws which retain the catch rod bracket to the bottom of the door.

24   Adjust the catch-to-striker engagement by sliding the bracket laterally. The catch should fully engage the striker.

25   Adjust the front and rear strikers as described in paragraph 10 through 16 of this Section.

26   *To adjust the door fore and aft,* partially open the door and remove the front latch striker and rear lock striker. Loosen the rear wedge assembly.

27   Remove the upper rear track cover.

28   Loosen the upper rear hinge striker.

29   Move the door assembly forward or rearward as necessary, then re-tighten the striker bolts.

30   Install the track cover and the front and rear strikers. Adjust the latch strikers and the wedge as described in paragraph 10 through 19 of this Section.

31   All bolts and nuts must be finally tightened to the specified torque.

15 Sliding side doorlatch and hinge – removal and installation

1   *To remove the front latch* assembly, withdraw the trim panel (where applicable) and remove the access panel.

2   Unscrew the door lock knob and then disconnect the rear latch

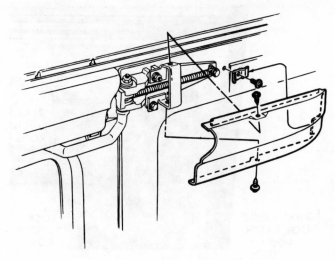

Fig. 12.11 Sliding side door upper hinge cover

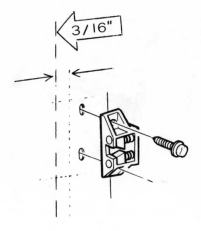

Fig. 12.12 Adjustment diagram for sliding side door wedge

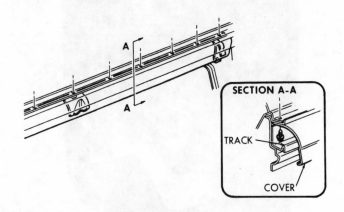

SECTION A-A

TRACK

COVER

Fig. 12.13 Sliding side door rear track cover

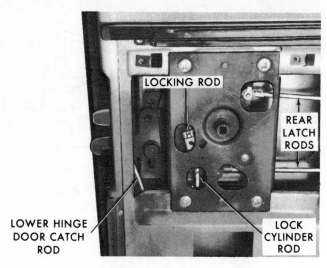

Fig. 12.14 Sliding side door front latch

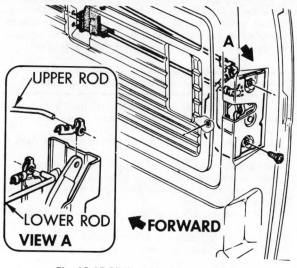

Fig. 12.15 Sliding side door rear latch

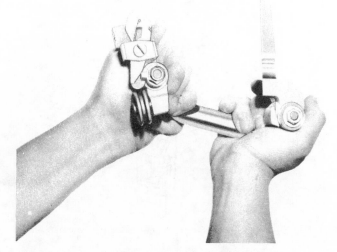

Fig. 12.16 Checking sliding side door upper rear hinge for cam engagement before installing

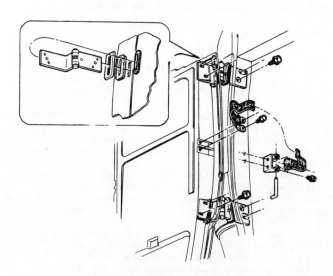

Fig. 12.17 Rear door hinges and check strap

17.2 View of typical door lock cylinder and exterior handle retaining screw from inside door cavity

rods, the lock cylinder rod and the door lock rod.

3   Remove the door handle and the screws which attach the latch assembly to the door.

4   Slide the latch rearward and lift it at the front. Disconnect the rod which leads to the lower hinge door catch and remove the latch.

5   *Access to the rear latch* is obtained as described in paragraph 1. Disconnect the rear latch rod from the front latch then extract the rear latch screws.

6   Slide the rear latch toward the front of the door until the rod clips are exposed, disconnect the clips and withdraw the latch.

7   *To remove the upper rear hinge,* detach the hinge cover and the rear track cover. Open the door and disengage the spring from the bolt. Now close the door and remove the hinge.

8   Installation of all components is a reversal of removal but the upper rear hinge must only be installed when the lower latch has engaged the cam (Fig. 12.16).

9   Carry out the adjustments as necessary and as described in Section 14.

10   All bolts and nuts must be finally tightened to the specified torque.

16 Rear door – removal, installation and adjustment

1   Open the door and support it on blocks or stands using pads of rag to prevent damage to the paintwork.

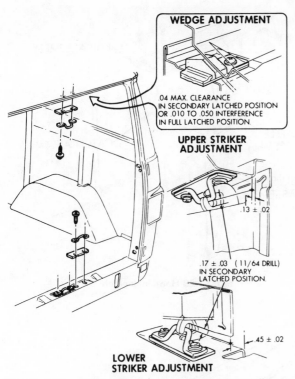

Fig. 12.18 Rear door striker and wedge adjustment diagram

2   Pull out the check strap release pin.

3   Remove the bolts which hold the hinges to the door. Mark the position of the hinge plates before removing the bolts.

4   Remove the door.

5   Install by reversing the removal procedure; adjustment can be made by moving the door within the limits of the oversize hinge bolt holes.

6   The striker and wedge should be adjusted to provide positive closure using shims if necessary under the wedge.

17   Rear door outside handle and lock cylinder – removal and installation

1   Remove the door interior trim panel, then unscrew the retaining screws and withdraw the handle and gaskets.

2   The lock cylinder can be removed after the remote control upper and lower latch rods have been disconnected. Pull out the lock cylinder retaining clip and remove the cylinder (photo).

3   Installation is a reversal of removal but grease the handle plunger contact point.

18   Hood – removal, installation and adjustment

1   Open the hood and mark the position of the hinge plates in relation to the underside of the hood.

2   Remove the bolt from one end of the hood support rod and then, with the help of an assistant, unscrew the hinge bolts at the hood end and lift the hood away.

3   Install and adjust if necessary by moving the hood within the limit of the oversize hinge bolt holes.

19   Hood lock – removal, installation and adjustment

1   The hood lock device may be directly lever-operated from the front of the radiator grille or remotely controlled from inside the vehicle by a cable release, depending on the date of production.

2   The catch or locking bolt mounting plates should be marked in respect of position before unbolting and removing them.

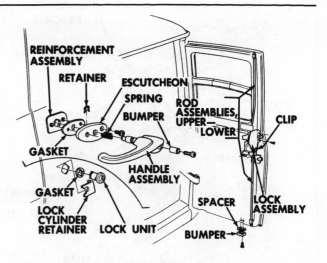

Fig. 12.19 Rear door exterior handle and lock cylinder (early models)

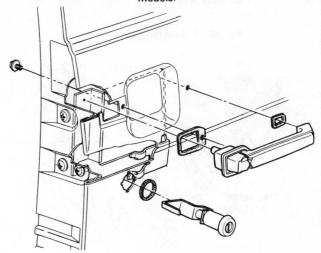

Fig. 12.20 Rear door exterior handle and lock cylinder (later models)

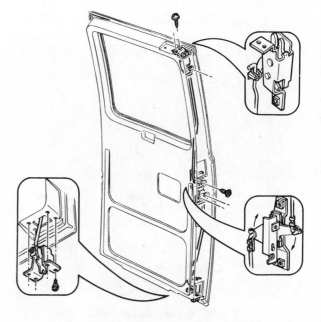

Fig. 12.21 Rear door remote control and latch

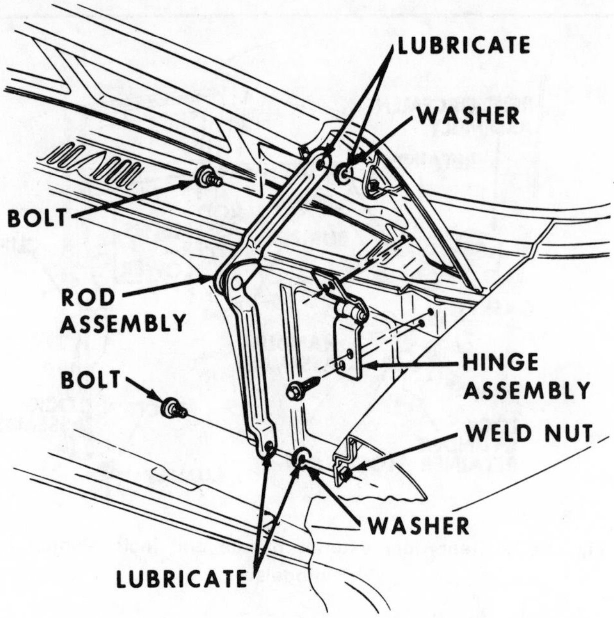

Fig. 12.22 Hood hinge and support rod

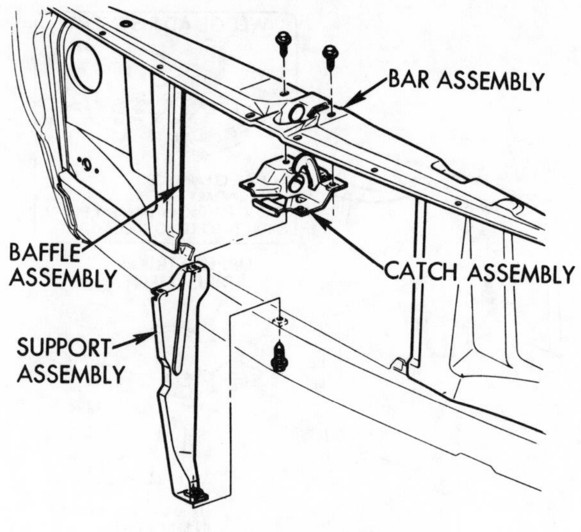

LUBRICATE
WASHER
BOLT
ROD ASSEMBLY
BOLT
HINGE ASSEMBLY
WELD NUT
WASHER
LUBRICATE

Fig. 12.23 Hood lock catch

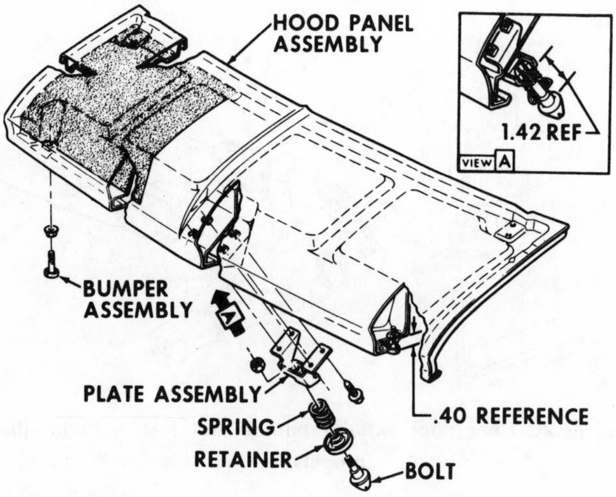

BAR ASSEMBLY
BAFFLE ASSEMBLY
CATCH ASSEMBLY
SUPPORT ASSEMBLY

Fig. 12.24 Hood latch and bumpers

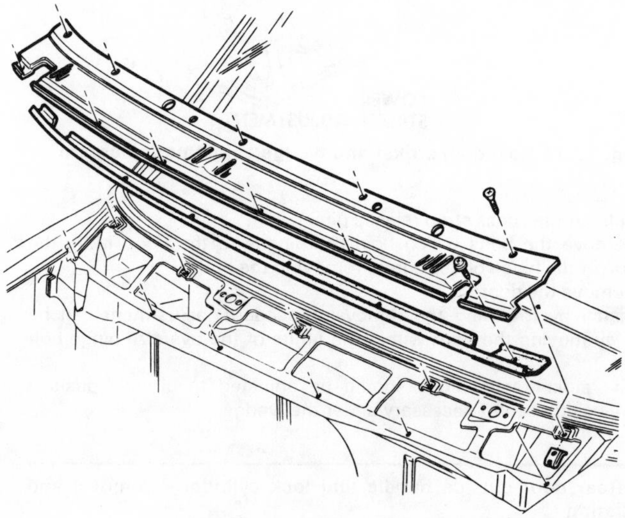

HOOD PANEL ASSEMBLY
1.42 REF
VIEW A
BUMPER ASSEMBLY
PLATE ASSEMBLY
SPRING
RETAINER
BOLT
.40 REFERENCE

Fig. 12.25 Cowl ventilator grille

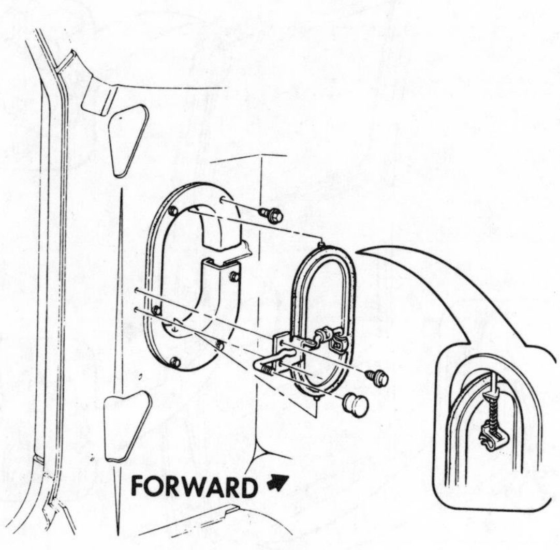

Fig. 12.26 Side cowl ventilator

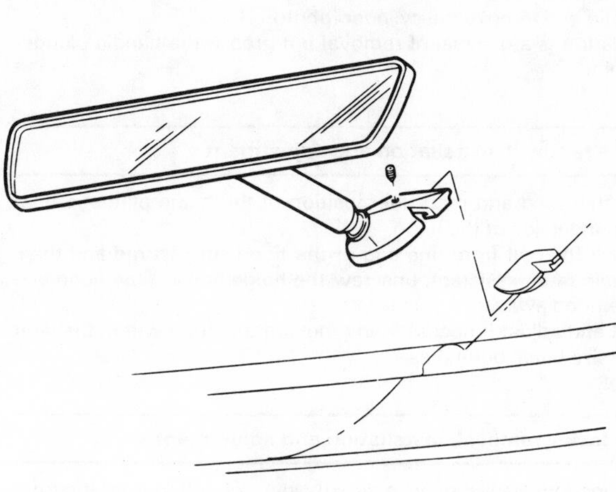

FORWARD

Fig. 12.27 Interior rear view mirror

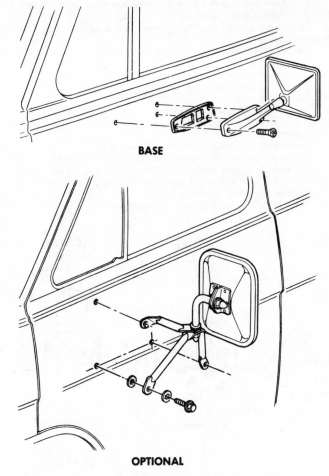

BASE

OPTIONAL

Fig. 12.28 Exterior rear view mirror

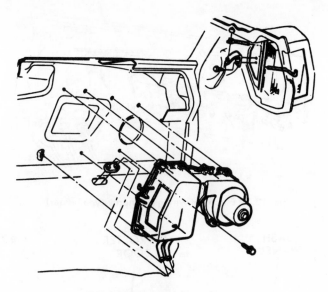

Fig. 12.29 Economy-type heater

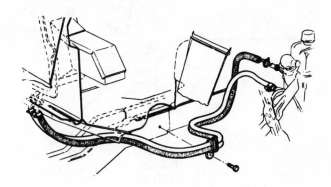

Fig. 12.30 Heater hose routing (economy-type heater)

3   Should adjustment be required to obtain positive closure, first make sure that the lock bolt enters the center of the elongated guide in the catch. Now adjust the lock bolt for length to ensure smooth closure. This will have to be done in conjunction with the bumpers which will have to be screwed in or out to compensate for any adjustment of the lock bolt.

20 Cowl ventilator grille – removal and installation

1   Remove the windshield wiper blades.
2   Unscrew and remove the grille retaining screws (Fig. 12.25).
3   Lift away the grille and seal.
4   The side cowl ventilator can be removed by extracting the screws which hold the valve guide to the panel. The valve assembly can be removed by depressing the pins at the top and bottom of the valve (Fig. 12.26).
5   Installation is a reversal of removal.

21 Rear view mirrors – removal and installation

1   The interior mirror is held to its mounting plate by a grub-screw which should be unscrewed to remove the mirror assembly.
2   The exterior mirror may be one of two types secured by screws installed from outside the vehicle.

22 Heater (economy models through 1970) – removal and installation

1   This type of heater is mounted on the toe-board inside the vehicle.
2   *To remove the blower,* disconnect the battery ground cable, unclip

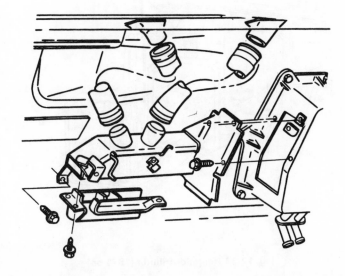

Fig. 12.31 Defroster hoses (economy-type heater)

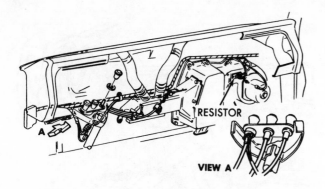

Fig. 12.32 Electrical wiring (economy-type heater)

the wire from the blower flange terminal and then mark the motor flange in relation to the casing.

3   Extract the blower mounting screws and pry the blower flange from the casing.

4   Disconnect the blower fan from the motor shaft by unscrewing the nut.

5   *To remove the heater core,* drain the cooling system and disconnect the heater hoses below the toe-pan.

6   Remove the glovebox.

7   Disconnect the blower motor wire.

8   Disconnect the defroster and air door control cables at the distributor duct.

9   Remove the distributor duct mounting screws.

10 Disconnect the defroster hoses from the distributor duct.

11 Remove the screws which hold the heater case to the toe-pan and then lower the case, sliding the core tubes through the toe-pan.

12 Remove the temperature door cable.

13 Remove the core by unscrewing the retainers.

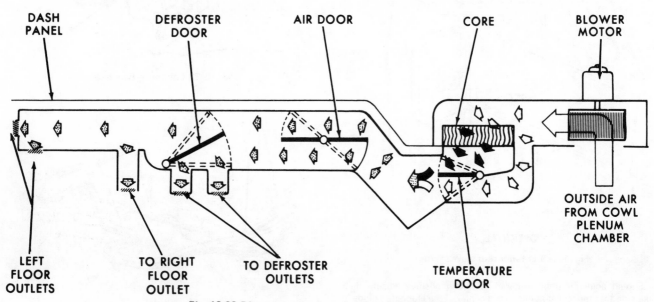

Fig. 12.33 Diagrammatic view of airflow (heater 1971 on)

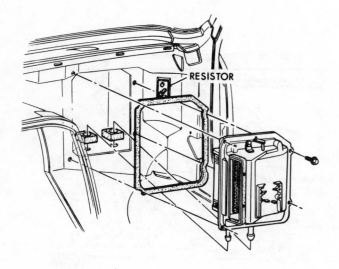

Fig. 12.34 Heater distributor (1971 on)

14 The core may be reverse-flushed to clean it as described for the radiator in Chapter 2. If it is completely blocked or leaking, it is recommended that a new or reconditioned unit is obtained.

15 Reassembly and installation are reversals of dismantling and removal, but make sure that the open end of the blower fan is away from the motor and don't forget to fill the cooling system.

23 Heater controls (economy models through 1970) – removal, installation and adjustment

1   Pull off the knobs from the control shafts, then unscrew the control nuts and escutcheons. The control can then be removed from its mounting plate.

2   *The heat/fan control* is removable after disconnecting the blower wiring connector.

3   *The air or defroster control* cable is simply disconnected from the operating lever or duct.

4   *The temperature control* can be removed after the withdrawal of the glovebox.

5   *The heater resistor* can be removed by disconnecting its wiring harness and unscrewing it from the heater casing.

6   Installation in all cases is a reversal of removal; no adjustment is required at the control cables as they are of fixed length.

24 Heater (1971 on) – removal and installation

1   The heater assembly is attached to the dash panel on the right

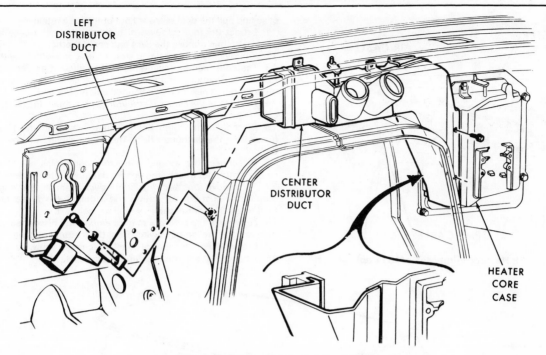

Fig. 12.35 Heater distribution ducts (1971 on)

side of the vehicle. The blower and air inlet assembly and coolant hoses are located on the forward side of the dash panel while the heater core and air distributor duct are on the passenger side.

2   *To remove the blower,* disconnect and remove the battery.
3   Disconnect the blower lead.
4   Remove the blower mounting screws and withdraw the motor and fan. The flange sealing strip may need cutting through to do this.
5   The fan can be removed from the motor shaft after the nut has been unscrewed.
6   *To remove the heater core and distributor,* disconnect the battery ground cable.
7   Place a suitable container under the heater core, quickly disconnect the coolant hoses from the core and tie them up as high as possible. Allow the coolant in the core to drain into the container.
8   Disconnect the right air distributor hose from the heater casing and twist it up out of the way.
9   Disconnect the control cable from the temperature door.
10 Extract the screws which hold the distributor duct to the heater

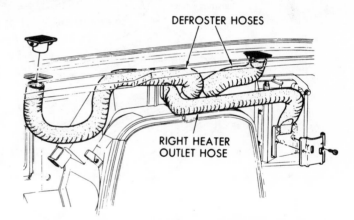

Fig. 12.36 Heater defroster hoses (1971 on)

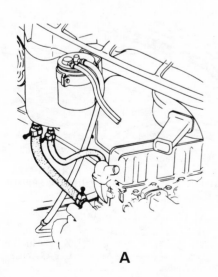

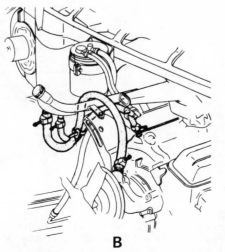

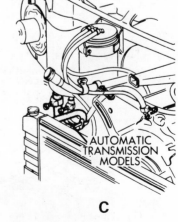

A   B   C

Fig. 12.37 Heater hose routing

A In-line engine   *B V8 engines*   *C Models with automatic transmission*

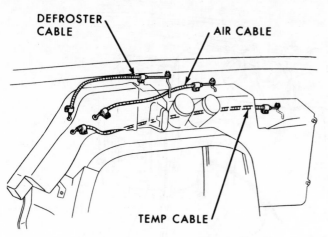

Fig. 12.38 Heater control cables (1971 on)

case and pull the duct rearward out of the case retainer.

11　Extract the four screws which attach the heater case to the dash panel and then remove the case and core together.

12　Remove the core retaining strap screws and withdraw the core.

13　The core may be reverse flushed to clean it as described for the radiator in Chapter 2. If it is completely blocked or leaking, it is recommended that a new or reconditioned unit is obtained.

14　*To remove the center distributor duct,* remove the heater case and core as just described.

15　Disconnect the right heater outlet hose and the two defroster hoses from the distributor duct. The engine cover must be removed to do this.

16　Disconnect the air and defroster door cables and then pull the center distributor duct to the right and remove it from the vehicle.

17　*To remove the left distributor duct,* remove the engine cover, remove the duct bracket screws and withdraw the duct taking care not to damage the control cables which run below it.

18　*To remove the control cable assembly,* first disconnect the battery, then remove the ignition switch from the instrument panel.

19　Extract the heater control panel attachment screws and then lower the panel until the control cables are accessible.

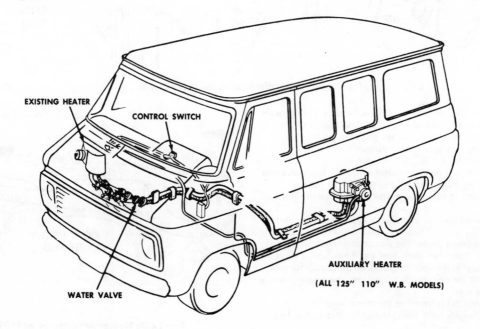

Fig. 12.39 Auxiliary heater

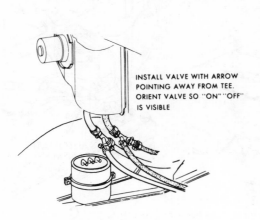

Fig. 12.40 Auxiliary heater water valve

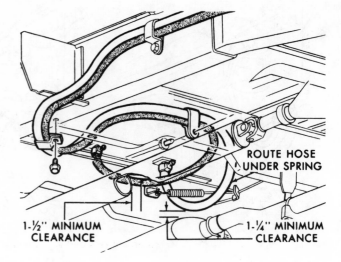

Fig. 12.41 Auxiliary heater hose routing

20 Disconnect the control cables, the lighting bulb, the blower switch lead and then withdraw the control assembly.

21 *To remove the blower resistor,* extract the mounting screws and remove it from its location just above the heater distributor.

22 Installation of all components is a reversal of removal, but make sure that the routing of the heater hoses is in accordance with the appropriate diagram. Make sure that the cables are adjusted to provide full opening and closure of the various air flaps and doors. To adjust the effective length of the cables, turn the mounting clip on the cable while holding the cable still with a pair of pliers (Figs. 12.37 and 12.38).

25 Auxiliary heater for rear compartment

1 On some later models an optional heater can be installed to provide additional heating in the rear of the vehicle (Figs. 12.39, 12.40 and 12.41).

2 The unit is independent of the standard heater and incorporates its own controls and components. The water valve located in the engine compartment should be turned off in the summer period.

26 Air conditioning system – description and precautions

1 When installed, this optional system performs both the heating and cooling functions. Although some systems operate independently, (they are known as a 'parallel system'), an overhead system may be installed which does not operate independently and operates on recirculated air only (Figs. 12.42, 12.43 and 12.44).

2 The main units of the system comprise the evaporator, an engine driven compressor and the condensor.

3 In view of the toxic nature of the chemicals and gases employed in the system, no part of the system must be disconnected by the home mechanic. Due to the need for specialized evacuating and charging equipment, such work should be left to your GM dealer or a refrigeration specialist.

4 The compressor may be dismounted (not disconnected) and moved to one side for engine removal as described in Chapter 1 but this, and the checks and maintenance operations described in the next Section, should be the limit of work undertaken by the home mechanic.

27 Air conditioner – checks and maintenance

1 Regularly inspect the fins of the condenser (located ahead of the radiator) and if necessary, brush away leaves and bugs.

2 Clean the evaporator drain tubes free from dirt.

3 Check the compressor drivebelt tension and if necessary, adjust the idler pulley to provide a total deflection of between $\frac{3}{8}$ and $\frac{1}{2}$ inch at the center of its longest run.

4 Check the condition of the system hoses and, if there is any sign of deterioration or hardening, have them renewed by your dealer.

5 Every 6000 miles have the system checked for low oil or refrigerant levels by your GM dealer.

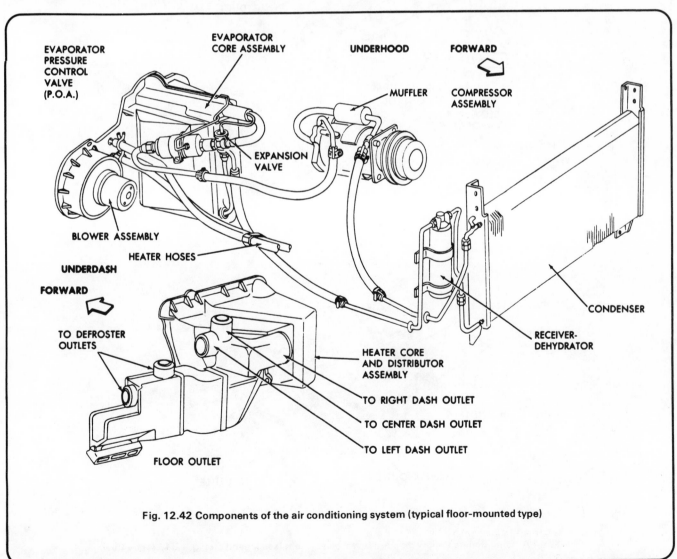

Fig. 12.42 Components of the air conditioning system (typical floor-mounted type)

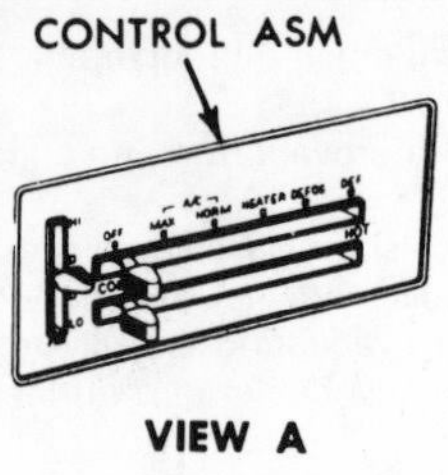

CONTROL ASM

VIEW A

Fig. 12.43 Air conditioning airflow diagram (floor mounted)

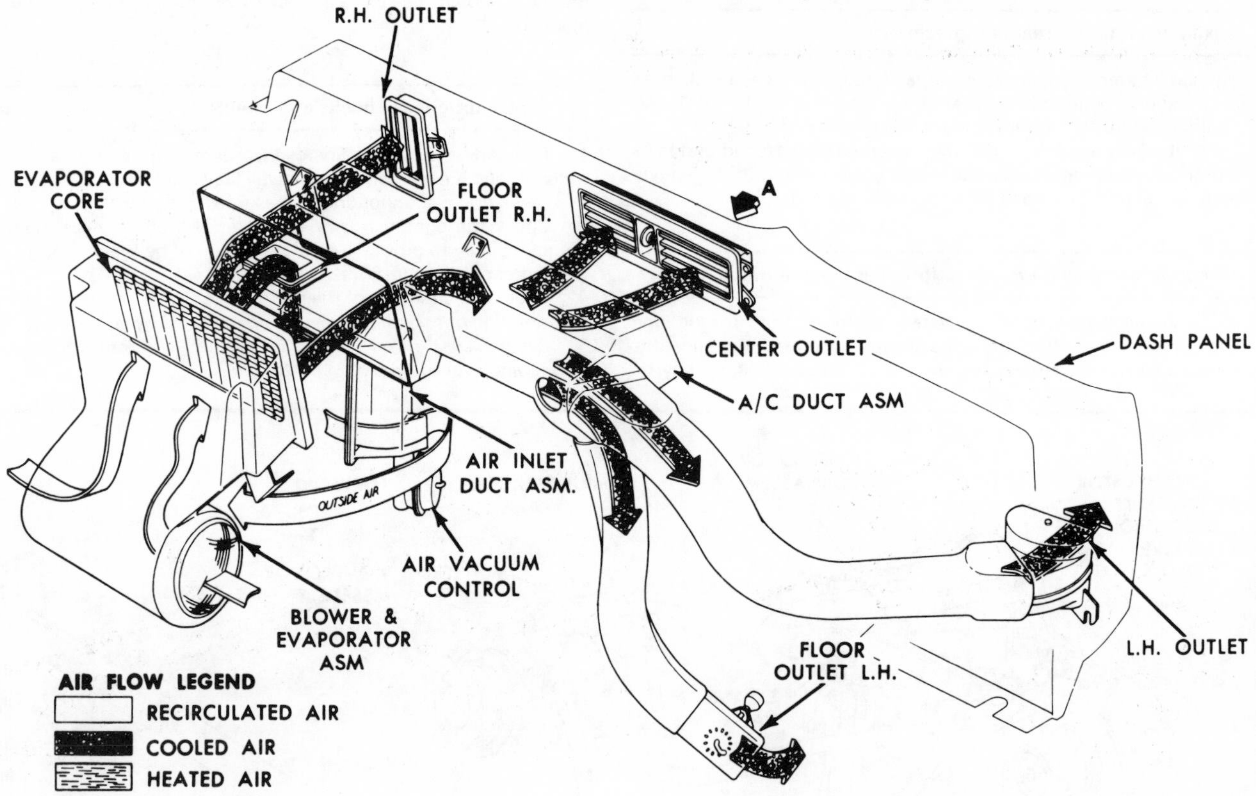

R.H. OUTLET

EVAPORATOR
CORE

FLOOR
OUTLET R.H.

A

CENTER OUTLET

DASH PANEL

A/C DUCT ASM

AIR INLET
DUCT ASM.

OUTSIDE AIR

AIR VACUUM
CONTROL

BLOWER &
EVAPORATOR
ASM

FLOOR
OUTLET L.H.

L.H. OUTLET

AIR FLOW LEGEND
RECIRCULATED AIR
COOLED AIR
HEATED AIR

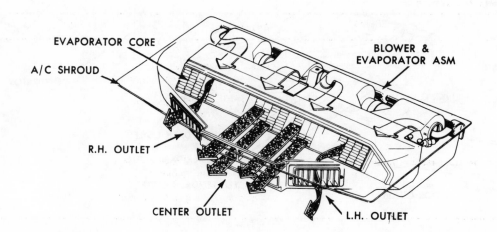

EVAPORATOR CORE

BLOWER &
EVAPORATOR ASM

A/C SHROUD

R.H. OUTLET

CENTER OUTLET

L.H. OUTLET

Fig. 12.44 Air conditioning airflow diagram (overhead system (see legend on Fig. 12.43 for air flow))

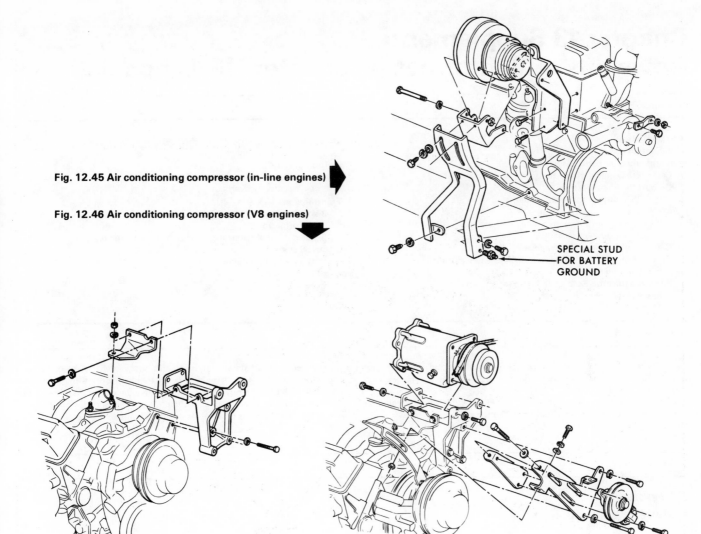

Fig. 12.45 Air conditioning compressor (in-line engines)

Fig. 12.46 Air conditioning compressor (V8 engines)

SPECIAL STUD
FOR BATTERY
GROUND

28 Fault diagnosis – heating system

Symptom	Reason/s
Insufficient heat	Faulty coolant reservoir cap
	Faulty thermostat in cooling system
	Kink in heater hose
	Faulty control lever or cable
	Heater core blocked
	Blower fuse blown
	Low coolant level
Inadequate defrosting or general heat circulation	Incorrect setting of deflector doors
	Blocked plenum chamber
	Disconnected ducts
	Carpet obstructing air flow at outlet

Chapter 13 Supplement:
Revisions and information on later USA models

Contents

1 Introduction

This supplementary Chapter covers changes made in the Chevrolet and GMC vans during the 1979 through 1985 model years, and the procedures affected by those changes.

Operations that are not included in this Chapter are the same or similar to those described for the 1978 model found in the first 12 Chapters of this manual.

The recommended way of using this supplement is, prior to any operation, check here first for any relevent information pertaining to your model. After noting any model differences, particularly in the Specifications Section, you can then follow the appropriate procedure, either listed in this Chapter or one of the preceding 12.

2 Specifications

Fuel system
Carburetor application

	250 cu in	305 cu in	350 cu in	400 cu in
1979	1ME or 2SE	M2M	M2M or M4M	M4M
1980	2SE	M2M	M2M or M4M	M4M
1981	2SE	M2M or M4M	M2M or M4M	—
1982	2SE	M4M	M4M	—
1983	E2SE or 2SE	E4ME or M4M	E4ME or M4M	—
1984	E2SE or 2SE	E4ME or M4M	E4ME or M4M	—
1985	E2SE or 2SE	E4ME or M4M	E4ME or M4M	—

Idle speed settings

Note: *In the following tables 'High' indicates the carburetor setting for fast idle in Neutral and 'Low' indicates the final carburetor idle speed. If there is a discrepancy between the idle rpm settings given here and those specified on the individual vehicle decal, (located under the hood), the figures on the decal should be followed.*

	250 cu in		305 cu in		350 cu in		400 cu in	
	High	Low	High	Low	High	Low	High	Low
1979								
Federal MT	1800	750	1300	600	1300	700	—	—
AT	2000	600	1600	500	1600	500	1600	500
California MT	2100	750	—	—	1600	700	—	—
AT	2100	600	—	—	1600	500	1600	500
1980								
Federal MT	2000	750	1300	600	1300	700	—	—
AT	2200	650	1600	500	1600	500	1600	500
California MT	2000	750	—	—	1600	700	—	—
AT	2200	600	—	—	1600	500	1600	500
1981								
Federal MT	2000	750	1300	600	1300	700	—	—
AT	2200	650	1600	500	1600	500	—	—
California MT	2000	750	—	—	1900	700	—	—
AT	2200	650	—	—	1800	550	—	—

1982
Refer to the Emission Control information label in the engine compartment for 1982 specifications.

Carburetor specifications — Rochester M2M series

	1979	1980	1981
Float level	15/32 in	7/16 in	13/32 in
Pump rod (inner hole)	13/32 in	9/32 in	5/16 in
Fast idle cam	38°	38°	38°
Front vacuum break	29°	29°	25°
Unloader	—	—	38°

Carburetor specifications — Rochester 2SE

For location of carburetor part numbers, see *Carburetor Identification*

	1979	1980	1981	1982
Float level	1/8 in	1/8 in	3/16 in	3/16 in
Air valve rod	0.040 in	2°	1°	1°
Fast idle cam (choke rod)	17°	17°	15°	15°
Primary vacuum break	17059641 17059643 17059765 17059767 } 23.5°	17080720 17080722 } 20° 17080721 17080723 } 23.5°	17081629 — 24° 17081720 17081721 17081725 17081726 17081727 } 30°	17082482 — 23° 17082341 17082342 17082344 17082345 } 30° 17082431 17082433 } 24° 17082486 17082487 17082488 17082489 } 28°
All others	20°	22°	26°	26°
Secondary vacuum break	37°	35°	17081629 — 34° 17081720 17081721 17081725 17081726 17081727 } 37°	17082341 17082342 17082344 17082345 } 37°
All others	37°	35°	38°	38°
Unloader	49°	41°	17081720 17081721 17081725 17081726 17081727 17081629 } 41°	42°
All others	49°	41°	38°	42°

Carburetor specifications — Rochester M4M (1979)

For location of carburetor part numbers, see *Carburetor Identification* (dimensions in inches)

Float level
17059212	7/16
17059512	13/32
17059520 17059521	3/8
All others	15/32

Pump rod
17059377 17059527 17059378 17059528	9/32 outer hole
17059212 17059213 17059215 17059229 17059510 17059512 17059513 17059515 17059520 17059521 17059529	9/32 inner hole
All others	13/32 inner hole

Fast idle cam
17059213 17059215 17059229 17059513 17059515 17059529	37°
All others	46°

Carburetor specifications — Rochester M4M (1979) continued

Front air valve rod	0.015
Rear air valve rod	0.015
Front vacuum break	
17059212 17059512	24°
17059501 ... ... 17059520 17059521	28°
17059509 ... ... 17059510 17059586 17059588	30°
All others	23°
Rear vacuum break	
17059363 ... ... 17059366 17059368 17059377 17059378 17059503 17059506 17059508 17059527 17059528	26°
All others	23°
Air valve spring	
17059212 17059512	3/4 in
17059213 ... ... 17059215 17059229 17059513 17059515 17059529	1.0 in
All others	7/8 in
Unloader	
17059212 ... ... 17059213 17059215 17059229 17059512 17059513 17059515 17059529	40°
All others	42°

Carburetor specifications — Rochester M4M (1980)

For location of carburetor part numbers, see *Carburetor Identification*

Float level	
17080213 ... ... 17080215 17080513 17080515 17080229 17080529	3/8 in
All others	15/32 in
Pump rod	9/32 inner hole
Fast idle cam	
17080213 ... ... 17080215 17080513 17080515 17080229 17080529	37°
All others	46°
Front air valve rod	0.015 in
Rear air valve rod	0.025 in
Front vacuum break	
17080212 17080512	24°
All others	23°
Rear vacuum break	
17080290	26°

17080291	
17080292	
17080503	
17080506	
17080508	
17080212	30°
17080512	
17080213	
17080215	
17080513	
17080515	
17080229	
17080529	
All others	23°
Unloader	
17080212	40°
17080512	
17080213	
17080215	
17080513	
17080515	
17080229	
17080529	
All others	42°
Air valve spring	
17080212	3/4 in
17080512	
17080213	1.0 in
17080215	
17080513	
17080515	
17080229	
17080529	
All others	7/8 in

Carburetor specifications — Rochester M4M (1981)

For location of carburetor part numbers, see *Carburetor Identification*

Float level	
17080212	3/8 in
17080213	
17080215	
17080298	
17080507	
17080512	
17080513	
17081200	15/32 in
17081201	
17081205	
17081206	
17081220	
17081226	
17081227	
All others	13/32 in
Pump rod	
17081524	5/16 outer hole
17081526	
All others	9/32 inner hole
Fast idle cam	
17080213	37°
17080215	
17080298	
17080507	
17080513	
All others	46°
Front air valve rod	0.025 in
Rear air valve rod	0.025 in
Rear vacuum break	
17081200	23°
17081201	
17081205	
17081206	
17081220	
17081226	
17081227	

Carburetor specifications — Rochester M4M (1981) continued

Rear vacuum break (continued)

17081290	24°
17081291	
17081292	
17081506	36°
17081508	
17081524	
17081526	
All others	30°

Front vacuum break

17080212	24°
17080512	
17081200	
17081226	
17081227	
17081524	25°
17081526	
All others	23°

Air valve wind-up

17080213	1.0 in
17080215	
17080298	
17080507	
17080212	3/4 in
17080512	
17080513	
All others	7/8 in

Unloader

17080212	40°
17080213	
17080215	
17080298	
17080507	
17080512	
17070513	
17081506	36°
17081508	
17081524	38°
17081526	
All others	42°

Carburetor specifications — Rochester M4M (1982)

For location of carburetor part numbers, see *Carburetor Identification*

Float level

17080212	3/8 in
17080213	
17080215	
17080298	
17080507	
17080512	
17080513	
17082213	
17082513	
All others	13/32 in

Pump rod

17082524	5/16 outer hole
17082526	
All others	9/32 inner hole

Fast idle cam

17080213	37°
17080215	
17080298	
17080507	
17080513	
17082213	
17082513	
All others	46°

Air valve rod ... ... | 0.025 in

Front vacuum break

17082230	26°
17082231	
17082234	
17082235	

17082524	...	...	...	...	...	...	...	...	25°
17082526								
17082506	...	...	...	...	...	...	...	...	23°
17082508								
17082513								
17080513								
17082213								
17080213								
17080215								
17080298								
17080507								
All others	...	...	...	...	...	...	...	...	24°

Rear vacuum break

17082220	...	...	...	....	...	...	...	...	34°
17082221								
17082222								
17082223								
17082224								
17082225								
17082226								
17082227								
17082290								
17082291								
17082292								
17082293								
17082230	...	...	...	...	...	...	...	...	36°
17082231								
17082234								
17082235								
17082524								
17082526								
17082293								
17082506								
All others	...	...	...	...	...	...	...	...	30°

Air valve wind-up

17080212	...	...	...	...	...	...	...	...	3/4 in
17080512								
17080513								
17080213	...	...	...	...	...	...	...	...	1.0 in
17080215								
17080298								
17080507								
17082213								
All others	...	...	...	...	...	...	...	...	7/8 in

Unloader

17080212	...	...	...	...	...	...	...	...	40°
17080213								
17080215								
17080298								
17080507								
17080512								
17080513								
17082213								
All others	...	...	...	...	...	...	...	...	39°

Carburetor specifications — Rochester 2SE — 1983, 1984 (dimensions in inches)

For location of carburetor part numbers, see Carburetor Identification

Float level	...	...	...	...	...	...	...	...	...	3/16
Air valve rod	...	...	...	...	...	...	...	...	1°
Fast idle cam (choke rod)		...	...	...	...	...	...	15°
Primary vacuum break	...	...	...	...	...	...	...	17083410

Primary vacuum break:

17083410
17083412
17083414 } 23°
17083416

17083411
17083413
17083415
17083417
17083419 } 26°
17083421
17083425
17083427

```
                                                      17083423 ⎫
                                                      17083429 ⎪
                                                      17083560 ⎬ 28°
                                                      17083562 ⎪
                                                      17083565 ⎪
                                                      17083569 ⎭
```

Secondary vacuum break ... ... 38°
Unloader ... ... 42°

1984
Float level ... ...
```
                                                      17084348 ⎫
                                                      17084349 ⎪
                                                      17084350 ⎪
                                                      17084351 ⎪
                                                      17084352 ⎪
                                                      17084353 ⎪
                                                      17084354 ⎪
                                                      17084355 ⎬ 11/32
                                                      17084410 ⎪
                                                      17084412 ⎪
                                                      17084425 ⎪
                                                      17084427 ⎪
                                                      17084560 ⎪
                                                      17084562 ⎪
                                                      17084569 ⎭
                                                      17084360 ⎫
                                                      17084362 ⎬ 5/32
                                                      17084364 ⎪
                                                      17084366 ⎭
                                                      17084390 ⎫
                                                      17084391 ⎬ 7/16
                                                      17084392 ⎪
                                                      17084393 ⎭
```
Air valve rod ... ... 1°
Fast idle cam (choke rod) ... ...
```
                                                      17084348 ⎫
                                                      17084349 ⎪
                                                      17084350 ⎪
                                                      17084351 ⎪
                                                      17084352 ⎪
                                                      17084353 ⎬ 22°
                                                      17084354 ⎪
                                                      17084355 ⎪
                                                      17084360 ⎪
                                                      17084362 ⎪
                                                      17084364 ⎪
                                                      17084366 ⎭
                                                      17084390 ⎫
                                                      17084391 ⎬ 28°
                                                      17084392 ⎪
                                                      17084393 ⎭
                                                      17084410 ⎫
                                                      17084412 ⎪
                                                      17084425 ⎪
                                                      17084427 ⎬ 15°
                                                      17084560 ⎪
                                                      17084562 ⎪
                                                      17084569 ⎭
```
Primary vacuum break ... ...
```
                                                      17084348 ⎫
                                                      17084349 ⎪
                                                      17084350 ⎪
                                                      17084351 ⎪
                                                      17084352 ⎪
                                                      17084353 ⎪
                                                      17084354 ⎪
                                                      17084355 ⎬ 30°
                                                      17084360 ⎪
                                                      17084362 ⎪
                                                      17084364 ⎪
                                                      17084366 ⎪
                                                      17084390 ⎪
                                                      17084391 ⎪
                                                      17084392 ⎪
                                                      17084393 ⎭
                                                      17084410 ⎫
                                                      17084412 ⎬ 23°
```

	17084425 } 26°
	17084427
	17084560
	17084562 } 24°
	17084569
Secondary vacuum break	17084348
	17084349
	17084350
	17084351 } 32°
	17084360
	17084362
	17084352
	17084353
	17084354 } 35°
	17084355
	17084364
	17084366
	17084390
	17084391
	17084392 } 38°
	17084393
	17084410
	17084412
	17084425 } 36°
	17084427
	17084560
	17084562 } 34°
	17084569
Unloader	17084348
	17084349
	17084350
	17084351
	17084352
	17084353
	17084354 } 40°
	17084355
	17084360
	17084362
	17084364
	17084366
	17084390
	17084391
	17084392
	17084393 } 38°
	17084560
	17084562
	17084569
	17084410 } 42°
	17084512

Carburetor specifications — Rochester E2SE — 4.1L engine (dimensions in inches)

For location of carburetor numbers, see Carburetor Identification

1983

Float level	11/32
Air valve rod	1°
Fast idle cam (choke rod)	15°
Primary vacuum break	26°
Secondary vacuum break	38°
Unloader	42°

1984

Float level	17084356
	17084357
	17084358
	17084359 } 9/32
	17084632
	17084633
	17084635
	17084636
	17084368
	17084370 } 1/8
	17084542

	17084430 ⎫
	17084431 ⎬ 11/32
	17084434 ⎪
	17084435 ⎭
	17084534 ⎫
	17084535 ⎪
	17084537 ⎬ 5/32
	17084538 ⎪
	17084540 ⎭
Air valve rod	1°
Fast idle cam (choke rod)	17084356 ⎫
	17084357 ⎪
	17084358 ⎬ 22°
	17084359 ⎪
	17084368 ⎪
	17084370 ⎭
	17084430 ⎫
	17084431 ⎬ 15°
	17084434 ⎪
	17084435 ⎭
	All others — 28°
Primary vacuum break	17084430 ⎫
	17084431 ⎬ 26°
	17084434 ⎪
	17084435 ⎭
	All others — 25°
Secondary vacuum break	17084356 ⎫
	17084357 ⎪
	17084358 ⎬ 30°
	17084359 ⎪
	17084368 ⎪
	17084370 ⎭
	17084430 ⎫
	17084431 ⎬ 38°
	17084434 ⎪
	17084435 ⎭
	All others — 35°
Unloader	17084356 ⎫
	17084357 ⎪
	17084358 ⎬ 30°
	17084359 ⎪
	17084368 ⎪
	17084370 ⎭
	17084430 ⎫
	17084431 ⎬ 42°
	17084434 ⎪
	17084435 ⎭
	All others — 45°

Carburetor specifications — Rochester M4M — 1983 (dimensions in inches)

For location of carburetor part numbers, see Carburetor Identification

5.0L engine

Float level	13/32
Pump rod	9/32 (inner)
Fast idle cam	46°
Air valve rod	0.025 in.
Front vacuum break	—
Rear vacuum break	24°
Air valve wind-up (turns)	7/8
Unloader	39°

7.4L engine

Float level	3/8
Pump rod	9/32 (inner)
Fast idle cam	46°
Air valve rod	0.025 in.
Front vacuum break	24°
Rear vacuum break	30°
Air valve wind-up (turns)	3/4
Unloader	40°

5.7 engine

Float level   17080201
17080205
17080206
17080290 } 15/32
17080291
17080292

17080213
17080298
17080507
17080513 } 3/8
17083298
17083507

17082213 — 9/32
All others — 13/32

Pump rod ...   .   9/32 (inner)

Fast idle cam   17080213
17080298
17080507
17080513 } 37°
17082213
17083298
17083507

All others — 46°

Air valve rod ...   .   0.025 in.

Front vacuum break ...   .   23° if equipped

Rear vacuum break   17080201
17080205 } 23°
17080206

17083290
17083291
17083292 } 24°
17083293

17080290
17080291
17080292 } 26°
17083234
17083235

All others — 30°

Air valve wind-up (turns)   17080213
17080298
17080507
17080513 } 1
17082213
17083298
17083507

All others — 7/8

Unloader   17080201
17080205
17080206
17080290 } 42°
17080291
17080292

...   .   17083234
17083235
17083290
17083291 } 39°
17083292
17083293

All others — 40°

Carburetor specifications — Rochester M4M — 1984 (dimensions in inches)

For location of carburetor part numbers, see Carburetor Identification

Float level   17080212
17080213
17080298
17082213 } 3/8
17083298
17084500
17084501
17084502

All others — 13/32

Pump rod ...   .   9/32 (inner)

Fast idle cam ... ...
17080213
17080298
17080507
17080513 ⎬ 37°
17082213
17083298
17083507
All others— 46°

Air valve rod ... ... 0.025 in
Front vacuum break ... ... 23° if equipped
Rear vacuum break ... ...
17084226
17084227 ⎬ 24°
17084290
17084292

17080212
17080213
17080298
17082213
17083298 ⎬ 30°
17084500
17084501
17084502
All others— 26°

Air valve wind-up (turns)... ... ...
17080212
17080213
17080298
17082213 ⎬ 1
17083298
17084500
17084501
All others— 7/8

Unloader ... ...
17080212
17080213
17080298
17082213
17083298 ⎬ 40°
17084500
17084501
17084502
All others— 39°

Carburetor specifications — Rochester M4M — 1985 (dimensions in inches)
For location of carburetor part numbers, see Carburetor Identification

Float level ... ...
17080212
17080213
17080298
17082213
17084500 ⎬ 3/8
17084501
17084502
17085000
17085001
All others— 13/32

Fast idle cam ... ...
17080213
17080298
17082213 ⎬ 37°
17083298
17084500
17084501

17080212
17084502
17085000
17085001
17085003
17085004
17085206
17085212
17085213
17085215 ⎬ 46°
17085228
17085229
17085235
17085290
17085291

Fast Idle Cam Continued

	17085292
	17085293
	17085294
	17085298
	All others— 20°

Front vacuum break (if equipped) ... ...

	17080212
	17084502 } 24°
	17085000
	17080213
	17080298
	17082213
	17083298
	17084500
	17084501 } 23°
	17085001
	17085003
	17085004
	17085212
	17085213
	All others— 26°

Rear vacuum break ... ...

	17080212
	17080213
	17080298
	17082213
	17083298
	17084500 } 30°
	17084501
	17084502
	17085000
	17085001
	17085205
	17085208 } 38°
	17085210
	17085216
	17085209
	17085211
	17085217
	17085219
	17085222 } 36°
	17085223
	17085224
	17085225
	17085226
	17085227
	17085228 } 24°
	17085229
	17085290
	17085292
	All others— 26°

Air valve wind-up (turns)... ... ...

	17080213
	17080298
	17082213 } 1
	17083298
	17084500
	17084501
	17085001— 1
	17080212— 3/4
	17085217
	17085219
	17085222 } 1/2
	17085223
	17085224
	17085225
	All others— 7/8

Unloader ... ...

	17080212
	17080213
	17080298
	17082213
	17083298 } 40°
	17084500
	17084501
	17084502
	17085000
	17085001

17085003	
17085004	35°
17085213	
17085125	
17085220	
17085221	
17085226	
17085227	32°
17085230	
17085231	
17085238	
17085239	
All others— 39°	

Carburetor specifications — Rochester E4M — 1983 (dimensions in inches)

For locations of carburetor part numbers, see Carburetor Identification

5.7L and 5.0L engines with a front vacuum break

Float level	7/16
Fast idle cam	20°
Front vacuum break	27°
Rear vacuum break	36°
Air valve wind-up(turns)	7/8
Unloader	36°

5.0L engine

Float level	11/28
Fast idle cam	20°
Rear vacuum break	27°
Air valve wind-up(turns)	7/8
Unloader	38°

Carburetor specifications — Rochester E4M — 1984 (dimensions in inches)

For locations of carburetor part numbers, see Carburetor Identification

Float level	17084507 17084509 17084525 14/32 17084527 All others— 11/32
Fast idle cam	17084205 38° 17084209 All others— 20°
Front vacuum break	17084525 25° 17084527 All others— 27°
Rear vacuum break	36° if equipped
Air valve wind-up(turns)	17084507 17084509 17084525 1 17084527 All others— 7/8
Unloader	17084507 17084509 17084525 36° 17084527 All others— 38°

Ignition system

Distributor application

Year and engine	Dist. No.	Centrifugal advance (crank degrees @ engine rpm)	Vacuum advance (crank degrees @ inches of vacuum)	Ignition timing at engine idle (degrees BTDC)	Spark plug type and gap
1979					
250 cu in (Federal)	1110717	0 @ 1100 14 @ 2300 24 @ 4100	0 @ 4 18 @ 12	10	R46TS (0.035)
250 cu in (California)	1110749	0 @ 1100 7 @ 2300 16 @ 4200	0 @ 4 10 @ 8	10	R46TS (0.035)

Distributor application (continued)

Year and engine	Dist. No.	Centrifugal advance (crank degrees @ engine rpm)	Vacuum advance (crank degrees @ inches of vacuum)	Ignition timing at engine idle (degrees BTDC)	Spark plug type and gap
1979 (continued)					
250 cu in (California)	1110717	0 @ 1100 14 @ 2300 24 @ 4100	0 @ 4 18 @ 12	6 (MT) 8 (AT)	R46TS (0.035)
305 cu in (Federal)	1103381	0 @ 1200 8 @ 2000 20 @ 4200	0 @ 3 20 @ 7.5	6	R45TS (0.045)
305 cu in (Federal)	1103369	0 @ 1200 8 @ 2000 20 @ 4200	0 @ 3 16 @ 6.5	6	R45TS (0.045)
350 cu in	1103375	0 @ 1150 17 @ 2900 22 @ 4200	0 @ 4 10 @ 8	4	R44T (0.045)
350 cu in (Federal)	1103372	0 @ 1100 12 @ 1600 16 @ 2400 22 @ 4600	0 @ 4 14 @ 8	8	R45TS (0.045)
350 cu in	1103302	0 @ 1100 12 @ 1600 16 @ 2400 22 @ 4600	0 @ 6 15 @ 12	8	R45TS (0.045)
350 cu in	1103339	0 @ 1100 12 @ 1600 16 @ 2400 22 @ 4600	0 @ 4 10 @ 8	8	R45TS (0.045)
350 cu in (Federal)	1103353	0 @ 1100 12 @ 1600 16 @ 2400 22 @ 4600	0 @ 4 20 @ 10	8	R45TS (0.045)
350 cu in (California)	1103286	0 @ 1100 12 @ 1600 16 @ 2400 22 @ 4600	0 @ 4 18 @ 12	8	R45TS (0.045)
400 cu in	1103375	0 @ 1150 17 @ 2900 22 @ 4200	0 @ 4 10 @ 8	4	R44T (0.045)
400 cu in	1103301	0 @ 1000 8 @ 1600 19 @ 3450	0 @ 4 10 @ 8	4	R45TS (0.045)
1980					
250 cu in (Federal)	1110717 1110755	0 @ 1100 14 @ 2300 24 @ 4100	0 @ 5 16 @ 11.5	10	R46TS (0.035)
250 cu in (California)	1110747	0 @ 1100 14 @ 2300 24 @ 4100	0 @ 4 15 @ 12	10	R46TS (0.035)
250 cu in (California)	1110749	0 @ 1100 7 @ 2300 16 @ 4200	0 @ 4 10 @ 8	10	R46TS (0.035)
250 cu in (California)	1110717	0 @ 1100 14 @ 2300 24 @ 4100	0 @ 4 18 @ 12	8	R46TS (0.035)

Year and engine	Dist. No.	Centrifugal advance (crank degrees @ engine rpm)	Vacuum advance (crank degrees @ inches of vacuum)	Ignition timing at engine idle (degrees BTDC)	Spark plug type and gap
305 cu in (Federal)	1103381	0 @ 1200 8 @ 2000 20 @ 4200	0 @ 3 20 @ 7.5	8	R45TS (0.045)
305 cu in (Federal)	1103369	0 @ 1200 8 @ 2000 20 @ 4200	0 @ 3 16 @ 6.5	8	R45TS (0.045)
350 cu in	1103436	0 @ 1100 12 @ 1600 16 @ 2400 22 @ 4600	0 @ 3 10 @ 7.5 2 @ 7.5 (K series)	8	R45TS (0.045)
350 cu in	1103372	0 @ 1100 12 @ 1600 16 @ 2400 22 @ 4600	0 @ 4 14 @ 8	8	R45TS (0.045)
350 cu in	1103339	0 @ 1100 12 @ 1600 16 @ 2400 22 @ 4600	0 @ 4 10 @ 8	6 8 (Calif.)	R45TS (0.045)
350 & 400 cu in (Federal)	1103375	0 @ 1150 17 @ 2900 22 @ 4200	0 @ 4 10 @ 8	4	R44T (0.045)
350 & 400 cu in (California)	1103420	0 @ 1800 24 @ 4000	0 @ 10 10 @ 13	6	R44T (0.045)
350 cu in (Federal)	1103439	0 @ 1000 8 @ 1600 19 @ 3450	0 @ 4 14 @ 8	4	R44T (0.045)
400 cu in (California)	1103423	0 @ 1000 8 @ 1600 19 @ 3450	0 @ 4 15 @ 10	4	R45TS (0.045)

1981

Year and engine	Dist. No.	Centrifugal advance (crank degrees @ engine rpm)	Vacuum advance (crank degrees @ inches of vacuum)	Ignition timing at engine idle (degrees BTDC)	Spark plug type and gap
250 cu in (Federal)	1110589	0° @ 1100 14° @ 2300 24° @ 4100	0 @ 3 16 @ 6.5	8 (AT) 10 (MT)	R46TS (0.035)
250 cu in (Nationwide)	1110749	0° @ 1100 7° @ 2300 16° 4200	0 @ 4 10 @ 8	10	R46TS (0.035)
305 cu in (Federal)	1103369	0° @ 1200 8° @ 2000 20° 4200	0 @ 3 16 @ 6.5	8	R45TS (0.045)
305 cu in (Federal)	1103381	0° @ 1200 8° @ 2000 20° @ 4200	0 @ 3 10 @ 7.5	8	R45TS (0.045)
305 cu in (Federal)	1103464	— —	— —	6 (MT) 4 (AT)	R45TS (0.045)
350 cu in (Federal)	1103353	0° @ 1100 12° @ 1600 16° @ 2400 22° @ 4600	0 @ 4 20 @ 10	8	R45TS (0.045)
350 cu in (California)	1103433	0° @ 1100 12° @ 1600 16° @ 2400 22° @ 4600	0 @ 4 15 @ 12	8	R45TS (0.045)

Distributor application

Year and engine	Dist. No.	Centrifugal advance (crank degrees @ engine rpm)	Vacuum advance (crank degrees @ inches of vacuum)	Ignition timing at engine idle (degrees BTDC)	Spark plug type and gap
1981 (continued)					
350 cu in (Federal)	1103375 (Vac model 620)	0° @ 1150 17° @ 2900 22° @ 4200	0 @ 4 14 @ 8 0 @ 3 16 @ 6.5	4	R44T
350 cu in (California)	1103420	0° @ 1800 24° @ 4000	0 @ 10 10 @ 13	6	R44T (0.045)
350 cu in (Federal)	1103375 (Vac model 681)	0° @ 1150 17° @ 2900 22° @ 4200	0 @ 4 10 @ 8	4	R44T (0.045)
350 cu in (California)	1103420	0° @ 1000 17° @ 1600 22° @ 4200	0 @ 4 15 @ 10	6	R44T (0.045)

1982 through 1985

Ignition specifications are not given for these years. Refer to the Emission Control Information label located under the hood.

Transmission

Torque specifications

3-speed manual transmission (77 mm Tremec)						Ft-lb
Drive gear retainer-to-case bolts	...	...	...	...	...	35
Cover-to-case bolts	...	...	...	...	...	30
Extension-to-case bolts	...	...	...	...	...	45
Shift lever-to-shifter shaft bolts	...	...	...	...	...	25
Lubrication filler plug	...	...	...	...	...	15
Transmission-to-clutch housing bolts	...	...	...	...	...	75
Crossmember-to-frame nuts	...	...	...	...	...	65
Crossmember-to-mount bolts	...	...	...	...	...	45
2-3 crossover shaft bracket retaining nut	...	...	...	...	18
1-reverse swivel attaching bolt	...	...	...	...	...	20
Mount-to-transmission bolt	...	...	...	...	...	35

3 Fuel and emission control systems

Carburetor — general information

Rochester 2SE/E2SE carburetor

1 This carburetor is a two-barrel, two-stage carburetor of downdraft design. The primary side uses a triple venturi system. The secondary stage has a single large bore with a single tapered metering rod. On E2SE models, a mixture control solenoid is incorporated into the air horn to work in conjunction with the C-4 emissions control system.

2 An automatic choke system is incorporated, using an electrically heated thermostatic choke coil that is mounted on the secondary side of the carburetor.

3 A check valve is mounted in the fuel inlet line and is used to shut off fuel flow to the carburetor and prevent fuel leaks in case of a vehicle roll-over.

Rochester M2M series carburetor

4 This is a downdraft single stage unit using a triple venturi system. It is designed after the primary side of the M4M Rochester carburetor.

5 The M2ME carburetors used on air conditioned vehicles have an electrically operated air conditioner idle speed solenoid which maintains proper idle speed when the air conditioner is being used.

Rochester E4ME series carburetor

6 Later models using the Rochester E4M Varajet carburetors are very similar to earlier models except for the changes due to increased emissions restrictions. General Motors has integrated the operation of these carburetors with the emissions systems through the use of a mixture control solenoid mounted in the float bowl. The solenoid works in concert with the Electronic Control Module (ECM) and oxygen sensor of the C-4 system, described later in this Chapter, and maintains the proper fuel/air mixture for optimum driveability while maintaining low emissions.

Carburetor identification

7 The M4M/E4M carburetor has an identification number stamped on the vertical portion of the float bowl, near the secondary throttle lever.

8 The model E2SE/2SE carburetor has a model identification number stamped vertically on the float bowl in a flat area adjacent to the vacuum line.

9 The M2M model carburetor has a model identification number stamped vertically on the left rear corner of the float bowl.

2SE/E2SE carburetor — adjustment

Float adjustment

10 Hold the float retainer firmly in place while gently pushing the float against the needle.

11 Measure the height of the float at the furthest point from the float hinge pin at the toe of the float.

12 If necessary, remove the float and bend the float arm up or down to adjust. Always visually check the float alignment after adjustment.

Pump adjustment

13 Make sure the fast idle screw is off of the steps of the fast idle cam and that the throttle valves are completely closed.

14 Measure the distance from the air horn casting surface to the top of the pump stem.

15 The pump adjustment should not be changed from the original factory setting unless your measurement shows that it is out of specification. If it is necessary to adjust, remove the pump lever retaining screw and washer and remove the pump lever by rotating the lever to remove it from the pump rod. Place the lever is a soft-jawed vise, protecting it from damage, and bend the end of the lever nearest the neck down section. **Note:** *Do not bend the lever in a side-ways or twisting motion.*

16 Reinstall the pump lever, washer and retaining screw and re-check the pump adjustment.

17 Tighten the retaining screw securely after the pump adjustment is correct.

18 Open and close the throttle valves, checking the linkage for freedom of movement and observing pump lever alignment.

Fast idle adjustment (bench setting)

19 Place the fast idle screw on the highest step of the fast idle cam.

20 Turn the fast idle screw in or out the number of turns specified on the Emission Control Information label located under the hood.

Choke coil lever adjustment

21 Obtain a choke thermostatic cover rebuild kit and remove the choke cover and coil assembly as per the instructions in the rebuild kit.

22 Place the fast idle screw on the high step of the fast idle cam.

23 Push on the intermediate choke lever until the choke valve is completely closed.

24 Insert a twist drill of the specified thickness into the hole provided.

25 The edge of the choke coil lever should just make contact with the side of the twist drill.

26 Bend the intermediate choke rod to adjust the choke coil lever as necessary.

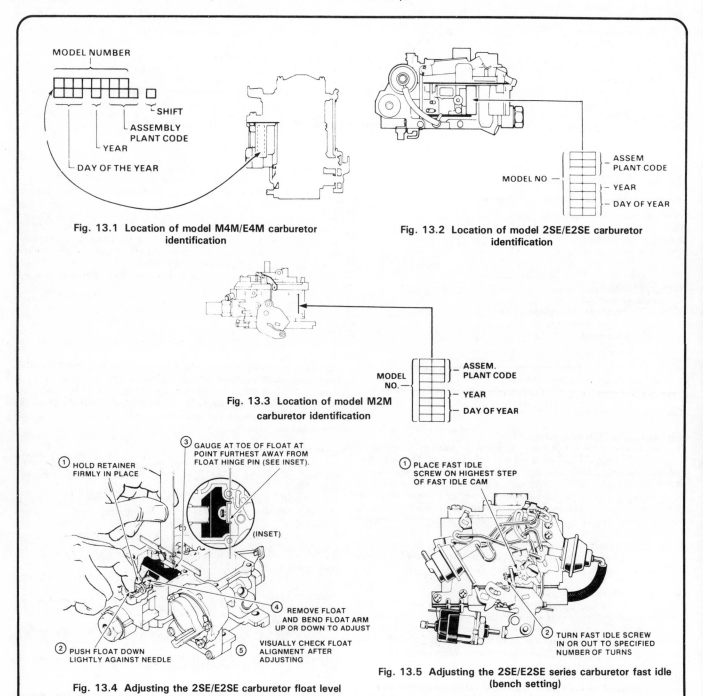

Fig. 13.1 Location of model M4M/E4M carburetor identification

Fig. 13.2 Location of model 2SE/E2SE carburetor identification

Fig. 13.3 Location of model M2M carburetor identification

Fig. 13.4 Adjusting the 2SE/E2SE carburetor float level

Fig. 13.5 Adjusting the 2SE/E2SE series carburetor fast idle (bench setting)

Fast idle cam (choke rod) adjustment

27 Choke coil lever and fast idle adjustments must be made before proceeding.

28 With the choke valve completely closed, place a magnet squarely on top of it, then mount choke valve measuring tool (No. J-26701) or an angle gauge to the magnet so that the rotating degree scale reads zero and the leveling bubble is centered.

29 Rotate the scale so that the degree specified for adjustment is opposite the pointer.

30 Place the fast idle screw on the second step of the cam against the rise of the high step.

31 Close the choke by pushing on the intermediate choke lever.

32 Push on the vacuum break lever toward the open choke position until the lever is against the rear tang on the choke lever.

33 Bend the fast idle cam rod until the bubble is centered, to make the necessary adjustment.

34 Remove the gauge and magnet.

Air valve rod adjustment

35 Attach a choke valve measuring gauge or angle gauge as described in *Fast idle cam adjustment*.

36 Rotate the scale so that the degree specified for adjustment is opposite the pointer.

37 Using a vacuum pump of some sort, seat the vacuum diaphragm.

38 Rotate the air valve in the direction of the open air valve by applying a light pressure to the air valve shaft.

39 To adjust, bend the air valve rod until the bubble on the angle gauge is centered.

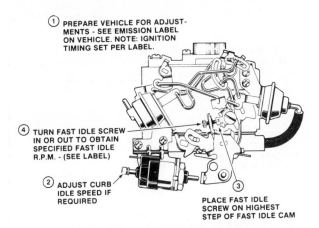

① PREPARE VEHICLE FOR ADJUSTMENTS - SEE EMISSION LABEL ON VEHICLE. NOTE: IGNITION TIMING SET PER LABEL.

④ TURN FAST IDLE SCREW IN OR OUT TO OBTAIN SPECIFIED FAST IDLE R.P.M. - (SEE LABEL)

② ADJUST CURB IDLE SPEED IF REQUIRED

PLACE FAST IDLE SCREW ON HIGHEST STEP OF FAST IDLE CAM

Fig. 13.6 Adjusting the 2SE/E2SE series carburetor fast idle (on vehicle)

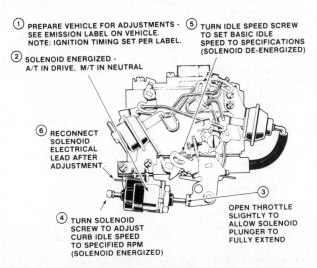

① PREPARE VEHICLE FOR ADJUSTMENTS - SEE EMISSION LABEL ON VEHICLE. NOTE: IGNITION TIMING SET PER LABEL.

⑤ TURN IDLE SPEED SCREW TO SET BASIC IDLE SPEED TO SPECIFICATIONS (SOLENOID DE-ENERGIZED)

② SOLENOID ENERGIZED - A/T IN DRIVE, M/T IN NEUTRAL

⑥ RECONNECT SOLENOID ELECTRICAL LEAD AFTER ADJUSTMENT

④ TURN SOLENOID SCREW TO ADJUST CURB IDLE SPEED TO SPECIFIED RPM (SOLENOID ENERGIZED)

③ OPEN THROTTLE SLIGHTLY TO ALLOW SOLENOID PLUNGER TO FULLY EXTEND

Fig. 13.7 Adjusting the 2SE/E2SE series carburetor idle speed (on vehicle)

Primary side vacuum break adjustment

40 Attach a choke valve measuring gauge or angle gauge as described in *Fast idle cam adjustment*.

41 Rotate the scale so that the degree specified for the adjustment is opposite the pointer.

42 Seat the choke vacuum diaphragm using an outside vacuum source.

43 Hold the choke valve towards the closed position by pushing on the intermediate choke lever.

44 To adjust, bend the vacuum break rod until the bubble on the angle gauge is centered.

45 Remove the gauge.

Secondary vacuum break adjustment

46 Mount a choke valve measuring gauge or angle gauge on the carburetor as described in *Fast idle cam adjustment*.

47 Rotate the scale so that the degree specified for adjustment is opposite the pointer.

48 Using an outside vacuum source, seat the diaphragm. On models with an air bleed, plug the end cover with a piece of masking tape. Remove the tape after the adjustment.

49 While reading the angle gauge, lightly push clockwise on the intermediate choke lever (in the direction of the closed choke valve) and hold in position with a rubber band.

50 To adjust, bend the vacuum break rod until the bubble in the angle gauge is centered. On later models use a 1/8 in hex wrench and turn the screw in the rear cover until the bubble is centered. Remove the angle gauge.

Unloader adjustment

51 Use a choke valve measuring gauge or appropriate angle gauge and mount it as described in *Fast idle cam adjustment*.

52 Rotate the scale so that the degree specified for adjustment is opposite the pointer.

53 Install the choke thermostatic cover and coil assembly in the housing. Align the index mark with the specified point on the housing.

54 Hold the primary throttle valve wide open. Close the choke valve by pushing clockwise on the intermediate choke lever. If the engine is warm, hold it in position with a rubber band.

55 Bend the tang to adjust the unloader until the bubble in the gauge is centered.

56 Remove the gauge.

Secondary lockout adjustment

57 Hold the choke valve wide open by pushing counterclockwise on the intermediate choke lever.

58 Open the throttle lever until the end of the secondary actuating lever is opposite the toe of the lockout lever.

59 Insert the specified size twist drill and measure the clearance.

60 If necessary to adjust, bend the lockout lever tang contacting the fast idle cam.

Fast idle adjustment (on vehicle)

61 Refer to the Emission Control Information label. Set the ignition timing as per the label and prepare the vehicle for adjustments.

62 Adjust the curb idle speed if required.

63 Place the fast idle screw on the highest step of the fast idle cam.

64 Turn the fast idle screw in or out to obtain the specified fast idle rpm (see the label).

Idle speed adjustment

65 Prepare the vehicle for adjustments as per the Emission Control Information label on the vehicle.

66 An assistant will be needed to keep pressure on the brake while the idle is adjusted.

67 With the solenoid energized, put an automatic transmission equipped vehicle in Drive or a manual transmission equipped vehicle in Neutral. Switch the air conditioner Off, if equipped.

68 Open the throttle slightly to allow the solenoid plunger to fully extend.

69 Turn the solenoid screw to adjust the curb idle speed to the specified rpm.

70 Disconnect the solenoid and turn the idle speed screw to set the base idle speed to Specifications.

71 Reconnect the solenoid electrical lead after the adjustment.

M2M carburetor — adjustment

Float adjustment

72 Hold the float retainer firmly in place and gently push down on the float against the needle.

73 Measure from the top of the casting to the top of the float, at a point 3/16 in back from the end of the float, at the toe.

74 If adjustment is necessary, remove the float and bend the float arm up or down as necessary.

75 Reinstall the float and visually check the alignment and recheck the float setting.

Pump adjustment

76 With the throttle valves completely closed, make sure the fast idle cam follower lever is off the steps on the fast idle cam.

77 Insert an appropriate size twist drill into the specified hole of the pump lever.

78 Measure from the top of the choke valve wall, next to the vent stack, to the top of the pump stem as specified.

79 If adjustment is necessary, support the pump lever with a screwdriver while bending the lever.

Choke coil lever adjustment

80 The procedure is the same as that for the adjustment of the 2SE carburetor.

Fast idle adjustment — bench setting

81 Hold the cam follower on the highest step of the fast idle cam.

82 Turn the fast idle screw out until the primary throttle valves are closed. Turn the screw in to contact the lever, then turn the screw in two complete turns.

Fast idle cam adjustment

83 This procedure is very similar to that used to adjust the 2SE carburetor. Refer to steps 27 through 34.

84 After Step 30, close the choke by pushing upward on the choke coil lever or vacuum break lever tang. Hold in that position with a rubber band.

85 To adjust, bend the tang on the fast idle cam until the bubble on the angle gauge is centered.

86 Remove the angle gauge.

Front vacuum break adjustment

87 This procedure can be carried out the same as the *Primary side vacuum break adjustment* described in Steps 40 through 45 for the 2SE carburetor.

Automatic choke coil adjustment (1979)

88 Place the cam follower on the highest step of the cam.

89 Loosen the three retaining screws on the choke housing.

90 Rotate the cover and coil assembly counterclockwise until the choke valve just closes.

91 Line the mark on the cover with the point on the housing that is one notch to the lean side. **Note:** *Make sure the slot in the lever engages with the coil tang.*

Unloader adjustment (1980 through 1982)

92 This procedure is very similar to that for the 2SE carburetor. Refer to Steps 51 through 56.

93 Hold the throttle valves wide open.

94 With the engine warm, close the choke valve by pushing up on the tang on the vacuum break lever. Hold in this position with a rubber band.

95 To adjust, bend the tang on the fast idle lever until the bubble in the angle gauge is centered.

96 Remove the gauge.

Idle adjustment

97 The procedure is very similar to that described for the 2G carburetor. Refer to Section 14, paragraphs 2 through 27 of Chapter 3.

Fast idle adjustment

98 The procedure for this is the same as that used on the 2SE carburetor.

2SE carburetor — overhaul

Removal and installation

99 If the carburetor is to be rebuilt by a professional repair shop,

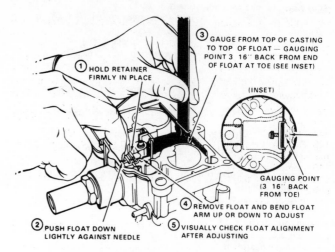

Fig. 13.8 Adjusting the M2M series carburetor float level

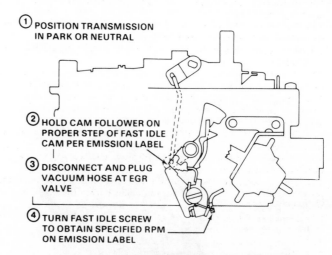

Fig. 13.9 Adjusting the M2M series carburetor fast idle (on vehicle)

much money can be saved if it is first removed at home.

100 If the carburetor is being overhauled, check on the availability of a rebuild kit which will contain all the necessary parts for the job. Do this before the carburetor is removed to prevent the car from being disabled as the parts are received.

101 Allow the engine to completely cool, as you will be working on areas which can cause serious burns to the skin if touched when hot. Also, fuel will more than likely be spilled and should not come into contact with hot parts.

102 Disconnect the negative battery cable at the battery.

103 Remove the air cleaner.

104 Disconnect the fuel inlet line from the inlet nut.

105 Disconnect the PCV hose from its carburetor fitting.

106 Disconnect all vacuum hoses from the carb. As you disconnect them, label the hoses as to their position, so there will be no confusion during installation.

107 Disconnect all electrical leads and connectors. Again, label them as they are removed to eliminate confusion during installation.

108 Disconnect the accelerator linkage from the carburetor.

109 Remove any other hoses or lines attached to the carb.

110 Remove the four carb mounting nuts.

111 Lift off the carburetor.

112 Remove the carburetor base gasket.

113 If the carburetor needs to be disassembled or overhauled, refer to the following procedure.

114 Before installing the carburetor, check that the four mounting studs are in good shape and their threads are not damaged. Run the carb nuts over the studs to make sure they can be installed easily.

115 Installation is the reverse of the removal procedure.

Disassembly

116 Prior to disassembling the carburetor, purchase a carburetor re-build kit for your particular model. This kit will have all of the necessary replacement parts for the overhaul procedure.

117 It will be necessary to have a relatively large, clean workshop to lay out all of the parts as they are removed from the carb. Many of the parts are very small and thus can be lost if the work space is cluttered. Work slowly through the procedure and if at any point you feel the reassembly of a certain component may prove confusing, stop and make a rough sketch or apply identification marks. The time to think about reassembling the carburetor is when it is being taken apart.

118 Remove the gasket from around the top of the air horn. Remove the fuel inlet nut along with the fuel filter.

119 Remove the pump lever attaching screw.

120 Disconnect the pump rod from the pump lever and remove the pump lever.

121 Disconnect the vacuum break diaphragm hose from the throttle body.

122 Remove the screws that secure the idle speed solenoid/vacuum break diaphragm bracket.

123 Lift off the idle speed solenoid/vacuum break diaphragm assembly and disconnect the air valve rod from the outside vacuum break plunger.

124 Disconnect the vacuum break rod from the inside vacuum break diaphragm plunger.

125 Pry off the clip that secures the intermediate choke rod to the choke lever and separate the rod from the lever.

126 Remove the screws that secure the vent/screen assembly to the air horn and lift off the assembly.

127 Remove the screws that secure the mixture control solenoid and, using a slight twisting motion, lift the solenoid out of the air horn.

128 Remove the seven screws that secure the air horn to the float bowl. If so equipped, the hot idle compensator must be removed to gain access to the short air horn screw.

129 Rotate the fast idle cam upwards, lift off the air horn and discon-nect the fast idle cam rod from the fast idle cam.

130 Disengage the fast idle cam rod from the choke lever and save the bushing for reassembly.

131 The pump plunger will probably come out with the air horn and must be removed. If not, remove the plunger from the pump well in the float bowl.

132 Compress the pump plunger spring and remove the spring retainer clip and spring from the piston.

133 Remove the air horn gasket from the float bowl.

134 Remove the pump return spring from the pump well.

135 Remove the plastic filler block that covers the float valve.

136 Remove the float assembly and float valve by pulling up on the retaining pin.

137 Using needle-nosed pliers, pull out the white plastic retainer and remove the pump discharge spring and check ball. Do not pry on the retainer to remove it as this will damage the sealing surface around it.

138 Remove the screws that secure the choke housing to the throttle body.

139 Remove the four screws that attach the float bowl to the throttle body.

140 Separate the float bowl from the throttle body.

141 Carefully file off the heads of the pop-rivets that secure the choke cover to the choke housing and remove the cover. Tap out the remainder of the rivets.

142 Remove the choke coil lever screw and lift out the lever.

143 Remove the intermediate shaft and lever assembly by sliding it out the lever side of the float bowl.

144 The plug covering the idle mixture needle should not be removed unless the needle needs replacing or normal cleaning procedures fail to clean the idle mixture passages. If removal is necessary, use a punch at the locater point and break out the throttle body casting, then drive out the plug. Finally, remove the needle and spring.

145 Further disassembly of the air horn, float bowl and throttle body is not necessary for normal cleaning purposes.

Cleaning and inspection

146 Clean the air horn, float bowl, throttle body and related compo-nents with clean solvent and blow them out with compressed air. A can of compressed air can be used if an air compressor is not available. Do not use a piece of wire for cleaning the jets and passages.

147 The idle speed solenoid, mixture control solenoid, electric choke, pump plunger, diaphragm, plastic filler block and other electrical,

rubber and plastic parts should *not* be immersed in carburetor cleaner, as they will harden, swell or distort.

148 Make sure all fuel passages, jets and other metering parts are free of burrs and dirt.

149 Inspect the upper and lower surfaces of the air horn, float bowl and throttle body for damage. Be sure all material has been removed.

150 Inspect all lever holes and plastic bushings for excessive wear or out-of-round conditions and replace if necessary.

151 Inspect the float valve and seat for dirt, deep wear grooves and scoring and replace if necessary.

152 Inspect the float valve pull clip for proper installation and adjust if necessary.

153 Inspect the float, float arms and hinge pin for distortion or binding and correct or replace as necessary.

154 Inspect the rubber cup on the pump plunger for excessive wear or cracking.

155 Check the choke valve and linkage for excessive wear, binding or distortion and correct or replace as necessary.

156 Inspect the choke vacuum diaphragm for leaks and replace if necessary.

157 Check the choke valve for freedom of movement.

Reassembly

158 Prior to reassembling the carburetor, compare all old and new gaskets back-to-back to be sure they match perfectly. Check especially that all the necessary holes are present and in the proper position in the new gaskets.

159 If the idle mixture needle and spring have been removed, reinstall by lightly seating the needle, then back it off three turns. This will provide a preliminary idle mixture adjustment. Final idle mixture adjustment must be made on the car.

160 Install a new gasket on the bottom of the float bowl. Mount the throttle body on the float bowl so that it is properly fitted over the locating dowels on the bowl, and reinstall the four attaching screws, tightening them evenly and securely. Be sure that the steps on the fast idle cam face toward the fast idle screw on the throttle lever when installed.

161 Inspect the linkage to make sure that the lockout tang properly engages in the slot of the secondary lockout lever and that the linkage moves freely without binding.

162 Install the choke housing onto the throttle body making sure the locating lug on the rear of the housing sits in its recess in the float bowl.

163 Install the intermediate choke shaft and lever assembly into the float bowl by pushing it through from the throttle lever side.

164 Position the intermediate choke lever in the 'up' position and install the thermostatic coil lever onto the end sticking into the choke housing. The coil lever is properly aligned when the coil pick-up tang is in the 12 o'clock position. Install the attaching screw into the end of the intermediate shaft to secure the coil lever.

165 Three self-tapping screws supplied in the overhaul kit are used in place of the original pop-rivets to secure the choke cover and coil assembly onto the choke housing. Start the three screws into the housing, checking that they start easily and are properly aligned then remove them again.

166 Place the fast idle screw on the highest step of the fast idle cam, then install the choke cover onto the housing, aligning the notch in the cover with the raised casting projection on the housing cover flange.

167 When installing the cover, be sure the coil pick-up tang engages the inside choke lever.

168 With the choke cover installed, install the three self-tapping screws and tighten securely.

169 Install the pump discharge check ball and spring in the passage next to the float chamber, then place a new plastic retainer in the hole so that its end engages the spring and tap it lightly into place until the retainer top is flush with the bowl surface.

170 Install the main metering jet into the bottom of the float chamber.

171 Install the float valve seat assembly with its gasket.

172 To make float level adjustments easier, bend the float arm upward slightly at the notch.

173 Install the float valve onto the float arm by sliding the lever under the pull clip. The correct installation of the pull clip is to hook the clip over the edge of the float on the float arm facing the float pontoon.

174 Install the float retaining pin into the float arm, then install the float assembly by aligning the valve into its seat and the float retaining pin into its locating channels in the float bowl.

175 Adjust the float level in the following manner: While holding the float retaining pin firmly in place, push down on the float arm at its outer end, against the top of the float valve, so that the top of the float is the specified distance from the float bowl surface. Bend the float arm as necessary to achieve the proper measurement by pushing down on the pontoon. See Specifications for the proper float measurement for your car. Check the float level visually following adjustment.

176 Install the power piston spring into the piston bore. If the metering rod has been removed from the power piston assembly, re-install the rod into its holder, making sure the spring is on top of the arm. Then install the assembly into the float bowl. Use care when installing the metering rod into the main metering jet so as not to damage the metering rod tip. Press down firmly on the power piston's plastic retainer until it is firmly seated in its recess and the top is flush with the top of the bowl casting. Light tapping may be required.

177 Install the plastic filler block over the float valve so that it is flush with the float bowl surface.

178 Install a new air horn gasket on the float bowl.

179 Install the pump return spring in the pump well.

180 Reassemble the pump plunger assembly, lubricate the plunger cap with a thin coat of engine oil, and install the pump plunger into the pump well.

181 Remove the old pump plunger seal and retainer in the air horn. Install a new seal and retainer and lightly stake the retainer in three places other than the original staking locations.

182 Install the fast idle cam rod into the lower hole of the choke lever.

183 Prior to installing the air horn, apply a light coating of silicone grease or engine oil to the pump plunger stem to aid in slipping it through its seal in the air horn.

184 Rotate the fast idle cam to the 'up' position so it can be engaged with the lower end of the fast idle cam rod and, while holding down on the pump plunger assembly, carefully lower the air horn onto the float bowl, guiding the pump plunger stem through its seal.

185 Install the seven air horn attaching screws and lock washers, tightening them in the proper sequence as shown.

186 With a new gasket in place, install the mixture control solenoid, lining up the stem with the recess in the float bowl and evenly tightening the retaining screws. If so equipped, install a new seal in the recess of the float bowl and the hot idle compensator valve.

187 Install the vent/screen assembly onto the air horn.

188 Install a plastic bushing in the hole in the choke lever, with the small end facing outward. Then with the intermediate choke lever at the 12 o'clock position, install the intermediate choke rod in the bushing. Install a new retaining clip on the end of the rod. An effective way of doing this is to use a broad flat-head screwdriver and a 3/16-in socket. Make sure the clip is not seated tightly against the bushing and that the linkage moves freely.

189 Engage the vacuum break rod with the inside vacuum break diaphragm plunger and the air valve rod with the outside plunger and mount the idle speed solenoid/vacuum break diaphragm assembly to the car.

190 Engage the pump rod with the pump rod lever and mount the pump lever on the air horn with its washer between the lever and the air horn.

191 Reconnect the vacuum break diaphragm hose to its fitting on the carb body.

192 Install the fuel filter so that the hole faces toward the inlet nut.

193 Place a new gasket on the inlet nut and install, torquing it to specs. Be careful not to overtighten the nut, as this could damage the gasket causing a fuel leak.

194 Install a new gasket on the top of the air horn.

M2M carburetor — overhaul

195 When a carburetor develops faults after a considerable mileage, it is usually more economical to replace the complete unit, rather than to completely dismantle it and replace individual components. Where, however, it is decided to strip and rebuild the unit, first obtain a repair kit which will contain all the necessary gaskets and other needed items and proceed in the following sequence.

196 Remove the solenoid (if equipped) from the float bowl. Screws secure the solenoid and bracket assembly. Do not immerse the solenoid in any type of carburetor cleaner.

197 Remove the choke lever at the top of the carburetor by removing the retaining screw. Then rotate the choke lever to remove the choke rod from its slot in the lever.

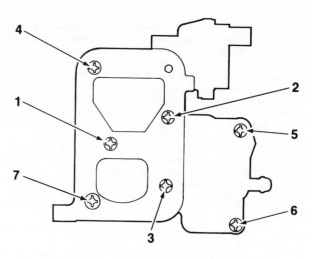

Fig. 13.10 Tightening sequence for the 2SE/E2SE series carburetor air horn

198 To remove the choke rod from the lower lever, hold the lower lever outward and twist the choke rod in a counterclockwise direction.

199 Note the position of the accelerator pump rod on its lever. Then remove the pump lever by driving the pivot pin inwards slightly until the lever can be removed from the air horn.

200 Remove the seven screws which attach the top air horn assembly to the bowl. Two of them are countersunk near the center of the carburetor. Lift the air horn straight up and off the float bowl.

201 From the air horn assembly, remove the vacuum break hose followed by the vacuum break control and bracket assembly. Do not immerse the vacuum break assembly in carburetor cleaner.

202 Lift the air horn gasket from the top of the float bowl assembly being careful not to distort the spring holding the main metering rods in place.

203 Remove the pump plunger from the pump well. Following the plunger from the well will be the plunger return spring.

204 Remove the power piston and metering rods from the well. Do this by pressing down on the piston and releasing it quickly with a snap. This procedure may have to be repeated many times. Do not remove the piston with pliers on the metering rod hanger. The A.P.T. metering rod adjustment screw is pre-set and should not be changed. If float bowl replacement is necessary the new float bowl will be supplied with a new A.P.T. metering screw.

205 Remove the metering rods from the power piston by disconnecting the spring from the top of each rod. Rotate the rod to remove from the hanger, then remove the plastic filler block over the float valve.

206 Remove the float assembly and float needle by pulling up on the retaining pin. Also remove the needle, seat and gasket.

207 Remove the pump discharge check ball retainer and check ball. Then remove the pump well fill shot baffle.

208 After drilling out the retaining rivits in the choke cover, remove the choke assembly and gasket from the main housing. Do not remove the baffle beneath the choke cover coil.

209 Remove the choke housing retaining screw inside the housing, then invert the float bowl and remove the lower choke lever from inside the cavity.

210 To remove the intermediate choke shaft, remove the retaining screw inside the choke housing and the coil lever from the flats on the shaft. Slide the intermediate shaft outward and remove the fast idle cam from the shaft.

211 Remove the cup seal from the float bowl insert. Do not remove the insert itself.

212 From the float bowl assembly, remove the fuel inlet nut, gasket, check valve filter and spring.

213 The throttle body can be separated from the float bowl by removing the attaching screws.

214 Remove the pump rod from the throttle lever.

215 Do not remove the plugs covering the idle mixture needles unless it is necessary to replace the mixture screws. The mixture passages should clean with normal soaking and air pressure.

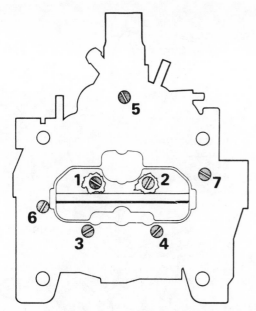

Fig. 13.11 Tightening sequence for the M2M series carburetor air horn

216   Clean all metal parts in a suitable cold solvent. Do not immerse rubber parts, plastic parts, the vacuum break assembly or the idle stop solenoid. Do not probe the jets, but blow through them with clean, dry compressed air. Examine all fixed and moving parts for cracks, distortion, wear and other damage. Replace all parts as necessary. Discard all gaskets and the fuel inlet filter.

217   Assembly is essentially the reverse of the removal procedure, but the following points should be noted:

a) Do not install the choke coil cover assembly until the inside coil lever is adjusted. With the fast idle cam follower on the high step, push up on the coil tang until the choke valve is closed. Insert a 0.0120-inch plug gauge and bend the choke rod near the lever until the lower edge of the lever just contacts the plug gauge.

b) With the float bowl components assembled, adjust the float level. Hold down the float retainer firmly and push the float down tightly against the needle. Measure from the top of the float bowl (without gasket) to the top of the float, about 3/16-in back from toe. Bend the float arm as necessary.

c) Tighten the seven air horn attaching screws evenly in the sequence given.

E4ME/E4MC carburetor — adjustment

218   Except where noted, adjustments are the same as for earlier models. Carburetors used with the C4 system do not require adjustment of the pump rod.

Float level adjustment

219   Hold the float retainer firmly in place, push the float down until it lightly contacts the needle and measure the float level with the gauge. The gauging point is 3/16-inch back from the toe of the float as shown in the illustration.

220   On carburetors used with the C4 system, the float should be adjusted if the height varies from that shown in the Specifications Section of this Chapter by plus or minus 1/16-inch.

221   If the level is too high, hold the retainer in place and push down on the center of the float pontoon until the specified setting is obtained.

222   If the level is too low on non-solenoid carburetors, remove the power piston, metering rods, plastic filler block and the float. Bend the float arm up to adjust. Reinstall the parts and visually check the alignment of the float.

223   If the level is too low on solenoid equipped carburetors, remove the metering rods and the solenoid connector screw. Count and record for use at the time of reassembly, the number of turns necessary to lightly bottom the lean mixture screw. Back the screw out and remove it, the solenoid, connector and float. Bend the float arm up to adjust. Install the parts and reset the mixture screw to the recorded number of turns.

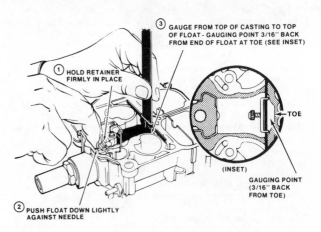

Fig. 13.12 Float level adjustment

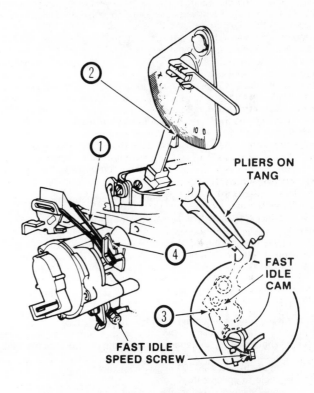

Fig. 13.13 1983 thru 1985 choke rod adjustment

Choke rod adjustment (1983 though 1985)

224   Attach a rubber band to the green tang of the intermediate choke shaft as shown in the illustration.

225   Close the choke valve by opening the throttle and install a choke angle gauge such as GM tool J-26701 and set the angle to specification.

226   Place the cam follower on the second step of the cam, against the high step, and if the follower does not contact the cam, turn the fast idle speed screw in until it does. The final fast idle adjustment must be made according to the information on the Emissions Control Information label under the hood.

227   Bend the fast idle cam tang until the bubble is centered.

Front vacuum break adjustment (1983 through 1985)

228   Attach a rubber band to the green tang of the intermediate choke shaft and open the throttle to allow the choke valve to close, then install the GM J-26701 gauge tool and set the vacuum break to the specified adjustment.

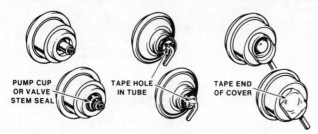

Fig. 13.14 Methods of plugging the vacuum delay air bleed

PUMP CUP OR VALVE STEM SEAL   TAPE HOLE IN TUBE   TAPE END OF COVER

1   Rubber band attached to the intermediate choke shaft green tang
2   Angle gauge set to specification
3   Air valve rod

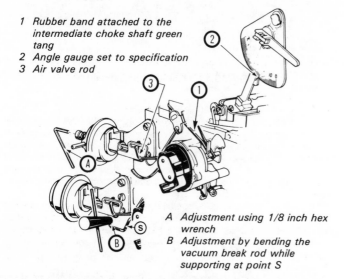

A   Adjustment using 1/8 inch hex wrench
B   Adjustment by bending the vacuum break rod while supporting at point S

Fig. 13.16 Rear vacuum break adjustment

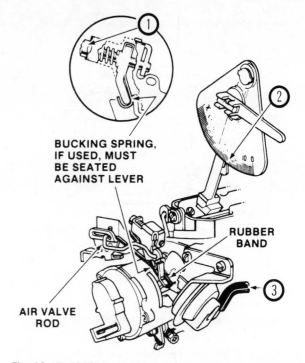

BUCKING SPRING, IF USED, MUST BE SEATED AGAINST LEVER

RUBBER BAND

AIR VALVE ROD

Fig. 13.15 1983 thru 1985 front vacuum break adjustment

1   Adjustment screw
2   Vacuum port
3   Adjustment gauge set to specification

229   Apply at least 18 in Hg of vacuum to retract the vacuum break plunger. Plug any air bleed holes.
230   On 4-barrel carburetors, the air valve rod can sometimes restrict the plunger from retracting completely and it might be necessary to bend the rod slightly. The final rod clearance must be set after the vacuum break adjustment has been made.
231   With the vacuum applied, adjust the screw until the bubble is centered.

Rear vacuum break adjustment (1983 through 1985)
232   Attach a rubber band to the green tang of the intermediate choke shaft as shown in the illustration, and open the throttle until the choke valve closes.
233   Set up the GM J-26701 angle gauge tool on the carburetor and set the angle to specification.
234   Apply vacuum to retract the vacuum break plunger, making sure to plug any bleed holes.
235   On 4-barrel carburetors, the air valve rod can sometimes restrict the plunger from retracting completely. If necessary, bend the rod at the point indicated in the illustration to allow full travel of the plunger.
236   To center the bubble, either of two methods can be used. With the vacuum applied, use a 1/8-inch hex wrench to turn the adjustment screw (A in the illustration). Alternatively, support the vacuum break rod at point S and bend the rod (B in the illustration) with the vacuum applied.

Choke unloader adjustment
237   Attach a rubber band to the green tang of the intermediate choke shaft as shown in the illustration and open the throttle to allow the choke valve to close.
238   Install the GM angle gauge tool J-26701 and set the angle to specification. Hold the secondary lockout lever away from the pin as shown in the illustration.
239   Hold the throttle lever in the wide open position and bend the fast idle lever tang until the bubble is centered.

Idle speed adjustment — preparation
240   Prior to idle speed adjustment, the engine must be at normal

1   Rubber band attached to the intermediate choke shaft green tang
2   Angle gauge set to specification
3   4-barrel carburetor secondary lockout lever and pin
4   Adjustment is made by bending the fast idle lever tang

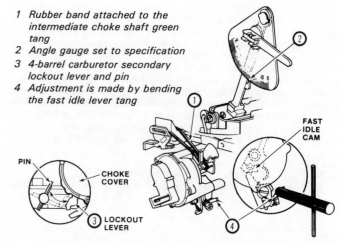

FAST IDLE CAM

PIN

CHOKE COVER

LOCKOUT LEVER

Fig. 13.17 Choke unloader adjustment

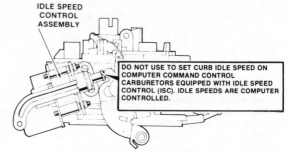

IDLE SPEED CONTROL ASSEMBLY

DO NOT USE TO SET CURB IDLE SPEED ON COMPUTER COMMAND CONTROL CARBURETORS EQUIPPED WITH IDLE SPEED CONTROL (ISC). IDLE SPEEDS ARE COMPUTER CONTROLLED.

Fig. 13.18 Idle speed control used on C-4 system equipped carburetors

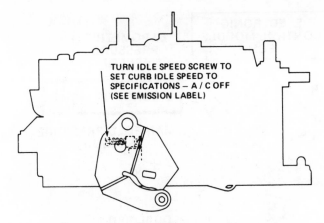

Fig. 13.19 Non-solenoid equipped curb idle speed adjustment

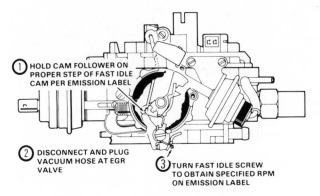

Fig. 13.21 Fast idle speed adjustment

operating temperature and the ignition timing set to the specification on the Emissions Control Information label.

241   Some models equipped with the C4 system use an idle speed control (ISC) assembly mounted on the carburetor, which is controlled by the ECM. Do not attempt to adjust the idle on the idle speed control. Adjustment of the idle speed control assembly should be left to your dealer or a properly equipped shop.

Curb idle speed adjustment (non-solenoid equipped)
242   With the air conditioner off, adjust the curb idle screw to the specifications on the Emissions Control Information label as shown in the illustration.

Curb idle speed adjustment (solenoid equipped)
243   Adjust the curb idle as described in the previous Step, then with the air conditioner on, the compressor lead disconnected at the compressor, the solenoid energized and the transmission in Neutral (manual) or Drive (automatic), open the throttle slightly to completely extend the solenoid plunger.
244   Adjust the curb idle to the specified rpm by turning the solenoid screw.
245   Reconnect the air conditioner compressor after adjustment.

Fast idle speed adjustment (non-solenoid equipped)
246   With the transmission in Park (automatic) or Neutral (manual), hold the cam follower on the step specified on the Emissions Control Information label as shown in the illustration. Turn the screw to obtain the correct fast idle speed.

Fast idle speed adjustment (solenoid equipped)
247   With the transmission in Park (automatic) or Neutral (manual), hold the cam follower on the step of the fast idle cam specified on the Emissions Control Information label.
248   Disconnect the vacuum hose at the EGR valve and plug it, then turn the fast idle screw, as shown in the illustration, untill the RPM is to specification. (See the emissions label for the proper specification).

Carburetor overhaul (Rochester E4ME)
249   Because of the complexity of this particular carburetor and the

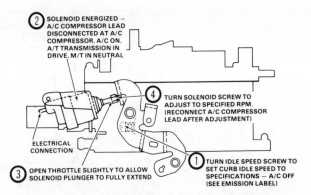

Fig. 13.20 Solenoid equipped curb idle speed adjustment

special tools required to overhaul and adjust it, it is recommended that major service work be left to a dealer service department or a carburetor specialist.

C-4 system description and maintenance
250   This system first became available on the 1980 California model and is used on all 1981 models, (a modified version is used on later models). The computer system controls exhaust emissions while retaining drivability by maintaining a continuous interaction between all of the emissions systems. Any malfunction in the computer system is signaled by a 'check engine' light on the dash which goes on and remains lit until the malfunction is corrected.
251   The computer controlled catalytic converter system requires special tools for maintenance and repair, so any work on it should be left to your dealer or a qualified technician. Although complicated, the system can be understood by examining each component and its function.

Electronic control module (ECM)
252   The electronic control module (ECM) is essentially a small onboard computer located under the dash which monitors up to 15 engine/vehicle functions and controls as many as 9 different operations. The ECM contains a programmable read only memory (PROM) calibration unit which tailors each ECM's performance to conform to the vehicle. The PROM is programmed with the vehicle's particular design, weight, axle ratio, etc. and cannot be used in another ECM in a car which differs in any way.
253   The ECM receives continuous information from the computer system and processes it in accordance with PROM instructions. It then sends out electronic signals to the system components, modifying their performance.

Oxygen sensor (OS)
254   The oxygen sensor (OS) is mounted in the exhaust pipe, upstream of the catalytic converter. It monitors the exhaust stream and sends information to the ECM on how much oxygen is present. The oxygen level is determined by how rich or lean the fuel mixture in the carburetor is.

Mixture control solenoid
255   This controls the fuel flow through the carburetor idle and main metering circuits. The solenoid cycles 10 times per second, constantly adjusting the fuel/air mixture. The ECM energizes the solenoid on information it receives from the oxygen sensor to keep emissions within limits.

Coolant sensor
256   This sensor in the coolant stream sends information to the ECM concerning engine temperature. The ECM can then vary the fuel/air ratio for conditions such as cold start. The ECM can also perform various switching functions on the EGR, EFE and AIR management systems, according to engine temperature. This feedback from the coolant sensor to the ECM is used to vary spark advance and activate the hot temperature light.

Pressure sensors
257   The ECM uses the information from various pressure sensors to adjust engine performance. The sensors are: barometric pressure sensor (BARO), manifold absolute pressure (MAP) sensor and the throttle position sensor (TPS) as well as the above mentioned coolant sensor.

Barometric pressure sensor (BARO)
258   Located in the engine compartment, the barometric pressure

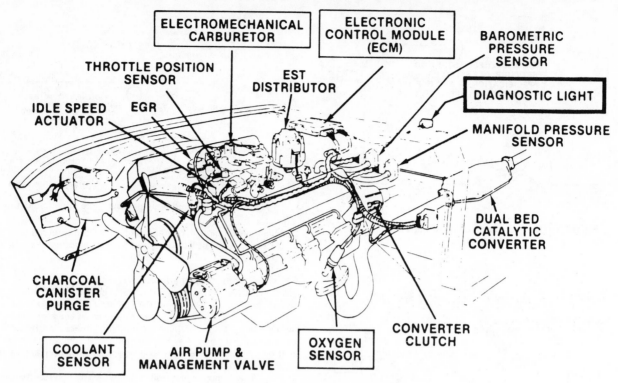

Fig. 13.22 C-4 system component layout

sensor provides a voltage to the ECM indicating ambient air pressure which varies with altitude. Not all vehicles are equipped with this sensor.

Manifold absolute pressure (MAPS)

259   Also located in the engine compartment, the MAPS senses engine vacuum (manifold) pressure. The ECM uses this information to adjust fuel/air mixture and spark timing in accordance with driving conditions.

Throttle position sensor (TPS)

260   Mounted in the carburetor body, the TPS is moved by the accelerator pump and sends a low voltage signal to the ECM when the throttle is closed and a higher voltage when it is opened. The ECM uses this voltage feed to recognize throttle position.

Idle speed control (ISC)

261   The idle speed control maintains low idle without stalling under changing load conditions. The ECM controls the idle speed control motor on the carburetor to adjust the idle.

Electronic spark timing (EST)

262   The high energy ignition (HEI) distributor used with this system has no provision for centrifugal or vacuum advance of spark timing. This is controlled electronically by the ECM (except under certain conditions such as cranking the engine).

263   The EGR, EFE and fuel evaporative systems explained elsewhere in this Chapter are also controlled by the ECM in the computer controlled catalytic converter system.

Air injection reactor

264   When the engine is cold, the ECM energizes an air switching valve which allows air to flow to the exhaust ports to lower carbon monoxide (C) and hydrocarbon (HC) levels in the exhaust.

Exhaust gas recirculator (EGR)

265   The ECM controls the ported vacuum to the EGR with a solenoid valve. When the engine is cold, the solenoid is energized to block vacuum to the EGR valve until the engine is warm.

Evaporative emission system

266   When the engine is cold or idling, the ECM solenoid blocks vacuum to the valve at the top of the charcoal canister. When the engine is warm and at a specified rpm, the ECM de-energizes the valve, releasing the collected vapors into the intake manifold.

Early fuel evaporation (EFE)

267   The ECM controls a valve which shuts off the system until the engine is warm.

Computer controlled catalytic converter system circuit check

268   With the proper equipment, the computer controlled system can

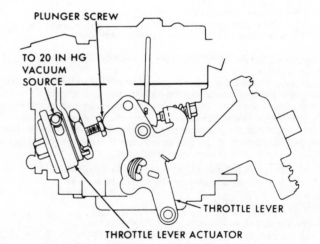

Fig. 13.23 Adjusting a typical TRC system

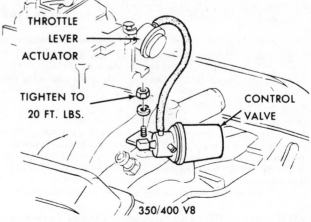

Fig. 13.24 A typical trc system

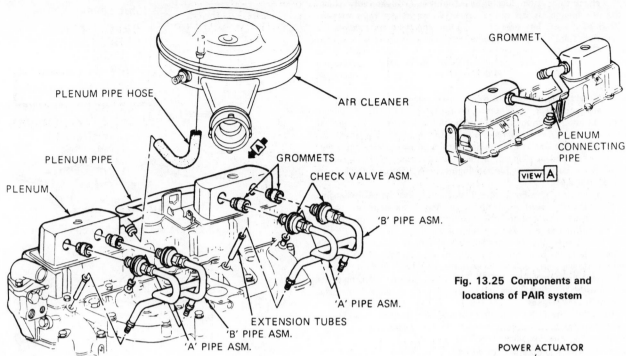

PLENUM PIPE HOSE

AIR CLEANER

PLENUM PIPE

PLENUM

GROMMETS

CHECK VALVE ASM.

'B' PIPE ASM.

'A' PIPE ASM.

EXTENSION TUBES
'B' PIPE ASM.
'A' PIPE ASM.

GROMMET

PLENUM CONNECTING PIPE

VIEW A

Fig. 13.25 Components and locations of PAIR system

be used to diagnose malfunctions within itself. The 'check engine' light can flash trouble codes stored in the ECM 'trouble code memory' As stated before, this diagnosis should be left to your dealer or a qualified technician because of the tools required and the fact that ECM programming varies from one model vehicle to another.

Throttle Return Control (TRC) system — description and maintenance

269 This system is used on vehicles with heavy duty emissions. Its purpose is to open the throttle lever slightly when coasting to reduce the emission of hydrocarbons.
270 Periodically check the security of the vacuum hose and the adjustment of the actuator.
271 To check the actuator valve, disconnect the hose from the valve and connect the valve to an external vacuum source such as a suction pump.
272 Have the engine idling at normal operating temperature, with the transmission in Neutal or P.
273 Apply a vacuum pressure of 20 in Hg to the actuator and then manually open the throttle slightly and let it close again against the actuator plunger. Record the engine rpm which should be approximately 1500 rpm. If it is not, turn the screw on the plunger and repeat the check.

Pulse Air Injection Reactor (PAIR) system — description and maintenance

274 The PAIR system consists of four pulse air valves. the combustion of the engine creates a pulsating flow of exhaust gases which are either of a positive or negative pressure. A positive pressure will force the check valve closed and no exhaust gas will flow past the valve into the fresh air supply line. A negative pressure at the pulse air valves will result in the flow of fresh air into the exhaust system.
275 Inspect the pulse air valves, pipes, grommets and hose for leaks and cracks and replace as required.
276 Apply 1.5 in Hg of vacuum at the grommet end of the valve. There will be an allowable drop to 0.5 in Hg in two seconds. If the vacuum drops in less than two seconds replace the valve and/or the hose. **Note:** *Be sure the leak is not in the hose or connection before replacing the valve with a new one.*
277 To replace the pulse air valve, remove the air cleaner and disconnect the rubber hose from the plenum connecting pipe.
278 Disconnect the four pipe check valve fittings at the cylinder head and remove the check valve pipes from the plenum grommets.

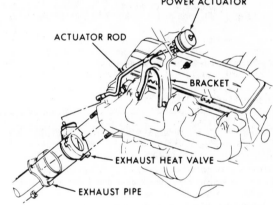

POWER ACTUATOR

ACTUATOR ROD

BRACKET

EXHAUST HEAT VALVE

EXHAUST PIPE

Fig. 13.26 Components and locations of typical EFE system

279 Disconnect the check valve from the check valve pipe.
280 Assemble the check valves to the check valve pipes on a workbench before reinstalling them.
281 Install the pipe check valve assemblies on the cylinder head and finger-tighten the fittings.
282 Using a large wrench or similar tool as a lever, align the check valve with the plenum grommet. Then, using the palm of your hand, install the check valve into the grommet. Use rubber lubricant on the grommets to ease assembly.
283 Tighten the fittings to the specified torque and reinstall the air cleaner and hose.

Early Fuel Evaporation (EFE) system — description and maintenance

284 This system improves cold engine warm-up and driveability by routing hot exhaust gases under the base of the carburetor which results in better atomization of fuel and reduced exhaust emission.
285 The system consists of a vacuum controlled actuator which is linked to a stainless steel exhaust heat valve and a method of controlling the vacuum source.
286 On in-line engines, the vacuum is controlled according to oil temperature, while on V8 engines, the vacuum is controlled by a coolant temperature switch.
287 Maintenance consists of inspecting all hoses for security of connection and for splits. Move the exhaust valve by hand. If it is stiff to operate or seized, free it with special GM heat valve lubricant.

288 To check this system, locate the actuator and rod assembly which, on the V8 engine, is on a bracket attached to the right exhaust manifold or on the left side of the in-line engine, connected to the exhaust manifold. With the engine cold, have an assistant start the engine. Observe the movement of the actuator rod which leads to the heat valve inside the exhaust pipe. It should immediately operate the valve to the closed position. If this is the case, the system is operating correctly.

289 If the actuator rod did not move, disconnect the vacuum hose at the actuator and place your thumb over the open end. With the engine cold and at idle, you should feel a suction indicating proper vacuum. If there is vacuum at this point, replace the actuator with a new one.

290 If there is no vacuum in the line, this is an indication that either the hose is crimped or plugged, or the thermal vacuum switch threaded into the water outlet is not functioning properly. Replace the hose or switch as necessary.

291 To make sure the Early Fuel Evaporation System is disengaging once the engine has warmed, continue to observe the actuating rod as the engine reaches normal operating temperature. The rod should again move, indicating the valve is in the open position.

292 If after the engine has warmed, the valve does not open, pull the vacuum hose at the actuator and check for vacuum with your thumb. If there is no vacuum, replace the acutator. If there is vacuum, replace the Thermal Vacuum Switch (TVS). The TVS is mounted on the water outlet housing on V8 engines and to the block, just above the starter motor, on in-line engines.

293 To replace the TVS, drain the engine coolant until the fluid level is below the engine water outlet (thermostat) housing (V8 only).

294 Disconnect the hoses from, the TVS.

295 Apply a soft setting sealant uniformly to the threads of the new TVS. Be careful that none of the sealant gets on the sensor end of the switch.

296 Install the switch and tighten to specifications.

297 Connect the vacuum hoses to the switch in their original positions.

298 Add coolant as necessary on V8 engines.

4 Ignition system

1979 through 1982 vehicles with 6-cylinder engines have the ignition coil mounted, in compact form, to the distributor (the same as the V8 engine described in Chapter 4).

Distributor — general description

1   Later model distributors vary somewhat from those described in Chapter 4. Most later distributors are not equipped with vacuum advance units, as advance is controlled by the Electronic Control Module (ECM).

Distributor — overhaul

2   Unplug the electrical connector(s), disengage the latches and remove the distributor cap.

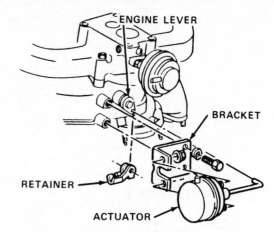

Fig. 13.27 EFE system on 250 cu in engine

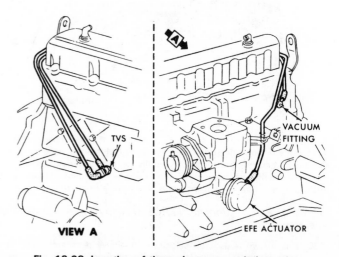

Fig. 13.28 Location of thermal vacuum switch on six cylinder EFE system

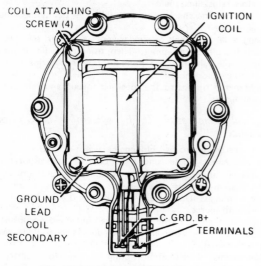

Fig. 13.29 Ignition coil in cap removal

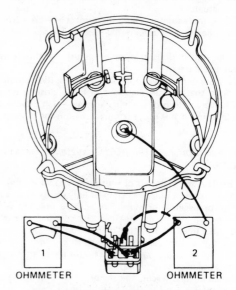

Fig. 13.30 Testing the coil in cap coil

1 With the ohmmeter connected, the reading should be very near zero
2 Connect the ohmmeter as shown, using the High scale (the coil is faulty if both readings are infinite

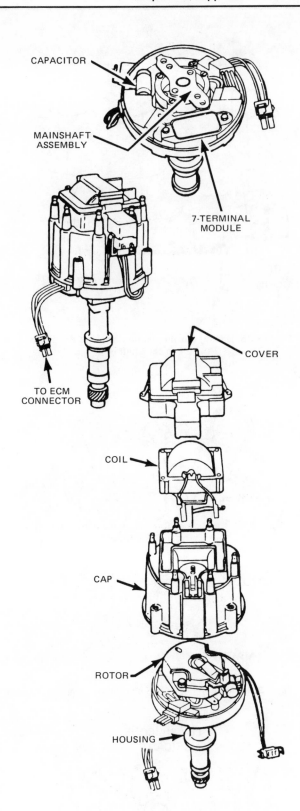

Fig. 13.31 Disributor component layout

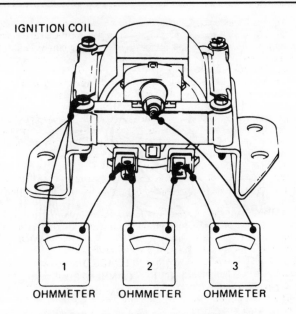

Fig. 13.32 Testing the seperate ignition coil

1 On the High scale, the reading
   should be very high (infinite) or
   there is a fault in the coil
2 On the low scale, the reading
   should be very low or zero (if it is
   high, the coil is faulty
3 On the High scale, the reading
   should not be infinite (if it is
   replace the coil)

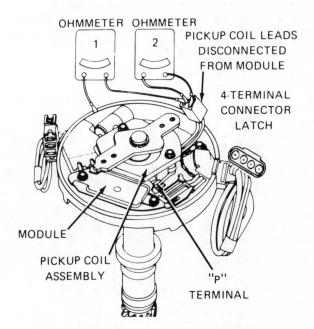

Fig. 13.33 Testing the pick-up coil (coil in-cap distributor)

3   Test the ignition coil by referring to the appropriate illustration (separate illustrations for remote coil and coil-in-cap).

4   To remove the cap-installed ignition coil, remove the coil cover screws, then lift off the cover, followed by the coil mounting screws. Separate the coil from the cap and remove the coil arc seal. Clean the cap carefully with a soft cloth and inspect it for cracks and damage.

5   To test the pick-up coil, remove the rotor and pickup leads and connect an ohmmeter as shown in the accompanying illustrations.

6   With the ohmmeter attached as shown in Step 1 in the illustrations, the reading should be infinite. With the ohmmeter attached as shown in Step 2, the reading should be between 500 and 1500 ohms. Replace the coil with a new one if it fails either test.

7   Place the distributor in a vise, using blocks of wood to protect it.

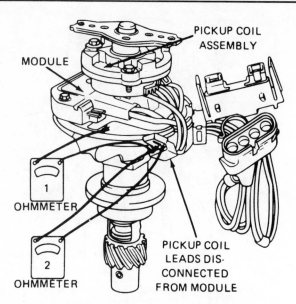

Fig. 13.34 Testing the pick-up coil on a distributor with a separately mounted coil

8   Mark the relative positions of the gear and shaft. Drive the roll pin out as shown in the illustration. Remove the gear and pull the shaft from the distributor housing.

9   On distributors with the ingition coil in the cap, remove the aluminum shield for access to the pick-up coil and module. The pickup coil can be lifted out after removal of the C washer. Remove the two screws and lift the module, capacitor and harness assembly from the distributor base. When installing, apply a coat of silicone lubricant under the module.

10   On distributors with separately mounted ignition coils, remove the C washer and lift out the pick-up coil assembly. Unplug the harness, remove the two screws and lift the module from the base. Apply silicone lubricant to the distributor base under the module prior to installation.

11   Wipe the distributor base and module with a clean cloth and inspect it for cracks and damage.

12   Reassembly is the reverse of the disassembly procedure. Be sure to apply a coat of silicone lubricant to the distributor base under the module. After reassembly, spin the distributor shaft to make sure there is no contact by the pick-up coil and teeth.

---

5 Transmission

3-speed manual transmission (Tremec) — general information

On the model years 1979 through 1982 a heavy-duty 3-speed manual tramsmission was offered. It has an identification number stamped on the top side of the left attachment case. This transmission is synchronized in all forward gears, similar to the transmissions described in Chapter 6.

77 mm 3-speed transmission

Transmission overhaul

1   Shift the transmission into Neutral and raise the vehicle for access beneath. Set firmly on stands.

2   Drain the oil and remove the transmission as described in Sections 7 and 8 of Chapter 6.

3   Unbolt the top cover and remove it along with the gasket from the case.

4   Lift out the long spring that holds the detent plug in the case and, using a small magnet, remove the detent plug.

5   Unbolt the extension housing and remove it along with the gasket.

6   Apply pressure to the speedometer gear retainer and remove the speedometer drivegear retainer from the output shaft.

7   Remove the fill plug from the right side of the case. Working through the plug hole, use a 3/16 in pin punch and drive out the countergear roll pin. Let the pin drop, it can be retrieved at a later time.

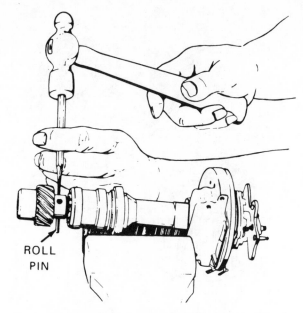

Fig. 13.35 Driving out the pin retaining the distributor gear to the shaft

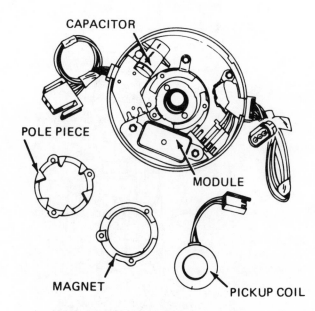

Fig. 13.36 Ignition coil-in-cap distributor component layout

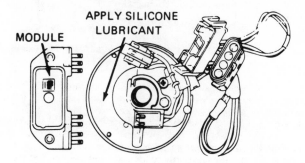

Fig. 13.37 Removal or installation of the module on a distributor with a seperately mounted ignition coil

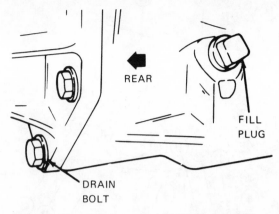

Fig. 13.38 Location of drain bolt and fill plug (77 mm transmission)

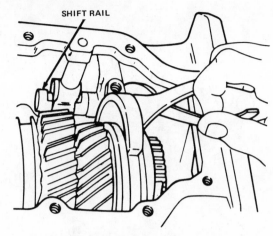

Fig. 13.39 Turn the shift rail 90° with pliers (77 mm transmission)

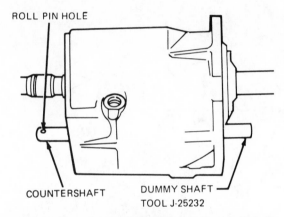

Fig. 13.40 Insert dummy shaft to remove the countershaft (77 mm transmission)

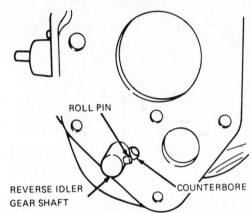

Fig. 13.41 Positioning of the roll pin in the idler gear shaft in relation to the counterbore in the transmission case (77 mm transmission)

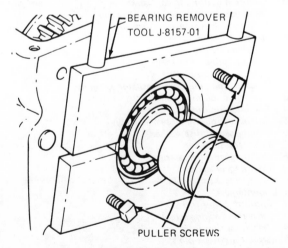

Fig. 13.42 Using the special tool to remove the rear bearing (77 mm transmission)

8   Insert dummy shaft tool No. J25232 into the hole at the front of the case. Lightly tap on the tool to push the countershaft out the rear of the case. Allow the countergear to lie at the bottom of the case.

9   With a punch and hammer, put alignment marks in the front bearing retainer and transmission case to ensure correct reassembly. Remove the front bearing retainer and gasket.

10 Remove the snap-ring that holds the front bearing and the clutch gear shaft in place.

11 Using special tool No. J6654-01 and tool No. J8433-1, remove the clutch shaft front bearing.

12 Remove the snap-rings from the rear bearing and from the output

shaft. It may be necessary to place a piece of barstock or a screwdriver between the 1st/Reverse sleeve and gear assembly and the transmission case. This will hold the output shaft assembly in place while removing the rear bearing.

13 Use special tool No. J8157-01 or an equivalent puller to remove the rear bearing from the output shaft.

14 Remove the set screw from the 1st/Reverse shift fork and push the shift rail out of the case.

15 Push the 1st/Reverse sleeve and gear all the way to the front and rotate the 1st/Reverse shift fork upward and out of the case. Remove the 1st/Reverse detent plug from the case.

16 Push the 2nd/3rd shift fork to the back to gain access to the set screw. Remove the set screw. Next, twist the shift rail 90° with pliers to clear the bottom detent plug and, using a magnet, remove the inner lock plug.

17 Insert a 1/4 inch diameter punch through the access hole in the rear of the case to drive out the shift rail and expansion plug located in the shift rail bore at the front of the case.

18 Turn the 2nd/3rd shifter fork upward and lift it out of the case.

19 Remove the bottom detent plug and its short detent spring from the case.

20 Disengage the clutch gear from the output shaft and remove the output shaft assembly. To do this, tilt the splined end of the shaft downward and lift the gear end upward and out of the case. At the right-rear end of the case there is a notch through which the 1st and Reverse sleeve and gear must pass.

21 Lift the clutch gear through the top of the case.

22 Remove both shifter fork shafts.

23 Remove the countergear, thrust washer and roll pin with the tool still in place.

24 Tap the end of the idler gear shaft with a hammer until the end with the roll pin clears the counter bore in the rear of the case. Remove the shaft, the Reverse idler gear and the thrust washer.

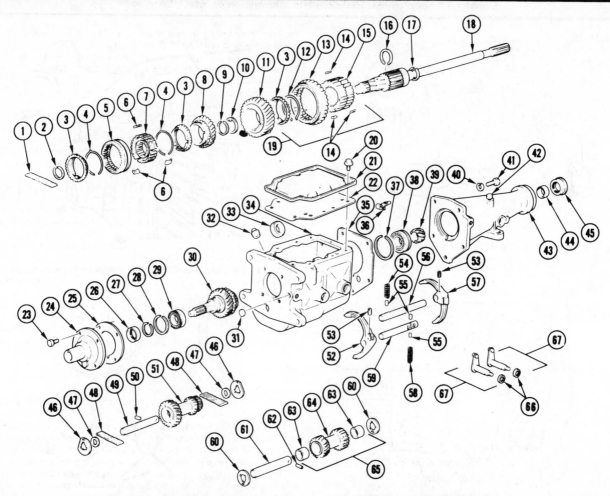

Fig. 13.43 Exploded view of 77 mm 3-speed transmission

1   Mainshaft roller bearings
2   2nd/3rd synchronizer retaining ring
3   Synchronizer blocker rings
4   2nd/3rd synchronizer spring
5   2nd/3rd synchronizer sleeve
6   2nd/3rd synchronizer keys
7   2nd/3rd synchronizer hub
8   2nd speed gear
9   1st speed gear retaining ring
10   1st speed gear tabbed washer
11   1st speed gear
12   Reverse synchronizer spring
13   1st/Reverse synchronizer sleeve and gear
14   Reverse synchronizer hub
15   1st/Reverse synchronizer hub
16   1st/Reverse synchronizer retaining ring
17   Rear bearing retaining ring
18   Transmission mainshaft
19   Reverse synchronizer assembly
20   Access cover bolts
21   Access cover
22   Access cover gasket
23   Bearing retainer-to-case bolts
24   Bearing retainer clutch gear
25   Gasket clutch gear bearing retainer
26   Seal assembly clutch gear bearing retainer
27   Clutch gear bearing retaining ring
28   Clutch gear bearing lock ring
29   Clutch gear bearing assembly
30   Clutch gear
31   Expansion plug
32   Filler plug
33   Transmission case magnet
34   Case

35   Extension housing-to-case gasket
36   Speedometer driver gear retaining clip
37   Transmission rear bearing lock ring
38   Mainshaft bearing assembly
39   Speedometer drive gear
40   Extension-to-case washer
41   Extension-to-case bolt
42   Transmission extension ventilator assembly
43   Extension housing assembly
44   Extension housing bushing
45   Extension housing oil seal assembly
46   Countergear thrust washer
47   Countergear spacer
48   Countergear roller bearings
49   Countergear shaft
50   Countergear spring pin
51   Countergear
52   2nd/3rd shifter fork
53   Shift fork locking screw
54   1st/2nd shifter interlock spring
55   Shifter interlock pin
56   1st/Reverse shift rail
57   1st/Reverse shift fork
58   2nd/3rd shifter interlock spring
59   2nd/3rd shift rail
60   Reverse idler gear thrust washer
61   Reverse idler gear shaft
62   Spring pin, idler gear shaft
63   Reverse idler gear bushing
64   Reverse idler gear
65   Reverse idler gear assembly
66   Seal, transmission shifter
67   Transmission shifter shaft and lever assembly

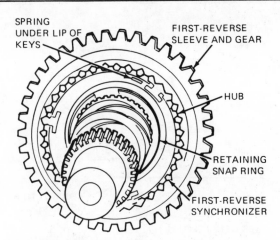

Fig. 13.44 77 mm transmission 1st/Reverse synchronizer
assembly

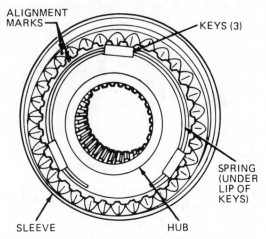

Fig. 13.45 77 mm transmission 2nd/3rd synchronizer assembly

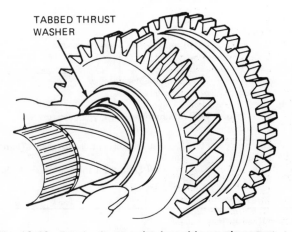

Fig. 13.46 Put the thrust washer in position on the output
shaft (sharp edge facing out) (77 mm transmission)

25 Remove the clutch shaft roller bearing or countergear needle bearing or anything else that may have fallen into the case during disassembly.
26 The mainshaft should only be disassembled if a press or bearing puller is available. Otherwise, take the assembly to your GM dealer. Be careful to keep all components separated in order to easily reassemble.
27 Remove the front output shaft snap-ring and lift out the 2nd/3rd synchronizer assembly and 2nd gear. Place alignment marks on the hub and sleeve for ease in reassembly.

28 After removing the snap-ring and tabbed thrust washer from the shaft, remove 1st gear and the blocking ring.
29 Make a note of the position of the springs and keys in the Reverse hub and place alignment marks on the hub and sleeve for correct reassembly.
30 Remove the 1st/Reverse hub retaining snap-ring then separate the sleeve gear spring and three keys from the hub.
31 Separate the hub from the output shaft using an arbor press.
32 Clean all components in solvent and dry thoroughly. Check the gears for wear or chipped teeth. Check the bearings for smoothness of operation inside the race. If there has been a history of noisy gear shifts or the synchro facility could easily have been 'beaten' then replace the appropriate synchro unit.
33 If the bushing in the rear extension requires replacement, drive the rear seal out, then drive the bushing out using tubular drifts. Using a socket or the correct size drift, drive a new bushing in from the rear. Lubricate the inside diameter of the bushing and install the new rear seal using an appropriate tubular drift.
34 Clean the transmission case inside and out and check for cracks, particularly around the bolt holes.
35 Extract the clutch bearing retainer seal and drive in a new one.
36 Commence rebuilding the transmission by first reassembling the mainshaft.
37 Fit the 1st/Reverse synchronizer hub onto the output shaft splines. The slotted end of the hub should face the front of the shaft. Use an arbor press to complete the hub installation onto the shaft. In the most rearward groove, install the retaining snap-ring. Note: *A press must be used, do not try to drive the hub onto the shaft with a hammer.*
38 Slip the 1st/Reverse sleeve and gear half-way onto the hub with the gear end of the sleeve facing the rear of the shaft. Align the sleeve and the hub with the marks made during disassembly.
39 Place the spring in the 1st/Reverse hub making sure that the spring is bottomed in the hub and covers all three key slots. Place the three synchronizer keys in the hub with the small end of the key in the hub slot and the large end inside the hub. Push the keys all the way into the hub so that they seat on the spring, then slide the 1st/Reverse sleeve and gear over the keys until the keys engage in the synchronizer sleeve.
40 Install the 1st gear blocking ring to the tapered surface of the gear and insert the 1st gear onto the output shaft. Rotate the gear until the notches in the blocking ring engage with the keys in the 1st/Reverse hub.
41 With the sharp edge facing out, install the tabbed thrust washer and retaining snap-ring onto the output shaft.
42 Attach the 2nd gear blocking ring to the tapered surface of the 2nd gear and install the 2nd gear onto the output shaft with the tapered surface facing the front of the shaft.
43 Install the 2nd/3rd synchronizer assembly to the output shaft. Make sure the flat portion of the synchronizer hub faces the rear. Turn the 2nd gear until the keys in the 2nd/3rd synchronizer assembly engage with the notches in the locking ring. To ease assembly, tap the synchronizer with a plastic hammer.
44 Install the retaining snap-ring on the output shaft and measure the endplay between the snap-ring and the 2nd/3rd synchronizer hub. If the endplay exceeds 0.014 inch, replace the thrust washer and all snap-rings on the output shaft assembly.
45 Smear petroleum jelly over the transmission case Reverse idler gear thrust washer and position the thrust washer in the case. Be sure to engage the thrust washer locating tabs into the locating slots in the case.
46 With the helical cut gears toward the front of the case, install the Reverse idler gear. From the rear of the case, install the Reverse idler gear shaft, aligning the gear bore thrust washer in case bores. Align and seat the roll pin, in the shaft, into the counter bore in the rear of the case.
47 Measure the endplay between the Reverse idler gear and the thrust washer. If the play exceeds 0.018 inches, remove the idler gear and replace the thrust washer.
48 Apply a thick coat of heavy grease to the bore of the countergear and insert dummy shaft No. J25232, then load a row of 25 needle bearings into each end of the gear. Next, install one needle bearing retainer on each end of the gear to hold the needle bearings in place.
49 Cover the countergear thrust washer with petroleum jelly and position it in the case. Be sure to engage the locating tabs on the thrust washer into the locating slots in the case.
50 Slip the countershaft through the bore at the rear of the case just far enough to hold the rear thrust washer in position when the countergear is installed.

51 Insert the countershaft into the countergear, aligning the bore in the countergear with the countershaft and the front thrust washer. Before the countershaft is completely installed, make sure that the roll pin in the countershaft is aligned with the hole in the case. When the holes are aligned, remove tool No. J25232 from the countergear and tap the countershaft into place.

52 Measure the countershaft endplay between the thrust washer and countergear with a feeler gauge. If the endplay exceeds 0.018 inches, remove the gear and replace the thrust washer.

53 When the correct endplay is obtained, install the roll pin in the case.

54 Place the shorter detent spring into its bore in the case. The spring should fit into place at the bottom of the 2nd/3rd shift rail bore. Next, install the lower detent plug in the detent bore, on top of the spring.

55 Install the shifter fork shafts in their case bores with the pivot lug facing up. **Note:** *Shifter fork shafts are interchangeable.*

56 Apply petroleum jelly or equivalent light grease to the clutch shaft bore and install the 15 roller bearings. Do not use heavy chassis grease as it could plug the lubricant holes.

57 Attach the blocking ring to the clutch gear and place the gear through the top of the case into position in the front case bore.

58 Place the 1st/Reverse sleeve and gear in its Neutral (centered) position on the hub. Install the output shaft assembly in the case. Be careful so the gear end of the sleeve will clear the notch in the top of the case.

59 Engage the output shaft to the clutch gear.

60 Slide the 2nd/3rd sleeve to the rear until it is in its 2nd gear position and place the 2nd/3rd shift fork in the groove of the sleeve. Be sure the shift fork set screw hole is facing upward. **Note:** *The 2nd/3rd fork is the smaller of the two shift forks.*

61 Engage the 2nd/3rd shift fork in the shift fork shaft.

62 Slide the 2nd/3rd shift rail (with the tapered end facing the front of the case) through the front case bore and into the shifter fork.

63 Rotate the shift rail until the detent notches in the rail face down. Depress the lower detent plug with a Phillips screwdriver and push the shift rail into the rear bore. Push the rail inward until the detent plug engages the forward notch in the shift rail (the second gear position).

64 Install the set screw to attach the fork to the rail and move the 2nd/3rd synchronizer to the Neutral (centered) position.

65 Insert the interlock plug into the detent bore. The top of the plug should be slightly below the surface of the 1st/Reverse shift rail bore.

66 Slide the 1st/Reverse synchronizer forward to the 1st gear position. Place the 1st/Reverse shifter fork (with the set screw hole facing up) in the groove of the sleeve. Engage the fork with the shifter fork shaft, then slide the 1st/Reverse shift rail through the rear case bore and shifter fork.

67 Rotate the shift rail until the detent notches in the rail face upward. Align the set screw bore in the shift rail with the set screw hole in the fork and secure with the set screw. Place the 1st/Reverse sleeve and gear into the Neutral (centered) position.

68 Install the large snap-ring on the front bearing.

69 Install the front bearing on the clutch gear shaft by hand. Drive the bearing onto the clutch shaft using an appropriate tubular drift.

70 Install a small snap-ring on the clutch gear shaft.

71 Place the bearing retainer gasket on the case (be sure the oil return hole on the case is not blocked).

72 Align the marks made during disassembly on the front bearing retainer and the transmission case and check that the oil return slot in the cap is aligned with the oil return hole in the case. Attach the bolts and tighten them to the specified torque.

73 Install the large snap-ring on the rear bearing.

74 Install the rear bearing on the output shaft by hand. Drive the bearing onto the shaft and into the case with the appropriate size tubular drift. Make sure the snap-ring groove is facing the rear of the shaft.

75 Install the small snap-ring on the output shaft to hold the rear bearing in place.

76 In the hole provided in the output shaft, engage the speedometer gear retainer. Slide the speedometer gear over the output shaft and into position with the retainer plate facing forward.

77 Place the new extention housing gasket on the case and install the extention housing. Tighten the bolts to the specified torque.

78 Insert the expansion plug into the 2nd/3rd shift rail bore in the front of the case. When the plug is fully seated in its bore it should be approximately 1/16th inch below the front face of the case.

79 Install the upper detent plug in the detent bore, then install the long detent spring on top of the plug.

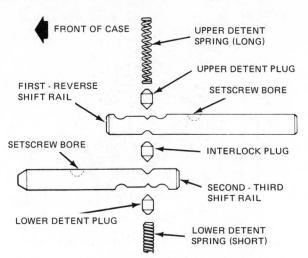

Fig. 13.47 Positioning of the detent plugs and springs in relation to the shift rails during installation (77 mm transmission)

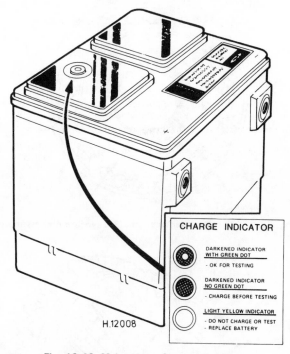

Fig. 13.48 Maintenance-free type battery

80 Place a new gasket on the case and install the top cover. Tighten the bolts to the specified torque.

81 Fill the transmission with oil and install the transmission fill plug. Tighten it to the specified torque.

6   Electrical system

Battery maintenance

1 On all models built between 1979 and 1982, a Delco (Freedom) maintenance-free type battery is installed as original equipment. These batteries require no filling-up of the cells, since they are sealed. A charge indicator is built into the top of the battery.

Battery – charging

2 Check the charge indicator on the top of the battery and charge only if the window is darkened. The Delco sealed battery can be charged the same as a conventional battery (described in Chapter 10, Section 5).

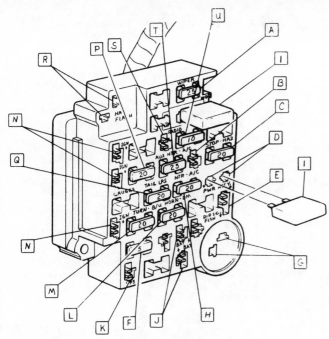

Fig. 13.49 Typical fuse box

1　Circuit breaker
A　Fuse-windshield wiper
B　Receptacle-ignition ACC, radio and auxiliary battery
C　Fuse-stop and traffic hazard lamps
D　Power accessory
E　Receptacle-power door locks
F　Fuse-instrument panel lamps
G　Receptacle-direction signal lamp flasher
H　Fuse-heater and A/C
J　Receptacle-battery, lighter, radio capacitor, clock, H/L warning
K　Receptacle-panel lamps, radio dial, transmission indicator lamp and tilt wheel
L　Fuse-horn
M　Fuse-direction signal and back-up lamps
N　Receptacle-ignition automatic transmission, cruise control, pulse wiper, transmission indicator lamps
P　Fuse-gauges
Q　Fuse-tail lamps
R　Receptacle-traffic hazard flasher
S　Receptacle-ignition/ACC, rear A/C, auxiliary heater
T　Fuse-auxiliary heater and A/C
U　Fuse-radio

3　If the window is clear or light yellow, DO NOT charge. This condition indicates that the fluid level is below the bottom of the hydrometer. Charging or jumping a battery in this condition could result in a battery explosion causing serious injury (particularly to the

eyes). Replace the battery with a new unit.

Fuse box

4　1979 through 1982 models use a different style of fuses than earlier models. The new fuses still work the same as before and are located just beneath the dash on the driver's side, but instead of using clear glass capsules to house the fuse, the new fuses are housed in colored transparent plastic. The new fuses are easier to remove and replace then the glass fuses, but they must be removed to see if they are 'blown'.

5　The fuse block on some 1983 through 1985 models is a swing-down unit located in the underside of the instrument panel adjacent to the steering column. Access to the fuse block on some models is gained through the glove box. Consult your owner's manual for the location on your vehicle.

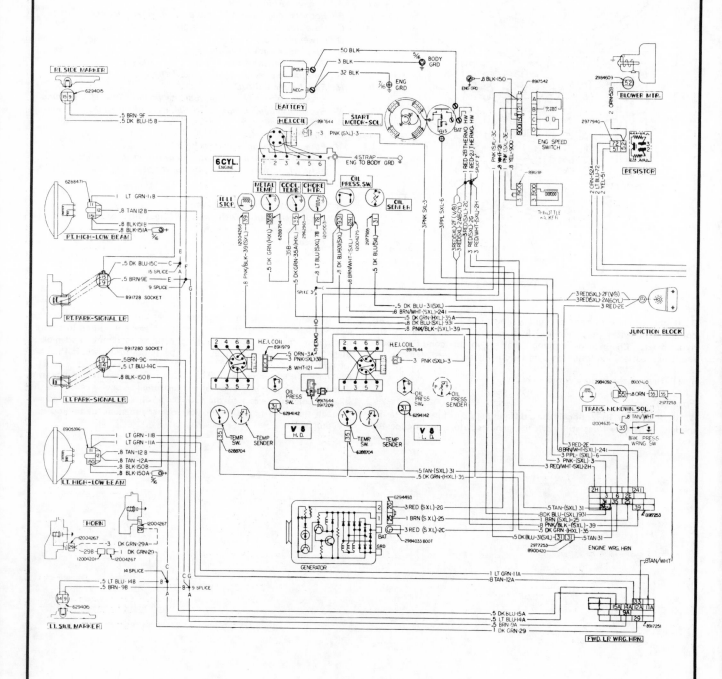

Fig. 13.50 1979 and 1980 models (1 of 5)

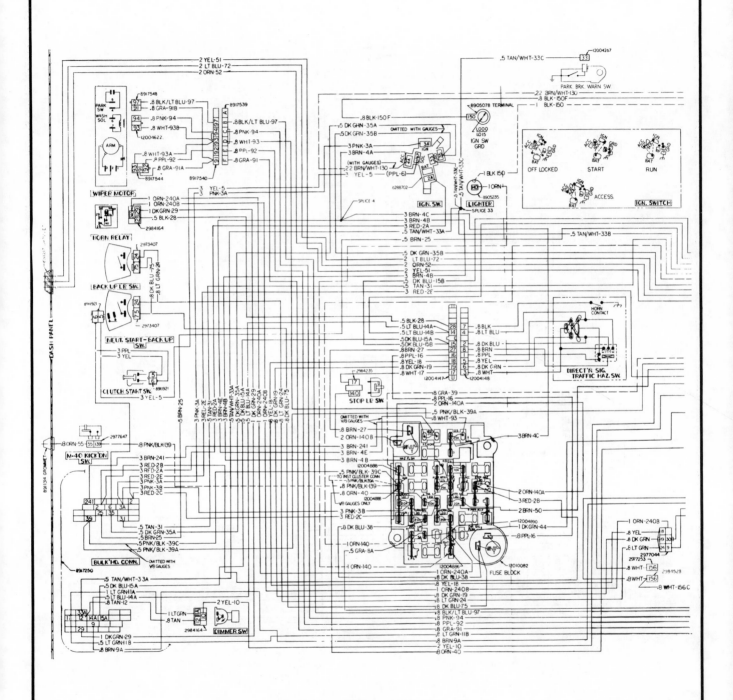

Fig. 13.51 1979 and 1980 models (2 of 5)

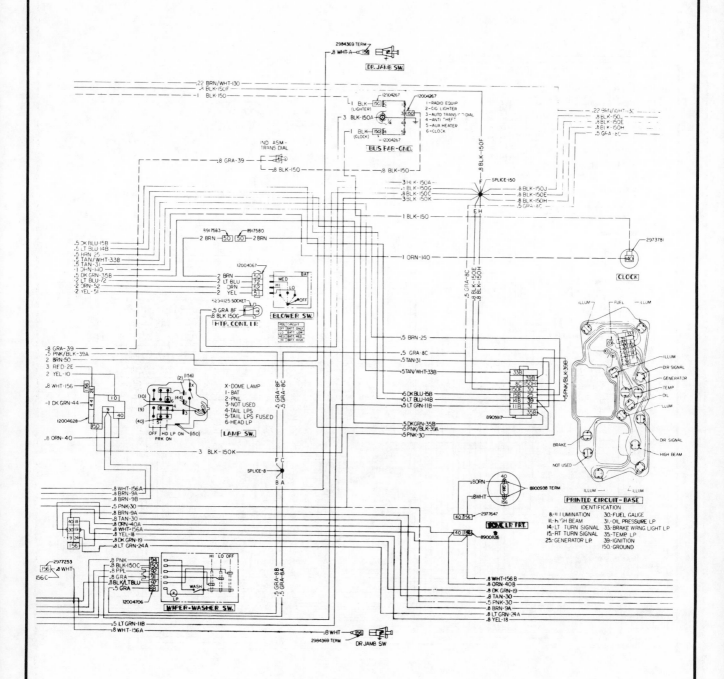

Fig. 13.52 1979 and 1980 models (3 of 5)

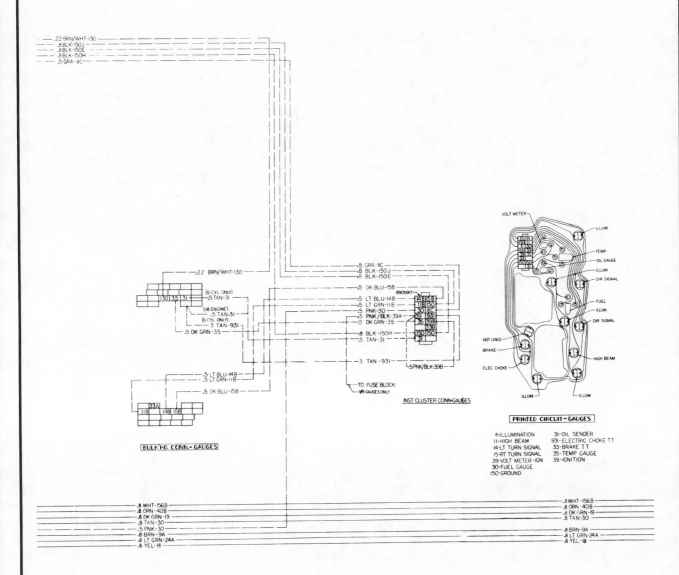

.22 BRN/WHT-130
.8 BLK-150J
.8 BLK-150E
.8 BLK-150H
.5 GRA-8C

.22 BRN/WHT-130

(6 CYL ONLY)
.5 TAN-31
(V8 ENGINE)
.5 TAN-31
(6 CYL ONLY)
.3 TAN-931
.5 DK GRN-35

130 | 35 | 31

.5 LT BLU-14B
.5 LT GRN-11B
.5 DK BLU-15B

33A
11B | 14B | 15B

BULK'HD. CONN.- GAUGES

.5 GRA-8C
.8 BLK-150 J
.8 BLK-150E
.5 DK BLU-15B
.5 LT BLU-14B
.5 LT GRN-11B
.5 PNK-30
.5 PNK/BLK-39A
.5 DK GRN-35
.8 BLK-150H
.5 TAN-31

.3 TAN-931

.5 PNK/BLK-39B

TO FUSE BLOCK
V8 GAUGES ONLY

14|8|15 B
11B|150
30|8 C
39 | 931
35 |39 B
|33|
150|150
31

8905917

INST CLUSTER CONN-GAUGES

VOLT METER
ILLUM
TEMP
OIL GAUGE
ILLUM
DIR SIGNAL
FUEL
ILLUM
DIR SIGNAL
NOT USED
BRAKE
HIGH BEAM
ELEC CHOKE
ILLUM
ILLUM

PRINTED CIRCUIT - GAUGES

8-ILLUMINATION
11-HIGH BEAM
14-LT TURN SIGNAL
15-RT TURN SIGNAL
39-VOLT METER-IGN.
30-FUEL GAUGE
150-GROUND

31-OIL SENDER
931-ELECTRIC CHOKE T.T.
33-BRAKE T T
35-TEMP GAUGE
39-IGNITION

.8 WHT-156B
.8 ORN-40B
.8 DK GRN-19
.8 TAN-30
.5 PNK-30
.8 BRN-9A
.8 LT GRN-24A
.8 YEL-18

.8 WHT-156B
.8 ORN-40B
.8 DK GRN-19
.8 TAN-30

.8 BRN-9A
.8 LT GRN-24A
.8 YEL-18

Fig. 13.53 1979 and 1980 models (4 of 5)

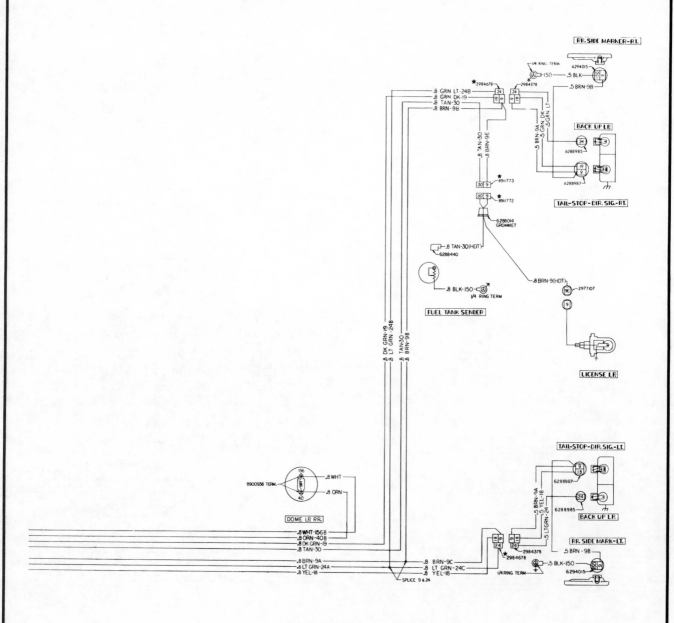

Fig. 13.54 1979 and 1980 models (5 of 5)

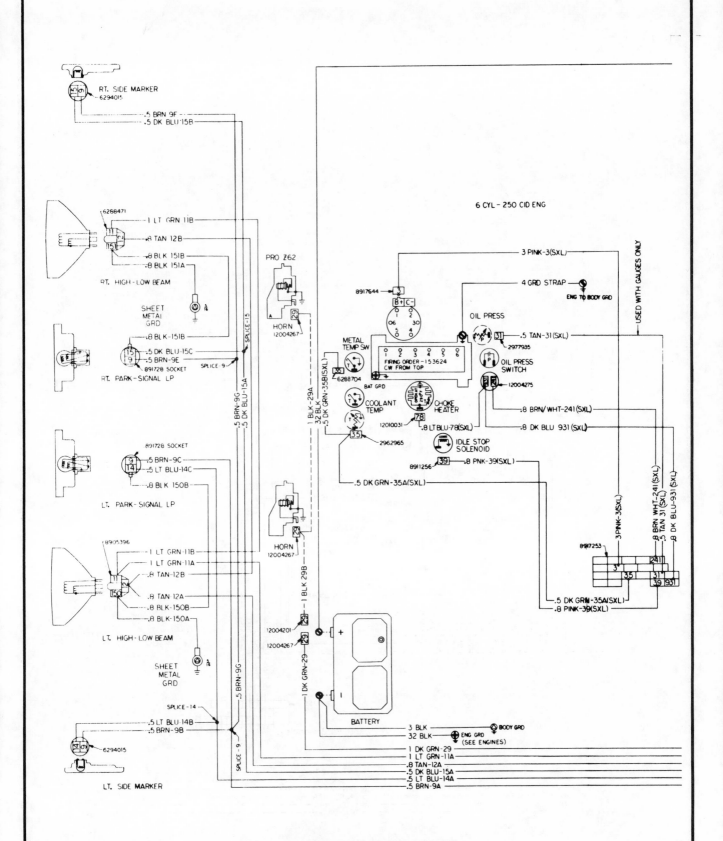

Fig. 13.55 1981 and 1982 models (1 of 8)

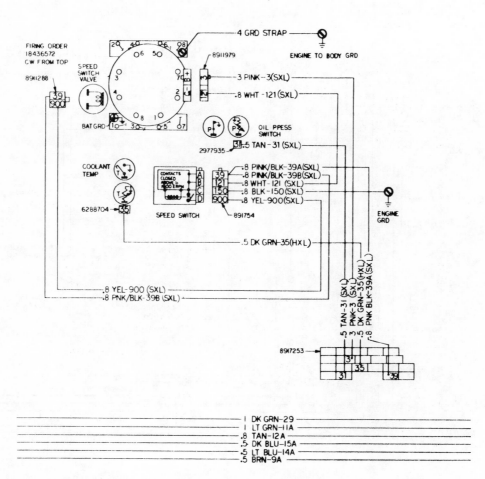

V/8 — ENGINE
HEAVY DUTY TRUCK

Fig. 13.56   1981 and 1982 models (2 of 8)

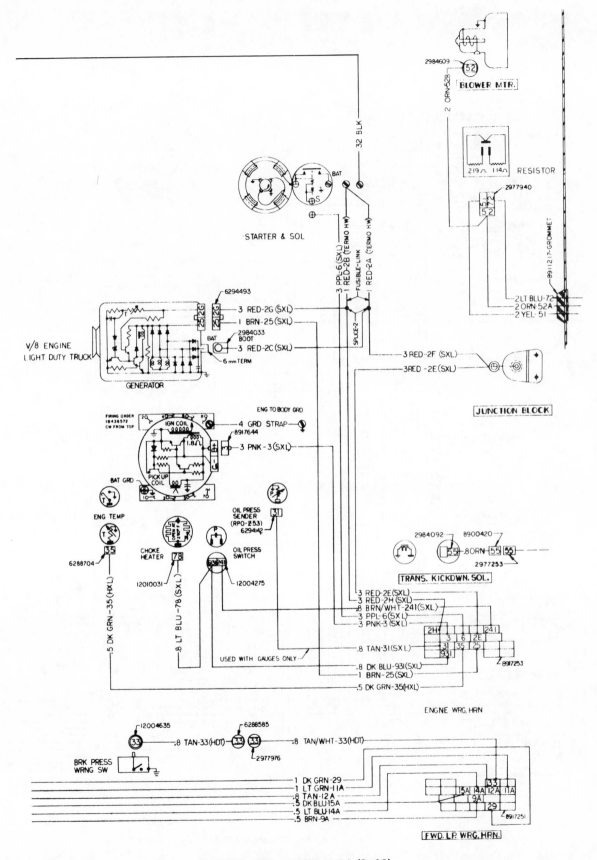

Fig. 13.57 1981 and 1982 models (3 of 8)

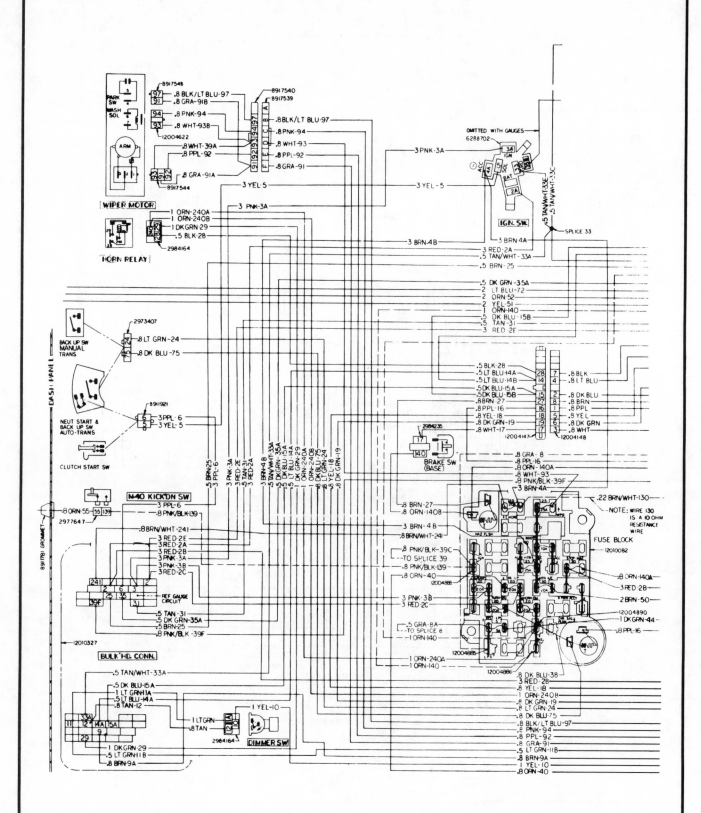

Fig. 13.58   1981 and 1982 models (4 of 8)

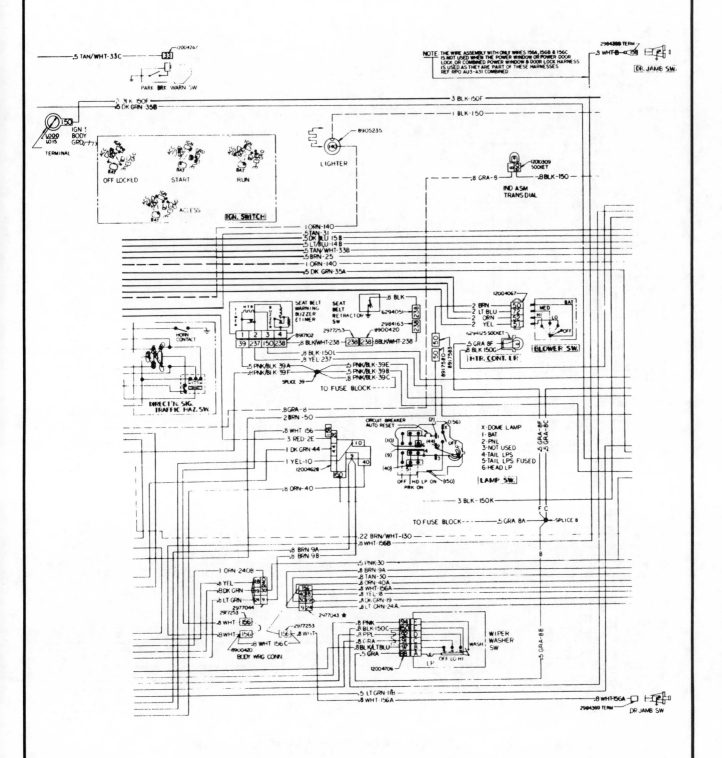

Fig. 13.59 1981 and 1982 models (5 of 8)

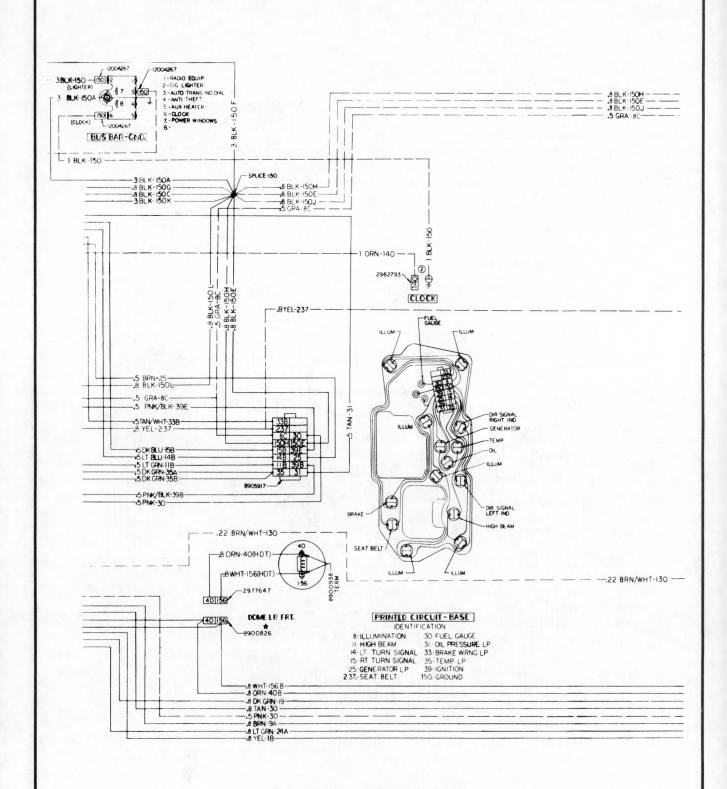

Fig. 13.60 1981 and 1982 models (6 of 8)

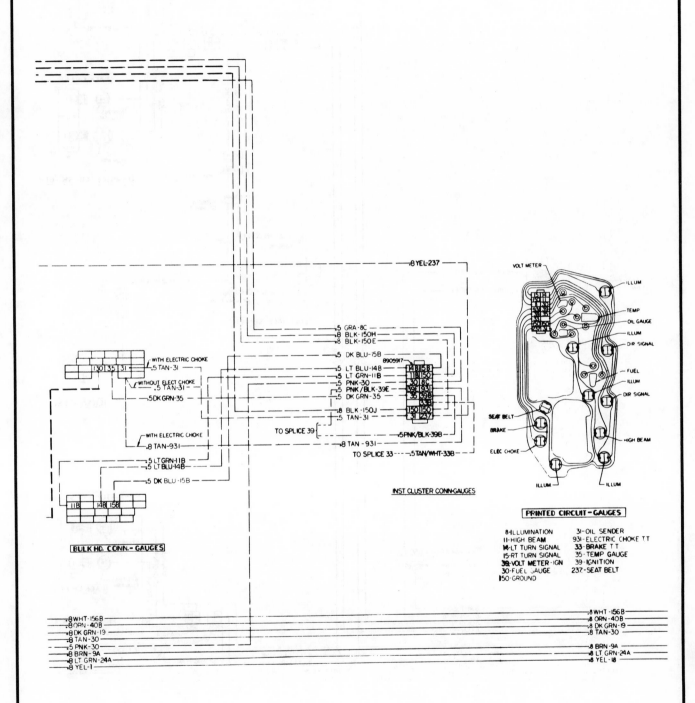

Fig. 13.61   1981 and 1982 models (7 of 8)

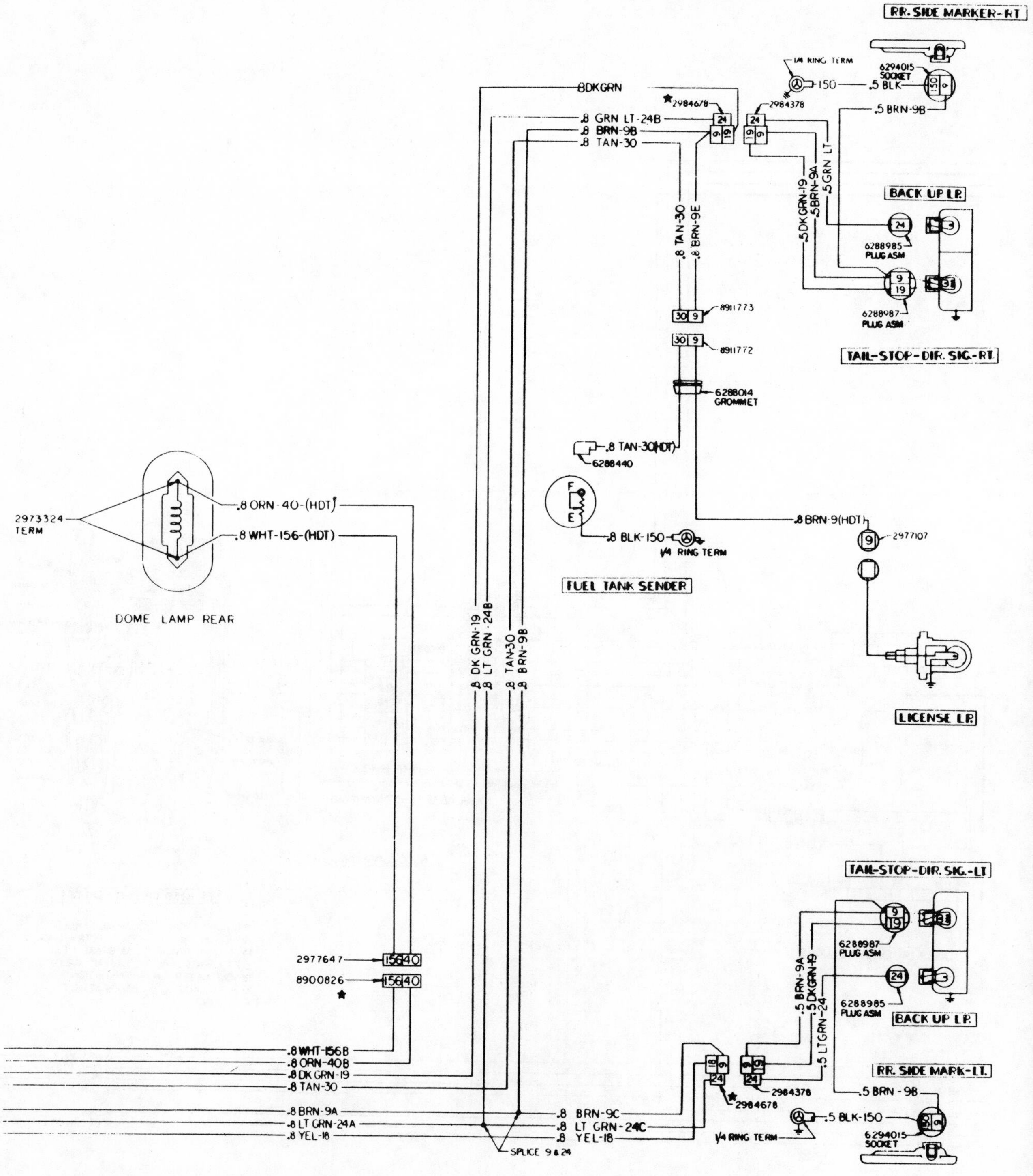

RR. SIDE MARKER-RT

14 RING TERM

2984678

6294015 SOCKET

.5 BLK

.5 BRN-9B

8 DK GRN

.8 GRN LT-24B
.8 BRN-9B
.8 TAN-30

2984378

150

BACK UP LP.

.8 TAN-30
.8 BRN-9E

.5 DK GRN-19
.5 GRN LT
.5 BRN-9A

6288985 PLUG ASM

6288987 PLUG ASM

8911773

8911772

6288014 GROMMET

TAIL-STOP-DIR. SIG.-RT

.8 TAN-30 (HDT)
6288440

F
E

.8 BLK-150

1/4 RING TERM

.8 BRN-9 (HDT)

2977107

FUEL TANK SENDER

2973324 TERM

.8 ORN-40-(HDT)

.8 WHT-156-(HDT)

DOME LAMP REAR

LICENSE LP.

.8 DK GRN-19
.8 LT GRN-24B
.8 TAN-30
.8 BRN-9B

2977647   156 40

8900826   156 40

.8 WHT-156B
.8 ORN-40B
.8 DK GRN-19
.8 TAN-30

.8 BRN-9A
.8 LT GRN-24A
.8 YEL-18

.8 BRN-9C

.8 LT GRN-24C
.8 YEL-18

SPLICE 9 & 24

2984378

2984678

1/4 RING TERM

TAIL-STOP-DIR. SIG.-LT

6288987 PLUG ASM

.5 BRN-9A
.5 DK GRN-19
.5 LT GRN-24

6288985 PLUG ASM

BACK UP LP.

RR. SIDE MARK-LT.

.5 BRN-9B

.5 BLK-150

6294015 SOCKET

Fig. 13.62   1981 and 1982 models (8 of 8)

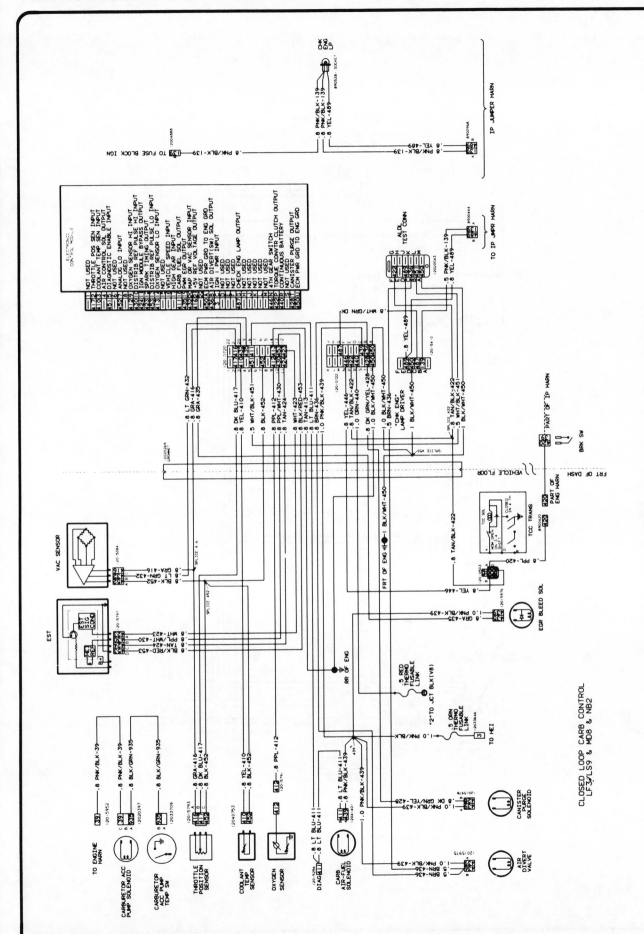

Fig. 13.63 1983 through 1985 — Closed loop carburetor control system

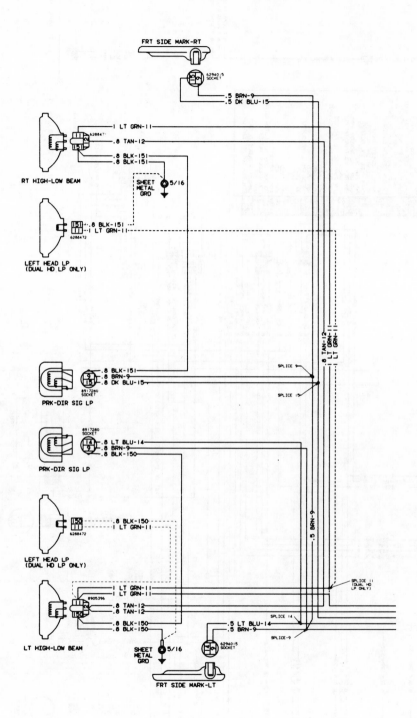

Fig. 13.64 1983 through 1985 (1 of 9)

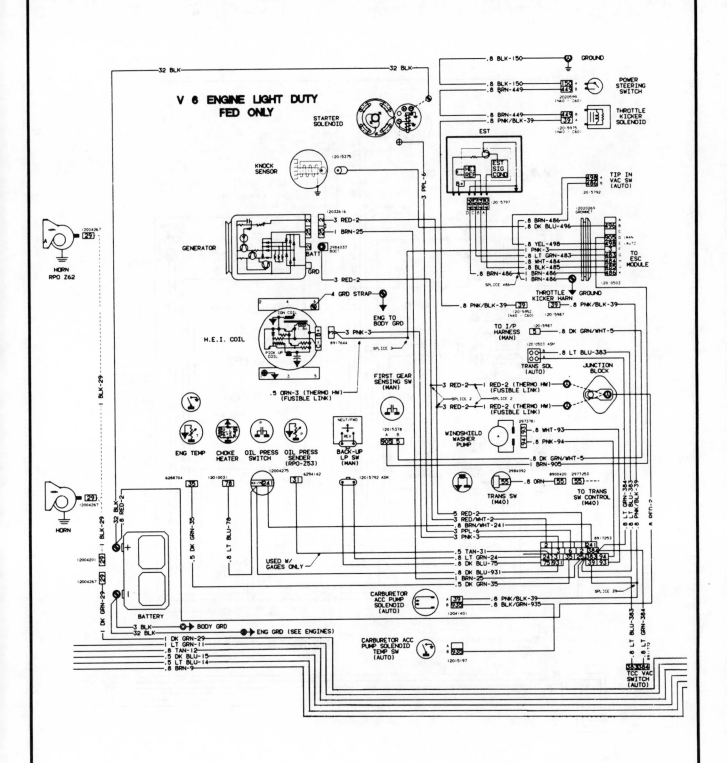

Fig. 13.65 1983 through 1985 (2 of 9)

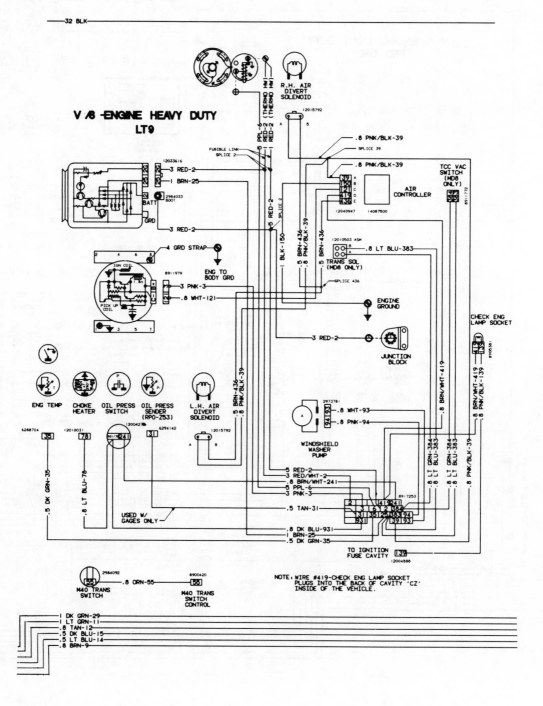

Fig. 13.66 1983 through 1985 (3 of 9)

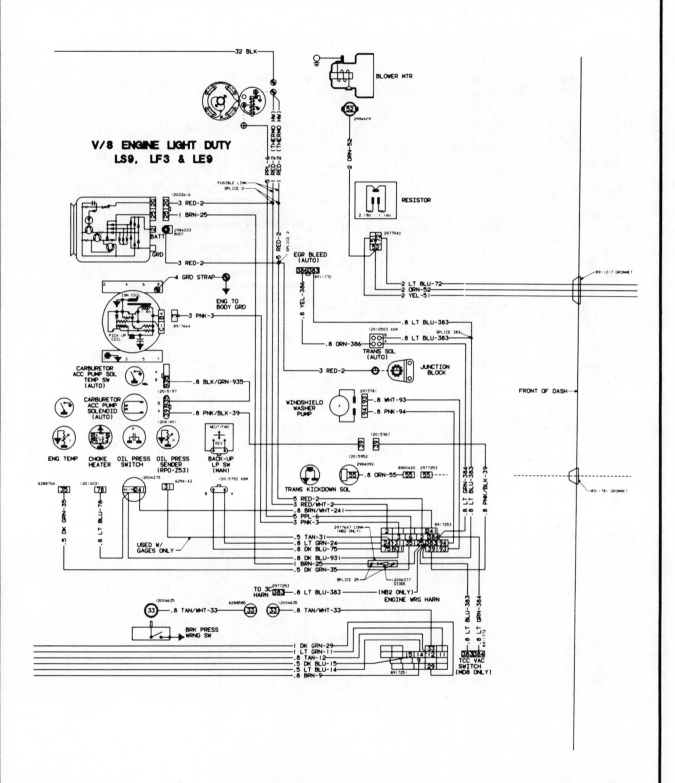

Fig. 13.67 1983 through 1985 (4 of 9)

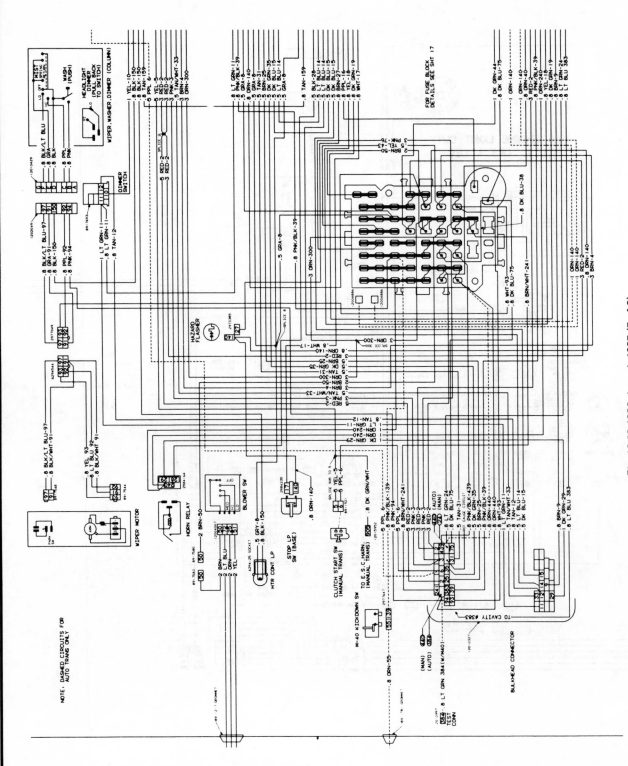

Fig. 13.68 1983 through 1985 (5 of 9)

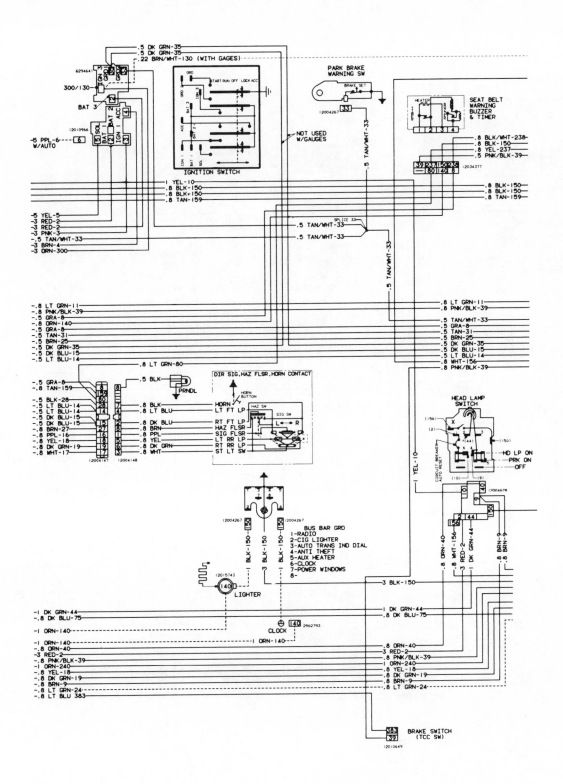

Fig. 13.69 1983 through 1985 (6 of 9)

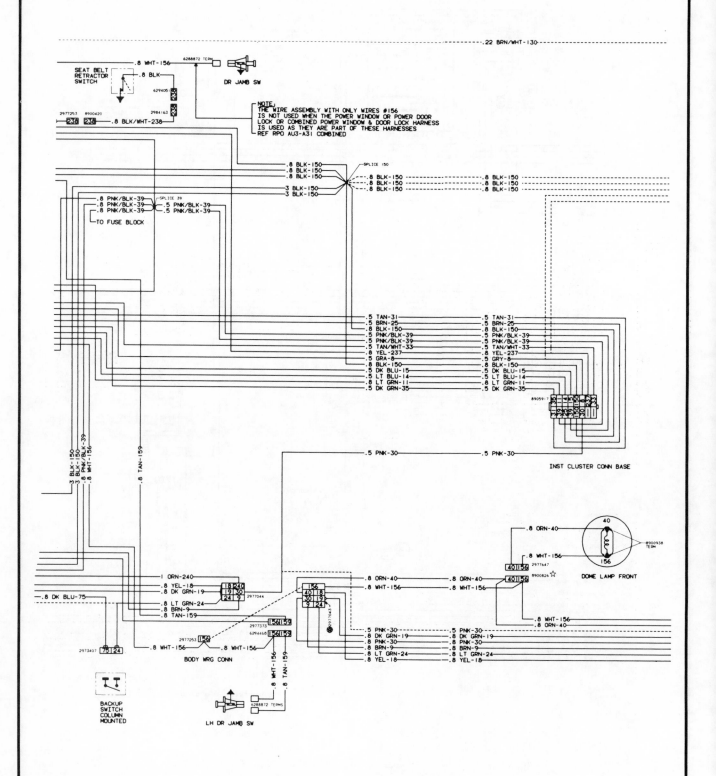

Fig. 13.70 1983 through 1985 (7 of 9)

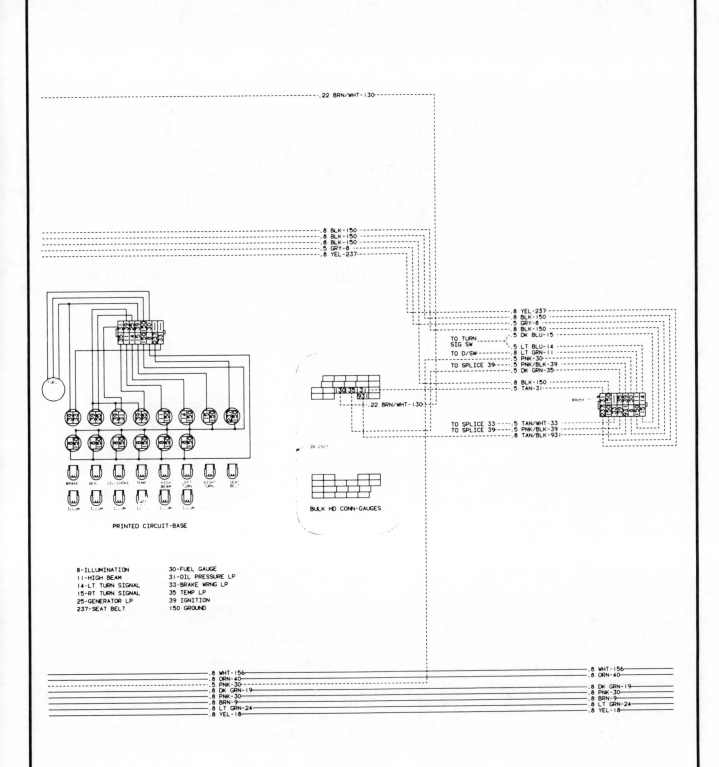

Fig. 13.71 1983 through 1985 (8 of 9)

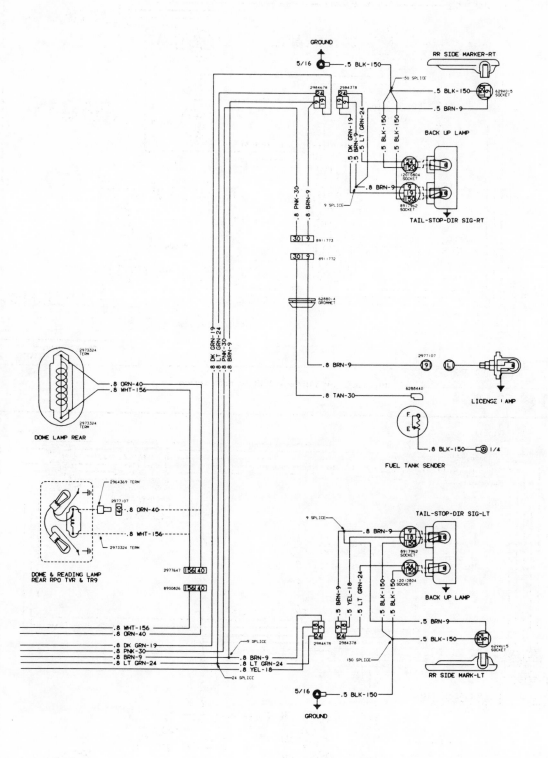

Fig. 13.72 1983 through 1985 (9 of 9)

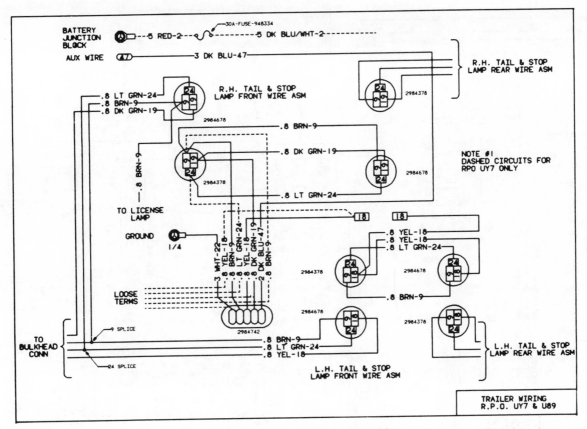

Fig. 13.73 1983 through 1985 — trailer wiring

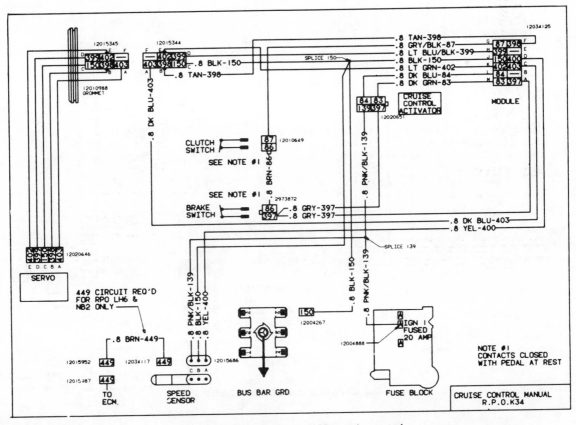

Fig. 13.74 1983 through 1985 — cruise control

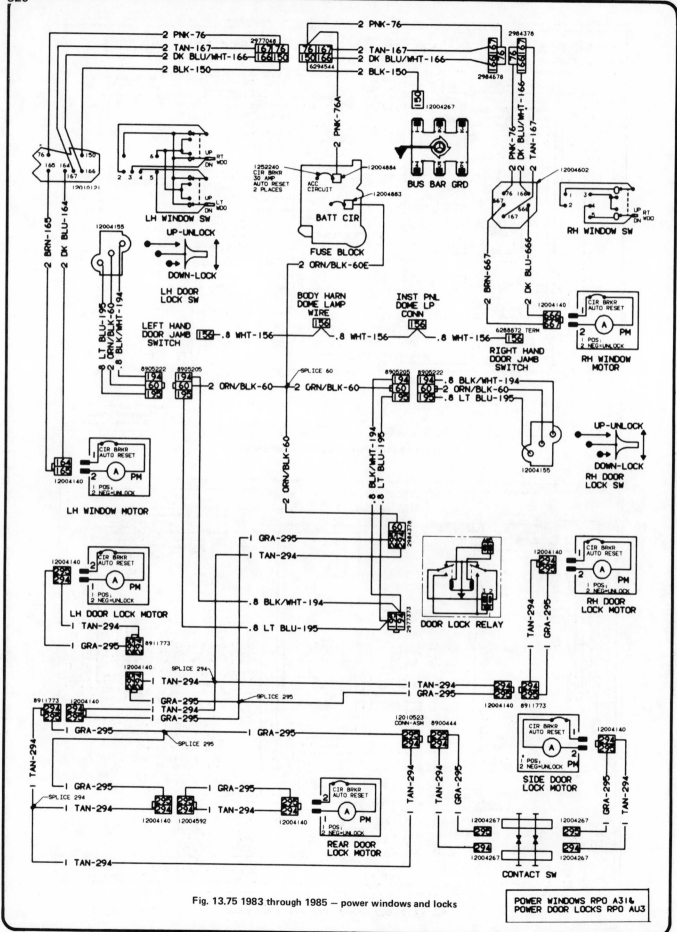

Fig. 13.75 1983 through 1985 — power windows and locks

POWER WINDOWS RPO A31&
POWER DOOR LOCKS RPO AU3

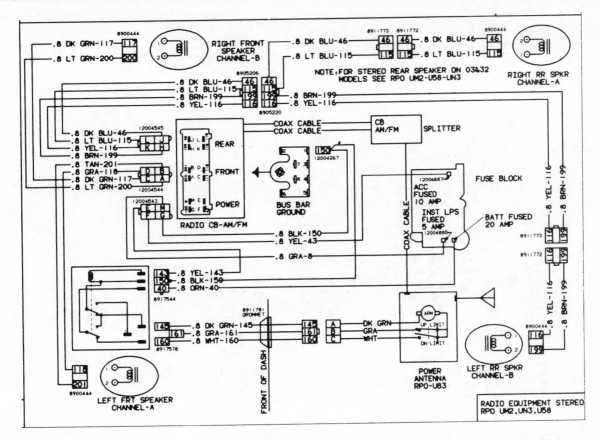

Fig. 13.76 1983 through 1985 — stereo radio

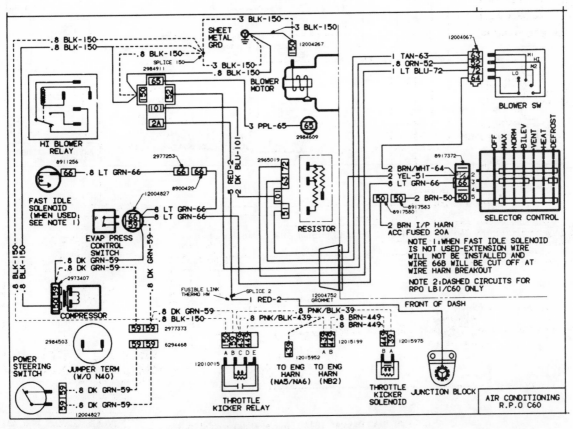

Fig. 13.77 1983 through 1985 — air conditioning

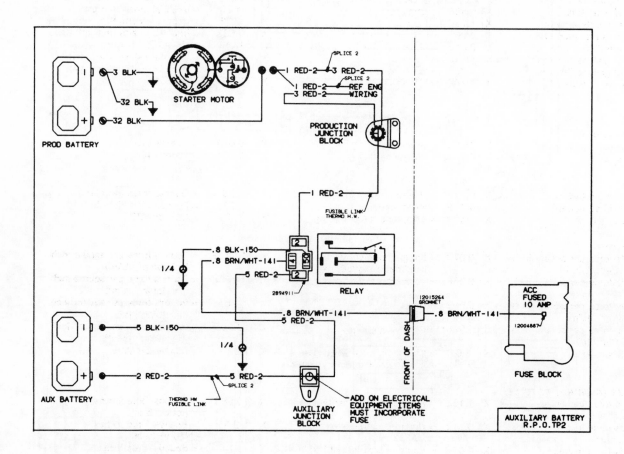

Fig. 13.78 1983 through 1985 — auxiliary battery

Conversion factors

Length (distance)					
Inches (in)	X 25.4	= Millimetres (mm)	X	0.0394	= Inches (in)
Feet (ft)	X 0.305	= Metres (m)	X	3.281	= Feet (ft)
Miles	X 1.609	= Kilometres (km)	X	0.621	= Miles
Volume (capacity)					
Cubic inches (cu in; in^3)	X 16.387	= Cubic centimetres (cc; cm^3)	X	0.061	= Cubic inches (cu in; in^3)
Imperial pints (Imp pt)	X 0.568	= Litres (l)	X	1.76	= Imperial pints (Imp pt)
Imperial quarts (Imp qt)	X 1.137	= Litres (l)	X	0.88	= Imperial quarts (Imp qt)
Imperial quarts (Imp qt)	X 1.201	= US quarts (US qt)	X	0.833	= Imperial quarts (Imp qt)
US quarts (US qt)	X 0.946	= Litres (l)	X	1.057	= US quarts (US qt)
Imperial gallons (Imp gal)	X 4.546	= Litres (l)	X	0.22	= Imperial gallons (Imp gal)
Imperial gallons (Imp gal)	X 1.201	= US gallons (US gal)	X	0.833	= Imperial gallons (Imp gal)
US gallons (US gal)	X 3.785	= Litres (l)	X	0.264	= US gallons (US gal)
Mass (weight)					
Ounces (oz)	X 28.35	= Grams (g)	X	0.035	= Ounces (oz)
Pounds (lb)	X 0.454	= Kilograms (kg)	X	2.205	= Pounds (lb)
Force					
Ounces-force (ozf; oz)	X 0.278	= Newtons (N)	X	3.6	= Ounces-force (ozf; oz)
Pounds-force (lbf; lb)	X 4.448	= Newtons (N)	X	0.225	= Pounds-force (lbf; lb)
Newtons (N)	X 0.1	= Kilograms-force (kgf; kg)	X	9.81	= Newtons (N)
Pressure					
Pounds-force per square inch (psi; lbf/in^2; lb/in^2)	X 0.070	= Kilograms-force per square centimetre (kgf/cm^2; kg/cm^2)	X	14.223	= Pounds-force per square inch (psi; lbf/in^2; lb/in^2)
Pounds-force per square inch (psi; lbf/in^2; lb/in^2)	X 0.068	= Atmospheres (atm)	X	14.696	= Pounds-force per square inch (psi; lbf/in^2; lb/in^2)
Pounds-force per square inch (psi; lbf/in^2; lb/in^2)	X 0.069	= Bars	X	14.5	= Pounds-force per square inch (psi; lbf/in^2; lb/in^2)
Pounds-force per square inch (psi; lbf/in^2; lb/in^2)	X 6.895	= Kilopascals (kPa)	X	0.145	= Pounds-force per square inch (psi; lbf/in^2; lb/in^2)
Kilopascals (kPa)	X 0.01	= Kilograms-force per square centimetre (kgf/cm^2; kg/cm^2)	X	98.1	= Kilopascals (kPa)
Torque (moment of force)					
Pounds-force inches (lbf in; lb in)	X 1.152	= Kilograms-force centimetre (kgf cm; kg cm)	X	0.868	= Pounds-force inches (lbf in; lb in)
Pounds-force inches (lbf in; lb in)	X 0.113	= Newton metres (Nm)	X	8.85	= Pounds-force inches (lbf in; lb in)
Pounds-force inches (lbf in; lb in)	X 0.083	= Pounds-force feet (lbf ft; lb ft)	X	12	= Pounds-force inches (lbf in; lb in)
Pounds-force feet (lbf ft; lb ft)	X 0.138	= Kilograms-force metres (kgf m; kg m)	X	7.233	= Pounds-force feet (lbf ft; lb ft)
Pounds-force feet (lbf ft; lb ft)	X 1.356	= Newton metres (Nm)	X	0.738	= Pounds-force feet (lbf ft; lb ft)
Newton metres (Nm)	X 0.102	= Kilograms-force metres (kgf m; kg m)	X	9.804	= Newton metres (Nm)
Power					
Horsepower (hp)	X 745.7	= Watts (W)	X	0.0013	= Horsepower (hp)
Velocity (speed)					
Miles per hour (miles/hr; mph)	X 1.609	= Kilometres per hour (km/hr; kph)	X	0.621	= Miles per hour (miles/hr; mph)
Fuel consumption*					
Miles per gallon, Imperial (mpg)	X 0.354	= Kilometres per litre (km/l)	X	2.825	= Miles per gallon, Imperial (mpg)
Miles per gallon, US (mpg)	X 0.425	= Kilometres per litre (km/l)	X	2.352	= Miles per gallon, US (mpg)

Temperature

Degrees Fahrenheit = (°C x 1.8) + 32

Degrees Celsius (Degrees Centigrade; °C) = (°F - 32) x 0.56

**It is common practice to convert from miles per gallon (mpg) to litres/100 kilometres (l/100km), where mpg (Imperial) x l/100 km = 282 and mpg (US) x l/100 km = 235*

Index

Printed by
J H Haynes & Co Ltd
Sparkford Nr Yeovil
Somerset BA22 7JJ England